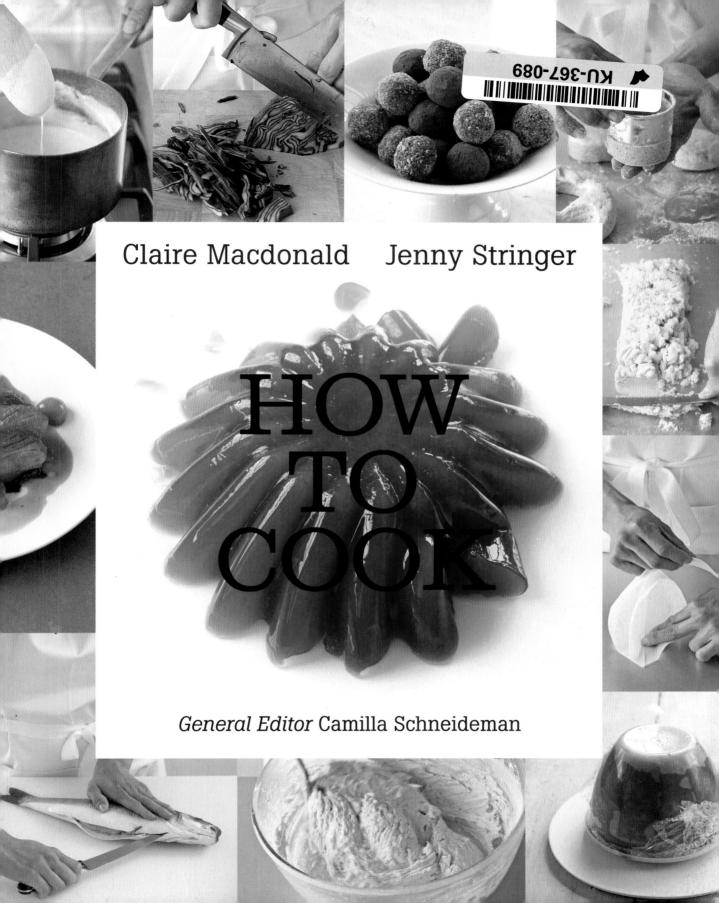

Claire Macdonald   Jenny Stringer

HOW TO COOK

General Editor Camilla Schneideman

Editorial director Anne Furniss
Creative director Helen Lewis
Project editor Janet Illsley
Design and art direction Gabriella Le Grazie
Photographer Peter Cassidy
Food stylist Emily Quah
Leiths consultant Claire Macdonald
Copy editor Sally Somers
Props stylist Cynthia Inions
Indexer Hilary Bird
Proofreader Kathy Steer
Production Aysun Hughes, Vincent Smith

First published in 2013 by
Quadrille Publishing Limited
Alhambra House, 27–31 Charing Cross Road
London WC2H 0LS
www.quadrille.co.uk

Text © 2013 Leiths School of Food and Wine
Photography © 2013 Peter Cassidy
Design and layout © 2013 Quadrille Publishing Limited

Cataloguing in Publication Data: a catalogue record for
this book is available from the British Library.

ISBN 978 1 84949 319 2

Printed in China

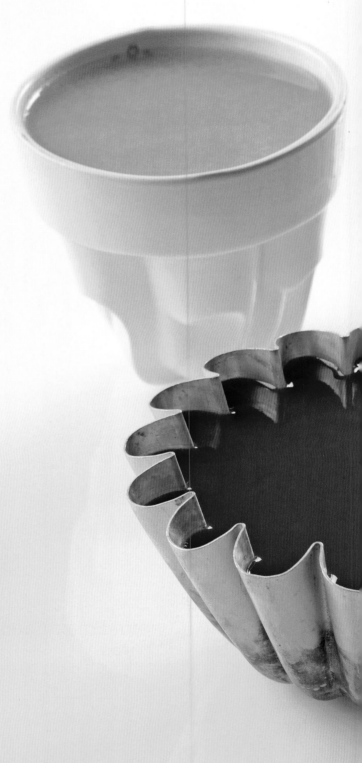

NOTES

All spoon measures are level unless otherwise stated:
1 tsp = 5ml spoon; 1 tbsp = 15ml spoon.

Use medium eggs unless otherwise suggested.
Anyone who is pregnant or in a vulnerable health
group should avoid recipes that use raw egg whites
or lightly cooked eggs.

Use fresh herbs unless otherwise suggested.

If using the zest of citrus fruit, buy unwaxed fruit.

Timings are guidelines for conventional ovens.
If you are using a fan-assisted oven, set your oven
temperature approximately 15°C (1 Gas mark) lower.
Use an oven thermometer to check the temperature.

Quadrille
PUBLISHING

Photography Peter Cassidy

Contents

Introduction

The hallways of Leiths echo with the footsteps of aspiring cooks, chefs, food professionals and restaurateurs. They are the food stylists and writers of tomorrow, the family cooks of the future and everything in between. Linking them together, whether they are here for a day or a year, is the desire to cook well, without fuss but with success.

Back in 1975, when Prue Leith founded a cookery school with Caroline Waldegrave at the helm, their mission was to inspire and educate a generation of cooks who would see past the fripperies of frills and fancy presentation. With good ingredients at its core, the school sought to train students to cook delicious, unpretentious food.

Our subsequent expansion and a change of location have done nothing to dilute this. The school in its current West London location accommodates 96 aspiring professionals daily; a separate group of keen enthusiasts assembles in the upstairs kitchen, knives at the ready, hoping to refine their knife skills, or become even better bakers.

During its long history, Leiths has seen Britain fall in love with food. In the seventies, home cooking was, if you were lucky, good but plain. Garlic, olive oil and pasta were exotic ingredients and spices sparingly used. The advent of processed food meant that convenience was around the corner, and the growing feminist movement gave permission to women to cast off their aprons. Restaurants were dominated by a desire to embellish and impress, more with fancy presentation than flavour. It was all a bit of a mess.

Despite the confusion, those with a true appreciation of good food and cooking soldiered on. Elizabeth David, who had awoken post-war taste buds with her sunny descriptions of Mediterranean food, continued to inspire those that she had converted. Leiths embraced classical technique but also found inspiration in foreign cuisine and ingredients. A career in cooking started to become appealing, and the school thrived.

Nearly forty years on, good food is reaching the masses. Although convenience food has taken root, the consumer has become more aware, less accepting and wants to know what lies hidden under the label. Chefs, once the prisoners of hot kitchens, have emerged into the light and become household names. Ingredients are heroes. There is an instinctive desire to reconnect with proper home cooking. Baking is a national obsession and cooking a great dinner is no longer seen as a mundane chore.

For Leiths, Britain's food obsession makes for exciting times. For the aspiring food professional, there are a myriad of different careers to pursue. Not just cooking food, but writing about it, developing and teaching people about it. Home cooks are becoming more inquisitive and adventurous. Not just about survival, cooking is, for many, a hobby, and for others an obsession. Students want to know why bread rises, how to make the shortest pastry and whether pomegranate molasses can be substituted for lemon juice.

Entertaining at home no longer means white tablecloths, best cutlery and fancy food. There is a simple approach to entertaining which feels more inclusive, and reflects the ethos at the heart of Leiths, that 'good cooking is enjoyable and rewarding for everyone – not least the cook.'

In order to gain real pleasure from cooking, it is vital that you gain confidence in the kitchen. *Leiths How to Cook* has been written to that end. With the help of this book, even the most beginner cook can build up a repertoire, not just of recipes, but of skills. Once mastered, each technique can be applied across different recipes, and with time, you will create a toolbox of skills to accompany you on any of life's culinary adventures. The recipes in this book are a combination of the classic and the new, and have been inspired by the wonderful mixture of cultures that influence the way we eat today. They have been thoroughly tested by our teachers, and many have been rubber stamped by our students too.

We hope that this book will help you to find the real pleasure in cooking, and that the next generation of cooks will be excited, and never intimidated by the kitchen. With a few good ingredients and a toolbox of skills, the kitchen really can be your oyster.

Camilla Schneideman

Acknowledgements

This book was written on behalf of Leiths School of Food and Wine by Claire Macdonald, Jenny Stringer and Camilla Schneideman. They are the School Principal, Deputy Managing Director and Managing Director respectively and all graduates of the Leiths Diploma in Food and Wine.

We are extremely fortunate to be surrounded by a wealth of creative and technical talent at Leiths and would like to thank all those who have donated recipes, tested recipes or helped to prepare for the photographs in this book. They are too numerous to mention by name as generations of Leiths cooks have added their own dishes to our courses, which have been adapted over the years; many are here in their current incarnation.

Thank you to Quadrille who, with our Editorial Director Anne Furniss and Creative Director Helen Lewis, have been wonderfully supportive, and to Heather Holden Brown for introducing us. Thank you to Peter Cassidy for photographs which are instructive as well as beautiful, no mean feat, and Emily Quah for her styling, expertise and calm good humour throughout the food photography process. Thanks, also to Sally Somers, for her skillful and thorough editing.

Finally a huge thank you must go to Janet Illsley our editor, and to Gabriella Le Grazie our designer. Janet's contribution to the manuscript has been immense. We know we are incredibly lucky to have worked with someone with so much knowledge, so much patience and who has been so committed to making this book something that will make such a difference to life here at Leiths school, as well as help those learning to cook at home. Gabriella, as well as being fantastically creative with the design of the book, has had such a practical approach to the project that the seemingly impossible photography programme has actually worked, and worked beautifully.

Lastly, thank you to all of the students who have attended Leiths courses over the decades, who have challenged us, encouraged us, road-tested our recipes in real life and kept us on our toes. This book is for you, and the generations of cooks to come.

The authors

Claire Macdonald trained at Leiths before gaining experience in the restaurant world. Finding that her true passion was for teaching, Claire returned to Leiths. She has been Principal of the school since 2007. Claire lives in central London.

Jenny Stringer trained at Leiths and was a private chef to HRH The Prince of Wales, cooking at Highgrove, St James's Palace and the Royal Yacht before returning to Leiths as a teacher. She was the Principal of the school for 5 years, then returned as Deputy Managing Director in 2010. Jenny co-authored *Leiths Simple Cookery*, published in 2007. Jenny lives in Bromley with her husband and two sons.

Camilla Schneideman, a graduate of Leiths School of Food and Wine, worked in restaurants before establishing the successful Café Divertimenti, Divertimenti Cookery School and the Lemon Tree Cookery School. Camilla is the author of *The Divertimenti Cookbook*, published in 2007. She returned to Leiths as Managing Director in 2008. Camilla lives in Acton with her husband and two children.

Vegetables

Vegetables are diverse and offer endless possibilities in the kitchen. Become aware of their seasonality, so you can cook and enjoy them at their best. Choose vegetables that look in peak condition, with no wilting or discoloured leaves, or signs of damage or bruising. Most varieties should be washed first. You will find vegetables easy to prepare if you use a sharp knife and develop good knife skills. Don't prepare them too far in advance and leave them immersed in water or some of their valuable vitamins will leach out and be lost. The vegetables included in this chapter are the ones we most often use at Leiths.

Onions

Onions are included in many savoury dishes. Yellow onions are the most versatile; white and red onions are valued for their mildness. Shallots and spring onions (also called salad onions) are members of the onion family too. Shallots are valued for their mild, sweet flavour and are used whole in casseroles as well as sliced and chopped for all manner of dishes. Choose firm onions with a thin, papery skin.

Preparing onions or shallots for slicing and dicing

1 Cut a small slice off the top of the onion so it can stand upright. Trim a little off the hairy part of the root but keep the root intact (as this holds the onion together when you are cutting it).

2 Stand the onion with the trimmed top surface down. Using a large, sharp knife (for onions, a small knife for shallots), cut down through the onion to halve it.

3 Peel each onion half and discard the skin. It is also a good idea to remove the first of the inner pale leaves of the onion as these tend to be leathery and do not break down during cooking.

Slicing onions

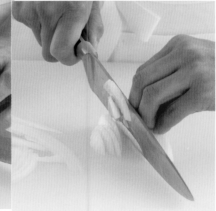

1 Place the onion rounded side up on the board with the root end furthest from your chopping hand. With your hand in a claw shape and the tips of your fingers bent, hold the onion lightly. Your thumb will support the root end.

2 Slice the onion in a rocking action, keeping the tip of the knife in contact with the board as you draw it down to cut through the onion.

3 As you reach the root end of the onion, turn the onion onto the largest flat side and slice again, ensuring no onion is wasted.

Dicing onions

1 Halve and peel your onion. With the flat side down and the root end away from you, slice through the onion vertically, towards the root, but not right through it (to keep it intact). For fine dice ensure the cuts are close together.

2 Slice horizontally through the onion once or twice, again not right through the root, but very close to it, keeping the knife slightly angled towards the board for safety.

3 Now move the onion so that the root end is on your left and proceed as for slicing an onion. It may be a little more difficult, but try to hold the onion together in your other hand 'claw' to protect your fingertips and fingernails.

Cooking onions

When onions are used to flavour a dish, they are usually cooked gently at first in a little butter or oil (ie sweated). We lay a greaseproof paper 'cartouche' on top of sweating onions to minimise evaporation. Similarly, we place one over braising vegetables and poaching fruit to keep them immersed in the liquid or fat. Dampening the cartouche helps to maintain a moist environment. Dry cartouches are used too, when baking pastry blind (see page 482), for example.

Making a cartouche

1 To make a cartouche, cut a square or round of greaseproof paper and fold into segments, the shape of an elongated triangle. Trim the triangle to a fraction larger than the radius of your pan.

2 Unfold the paper into a circle that should fit snugly inside the saucepan on top of the onions.

3 Crumple the cartouche and dampen under cold water before use. The crumpling helps the greaseproof paper hold a little more water. Lay on top of the ingredient(s) to be cooked.

Sweating onions

This technique describes the cooking process of softening an onion and drawing out its natural sweetness without allowing it to take on any colour. The onions are gently sweated in a little oil or butter. Using a dampened cartouche (see page 13) helps the sweating process and seals in the juices.

1 In a suitably sized saucepan, melt a nut of butter or a little oil. Put the onions in the saucepan and place a dampened cartouche on the surface, in contact with the onions. Cover with a tight-fitting lid, place over a very gentle heat and allow the onions to 'sweat'.

2 Check the onions occasionally, especially if a lot of steam is escaping. If the cartouche is dry, re-dampen it and return it to cover the onions. If any onions have browned on the bottom of the pan, don't stir them in. Discard them and use a clean saucepan to continue sweating.

3 After 10–15 minutes, check the onions again. They will be ready when they have lost volume and become translucent. If you squeeze a piece of onion between your fingers there should be no resistance. If you taste a piece, it will have a sweet, mild flavour.

Caramelising onions

Follow the same procedure as for sweating onions, and when the onions are almost soft, remove the lid and cartouche and turn the heat up a little to medium to evaporate the water from the onion juices. What will be left will be the butter or oil and the onions' natural sugars, which will begin to caramelise to a rich colour and flavour as the onions are cooked further. Do not be tempted to turn the heat up too much as the onions may scorch, resulting in a harsh, burnt flavour.

A note on sweating and caramelising other vegetables...
Other vegetables can be sweated and caramelised in the same way. Once they have been sweated, a little sugar can be added to aid the caramelisation process.

Caramelised onion confit

Makes 300ml
3 medium onions
30g butter
2–3 tbsp soft light brown sugar
75ml red wine
Few thyme sprigs
Salt and freshly ground black pepper

1 Halve, peel and thinly slice the onions. Heat the butter in a frying pan and add the onions. Cover with a damp cartouche and lid and sweat the onions until softened, about 10–15 minutes.

2 Remove the lid and cartouche, turn up the heat to medium, stir in the sugar, to taste, and continue cooking for 10–15 minutes until the onions are golden brown.

3 Stir in the wine and cook gently until it has mostly evaporated and the onions are a deep brown colour. This can take up to 15 minutes.

4 Finely chop enough thyme leaves to give you ¼–½ tsp and stir them into the confit. Season with salt and pepper to taste and allow to cool. Use the caramelised onion confit as a garnish for meat and poultry dishes and terrines.

French onion soup

Serves 4
4 medium onions
1 garlic clove
50g butter
1 tsp plain flour
1 litre brown beef stock or brown
  chicken and veal stock (see page 98)
Salt and freshly ground black pepper

For the croûtons
60g Gruyère cheese
1 tsp Dijon mustard
½ baguette

1 Halve, peel and thinly slice the onions. Peel and crush the garlic.

2 Melt the butter in a large, heavy-based saucepan. Add the onions, cover with a damp cartouche (see page 13) and cook over a gentle heat, checking from time to time, until they are well softened and turning golden brown. This can take up to an hour and cannot be rushed as it is this initial gentle cooking and caramelisation that helps to give the soup its rich flavour.

3 Increase the heat and add the garlic to the pan. Cook for 1 minute and then add the flour. Cook for a further minute, stirring continuously.

4 Add the stock and bring to the boil, stirring to make sure the flour does not set in lumps. Season lightly with salt and pepper. Lower the heat and simmer for 20 minutes, adding a little water during cooking if the soup becomes too thick.

5 Meanwhile, heat the oven to 200°C/gas mark 6 or heat the grill to high.

6 For the croûtons, grate the Gruyère finely and mix it with the mustard. Cut 4 slices of the bread on the diagonal, about 1.5–2cm thick, and spread with the Gruyère mixture. Adjust the seasoning, then ladle the soup into 4 ovenproof soup bowls and place a piece of bread on each, cheese side up.

7 Put the soup bowls on a baking sheet in the oven until the cheese is golden brown and bubbling. Alternatively, grill the slices of bread topped with cheese until golden, then float one on each bowl of soup.

Shallot purée

Makes 300–400ml
1kg banana shallots
3 garlic cloves
50g butter
2 thyme sprigs
Salt and ground white pepper

1 Halve, peel and finely dice the shallots. Bash the unpeeled garlic cloves with the flat side of a large knife so that they split but do not fall apart (as shown).

2 Melt the butter in a saucepan, add the shallots, garlic and thyme and cover with a damp cartouche (see page 13). Sweat over a gentle heat until the shallots are completely soft and colourless. The garlic and thyme flavours will infuse into the shallots during the sweating process.

3 Remove the cartouche, the thyme and garlic, and allow any excess moisture to evaporate over the same gentle heat. Take care that the shallots do not brown.

4 In a blender or small food processor bowl, purée the shallots until completely smooth, then pass through a fine sieve. If the purée is still a little watery, return it to the saucepan and place over a low to medium heat until the excess water has evaporated.

5 Season the shallot purée with a little salt and pepper to taste. Serve as an accompaniment to red meat and poultry dishes.

Carrots

This versatile root adds sweetness to stocks and stews; is steamed, sautéed or roasted as a side dish; or served raw grated in salads. Carrots work well with parsley and thyme, and aromatic spices such as cumin, coriander and cinnamon. Choose firm, unblemished carrots.

Blocking carrots

Wash and peel the carrot and trim off the top end. Cut the carrot into 4 finger-width pieces. Cut off a side of the carrot. Turn it and repeat on all other sides to create a rectangular block of carrot. (Reserve any trimmings for stock.)

Batons

Cut the blocked carrot into batons or sticks, 5–6.5cm long and approximately 1cm square. For smaller batons, or allumettes, cut each large baton lengthways into 4 thinner sticks, about 5mm square.

Julienne

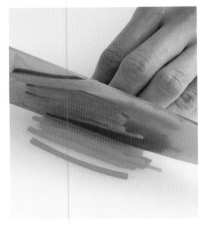

Cut the blocked carrot into very thin slices (1–2mm thick) and stack them neatly. Slice through the carrot as uniformly as possible to create julienne.

Dice and brunoise

Cut across batons to form uniform dice (left); the carrot should be perfectly square in shape. Cut across allumettes to form brunoise (right). Cut across julienne to form fine brunoise (top).

Turning carrots

1 Peel and block the carrots. Remove each corner, then holding the carrot in your hand, insert a small, sharp knife quite deep at the end of the block, then draw the knife gradually up towards you until you reach the middle of the block, then down and away towards your thumb.

2 Trim the remaining sides in the same way to create the basic 5- or 7-sided barrel shape. Use trimmings in stocks and soups. Turned vegetables are consistent in size for even cooking and elegant presentation. Any firm vegetable can be turned and with some (such as courgettes), the skin is retained on one side to provide colour.

Vichy carrots

Serves 4

6–8 carrots, depending on size
15g butter
⅛ tsp salt
1 tsp caster sugar
Few mint sprigs
Few parsley sprigs
Freshly ground black pepper

1 Peel the carrots and cut them into batons (see left).

2 Put the butter, salt and sugar in a saucepan and heat gently to melt the butter. Don't add more salt, as the liquid will all evaporate, over-salting the dish. Stir in the carrots and add enough water to come halfway up the carrots.

3 Increase the heat to medium and put the lid on, leaving a small gap for steam to escape. Simmer until the carrots are tender and most of the water has evaporated.

4 Turn down the heat and remove the lid. Allow the remaining liquid to reduce to a glaze, stirring to make sure the carrots are evenly coated and don't burn.

5 Finely chop enough mint and parsley leaves to give you ¼ tsp of each. Season the carrots with pepper, stir in the herbs and serve.

Carrots with raisins, walnuts and sherry vinegar

Serves 4

25g raisins
4 carrots
2 garlic cloves
1–2 tbsp olive oil
25g walnuts
20g butter
50ml sherry vinegar, or to taste
Small handful of flat-leaf parsley
Sea salt and freshly ground black pepper

1 Soak the raisins in boiling water for 30 minutes. Peel the carrots and cut them on the diagonal into slices 7–8mm thick. Bash the unpeeled garlic cloves with the flat side of a large knife so that they split but do not fall apart.

2 Heat the olive oil in a large frying pan over a medium heat. Add the garlic and allow it to start sizzling before adding the carrots and a small pinch of salt. Increase the heat and cook for 5 minutes, or until starting to turn brown, stirring frequently.

3 Roughly chop the walnuts and add them to the pan. Continue cooking for a further 5 minutes, adding a splash of water if there is any danger of the carrots burning before they have softened sufficiently. Remove the garlic.

4 Drain the raisins and stir through the carrots with the butter and sherry vinegar to taste. Season with pepper and reheat. Roughly chop enough parsley leaves to give you 1 tbsp, and stir through the carrots.

Sautéed carrots with cumin

Serves 4

4 carrots
1–2 tbsp olive oil
2 garlic cloves
1 tsp ground cumin
10g butter
Small handful of flat-leaf parsley
Sea salt and freshly ground black pepper

1 Peel the carrots and cut them on the diagonal into slices 7–8mm thick.

2 Heat the olive oil in a large frying pan over a medium heat. Bash the unpeeled garlic cloves with the side of a large, sharp knife so they split but do not fall apart.

3 Add the garlic to the pan and allow it to start sizzling in the oil before adding the carrots. Increase the heat and cook for about 5 minutes, or until the carrots are starting to turn brown, stirring frequently.

4 Reduce the heat and stir in the cumin and a pinch of salt. Cook for a further 5 minutes or until the carrots are tender. Add a splash of water if there is any danger of them burning before they have softened sufficiently. Remove the garlic.

5 Stir in the butter to glaze, and season with pepper. Roughly chop enough parsley leaves to give you 1 tbsp, and stir through the carrots.

Variations

Replace the cumin with other spices, such as ras-al-hanout for Moroccan-style carrots, or five-spice powder for Chinese-style carrots.

Celery and celeriac

Celery and celeriac are often thought to be from the same plant, which they are not, although they are from the same family, hence the similarity in flavour. With celery it is the stalks that are prized, both white and green, whereas with celeriac it is the root that's eaten. Celery and celeriac can be eaten both raw and cooked, but they are not interchangeable. Celery works well with citrus fruit and goat's and blue cheeses, while celeriac pairs well with mustard and garlic.

Choose straight, firm stalks of celery. When selecting celeriac, avoid very large ones which may be woolly and hollow.

Celeriac rémoulade

Serves 4–6
1 lemon (for acidulating)
½ medium celeriac

For the rémoulade
10g capers
1 anchovy fillet in oil (optional)
60ml mayonnaise (see page 116)
½ tsp Dijon mustard
Few chervil sprigs
Squeeze of lemon juice
Salt and freshly ground black pepper

1 Juice the lemon. Peel the celeriac and cut it into julienne (as for carrot julienne, see page 16), or use a mandolin. Submerge the celeriac in cold water acidulated with the lemon juice (see below) before and after it is prepared.

2 To make the dressing, rinse, drain and finely chop the capers. Drain and finely chop the anchovy fillet, if using. Add these to the mayonnaise along with the mustard. (You can add more or less of these flavouring ingredients, to taste.) Finely chop enough chervil leaves to give you 1 tsp and stir through the sauce along with the drained and dried celeriac.

3 Add the celeriac to the sauce swiftly to prevent it from discolouring. Season to taste with salt and pepper and a squeeze of lemon juice.

Variation

Celeriac and apple rémoulade Replace half the celeriac with Granny Smith apples. Peel, core and cut into julienne. Add to the dressing with the celeriac.

Oxidisation and discolouration

Some vegetables and fruit, once peeled or cut (exposing their flesh to the air), oxidise and discolour very quickly. When preparing vegetables such as celeriac, artichokes, potatoes, parsnips and salsify, and fruit such as apples, pears and avocados, use a stainless steel knife and something acidic, such as vinegar and lemon juice, to help prevent discolouring.

As soon as the vegetable or fruit is cut, rub a little acidity on the cut side or submerge it immediately in acidulated water (water to which a splash of vinegar or the juice of a lemon has been added). Potatoes, parsnips, apples and pears can be submerged in just water.

Often recipes will ask for vegetables to be cooked in acidulated water for the same reason. Lemon juice or vinegar is generally used. An alternative is to use a 'blanc': water to which both acid and a little flour has been added. Make a soft paste of 3 tbsp water and 1 tbsp plain white flour and slake the paste (see page 111) into 1 litre salted simmering water, before adding the juice of ½ lemon.

Celeriac purée

Serves 4

1 lemon (for acidulating)
350g celeriac
150g floury potatoes
50ml double cream or crème fraîche
25–50ml milk
15g butter
Salt and ground white pepper

1 Juice the lemon. Peel the celeriac and cut it into 5cm chunks. Submerge the celeriac in cold water acidulated with the lemon juice until you are ready to cook it.

2 Peel the potatoes, cut into chunks the same size as the celeriac and put them into a small saucepan. Cover the potatoes with salted water, bring to the boil, then lower the heat and simmer for 15 minutes, or until tender.

3 Put the celeriac chunks in a separate saucepan, cover with salted water, add a little lemon juice and bring to the boil. Reduce the heat and simmer until tender. The celeriac will not cook in the same time as the potato, which is why they are best cooked separately.

4 When a cutlery knife can easily be pushed through the potato and celeriac chunks, drain well, keeping them separate, and allow to steam-dry in colanders for a minute or so. Mash the potato using a potato ricer or by pushing through a sieve with a non-metal spoon. Mash the celeriac either with a potato ricer or by blending in a food processor. Combine the two vegetables in a clean saucepan.

5 Over a gentle heat, stir in the cream with enough milk to reach your desired consistency. Stir in the butter and allow to melt. Season well with salt and pepper.

Variations

You can make purées from many other vegetables in this way, using as much or as little potato to give a smooth texture as you wish. In most cases potato is not even required. Jerusalem artichoke, carrot, parsnip, sweetcorn, cauliflower and asparagus purées all work well and can be puréed in a food processor for speed.

A note on puréeing potato...

Potato cannot be mashed or puréed in a food processor as the texture will become gluey owing to the vegetable's high starch content.

Celery braised in cider

Serves 4

1 head of celery
1 garlic clove
1 tbsp olive oil
10g butter
1 rasher of smoked streaky bacon
125ml dry cider
125ml chicken and veal stock
  (see page 96)
1 bay leaf
1 thyme sprig
Salt and freshly ground black pepper

1 Heat the oven to 180°C/gas mark 4.

2 Prepare the celery by removing any damaged or discoloured outer stalks and, with a small knife, shave off as much of the root as possible, keeping the stalks attached. Cut off the top half of the head (keep these loose stalks for stock). De-string the remaining celery with a vegetable peeler and cut lengthways into quarters. Bash the unpeeled garlic clove with the flat side of a large knife.

3 Put the olive oil and butter into a flameproof casserole or roasting tin (that will later hold the celery fairly snugly in a single layer) and heat over a medium heat. Add the garlic and bacon and cook until they brown and the bacon fat starts to render. Remove from the heat.

4 Combine the cider and stock, season and add the bay leaf and thyme. Add to the casserole with the celery. Cover tightly with foil, transfer to the oven and bake for 1–1½ hours, or until the celery is completely tender.

5 Remove the bay leaf, thyme sprig, garlic and bacon, and discard. If there is a lot of juice, let the dish gently bubble on the hob to reduce it and concentrate the flavour. Adjust the seasoning if necessary.

Globe and Jerusalem artichokes

These vegetables are not related. Globe artichokes, which are in season from June to August, belong to the thistle family, while Jerusalem artichokes, available January to February, are knobbly tubers of the sunflower family. These do not, as their title suggests, originate from the Middle East but take their name from the Italian 'girasole' meaning sunflower. They are prepared and cooked very differently from globe artichokes.

Cooking and serving globe artichokes whole

1 As close to the underside of the artichoke bulb as possible, score all around the stem to a depth of about 1mm. Holding the stem over the edge of a board or table, gently lever the stem downwards.

2 Now turn the artichoke a little and repeat this action again and again until the stem can be pulled free of the bulb. This helps to remove some of the coarse fibres in the bottom of the heart.

3 Trim the top third of the bulb away. Then trim the tops of the remaining leaves to remove the spiky points. The outer, very coarse bottom leaves can be pulled away completely.

4 As you finish preparing each artichoke to this stage, put it into in a bowl of acidulated water (cold water with the juice of 1 lemon or 2 tbsp white wine vinegar added, see page 18).

5 Drain the artichokes and immerse them in a large pan of simmering, acidulated and seasoned water. It may be necessary to weight down the artichokes with a plate or to cover them with a cartouche (see page 13), to keep them submerged. Cook the artichokes for about 15–20 minutes until one of the inner leaves can be pulled away easily.

6 Remove the artichokes from the water and place them upside down in a colander or on a wire rack to drain well.

7 Once the artichokes are cool enough to handle, the chokes need to be removed: turn an artichoke the right way up and gently tug on the inner purple/yellow leaves towards the centre. If you can get a good hold of all these leaves in one go, all the better. Carefully pull these leaves out and reserve them.

8 Using a teaspoon, carefully scrape at the hairy choke that lies on top of the heart. Try not to dig too deep or you will remove some of the heart.

9 Continue scraping until all the choke has been removed. Repeat with the remaining artichokes. Return the centre leaves to the artichokes. Serve on large plates, with a beurre blanc (see page 122), French dressing (see page 125), or melted butter seasoned with salt, freshly ground black pepper and lemon juice.

To turn globe artichokes for braising

Follow steps 1 and 2, above. Pull away the coarse outer leaves until only the pale yellow leaves remain. Cut off the top third to two-thirds of the artichoke, then, using a small, sharp knife or swivel peeler, carefully shave off any remaining outer leaves of the artichoke surrounding the heart. Take care not to shave the heart itself and try to maintain the natural shape of the artichoke. As more of the heart is exposed, work quickly to prevent discolouring. Place each prepared artichoke in acidulated water, as in step 4, above. While the choke can be scraped out at this stage, it is often removed after cooking as it is easier.

1 Levering the artichoke stem on the edge of the table.

2 Pulling the stem free from the bulb.

3 Pulling away the coarse bottom leaves.

4 Immersing the prepared artichokes in acidulated water.

5 Pulling away an inner leaf to check that the artichoke is cooked.

6 Draining the artichokes upside down in a colander.

7 Pulling out the inner leaves from the middle to expose the choke.

8 Scooping out the hairy choke.

9 The artichoke with its choke fully removed.

Braised artichokes

Makes 4
1 lemon (for acidulating)
4 artichokes
1 onion
1 carrot
1 celery stick
2 garlic cloves
5 tbsp olive oil
100ml white wine
500ml chicken and veal stock
  (see page 96)
1 bay leaf
Few thyme sprigs
Few black peppercorns
Salt

1 Juice the lemon. Turn the artichokes (see page 20) and immerse them in cold water acidulated with the lemon juice. Halve, peel and finely slice the onion. Wash and peel the carrot, wash the celery and slice both thinly. Peel and crush the garlic.

2 Heat the olive oil in a saucepan large enough to fit the artichokes in a single layer (when they are added later). Add the onion, carrot and celery, cover and sweat for 10–15 minutes, or until soft, then add the garlic and cook for 1 minute.

3 Add the wine and stock, herbs, peppercorns and some salt. Bring to a simmer, then submerge the artichokes in the braising liquor. Add some water if the liquor does not cover the artichokes. Use a cartouche (see page 13) if the artichokes rise to the surface. Cover and cook at a gentle simmer until the hearts are just tender, about 20–25 minutes, using a cutlery knife to check the tenderness.

4 Once the artichokes are cooked, take the pan off the heat and leave them to cool in the liquor. Once cool, remove the artichokes, carefully scrape the choke away and discard. The artichoke hearts are now ready for use, but can be kept in the braising liquor, in the fridge, for a few days.

Preparing baby artichokes for braising
The choke and stem of baby artichokes are soft, and the whole artichoke is often eaten raw or cooked. For cooking, leave the stem on, but trim the length to 3–4cm. Remove the leaves until only the pale yellowy purple leaves remain, then trim a third off the top of the bulb. Turn the base of each baby artichoke (see page 20) and keep in acidulated water until ready to braise, as for large artichokes. They will only take about 8–12 minutes to cook, depending on size.

If preferred, prior to braising, halve the artichoke through the stem and remove the choke with a teaspoon.

Fried baby artichokes with aioli

Serves 4
12 braised baby artichokes (see above)
Oil for deep-frying
4–5 tbsp plain flour, mixed with a pinch
  of salt
Coarse sea salt
Aioli (see page 117), to serve

1 Remove the artichokes from the braising liquor and leave them to drain, stalk side uppermost, in a colander or on a wire rack.

2 Heat the oil in a deep-fat fryer to 190°C, or until a small piece of bread browns in about 40 seconds.

3 Dry the artichokes well, cutting some of them in half to reveal their pretty insides if you like. Toss them in the seasoned flour, dusting off all the excess; this works well if you shake the artichokes in a sieve.

4 Deep-fry 6 artichokes at a time, for 2–3 minutes until they are golden brown and the leaves are crisp. Drain well on kitchen paper.

5 Pile the baby artichokes onto a serving plate. Sprinkle with sea salt and serve with the aioli (as shown).

Artichoke salad with hot bacon and mustard vinaigrette

Serves 4
4 braised artichoke hearts (see page 23)
4 rashers of streaky bacon
1 garlic clove
5 tbsp olive oil
1 tsp wholegrain mustard
1 tbsp red wine vinegar
100g mixed salad leaves
Salt and freshly ground black pepper

1 Cut each artichoke into 6 or 8 wedges, depending on their size. Derind the bacon rashers and cut into strips. Peel and crush the garlic.

2 Heat 2 tbsp of the olive oil in a frying pan, add the bacon and fry over a medium heat until lightly browned but not very crisp (or it will end up being tough). Add the garlic to the pan with the artichoke hearts and continue to fry for 2 minutes, stirring gently to make sure the garlic does not burn.

3 For the vinaigrette, in a small bowl, whisk together the mustard and wine vinegar, then gradually whisk in the remaining oil and season with salt and pepper.

4 Tip the dressing into the pan with the artichokes, then quickly stir through the salad leaves and pile onto 4 serving plates.

Jerusalem artichoke soup

Serves 4
1 small onion
60g butter
500ml milk
1 lemon (for acidulating)
600g Jerusalem artichokes
300ml chicken and veal stock
   (see page 96) or water
Salt and ground white pepper
Truffle oil, to drizzle

1 Halve, peel and finely slice the onion. Melt the butter in a saucepan, add the onion, cover and sweat until soft.

2 In another pan, scald the milk by heating it until it is steaming. Just before it bubbles, remove from the heat and leave it to cool.

3 Juice the lemon. Peel the artichokes and immerse them in cold water acidulated with the lemon juice.

4 When the onion is soft, drain and slice the artichokes and add them to the saucepan. Cook the artichokes gently for 10 minutes, stirring occasionally, to ensure the onion does not brown.

5 Add the milk and stock and season lightly with salt and pepper. Simmer very gently for 20 minutes without letting it boil, as this may cause the milk to curdle. To check that the artichokes are tender, insert a cutlery knife. When they are ready, remove from the heat and leave to cool a little.

6 Purée the soup in a blender, in batches, until completely smooth, then push through a sieve into a clean pan using a wooden spoon. Adjust the consistency with stock or water and check the seasoning; this soup needs to be generously seasoned. Reheat gently, as necessary. Serve lightly drizzled with truffle oil.

Variation

Jerusalem artichoke purée Follow the above recipe, but only add one-third to half the cooking liquor when blending the artichokes, to give a stiffer consistency.

A note on choosing Jerusalem artichokes...
Look for the least knobbly tubers and choose ones with a fairly regular shape, which are easier to peel. Their skins can be cream or a purple colour.

Asparagus

Homegrown asparagus is available for just 6 weeks of the year, during May and June. It has a superb flavour, far superior to that of imported asparagus, so don't miss out on its short season. Both green and white varieties are available. White asparagus is pale because it is kept covered with soil as it grows. It is more tender than green asparagus and has a much milder flavour.

Choose spears that are straight and firm. With white asparagus, opt for plump stalks. Young, thin green spears don't need peeling, but the lower half of thicker asparagus spears should be peeled.

Preparing asparagus

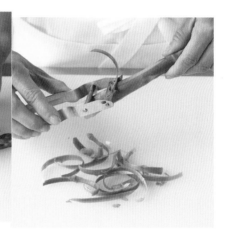

1 Bend the lower end of the asparagus stalk until it snaps. Discard the lower woody end.

2 Trim the spears with a sharp knife so they are all the same length.

3 If the spears are thick, peel away the skin from the lower half with a swivel peeler.

Griddled asparagus

Serves 4

700g asparagus, or at least 3–4 large
  spears per person
2 tbsp extra virgin olive oil, plus extra
  to drizzle
50g Manchego or Pecorino cheese
Salt and freshly ground black pepper

1 Wash and prepare the asparagus (as above), dry and turn through the olive oil in a bowl to coat fully. Shave the Manchego, using a swivel vegetable peeler.

2 Heat a griddle pan over a medium to high heat and griddle the asparagus in batches for 5–8 minutes, depending on size. Turn the asparagus occasionally to allow it to caramelise on all sides and cook evenly until tender.

3 Pile the asparagus onto a plate, drizzle with a little extra olive oil and sprinkle over some cheese shavings. Season with salt and pepper.

Variation

Griddled asparagus with roasted vine tomatoes Omit the cheese shavings. Place 4 small vines of cherry tomatoes in a roasting tin. Drizzle with 1–2 tbsp extra virgin olive oil and sprinkle with salt and pepper. Roast in an oven preheated to 200°C/gas mark 6, for 15–20 minutes until the tomatoes are just softening and their skins are just starting to burst. Combine with the asparagus once griddled and use the oil and tomato juices to drizzle over the asparagus and tomatoes.

Asparagus with hollandaise sauce

Serves 4

700g asparagus, or at least 3–4 large
  spears per person
1 quantity freshly made hollandaise
  (see page 120)
Sea salt and freshly ground black pepper

1 Prepare the asparagus spears by snapping off the woody ends, trimming the spears to the same length and peeling the lower half of the spears if they are thick (see page 25).

2 Keep the hollandaise warm in a bain marie off the heat.

3 Bring salted water to the boil either in an asparagus cooker, or in a deep sauté pan. If using an asparagus cooker, put the asparagus in stalk end downwards so the delicate tips stand proud and cook in the steam. Otherwise, lie the spears down in the pan, bring back to the boil, then lower the heat and simmer for 3 minutes or until the stem is just tender. Use the tip of a cutlery knife to check.

4 Remove the asparagus spears with a slotted spoon and drain well on kitchen paper. Pile onto individual plates and sprinkle with salt and pepper. Serve with the hollandaise sauce.

Variations

Asparagus with herby hollandaise Add about ½–1 tbsp coarsely chopped herbs such as parsley, chives, mint and tarragon to the hollandaise.

Asparagus with hollandaise and soft-boiled eggs Place a peeled, soft-boiled egg on top of each asparagus serving, before spooning over the hollandaise.

Asparagus with crushed Jersey Royals and hollandaise Boil or steam 150g Jersey Royals or small new potatoes until tender. While still hot, crush with a fork to break into fairly large pieces. Sauté in a frying pan in a little butter until browning and crisp, and spoon over the asparagus before the hollandaise.

Asparagus and samphire with brown shrimps and new potatoes

Serves 4

200g small new potatoes, ideally
  Jersey Royals
250g fine asparagus spears
150g fresh samphire
Handful of tarragon sprigs
2 x 57g tubs of potted shrimps
30g butter
Squeeze of lemon juice
Salt and freshly ground black pepper

1 Put the potatoes into a pan of simmering salted water, bring back to the boil, then lower the heat and simmer for about 15 minutes until they are tender. Drain and allow them to steam-dry in a colander.

2 Meanwhile, prepare the asparagus spears by snapping off the woody ends, trimming the spears to the same length and peeling the lower half of the spears if they are thick (see page 25). Cut the spears in half lengthways. Bring a pan of salted water to the boil and blanch the asparagus spears for 1 minute, then refresh in cold water and drain them.

3 Wash the samphire, picking off and discarding any coarse ends. Pick the tarragon leaves off their stalks. Cut the cooked potatoes into halves or quarters, depending on their size.

4 Heat a large, heavy-based frying pan over a medium heat. Add the potted shrimps with all their butter and the extra butter. When the butter has melted, remove the shrimps with a slotted spoon. Increase the heat and add the potatoes, asparagus and samphire. Stir-fry for 2 minutes until it is all piping hot.

5 Return the shrimps to the pan and stir in the tarragon. Season generously with salt and pepper and add a squeeze of lemon juice to taste. Pile onto a serving dish or individual plates.

Note You can use 500g whole cooked brown shrimps and 50g butter in place of the potted shrimps. You will need to peel the shrimps before using.

Aubergine

This vegetable is highly prized in Mediterranean, Middle Eastern and Indian cookery. When buying, look for smooth, shiny, unblemished skins and select aubergines that feel heavy. Aubergines must be cooked through, at which point they become creamy and delicious. Prone to soaking up water and oil, they sometimes need to be degorged before cooking (see below). Once degorged, they are ideal for mixing with many other flavourful ingredients such as tomato, garlic and spices, whose flavours they will absorb.

Aubergine and panch phoran pie

Serves 6–8
2 large aubergines
2 large red peppers
3 large potatoes
3 onions
Small bunch of coriander
5–6 tbsp olive oil
2 garlic cloves
2cm piece of fresh root ginger
1½ tsp ground turmeric
1½ tsp ground cumin
1½ tsp ground coriander
½ tsp chilli powder
2 tsp panch phoran
100g tomato purée
150–200ml water
75g butter
1 packet of filo pastry, about 225g
Salt and freshly ground black pepper

1 Prepare the vegetables: cut the aubergines into 2cm cubes and the red peppers into similar-sized squares. Peel the potatoes and cut them into 2cm cubes. Halve, peel and finely slice the onions. Chop the coriander leaves and set aside.

2 Heat 1–2 tbsp olive oil in a frying pan and fry the aubergines and peppers, in batches to avoid overcrowding, over a medium heat until lightly coloured, adding more oil to the pan as necessary.

3 Meanwhile, heat 2 tbsp olive oil in a large frying pan. Add the potatoes and cook over a low heat for 10 minutes, then add the onions. Cook until both are soft and lightly golden.

4 In the meantime, peel and crush the garlic, and peel and grate the ginger. Add both to the potato mixture and cook for 1 minute. Add the turmeric, cumin, coriander, chilli and panch phoran and cook over a medium heat until the mustard seeds start to 'pop'.

5 Add the aubergine and red pepper to the pan with the tomato purée. Season well with salt and pepper and stir in enough water so it is not too thick to simmer. Bring to a simmer and cook gently for 30 minutes to let the flavours develop, adding a little extra water during cooking if necessary. Take off the heat and leave to cool, then stir in the coriander. Meanwhile, heat the oven to 200°C/gas mark 6.

6 Melt the butter. Pile the vegetable mixture into a rectangular baking dish, about 30 x 20cm. Cover with 5 or 6 layers of filo pastry, brushing each sheet with melted butter and crumpling the top layer for a decorative effect. Bake in the oven for 30 minutes, or until the filling is hot and the filo is a deep golden colour and crisp.

A note on panch phoran...
This is a Bengali five-spice mix of cumin, fennel, nigella, fenugreek and mustard seeds.

Degorging
This is the process of salting to extract water from vegetables with a high water content. It is no longer necessary to degorge cultivated aubergines to extract bitter juices but degorging can be applied to aubergines, courgettes and potatoes to prevent excess oil absorption during cooking. To degorge, spread the vegetable slices out in a colander over a bowl and salt lightly. Leave for 15–30 minutes (just 10 minutes for potatoes or they will discolour). During this time the salt extracts some water, which drains away. The vegetables can then be squeezed to remove any excess moisture, or if you feel the vegetables may be over-salted, rinse and dry well before proceeding with the recipe.

Fried aubergines with garlic and minted yoghurt

Serves 4
2 large aubergines
2 garlic cloves
Olive oil for frying
Salt and freshly ground black pepper

For the minted yoghurt
Handful of mint sprigs
300g Greek yoghurt
2 tsp pomegranate molasses

1 Cut the aubergines into 1cm thick slices, either lengthways or horizontally. Place in a colander and sprinkle lightly but evenly with salt (about 1 tsp). Leave to degorge (see page 28) for about 30 minutes, then rinse quickly with cold water and pat dry with kitchen paper. Meanwhile, peel and crush the garlic.

2 Heat 2 tbsp olive oil in a large frying pan. You will need to fry the aubergines in 2 or 3 batches, depending on your pan. Add the first batch and fry over a medium heat for 3–4 minutes until golden brown, then repeat on the other side. Remove from the pan and repeat with the remaining slices, heating more oil for each batch.

3 Return all the fried aubergine to the pan and add the garlic. Cook, stirring gently so the slices do not break up, for 2 minutes. Season to taste.

4 Chop or chiffonade (see page 89) enough mint leaves to give you 2 tbsp. Put the yoghurt in a bowl, drizzle over the molasses and sprinkle on the mint. Fold gently to give a marbled effect. Serve the aubergine slices with the yoghurt mixture, garnished with extra mint leaves.

Note This is also delicious served with tomato and basil salsa (see page 127) in place of the minted yoghurt.

Moutabal

Serves 4
2 aubergines
4 garlic cloves
2 tbsp olive oil
1 tbsp tahini
3 tbsp Greek yoghurt
1 tsp pomegranate molasses
½ lemon, or to taste
Salt and freshly ground black pepper
½ tbsp flat-leaf parsley leaves, to finish

Moutabal is a Middle Eastern aubergine dip often served as part of a selection of mezze dishes.

1 Heat the oven to 190°C/gas mark 5.

2 Prepare the aubergines by cutting a very shallow incision through the skin of each aubergine, 1–2mm deep, from the stem end to the bottom, every 2–3cm around the aubergine. This will make them easier to peel after cooking.

3 Place each scored aubergine directly on the gas hob with the heat turned up high (or place under a hot grill). Turn every few minutes using tongs (as shown), until all the skin is black and blistered, then transfer to a baking sheet.

4 Brush the unpeeled garlic cloves with a little of the olive oil and put them on the baking sheet with the aubergines. Bake in the oven until the aubergines and the garlic cloves are all completely soft, about 30 minutes. The garlic may be soft before the aubergine, in which case remove it from the tray and leave the aubergines to cook for longer.

5 Squeeze the garlic cloves to extract the soft interior and discard the skin; set aside until needed.

6 Once the aubergines are soft, leave to cool a little, then peel off the skin, cut off the stalk and discard. Roughly chop the flesh, put it in a sieve and allow to drain for 15–20 minutes to remove any excess water.

7 Once drained, place the aubergine flesh in a food processor and add the garlic, remaining olive oil, tahini, yoghurt and pomegranate molasses. Pulse until the mixture is well blended but not completely smooth.

8 Scoop the mixture into a bowl. Juice the ½ lemon. Flavour the mixture with lemon juice, salt and pepper to taste. Serve the moutabal garnished with whole or torn parsley leaves.

Avocado

Depending on the variety, a ripe avocado has either green or darkish brown skin. The skin of the common Hass variety is green when under-ripe, then becomes pitted and almost black when fully ripened. A ripe avocado yields gently to a little pressure when held. Prone to bruising, avocados must be treated carefully when prepared. They also discolour (oxidise) easily (see page 18), so cut sides should be rubbed with a little lemon juice if they are not being served immediately.

Preparing avocados

  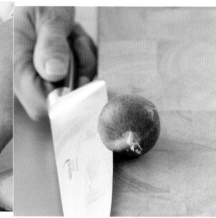

1 Halve the avocados and remove the stone by placing each avocado half on a board and firmly inserting a large, sharp knife in the stone, keeping your fingers well away.

2 Twist the knife, which should help to release the stone. Lift the stone out of the avocado half.

3 Drag the knife against the side of the board to release the stone from the knife.

Guacamole

Serves 4
1 spring onion
1 garlic clove
1 green chilli
Small bunch of coriander
½ lime, plus extra to taste (optional)
2 ripe avocados
Salt and freshly ground black pepper

1 Finely slice the spring onion, including plenty of the green part. Peel and crush the garlic, finely chop the chilli and chop enough coriander leaves to give you 2 tbsp. Juice the ½ lime.

2 Halve the avocados and remove the stones (see above). Mash the flesh in the skin with a fork, which ensures you get all the best green coloured flesh away from the skin. Scoop the avocado flesh into a bowl and stir in the lime juice, which will stop it turning brown.

3 Stir through the prepared spring onion, garlic, chilli and coriander to taste.

4 Season the guacamole with plenty of salt and pepper and add more lime juice to taste if required. Garnish with extra coriander leaves and serve at room temperature. If not serving immediately, cover the surface closely with cling film, before you add the coriander leaves, then refrigerate until needed.

Avocado and spring onion salad with soy and mirin dressing

Serves 4
¼ iceberg lettuce
4 spring onions
2 avocados, ripe but not overly soft

For the dressing
½ lemon
2 tbsp light soy sauce
2 tsp mirin
1 tsp wasabi paste
Pinch of Chinese five-spice powder
1 tbsp toasted sesame oil
2 tbsp sunflower oil

1 First make the dressing. Finely grate the zest from the lemon and squeeze enough juice to give you 1 tbsp. Whisk the lemon zest and 1 tbsp juice together with the rest of the ingredients, adding more soy, lemon juice or five-spice powder to taste if desired.

2 Wash and dry the lettuce leaves and tear into bite-sized pieces. Slice the spring onions finely on the diagonal, using as much of the green as possible.

3 Halve the avocados and remove the stones (see page 31), then peel and cut into even slices or chunks.

4 Place the salad ingredients in a bowl and toss gently with the dressing, taking care not to mash the avocado.

Avocado fattoush with za'atar crisps

Serves 4
1 lemon
120ml olive oil
Small bunch of mint
Small bunch of flat-leaf parsley
1 Little Gem lettuce
4 spring onions
1 small cucumber
4 tomatoes
1 large, ripe avocado
Sea salt and freshly ground black pepper

For the za'atar crisps
2 pitta breads
Za'atar, to sprinkle
Olive oil, for brushing

1 Heat the oven to 200°C/gas mark 6.

2 Finely grate the zest from half of the lemon; halve the lemon and squeeze the juice from both halves. Put the lemon zest and juice in a bowl with some salt and pepper. Whisk in the olive oil. Roughly chop half the mint and parsley leaves and add them to the dressing. Chiffonade the remaining herbs (see page 89) and the lettuce leaves and set aside.

3 Slice the spring onions on the diagonal, including plenty of the green part. Peel, halve, deseed and dice the cucumber. Dice the tomatoes. Add the spring onions, cucumber and tomatoes to the dressing.

4 For the za'atar crisps, lightly toast the pitta breads in a toaster or under the grill, until puffing up but not too brown. Cut all around the edge and split them open. Lay the flat pieces on a baking sheet and brush with olive oil. Sprinkle with a little za'atar and bake for 5 minutes, or until crisp and brown. Break or cut into pieces.

5 When ready to serve, halve the avocado and remove the stone (see page 31), then peel each half and cut the flesh into chunks. Add to the salad with the lettuce and remaining herbs and toss through, then adjust the seasoning.

6 Pile the fattoush onto individual serving plates and top with the za'atar crisps. This is also delicious served with plain grilled chicken or fish, brushed with oil and sprinkled with za'atar or sumac before cooking.

A note on za'atar...
This Middle Eastern condiment is a mixture of sesame seeds, dried herbs and ground sumac (a lemony flavoured spice). To make your own, lightly toast 2 tbsp sesame seeds in a dry frying pan over a low to medium heat. Tip onto a plate and set aside to cool. Put the cooled sesame seeds in a small food processor bowl with 50g sumac, 2 tbsp dried thyme, 1 tbsp dried oregano, ½ tbsp dried marjoram and 1 tsp coarse sea salt and pulse until ground to a coarse consistency. Za'atar is delicious as a dip for crudités or stirred through yoghurt to make a sauce for grilled meats. Makes 150–200g.

Beans, mangetout, sugar snaps, peas and broad beans

When choosing green beans, whether fine or runner, select those that snap easily and are crisp and juicy. Mangetout and sugar snaps should also be crisp and firm. Peas in their pods, in season from June to September, should be chosen for the pods' bright green satiny colour. They should be round and full. Petit pois are just very young peas. Broad beans, in season from May to June, should have pale green pods with a satiny bloom, and feel soft and tender.

Preparing beans, mangetout and sugar snaps

Fine green beans require topping only. If young and tender they can be left whole.

Runner beans need to be topped and the string running the length of the bean removed either by pulling or cutting off.

Mangetout and sugar snaps also require topping and de-stringing. These are both more tender than green and runner beans and only require brief cooking.

Preparing peas and broad beans

1 To pod broad beans (or peas), squeeze the pod until it 'pops'.

2 Run your finger down the inside of the pod to release the beans (or peas) into a bowl.

3 Unless very young, broad beans also need to have their pale outer skin removed. Blanch for 30 seconds (see page 34), then refresh. Pinch the end of the skin to release the bean.

Blanching and refreshing vegetables

Vegetables are blanched for a variety of reasons – to partially cook them to reduce their final cooking time, to set their colour, to soften their texture or to remove strong flavours or bitterness. Soft fruits such as tomatoes and peaches, as well as shallots and baby onions, are blanched to make them easier to peel. Vegetables should be of the same size to ensure even cooking.

Blanching requires plunging the vegetable or fruit into boiling, usually salted, water, bringing the water back to the boil as swiftly as possible, cooking for the required amount of time (taken from the point of return to the boil), then removing the vegetables or fruit and submerging them immediately into ice-cold water to stop the cooking process and set the colour. As soon as the vegetables are cool, remove them from the cold water to prevent them from absorbing water, and leave to drain thoroughly.

Don't blanch too many vegetables at one time, as this will lower the temperature of the water too much; instead blanch in batches.

Vegetables are sometimes blanched, but not refreshed, when they are added to other ingredients and the dish is cooked further, for example roast parsnips.

1 Plunge the vegetable into a pan of boiling water (usually salted) and return to the boil as quickly as possible.

2 Have ready a bowl of cold water with ice cubes added. After the required blanching time, remove the vegetables from the boiling water and immerse in the ice-cold water to refresh.

3 As soon as the vegetables are cold, remove them from the water with a slotted spoon and drain thoroughly.

Fine green beans with almonds

Serves 4
250g fine green beans
10g butter
15g flaked almonds
Salt and freshly ground black pepper

1 Top the green beans. Bring a large pan of salted water to the boil, add the beans and cook for about 4 minutes, or until they are nearly tender and starting to lose their 'squeakiness'.

2 Meanwhile, melt the butter in a frying pan and when it foams, stir in the flaked almonds. Cook until the almonds start to lightly brown, then, to ensure they colour evenly, remove from the heat and stir continuously as they finish browning.

3 Drain the green beans and stir into the buttery almonds. Season well with salt and pepper.

Note You can use finely sliced runner beans instead of green beans for this recipe and the variations below.

Variations

Fine green beans with tarragon and garlic Omit the almonds and cook a crushed ½ garlic clove in the butter until lightly golden. Stir 2 tbsp roughly chopped tarragon in with the beans.

Fine green beans with hazelnuts and lemon Use roughly chopped skinned hazelnuts in place of the almonds, and add ½ tsp finely grated lemon zest at the end, with a squeeze of lemon juice to taste.

Fine green bean and tomato salad with salsa verde

Serves 4
250g fine green beans
125g cherry tomatoes

For the salsa verde dressing
½ shallot
40ml white wine vinegar
50ml olive oil
1 tbsp capers
½ lemon
Small bunch of parsley
½ tsp caster sugar
Salt and freshly ground black pepper

1 Top the green beans. Bring a large pan of salted water to the boil, add the beans and blanch for 3–4 minutes, then refresh them in cold water. Drain well and pat dry with kitchen paper.

2 Cut the cherry tomatoes into halves or quarters, depending on their size; set them aside.

3 To make the salsa verde dressing, peel and finely chop the shallot, place in a large bowl and whisk in the wine vinegar and olive oil. Rinse, drain and finely chop the capers. Finely grate the zest from the lemon and squeeze the juice; set aside. Finely chop enough parsley leaves to give you 2 tbsp, then stir into the dressing with the capers and lemon zest. Season with the sugar, and salt and pepper.

4 Add the tomatoes and beans to the dressing in the bowl and toss to make sure everything is well coated. Add lemon juice to taste and adjust the seasoning.

Variation

Fine green bean salad with coriander and chilli Omit the lemon zest and capers. To the dressing, add the finely grated zest of ¼ lime, ¼ red chilli, finely chopped, and 1½ tbsp chopped coriander leaves.

Broad bean, pea, feta and mint salad

Serves 4
1 onion
2 tbsp olive oil
2kg broad beans in pods (to yield about 500g podded)
1kg peas in pods (to yield about 350g podded)
50g feta
½ lemon
10–12 mint leaves
Salt and freshly ground black pepper

1 Halve, peel and finely slice the onion. Heat 1 tbsp of the olive oil in a small saucepan over a low to medium heat, add the onion, cover and sweat for 4–5 minutes, then remove the lid and allow to caramelise until golden. Remove from the heat and set aside to cool.

2 Pod and blanch the broad beans in boiling salted water for 3–4 minutes, then refresh in cold water and skin them. Pod the peas, blanch for 1–3 minutes until tender, then refresh in cold water.

3 Crumble the feta. Finely grate the zest from the lemon and squeeze the juice. Chiffonade the mint leaves (see page 89).

4 Combine the onion, broad beans, peas, feta, mint, remaining olive oil and the lemon zest in a bowl. Season with the lemon juice, and salt and pepper to taste.

Variations

Broad bean, pea, Jersey Royal and ham hock salad Replace half the broad beans and the feta with 200g boiled, small, new season Jersey Royal potatoes, halved if necessary, and 100g shredded, cooked ham hock.

Broad bean, pea, Jersey Royal and chorizo salad Replace half the broad beans and feta with 200g boiled, small, new season Jersey Royal potatoes, halved if necessary, and 100g peeled and sliced cooking chorizo. Fry the chorizo slices until crisp, cool slightly, then crumble and add to the salad with 1 tbsp coarsely chopped flat-leaf parsley and ½ tbsp finely shredded preserved lemon.

Braised peas and baby onions

Serves 4
150g baby onions
1 garlic clove
30g butter
250g peas, shelled or frozen
100ml water
1 tsp caster sugar
Few mint sprigs
Small handful of flat-leaf parsley sprigs
Salt and freshly ground black pepper

1 Heat the oven to 170°C/gas mark 3.

2 Blanch the onions in boiling water for about 15 seconds, then remove and allow to cool (this will make them much easier to peel). Peel the onions and trim the fibres off the root but leave the onion intact. Peel and chop the garlic.

3 Melt the butter in an ovenproof casserole which has a tight-fitting lid. Add the onions and cook gently for 5 minutes so they start to soften but not brown.

4 Add the garlic and cook for 1 minute, then stir in the peas, water, sugar, mint and a few of the parsley sprigs. Season well with salt and pepper.

5 Cover the pea and onion mixture with a damp cartouche (see page 13) and, if the lid is not tight-fitting, use foil or 'luting' paste (see page 448) to ensure the pan is well sealed. Braise in the oven for about 1 hour until the peas are completely soft and the onion is tender.

6 Check the seasoning of the liquid and remove the herb sprigs, squeezing out any juice. Chop enough leaves of the remaining parsley sprigs to give you 1 tbsp and stir through the braised peas and onions just before serving.

Note The juices can be reduced to a stronger flavour through gentle boiling. Strain and reserve the peas and onions first or they will overcook in the reducing juices. Add them back to the juices once the desired flavour is reached.

Beetroot and parsnips

Like carrots, these two root vegetables are prized for their sweetness. Beetroots are, of course, commonly dark red, but they are also available in other colours, including golden yellow and pink and white candy striped. Ruby red beetroot, with its capacity to 'bleed' very easily, should be kept separate from other vegetables when preparing and cooking, as it will turn everything a vibrant pink.

Choose firm, unwrinkled parsnips and beetroot. When you are buying parsnips choose small or medium ones, as the larger ones tend to have a more woody interior.

Salad of beetroot, goat's cheese and candied pecans

Serves 4
2 crottin goat's cheeses (firm, small individual cheeses)
Small handful of thyme sprigs
2–3 tbsp olive oil, plus extra to drizzle
500g uncooked baby beetroot
100g lamb's lettuce

For the candied pecans
100g pecan nut halves
1 tbsp icing sugar
Pinch of ground cinnamon
Pinch of cayenne pepper
Olive oil, to drizzle

For the dressing
1 tsp Dijon mustard
1 tbsp red wine vinegar
2 tbsp olive oil
Sea salt and freshly ground black pepper

1 Heat the oven to 200°C/gas mark 6.

2 Cut the crottins in half horizontally and place in a bowl. Finely chop enough thyme leaves to give you 2 tsp and stir into the oil. Trickle the thyme flavoured oil over the goat's cheese and set aside.

3 Wash the beetroot and cut off the tops, leaving about 1cm tufty stem still attached, then trim the root (as shown). Place the beetroot in a bowl and toss in enough olive oil to coat. Season generously with salt and pepper and add a few thyme sprigs.

4 Tip the beetroot into a roasting tin lined with foil and roast for 45–60 minutes, or until tender. Check for tenderness with the point of a cutlery knife. When the beetroot is tender, allow it to cool a little, then slip the skins off with your fingers (as shown). They are easier to peel from the root end to the stalk. Cut into halves or wedges, depending on their size.

5 While the beetroot is cooking, prepare the candied pecans. Put the pecans into a bowl, pour boiling water over them, then drain well. Sift the icing sugar, cinnamon and cayenne together into another bowl, add the pecans and toss them in the icing sugar mixture. Line a baking sheet with silicone paper, lay the nuts out on the paper and drizzle with olive oil. Bake in the oven for 5 minutes, or until golden brown. They may need to be turned over once when they have just started to brown.

6 To make the dressing, mix the mustard and wine vinegar together in a small bowl and season well with salt and pepper. Whisk in the 2 tbsp olive oil. Taste and adjust the seasoning.

7 When ready to serve, heat the grill to its highest setting. Place the 4 half crottins on a baking sheet, sprinkle with pepper and grill until hot (or use a blow torch). Toss the lamb's lettuce in the dressing and pile onto 4 plates. Arrange the beetroot and pecan nuts over the lettuce and top each with a grilled goat's cheese half.

Note The cheese can be marinated in advance for a more distinct flavour.

Hot raw beetroot with black pepper and lemon

Serves 4
500g uncooked beetroot
¼–½ lemon, to taste
60g butter
Salt and freshly ground black pepper

1 Peel the beetroot using a vegetable peeler, wearing rubber gloves as the colour will stain your hands.

2 Cut the beetroot into julienne (as for carrot julienne, see page 16), use a mandolin with a julienne cutter or grate coarsely. Squeeze the juice from the lemon and set aside.

3 Melt the butter in a large, heavy-based frying pan over a high heat until foaming. Add the beetroot and sauté for 2–3 minutes, by which time it will be hot and dry but not cooked through. Season well with salt, plenty of pepper and lemon juice to taste.

Variations

Horseradish and dill beetroot Add 1–2 tbsp grated horseradish and 1 tbsp dill to the beetroot with the lemon juice.

Mustard beetroot Add 1 heaped tsp wholegrain mustard when adding the beetroot to the pan.

Roast parsnips

Serves 4
3–4 parsnips
Oil, goose fat, or fat from a roast joint
Salt and freshly ground black pepper

1 Heat the oven to 200°C/gas mark 6.

2 Wash and peel the parsnips, then cut them into even-sized chunks. The easiest way to do this is to cut them across in half, then cut the thicker end into quarters and the thinner end lengthways in half again.

3 Put enough oil or fat (or a combination of the two) into a roasting tin large enough to hold the parsnips in a single, not tightly packed layer to give a depth of 2–3mm. Put in the oven to heat.

4 Meanwhile, blanch the parsnips in boiling water for 5 minutes, or until they are beginning to soften. Drain well and allow them to steam-dry for a few minutes. Season with salt and pepper.

5 When the oil is piping hot, remove the roasting tin from the oven and add the parsnips (they should sizzle). Roast in the oven for about 30 minutes, or until crisp and golden, turning them occasionally as they roast, to ensure an even colour.

Variations

Honey roast parsnips Drizzle 1 tbsp clear honey over the parsnips when they have just started to brown, and turn them every 10 minutes or so until golden, to prevent the honey burning.

Parmesan and thyme crusted parsnips Toss the blanched, drained parsnips in a mixture of 30g grated Parmesan and ½ tsp chopped thyme. Season with plenty of salt and pepper before roasting.

Roast celeriac Peel and cut 500g celeriac into 4–5cm chunks, cook in acidulated water (water to which a splash of vinegar or the juice of a lemon has been added) for 5 minutes, then proceed as for the roast parsnips.

Roast beetroot Scrub 500g beetroot well to remove grit, cut into wedges, then toss in oil and roast without blanching. They will take about 45–60 minutes; test with the point of a cutlery knife for tenderness.

Broccoli and cauliflower

These vegetables are from the same family. When choosing broccoli or cauliflower look for a firm, tight compact head and stem. Broccoli should be a deep green colour; cauliflower should be pale white or creamy; avoid any with discoloured patches. Sprouting broccoli, available during February and March, has smaller heads and a longer, leafier stem. Tenderstem broccoli, as the name suggests, has a very tender stem and a mild flavour.

It is very easy to overcook broccoli and cauliflower, particularly as their florets and stems have different cooking times. Broccoli florets tend to fall apart very easily and lose their vibrant green colour, so take care when cooking them.

Steaming broccoli

1 To prepare a head of broccoli (about 550g), cut off and reserve the thick stalk. Trim the florets neatly, ideally at an angle. If the florets are very large, halve them. Trim the reserved stalk and cut into batons (as for carrot batons, see page 16).

2 Prepare a steamer, ensuring the water is gently boiling when the broccoli is placed in the basket. Place the stem batons in first, cover and steam them for a minute or two before adding the rest of the broccoli, ideally in one layer. Sprinkle lightly with salt and put the lid back on.

3 Steam for 4–6 minutes, until the stem is just tender when tested with a cutlery knife. The florets will be cooked when the stem is tender.

Steaming

Steaming is the cooking of food in hot vapours over boiling liquid, usually so the food never comes into contact with the liquid. Steaming can be either direct or indirect.

Direct steaming is when the food, placed in a steamer basket, comes into direct contact with the steam. It is a very 'clean' and healthy way of cooking as no fat is required, there is no browning, and any loss of flavour, vitamins or minerals is minimal, as the ingredients are not submerged in liquid into which the flavour, vitamins and minerals can be transferred. Most vegetables, fish and poultry are suitable for steaming.

Indirect steaming involves placing the food in a container first, before steaming. This process takes longer as the heat has to penetrate the container first, before coming into contact with the food. This method is used for steamed puddings (see page 546).

Stir-fry of tenderstem broccoli, chilli, garlic and lemon

Serves 4
500g tenderstem broccoli
1–2 red chillies, depending on their heat
1 garlic clove
2cm piece of fresh root ginger
1 lemon
1 tbsp sunflower oil
2 tbsp sesame oil
2 tbsp light soy sauce, or to taste
1 tbsp mirin (rice wine)

1 Trim the broccoli to remove any very coarse stem at the base. Bring a pan of water to the boil, add the broccoli and blanch for 2 minutes, then refresh in cold water and drain very well.

2 Finely slice the chilli(es), peel and finely slice the garlic, and peel and grate the ginger. Finely grate the zest from the lemon and squeeze the juice from one half.

3 Heat both oils in a wok until they start to smoke, then add the chilli(es), ginger and garlic. Stir briefly, then add the broccoli and stir until it is heated through and starts to char slightly. Before the garlic gets too dark, add the soy sauce, mirin, lemon zest and half the lemon juice. Allow to bubble and reduce briefly so the sauce clings to the broccoli.

4 Taste and add more soy sauce or lemon juice as required.

Variation

Stir-fry of broccoli with sesame seeds Omit the chilli and ginger and add 1 tbsp lightly toasted sesame seeds to the broccoli at the end of cooking.

Purple sprouting broccoli with salsa verde butter sauce

Serves 4
500g purple sprouting broccoli
Salt and freshly ground black pepper

For the sauce
2 garlic cloves
3–4 anchovy fillets in oil
2 tbsp baby capers
Large bunch of flat-leaf parsley
Small bunch of mint
100g butter
1–2 tsp Dijon mustard
Squeeze of lemon juice

1 For the sauce, peel and crush the garlic, drain and roughly chop the anchovies, and rinse and drain the capers. Roughly chop the parsley and mint (you need about 3 times as much parsley as mint).

2 Bring a large pan of salted water to the boil. Trim any coarse stalks from the broccoli. Add the broccoli to the boiling water and simmer until it is becoming tender, about 2–3 minutes.

3 While the broccoli is cooking, heat the butter in a large frying pan or wok until beginning to brown, then add the garlic, anchovies and capers and cook for 1 minute. Remove from the heat and stir in the mustard, a little squeeze of lemon juice to taste, then the chopped herbs.

4 Drain the broccoli in a colander as soon as it is ready and, while still warm, toss with the dressing and season to taste with salt and pepper. Serve at once.

Boiling and simmering

In these methods of cooking, food is submerged fully in liquid, more often than not water. It is either cooked at a fast and vigorous bubbling, known as a rolling boil, or at a gentle bubbling, known as simmering.

Salting water for cooking vegetables

The ratio of salt to water when cooking vegetables is generally 1 tsp salt to 1 litre water.

Boiling

When quick cooking is required of a fairly robust ingredient, such as cauliflower or some pulses, then you need a high heat initially to bring the water to a rapid boil. Add the food when the water comes to the boil, then keep the heat high while the water returns to a rolling boil.

For most foods, you then turn down the heat to a gentle boil (with not quite so rapid bubbling).

For rice and pasta, you need a rolling boil throughout the cooking process, as the rapid movement of the water also helps to prevent the grains or pasta sticking together, with the surface starch rapidly washed off into the water.

Root vegetables require a lid, other vegetables do not, especially vibrantly coloured vegetables which would lose colour if cooked with a lid on.

A gentle boil, with no lid, is also used to evaporate moisture when necessary, for example when reducing stocks and sauces.

Simmering

Simmering is the continuous breaking of the surface of a liquid with small bubbles. As with boiling, the liquid is initially brought up to a rapid bubbling (a boil), then immediately the heat is turned down to low to medium, to allow for gentler cooking. Simmering is used for slow cooking, where the ingredient(s) will need a fairly long time to soften and/or develop flavour, or they are are prone to breaking up easily. Pulses and sauces, such as tomato and ragù, are simmered.

Poaching (see page 539) is gentler than simmering and used for delicate foods, such as eggs, fish and chicken breasts.

Cauliflower cheese

Serves 4
1 large cauliflower
50g cheese, either Gruyère, strong
   Cheddar, Parmesan or a mixture
20g butter
20g plain flour
Pinch of English mustard powder
Pinch of cayenne pepper
300ml milk
1 tbsp dried white breadcrumbs
Salt and ground white pepper

1 Cut the cauliflower into even-sized florets. Bring a large pan of salted water to the boil and cook the cauliflower until just tender, about 4 minutes. Drain well.

2 Meanwhile, make the cheese sauce. Grate the cheese and set aside. Melt the butter in a heavy-based saucepan over a gentle heat, then stir in the flour, mustard and cayenne. Mix to a smooth paste and cook for 1 minute.

3 Remove the saucepan from the heat and gradually start to add the milk, a little at a time, stirring and incorporating it well into the roux as you add it. As more of the milk is added, the sauce will start to loosen and thin. Once a third to half of the milk has been incorporated off the heat, add the remaining milk in generous additions and return the saucepan to the heat.

4 Increase the heat to medium to high and stir the sauce constantly as you bring it to the boil. Then turn down the heat and simmer for 2 minutes.

5 Meanwhile, heat the grill to its highest setting.

6 Off the heat, stir all but 2 tbsp of the grated cheese into the sauce, allowing it to melt in the heat of the sauce. Taste and season with salt and pepper and then stir in the drained cauliflower until it is well coated with sauce.

7 Transfer to an ovenproof dish, placing the more attractive florets uppermost and spooning over any remaining sauce. Mix the breadcrumbs with the remaining cheese and sprinkle over the top. Grill until the topping is golden and bubbling.

Note If making the cauliflower cheese in advance, cool it once assembled and refrigerate. Before serving, bake in an oven preheated to 180°C/gas mark 4 for about 30 minutes until golden.

Variations

Cauliflower cheese with pancetta and Parmesan Cut 100g derinded pancetta into cubes and fry over a moderate heat until golden brown, then stir into the sauce with the cauliflower. Use 50g grated Parmesan in place of the above breadcrumb and cheese topping.

Broccoli gratin with blue cheese Use broccoli in place of the cauliflower. Stir 25g grated Cheddar into the sauce and cool slightly before adding 25g crumbled blue cheese, which should not entirely melt. Sprinkle with the mixed crumbs and 2 tbsp grated cheese and proceed as for the main recipe.

Baked leeks with cheese Use 2–3 leeks in place of the cauliflower. Cut the leeks into 5cm lengths and wash them well. Boil until tender, about 6 minutes, then drain well. Proceed as for the main recipe.

Roasted cauliflower with beurre noisette, almonds and sherry vinegar

Serves 4
1 medium cauliflower
2 tbsp olive oil
50g butter
50g Marcona almonds
½ tbsp sherry vinegar, or to taste
Salt and freshly ground black pepper

1 Heat the oven to 200°C/gas mark 6.

2 Break the cauliflower into large bite-sized florets and toss in a bowl with the olive oil and a little seasoning. Transfer to a roasting tin and roast in the oven for 20 minutes, turning occasionally to encourage even browning.

3 When the cauliflower is almost tender (test the stem with the point of a cutlery knife), add the butter. Allow it to melt and continue to roast the cauliflower for a further 10 minutes, basting with the butter occasionally. Meanwhile, slice the almonds into slivers.

4 When the butter becomes a light beurre noisette (see page 114), add the slivered almonds and return to the oven to allow them to toast in the butter for a further 5 minutes, basting the cauliflower once or twice.

5 Add the sherry vinegar to taste and adjust the seasoning. Pile the cauliflower and almonds into a serving dish and spoon over the beurre noisette.

Variations

Add 50g chopped or shredded Ibérico ham with the butter. You can also add ½ tbsp baby capers with the sherry vinegar.

Cauliflower soup with truffle oil

Serves 4
1 small cauliflower
1 small onion
1 celery stick
1 garlic clove
1 small floury potato
30g butter
750ml chicken and veal stock (see page 96) or vegetable stock (see page 101)
150ml double cream
Salt and ground white pepper
Truffle oil, to finish

1 First prepare the vegetables. Cut the cauliflower into florets, discarding only the central core. Halve, peel and finely slice the onion, de-string and finely slice the celery, and peel and crush the garlic. Peel and cut the potato into 2cm dice.

2 Melt the butter in a heavy-based saucepan, add the onion and celery, cover and sweat over a gentle heat until softened. Add the cauliflower and garlic and cook for 2 minutes.

3 Add the potato and stock and season lightly with salt and pepper. Simmer until the cauliflower and potato are soft, about 15–20 minutes. Push a piece of potato against the side of the saucepan; if cooked, it will break up easily.

4 Allow the soup to cool slightly, before blitzing in a blender until smooth. Pass the soup through a sieve into a clean saucepan. Add the cream and more stock if necessary to loosen the soup to the consistency of single cream. Taste and adjust the seasoning and serve drizzled with a little truffle oil.

Variation

Spiced cauliflower soup Omit the truffle oil. Add ¼ tsp each of ground turmeric, chilli powder, ground coriander and cumin, and a pinch of asafoetida, with the cauliflower. Omit the cream and increase the stock to 1 litre. Serve the soup garnished with coriander sprigs, with hot naan bread on the side.

Chicory, leeks and fennel

More often used in salads, chicory (also known as Belgian endive) is also good braised and served with rich meats, as its natural slight bitterness helps to act as a foil to the richness of the meat. Look for tight, crisp pear-shaped chicory. Radicchio is an Italian red-leafed chicory; there are several varieties including Treviso, which closely resembles chicory in shape.

Leeks have a delicate oniony flavour. They are most often eaten cooked, and lend themselves well to chicken, fish, egg and creamy dishes. Look for firm, straight, medium-sized leeks, as larger, old leeks can have a woody core. It is essential to wash leeks thoroughly as they harbour grit in their green tops, between the tightly packed leaves. It is better to wash them after cutting as the grit between the layers is difficult to remove when the leeks are whole.

Fennel has a distinctive aniseed flavour. It is eaten both raw, in salads, and cooked and eaten on its own, or used to flavour dishes. Choose rounded bulbs that are white, with tight leaves.

Chicory tatin

Serves 4
200g puff pastry (see page 508, or use ready-made)
4 small heads of chicory
1 orange
1 tbsp olive oil
½ tsp ground coriander
30g unsalted butter
1 tbsp caster sugar
Salt and freshly ground black pepper

1 Heat the oven to 180°C/gas mark 4. Roll out the pastry to a circle just bigger than a 15cm frying pan, 3mm thick. Chill on a baking sheet.

2 Cut the chicory in half through the root. Squeeze the juice from the orange.

3 Place the chicory in a roasting tin and sprinkle with the orange juice, olive oil and coriander. Season with salt and pepper. Cover with foil and roast in the oven for 15–20 minutes until tender.

4 Turn the oven setting up to 200°C/gas mark 6. Melt the butter in a 15cm non-stick ovenproof frying pan and stir in the sugar. Drain the chicory and arrange in the pan, cut side down, ensuring it is tightly packed. Cook over a medium heat for 5–10 minutes to caramelise the chicory.

5 Place the chilled pastry disc over the chicory, tucking the edges down inside the pan around the chicory.

6 Bake on the top shelf of the oven for about 30 minutes until the pastry is risen and golden.

7 Allow the tatin to rest briefly before inverting a plate over the pan, carefully turning the pan upside down and lowering it to the table. Leave the frying pan in place for a minute or two, then carefully remove.

Variation
Chicory and walnut tatin Prepare 75g candied walnuts (as for candied pecans, see page 38, step 5, using 2 tsp icing sugar and a small pinch each of the spices). After the chicory has been caramelised, tuck the candied walnuts around the chicory flat side up, then proceed as for the main recipe.

Buttered leeks

Serves 4
3 large leeks
30g butter
1 thyme sprig
Salt and freshly ground black pepper

1 Cut the roots off the leeks and trim away the very coarse green leaves. Cut the leeks in half lengthways and remove the outer layer. With the flat side down on the board, cut the leeks into 1cm slices.

2 Put the leeks into a large bowl of cold water, swirl them round and allow them to soak for a few minutes before draining. Repeat this with fresh water until there is no grit left in the bowl. Drain well.

3 Heat the butter in a medium saucepan and add the leeks, stirring well to coat them in the butter. Season well with salt and pepper and add the thyme. Cover the pan with a lid and cook over a gentle heat for 10–15 minutes, or until tender. Discard the thyme sprig, taste and adjust the seasoning before serving.

1 Cutting the halved leeks into slices.

2 Washing the sliced leeks to get rid of all grit.

3 Stirring the leeks to coat them in the butter.

Roasted leeks with lemon and pine nuts

Serves 4
6 small leeks
1 lemon
Small handful of flat-leaf parsley
30g pine nuts
6 tbsp olive oil
Salt and freshly ground black pepper

1 Heat the oven to 170°C/gas mark 3.

2 Cut the green tops off the leeks, remove the outer layer and trim off the root end, keeping the leek intact. Cut the leeks in half lengthways through the root and soak in a bowl of cold water for 5–10 minutes.

3 Meanwhile, finely grate the zest from the lemon and squeeze the juice. Coarsely chop enough parsley leaves to give you 1 tbsp. Scatter the nuts on a baking tray, toast in the oven until golden, about 5 minutes, then tip onto a plate; leave to cool.

4 Drain the leeks, add to a large pan of boiling water and boil for 2 minutes. Drain and place in a shallow roasting tin, cut side up. Drizzle over the olive oil, sprinkle with a little salt and roast in the oven for 40–50 minutes until tender.

5 Remove the leeks to a serving plate and keep warm. Taste the pan juices, add a little lemon zest and juice to taste and season with salt and pepper. Add the pine nuts and chopped parsley, then pour the dressing over the roasted leeks and serve immediately, as a starter or side dish.

Vichyssoise

Serves 4
700g leeks
2 small onions
75g butter
350g floury potatoes
750ml chicken and veal stock (see page 96) or vegetable stock (see page 101)
120ml double cream
300–400ml milk
Salt and ground white pepper

To finish
Few chives
4 tbsp crème fraîche

1 Cut the roots off the leeks and chop off the coarse green tops, leaving just the white parts. Remove the outer layer, then finely slice the white parts and weigh them; you should have about 500g. Wash them well in several changes of water until there is no trace of grit.

2 Halve, peel and finely slice the onions. Melt the butter in a large, heavy-based saucepan over a low heat and add the onions and leeks. Cover and sweat gently until very soft but not coloured, at least 20–30 minutes.

3 Meanwhile, peel and finely dice the potatoes. Add to the sweated leeks and onions with the stock and a little seasoning, then simmer for 10–15 minutes, or until the potato is cooked; a piece pushed against the side of the pan will break up easily.

4 Add the cream and cook for a further 2 minutes, then allow to cool. Blitz the soup in a blender until very smooth, then pass through a fine sieve into a bowl. Stir in enough milk to achieve a single cream consistency. Allow to cool, then chill.

5 Adjust the seasoning when the soup is chilled. Just before serving finely chop the chives and stir through the soup. Divide between soup plates and top each portion with a quenelle (see page 301), or spoonful, of crème fraîche.

Variations

Vichyssoise with poached egg Serve the soup hot with the chopped chives stirred through, topping each portion with a small poached egg (see page 146).

Vichyssoise with smoked haddock Serve the soup hot with the chopped chives stirred through. Scatter each portion with flakes of hot poached smoked haddock (see page 320).

Steamed baby leeks with tomato and shallot vinaigrette

Serves 4
500g baby leeks

For the tomato and shallot vinaigrette
2 tomatoes
½ shallot
1 garlic clove
1 tbsp red wine vinegar
3 tbsp olive oil
Few tarragon sprigs
Salt and freshly ground black pepper

1 Trim any fibres from the roots of the leeks and cut off the very tips, but leave most of the green parts attached. Wash the leeks in cold water to remove any grit.

2 To make the vinaigrette, plunge the tomatoes into boiling water for 10 seconds, then refresh in cold water, dry and peel. Quarter and deseed the tomatoes, then cut into fine dice (concasse) and set aside.

3 Halve, peel and finely dice the shallot, peel and crush the garlic, and put them both into a small bowl with the wine vinegar for 10–15 minutes to allow the shallot to soften. Season well with salt and pepper, then whisk in the olive oil. Roughly chop enough tarragon leaves to give you ½ tbsp and add to the dressing; reserve the stalks. Stir in the tomato concasse.

4 Steam the leeks (see page 41) with some of the tarragon stalks for 5–6 minutes, or until just tender. Discard the tarragon stalks.

5 Arrange the leeks in a serving dish or on individual plates and drizzle with the tomato and shallot vinaigrette.

Fennel salad with blood orange, watercress and black olives

Serves 4
2 fennel bulbs
3 blood oranges
½ garlic clove
1 tsp Dijon mustard
1 tsp clear honey
½ tbsp white wine vinegar
3 tbsp olive oil
100g watercress
50g pitted black olives
Salt and freshly ground black pepper

1 Trim the root and coarser tops of the fennel, but reserve the fronds. Remove any tough outer leaves and slice the remaining fennel very thinly.

2 Finely grate the zest of 1 orange, then segment all 3 oranges (see page 530); set aside, reserving any juice.

3 Peel and crush the garlic and put into a large bowl with the mustard, orange zest and honey. Whisk in the wine vinegar and reserved orange juice and season with salt and pepper, then whisk in the olive oil.

4 Toss the sliced fennel in the dressing and leave to marinate in a cool place for at least 20 minutes before assembling the salad.

5 Just before serving, wash the watercress and remove any discoloured leaves or tough stalks. Toss with the fennel and gently stir through the orange segments and olives, making sure everything is lightly coated in dressing. Taste the salad and adjust the seasoning if necessary. Serve garnished with the reserved fennel fronds.

Note If blood oranges are not available, use navel oranges and add the juice of ½ lemon to the dressing.

Braised fennel with lemon thyme

Serves 4
2 large fennel bulbs
2 tbsp olive oil
75ml dry white wine
100ml well-flavoured chicken and veal stock (see page 96) or vegetable stock (see page 101)
1 garlic clove
1 lemon
2 small lemon thyme sprigs
Salt and freshly ground black pepper

1 Heat the oven to 190°C/gas mark 5.

2 Trim the roots of the fennel bulbs but leave them intact, then cut the fennel vertically through the root into 6–8 wedges, depending on size.

3 Heat the olive oil in a casserole and, over a medium heat, lightly brown the fennel wedges in batches. Add the wine and stock, bring to the boil and then remove from the heat.

4 Bash the unpeeled garlic clove with the flat side of a large knife and add it to the casserole. Finely pare a long strip of zest from the lemon, using a vegetable peeler, and add to the casserole with the lemon thyme. Season lightly with salt and pepper.

5 Cover the casserole dish with a tight-fitting lid or foil and cook in the oven for 30–35 minutes, or until the fennel is tender. Use the point of a cutlery knife to test the fennel; it should meet with no resistance.

6 Remove the garlic, lemon zest and thyme. Taste the braising liquor: if it is too weak, reduce it until the flavour intensifies. Adjust the seasoning.

Variation

Braised fennel with pancetta and Parmesan Use thyme rather than lemon thyme. Add 1–2 tbsp finely grated Parmesan cheese to 1 quantity ciabatta and pancetta crumb (see page 216) and sprinkle over the braised fennel before serving. Place briefly under a hot grill to allow the Parmesan to melt a little, if you like.

Chillies and Peppers

Both chillies and peppers belong to the capsicum family. Chillies can vary in heat, depending on the variety and growing conditions, while peppers, also known as bell peppers, are firm fleshed and sweet. Of the most widely available chillies, the smaller ones tend to be hotter than the larger ones, and in all cases, the heat is concentrated in the white membranes, or ribs, and seeds. When choosing chillies and peppers, look for shiny, plump ones, with no soft spots.

Deseeding chillies

Cut the chilli in half lengthways through the stem. Scrape away the seeds and pale ribs with a teaspoon and discard (if extra heat is required, leave the seeds and ribs in).

Dicing chillies

Make parallel cuts down the full length of the chilli, keeping the stem end intact. For fine dice, make the cuts as close together as possible. Now holding the stem end, slice across the chilli.

Slicing chillies

Slice across the chilli into fine julienne strips. Be careful not to wipe your face or eyes with a hand that has touched chilli as it is a strong irritant. Wash your hands after preparing chillies.

Coring whole peppers

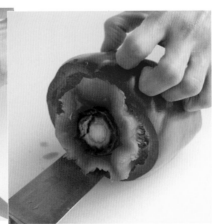

1 Slice off the top and stem. Measure a 4-finger length towards the base of the pepper and cut off the tapering end. (Keep these pieces as they can often be cut up and used too.)

2 To remove the core and seeds, cut through the pepper and carefully slice through the inner pale ribs, removing the core and seeds at the same time.

Slicing peppers

Ensure the pepper flesh is the thickness you require. If not, you may need to trim the inside of the pepper a little. Cut the pepper into batons or fine julienne (see slicing chillies, above).

Peeling peppers

Peppers are left with their skin intact in many dishes for texture, and to help them hold their shape during cooking, but certain recipes require peppers to be peeled. This can be done simply by using a vegetable peeler. However, roasting or blistering the skin is a more effective technique and has the added advantage of lending flavour to the finished dish.

1 Preheat the grill to high. Quarter, core and deseed the pepper. Flatten each quarter and place skin side up on a baking sheet under the grill until the skins are blistered and blackened.

2 Put the peppers in a bowl and cover with cling film or place in a plastic bag and seal. As the peppers cool, the steam will help to release the skins.

3 Once cool, the skins can be easily pulled away from the pepper flesh.

Skinning a pepper whole

Place the whole pepper on an open gas flame (as shown) or beneath a grill and turn occasionally to ensure all sides are blackened. Allow the pepper to cool in the same way as above, then rub the skin away, cut the pepper in half and pull away the stem and seeds. The pepper is now ready to use.

Note Whole peppers can also be placed in a roasting tin and roasted in an oven preheated to 200°C/gas mark 6 for 20–25 minutes. The skin doesn't fully blacken, but the roasting process does help to release the skin, which can then be pulled away once the pepper is cool. This method cooks the pepper flesh and softens it, so it can be used for recipes where cooked/softened peppers are required.

Stir-fry of sweet peppers with chilli and ginger

Serves 4
1 red, 1 orange and 1 yellow pepper
1 red onion
6 spring onions
1 garlic clove
2cm piece of fresh root ginger
1 red chilli
2 tbsp sesame oil
2 tbsp groundnut oil
1 tbsp dark soy sauce
1 tbsp Shaoxing rice wine
1 tsp clear honey

1 Prepare all the vegetables. Core, deseed and slice the peppers into 5mm thick slices. Halve and peel the red onion, cut off the root and top and cut into wedges the same width as the pepper slices. Slice the spring onions, discarding only their root and the very end of the green tips. Peel and crush the garlic, peel and grate the ginger and slice the red chilli finely.

2 Heat the oils in a wok until they start to smoke. Add the red onion and stir-fry over a high heat for 1 minute. Add the sliced peppers and continue to stir-fry until they are just starting to brown. Add the garlic, ginger and chilli and cook for a further minute.

3 Add the soy sauce, rice wine and honey, along with the spring onions, and stir until everything is well coated. Taste and adjust the flavour as required. Serve at once.

Red ratatouille

Serves 4
2 red onions
1 garlic clove
1 red pepper
1 aubergine
3–4 tbsp olive oil
400g tin chopped tomatoes
Pinch of caster sugar
Pinch of ground coriander
Small bunch of purple basil
Salt and freshly ground black pepper

1 Halve, peel and finely slice the onions; peel and crush the garlic. Cut the red pepper into 1.5cm dice and the aubergine into 1.5cm chunks.

2 Heat 2 tbsp olive oil in a large saucepan, add the onions and cook over a low to medium heat until soft but not brown. Add the garlic and cook for 1 minute. Add the red pepper and aubergine and continue to cook until they start to soften, adding more oil to the pan as necessary.

3 Add the tomatoes, sugar, coriander and some salt and pepper. Add a few basil stalks, cover and simmer for about 20 minutes until all the vegetables are cooked.

4 Uncover, increase the heat and reduce the juices slightly. Discard the basil stalks. Check the seasoning. Tear a handful of basil leaves into the ratatouille and stir in.

Chilli, coriander and mint salad

Serves 4
½ red chilli
1 garlic clove
1 lemongrass stalk
1cm piece of fresh root ginger
½ lime
1 tbsp soy sauce
½–1 tsp palm or caster sugar
3 tbsp sunflower oil
1 cos lettuce
¼ cucumber
3 spring onions
Large handful of coriander leaves
Large handful of mint leaves

1 For the dressing, halve, deseed and finely chop the chilli. Peel and crush the garlic. Remove the outer leaves of the lemongrass and trim off the coarse green tops. Cut the lemongrass in half lengthways, slice thinly into half moons and chop very finely. Peel and grate the ginger.

2 Squeeze the juice from the ½ lime and put 1 tbsp into a small bowl with the soy, sugar and oil. Add the chilli, garlic, lemongrass and ginger and stir to combine. Taste and adjust the seasoning, adding more lime juice or sugar as necessary.

3 Wash, dry and cut the lettuce into 4–5mm wide strips. Halve the cucumber lengthways and scoop out and discard the seeds, then cut into thin slices on the diagonal. Trim and thinly slice the spring onions on the diagonal, retaining as much of the green as possible.

4 Place the lettuce, cucumber, spring onions, coriander and mint leaves in a large bowl and pour over the dressing. Toss to combine and serve immediately.

Leafy greens

This group includes a large variety of vegetables. The most common are cabbages, both green and red, kale, spinach, spring greens and Asian greens. When young they can be eaten raw, but they do lend themselves to cooking, their robust flavours making them the ideal partner to strong flavours such as garlic, chilli, cheeses and bacon. As they become older, blanching helps to soften them before further cooking. It also sets their colour and often removes any bitterness.

Savoy cabbage with pancetta

Serves 4
1 small Savoy cabbage
150g pancetta
20g butter
2 tbsp dry white wine
50ml chicken and veal stock (see page 96) or vegetable stock (see page 101)
Salt and freshly ground black pepper

1 Cut the cabbage into quarters. Discard the outermost leaves only and cut out and discard the core. Shred the cabbage finely or tear into largish pieces. Derind the pancetta and cut into lardons.

2 Gently fry the pancetta in a large, dry saucepan until releasing its fat and lightly golden. Add the butter and let it melt. Add the cabbage and sauté for 2 minutes.

3 Add the wine and stock and season lightly with salt and pepper. Put the lid on and cook over a low heat for 5 minutes, or until the cabbage is just tender and still retaining its colour. Remove the lid and turn the heat up to bubble away the liquid until syrupy. Adjust the seasoning and serve.

Bubble and squeak with spring greens

Serves 4
2 large floury potatoes
250g spring greens (or cabbage)
Small handful of chives, parsley or tarragon
60g butter
Salt and freshly ground black pepper

1 Peel and halve the potatoes. Put them into a saucepan, add enough salted water to just cover them and bring to the boil. Lower the heat and simmer for 15–20 minutes until tender.

2 Bring another pan of salted water to the boil. Remove any coarse leaves and stems from the spring greens and roughly slice them. Blanch for 4 minutes, then refresh under cold water. Drain well, cool and squeeze out excess water.

3 Drain the potatoes and crush them so they are just starting to break up, then leave to cool. Chop enough of your chosen herb to give you 1–2 tbsp. Stir the greens and herbs into the potatoes and season well with salt and pepper.

4 In a heavy-based frying pan, melt half the butter over a medium heat, and when foaming add the potato mixture. Press it down with a palette knife and cook until a golden crust has formed on the underside (lift the edge with the knife to check).

5 Invert the bubble and squeak onto a baking sheet. Add the remaining butter to the pan and allow to melt, then slide the cake back into the pan. Cook until the second side is golden brown, cut into wedges and serve.

Note Bubble and squeak is usually made to use up leftovers, mixing together equal quantities of cold, leftover mashed potatoes and green vegetables.

Variation

Bubble and squeak cakes Add 1 beaten egg to the mixture in step 3. With floured hands, shape into patties of the required size. Dust well with flour and fry in butter until golden all over.

Red cabbage with chestnuts and bacon

Serves 4

1 large red cabbage
6 rashers of smoked streaky bacon
2 red onions
4 tbsp olive oil
2 garlic cloves
200g peeled, roasted vacuum-packed
  chestnuts
100ml red wine
4 tbsp balsamic vinegar
1–2 tbsp soft light brown sugar
Salt and freshly ground black pepper

1 Discard the outer leaves from the cabbage and cut it into quarters through the stalk. Remove and discard the core and shred the cabbage finely (as shown).

2 Derind the bacon rashers and cut into strips. Halve, peel and finely slice the onions. Heat the olive oil in a large frying pan, add the bacon and onions and fry over a medium heat until they are starting to turn brown. Peel and crush the garlic, add to the pan and cook for 1 minute.

3 Add the cabbage and stir so that it is evenly coated in the oil. Crumble the chestnuts into large chunks and add to the cabbage with the wine and balsamic vinegar. Cook for 10–15 minutes, or until the cabbage has softened and the raw flavour of the alcohol has cooked away.

4 Season the cabbage with sugar, salt and pepper to taste before serving.

Variation

Brussels sprouts with chestnuts and pancetta Use 500g Brussels sprouts in place of the red cabbage and 75g pancetta, cut into lardons, instead of bacon. Omit the wine, balsamic vinegar and sugar. Trim off the outer leaves of the sprouts, if necessary, and trim the root end, leaving the sprout intact. If they are large, cut in half lengthways. Cook in simmering salted water for 2 minutes until just tender, then drain and refresh in cold water. Add to the frying pan as for the cabbage and sauté for 2–3 minutes over a medium heat, to heat through. Don't let the pancetta and onions brown too much. Taste and season with salt and black pepper and a little sherry vinegar, then serve.

Braised red cabbage and apple

Serves 4

1 red cabbage
1 red onion
2 dessert apples
75ml red wine
45ml red wine vinegar
150ml water
2 tbsp soft dark brown sugar
¼ tsp freshly ground nutmeg
¼ tsp ground cinnamon
Small pinch of ground cloves
40g butter
Salt and freshly ground black pepper

1 Remove the outer leaves from the cabbage. Cut into quarters through the stalk, remove and discard the core and shred the cabbage finely (as shown). Halve, peel and slice the onion.

2 Peel, core and thinly slice the apples, and put them with the cabbage and onion into a heavy-based saucepan.

3 Add the wine, wine vinegar, a little seasoning and the water and stir well. Bring to the boil, then turn down the heat to low and cover with a lid. Simmer for 1 hour, stirring occasionally to make sure the cabbage does not burn on the bottom of the pan. Add a little more water if necessary.

4 Add the sugar and spices, cover and continue to cook for a further 30 minutes, or until the cabbage is tender and the onion and apples have softened.

5 Just before serving, taste and adjust the seasoning. Stir through the butter and allow it to melt and give the cabbage a shine.

Note This can also be made by mixing all the ingredients together in a casserole, covering with a tight-fitting lid and cooking in an oven preheated to 150°C/ gas mark 2 for 2 hours.

Sweet dill slaw

Serves 4–6
1 carrot
1 small beetroot
200g celeriac
1 Cox apple
¼ small red cabbage
4 tbsp cider vinegar
1 tbsp maple syrup
2 tbsp rapeseed oil
Small bunch of dill
Salt and freshly ground black pepper

1 Peel and coarsely grate the carrot, beetroot, celeriac and apple, or cut into julienne (as for carrot julienne, see page 16), or use a mandolin with a julienne cutter. Remove the outer leaves from the cabbage, cut out and discard the core and shred the cabbage finely. Mix everything together in a bowl.

2 For the dressing, whisk together the cider vinegar, maple syrup and rapeseed oil.

3 Pour the dressing over the vegetables and stir well. Finely chop enough dill leaves to give you 3 tbsp, stir into the slaw and season to taste with salt and pepper. More cider vinegar or maple syrup can be added if necessary to balance the flavour.

Kale with garlic and chilli

Serves 4
400g kale
2 garlic cloves
1 red chilli
2 tbsp olive oil
Salt and freshly ground black pepper

1 Prepare the kale by stripping the curly leaves from the stalk either by pulling them off, if young and tender, or cutting them off. Leave the curly leaves as whole as possible. Peel and crush the garlic, and halve, deseed and finely chop the chilli.

2 Bring a large pan of salted water to the boil, add the kale and blanch for 2–3 minutes, until just starting to soften, then refresh in cold water and drain well, squeezing out any excess water.

3 In a large frying pan, heat the olive oil with the crushed garlic until it starts to sizzle. Add the chilli and kale and stir-fry until very hot, about 2 minutes. Season with plenty of salt and pepper.

Variation

Kale with garlic, anchovy and chilli Add 3 chopped anchovies in oil, drained and chopped, to the garlic when frying.

Wilted spinach

Serves 4
1.5kg large leaf spinach
20g butter
Pinch of freshly grated nutmeg
Salt and freshly ground black pepper

1 Prepare the spinach by tearing out all the coarse stalks and stems. Wash the spinach in several changes of water until it is completely free of grit.

2 Heat a large, heavy-based saucepan until hot. Add enough of the spinach, with just the water clinging to the leaves after washing, to loosely fill the pan, then cover with a lid. The spinach cooks in the steam from the water it was washed in. You may need to do this in batches, as the spinach will not wilt properly if the pan is overfilled. Stir every 30 seconds or so until all the spinach has completely wilted.

3 Transfer the wilted spinach to a sieve to drain, pressing out as much liquid as possible with the underside of a ladle.

4 Chop the spinach roughly if required. Heat the butter in a large frying pan until foaming, then add the spinach and sauté briefly, adding a little nutmeg and salt and pepper to taste. Stir well to ensure the seasoning is well distributed.

Note Young leaf spinach can be wilted without removing the stalks.

Chinese broccoli with oyster sauce

Serves 4

500g Chinese broccoli (Gai Lan)
1 garlic clove
1cm piece of fresh root ginger
1 tbsp groundnut oil
6 tbsp oyster sauce
1 tbsp rice wine vinegar
1½ tbsp water
Salt

1 Prepare the Chinese broccoli by trimming the stems to remove the dry end. Bring a large pan of salted water to the boil. Add the broccoli, bring back to the boil and cook for 3–4 minutes.

2 Meanwhile, for the sauce, peel and crush the garlic; peel the ginger and cut into fine julienne. Heat the oil gently in a saucepan, add the garlic and ginger and cook for 30 seconds until sizzling. Add the oyster sauce, rice wine vinegar and water, and stir well. Bring the sauce to a simmer and add a little more water if it is very thick.

3 Drain the broccoli, place in a serving dish and pour the sauce over it to serve.

Stir-fry of Asian leaves

Serves 4

750g Asian leaves, such as pak choi, choi sum, mizuna or Chinese mustard greens
3 garlic cloves
1 green chilli (optional)
1 tbsp groundnut oil
2 tbsp light soy sauce
2 tbsp Shaoxing rice wine
1 tbsp toasted sesame oil

1 Wash the leaves and cut off and discard any tough or woody pieces of stalk. Chop the leaves roughly. Peel and finely slice the garlic, and slice the chilli, if using.

2 Heat the oil in a wok until smoking. Add the chilli and garlic and cook for 10 seconds. Add the greens and cook for 3–4 minutes, or until they have wilted.

3 Add the soy sauce, rice wine and sesame oil and continue to stir-fry until the liquid bubbles. The greens should be tender but still retaining a little crunch. Serve at once.

Note If the Asian greens have coarse stems, heat a saucepan of boiling water and blanch them for 1 minute, then refresh in cold water and drain well, before you stir-fry them.

Stir-frying

Stir-frying is a very quick method of cooking over a high heat, usually in a wok. This provides a large surface area at an evenly high temperature over which the ingredients can be spread to cook quickly. Thus, they retain their flavour, colour and texture. A deep frying pan or sauté pan works very well too, if a wok is not available. Be careful not to overcrowd the pan, as it is essential that the ingredients have room to fry, or they will stew.

The ingredients must be moved constantly so they come into contact with the hot surface of the wok only briefly before being turned to allow another side to be heated and cooked. This helps to ensure even cooking. A wok spoon or similar large metal spoon helps to keep the ingredients moving. A wok with a handle can also be shaken.

When stir-frying meat and vegetables together in a dish the meat is often stir-fried first to achieve some surface colour, then removed before the firmer vegetables are stir-fried. The meat is then added back to cook through and the more tender vegetables are added last, along with any final seasonings.

Lettuce and other salad greens

Choose salad leaves that are fresh and crisp, not limp, and avoid leaves that show signs of discolouring at the edges. Allow 20–25g salad leaves per person, or a generous handful.

Preparing salad leaves

It is important to wash the delicate leaves carefully so they are not bruised. Fill a bowl or sink with cold water and gently lower the leaves into it. Do not run water from the tap onto the leaves. Move the leaves through the water to remove any grit, then lift them out, drain and dry them gently in a salad spinner. The leaves must be properly dried or the dressing will not cling to the leaves and will be diluted by the excess water.

Washed salad leaves can be stored in the fridge wrapped in a damp tea towel to prevent them from wilting. To revitalise salad leaves that are just starting to wilt, immerse them in a bowl of water, chilled with a handful of ice cubes, until they crisp up, then drain them.

Smaller young, tender leaves can be served whole. Leaves should all be small enough to be eaten in one mouthful and to be easy to eat with a fork. Larger salad leaves should be picked before serving. Picking salad leaves involves ripping the leaves into bite-sized pieces, discarding large or tough stems from the leaf. If you are hoping to pile up leaves for presentation purposes, smaller pieces of leaves will hold the shape of the pile much better than larger ones.

Choosing salad leaves

When assembling a mixed leaf salad, consider the flavours and textures of the individual leaves. Some add peppery or bitter flavours while others are used for their crunch. Romaine, cos and iceberg are crisp with a mild flavour, whereas Webbs and oak leaf lettuce are soft with a mild flavour, and lamb's lettuce (or mâche), baby spinach and sorrel are more intensely flavoured. Rocket and watercress are peppery, while radicchio, chicory and curly endive (or frisée) are bitter leaves. A combination of bitter or peppery and mild-flavoured leaves often works well. Soft herbs are added for flavour, and herby salads are good with plain grilled fish or chicken, but can overshadow the other flavours on the plate if used in excess.

Braised baby gem hearts

Serves 4
2 Baby Gem lettuce hearts
½ orange
30g butter
200ml chicken and veal stock
  (see page 96)
Salt and white pepper

1 Wash the lettuce hearts and cut them in half, through the stalk, keeping each half intact. Squeeze the juice from the ½ orange.

2 Melt the butter in a frying pan. Place the lettuce flat side down in the pan and gently fry over a medium heat until the cut sides are evenly caramelised.

3 Season the stock with salt and pepper and add to the pan with the orange juice so the liquid comes about halfway up the lettuce. Turn down the heat, cover and cook gently until the lettuce is just wilted and tender, but still holding its shape.

4 Drain the lettuce thoroughly, reserving the braising liquor. Keep the lettuce warm while you reduce the braising liquor to concentrate the flavour. Serve the lettuce with a little of the reduced liquor.

Mushrooms

Many different types of mushroom – cultivated and wild – bring a savoury flavour to cooking. Cultivated mushrooms have a milder taste than wild ones. Dried wild mushrooms have a very intense flavour and should be used sparingly. The main season for wild mushrooms is from September to November. Not all wild mushrooms are edible, so only gather them from the wild if you are absolutely sure you can identify them.

Mushrooms don't keep well, so buy them as you need them and avoid any that look slightly damp and slimy.

Preparing mushrooms

Cultivated mushrooms Simply wipe with dampened kitchen paper, trimming off the stem end if necessary. Unless old, with tough thick skins, mushrooms do not need peeling.

Wild mushrooms Trim off the sandy stalk end and brush with a soft brush to remove any grit and sand. If they are very gritty, quickly dunk in cold water, then dry well. Don't leave them to soak – they will absorb water like a sponge.

Try to keep small mushrooms whole and tear large mushrooms into bite-sized pieces. Note that some mushrooms, such as pied de mouton, might need a little scraping of the fine fibres beneath the cap.

Sauté of wild mushrooms and hazelnuts

Serves 4
50g skinned hazelnuts
500g wild mushrooms, such as
 chanterelle, blewitt, pied de mouton
1 garlic clove
Few thyme sprigs
30g butter
10ml hazelnut oil
Squeeze of lemon juice
Salt and freshly ground black pepper

1 Heat the oven to 180°C/gas mark 4. Place the hazelnuts on a baking sheet and toast in the oven for 5–10 minutes until lightly coloured, making sure they do not over-colour. Tip onto a plate to cool, then roughly chop.

2 Prepare the mushrooms and set aside (see above). Peel and crush the garlic and chop enough thyme leaves to give you 1 tsp.

3 Melt the butter in a large frying pan and add the hazelnut oil. Sauté the mushrooms quickly. It is important this is done over a high heat to ensure the mushrooms take on colour and do not sweat, release moisture and become slimy.

4 Add the garlic, thyme and hazelnuts and stir, allowing the heat to draw out the flavours. Cook for another minute. Taste and season with salt and pepper and a little lemon juice. Serve immediately. This works well as an accompaniment to steaks or with soft polenta.

Mushrooms on sourdough toast with deep-fried poached duck eggs

Serves 4

400–500g wild mushrooms
1 shallot
1 garlic clove
Handful of flat-leaf parsley
4 duck eggs
4–5 tbsp plain flour, seasoned with
    salt and pepper
4–5 tbsp panko breadcrumbs
1 egg, beaten
Oil for deep-frying
50g butter
100ml double cream
Squeeze of lemon juice
4 slices of sourdough bread
Salt and freshly ground black pepper
Truffle oil, to finish

1 Heat the oven to 120°C/gas mark ½.

2 Prepare the mushrooms (see page 63) and set aside. Halve, peel and finely chop the shallot; peel and crush the garlic; coarsely chop enough parsley leaves to give you 1–2 tbsp and set aside.

3 Poach the duck eggs, refresh in cold water and drain well (see page 146). Put the seasoned flour and breadcrumbs on separate plates, and coat the poached duck eggs first in the flour, then dip into the beaten egg and finally coat in the breadcrumbs, then chill.

4 Fill a saucepan one-third full with oil and heat gently to about 193°C, or until a small piece of bread dropped into the oil browns in 30 seconds (see page 72).

5 Meanwhile, melt the butter in a large frying pan and sauté the shallot and garlic for 1 minute. Increase the heat, add the mushrooms and sauté quickly for 3–4 minutes until they take on some colour. Season lightly.

6 While the mushrooms are sautéeing, deep-fry the coated eggs in the hot oil, in 2 batches if necessary, for 2–3 minutes until the panko crumbs are golden and crisp. Drain on kitchen paper, salt lightly and keep warm in the low oven.

7 Lower the heat under the mushroom pan and stir through the cream, adding a splash of water if the cream starts to thicken too quickly.

8 Taste the mushrooms, adjust the seasoning and add a squeeze of lemon juice. Stir through the parsley.

9 Toast the sourdough bread and place one slice on each plate. Divide the mushrooms between the sourdough slices, pour over any remaining sauce and place a deep-fried duck egg on top. Drizzle the mushrooms with a few drops of truffle oil and serve.

Variations

Mushrooms on toast with fried eggs Top the mushrooms with a classic fried egg (see page 150) rather than the duck egg.

Mushrooms with Parmesan risotto Omit the sourdough toast and duck eggs. Serve the mushrooms with a Parmesan risotto (see page 188).

A note on seasoned flour...

Seasoned flour is used for coating prior to frying. Season the flour well with salt and freshly ground black pepper, mix thoroughly and put on a plate. Sometimes cayenne, mustard powder or other spices are added for extra flavour. As a rough guide, season 100g flour with ½ tsp salt and ¼ tsp pepper.

Individual mushroom and onion confit Charlottes

Serves 6
100g butter
25g dried porcini
18 small to medium chestnut mushrooms
Few thyme sprigs
½ shallot
½ garlic clove
50ml red wine
22 thin slices of white bread
1 quantity caramelised onion confit
  (see page 14)
125ml Madeira
200ml strong vegetable stock (see
  page 101)
A little cornflour
Salt and freshly ground black pepper
Watercress sprigs, to finish

1 Heat the oven to 200°C/gas mark 6. Melt 25g of the butter in a small saucepan; keep it warm.

2 Soak the dried porcini in boiling water for 30 minutes to rehydrate. Ensure they are fully submerged, but with only just enough water to cover them.

3 Remove the stalks from the chestnut mushrooms and reserve them. Wipe the mushroom caps to remove any grit. Brush them with some of the melted butter and place rounded side down on a baking sheet. Finely chop enough thyme leaves to give you ½ tsp and sprinkle over the mushrooms. Season with salt and pepper. Roast in the oven until the mushrooms are tender, about 20–30 minutes.

4 Chop the reserved mushroom stalks finely. Peel and finely dice the shallot, and peel and crush the garlic. Drain the porcini, reserving the soaking liquor, and chop them finely.

5 Heat 25g butter in a frying pan and, when foaming, add the shallot and sauté for 2 minutes, then add the garlic and cook for 1 minute. Increase the heat and add the chopped mushrooms and porcini and sauté quickly until they have lost volume and all the water they release has evaporated. Add the wine and reduce the liquid to ½ tbsp. Season with salt and pepper.

6 Melt the remaining butter and brush 6 dariole moulds or deep ramekins with butter twice, allowing the first coating to set before re-buttering.

7 Use 12 slices of the bread to cut out 6 small discs of bread to fit in the bottom of each dariole, and 6 larger discs to be used to cover the filling once the Charlottes are assembled. Cut the crusts off the remaining 10 slices of bread and cut them into quarters, then cut each quarter into 2 on a slight diagonal (as shown). Brush the bread pieces with the melted butter.

8 Lay a small disc in the bottom of each of the 6 darioles, then place the irregular pieces of bread around the sides of the dariole, placing the narrow end towards the bottom and overlapping each piece slightly (as shown).

9 Layer the roasted mushrooms rounded side down in the darioles, alternating with the sautéed mushroom mixture and caramelised onion confit, until they are almost full. You should fit 3 mushrooms in each. Top with the remaining large discs of bread (as shown) and press down slightly to help seal.

10 Stand the darioles on a baking sheet and bake in the oven for 25–30 minutes until the bread is golden and crisp.

11 Meanwhile, to make the sauce, strain the reserved mushroom liquor through a piece of muslin to remove any grit. Pour the Madeira into a small saucepan and reduce by two-thirds. Add 125ml of the mushroom soaking liquor and all the vegetable stock and simmer gently for 10–15 minutes until the flavours are combined. You might need to add a little more mushroom liquor. Taste the sauce and adjust the seasoning. Slake the cornflour with a little water (see page 111), stir into the sauce and cook for a minute or two to thicken it slightly, to a light, syrupy consistency.

12 When the Charlottes are cooked, allow them to rest for 2–3 minutes before inverting them onto serving plates. Spoon a little of the sauce around the Charlottes and serve garnished with watercress.

Potatoes

Potatoes lend themselves particularly well to absorbing flavours and complementing textures. There are many common varieties available through the year. Their texture on cooking varies, ranging from waxy potatoes, which hold their shape, through creamy to floury varieties, which soften and have a fluffy texture. Different potatoes are suited to different cooking methods. King Edward, Maris Piper and Desiree are popular maincrop varieties; these have a floury texture and are best for roasting and mash. Jersey Royals, the most highly prized of the new potatoes, are in season from April to June; these are best simply boiled.

When buying potatoes select those with tight skins, avoiding any that are soft, sprouting or have green patches. For new potatoes, the skin should be easy to rub off or already flaking.

Sweet potatoes have a yellowish or pinkish skin and the flesh ranges from white to deep orange. As their name implies, they have a sweet flavour and are excellent roasted with other vegetables or puréed.

Boiled new potatoes

Serves 4
500g new potatoes
Salt

1 Wash the potatoes well. If the skins are not very tender and new, remove them by scraping them off with a small knife.

2 Place the potatoes in a pan of boiling salted water and boil gently until tender, about 10–15 minutes. They are cooked when a cutlery knife inserted into the centre of the potato passes through easily. Drain the potatoes in a colander.

Steamed new potatoes

Serves 4
500g Jersey Royal or other new potatoes
Salt and freshly ground black pepper

1 Wash the potatoes well to remove any grit. It is not necessary to peel them if they are very young.

2 Put the potatoes in the steamer and season with salt and pepper. Steam over a medium heat until tender when pierced with a cutlery knife, about 15–20 minutes.

Variations

Herb buttered steamed potatoes Once steamed, turn the potatoes in 30g butter and ½ tbsp chopped herbs such as parsley, chives, thyme or mint.

Crushed potatoes with chorizo Fry 75g thickly sliced cooking chorizo in a small frying pan until starting to crisp at the edges. Remove from the pan, reserving the oil, allow to cool, then crumble. After steaming the potatoes, crush them gently in a bowl. Add the chorizo and reserved oil, mix through, then taste and season.

Salad of Jersey Royals with radish and mint While the potatoes are still warm, turn them through a tomato and shallot vinaigrette (see page 51), so that the potatoes absorb the flavour of the vinaigrette. Add 8–10 thinly sliced radishes and ½ tbsp chiffonaded mint (see page 89).

Mashed potatoes

Serves 4
700g (2 large) floury potatoes
85–100ml milk
60g butter
Salt and ground white pepper

1 Wash and peel the potatoes and cut them into large, uniform-sized chunks. Put them in a saucepan of salted cold water. Bring the water to the boil, turn the heat down to a gentle boil and cover with a lid. Cook the potatoes until a cutlery knife inserted into the potato passes through easily.

2 Drain the potatoes well and sit them in a colander over the pan to steam-dry for 2–3 minutes.

3 While still warm, pass the potatoes through a sieve, ricer or mouli one piece at a time. Try not to allow the potatoes to cool down or to overwork them as they may become gluey.

4 Return the potatoes to the pan and draw them to one side. Add the milk and butter to the other side of the pan. Season the milk with salt and pepper and return the pan to the heat, allowing the butter to melt into the milk as it heats.

5 Once the butter has melted and the milk is just coming to the boil, remove the pan from the heat and slowly beat the milk and melted butter into the potato to create a soft, light, fluffy mash. Taste and adjust the seasoning.

Note To prepare mashed potatoes in advance (up to 3 hours ahead), follow the method to the end of step 3, then put into a bowl and cover with cling film. When ready to serve, heat the milk and butter and combine.

Variations

Roasted garlic mash Roast 5–6 unpeeled garlic cloves in an oven preheated to 200°C/gas mark 6 until soft, about 30 minutes. Squeeze the softened garlic from the skins and add to the potatoes before you sieve or rice them.

Mustard mash Stir 1–2 tbsp wholegrain mustard into the mash.

Horseradish mash Stir 2–3 tbsp hot horseradish sauce or creamed horseradish into the mash.

Lemon and olive oil mash Use olive oil in place of the milk, omit the butter and add the finely grated zest of ¼ lemon to the mash.

Herb mash Stir 1–2 tbsp chopped herbs such as chives, parsley or chervil through the mash.

Saffron mash Add 4–6 saffron strands to the milk when heating to infuse, before combining with the mash.

Sweet potato mash Use sweet potatoes rather than standard ones. Bake them whole on a baking sheet, in an oven preheated to 200°C/gas mark 6 for 30–40 minutes until soft. Allow to cool slightly before cutting in half and scooping the cooked flesh into a food processor. Blend with 30g butter and 50ml crème fraîche.

Fondant potatoes

Serves 4
4 large potatoes
60g butter
2 bay leaves
200ml chicken and veal stock
  (see page 96)
Salt and freshly ground black pepper

1 Wash and peel the potatoes, then shape them into 4 cylinders, about 3 x 4cm (or any size you like, depending on what you are serving them with), trimming them as necessary.

2 Melt the butter in a sauté pan, add the potatoes and brown lightly on both flat sides. Add the bay leaves, stock and seasoning and cover with a damp cartouche (see page 13). Cook gently over a low heat for about 35–45 minutes, turning the potatoes after 20 minutes, until the stock has been absorbed and the potatoes are tender. Carefully transfer the potatoes to a serving dish.

Sauté potatoes

Serves 4
3 large or 4 medium floury potatoes
1 tbsp olive oil
50g butter
Few rosemary sprigs
Salt and freshly ground black pepper

1 Wash the potatoes, but do not peel them. Put them in a saucepan of salted cold water. Only cut the potatoes in half if they will not fit into the pan or if they are very different sizes. Bring to the boil, turn the heat down to a gentle boil and cover. Cook until a cutlery knife inserted into the centre of a potato passes through easily.

2 When the potatoes are cooked, drain and leave to steam-dry in a colander. While they are still hot, peel and break them into bite-sized pieces; you might want to wear rubber gloves to do this. Do not worry if the potatoes are rough edged and crumbly, this is good; the crumblier the better. The potatoes must not be allowed to cool down completely or the starch sets.

3 Heat the olive oil in a non-stick frying pan, add the butter and, when foaming, add the warm potatoes. Turn them through the fat to coat them evenly. Season with salt and pepper, add the rosemary sprigs and cook over a gentle heat, allowing them to absorb a little of the fat. Once coloured on one side, turn the potatoes, leaving them to colour on the next side. Continue with this process until the potatoes are an even golden colour all over; this can take 30–40 minutes.

Note The browning process cannot be done over a high heat; it is a long, slow process, allowing the potato to absorb the butter as it colours, crisping the exterior and keeping the interior of the potato light, tender and fluffy.

To prove or season a pan to make it non-stick
If you do not have a non-stick frying pan in your kitchen, it is possible to render one non-stick. Place 1 tbsp each of salt and vegetable oil in a medium to large frying pan and heat over a medium to high heat until just starting to smoke. Remove from the heat and allow to cool. Pour off the oil and salt, then, using kitchen paper, scrub the base and sides of the pan vigorously. The salt acts as an abrasive and removes particles that can cause sticking. Wipe out all the salt and your frying pan is ready to use as a non-stick pan. Don't be tempted to wash the pan after proving or the non-stick effect will be destroyed.

Rosti

Serves 4–6
4–5 large floury potatoes
75g butter
Salt and ground white pepper

1 Wash and peel the potatoes, then grate coarsely. Alternatively, use a mandolin with a julienne cutter. Transfer the potatoes to a sieve set over a bowl, spreading them out as much as possible, and sprinkle with ¼ tsp salt. Allow them to sit for 10 minutes for the salt to draw out the moisture (ie degorge, see page 28). Do not leave them any longer or the potatoes will start to oxidise and turn grey.

2 Heat the oven to 180°C/gas mark 4, and if you are not using an ovenproof frying pan, put a baking sheet in to heat.

3 Tip the potatoes onto a clean tea towel and wring out any excess moisture, to make them as dry as possible. Season with white pepper.

4 In a 15–18cm non-stick (ideally ovenproof) frying pan, melt half the butter, and as it begins to foam pack the potatoes into the pan in a thick (2.5–3cm) layer. Use a palette knife to shape the edges and press down on the potato to compact it as much as possible, or the rosti will not hold together. Give the pan a shake to ensure the potato is not sticking.

5 Cook gently over a low to medium heat until the potato is a deep golden colour underneath (check by lifting the edge slightly with a palette knife).

6 To turn the potato over, invert a plate over the potato and turn the frying pan upside down. Return the frying pan to the hob and melt the remaining butter. Once foaming, slide the rosti back into the pan and repeat the browning process on the second side.

7 When the rosti has been browned on both sides, transfer it to the oven (or slide it onto a hot baking sheet if your pan is not ovenproof) to cook through, about 20–25 minutes. Use a cutlery knife to check the tenderness of the potato. There should be no resistance when the knife is inserted.

8 Carefully slide the rosti onto a serving plate or board and cut into wedges to serve. The exterior should be golden and crisp and the inside should be soft.

Variations

Individual rostis Use half the butter. Place 4 metal cutters of the same size in a large frying pan and pack the potato into each cutter. Once browned on one side, carefully turn the rosti and cutter over to retain the shape and brown on the other side. The rosti might still need to be transferred to the oven to finish the cooking if the middle is not quite cooked through.

Herb rosti Add ½ tsp chopped thyme, rosemary or other herb of your choice to the raw potato when seasoning.

Onion rosti Sweat a diced onion and add this to the raw potato when seasoning.

Bacon and onion rosti Fry 75g chopped streaky bacon until golden, remove from the pan and sweat a diced onion in the rendered fat. Proceed as for the main recipe, adding both the bacon and onion to the raw potato.

Root vegetable rosti Any root vegetable can be used to make rosti. Other root vegetables don't have as much starch as potatoes, but a good packing of the vegetables should be enough to hold them together. Or use a combination of half potato and half another root vegetable, such as parsnip.

Chips

Serves 4
3 large floury potatoes
Oil for deep-frying
Salt

For this method of making chips the potatoes are fried twice. The initial frying, at a low temperature, is to cook but not colour the chips; this can be done in advance. The second frying, at a higher temperature, heats the chips, crisps them and turns them a golden colour.

1 Wash the potatoes, peel and cut into batons, 5cm long and 1cm thick (as for carrot batons, see page 16). Immerse in a bowl of cold water until ready to cook. This removes excess starch and prevents the chips sticking together when frying.

2 One-third fill a large, deep, heavy saucepan with oil, and heat to 193°C, or until a small piece of bread dropped into the oil sizzles gently and browns in 30 seconds (see below).

3 Drain and dry the potatoes thoroughly. You will need to fry them in batches or they may stick together. Lower a handful into the hot oil in a basket and fry for 7–8 minutes until the potato is soft, but has not taken on any colour. Remove the chips and drain them well on kitchen paper. Repeat with the remaining potato.

4 When ready to serve, heat the oil again to 195°C, or until a small piece of bread sizzles and browns in 20 seconds. Fry the chips again, in batches, until they are crisp, golden and piping hot. Drain on kitchen paper and sprinkle lightly with salt.

Deep-frying

Deep-frying is an extraordinarily fast method of cooking small pieces of food, as the oil reaches such a high temperature. The best oils to use are flavourless, such as a peanut, sunflower or vegetable oil.

In some cases the food is in the hot oil for such a short time that it does not require a coating. However, most foods are panéed in flour, then egg and finally breadcrumbs, or coated in an egg and flour batter, to protect them from the fierce heat of the oil, preventing overcooking and spluttering of moisture into the oil from the food. While the coating cooks to a crisp golden colour, the food inside remains tender and moist.

The coating also helps to prevent a transfer of flavour from the food to the oil, which means the oil can be used again, except in the case of fish. When the oil has been used to fry fish, it must either be discarded or used only for fish thereafter. After use, leave the oil to cool, then strain it to remove any cooked bits of food before storing or using again. Oil should only be re-used 3 or 4 times.

Oil temperatures for deep-frying

If your deep-fat fryer is not thermostatically controlled, use a piece of bread to test the temperature of the oil. If a small piece of bread browns in:

- 60 seconds, then the oil is moderate, about 182°C
- 40 seconds, the oil is moderately hot, about 190°C
- 30 seconds, the oil is hot, about 193°C
- 20 seconds, then it is very hot, about 195°C
- 10 seconds, the oil is dangerously hot and should be cooled down.

Safety

While deep-frying, take the following precautions: only fill the saucepan one-third full of oil and turn the pan handles inwards. Dry food thoroughly before frying where appropriate, deep-fry in small batches and lower food into the hot oil carefully. Avoid moving a container or pan of hot oil; if in doubt, turn off the heat source.

Matchstick potatoes

Serves 4
2 large floury potatoes
Oil for deep-frying
Cornflour
Salt

1 Wash and peel the potatoes, then block them (as for carrots, see page 16). Cut the potatoes into allumettes (as for small carrot batons, see page 16) and place in a bowl of cold water.

2 One-third fill a large, deep, heavy saucepan with oil and heat to 190°C, or until a small piece of bread dropped into the oil sizzles gently and browns in 40 seconds.

3 Drain and dry the potatoes thoroughly, then toss them in the cornflour (which helps to retain crispness), ensuring any excess cornflour is removed, so only a very thin layer remains on the potato. Placing the potatoes in a sieve and shaking helps to remove excess cornflour.

4 Place a very small amount of potatoes at a time in the hot oil; too many will stick together. Fry them for 5–6 minutes until the potato is soft and golden in colour, then remove and drain them well on kitchen paper. Repeat with the remaining matchstick potatoes. Season sparingly with salt and serve at once.

Game chips

Serves 4
2 medium floury potatoes, of similar size
Oil for deep-frying
Salt

1 Wash and peel the potatoes, then shape each into a cylinder, similar in diameter. Slice them into very thin rounds, using a mandolin or very sharp knife. Soak in cold water for 10 minutes to remove some of the surface starch.

2 Dry the potato slices thoroughly in a clean tea towel.

3 One-third fill a large, deep, heavy saucepan with oil. Heat the oil gently to 193°C. To test the temperature add a potato slice or two; if the potatoes rise to the surface within a minute or so, the oil is ready. Alternatively, drop a small piece of bread in the oil; it should sizzle gently and brown in 30 seconds.

4 Fry the game chips in small batches. Lower the first batch into the hot oil and gently move them around with a slotted metal spoon to prevent them from sticking together. As the potato slices cook and dry out, they will rise to the surface. Allow them to cook a little longer until they are crisp and light golden.

5 Using the slotted spoon, remove the potato slices from the oil, drain on kitchen paper and sprinkle lightly with salt. Repeat with the remaining potato slices.

6 Serve immediately or keep the chips crisp in a warm oven with the door ajar until you are ready to serve. As the name suggests, these are traditionally served with roasted game birds.

Variations

Parsnip, carrot, beetroot and Jerusalem artichoke crisps Most root vegetables can be successfully made into crisps. Slice them very finely, on a mandolin if possible, and they will take 2–3 minutes to cook. If frying a mixture of vegetable crisps, cook beetroot last as the colour will stain the oil.

Roast potatoes

Serves 4
3 large floury potatoes
75g duck fat (or 3 tbsp oil plus
    30g unsalted butter)
Salt

1 Heat the oven to 200°C/gas mark 6.

2 Wash and peel the potatoes, then cut into 4–5cm chunks. Place them in a saucepan and add enough salted cold water to just cover. Bring to the boil, lower the heat and simmer for 5 minutes. Test with a cutlery knife; it should pass easily through the outer 1cm of potato flesh.

3 Meanwhile, put the duck fat in a large roasting tin and heat it in the oven while the potatoes are simmering.

4 Drain the potatoes well and let them steam-dry in the pan for 2–3 minutes. Once dried, shake them well in the pan to break up the outside. The crumblier the outside the crisper the potatoes will be. Do not allow the potatoes to get cold.

5 Remove the roasting tin from the oven and carefully add the hot potatoes to the hot fat. Give them plenty of space; overcrowding them means they will steam, not roast. The potatoes should sizzle vigorously. Turn them in the hot fat and season with salt. Return the tin to the oven and roast for 50–60 minutes, turning and basting the potatoes every 10–15 minutes to ensure even colouring.

6 The potatoes should be golden and crisp on the outside and fluffy and tender on the inside. They are ready when a cutlery knife inserted into the middle of a potato passes through easily. Drain on kitchen paper and keep warm.

Note Roast potatoes can be lightly browned and taken out of the oven up to 2 hours in advance. Return them to the top shelf of the oven to finish browning 30 minutes before serving. This can help when trying to get all the elements of a roast ready at once.

Variations

Roast new potatoes New potatoes can be roasted in their skins. Wash and scrub them well and coat them in a little olive oil. Roast them in the top third of the oven at 200°C/gas mark 6 for 40–50 minutes, or until they 'give' when pressed firmly.

New potatoes baked en papillote Turn 500g new potatoes in 1 tbsp olive or sunflower oil. Add 2 bashed garlic cloves, a few thyme or rosemary sprigs and some salt and pepper. Encase in an en papillote case (see page 286) and bake in the oven at 200°C/gas mark 6 for 45–50 minutes. They are cooked when the potatoes 'give' when pressed through the greaseproof paper and the paper is very brown.

Roast sweet potatoes Wash, scrub and dry 3 medium-sized sweet potatoes. Cut them into 4cm chunks, leaving the skins on. Turn them in 2 tbsp olive oil and season with salt and pepper. Tip them onto a baking tray (lining this with baking parchment saves washing up later). Bake in the top third of the oven at 200°C/gas mark 6 for about 40 minutes, or until the potatoes are golden on the outside and a cutlery knife inserted into the middle of a potato passes through easily.

Boulangère potatoes

Serves 4

2 large floury potatoes
1 onion
50g butter
200–300ml chicken and veal stock
  (see page 96)
Salt and freshly ground black pepper

1 Heat the oven to 190°C/gas mark 5. Butter a shallow ovenproof dish.

2 Wash and peel the potatoes, then slice them thinly, ideally using a mandolin.

3 Halve, peel and slice the onion. Place in a pan with the butter, cover and sweat over a gentle heat until soft.

4 Heat the stock in a small pan. Layer the potatoes and onion in the prepared dish, seasoning each layer, then pour in enough hot stock to come just below the surface of the potatoes. Cover with foil and bake in the oven for 45 minutes.

5 Remove the foil and bake for a further 45 minutes, basting occasionally, until the stock has been absorbed by the potatoes, they have taken on a golden colour and are cooked. Check by inserting a cutlery knife; it should pass through easily.

Variation

Cut the potatoes in half, then slice, keeping the slices together and fanning them out. Continue as above, but to assemble lay all the onion in a roasting tin. Place the potatoes on top of the onion and pour in enough stock to come about two-thirds of the way up the potatoes. Bake as above. Each potato fan is a portion.

Pommes Anna

Serves 4–6

3 large floury potatoes
75g clarified butter (see below)
Freshly grated nutmeg
Salt and freshly ground black pepper

1 Wash and peel the potatoes, then slice very thinly using a mandolin, or by hand.

2 Heat the oven to 180°C/gas mark 4. Melt the clarified butter in a small saucepan.

3 Brush a 15cm non-stick ovenproof frying pan with the melted butter and arrange a layer of overlapping potato slices on the bottom of the pan. This will become the presentation side, so it needs to be neat. Brush the potatoes with a little butter and season well with salt, pepper and nutmeg.

4 Repeat this layering to use all the potato, making a cake about 2.5cm thick. Place the pan over a low to medium heat and allow the bottom layer of potato to turn golden and caramelise (check by lifting the edge with a palette knife); this can take up to 10 minutes. Shake the pan occasionally to ensure the potato is not sticking.

5 Once the cake is golden underneath and releases from the pan, place a disc of greased greaseproof paper on top and weight the potato down with a smaller lid. Place the pan on a baking sheet in the middle of the oven for 40–45 minutes, or until a cutlery knife inserted into the potato passes through easily.

6 Remove the small pan lid and greaseproof paper and invert a plate over the pan, then turn the plate the right way up, so the pan is now on top of the plate. Lower the plate to the table, leaving the pan over the potato cake for a couple of minutes and allowing it to self-release. Carefully remove the pan and serve.

Clarified butter

Clarified butter is butter from which the milk solids have been removed. It can be heated to a higher temperature than normal butter without burning. To prepare, put 250g butter into a fairly deep saucepan and place over a low to medium heat until simmering. Simmer for 10–15 minutes, then allow the butter to cool. The milk solids will have fallen to the bottom of the pan and on top will be left the clear, pure butter fat. Carefully pour this off, without allowing any milk solids to follow. Discard the solids.

Dauphinoise potatoes

Serves 6–8
5 medium floury potatoes
1 onion
30g butter
1 garlic clove (optional)
300ml double cream
100ml crème fraîche
300ml milk
Pinch of freshly grated nutmeg
Salt and freshly ground black pepper

1 Heat the oven to 170°C/gas mark 3.

2 Wash and peel the potatoes, then slice thinly, using a mandolin if you have one.

3 Halve, peel and thinly slice the onion. Melt the butter in a large saucepan, add the onion, cover and sweat until soft. Peel and crush the garlic, if using, then add it to the onion and cook for a further minute.

4 Add both creams, the milk and the nutmeg to the onion, and bring to a simmer. Add the potatoes with some salt and pepper and simmer for 10–15 minutes until the potatoes begin to soften, release their starch and the cream begins to thicken.

5 Transfer to a lightly buttered ovenproof dish, spreading the potatoes into an even layer. Bake in the oven for 1–1½ hours, or until tender and golden brown on top. The slower the cooking the better.

Variations

Any root vegetable can be used to make a dauphinoise. Potato has a high starch content which holds the dauphinoise together better than other root vegetables, but using a combination of potato and another root works well. Celeriac, sweet potato, Jerusalem artichoke and parsnip are all excellent with potato.

Sweet potato roasted with lemon, red onion and sweet paprika

Serves 6
4 sweet potatoes
2 lemons
2 red onions
12 garlic cloves
4 bay leaves
Small handful of thyme
1 tsp Spanish sweet paprika
½ tsp chilli powder
1 tbsp wholegrain mustard
4 tbsp olive oil
Sea salt and freshly ground black pepper

1 Preheat the oven to 200°C/gas mark 6.

2 Peel the sweet potatoes and cut into even-sized wedges. Cut the lemons into wedges, removing the seeds. Halve, peel and cut the red onions into wedges.

3 Add the sweet potato wedges to a saucepan of boiling water and parboil for 2 minutes. Drain well, then transfer to a large roasting tin with the lemons, onions, unpeeled garlic cloves and bay leaves.

4 Finely chop enough thyme leaves to give you 1 tsp. Mix the paprika, chilli powder, thyme, mustard and olive oil together in a small bowl. Pour over the vegetables, season with salt and pepper and toss well to coat.

5 Roast in the oven for 30–35 minutes until the sweet potato is tender and golden brown. Serve hot as an accompaniment (it is very good with a simple roast chicken) or at room temperature as a salad.

Variation

Sweet potato roasted with bay and orange Replace the lemons with 1 large orange. Omit the paprika, chilli powder and thyme. Use 6 bay leaves, fresh if possible, crumbled in your fingers to bring out more of their flavour. Use Dijon in place of the wholegrain mustard and proceed as for the main recipe.

Salsify and scorzonera

These are from the same family and share a similar flavour that is often likened to oyster or asparagus, which makes them a good accompaniment to fish or for use in salads. Salsify has a pale, brownish skin and a long, thin tapering shape, while scorzonera is more uniformly shaped throughout its length and has much darker skin. Both are available through the winter months.

Once peeled, they oxidise quickly and should be kept and cooked in lightly acidulated water (ie with a splash of vinegar or the juice of a lemon added). Alternatively, they can be cooked before peeling.

Sautéed salsify

Serves 4
1 lemon (for acidulating)
4–6 salsify, depending on size
30g butter
Salt and freshly ground black pepper

1 Juice the lemon. Wash the salsify well, peel and cut into 4 even lengths, discarding the tapering root end. Bring a saucepan of water (with the lemon juice added) to the boil. Add the salsify, bring back to the boil, then lower the heat and simmer until tender, about 5–10 minutes, depending on their thickness.

2 Drain well and dry and cut each piece again, if you wish, in half lengthways. The salsify can be set aside like this until ready to serve.

3 Shortly before you are ready to serve, heat a frying pan over a medium heat and melt the butter. When the butter is foaming, add the salsify and sauté for a few minutes until golden. Season well with salt and pepper.

Deep-fried scorzonera with a parsley, chive and walnut pesto

Serves 4 as a starter
1 lemon (for acidulating)
6 scorzonera
4–5 tbsp plain flour, seasoned with
  a pinch of salt
2 eggs, beaten
6 tbsp panko breadcrumbs
Oil for deep-frying

For the pesto
¼ large bunch of parsley
Handful of chives
1 garlic clove
25g walnuts
100ml olive oil
30g pecorino cheese
Salt and freshly ground black pepper

1 Juice the lemon. Wash the scorzonera well, peel and cut into 4 even lengths, discarding the root end. Bring a saucepan of water (with the lemon juice added) to the boil. Add the scorzonera, bring back to the boil, then lower the heat and simmer until tender, about 5–10 minutes, depending on thickness. A cutlery knife should pass through them easily. Drain well, pat dry and cut each piece again, if necessary, in half lengthways. Set aside.

2 To make the pesto, pick the parsley leaves from the stalks and roughly chop the chives. Peel the garlic and then blend with the herbs in a food processor to a coarse paste. Add the walnuts, blitz to combine, then slowly pour in the olive oil in a thin stream, with the motor running. Grate the pecorino, add to the pesto and blitz briefly. Taste and season with salt and pepper, then transfer to a small serving bowl; set aside.

3 Heat the oven to 120°C/gas mark ½. Toss the scorzonera in the seasoned flour and shake off the excess, toss it in the beaten egg until coated, then finally in the panko breadcrumbs. One-third fill a large, deep, heavy saucepan with oil and heat to 193°C, or until a small piece of bread sizzles gently and browns in 30 seconds.

4 Deep-fry the scorzonera in the hot oil in batches, until golden, about 2–3 minutes. Drain well on kitchen paper and season very lightly with salt. Keep warm in the oven with the door ajar while you deep-fry the remaining scorzonera.

6 Pile the scorzonera onto a plate and serve the pesto as a dipping sauce.

Sweetcorn

Sweetcorn is delicious served steamed or boiled with a little butter. Throw corn cobs onto a hot barbecue or grill them and the natural sugars begin to caramelise, transforming the vegetable into a perfect accompaniment to grilled meat or fish. The sweet flavour works well with chilli and it is a lovely addition to Asian or Mexican dishes.

To remove the kernels from a corn cob (before or after cooking), stand the cob on its end. Take a sharp knife, such as a small serrated knife, and cut down the length of the cob, removing the kernels in strips.

Sweetcorn soup

Serves 4

9 corn cobs
3 banana shallots
Small handful of chives
100g butter
6 slices of pancetta or smoked streaky
  bacon
900ml chicken and veal stock (see page
  96) or vegetable stock (see page 101)
300ml double cream
Salt and ground white pepper

1 Cut the sweetcorn kernels from the cobs, removing as much of the kernel as possible. Halve, peel and finely slice the shallots. Finely chop the chives and reserve for serving.

2 Heat the butter in a medium saucepan over a low heat and add the shallots. Cover with a damp cartouche (see page 13) and lid, and sweat until soft and translucent, about 10–15 minutes.

3 Meanwhile, heat the grill to its highest setting. Derind the pancetta slices and place on a lipped baking sheet. Grill until the fat is rendered and the pancetta is crisp. Set aside to cool, then crumble into small pieces and reserve for serving.

4 Remove the lid and cartouche from the shallots, add the corn kernels and cook over a low to medium heat for 10 minutes; do not let the shallots or corn brown.

5 Add the stock, season with a little salt and white pepper and simmer for 10 minutes until the corn is tender. Add half the cream and simmer for a further 5 minutes. Remove from the heat and set aside to cool a little.

6 Blitz the mixture in a blender until completely smooth, about 5 minutes, then pass through a fine sieve into a clean saucepan. Reheat gently, then taste and adjust the seasoning. Check the consistency; it should be that of single cream, so add a little of the remaining cream if necessary.

7 To serve, divide the soup between 4 bowls, swirl a little cream in the middle and sprinkle some crisp pancetta and chives on top.

Variation

Sweetcorn purée Omit the pancetta and chives and make the soup using just 300ml stock and 100ml cream, to create a thicker purée. This is delicious as an accompaniment to chicken or fish.

Courgettes and other squashes

Squashes fall into two categories: summer and winter varieties. Summer squashes, such as courgettes, have thin tender skins and do not require peeling before cooking and eating, but can be watery. Winter squashes, including pumpkins, have a tough exterior skin that is ideally removed before cooking, and denser flesh. They are not so prone to overcooking, but are more often fibrous.

Courgette fritters with dukkah

Serves 4
For the sauce
Few dill sprigs
150g Greek yoghurt
Salt and freshly ground black pepper

For the dukkah
50g skinned hazelnuts
30g sesame seeds
1 tbsp coriander seeds
1 tbsp cumin seeds
½ tsp salt flakes
1 tsp freshly ground black pepper

For the fritters
½ onion
½ tbsp olive oil, plus extra to drizzle
1 large courgette, about 250g
1 very small rosemary sprig
½ lemon
50g ricotta cheese
1 egg white, lightly whisked
4 tbsp plain flour
Oil for frying

1 To make the sauce, chop the dill finely and stir it into the Greek yoghurt. Season with salt and pepper and set aside.

2 For the dukkah, heat the oven to 180°C/gas mark 4. Place the hazelnuts on a baking sheet and roast in the oven for 10–15 minutes until lightly toasted. Tip onto a plate and set aside to cool.

3 Meanwhile, in a frying pan set over a medium heat, toast the sesame seeds until lightly coloured, then transfer to a bowl. Dry-fry the coriander and cumin seeds for 3–5 minutes, then add them to the sesame seeds.

4 Put the cooled hazelnuts in a small food processor bowl and blend until roughly chopped. Add the toasted ingredients, salt and pepper and blend again until the mixture resembles coarse breadcrumbs.

5 For the fritters, peel and finely slice the onion. Heat the olive oil in a small pan, add the onion, cover and sweat until soft. Transfer to a bowl.

6 Coarsely grate the courgette or cut into julienne. Place in the middle of a clean tea towel and wring out any excess moisture; it must be as dry as possible.

7 Finely chop the rosemary and finely grate the zest from the lemon. Add the courgette to the sweated onion, then add the ricotta, egg white, flour, lemon zest, rosemary and seasoning.

8 Heat ½–1cm oil in a non-stick frying pan. When hot, fry spoonfuls of the batter in the oil until pale golden and crisp, turning each fritter over to brown the other side. Take care not to let the oil get too hot. Drain the fritters on kitchen paper and season them lightly with salt.

9 Serve a couple of courgette fritters on each plate, with a spoonful of sauce, a drizzle of olive oil, and sprinkled with 2 tsp of the dukkah. They can also be served as an accompaniment to lamb or poultry dishes, in which case the sauce may not be necessary.

Note Dukkah is an Egyptian spice mix used as a dry dip. You will have more than you need for the fritters. Store the rest in an airtight container to serve later, with small pieces of rustic bread which are dipped into extra virgin olive oil, then into the dukkah.

Sautéed courgettes with shallots and garlic

Serves 4
3 shallots
2–3 tbsp olive oil
3–4 courgettes
1 garlic clove
½ lemon
Salt and freshly ground black pepper

1 Halve, peel and slice the shallots. Heat the olive oil in a frying pan, add the shallots, cover and sweat until soft. Remove from the pan and set aside, reserving any oil remaining in the pan.

2 Cut the courgettes on the diagonal into 1cm thick slices. Peel and crush the garlic. Finely grate the zest from the lemon.

3 Return the frying pan to a medium heat and fry the courgettes until golden brown. Try not to let them get too brown; a deep golden colour is ideal.

4 Add the garlic and the sweated shallots to the courgettes and continue to cook for 1 minute, then stir in the lemon zest and season well with salt and pepper. Serve at once.

Variations

Sautéed courgettes with shallots and pine nuts Just before serving, add 50g toasted pine nuts and ½ tbsp coarsely chopped marjoram leaves to the sautéed courgettes and toss through.

Sautéed courgettes with shallots, pine nuts and sun-blushed tomatoes Add a handful of sun-blushed tomatoes, with 30g black olives, to the variation above, and heat through.

Courgettes and spinach

Serves 4
3 courgettes
250g spinach
30g butter
Freshly grated nutmeg
Salt and freshly ground black pepper

1 Coarsely grate the courgettes, season with salt and leave them in a sieve or colander set over a bowl, to remove excess water (ie degorge, see page 28) for 1 hour.

2 Meanwhile, wash the spinach in several changes of water until it is completely clean. Drain and remove any tough central stalks.

3 Heat a large, heavy-based saucepan until hot. Add enough of the spinach to loosely fill the pan and cover with a tight-fitting lid. The spinach cooks in the steam from the water it was washed in. You may need to do this in batches as the spinach will not wilt properly if the pan is overfilled. Stir every 30 seconds or so until all the spinach has completely wilted.

4 Transfer the wilted spinach to a sieve and press out as much liquid as possible using the underside of a ladle, then coarsely chop.

5 Heat half the butter in a large, heavy-based frying pan until foaming. Squeeze any remaining excess liquid out of the courgettes, then mix them with the wilted spinach. Stir-fry half the mixture in the butter, adding a light grating of nutmeg and seasoning well with pepper; remove to a bowl. Repeat with the remaining butter and courgette and spinach mixture.

6 Return all the mixture to the pan. Check the seasoning and adjust as necessary. Serve at once.

Maple roasted butternut squash with sage and pine nuts

Serves 4

1 red onion
1 butternut squash
3 tbsp olive oil
30g pine nuts
50ml maple syrup
4–5 sage leaves
Salt and freshly ground black pepper

1 Heat the oven to 200°C/gas mark 6.

2 Halve and peel the red onion and trim away the fibres from the root. Cut the onion into thin wedges through the root, keeping them intact, making about 8–10 wedges. Peel and deseed the butternut squash and cut into 2–3cm dice.

3 Place the onion wedges and squash in a large roasting tin, ensuring they are not crowded, and drizzle over the olive oil. Season with salt and pepper, then turn the squash cubes through the oil and seasoning to ensure they are fully coated.

4 Roast in the oven for 30 minutes, turning occasionally to encourage even browning. Meanwhile, toast the pine nuts in a separate roasting tin in the oven for 5–10 minutes until just golden brown, then tip onto a plate.

5 Stir the maple syrup through the squash and onion, place the roasting tin over a medium to high heat on the hob and caramelise the squash evenly all over, stirring occasionally. This should take about 5–10 minutes.

6 Chiffonade the sage (see page 89) and stir it through the squash with the toasted pine nuts. Taste and adjust the seasoning. This can be served hot as an accompaniment or cooled to room temperature, combined with rocket or watercress and served as a salad.

Butternut squash, coconut and lemongrass soup

**Serves 6–8 as a starter
or 4 as a main course**

2 large onions
4 large garlic cloves
3 tbsp vegetable oil
1 medium-large butternut squash,
    about 1kg
4 lemongrass stalks
1½ x 400ml tins coconut milk
800ml vegetable stock (see page 101)
    or chicken and veal stock (see page 96)
8 fresh kaffir lime leaves or a few
    gratings of lime zest
4 tbsp nam pla (fish sauce), or to taste
Handful of coriander leaves

1 Halve, peel and dice the onions. Peel the garlic cloves and bash with the flat side of a knife.

2 Heat the oil in a large, heavy-based saucepan over a very low heat. Add the onions and garlic, cover and gently sweat until the onions are soft and beginning to caramelise, about 15 minutes. Meanwhile, peel, deseed and dice the squash.

3 When the onions are soft, take the whole lemongrass stalks and bash them using a pestle and mortar to release their flavour. Add two of them to the onions and cook briefly, then add the diced squash and cook, stirring, for a further 5 minutes.

4 Add the coconut milk and stock and bring to the boil. Lower the heat and simmer gently, uncovered, until the squash is soft, about 20 minutes.

5 Remove the lemongrass and blend the soup thoroughly using a hand-held stick blender, or in batches in a free-standing blender or food processor. For a really velvety finish, push the soup through a fine sieve, or chinois.

6 To serve, reheat the soup gently, adding the remaining 2 bashed lemongrass stalks. Remove from the heat. Tear the lime leaves in half to release their flavour and add them, or the lime zest, with the fish sauce. Taste, and add more fish sauce if necessary. Just before serving, remove the lime leaves and lemongrass. Chop the coriander leaves and scatter them over the soup to serve.

A note on using aromatics...

Most aromatics (lemongrass, lime leaves etc) have a very delicate flavour, and they can lose their freshness and flavour if they cook for too long. For this reason, in Asian cuisine they are often added at the end of cooking.

Marinated Mediterranean vegetables

Serves 4
1 aubergine
4–5 tbsp olive oil
2 red peppers
3 courgettes
2 onions
3 tomatoes
Few basil sprigs
Few mint sprigs
2–3 tbsp aged balsamic vinegar
Salt and freshly ground black pepper

1 Heat the grill to its highest setting.

2 Cut the aubergine in half lengthways and then across into slices 5mm thick. Brush with olive oil and grill on both sides until soft and dark brown. Transfer to a bowl.

3 Halve, quarter and deseed the peppers and grill, skin side up, until the skins are charred and blistered. Remove to a plastic bag to cool. Once cool, skin the peppers, cut them into wide strips and add to the aubergines.

4 Trim the courgettes, slice on the diagonal into 5mm thick slices and drizzle over 1–2 tbsp olive oil. Heat a griddle pan on a medium to high heat and griddle the courgette slices in batches, until browning but not fully softened. Add to the aubergines and peppers.

5 Halve, peel and cut the onions into 1cm thick wedges, turn them through the remaining olive oil and griddle until browning and starting to soften; add to the other vegetables.

6 Plunge the tomatoes into boiling water for 10 seconds, then refresh in cold water, drain, dry and peel them. Cut the tomatoes into quarters, deseed them and add to the other vegetables.

7 Tear 5–6 leaves each of basil and mint into the bowl, sprinkle over the balsamic vinegar and season with salt and pepper. Mix well and leave at room temperature for about 30 minutes to allow the flavours to infuse.

8 These vegetables are good served with any roasted or barbecued meats, such as a garlic and rosemary scented slow-roasted shoulder of lamb (see page 426).

Variations

Marinated Mediterranean vegetables with tomato and basil Prepare the vegetables as above to the end of step 6. Make 1 quantity of fresh tomato sauce (see page 128) and stir through the cooked vegetables with 2 tbsp chopped basil, omitting the balsamic vinegar. Serve hot.

Pesto marinated Mediterranean vegetables In place of the herbs and balsamic vinegar, stir 3 tbsp basil pesto (see page 126) into the warm vegetables and allow the flavours to infuse before serving. If you like, add 50g crumbled feta or coarsely grated Parmesan once the vegetables have cooled a little. Sprinkle with 2 tbsp toasted pine nuts just before serving.

Cumin marinated Mediterranean vegetables Omit the peppers, and use 5 courgettes. Prepare the vegetables as above to the end of step 6. Put 2 tbsp olive oil in a small saucepan and add 1 tsp ground cumin, 1 tsp nigella seeds and a pinch of chilli flakes. Place over a medium heat until the spices sizzle, about 1 minute. Add 1 tbsp red wine vinegar, a pinch of caster sugar and a further 1 tbsp olive oil. Season well with salt and pepper and pour over the vegetables. Stir in 2 tbsp coriander leaves and leave to stand for 30 minutes before serving.

Tomatoes

Tomatoes are widely available in a variety of shapes and sizes, from large beefsteak tomatoes through plum and salad varieties to cherry tomatoes. They have endless uses, both raw and cooked. Choose firm tomatoes with deep red skins and a definite tomato aroma. In winter when homegrown tomatoes are unavailable, tinned tomatoes are often a better option for cooking than imported fresh tomatoes.

Peeling tomatoes

Tomato skins are often removed as they can be indigestible. Plunge the tomatoes into boiling water for 10 seconds (no longer or the flesh will start to cook). Drain and refresh in cold water. Once cool, remove, dry and peel the tomatoes. Use as required.

Deseeding tomatoes

Quarter the peeled tomatoes through the core and, using a teaspoon, scoop out and discard the seeds and juice.

Tomato concasse

Stack the deseeded tomato quarters, slice lengthways and then across to create fine dice. Try not to crush the tomato as you cut, to ensure the dice retain their shape and don't turn into a mush.

Gazpacho

Serves 4

1.25kg (about 15 medium) ripe tomatoes
½ small onion
1 cucumber
1½ red peppers
2 garlic cloves
1 green jalapeño chilli (optional)
Small bunch of parsley
75ml olive oil
50ml tarragon vinegar
Caster sugar, salt and freshly ground
   black pepper

1 Peel and deseed the tomatoes (see above). Peel and coarsely dice the onion. Peel the cucumber. Cut off a quarter of the cucumber and reserve for the garnish. Halve the rest of the cucumber lengthways, scoop out the seeds and coarsely chop the flesh.

2 Core and deseed the red peppers, and set aside the half pepper. Peel and crush the garlic and roughly chop the chilli, if using, and the whole pepper.

3 Put the tomatoes, onion, chopped cucumber and pepper, garlic, chilli, if using, and the parsley leaves in a food processor and blend until smooth. Add the olive oil, vinegar and seasoning to taste, including a little sugar to balance the acidity of the tomatoes. Transfer to a bowl, cover and chill in the fridge for about 2 hours.

4 Before serving, deseed and very finely dice the rest of the cucumber and red pepper. Serve the gazpacho with the cucumber and pepper garnish.

Note Often bread is added to gazpacho to thicken it slightly. If you prefer a thicker consistency, add a slice of day-old white bread when blending the vegetables, but expect the bread to dilute the colour somewhat.

Heritage tomato salad

Serves 4

1–2 tbsp white wine vinegar
½ tsp caster sugar
6 tbsp olive oil
1 small banana shallot
Few oregano sprigs
8–10 heritage tomatoes (ideally
  a mixture of colours and sizes)
Sea salt and freshly ground black pepper

1 In a small bowl, combine the wine vinegar and sugar with some salt and pepper to make a vinaigrette. Stir well to allow the sugar to dissolve before slowly whisking in the olive oil.

2 Halve, peel and finely dice the shallot and chop enough oregano leaves to give you ½–1 tsp. Mix the shallot and oregano into the vinaigrette and set aside for 5–10 minutes to allow the flavours to blend.

3 Slice the tomatoes thinly through the equator so they still hold their shape. Pour the dressing over the tomatoes, making sure they are well coated. Adjust the seasoning and arrange on a plate.

Cherry tomato and grilled pepper salad

Serves 4

1 red pepper
1 yellow or orange pepper
250g cherry tomatoes, ideally a mixture
  of colours
1 tsp ground sumac
1 tsp ground cumin
Large pinch of smoked paprika
3 tbsp olive oil
1½ tbsp pomegranate molasses
Salt and freshly ground black pepper

1 Cut all the peppers into quarters, grill and skin them (see page 55). Cut the skinned peppers into even strips, about 5mm thick.

2 Cut the cherry tomatoes into halves or quarters, depending on their size. Mix them with the peppers.

3 In a small bowl, mix together the remaining ingredients except the salt and pepper, to make the dressing.

4 Toss the pepper and tomato mixture in the dressing. Season to taste with salt and pepper.

Italian tomato salad with crisp Parma ham

Serves 4

4 small plum tomatoes
2 tbsp olive oil
Handful of basil sprigs
4 slices of Parma ham
250g cherry tomatoes
40ml fresh tomato sauce (see page 128)
1 tbsp balsamic vinegar
Pinch of caster sugar
200g bag of mixed salad leaves
Salt and freshly ground black pepper

1 Heat the oven to 200°C/gas mark 6.

2 Cut the plum tomatoes in half lengthways, remove the green core and place them on a baking sheet cut side up. Sprinkle with ½ tbsp of the olive oil, tear some basil leaves over them and season well with salt and pepper. Bake in the oven for 15–20 minutes, or until the tops are browning but the tomatoes are still firm. Take out of the oven, release the tomatoes from the tray and leave to cool.

3 Lightly grease another baking sheet and lay out the slices of Parma ham. Bake them in the oven for about 10 minutes until very crisp, taking care not to let them get too dark. Remove them from the baking sheet and set aside.

4 Cut the cherry tomatoes into quarters.

5 For the dressing, put the fresh tomato sauce, balsamic vinegar and remaining 1½ tbsp olive oil in a small food processor bowl and whiz together. When smooth, season with the sugar and some salt and pepper, and transfer to a large bowl.

6 Toss the salad leaves, a handful of torn basil leaves and the cherry tomatoes in the dressing. Add the cooled, roasted plum tomatoes and turn them through gently. Plate the salad and finish with shards of the crisp Parma ham.

Baby vegetables

Baby vegetables are simple to cook and prepare. Served whole, they often require nothing more than a quick scrub, as their skins tend to be thinner, and therefore don't need to be removed. Baby courgettes are delicious served steamed, drizzled with olive oil and sprinkled with shredded mint and crumbled feta cheese.

Glazed baby vegetables

Serves 4
6 baby onions
8 baby carrots
6 baby parsnips
½–1 swede
40g butter
1 tbsp caster sugar
Small handful of flat-leaf parsley sprigs
Salt and freshly ground black pepper

1 Wash the vegetables well. Peel the onions, leaving them as natural looking as possible. Turn the swede (as for carrots, see page 16) into 8 pieces the same size as the other vegetables.

2 Place the turned swede and onions in a wide saucepan, in a single layer. Add the butter and sugar to the pan and enough water so it comes halfway up the sides of the vegetables. Season the vegetables with salt and pepper. Bring to a simmer and cook for 10–15 minutes.

3 Add the carrots and parsnips to the pan and cook for a further 15–20 minutes until all the vegetables are just tender, shaking the pan occasionally to ensure they are evenly coated in the glaze. Do not allow them to brown; if necessary add a little more water. By the time the vegetables are cooked, the water should have evaporated so the vegetables are coated only with the butter and sugar.

4 Taste and adjust the seasoning. Chop enough parsley leaves to give you ½ tbsp and stir it through the vegetables.

Roasted baby vegetables

Serves 4
8 baby leeks
8 baby onions
8 baby carrots
8 baby turnips
8 new potatoes
2 tbsp olive oil
3 tsp clear honey
Small handful of thyme sprigs
2 tsp white balsamic vinegar
Salt and freshly ground black pepper

1 Heat the oven to 220°C/gas mark 7.

2 Trim off a little of the green from the leeks and trim off the hairy root end. Place the leeks in a bowl of cold water for 5 minutes.

3 Bring a saucepan of water to the boil. Add the onions and boil for 1 minute, then remove with a slotted spoon and let cool. Peel and trim off the hairy fronds of the root end, keeping the onions intact and as natural looking as possible.

4 Drain the leeks and boil in the onion water for 30 seconds. Drain.

5 Trim off most of the green carrot tops, leaving about 2cm, and scrub under cold water with a new scourer. Scrub the turnips too. Halve the potatoes if large.

6 Put all the vegetables into a shallow roasting tin with the olive oil, 1 tsp of the honey, the thyme and some salt and pepper. Toss everything together so it is well coated, then spread out the vegetables in a single layer.

7 Roast in the oven for about 30 minutes until all the vegetables are tender, turning them once or twice so they brown evenly.

8 Remove from the oven, pick off and discard the thyme sprigs, then drizzle with the remaining honey and the balsamic vinegar. Taste and adjust the seasoning, sweetness and acidity, then transfer to a bowl and serve warm or hot.

Herbs

Herbs add flavour, colour and aroma to dishes. Whenever possible use fresh herbs, which have much more fragrance and vitality than dried. Their flavour comes from the essential oils in the leaves and stalks, which are released by heat or bruising.

Chopping herbs

1 Wash the bunch of herbs under cold running water and dry well. Pick off the leaves; the stalks can be used for infusing dishes. Place the leaves on a board and gather them together gently, without bruising, into a tight pack. Slice across them to start to reduce them in size.

2 Then, holding the knife in one hand, with the fingers of your other hand resting on the top third of the knife closest to the point, use the knife in a lever action to chop across the herbs.

3 Keep doing this, and scraping the herbs together, then chop across again. Continue in this manner until you have chopped the herbs to the required fineness.

To chiffonade herbs

This technique of finely shredding herbs is most successful with large soft herb leaves, such as basil or sage.

1 After washing and drying the herbs, pick the leaves and pile them on top of each other.

2 Then roll them up as tightly as possible, but without bruising them, and cut across the leaves to create a fine julienne of herb.

3 The herbs may need to be unrolled a little.

Parsley salad

Serves 4
Large bunch of flat-leaf parsley,
    about 90–100g
½ lemon
3 tbsp olive oil
½–1 tsp toasted sesame oil
½–1 tsp clear honey
Salt and freshly ground black pepper

1 Wash the parsley well and dry it. Pick the leaves from the stalks. The stalks can be kept for making stock rather than discarded.

2 Squeeze enough juice from the lemon to give you 1 tbsp and put it into a bowl. Add salt and pepper and mix in the remaining ingredients. The oil, acidity and sweetness of the dressing should be balanced, so taste it with the parsley and adjust the balance and seasoning as necessary.

3 Dress the parsley up to 30 minutes before serving to allow the flavours to blend; unlike most leaves, parsley can be dressed ahead without adversely affecting the texture or flavour.

Herb beignets

Makes about 15
Oil for deep-frying
30g cornflour
2 egg whites
Selection of large herb leaves, such as
    basil, parsley or sage
Salt and white pepper

1 One-third fill a large, deep heavy saucepan with oil and heat to 195°C, or until a small piece of bread dropped into the oil gently sizzles and browns in about 20 seconds.

2 To make the batter, mix the cornflour with the egg whites, and add salt and white pepper. Dip the herb leaves in the batter and immediately place in the hot oil, lowering them in with a slotted spoon. Turn carefully to ensure an even frying.

3 When the batter turns crisp and golden, remove the beignets and drain on kitchen paper. Sprinkle with a little salt and use as a garnish.

Deep-frying herbs
Some herbs, such as parsley, basil and sage can be successfully deep-fried for use as a garnish. The leaves can be kept on the stalks or picked off, depending on the desired effect. Because of their high water content, take care when deep-frying herbs as they will splutter when they are put in hot oil. Don't try to deep-fry too many at once. To deep-fry herbs, follow the recipe above, omitting the batter.

Herb oils

Herb oils can be used to flavour a dish and/or used as a garnish providing a little colour on a plate. Herbs will need to be blanched and refreshed to maintain their colour. Suitable herbs are chives, parsley and basil.

Chive, basil or parsley oil

Makes 300ml
Bunch of herb of your choice,
    about 40g
150ml sunflower oil
150ml olive oil
Salt

1 Blanch the herbs in boiling water for a few seconds only, until just wilted, then refresh in cold water and drain well. Place them in a blender with both oils and a little salt and blitz until the herbs are completely broken up and have almost become a purée.

2 Pour the oil into a bowl, cover with cling film and keep at room temperature for a few hours or overnight.

3 Strain the oil through a muslin-lined sieve to remove the herbs. Use as required.

Spices

Spices are dried seeds, roots or other vegetative substances that are used to flavour food. Generally pungent and highly flavoured, their addition can entirely transform a dish, giving it a unique personality. They are often used in combination, and different cuisines have their own particular spice mixes. In Indian, Southeast Asian and Middle Eastern cookery, spices are often cooked with the base ingredients of a dish, to provide a rounded flavour, and fresh herbs or aromatics are added at the last minute, to provide a burst of flavour before serving.

Using spices

Some recipes call for whole spices but where ground spices are required, for optimum flavour it is preferable to freshly grind whole spices yourself rather than use bought ready-ground spices. Grind them finely in a spice grinder (or a coffee grinder works just as well, but keep it purely for grinding spices). If all you can buy is ground spices, buy small quantities and use them relatively quickly, as their flavour intensity decreases over time.

Warming/toasting spices

Most recipes call for spices to be added at the beginning of a cooking process, whole or ground and either dry-fried/toasted in a frying pan or often sautéed in a little oil. This warming or toasting draws out the flavours of the spices and begins to reduce their 'rawness'. It ensures the flavours of the spices have time to develop and infuse into the other ingredients. Spices added at the end of cooking often leave the dish with a slightly bitter, raw spice flavour. However, there are some dishes that benefit from this.

Quantities

Spices can be very strong in flavour so follow recipes carefully when measuring to avoid over-spicing, which results in harsh, pungently flavoured dishes. Spices are used to complement, enhance and often to provide subtle warm overtones to a dish, but always keep in mind that the amount of spice can be varied to taste.

Harissa paste

Makes 120g
100g red chillies, to taste
1 red pepper
6 garlic cloves
1 tbsp cumin seeds
1 tbsp coriander seeds
1 tsp caraway seeds
½ tsp red wine vinegar
1 tsp salt
2–3 tbsp olive oil

This hot pepper spice paste is used extensively in North African cooking. It may be used as a rub for chicken and lamb before cooking, or added to couscous, soups and stews. Depending on the heat required, some of the chilli seeds can be retained. It can be stored in a clean scalded jar, covered with oil, in the fridge for up to 3 months.

1 Halve and deseed the chillies, then chop coarsely. Char the red pepper (see page 55), then skin, core, deseed and chop it roughly.

2 Peel and finely chop the garlic. Toast the spices in a frying pan over a low heat until the spices smell fragrant. Remove from the heat and allow to cool.

3 Place the chillies and peppers in a blender with the garlic, the toasted spices, red wine vinegar and salt and blend well until a smoothish paste is formed. Add olive oil as necessary to help blend the mixture.

Stocks & sauces

A wide range of sauces are covered in this section, from rich stock-based sauces that require care and time, to quick pan sauces that can be made while your meat or poultry is resting. Key skills include being able to make a clear, well-flavoured stock, and perfecting the art of thickening sauces without creating lumps. The classic, basic sauces are easily adapted to produce derivative sauces and variations (as indicated on page 102). Master the classics, try the derivatives and then experiment by adding your own choice of flavour combinations.

Stocks

Using good quality ingredients and a good technique will give you a high quality stock. And as stock is a vital component in many recipes, the quality of the finished dish is often dependent upon the quality of the stock used. Slow, gentle simmering is the secret to a fine stock.

For a simple stock, also described as a 'white stock', the bones and vegetables are simmered together with appropriate flavouring herbs and vegetables to produce a delicately flavoured stock. Veal, poultry, fish, shellfish and vegetable stocks are most often 'white stocks'.

For a brown stock, the bones and vegetables are browned before the stock is simmered. This results in a rich, strongly flavoured stock – useful for adding depth of flavour and colour to slow-cooked stews and braises. The browning process colours the bones and vegetables, and this colour is transferred to the stock on cooking. Importantly, the cooking of the bones also renders much of the fat from the bones, making it easier to remove (see dépouiller, page 97). Brown stocks are most often made from red meats, but you can also make brown poultry, game, fish, shellfish and vegetable stocks. Care must be taken to avoid scorching the bones and vegetables, which will infuse the stock with a bitter, burnt flavour.

The cooking time for stocks varies enormously, from 30 minutes for fish, shellfish and vegetable stocks to 5–6 hours for brown beef, veal and lamb stocks. Fish and shellfish bones, and shells, impart a bitter flavour to stocks if they are cooked for too long. Vegetable stocks need very little cooking as the flavour is quickly transferred to the water and, since vegetables contain little fat, stocks are easily skimmed.

Ingredients for stock making

Bones Fresh bones are ideal for stock making; the leftover bones from a roast can be used if you wish, although the flavour will be weaker. Veal bones are generally preferable for stock making as they impart a wonderful gelatinous quality and a clean, clear flavour.

Vegetables Onion, carrot and celery are commonly used. Starchy vegetables, such as potatoes, which can make the stock cloudy, should be avoided. When preparing a stock for a particular recipe, other vegetables can be added, such as fennel for a fish stock, but it's important that the flavour of the vegetables does not overwhelm the meat or fish flavour of the stock. Follow the guidelines in each recipe for the correct ratio of bones to vegetables, and consider the sweetness and the combination of the vegetables you are using: too many carrots can result in a very sweet stock, for example, and if you are adding leeks, then reduce the number of onions.

Aromatics Parsley, thyme and bay are the herbs most often added to stocks, but if the stock is being made for a specific recipe, then other herbs might be included. Generally, only the stalks of soft herbs such as parsley are used, as too many leaves can discolour the stock. Peppercorns complete the aromatic additions to classic stocks, but in Asian cooking, lemongrass, garlic, ginger and galangal are sometimes added.

Salt This should not be added when making stocks, as the stock may have to be reduced for use or storage and adding salt would result in over-seasoned dishes.

Water When this is added to bones and vegetables it should always be cold. If hot water is used it melts the fat immediately, which can cloud the stock. When cold water is added during simmering (a technique known as dépouiller, see page 97), it helps to solidify fat, which makes it easier to skim from the surface.

Chicken and veal stock

Makes 1 litre (in a 10-litre stockpot)
2kg raw chicken carcasses
1kg veal bones
3 onions
2 carrots
4 celery sticks
Handful of parsley stalks
Few thyme sprigs
2 bay leaves
Few black peppercorns
Handful of button mushrooms

1 Trim any excess fat from the chicken carcasses and cut them in half. Trim off excess fat from the veal bones. Peel the onions and carrots and cut them and the celery into large chunks. Put the veal and chicken in a tall stockpot and add enough cold water to cover. Place over a medium to high heat and bring slowly to the boil. Immediately turn the heat down and dépouiller the stock (see right).

2 Skim off the fat and scum that will have risen to the surface, until the stock is as clear as possible. Add the prepared vegetables, along with the aromatics, to the stockpot. Add more cold water to cover the bones and vegetables, then add the mushrooms. Simmer very gently for 2–3 hours, skimming occasionally.

3 Strain the stock carefully through a fine sieve into a clean pan and reduce over a medium heat to the required concentration of flavour for use. Alternatively, to store the stock, continue to reduce it until slightly 'sticky' when tested between thumb and finger. The stock can be cooled, refrigerated and kept for up to 3 days in the fridge, or frozen for up to 3 months.

1 Adding enough cold water to cover the veal bones and chicken carcasses.

2 Skimming off the fat and scum from the surface of the stock.

3 Testing the consistency of the reduced stock.

Variation

Chicken stock If you are unable to obtain veal bones, simply increase the quantity of chicken carcasses to 3kg.

....

A note on the strength of flavour...

If a recipe calls for a strong or well flavoured stock, simmer the finished stock rapidly over a medium heat to reduce it slightly and intensify the flavour.

Understanding more about stock...

Removing fat and impurities

Because raw bones are used in a 'white stock', all the fat still left on the bones melts as the stock comes up to the boil, and must be skimmed off. The dépouiller (see below) and skimming process for this type of stock is generally much lengthier than for brown stock (where the bones are roasted first), and as much as a quarter of the liquid can be skimmed from the pot to help in the removal of the fat and scum. Often a double dépouiller is needed, with any liquid removed replaced with cold water.

Dépouiller

This technique involves splashing a large amount of cold water into a stock (about 500ml for a 10-litre stockpot), generally as it is coming up to the boil. This helps to lower the temperature and most importantly to solidify fat and scum, lifting it to the surface ready for skimming. You can also dépouiller during the simmering process if there is a lot of fat and scum present.

Glace

A very well reduced stock is called a glace, or glace de viande (or meat or fish glaze). It has a very concentrated flavour and is used sparingly. A sauce or dish will sometimes need a little glace or glaze to be added towards the end of cooking to boost the flavour, such as a glace de viande for a béarnaise sauce. Sometimes it is added at the beginning, such as a fish glaze used in the reduction for a fish beurre blanc.

Take care when reducing stock for a glace that it is not over-reduced to the point where it catches and begins to burn, which will give it a bitter flavour; a glace should be very sticky to the touch (see page 98).

Storing stock

It is best to store frozen stock in small quantities so that only the required amount need be defrosted for use. Ice-cube trays are suitable for glace, as often only a very small amount is needed to 'lift' a dish or sauce.

Stocks cannot be refrigerated or frozen before they have cooled, so start making stocks that call for lengthy cooking early on in the day. If you need to hasten cooling, add a jug of ice to the stock to lower the temperature quickly.

When reheating the stock the following day, it must be brought back up to the boil before the temperature is turned down and the stock is simmered again. Don't be tempted to keep adding ingredients as this can present food safety issues if the stock is not brought properly back up to the boil after each addition.

Brown chicken and veal stock

**Makes about 1 litre
(in a 10-litre stockpot)**
2kg raw chicken carcasses
1kg veal bones
3 onions
2 carrots
4 celery sticks
3 tbsp vegetable oil
2 tsp tomato purée
Handful of parsley stalks
Few thyme sprigs
2 bay leaves
Few black peppercorns
Handful of button mushrooms

1 Heat the oven to 200°C/gas mark 6. Trim any excess fat from the chicken carcasses and cut them in half.

2 Place the chicken carcasses and veal bones in a large roasting tin and roast in the oven, turning occasionally to ensure even browning, for about 50–60 minutes, or until golden brown.

3 Meanwhile, cut the onions in half; the skin can be left on. Peel the carrots and cut them and the celery into large chunks. Heat the oil in a saucepan and brown the onions, carrots and celery over a medium to high heat. Although the vegetables can be browned in the oven, it is more efficient and more colour is achieved if they are browned on the hob.

4 Once the vegetables have browned, add the tomato purée and stir to caramelise it around the vegetables for 2–3 minutes.

5 Transfer the vegetables and browned bones to a tall stockpot and add enough cold water to cover. Place on a medium to high heat and bring slowly to the boil. Once boiling, immediately turn the heat down and dépouiller (see page 97).

6 Now skim off the fat and scum that will have risen to the surface. Replace any liquid removed with cold water.

7 Add the parsley, thyme, bay leaves and peppercorns. Add the mushrooms, halving any larger ones; they will absorb some surface fat as well as add flavour.

8 Simmer the stock very gently, uncovered, for 4–5 hours, skimming occasionally. If liquid is removed during the skimming process, replace it with cold water. The bones and vegetables should always be covered with liquid to ensure maximum flavour extraction.

9 Strain the stock carefully through a fine sieve into a clean pan and reduce over a medium heat to the required concentration of flavour for use. Alternatively, to store the stock, continue to reduce it until slightly 'sticky' when tested between thumb and finger. The stock can be cooled and refrigerated or frozen, then kept for up to 3 days in the fridge, and up to 3 months in the freezer.

Variations

Brown beef or lamb stock Beef or lamb bones can be substituted for the chicken bones in the main recipe. Cook the stock for a little longer, 5–6 hours, to allow as much extraction of flavour as possible; this will take longer than chicken because of the density of the bones.

Brown game stock Substitute any feathered game bones for the chicken. The flavour can be strong, so for a lighter game stock cook it for less time.

To make glace de viande or meat glaze...

To ensure you always have some glace to hand, reduce a sizeable amount of stock, such as 1 litre, and freeze what you don't need to use straight away in ice-cube trays.

Put brown chicken and veal stock in a deep frying pan or a saucepan and simmer until the stock is very well reduced to a thick, gelatinous consistency. When a little is tested between your thumb and fingertip it will feel very sticky (like Vaseline). It will taste too strong but this does not matter, as it will be diluted in the final sauce. Take care not to reduce it any further as the natural sugars in the stock will continue to caramelise and the glaze will burn. Strain the glace into a container or ice-cube tray. Once cool, it will be like a firm jelly.

1 Trimming excess fat from the chicken carcass.

2 The browned chicken and veal bones, ready for the stockpot.

3 Browning the onions, carrots and celery.

4 Caramelising the tomato purée.

5 Adding cold water to dépouiller the stock.

6 Skimming off the fat and scum from the surface.

7 Adding the aromatics and mushrooms.

8 Gently simmering the stock, ensuring the bones and vegetables are covered in liquid.

9 Testing the consistency of the reduced stock.

Fish stock

**Makes about 1 litre
(in a 10-litre stockpot)**
3kg fish bones, ideally from flat white
   fish (such as sole, brill or plaice)
1 onion
2 carrots
2 leeks
4 celery sticks
½ fennel bulb
Handful of parsley stalks
Few thyme sprigs
2 bay leaves
Few black peppercorns

1 Rinse the fish bones under cold water and cut off the heads from some of the frames (too many fish heads can cause bitterness in a stock). Cut the frames into large pieces, put into a tall stockpot and cover with cold water. Place on a medium to high heat and bring slowly to the boil. Meanwhile, peel the onion, carrots and leeks and cut them and the celery and fennel into thick slices.

2 As soon as the stock comes to the boil, turn the heat down and dépouiller (see page 97). Skim off the fat and scum that will have risen to the surface until the stock is as clear as possible. Add the vegetables and aromatics to the stockpot, and more cold water to cover the bones and vegetables. Simmer very gently for 20–30 minutes, skimming occasionally.

3 Strain the stock carefully through a fine sieve into a clean pan. Reduce over a medium heat to the required flavour concentration for use. Alternatively, to store the stock, continue to reduce it until a stronger concentration is achieved. The stock can be cooled and refrigerated or frozen, then kept for up to 3 days in the fridge or 3 months in the freezer.

1 The fish frames cut into manageable pieces for the stockpot.

2 Adding cold water to dépouiller the stock.

3 Straining the stock through a fine sieve.

Variations

Shellfish stock Proceed as for white fish stock, but substitute the fish bones with the same weight of crustacean shells, such as prawn, lobster and crab.

Brown fish/shellfish stock It is difficult to brown fish and shellfish bones, so you can brown just the vegetables lightly in 2–3 tbsp vegetable oil, then add them to the stock. A little more skimming will be required to remove the oil used.

Vegetable stock

**Makes about 1 litre
(in a 10-litre stockpot)**
6 onions
6 carrots
1 head of celery
4 leeks
Handful of parsley stalks
Few thyme sprigs
2 bay leaves
Few black peppercorns

1 Wash and peel the vegetables, as appropriate to each, and cut into large chunks. Place in a tall stockpot with the aromatics and cover with cold water. Place on a medium to high heat and bring slowly to a simmer. Reduce the heat and cook gently for 30 minutes, skimming as necessary. No fat is involved in making vegetable stock, so it is only scum that might rise to the surface.

2 Strain the stock carefully through a fine sieve and reduce to the required flavour concentration for use. Alternatively, to store the stock, continue to reduce it over a medium heat until a stronger concentration is achieved. The stock can be cooled and refrigerated or frozen then kept in the fridge for up to 3 days or the freezer for up to 6 months.

Variation

Brown vegetable stock Brown the vegetables in 2–3 tbsp vegetable oil until a deep golden colour all over. Make sure they brown rather than sweat or the stock will be too sweet, but also that they are not scorched, which will impart a bitter taste. After browning, add 2 tsp tomato purée to the vegetables and caramelise for 2–3 minutes before adding to the stockpot. A little more skimming will be required than for the main recipe, to remove the oil used to brown the vegetables.

Flour-thickened sauces

Flour-thickened sauces are generally roux-based sauces. The three most common rouxs are white, blond and brown. These are used to thicken various liquids to make white, velouté and espagnole sauces.

A roux is a mixture of (generally) equal quantities of flour and butter, which is cooked over a medium heat for a specified amount of time and to which a measured quantity of liquid, in the form of milk or stock, is added. Rouxs are cooked to varying degrees to achieve different effects and appearances; so a white roux is cooked for less time than a blond, and a brown for the longest.

Savoury sauces

Flour-thickened sauces	Derivatives
White sauce	Béchamel, Mornay, Parsley, Soubise
Velouté sauce	Chicken, Fish
Espagnole sauce	Madeira, Bordelaise, Chasseur

Emulsion sauces	Derivatives
Mayonnaise	Aioli, Gribiche, Mustard, Sweet miso, Tartare
Hollandaise	Béarnaise, Choron, Herby, Mousseline, Paloise
Beurre blanc	Mustard, Chicken, Fish

Composite/Other sauces
Reductions and Pan sauces Jus, Cream and Butter pan sauces
Flavoured butters Maître d'hôtel, Garlic etc
Vinaigrettes
Pestos and Salsas
Tomato sauces
Traditional sauces Apple, Mint, Cranberry and orange, Bread, Horseradish, Mustard, Rouille, Raita

White, blond and brown roux sauce bases

White sauce

Makes 300ml
20g butter
20g plain flour
300ml milk
Salt and ground white pepper

The most basic, but also the most common of all the roux-based sauces, the classic white sauce is used for a wide range of dishes – either as an integral part of the dish or as an accompanying sauce.

1 Melt the butter in a small saucepan over a gentle to medium heat, then add the flour. Cook the roux for 1 minute, stirring well with a wooden spoon to ensure even cooking.

2 Remove the pan from the heat and gradually add the milk, a little at a time, stirring and incorporating the milk well into the roux as it is added. It is important not to add the milk too quickly or lumps will result, which are difficult to beat out. As more of the milk is added the sauce will start to loosen and thin out. Once half has been incorporated, add the remaining milk in generous additions, and return the pan to the heat.

3 Increase the heat to medium to high and stir the sauce constantly as it comes to the boil (it has to boil in order to thicken). Once it has come to the boil, reduce the heat and simmer for 2 minutes. Season with salt and white pepper to taste.

1 Cooking the roux base.

2 Incorporating the milk into the roux.

3 Stirring the sauce constantly as it comes to the boil and thickens.

Variations

Béchamel sauce Heat the milk in a saucepan until scalding, then take off the heat and infuse with ¼ peeled onion, 1 bay leaf, 1 mace blade, a few parsley stalks and 4 white peppercorns. Allow the infused milk to cool and absorb the flavours, then strain before proceeding as for the main recipe. This sauce is generally used for lasagne.

Mornay sauce Reduce the butter and flour quantities to 10g each. Make the white sauce as above, adding a pinch each of mustard powder and cayenne pepper with the flour. After simmering the sauce for 2 minutes, remove it from the heat and add 75g grated strong Cheddar or Gruyère. Stir the cheese through the hot sauce to melt it. Season to taste. Do not reheat the sauce after the cheese is added as the cheese may become grainy, greasy or stringy. This classic sauce is used for macaroni cheese and cauliflower cheese.

Parsley sauce Heat the milk in a saucepan until scalding, then add ¼ onion and a bay leaf. Take off the heat and set aside to cool and absorb the flavours. Strain the infused milk and make the sauce as for the main recipe. Finally, stir in 1 tbsp finely chopped parsley. This sauce is often served with white fish.

Soubise sauce Sweat a very finely diced onion in 30g butter until it is very soft. Make a béchamel sauce and add the onion (soubise) and 50ml double cream. If a smoother texture is required the sauce can be processed in a blender. This sauce is typically served as an accompaniment to lamb.

Coating consistency

Recipes may ask for a 'coating consistency' sauce, which means that the finished sauce evenly coats and clings to the back of a wooden spoon (as shown). The white sauce recipe (left) results in a coating consistency.

If a recipe calls for different ratios of butter to flour to milk, then potentially a sauce of a different consistency is required. This should not affect the method you use; the resulting sauce will just be a little thinner or thicker depending on quantities.

Velouté sauce

Makes 300ml
20g butter
20g plain flour
300ml chicken and veal stock
  (see page 96)
2 tbsp double cream
Few drops of lemon juice
Salt and ground white pepper

A velouté sauce starts with a blond roux, uses stock as the liquid component, and is then enriched with cream. The roux is cooked until it is straw coloured and has taken on a biscuit aroma. A velouté sauce is usually made to accompany pale meats and fish.

1 Melt the butter in a small saucepan over a gentle to medium heat, then add the flour and cook the roux for 2–4 minutes, stirring frequently, until straw coloured and smelling biscuity.

2 Remove the pan from the heat and gradually add the stock, a little at a time, stirring and incorporating the stock well into the roux as it is added. Don't add the stock too quickly or lumps will result, which are difficult to beat out.

3 As more of the stock is added, the sauce will start to loosen and thin. Once half the stock has been added and incorporated, add the remaining stock in generous additions and return the pan to the heat.

4 Increase the heat to medium to high and stir the sauce constantly as it comes to the boil (the sauce has to boil in order to thicken). Once it has come to the boil, reduce the heat and simmer for 2 minutes. Add the cream and season with salt and white pepper. Now add a few drops of lemon juice to enhance the flavour.

Note Herbs are sometimes added to a finished velouté. However, if the stock being used has a good concentration and the sauce is seasoned correctly, it will be delicious without embellishment.

Variation

Fish velouté Use fish stock (see page 100) in place of the chicken and veal stock.

Brown/espagnole sauce

Makes 200–250ml

2 tbsp vegetable oil

50g unsmoked bacon

¼ carrot

¼ celery stick

½ onion, inner core discarded

¼ tsp tomato purée

2 tsp browned flour (see right)

600ml brown chicken and veal or beef
stock (see page 98)

Few button mushrooms

Bouquet garni (½ celery stick, 1 bay leaf,
1 thyme sprig and 1 parsley sprig
tied together)

Salt and freshly ground black pepper

Typically used for all types of meat, this sauce uses a brown stock and a brown roux. Because the flour loses some of its thickening ability in the longer cooking time, it lends texture and body, but not a full thickening quality, to the sauce.

1 Heat the oil in a sauté pan or frying pan. Derind and dice the bacon, add to the pan and fry lightly to render the fat. Once golden, transfer it to a bowl, leaving the fat in the pan, and set the bacon aside.

2 Wash and peel the vegetables and cut them into 1cm chunks. Reheat the fat in the frying pan and fry the carrot and celery over a medium heat until starting to shrivel and take on a little colour.

3 Add the onion and allow the vegetables to caramelise and become a deep golden colour. Take care not to scorch or over-brown them as the sauce will be bitter. Equally, don't sweat the vegetables or the sauce will be too sweet.

4 When the vegetables are browned, add the tomato purée, stir in and cook for 1 minute, then stir in the browned flour and cook for 1–2 minutes, stirring occasionally. Return the bacon to the pan, add the stock, mushrooms and bouquet garni and bring the sauce to a simmer.

5 Transfer the sauce to a saucepan and continue to cook gently for 1½–2 hours, skimming occasionally. Be careful to skim off only the fat or the sauce will be too thin. To ensure the vegetables are completely covered in liquid, a little extra water might need to be added during the cooking process.

6 Strain the sauce carefully through a chinois or fine sieve into a clean pan. Do not push the vegetables through or they may break up and turn the sauce cloudy. Taste and reduce the sauce to concentrate the flavour as required; it should be a lightly syrupy consistency. Season lightly with salt and pepper.

Variations

Bordelaise sauce Sweat 1 finely diced shallot in 10g butter. Once the shallot is very soft, add 350ml red wine (ideally a Burgundy) and reduce until syrupy, to about 2–3 tbsp. Add 200ml brown/espagnole sauce to the red wine reduction, with 1 bay leaf and 1 thyme sprig. Reheat and simmer gently for 5–10 minutes. Remove the bay leaf and thyme and discard. Season with salt and pepper. Monter the sauce (see page 111), by whisking in a nut of butter.

Chasseur sauce Reduce 250ml dry white wine until syrupy, to about 1–2 tbsp. Add 200ml brown/espagnole sauce to the reduced wine and set aside. Sweat 1 finely diced shallot in 15g butter. Add 40g finely sliced button mushrooms and sauté for 2–3 minutes, driving off the water released from the mushrooms. Add ½–1 tsp tomato purée and cook for 1 minute, then add the reduced wine sauce and stir well. Add 1 tsp finely chopped parsley and season with salt and pepper.

Madeira sauce Combine 5 tbsp Madeira with 1 tsp glace de viande (see page 98) and simmer until reduced by half. Add 200ml brown/espagnole to the Madeira reduction. Taste and season the sauce with salt and pepper. Monter the sauce (see page 111), by whisking in a nut of butter, to enrich it further and give it a shine, if you wish.

1 Gently frying the bacon to render the fat.

2 Frying the carrot and celery to colour lightly.

3 Caramelising the carrot, celery and onion to a deep golden colour.

4 Stirring the flour into the vegetables.

5 Skimming the fat from the surface of the sauce during simmering.

6 The finished sauce reduced to a light syrupy consistency and ready to use.

A note on browned flour...

To speed up the process of browning the roux, the flour is first browned in the oven. This result is the same as if the flour was browned in the fat. Put a few tablespoonfuls of plain flour into a small roasting tin and place in an oven preheated to 180°C/gas mark 4 for 15–20 minutes, stirring occasionally, until it is lightly browned.

Demi-glace

A demi-glace sauce is a richer brown/espagnole sauce. Combine equal parts of brown/espagnole sauce (see left) and brown chicken and veal or beef stock (see page 98) and reduce by half, then strain and season with salt and pepper.

Jus

Jus are stock-based reduction sauces. They are effectively 'double stocks' with the addition of extra flavouring ingredients, so the principles of stock making apply when you are making one. A jus is finally reduced to a complex, meaty savouriness, to accompany meat, poultry and game.

Chicken and thyme jus

Makes about 400ml
500g (about 10) chicken wings
2 tbsp sunflower oil
300ml dry white wine
400ml red wine
3 shallots
1 small carrot
1 leek
1 celery stick
2 tomatoes
2 garlic cloves
2 small thyme sprigs
1 bay leaf
1 parsley sprig
6 black peppercorns
3 litres chicken and veal stock
   (see page 96)
Salt and freshly ground black pepper

1 Prepare the chicken wings by cutting them through the joints into 2 or 3 pieces, which helps them to brown more evenly.

2 Heat the oil in a large pan and brown the chicken wings thoroughly over a medium heat. Meanwhile, reduce the white and red wines, in separate pans, by three-quarters. Peel and quarter the shallots; peel and slice the carrot; wash the leek and celery and cut into slices about 1–2cm thick.

3 Once the chicken wings are browned, lift them out of the pan and set aside. Add the shallots, carrot, leek and celery to the pan and brown evenly all over. Pour off the excess oil from the pan and deglaze with the reduced wines (see note). Return the chicken to the pan.

4 Quarter and deseed the tomatoes. Bash the unpeeled garlic cloves with the flat side of a large knife. Add the tomatoes and garlic to the pan with the other aromatics. Pour in the stock and bring slowly to the boil over a low to medium heat. Turn the heat down to low so the jus is just simmering and cook very slowly, uncovered, for 2–3 hours, skimming frequently.

5 Strain through a chinois or fine sieve into a clean saucepan, discarding the bones and vegetables.

6 Reduce the liquid gently to about 400ml or until you are happy with the flavour concentration. Strain the jus again through a chinois or fine sieve and season to taste with salt and pepper.

Note It is important that the wines are reduced well before being added, otherwise a slightly raw alcohol flavour will be evident in the finished sauce.

Variations

Any herb can be used to flavour the jus, depending on what it is being served with. Likewise, reduced fortified wines can be used in place of dry wines, but expect a slightly sweeter result.

Lamb and rosemary jus Use 500g browned lamb bones in place of the chicken wings, and substitute rosemary for the thyme, taking care with the amount of rosemary as it can lend a slightly bitter flavour to the jus if too much is used.

1 Cutting the chicken wings into pieces.　　2 Browning the chicken wings.　　3 Deglazing with the reduced wines.

4 Adding the tomatoes and aromatics.

5 Straining the jus through a fine chinois into a clean pan.

6 The reduced jus, ready to serve.

Deglaze

Deglazing requires the addition of a cold liquid to a hot pan in which meat or vegetables have been browned or cooked (and usually removed from). The liquid, generally water, but sometimes alcohol or vinegar, is brought to the boil, which lifts the sediment from the pan that was created during the browning or cooking process. Scraping the base of the pan with a wooden spoon helps to lift the sediment. The sediment is generally well flavoured and, once captured in the deglazing liquid, can then be used to impart flavour to a sauce.

Deglazing is also useful to clean a pan if the browning process has been done over too high a heat, causing scorching, or burning, of the sediment. Using this sediment in a sauce may cause bitterness, so if, after browning or cooking a piece of meat or fish you feel the heat has been too high and the bottom of the pan looks burnt, deglaze with water, bring to the boil, then pour the liquid (called the déglaçage) into a bowl. Allow it to cool, then taste it. If there is no bitterness it can be used in the sauce, otherwise discard it. The deglazing technique is particularly important when browning a large amount of meat in batches for stews.

Madeira jus

Makes about 250ml
2 chicken legs
2 tbsp sunflower oil
100g mushrooms
100g shallots
½ garlic bulb
1 thyme sprig
½ fresh bay leaf
1½ tbsp sherry vinegar
1½ tbsp Cognac
400ml Madeira
750ml chicken and veal stock
  (see page 96)
150ml water
4 dried morels
Few drops of lemon juice (optional)
Few drops of double cream (optional)
10g unsalted butter
Salt and freshly ground black pepper

1 Divide the chicken legs into thighs and drumsticks by cutting through the joint. Heat the oil in a frying pan and brown the chicken pieces over a medium heat.

2 Meanwhile, prepare the vegetables. Wipe the mushrooms and slice them. Halve, peel and slice the shallots and cut the head of garlic in half across the middle so the cloves are all halved.

3 When the chicken pieces are brown, remove to a plate and set aside. Add the mushrooms and shallots to the pan and sauté briefly before adding the garlic, thyme and bay leaf. Deglaze the pan with the sherry vinegar and reduce the liquid to 1–2 tsp. Add the Cognac and reduce this too, to 1–2 tsp.

4 Add the Madeira and reduce the liquid by two-thirds, until it has a syrupy appearance. Add the stock, water and dried morels, then return the browned chicken pieces to the pan. If the chicken and vegetables are not covered with liquid, add enough water to cover.

5 Bring to the boil, then turn down to a gentle simmer, skim well and cook gently for 20–30 minutes, skimming occasionally.

6 Strain the jus through a fine sieve, reserving the morels for the garnish, and return to a clean pan to reduce to about 250ml; the flavour shouldn't be too strong or intense.

7 When ready to use, heat the jus gently and add a few drops each of lemon juice and double cream to enrich it if you like. Taste and adjust the seasoning. Monter the sauce with the butter (see right).

Understanding more about sauces...

Thickening sauces

When making a sauce, a good concentration of flavour must first be achieved. Then you need to consider the consistency of the sauce. Most often in stock-based sauces if a suitably flavoured gelatinous stock has been used, then reducing the stock or sauce is often all that is required to achieve both a good concentration of flavour and a syrupy consistency. However, if after making a sauce it has a good concentration of flavour, but is thin, then a little thickening may be necessary to create a sauce with a syrupy consistency which will 'hold' better on a plate. Besides reducing the sauce, the following ways of thickening stock-based sauces can be applied:

Beurre manié

This is used to thicken an unknown quantity of liquid. Mix equal parts of softened butter and flour to a smooth paste. Whisk a little of this beurre manié (start with ½ tsp) into a simmering sauce. As the butter melts, it disperses the flour through the sauce and thickens it, without creating lumps.

Cornflour and arrowroot

Both of these work best when slaked into sauces. Slaking involves mixing the thickener (cornflour or arrowroot) with a little cold water (or sauce) to create a thin, smooth paste. This is then gradually whisked into the sauce a little at a time (½ tsp) and the sauce simmered to thicken. Both cornflour and arrowroot have a tendency to give a sauce a very gelatinous consistency, so you may only need a little. Avoid vigorous boiling after adding the thickening to a sauce as this can cause lumps, and strings if using arrowroot. Using cornflour or arrowroot as thickeners results in clear, rather than cloudy or opaque, sauces.

Monter au beurre

This involves incorporating butter into a sauce just before using it, either by whisking or by vigorously swirling the saucepan. The butter rounds out the flavour of the sauce and gives it a shine, but adding too much butter will thicken the sauce slightly too much. Take care also that the butter is fully incorporated into the sauce, or it will sit like a buttery slick on the surface.

Using cream in sauces

When using cream in sauces, choose those high in fat, such as double cream or full-fat crème fraîche. Some low-fat creams, including single cream, will split if boiled vigorously. Avoid adding too much cream, which can result in a cloying flavour and will dilute the base flavour; often just a little is enough. Used judiciously, cream adds richness and helps to achieve a rounder, more balanced flavour in a sauce; it can also be used to thicken sauces slightly.

Reheating and refreshing sauces

When reheating a sauce to serve, taste it and if the flavour is too strong, add a splash of water. Also, if you feel the sauce lacks the flavour of any herb used in the making, then a fresh sprig of the herb can be added at this stage to 'refresh' the flavour; remove it before serving.

Pan sauces

Pan sauces are made to capture the flavours remaining in a frying pan after meat or fish has been sautéed, by using the technique of deglazing to lift the sediment. By its nature, a pan sauce is very quick to prepare – it should be made within the time it takes for the meat or fish to rest, about 3–5 minutes. So it is important to have everything you need to hand.

We generally classify pan sauces into 3 types: stock-, cream- and butter-based.

Stock pan sauces

Steak with a red wine sauce

Serves 4

4 steaks, about 2.5cm thick, the cut of your choice

Oil and clarified butter (see page 75), to fry the steaks

1 orange

200ml red wine

1 thyme sprig

200ml well-flavoured, gelatinous brown chicken and veal stock (see page 98)

Salt and freshly ground black pepper

1 Cook the steaks in a sauté pan, in oil and clarified butter heated until foaming, according to your preference (see page 411), then remove from the pan and set aside to rest for 3–4 minutes.

2 While the steaks are cooking, finely pare a strip of zest from the orange with a vegetable peeler.

3 Deglaze the sauté pan with the wine, scraping the base well. Add the thyme and orange zest and let bubble to reduce by at least two-thirds.

4 Add the stock and bring back to the boil, then turn the heat down and simmer for 2–3 minutes. Taste and season with salt and pepper.

5 Strain the sauce into a jug and pour around the steaks to serve.

Variations

Madeira sauce Omit the orange zest and substitute Madeira for the red wine. Reduce to 50ml before adding the stock and seasoning. A knob of butter (10g) can be used to monter the sauce (see page 111). This sauce works well with beef or veal steaks, or chicken breasts.

Port and wild mushroom sauce After removing the cooked steaks, add 30g butter to the sauté pan and sauté 225g prepared wild mushrooms (see page 63) until golden. Remove the mushrooms and set aside. Add 200ml port to the pan and reduce by two-thirds. Finally, add the stock and simmer until syrupy, then season and return the mushrooms to the pan to reheat. This sauce works well with beef steaks, chicken or game.

Cream pan sauces

Breast of guinea fowl with a white wine and tarragon sauce

Serves 4

4 guinea fowl supremes, each about
170g, skin on (prepared as for chicken
supremes, see page 344)

20g butter

100ml dry white wine

200ml well-flavoured chicken and veal
stock (see page 96)

2–3 tbsp double cream

Few tarragon sprigs

Salt and freshly ground black pepper

1 Season the guinea fowl supremes with salt and pepper. Melt the butter in a frying pan over a low to medium heat, then add the guinea fowl, skin side down. Cook over a low to medium heat to render the fat beneath the skin. This will help to caramelise and crisp the skin.

2 Once the fat is rendered and the skin browned, turn the guinea fowl over, reduce the heat and continue to cook until the supremes are cooked through, about 10 minutes. Remove the guinea fowl to a warmed plate and leave to rest in a warm place while you finish the sauce.

3 Pour off the excess fat from the pan and deglaze with the wine. Reduce to 1–2 tbsp. Add the stock and reduce by half. Stir in the cream and simmer for 2–3 minutes. Coarsely chop enough tarragon leaves to give you 1 tsp, and add to the sauce. Taste and season with salt and pepper, then serve.

Butter pan sauces

Pan-fried fillet of sea bass with a butter sauce

Serves 4

80g butter

4 sea bass fillets, skin on

1 tsp lemon juice

1 tsp water

Salt and ground white pepper

1 Melt 20g of the butter in a frying pan and pan-fry the sea bass fillets until just cooked (see note on page 295). Lift out onto a warmed plate and keep warm.

2 Lightly wipe out the pan with kitchen paper and melt the remaining butter in it. When foaming, add the lemon juice and water. Taste the sauce, season with salt and pepper and serve with the fish.

Variations

Herb butter pan sauce Stir 2 tsp chopped herbs through the finished sauce before serving. Choose soft herbs such as parsley, chives, dill, tarragon or chervil.

Beurre noisette sauce Follow the main recipe, but allow the butter to become beurre noisette (see below) before adding the lemon juice and water. You can also add 1 tbsp chopped, rinsed capers and/or 1 tbsp chopped herbs. If adding capers, reduce the amount of lemon juice and salt added to the sauce.

....

Balancing flavour in butter pan sauces

When butter is the main ingredient, the sauce can be cloying if the butter isn't balanced with a little acidity and seasoning. Usually some lemon juice, wine or a mild vinegar is added to counteract the 'fattiness' of the butter and to give a better mouth feel. Seasoning also helps to balance the richness.

....

Beurre noisette

Butter contains milk solids and, when it melts over a medium heat for long enough, the milk solids will separate from the butter fat and fall to the bottom of the pan. If you heat the butter a little longer, the milk solids will begin to cook and change colour to a delicate brown, then a deeper golden brown, becoming 'beurre noisette'. The aroma coming off the butter as this happens is nutty, hence the 'noisette' name. Avoid taking the butter too far before adding the lemon juice, as once burnt it will taste bitter.

Flavoured butters

These versatile butters are easy to make as they are simply softened butter with flavouring ingredients added. They are generally served cool or at room temperature, complementing meat, poultry, fish and vegetables dishes. They can also be used in place of plain butter on bread or toast, or to add additional flavour to sauces.

Maître d'hôtel butter

Makes 60g
60g butter, at room temperature
Few parsley sprigs
½ lemon
Salt and freshly ground black pepper

1 Cream the butter in a bowl until completely soft. Finely chop enough parsley leaves to give you 1 tsp. Squeeze about 1 tbsp juice from the lemon.

2 Beat the parsley into the butter with about 2 tsp lemon juice. Season well with salt and pepper, taste and add a little more lemon juice if desired.

3 Lay out a sheet of cling film on a work surface. Spoon the softened butter onto the cling film. Use the cling film to shape the butter into a sausage shape, twisting both ends to make a tidy, smooth roll. Chill the butter until firm.

4 To serve, unwrap and cut the butter into slices. Melt on top of steaks or use as required.

Variations

Garlic butter Peel and crush ½–1 garlic clove and mix it into the softened butter. Depending on what the butter is to be used for, the parsley and lemon juice can be included or omitted.

Herbed butter Instead of the 1 tsp parsley, beat 2 tsp chopped, mixed soft herbs, such as chervil, parsley, tarragon or dill, into the softened butter. Add the lemon juice only if the acidity is needed in the final flavour of the butter.

Blue cheese butter Omit the parsley. Beat 15g strongly flavoured blue cheese, such as Roquefort or Gorgonzola, into the softened butter.

Tarragon and watercress butter Omit the parsley. Pick the leaves of 2 tarragon sprigs and 2 watercress sprigs and blanch in boiling water for 30 seconds, then refresh in cold water and dry on kitchen paper. Finely chop the blanched tarragon and watercress with a spring onion and beat into the softened butter.

Emulsions

Emulsions are created when two substances are combined in such a way that they result in a smooth, slightly thickened mixture, where naturally they would separate. Vigorous whisking and the correct temperature of the ingredients are both factors that help to encourage and create emulsions, as are natural emulsifiers (certain ingredients that aid the process), which include egg yolk, mustard and seasoning.

Stable emulsions hold their form, unless the oil is added too quickly (as can happen with mayonnaise) or the emulsion is overheated (a danger with hollandaise and beurre blanc), whereas unstable emulsions (such as vinaigrettes, see page 124) separate on standing.

In classic sauce making, the three most commonly used stable emulsions are mayonnaise, hollandaise and beurre blanc.

Mayonnaise

Makes 300ml
2 egg yolks, at room temperature
Pinch of English mustard powder
300ml sunflower oil or a combination
  of sunflower and light olive oil
Lemon juice or white wine vinegar,
  to taste
Salt and white pepper

We use a basic ratio of 1 egg yolk to 150ml oil. A mild flavoured oil such as sunflower is preferable, as a strongly flavoured oil like extra virgin olive oil may overpower the dish it accompanies.

1 Put the egg yolks into a medium, fairly deep bowl and put a pinch of salt and mustard powder on top of the yolks. Using a wooden spoon, mix the egg yolks and seasoning together.

2 Hold a fork with your other hand, dip it into the oil and then drip the oil onto the egg yolks, while stirring the yolks at the same time. Add a third of the oil in this way.

3 Once a third of the oil has been added and the emulsion created, start adding the oil ¼ tsp at a time, still stirring as you add it. Then progress to ½ tsp oil at a time. If the mayonnaise becomes very thick and looks greasy, add ¼–½ tsp lemon juice, wine vinegar or warm water, depending on whether you think the mayonnaise needs acidity or not. This will make it less greasy, thin it and help it to absorb more oil.

4 Once half to two-thirds of the oil has been added, add the rest slowly in a thin stream and keep stirring. Try to incorporate all of the oil to balance the egg flavour.

5 Taste the mayonnaise. Season it with salt and white pepper, and add lemon juice or wine vinegar as needed to balance the oil and acidity.

6 You should now have a shiny, thick, smooth mayonnaise. If you are not using it immediately, cover the bowl with cling film and refrigerate.

Note This mayonnaise can be kept in the fridge for up to a week if stored in a screw-topped jar in the fridge.

1 Mixing the egg yolks and seasoning together.

2 Dripping the oil onto the egg yolks from a fork, while stirring.

3 Adding the oil ¼–½ tsp at a time, stirring continuously.

4 Adding the last of the oil in a steady stream.

5 Adding lemon juice to balance the acidity.

6 The finished shiny, thick, smooth mayonnaise.

Variations

Herb mayonnaise Add 3 tbsp chopped herbs (chervil, chives, parsley etc) to the finished mayonnaise.

Aioli Add 3 or 4 crushed garlic cloves to the egg yolks before starting to add the oil. If you prefer a milder garlic flavour, roast the garlic cloves in their skins in an oven preheated to 180°C/gas mark 4 for 20–30 minutes until soft. Release the softened garlic from the skin, crush and add to the yolks as for the raw garlic.

Gribiche sauce Soft-boil 2 eggs (see page 144) and use the soft-cooked yolks to create the emulsion. Finely chop the cooked egg white and add to the finished mayonnaise with 1 tbsp each of finely chopped capers and shallots and 1–2 tbsp chopped tarragon, chives, parsley or chervil, or a mixture. This sauce is traditionally served with fish or chicken.

Mustard mayonnaise Add 1 tsp Dijon mustard to the egg yolks with the salt instead of the mustard powder. Flavour the finished mayonnaise with 1–2 tbsp wholegrain mustard to taste.

(Continued overleaf)

Sweet miso sauce Mix together 1 tbsp white miso paste, 2 tsp wasabi paste, 2 tbsp lime juice, 2 tbsp water and 1 tsp soft light brown sugar, to form a smooth paste. Stir this into the finished mayonnaise. This is good served with griddled fish.

Tarragon sauce Add 3 tbsp chopped tarragon to the finished mayonnaise. Thin down to the required consistency with well-flavoured, cold chicken and veal stock (see page 96) or vegetable stock (see page 101). Lovely served with a chicken salad.

Tartare sauce To the finished mayonnaise, add 1–2 tbsp each of rinsed and finely chopped gherkins and capers and 1–2 tbsp each of finely chopped parsley and shallot. (The shallot can be strong so you might prefer to use just 1 tbsp.) This sauce is typically served with fish.

Creating the emulsion

This happens during the first few minutes of adding the oil to the egg yolk. A constant stirring with one hand and dripping oil in with the other is necessary to ensure that the oil is quickly and evenly dispersed into the yolks. If the oil is added too quickly there is a danger of curdling/splitting the sauce. Curdling happens when the yolks and oil separate and the stable emulsion you have created is destroyed.

Balancing the acidity

It is important to add enough acidity in the form of lemon juice or white wine vinegar to achieve a balance between the oil and acidity. The mayonnaise contains 300ml oil and 2 egg yolks. If there is not enough acidity the mayonnaise will taste flat and oily.

How to remedy curdled mayonnaise...

Start with a new egg yolk in a medium bowl. Slowly add the curdled mayonnaise, while stirring, until an emulsion is created again, then start to add the curdled mayonnaise a little more quickly until it is all incorporated. As you have now used 3 egg yolks you might need to add more oil, up to 150ml to balance the flavour.

To lighten mayonnaise...

Use 1 whole egg and 1 egg yolk for 300ml mayonnaise. Egg white contains a lot of water so it may take a little longer for the emulsion to be created and the mayonnaise to thicken, but it can give a less cloying taste.

Making mayonnaise in a food processor or blender

To ensure the blade is covered by the yolks and seasoning, use a small food processor bowl; at least double the quantities if using a blender. Switch the motor on and slowly add the oil in a single stream, but not too quickly or the mayonnaise may curdle. It should thicken quite quickly. Adjust the seasoning as necessary.

Hollandaise

Makes 250–300ml
For the reduction
50ml white wine vinegar
50ml water
6 black peppercorns
1 bay leaf
1 mace blade

For the sauce
150g unsalted butter, at cool
  room temperature
3 egg yolks
Few drops of lemon juice, to taste
Salt and ground white pepper

This method makes a wonderful thick, dense sauce that is perfect for coating eggs and fish, or serving with vegetables such as asparagus.

1 For the reduction, put the wine vinegar, water, peppercorns, bay leaf and mace in a small saucepan and bring to a simmer. Reduce the liquid by at least two-thirds, then strain to remove the peppercorns, bay and mace.

2 To make the sauce, cut the butter into 1cm cubes. Put the egg yolks, a cube of butter and a small pinch of salt in a small bowl. Using a wooden spoon, cream the butter into the egg yolks, add ½–1 tsp of the reduction and stir to combine.

3 Half-fill a roasting tin with water and set over a medium heat, to create a warm bain marie. Heat until the water is hand-hot (it should be comfortable to dip your fingers into). A bubble might occasionally rise to the surface, but if you have the water too hot, the sauce will curdle. Turn off the heat.

4 Stand the bowl containing the egg yolk, butter and reduction mixture in the bain marie, off the heat, and stir until the egg yolks visibly start to thicken.

5 Beat the remaining butter in, a cube at a time, making sure that the sauce has re-thickened before adding the next cube of butter. As more butter is added, the heat can be turned on to low (but take care that the water does not boil) and the butter can be added more quickly. If the sauce becomes very thick and appears greasy, add a little more reduction or cool water.

6 Once all the butter has been added, remove the bowl of sauce from the roasting tin, taste it and adjust the seasoning. To achieve a balanced flavour, you may need to add more reduction, lemon juice, salt and ground white pepper. The sauce can be kept for about 30 minutes before serving, by standing the bowl in a warm bain marie, off the heat.

Variations

Choron sauce Prepare as above and add ½–1 tsp tomato purée to the finished sauce. This can be served with fish or chicken.

Herb hollandaise Omit the mace from the reduction and add 1 small, chopped shallot and a few herb sprigs, such as parsley, chervil or chives. Proceed as for hollandaise and add ½–1 tsp freshly chopped herb (the same herb used to infuse the reduction) to the finished sauce. Season with lemon juice and cayenne pepper. This is not a classic variation but delicious nonetheless.

Mousseline sauce Make as for hollandaise and add 50ml lightly whipped cream to the finished sauce. Taste and adjust the seasoning. This can be served with fish or vegetable dishes.

Béarnaise sauce Omit the mace from the reduction and add 1 small, chopped shallot and a few tarragon and chervil sprigs. Proceed as for hollandaise and add ½–1 tsp each of chopped tarragon and chervil and 1 tsp of glace de viande (see page 98) to the finished sauce. A classic sauce to accompany steaks.

Paloise sauce Make as for béarnaise sauce, but substitute 2–3 tsp chopped or chiffonaded mint (see page 89) for the tarragon and chervil. A delicious variation of a béarnaise to serve with lamb.

1 Straining the reduction through a sieve.

2 Adding ½–1 tsp reduction to the creamed butter and egg yolks.

3 Testing the temperature of the bain marie.

4 Stirring the egg yolk, butter and reduction mix over the bain marie until it starts to thicken.

5 Beating in the remaining butter, one cube at a time.

6 Balancing the flavour of the sauce with a little more reduction, lemon juice and seasoning.

Making hollandaise in a double boiler

This makes a lighter, more mousse-like hollandaise. Sometimes referred to as the sabayon method, it is especially useful when making a larger quantity of sauce.

Make the reduction as for the main recipe. Pour water into a large saucepan to a depth of 5cm, then bring to a simmer. Select a bowl large enough to sit over the pan, with the base well above the water level. Put the egg yolks in the bowl with 1 tsp reduction and a pinch of salt. Whisk the egg yolks with a balloon whisk until light and fluffy. Meanwhile, melt the butter in a small saucepan over a medium heat. Still whisking the egg mousse, slowly pour in the butter. Try to avoid adding the milk solids as they can thin the sauce. Once it is all added, remove the bowl from the pan and season with more reduction or lemon juice, salt and white pepper.

Making hollandaise in a blender

Double the ingredient quantities (to ensure the blender blades are covered with egg yolk). Make the reduction. Place the egg yolks, 2 tsp reduction and a pinch of salt in the blender. Melt the butter in a small saucepan over a medium heat. Once the butter is just starting to separate and is bubbling, pour a little into the blender with the motor running. Add a little more butter and the emulsion should be created, with a definite change in the sound the blender motor makes, from a high-pitched whine to a lower, slightly labouring noise.

Continue to add the butter slowly in a thin stream until all but the milk solids are added. Avoid adding the milk solids as they can thin the sauce. Taste and season with more reduction, lemon juice, salt and ground white pepper.

Consistency

The emulsion is created as the butter is dispersed into the egg yolk. The sauce begins to thicken as the yolk reaches a high enough temperature to coagulate and thicken the sauce. You need to allow the sauce to thicken between each addition of butter or it will remain very thin. Start slowly, and as more and more of the butter is added the sauce will become thicker, and the butter can be added a little more quickly. Using the basic method, the finished consistency should hold itself on a spoon. It is possible to thicken the sauce at the end of the cooking process, with continued stirring and a gradual increase in temperature, but it requires care and patience not to overheat the sauce.

How to save a hollandaise on the verge of splitting...

If the sauce becomes very thick and appears greasy, it may be just about to split. Take the sauce off the heat and add a little reduction or water at room temperature, or a small piece of ice. Confine your stirring to the addition itself, gradually drawing in the rest of the splitting mixture. This should bring it back, loosen it and lighten the colour a little, allowing it to continue to absorb more butter.

How to remedy split hollandaise...

If the sauce has split completely, start with a fresh egg yolk in a medium bowl, add a little reduction and re-make using the split hollandaise in place of the butter. You will need to add more butter after adding all the split hollandaise, as there will now be 4 yolks in the sauce.

Beurre blanc

Makes 150–200ml
½ shallot
50ml white wine vinegar
50ml water
200g unsalted butter, chilled
Few drops of lemon juice
Salt and ground white pepper

1 Peel and finely dice the shallot and put it in a small saucepan with the wine vinegar and water. Place over a medium heat and slowly reduce the liquid by at least two-thirds. Strain to remove the shallots.

2 Cut the butter into 1cm cubes and keep chilled and firm. Put ¾ tbsp reduction in a small saucepan and, over a gentle heat, add a cube of cold butter. Using a small sauce whisk, incorporate the butter into the reduction as vigorously as you can. The sauce requires constant, vigorous whisking.

3 As the butter melts fully, add another cube of butter, repeating the vigorous whisking. Continue in this manner until the sauce is starting to thicken and at least half the butter has been added. Now the butter can be added a little more quickly, all the while ensuring the saucepan is not getting too hot, as overheating will split the sauce. Make sure the sauce heats up between additions of butter.

4 Once all the butter has been added, the sauce should be pale, with a creamy consistency. Taste and season with more reduction, lemon juice, salt and ground white pepper. The sauce will keep briefly, but not for long; it is usually made just before serving.

Variations

For a more classical version, substitute a dry white wine in the reduction for the wine vinegar.

Mustard beurre blanc Stir ½–1 tbsp wholegrain mustard into the finished sauce.

Chicken beurre blanc Substitute 100ml chicken and veal stock (see page 96) for the water in the reduction, and reduce to 1 tbsp.

Fish beurre blanc Proceed as for the chicken beurre blanc, but with fish stock (see page 100) instead of chicken and veal stock in the reduction.

....

Creating the emulsion

This is more difficult when making a beurre blanc, because no egg yolk is involved. The cold butter must be vigorously whisked into the reduction to disperse it as finely and evenly as possible as it slowly melts: this is what creates the emulsion. Butter that is not cold will melt too quickly and you will not be able to disperse it quickly enough into the reduction, resulting in a split or thin sauce.

For the sauce to thicken, the butter must not be added too quickly, which is why each cube of butter must be fully incorporated before the next is added. Adding the butter too quickly initially will result in a thin sauce that is difficult to thicken later on. Only once at least half the butter has been added and a double cream consistency has been achieved can the butter be added a little more quickly, but still carefully. Overheating the emulsion will split it.

....

Stabilising a beurre blanc

To stabilise a beurre blanc, once the reduction is made, add 1 tbsp double cream and reduce again by about half. Strain, then whisk the butter in.

....

Balancing the flavour of emulsion sauces

All the basic emulsion sauce recipes use fat, acidity and sometimes egg yolk. It is important in making and finishing the sauces that they are balanced in terms of flavour, even before other flavourings are added. Where egg yolk is included in the base, enough oil or butter must be added to balance the eggy flavour, which is especially noticeable with raw eggs. With so much oil or butter, enough acidity is required to balance the cloying nature of the fat.

Acidity is generally added in the form of vinegar or lemon juice. Reducing vinegar softens the harshness of it, but the underlying acidity base is still present. The process of balancing the flavour of the fat begins in the early stages of making the sauce, with the addition of a little reduction or lemon juice.

In the final balancing and seasoning of the sauce both reduction and lemon juice can be used, as well as salt and pepper, as the tastebuds react to different forms of acidity in different parts of the mouth.

If a sauce is a little too acidic, try adding a little more salt, and vice versa.

....

A note on unsalted butter...

It is very important to use unsalted butter in a hollandaise or beurre blanc, as salted butter will over-season the sauce.

Vinaigrettes

When making vinaigrettes it is important to balance the oil, acidity, flavours and seasoning. Dip one of the salad ingredients into the dressing to taste it to make sure the flavour and seasoning are right. The flavour of the leaf may affect the flavour of the dressing, and a slight adjustment of the balance and seasoning may be necessary.

The standard ratio of oil to acid in a dressing is 3 parts oil (often olive) to 1 part acid (usually wine vinegar), but this is entirely dependent on the type of oil and vinegar used, so tasting the dressing becomes that much more important, in order to achieve balance.

Because vinaigrettes are unstable emulsions, they will separate if left to stand for any length of time. A vigorous shake in a lidded jar will re-emulsify a separated vinaigrette – a simpler solution than that needed for a split stable emulsion, such as mayonnaise.

Seasoning should be added at the start, so it will flavour the whole vinaigrette rather than being held in suspension in the emulsion. And, of course, it can be adjusted at the end.

French dressing

Makes 50–60ml

1 tbsp white wine vinegar
3–4 tbsp olive or sunflower oil
  (see oils, below)
Salt and freshly ground black pepper

A simple, classic vinaigrette that, once learnt and mastered, can be adapted to suit whatever it is to be served with.

1 Put the wine vinegar, a pinch of salt and a few grinds of pepper in a small bowl.

2 Whisk in the oil gradually to form an emulsion. Taste the dressing and adjust the seasoning as necessary.

Variations

Herb dressing Whisk in 1 tsp finely chopped herbs, such as chives, parsley or basil.

Mustard dressing Whisk in ½–1 tsp Dijon or wholegrain mustard.

Garlic dressing Whisk in 1 crushed small garlic clove.

Honey and mustard dressing Whisk in ½ tsp clear honey and ½ tsp Dijon or wholegrain mustard.

Lemon, caper and parsley dressing Replace the vinegar with 1½ tbsp lemon juice and the finely grated zest of ½ lemon. Add ½–1 tsp each of finely chopped capers and parsley.

Hoisin dressing Substitute groundnut oil for sunflower and rice wine vinegar for white wine vinegar. Whisk in 1 tsp hoisin sauce and ½ tsp crushed garlic.

Miso dressing Substitute groundnut oil for sunflower and rice wine vinegar for white wine. Whisk in 2 tsp white miso, 1 tbsp mirin (rice wine) and ½ tsp toasted sesame oil. Add 1 tsp finely grated ginger and 1 very finely chopped spring onion.

Ginger and soy dressing Substitute groundnut oil for sunflower and rice wine vinegar for white wine vinegar. Add ½ tsp toasted sesame oil, ½ tsp finely grated ginger and its juice, 1 tsp soy sauce and ½ crushed garlic clove.

Emulsifiers in vinaigrettes

Vinaigrettes are generally unstable, which means that they separate on standing. Some ingredients, such as mustard, honey and seasoning, can temporarily emulsify a vinaigrette, while also enhancing the flavour.

Oils

For a simple dressing it is worth using an extra virgin olive oil for its flavour. However, if there are a lot of competing elements to the dish, you may want to use a milder, blended olive oil. Alternatively, try using more neutral oils such as sunflower, grapeseed, rapeseed or groundnut. When more strongly flavoured oils such as walnut or toasted sesame are used, they can be diluted by combining with a more neutral oil if desired.

Acidity

Vinegars are used to provide acidity in vinaigrettes and they vary greatly in smell and taste. Sherry vinegars are more robust than most wine vinegars and a good aged balsamic will provide sweetness as well as acidity. You can try substituting citrus juices, but they will not be as acidic as vinegars, so use a ratio of 2 parts oil to 1 part citrus.

Flavouring ingredients

A variety of ingredients such as herbs, spices and mustards can be added to vinaigrettes to lend flavour and texture. Carefully consider the ingredients the dressing is being used for; it needs to complement and enhance the ingredients, not overpower or dominate.

Pestos and raw sauces

Quick and easy to make, these sauces are either textured or blended until smooth. Made from fresh, generally raw ingredients, pestos and salsas provide a burst of flavour to accompany all manner of cooked meats, poultry, fish and vegetables, and of course pasta.

Basil pesto

Makes 150ml
2 garlic cloves
100g basil leaves and stalks
60g pine nuts
125–150ml olive oil, depending on
   the consistency required
60g Parmesan cheese
Salt

1 In a blender or small food processor bowl, whiz the garlic, basil and pine nuts together to a paste. You may need to add a little of the olive oil to help the blades purée the mixture. A little texture in pesto is desirable, so avoid blending the pesto to an overly smooth purée. Alternatively you can also use a pestle and mortar rather than a food processor, to give an even more textured finish.

2 Finely grate the Parmesan and add it to the blender. Pulse briefly to mix, then gradually pour in the olive oil with the motor running. Season with salt to taste. Transfer to a small bowl, cover and refrigerate until needed.

Variations

Parsley pesto Substitute roughly chopped parsley for the basil, 30g blanched almonds for the pine nuts, and strong Cheddar for the Parmesan.

Chilli and coriander pesto Substitute coriander for the basil, and add 2 chopped green chillies to the mixture in step 1 of the main recipe. (The chilli seeds are optional; include them for a more fiery pesto.)

Pouring pesto sauce Whisk a little warm water or stock into the finished pesto to give a coating consistency sauce to serve with pan-fried fish.

Salsa verde

Makes 150ml
Large bunch of flat-leaf parsley
Small bunch of mint
Small bunch of basil or tarragon
1 garlic clove
1 anchovy fillet in oil
1 tbsp capers
1 tsp Dijon mustard
About 75–100ml olive oil
Salt and freshly ground black pepper

1 Pick the herb leaves off the stalks and chop roughly. You will need about 4 tbsp parsley and 1–2 tbsp of a selection of the remaining herbs.

2 Peel and crush the garlic. Drain and roughly chop the anchovy fillet. Rinse and drain the capers. Add these ingredients to the herbs.

3 Either chop the mixture further by hand (using a mezzaluna if you have one), or briefly pulse in a food processor. Don't over-process as the salsa needs to have some texture. Transfer to a small bowl if you have chopped the mixture by hand.

4 Stir in the mustard, season well with salt and pepper and then whisk or pulse in the olive oil. Salsa verde is best used on the day it is made, but it can be kept in the fridge for a day or two. It is particularly good with grilled or barbecued meats or fish.

Tomato and basil salsa

Makes 150ml
1 shallot
1 tbsp red wine vinegar
3 tbsp extra virgin olive oil
Few basil sprigs
4 tomatoes
Salt and freshly ground black pepper

1 Halve, peel and finely chop the shallot. Put into a small bowl and mix in the wine vinegar, olive oil and a bashed basil stalk (to add flavour). Leave to stand for at least 10 minutes.

2 Blanch the tomatoes in boiling water for 10 seconds, then refresh in cold water, dry and peel. Quarter and deseed, then finely chop the tomatoes. Add them to the shallot mixture.

3 Finely shred or chiffonade a few basil leaves (see page 89), add to the salsa and season with salt and pepper to taste. Just before serving, discard the basil stalk.

Pineapple and chilli salsa

Serves 4
½ small red onion
2 limes
1 tomato
½ red pepper
½–1 red chilli
¼ ripe pineapple
Few coriander sprigs
1–2 tbsp olive oil
Salt

1 Peel and finely dice the red onion and put into a bowl. Finely grate the zest from one of the limes and squeeze the juice from both fruit. Add the lime zest and half the juice to the onion, saving the remainder for seasoning at the end.

2 Blanch the tomato in boiling water for 10 seconds, then refresh in cold water, dry and peel (or leave the skin on if you prefer). Quarter and deseed the tomato, then finely dice.

3 Using a swivel vegetable peeler, peel the red pepper and finely dice it. (For a deeper, more intense flavour, you can lightly blister the pepper over the gas flame before peeling, see page 55.) Deseed and finely chop the chilli.

4 Peel, core and finely dice the pineapple and coarsely chop the coriander leaves.

5 Stir the tomato, pepper, chilli, pineapple and coriander into the onion and lime mixture. Stir in the olive oil and season well with salt and more lime juice, if necessary. Leave to stand for 30 minutes to allow the flavours to develop.

Variation

Avocado and black bean salsa Omit the tomato, red pepper and pineapple. Add 1 ripe but firm avocado, cut into even dice, ½ x 400g tin black beans, drained and rinsed, and 1 thinly sliced spring onion.

Avocado sauce

Serves 4
1 ripe avocado
2 tbsp mayonnaise (see page 116)
1 lime
½ green chilli
½ bunch of coriander
1 tbsp olive oil
Salt, caster sugar and freshly ground
  black pepper

1 Put the avocado flesh and mayonnaise in a blender. Finely grate the zest from the lime and squeeze the juice. Add half the lime zest and juice to the blender.

2 Deseed and roughly chop the chilli, roughly chop the coriander stalks and add to the mixture with the olive oil. Blend until smooth.

3 Add more lime juice or water as required to make a light, coating consistency dressing. Season well with salt and pepper and a little sugar. Just before serving, coarsely chop a handful of the coriander leaves and stir through the salsa.

Tomato sauces

The natural acidity and texture of tomatoes make them ideal in sauces. All cooked tomato sauces should be rich in colour, full flavoured and have a good balance of acidity and sweetness. They freeze well, so it is worth making double the quantity and freezing half. When using tinned tomatoes, add a pinch of sugar to counteract any 'tinny' flavour and help balance the acidity.

Fresh tomato sauce

Makes 500ml
1 onion
2 garlic cloves
10 very ripe tomatoes
1 tbsp olive oil
1 tbsp tomato purée
1 tsp caster sugar
½ tsp dried thyme
Salt and freshly ground black pepper

1 Halve, peel and finely dice the onion. Peel and crush the garlic. Blanch the tomatoes in boiling water for 10 seconds, then refresh in cold water, dry and peel. Quarter and deseed, then roughly chop the tomatoes.

2 Heat the olive oil in a frying pan, add the onion and soften over a low to medium heat for 5–10 minutes, without colouring. Add the garlic and cook for 1 minute. Now add the tomatoes with the tomato purée, sugar, thyme and some seasoning.

3 Increase the heat and cook at a brisk simmer for 10–15 minutes to drive off any water released by the tomatoes. Taste and adjust the seasoning.

Variations

Tomato and herb sauce Use different herbs, such as dried oregano or marjoram, or fresh basil or chives, depending on how you intend to use the sauce.

Tomato and chilli sauce Add 1 finely diced red chilli when you add the garlic. In the absence of fresh chilli, use a good pinch of crushed dried chillies instead, but beware of their highly concentrated heat.

Sauce pizzaiola

Makes about 600ml
1 onion
2 tbsp olive oil
3–4 garlic cloves
2 x 400g tins plum tomatoes
2 tbsp tomato purée
1–1½ tsp dried oregano
1 tsp dried basil
1 bay leaf
2 tsp caster sugar
Salt and freshly ground black pepper

1 Halve, peel and finely dice the onion. Heat the olive oil in a saucepan, add the onion and cover with a cartouche (see page 13) and lid. Sweat until soft but not coloured. Peel and crush the garlic, add to the onion and cook for 1 minute.

2 Coarsely chop the tomatoes and add them and their juice to the pan, with the tomato purée, oregano, basil, bay leaf and sugar. Season with salt and pepper and bring to the boil, then turn down the heat and simmer gently for 50–60 minutes until reduced to a thick purée. Discard the bay leaf. Taste and adjust the seasoning.

3 The sauce can be left textured or puréed to a smooth consistency, depending on use. It is generally served with steak but makes an excellent simple pasta sauce too.

Variations

Roasted tomato sauce Substitute slow-roasted tomatoes for tinned: cut 1kg ripe tomatoes in half and place in a shallow roasting tin. Scatter over 5 diced shallots, 3 crushed garlic cloves, a few thyme sprigs, 75ml olive oil and seasoning. Slow-roast in an oven preheated to 120°C/gas mark ½ for 3–4 hours. Pick off the tomato skins and discard the thyme. The shallots and garlic can be included in the sauce.

Roasted tomato and red pepper sauce Add 2 roasted, skinned, deseeded and finely diced peppers to the roasted tomato sauce variation.

Traditional sauces

These are classic accompaniments to various meats, poultry, game and fish. They are also useful when a quick sauce is needed to enhance a simple dish. A grilled pork loin chop is transformed by a spoonful of apple sauce, while the addition of horseradish sauce to mash boosts a braised beef dish. Where a cooling effect is required, to rich, spiced lamb dishes for example, raita offers a soothing contrast.

Apple sauce

Makes 150–200ml
500g (2 medium) Bramley apples
3 tbsp water
2 tsp caster sugar
½ lemon

Cooking apples, such as Bramley, have a natural sharpness that eating apples lack. They make a delicious tart sauce, which acts as a foil to the richness of pork.

1 Wash, peel and core the apples, cut them into large chunks and put them into a medium saucepan with the water and sugar. Finely grate the zest from the lemon and add to the pan.

2 Cover and cook over a very gentle heat until the apples have softened and lost their shape. Stir to break them up, taste and add more sugar if necessary.

Variations

Apple and sage sauce Chiffonade 3–4 sage leaves (see page 89) and stir through the finished sauce.

Bramley and Cox apple sauce Once the Bramleys are soft, add 1 peeled, cored and very finely diced Cox apple. The Cox dice will hold their shape and give the sauce texture.

Bread sauce

Makes 300ml
1 large onion
6 cloves
300ml milk
1 bay leaf
10 white peppercorns or a pinch of
  ground white pepper
Pinch of freshly grated nutmeg
60–80g coarse fresh white breadcrumbs,
  depending on desired thickness
50g butter
Salt and ground white pepper

An ideal accompaniment to roast chicken and turkey.

1 Cut the onion in half, peel it and stud each half with the cloves. Place in a saucepan with the milk, bay leaf, pepper and nutmeg.

2 Scald the milk by heating it over a medium heat until steaming. Just before it bubbles, remove from the heat and leave to infuse for at least 30 minutes.

3 Strain the infused milk into a clean saucepan, discarding the aromatics. Reheat over a low to medium heat and add the breadcrumbs. The breadcrumbs will absorb the milk, thickening the sauce.

4 Stir the butter through the sauce to enrich it. If the sauce is too thick, add a little warm milk; it should be spoonable, but not runny. Taste and season generously. Serve warm.

Note You can make the sauce in advance, up the point where you have added the breadcrumbs and thickened the sauce. Cube the butter and dot it over the surface of the sauce, allowing it to melt and create a buttery film over the sauce. This will help to prevent a skin from forming. When ready to serve, reheat the sauce and stir the butter through. Taste and season.

Mint sauce

Makes 100ml
¼–½ bunch of mint
2 tbsp caster sugar
2 tbsp hot water
2 tbsp white wine vinegar

The classic accompaniment to roast lamb.

1 Wash the mint and dry it. Pick the leaves off the stalks and discard the stalks. Finely chop or chiffonade the mint leaves (see page 89) and place in a bowl with the sugar.

2 Add the hot water and leave to stand for 5 minutes to allow the sugar to dissolve. Add the wine vinegar and leave to infuse for a couple of hours. Taste and adjust the sauce with more sugar or vinegar before serving.

Cranberry and orange sauce

Makes 500ml
2 oranges
200g caster sugar
500g cranberries

This is traditionally served with roast turkey.

1 Finely pare the zest from 1 orange in broad strips, using a vegetable peeler, and then cut the zest into julienne (see page 531). Squeeze the juice from both of the oranges.

2 Put the orange juice, zest julienne and sugar in a heavy-based saucepan and heat gently to dissolve the sugar and soften the zest.

3 Add the cranberries to the saucepan and simmer very slowly until they are becoming tender and just starting to break up. Remove from the heat and let the sauce cool before serving.

Horseradish sauce

Makes 200ml
½ horseradish root
75ml double cream
75ml crème fraîche
1–2 tsp white wine vinegar
½ tsp English mustard
Salt, ground white pepper and
   caster sugar (optional)

A classic accompaniment for roast beef and beef steaks.

1 Wash, peel and finely grate the horseradish root; you will need about 2–3 tbsp grated horseradish.

2 Mix the grated horseradish, cream, crème fraîche, wine vinegar and mustard together in a bowl and leave to infuse for a few hours, or ideally overnight, to allow the strength of the horseradish to develop.

3 Season with salt, pepper and a little sugar to taste if required.

A note on fresh horseradish...

Fiendishly hot, horseradish is a creamy-coloured root that requires washing and peeling. Grate the outer, softer flesh first and use the inner root only if it is not too woody (as it can become, particularly late in the season).

Fresh horseradish root is not always available. When you do find it, grate it all and freeze any spare in small quantities. You can also buy it grated and preserved in small jars.

Mustard and dill sauce

Makes 120ml
½ bunch of dill
1 tbsp Dijon mustard
100ml sunflower oil
1½ tbsp white wine vinegar
1 tsp caster sugar
Salt and freshly ground black pepper

The classic accompaniment to gravadlax (cured salmon), this sauce also goes well with lamb.

1 Pick the dill leaves from the stalks and finely chop them, discarding the stalks. You need about 3–4 tbsp.

2 Place the mustard in a small bowl and gradually whisk in the oil, then the wine vinegar. Add the dill and sugar, taste and season well with salt and pepper.

Rouille

Makes about 150ml
3 garlic cloves
1 red chilli
1 green pepper
1 red pepper
100ml olive oil
2–3 tbsp fresh white breadcrumbs
Salt and freshly ground black pepper

The traditional accompaniment to bouillabaisse, this is a spicy sauce with a mayonnaise-like consistency.

1 Heat the oven to 200°C/gas mark 6. Roast the unpeeled garlic cloves until soft, about 20–30 minutes. Meanwhile, deseed and roughly chop the chilli (see page 54), and grill, skin and deseed the peppers (see page 55).

2 Squeeze the soft roasted garlic flesh out of the skins and put into a food processor. Add the chilli and peppers and process until smooth. With the motor still running, very slowly pour the olive oil into the purée.

3 Add enough breadcrumbs, pulsing to mix, to bind the rouille, and season with salt and pepper to taste.

Raita

Makes about 500ml
1 cucumber
1 tbsp vegetable oil
½ tsp black mustard seeds
½ tsp cumin seeds
Pinch of asafoetida
1 garlic clove
Bunch of mint or dill, or half of each
1 spring onion
500g natural yoghurt
Salt and freshly ground black pepper

A cooling yoghurt-based sauce/dip, typically served alongside spicy Indian curries and kebabs.

1 Cut off and discard both ends of the cucumber, then cut it in half lengthways. Scoop out and discard the seeds, using a teaspoon. Grate the cucumber, place it in a sieve or colander and sprinkle with 2 or 3 pinches of salt. Leave for 10–15 minutes to degorge (see page 28).

2 Heat the oil in a small pan and add the mustard and cumin seeds, and the asafoetida. Stir for 1 minute, or until their fragrance is released and the seeds begin to pop. Remove from the heat and set aside to cool.

3 Peel and crush the garlic. Chop enough mint or dill, or a mixture, to give you 4 tbsp. Finely chop the spring onion, discarding only the very coarsest green part and the root.

4 Put the yoghurt into a bowl. Squeeze out as much liquid as possible from the cucumber. Stir the garlic, herbs, spring onion and cucumber into the yoghurt.

5 Add the cooled spiced oil to the yoghurt mixture and stir. Season well with salt and plenty of pepper.

Egg-based sweet sauces

Egg-based sweet sauces have a reputation for being tricky to make. Undercook a custard, and it simply will not thicken. Overcook it and the egg yolks will 'scramble', giving the sauce an uneven, grainy texture. Practice and repetition, and a fair amount of stirring, are key to success and gaining confidence.

Crème anglaise

Makes 300ml

300ml whole milk
1 vanilla pod or a few drops of vanilla extract
4 small or 3 large egg yolks
1–2 tbsp caster sugar

This classic custard, thickened with egg yolk, is served with all manner of desserts, including crumbles, steamed puddings and fruit tarts. It is also used as the base for some ice creams and buttercreams. A good crème anglaise has the consistency of double cream and is thinner than a flour-thickened custard.

1 Put the milk in a saucepan. Cut the vanilla pod, if using, down one side, then scrape out all the seeds. Add the pod and seeds to the milk and place the pan over a medium heat. Scald, by gently heating until steaming (see below, right). Just before it bubbles, take off the heat and remove the vanilla pod and any skin that has formed.

2 Put the egg yolks and 1 tbsp of the sugar in a medium bowl and stir to mix. Pour in a little of the scalded milk and stir, then add the remaining milk gradually, stirring continuously until fully combined. Rinse out the saucepan used to scald the milk.

3 Return the milk and egg mixture to the cleaned pan. Place over a low to medium heat and stir continuously with a wooden spoon. First the custard will steam, which is an indication that it is about to thicken. Watch it carefully and keep stirring, getting the wooden spoon well into the corners.

4 To test if the sauce is thickened, remove it from the heat and draw the back of the spoon through the sauce. It should coat the back of the spoon evenly and not drop away and pool at the base of the spoon.

5 When you draw a clean finger down the back of the spoon through the custard the trail should remain. This indicates that the sauce is ready.

6 When this point is reached, immediately strain the sauce through a chinois or fine sieve into a bowl. Taste and add more sugar if necessary. Set aside to cool. If you are using vanilla extract, add a few drops now. To prevent a skin forming, place a disc of greaseproof paper on the crème anglaise, in direct contact with the surface.

Note For a thicker crème anglaise, use all double cream in place of the milk, or half of each.

Variations

Crème anglaise with liqueur Add ½–1 tbsp Calvados or Grand Marnier to the finished, thickened sauce.

Chocolate crème anglaise Melt 30g chopped good quality dark chocolate in the milk when heating it. You may need to whisk the sauce to encourage the chocolate to melt fully.

Coffee crème anglaise Substitute 30–50ml of the milk for a strong espresso.

1 Scraping the seeds from the vanilla pod.

2 Slowly stirring the hot milk into the egg yolks.

3 Stirring the custard continuously over a low to medium heat.

4 Checking to see if the sauce is thickening.

5 Drawing a finger down the back of the spoon to test if the sauce is thickened enough.

6 Straining the sauce through a chinois into a bowl.

Scalding

Milk is scalded by being brought up to a temperature just below boiling point. Small bubbles will appear on the surface, particularly at the edges, where it comes into contact with the saucepan.

Curdling

Only too high a heat will curdle a crème anglaise. This happens when the egg is heated to such a high temperature that it 'cooks' rather than thickens, resulting in flecks of cooked egg and causing the sauce to lose its velvety texture.

A note on undercooking...

If a crème anglaise is cooked at too low a temperature for too long, it will lose volume through water evaporation and develop a 'condensed milk' flavour.

Crème pâtissière

Makes 300ml

300ml whole milk

½ vanilla pod or a few drops
   of vanilla extract

3 egg yolks

50g caster sugar

15g plain flour

15g cornflour

Crème pâtissière is essentially a crème anglaise thickened with flour and cornflour, which makes it more stable and means it can be boiled. It is much thicker than a crème anglaise and is used in pâtisserie as a sweet filling, such as in éclairs and millefeuille, rather than as a sauce.

1 Put the milk in a saucepan. Cut the vanilla pod, if using, down one side, then scrape out all the seeds. Add the pod and seeds to the milk and place the pan over a medium heat. Scald, by gently heating it until steaming (see page 133). Just before it bubbles, take off the heat and remove the vanilla pod and any skin that has formed.

2 Put the egg yolks and sugar in a medium bowl and mix well. Add a splash of the scalded milk, then the flours. Mix well to combine and ensure there are no lumps. Gradually stir in the remaining milk.

3 Return the mixture to a clean saucepan and place over a low to medium heat. Bring to the boil, stirring continuously with a wooden spoon. It will go lumpy, but persevere and stir vigorously and it will become smooth. Turn the heat down and simmer for 2 minutes.

4 Remove from the heat and add the vanilla extract, if using. Transfer the crème pâtissière to a bowl and place a disc of greaseproof paper on top, in contact with the surface of the custard, to prevent a skin forming. Set aside to cool.

5 Once cool, transfer the crème pâtissière to a food processor fitted with the metal blade and blend until soft and smooth. It is now ready for use.

Variations

Almond crème pâtissière Stir 2 tbsp ground almonds and ½–1 tsp Amaretto, to taste, into the finished mixture.

Chocolate crème pâtissière Reduce the flour and cornflour to 10g each and melt 30g good quality dark chocolate in the milk when scalding. You may need to use a whisk to encourage the chocolate to melt fully into the milk.

Coffee crème pâtissière Replace 30–50ml of the milk with strong espresso coffee, depending on the intensity of flavour required.

Orange crème pâtissière Stir the finely grated zest of ½ orange and ½–1 tbsp Grand Marnier or Triple Sec, to taste, into the finished crème pâtissière.

....

For a lighter crème pâtissière...

If you need or prefer a lighter version, whip 100ml double cream until soft peaks form and fold into the finished, blended crème pâtissière.

Sabayon

Sabayon is an egg-based sauce that can be either sweet or savoury, although it is most often sweet. A light, foamy sauce, it is ideal for serving with poached fruit or summer berries.

Champagne sabayon

Makes 250ml
4 egg yolks
3 tbsp caster sugar
75ml Champagne
100ml double cream

1 Place the egg yolks, sugar and half the Champagne in a heatproof bowl big enough to sit over a saucepan of simmering water. Set the bowl over the pan, making sure the base of the bowl is not in direct contact with the water.

2 Using a hand-held electric whisk, whisk the mixture for up to 10 minutes until it has increased in volume and is light and mousse-like. Remove the bowl from the heat and continue to whisk until the mixture is cool (this will take several minutes).

3 Meanwhile, in a separate bowl, whip the cream to soft peaks, then fold the cream and the remaining Champagne into the sauce. Chill until ready to use.

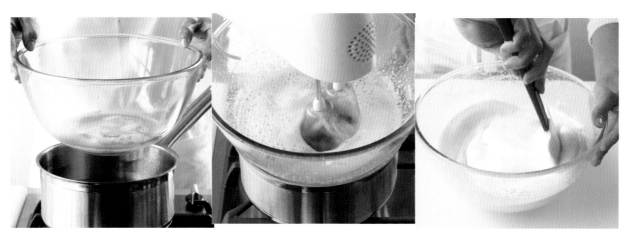

1 Placing the bowl of egg yolks, sugar and half the Champagne over a pan of simmering water.

2 Whisking the mixture over the heat until it is light and mousse-like.

3 Off the heat, folding in the whipped cream and remaining Champagne.

Variations

Pear sabayon Substitute 30ml Poire William liqueur for the Champagne.

Sauternes sabayon Substitute 50ml Sauternes for the Champagne and reduce the sugar to 2 tbsp.

Passion fruit sabayon Use 75ml passion fruit juice in place of the Champagne.

Savoury sabayon Omit the sugar and serve with pan-fried or steamed fish.

Stability

The mousse created by the whisking process is unstable. The addition of cream stabilises the sabayon to a degree, but it will still eventually separate, so use within a few hours. It is also possible to whisk a sabayon for too long over the heat, causing the mousse to collapse and become a sticky mass. To avoid this, as soon as a good volume is achieved, remove the bowl from the heat and whisk to cool down.

Fruit coulis

These simple uncooked fruit sauces are quick and easy to make and useful to serve with ice cream, mousses and other desserts. They are usually made with a sugar syrup, which helps to stop them separating.

Raspberry coulis

Makes 250ml
50g granulated sugar
75ml water
250g raspberries (fresh or defrosted frozen ones)
Squeeze of lemon juice (optional)

1 Put the sugar and water into a saucepan. Place over a low heat and dissolve the sugar, using the handle of a wooden spoon to gently agitate the sugar to prevent it from 'caking' on the bottom of the saucepan. Try to avoid splashing syrup up the sides of the pan.

2 Once the sugar is dissolved, use a pastry brush dipped in water to brush down the sides of the pan, to wash any remaining sugar crystals down into the syrup.

3 Turn the heat up, stop stirring from this point, and bring the syrup to the boil for 2 minutes, then remove from the heat and allow to cool slightly.

4 Put the raspberries into a food processor, pour on half the sugar syrup and blend to a purée.

5 Strain the coulis through a chinois or fine sieve into a bowl to remove the seeds.

6 Taste and adjust the consistency and sweetness with lemon juice or some of the remaining sugar syrup. The coulis should have a 'floodable' consistency.

Variations

Any soft fruit can be used to make a coulis, such as strawberries and blueberries. Fruit juice, sugar syrup or water can be used to thin the sauce.

Mango and passion fruit coulis

Makes 150ml
2 ripe passion fruit
1 large, ripe mango
75–100ml fresh orange juice
2–3 tsp icing sugar (optional)

1 Cut the passion fruit in half, scrape the seeds and juice into a sieve placed over a bowl, to extract just the juice, then discard the seeds. Peel the mango and cut the flesh from the stone, then cut it into large chunks.

2 Put the passion fruit juice and the mango into a food processor and blend to a smooth purée. Add enough orange juice to give a 'floodable' consistency (see step 6, right) and pass through a fine sieve into a bowl. The sweetness can be adjusted, if necessary, with icing sugar dissolved in a little water.

Melba sauce

Makes 200ml
250g fresh raspberries
30–50g icing sugar, to taste

1 Blend the raspberries and the icing sugar in a food processor until smooth, then pass through a fine sieve into a bowl. Adjust the consistency with a little warm water and the sweetness with a little water and icing sugar combined. The sauce can split on standing, so needs to be made shortly before serving.

1 Agitating the sugar as it dissolves to prevent it from caking on the bottom of the pan.

2 Brushing down the sides of the pan to wash down any sugar crystals.

3 Boiling the sugar syrup steadily.

4 Pouring the cooled sugar syrup onto the raspberries in the food processor, ready to purée.

5 Straining the coulis through a chinois to remove the seeds.

6 The finished raspberry coulis, with the correct 'floodable' consistency.

A note on seasoning a sweet dish...

Sugar is the usual sweet seasoning. When making a sauce such as a raspberry coulis, where the fruit is naturally quite sharp, enough sugar must be used to season the coulis to enhance the flavour of the raspberries and to balance their acidity. Always consider what the coulis is going to be served with too, when seasoning. If it will be served with something very sweet, the contrast will be too great if the raspberry coulis is under-sweetened and overly sharp.

Sugar syrups and caramels

Once dissolved and heated, sugar takes on almost magical qualities as it moves through the various stages towards caramelisation. At every stage, it has a different use, from stock syrup to deep caramel.

Stock syrup

Makes about 500ml
250g granulated sugar
500ml water

This is a basic syrup that can be made in a large volume and kept in the fridge for general purpose use, such as making coulis or macerating fruit.

1 Put the sugar and water in a medium saucepan. Place over a low heat to dissolve the sugar, using the handle of a wooden spoon to gently agitate it and prevent it from 'caking' on the bottom of the pan. Avoid splashing syrup up the sides.

2 Once the sugar has dissolved, use a pastry brush dipped in water to brush down the sides of the pan, to wash any remaining sugar crystals down into the syrup.

3 Turn the heat up and do not stir from this point. Bring the syrup to the boil and boil steadily for 5 minutes. Take off the heat, cool and keep covered until needed.

1 Agitating the sugar to stop it caking.   **2** Brushing down any sugar crystals.   **3** Boiling the sugar syrup.

Crystallisation
Sugar crystals attract each other. If there are a few crystals still present after the sugar has dissolved, when the syrup is boiled these crystals may contaminate the syrup and turn the dissolved sugar into crystals again, crystallising the entire syrup. If this happens the process will need to be started again with fresh ingredients.

Preventing crystallisation
A sound technique will prevent crystallisation. However, when sugar syrups are to be used for very sensitive recipes, then an interfering agent can be added to the syrup when dissolving the sugar. Interfering agents include glucose syrup or some form of acidity such as a few drops of lemon juice or a pinch of cream of tartar. These invert the sugar (sucrose), breaking it down into different sugars (glucose and fructose), which makes the mixture more stable and helps to prevent crystallisation.

Stages in sugar syrup concentration

When you are ready to use the syrup, bring it to the boil in a saucepan and boil for the length of time necessary for it to reach the correct temperature and required consistency. This will depend on what the syrup will be used for (see below).

Up until the 'soft ball' stage, test the consistency by using a teaspoon and your fingers, but take care as the syrup will be hot. Draw the syrup off the heat, dip the teaspoon in and take a little of the syrup between your thumb and forefinger, then test it (as shown).

From the soft ball stage the syrup will be too hot to use your fingers. Take a little of it with a teaspoon, drop into a jug of cold water, allow to cool, then take out and feel it.

Taking a syrup too far

If a syrup is taken to a stage too far, then it can be brought back by the addition of a good splash of water so the sugar density is diluted again. This can only be done if the syrup has not yet taken on colour. Once colour is achieved, the caramel can be stopped, but there is no going back to a previous stage.

A note on safety...

Great care should be taken when making and using sugar syrups. As shown in the table, the temperature of the syrup reaches well in excess of 100°C.

Sugar syrup stage	Temperature of the syrup	Testing the stage	Use
Vaseline	104°C	Slightly greasy, sticky feel	Syrup and sorbets
Short thread	108°C	Thread extends to 5–7mm	Syrup and sorbets
Long thread	110°C	Thread extends to 2cm	Syrup
Soft ball	115°C	Syrup balls, but is very soft	Fudge, fondant
Firm ball	120°C	Syrup balls with still some give	Mousse-based ice creams, Italian meringue
Hard ball	124°C	Syrup balls with no give	Marshmallows
Soft crack	138°C	Crack is sounded when hot syrup hits the cold water	Soft toffee
Hard crack	155°C 160°C	Crack is sounded when hot syrup hits the cold water. Syrup begins to take on a little colour	Hard toffee, some nougats Nougat
Spun sugar	152°C	Pale golden colour	Spun sugar
Caramel	194°C	Deep golden colour, quickly darkening on further heating	Sauce and flavourings

Caramel

Makes about 450g
A little oil
500g granulated sugar
250ml water

This will produce a brittle caramel that can either be broken into shards or drizzled onto an oiled baking sheet to harden and used for decoration.

1 Very lightly oil a baking tray. Put the sugar and water into a heavy-based saucepan. Place over a low heat and dissolve the sugar, using the handle of a wooden spoon to gently agitate the sugar to prevent it from 'caking' on the bottom of the saucepan. Try to avoid splashing syrup up the sides of the pan.

2 Brush down the sides of the pan with a pastry brush dipped in water to remove any sugar crystals, then bring the syrup to a gentle boil. Boil the syrup, without stirring, until it is an even, rich golden colour. It may be necessary to swirl the caramel to encourage even colouring.

3 Pour the caramel onto the oiled baking tray or quickly drizzle a pattern using a spoon. Wait for the caramel to cool completely and set before releasing it from the baking sheet and breaking it into pieces. It should be used soon after it is made as it will soon become sticky.

Controlling the cooking and colour of caramel

Making a caramel requires confidence and decisive action, which come with experience. As the sugar syrup begins to take on colour, turn the heat down a little to slow the caramelisation of the sugar and give you more control of the cooking. Don't walk away from it; sugar burns very quickly. As the sugar starts to caramelise you may need to give the saucepan a gentle swirl to ensure the sugar caramelises evenly.

As the sugar colours more it will begin to smoke lightly. Watch the caramel carefully. Remove the saucepan from the heat and swirl the caramel gently; this will help to reduce the size of the bubbles and allow you to see its true colour. If it is not the colour you require then return the saucepan to the heat and continue cooking.

When the caramel reaches a rich golden colour, it is ready and you must act quickly to take it off the heat and pour it out of the pan. Even off the heat the caramel will continue to deepen in colour, and too deep a colour will cause bitterness.

If you want to use the caramel to make a sauce, add water or cream to it to stop the cooking. It is best to have any liquid to hand and ready to use when you need it. The water needs to be poured onto the caramel when you think it is just a shade less than the desired colour, as the heat in the caramel will continue to colour it in the few seconds it takes to lift the liquid and pour it in. Stand well back when adding liquid to caramel, as it will splutter and spit alarmingly at first.

Caramel sauce

Makes about 500ml
500g granulated sugar
500ml water

This results in a liquid caramel sauce, with the addition of water stopping the cooking of the caramel.

1 Put the sugar and 250ml of the water into a heavy-based saucepan. Place over a low heat and dissolve the sugar, using the handle of a wooden spoon to gently agitate the sugar to prevent it from 'caking' on the bottom of the saucepan. Try to avoid splashing syrup up the sides of the pan.

2 After brushing down the sides of the pan with a pastry brush dipped in water, bring the syrup to a gentle boil, without stirring, and boil until a deep golden brown colour. You may need to swirl the pan very gently from time to time, but do not stir.

3 Immediately pour the remaining 250ml water into the caramel, taking care as it will splutter and spit. Swirl the caramel in the pan to dissolve it properly and return it to a low heat, if necessary, until fully dissolved.

4 Pour the caramel into a jug and cool until ready to use.

Variations

Lime caramel sauce Once the remaining water has been added, stir through the finely grated zest and juice of 2 limes. Strain before use.

Spiced caramel sauce Add to the finished caramel: 4 bay leaves, 4 star anise, 2 cinnamon sticks, 2 pared strips of lemon zest, 2 tbsp coriander seeds, crushed, and a 4cm piece of fresh root ginger, peeled and roughly chopped. Leave to infuse overnight and strain before use.

Butterscotch sauce Make a caramel as for the main recipe but using 150g sugar and 4 tbsp water. When it reaches the desired caramel colour, add 150ml double cream, in place of the water, to stop the cooking. Stir well to dissolve, then stir in 30g unsalted butter. Makes 250ml.

Salted butterscotch sauce Add ¼ tsp sea salt flakes to the cooled butterscotch sauce and stir to combine.

Making a dry caramel

It is possible to make a caramel without water. It is slightly quicker as the sugar does not need dissolving and the water does not need to be evaporated, but it calls for close attention. Caster, rather than granulated sugar is preferable, as the crystals are smaller and melt more quickly.

Sprinkle 200g caster sugar over the entire surface of a large, clean frying pan. Ideally the sugar should be no thicker than a few millimetres to ensure even colouring. Place the pan on a low to medium heat. The heat will start to melt the sugar at the edges, but leave it undisturbed. As more and more sugar melts and takes on colour, carefully swirl the pan to encourage even browning. You may need to use a fork to gently encourage the unmelted sugar to the outside of the pan to melt, but don't stir the sugar vigorously or it may crystallise. Eventually all the sugar should have melted and an even caramel formed. Act swiftly as the caramel will burn easily.

Eggs

A simple egg can be a dish in itself, embellished or left plain; boiled, fried, poached or scrambled. But that's only the beginning: eggs also play a vital role in cooking. Their ability to bind, thicken, set, enrich, leaven, clarify, emulsify and colour makes them a vital component in many savoury and sweet dishes. The common hen's egg is by far the most popular and most widely used in cooking. You may also come across duck and quail eggs. Duck eggs are larger than hen's eggs and have a richer and creamier taste, while delicate quail eggs are prized for their diminutive size and attractive speckled shells.

Boiled eggs

There are two ways to boil an egg: starting either in cold or simmering water. Whichever way you do it, the size of the egg will make a difference to the timings, so adjust for smaller or larger eggs (the timings below are for medium eggs).

Adding to simmering water

Remove the eggs from the fridge at least 15 minutes before cooking, or the shells may crack when they go into the water. Bring a saucepan of water to a simmer over a medium heat. Carefully lower the eggs into the pan using a tablespoon, ensuring they are covered with water. Time your eggs from the point the water begins to simmer (see below), cooking them at a gentle simmer.

As soon as soft- (or medium-soft-) boiled eggs are cool enough to handle, place in egg cups and tap around the shell with a teaspoon or the back of a knife to crack it, then peel off the top. Cut a slice off the top of the egg so you can dip toast soldiers into the warm soft yolk.

For hard-boiled eggs, tap them on a work surface to crack the shells, then peel.

Soft-boiled egg Allow 3½–4½ minutes.　　Medium soft-boiled egg Allow 5–6½ minutes.　　Hard-boiled egg Allow 8–9 minutes.

Adding eggs to cold water

Carefully place the eggs in a saucepan filled with enough cold water to cover them. Place the saucepan over a medium heat and bring to a simmer. Time your egg from the point the water begins to simmer (the first small bubbles rise), cooking them at a gentle simmer for ½–1 minute for a soft-boiled egg, 1½–2 minutes for a medium soft-boiled egg and 3–3½ minutes for a hard-boiled egg. Drain them as soon as the cooking time is up and run them under cold running water until just cool enough to peel, or until completely cold if you are serving the eggs cold.

A note on egg safety...

Eggs should always be kept in a cold place to retard bacterial growth, as they are susceptible to salmonella bacteria. However, some recipes, such as mayonnaise-based sauces or cakes, call for eggs at room temperature, so they should be removed from the fridge in time to lose their chill.

Thorough cooking kills bacteria, but anyone particularly vulnerable to contamination, such the young, old or infirm, and pregnant women, should avoid dishes involving raw or partly cooked eggs.

BLT salad with soft-boiled eggs

Serves 4
8 rashers of smoked streaky bacon
100g cherry tomatoes
4 eggs
½–¾ focaccia or ciabatta loaf
4–5 tbsp olive oil
4 tbsp mayonnaise (see page 116)
1–2 tbsp water
1 tbsp wholegrain mustard
150g mixed salad leaves, such as frisée,
  radicchio and curly lettuce
Salt and freshly ground black pepper

1 Heat the oven to 200°C/gas mark 6.

2 Derind the bacon rashers and stretch each one on a board with the back of a knife to make them even thinner, then place on a baking sheet with the tomatoes. Cook in the oven until the rashers are crisp and brown, removing the cherry tomatoes when they soften and begin to colour.

3 Put the eggs in a saucepan of cold water and place over a medium heat. Bring to a simmer and cook for 1½–2 minutes, depending on size, to medium soft-boil. Drain and refresh in cold water, then carefully peel.

4 To make the croûtons, cut the bread into 1.5cm cubes or tear into rustic pieces. Place in a bowl, drizzle over the olive oil and stir to ensure the bread is evenly and well coated in oil. Tip the bread onto an oven tray, spread out and cook in the oven, turning occasionally, until golden and crisp, about 10–15 minutes.

5 Whisk the mayonnaise, water and mustard together to a thick, pourable sauce and season to taste with salt and pepper. Carefully cut the soft-boiled eggs in half.

6 Break the bacon into pieces and put into a big bowl with the salad, mayonnaise sauce, tomatoes and some salt and pepper. Toss to mix, then pile into serving bowls and top with the croûtons and halved soft-boiled eggs.

Poached eggs

For best results, use very fresh, cold eggs straight from the fridge for poaching.

1 Break an egg into a small bowl. Fill a deep saucepan two-thirds full of water, add a little salt, place over a medium to high heat and bring to the boil.

2 Lower the heat, ensuring a few small bubbles are still rising and breaking the surface of the water. Swirl the water with a spoon to create a whirlpool.

3 Allow the whirlpool to almost subside, then pour the egg into the middle of the water.

4 As the egg sinks, the swirling water helps to wrap the white around the yolk. Poach for 2 minutes. If poaching ahead, lift out at this point with a slotted spoon. The white should be set and the yolk still very soft.

5 When ready to serve, lower the egg back into the water and cook for another 30 seconds, then lift the egg out and dab some kitchen paper under the slotted spoon to remove excess water.

6 Trim away any straggly white strands around the edge and serve. Repeat with the remaining eggs (see below).

Poaching a lot of eggs

Once you are confident, you can poach several eggs at a time. Until then, poach them one at a time for 2 minutes, so the white is just set but the yolk still very soft, then carefully lift into a bowl of cold water to stop the cooking process. When all the eggs are poached and in cold water, carefully lift out each one, trim as necessary and place in a bowl of fresh cold water. The eggs can be kept like this for a few hours.

When ready to serve, bring a saucepan of water to a gentle simmer and carefully place the eggs in the water for 30 seconds, to reheat and just start to set the yolk. Remove, dry the eggs (as above) and serve.

Eggs Benedict

Serves 4
1 quantity freshly made hollandaise
  (see page 120)
2 English muffins
4 thick slices of cooked ham
4 eggs, ideally cold
20g butter
Pinch of cayenne pepper (optional)

1 Keep the hollandaise warm in a bain marie off the heat, stirring occasionally. Heat the oven to 140°C/gas mark 1.

2 Split the muffins, toast lightly and keep warm. Place the ham slices on a plate, cover with a piece of slightly dampened greaseproof paper and warm in the oven.

3 Poach the eggs, trim and dry (see left). Place a toasted muffin half on each plate, spread with the butter, then top with a slice of ham. Place a poached egg on the ham, then spoon some hollandaise over the top. Serve immediately, sprinkled with a little cayenne pepper if you like.

Variations

Smoked salmon and egg muffins Replace the ham with 2–3 slices of smoked salmon per person, folded on the muffins under the egg. Sprinkle with 1 tsp chopped chives.

Smoked haddock and egg muffins Replace the ham with 100g smoked haddock per person, poached in milk for 3–5 minutes, then drained and dried.

Eggs Florentine Omit the ham. Wilt 500g washed spinach in a hot saucepan, squeeze out all the water, then reheat in 20g butter in a frying pan over a medium heat. Divide the spinach between the 4 muffins, then top with a poached egg and the hollandaise.

Salade tiède with poached eggs

Serves 4

4 eggs, ideally cold
1 head of curly endive
150g pancetta
2 garlic cloves
6 tbsp vegetable oil
2–3 tbsp sherry vinegar
½–1 tsp Dijon mustard
Handful of sourdough croûtons
  (see page 613)
Freshly ground black pepper

1 Poach the eggs for 2 minutes, then refresh in cold water (see page 146).

2 Discard the tough outer green leaves from the curly endive, pull apart the central pale leaves and break them into bite-sized pieces. Wash, dry well and transfer to a salad bowl.

3 Cut the pancetta into lardons and peel and crush the garlic.

4 Heat 1 tbsp of the oil in a frying pan, add the lardons and fry, stirring often, until golden, and the fat is rendered.

5 Lower the heat, add the garlic and cook for 30 seconds to soften, then add the remaining oil, with the sherry vinegar and mustard to taste. Season with pepper.

6 Heat a saucepan of water over a medium heat until simmering, then carefully add the eggs and reheat for 30 seconds. Remove with a slotted spoon and dab the underside of the spoon with kitchen paper to remove excess water.

7 Pour the dressing with the lardons over the endive, and toss to coat evenly. Divide the salad between individual plates. Place a poached egg on top, sprinkle over the croûtons and drizzle over any remaining dressing. Serve immediately.

Poached eggs on spicy pea and potato cakes

Serves 4

2 medium baking potatoes
2 green chillies
3 spring onions
½ lemon
Small bunch of coriander
100g frozen peas
50ml olive oil
½ tsp ground cumin
½ tsp ground coriander
½ tsp garam masala
2 tbsp chickpea flour
4 eggs
Salt and freshly ground black pepper

1 Peel the potatoes, cut into 3cm chunks and put into a large saucepan of salted cold water. Bring to the boil over a medium heat, then lower the heat and simmer until tender; a cutlery knife inserted into the potato should pass through easily.

2 Meanwhile, halve, deseed and finely chop the chillies. Slice the spring onions on the diagonal and squeeze the juice from the ½ lemon. Coarsely chop enough coriander leaves to give you 2 tbsp. Cook the peas in a separate pan of boiling water for 2–3 minutes until tender, then drain and set aside.

3 Drain the potatoes and return to the pan to steam-dry, then break them up coarsely with a fork and add the drained peas.

4 Heat 1 tbsp of the olive oil in a frying pan over a low to medium heat, add the chillies and spring onions and sauté for 1 minute. Add the dry spices, lower the heat and cook for a further 1 minute, then remove and set aside to cool.

5 Once cool, add the spice mixture to the potatoes and peas. Add the chickpea flour, lemon juice, coriander and salt and pepper to taste. Mix well, then divide into 8 portions and shape each into a flat disc about 7cm in diameter. Place on a baking tray lined with baking parchment and refrigerate for 30 minutes to firm up.

6 Heat the oven to 120°C/gas mark ½. Heat the remaining olive oil in a non-stick frying pan over a low to medium heat and fry the potato cakes, in batches, for 2–3 minutes each side until hot all the way through and browned and crisp on both sides. Transfer each batch to a tray lined with kitchen paper and keep warm in the oven while you fry the remaining cakes and poach the eggs (see page 146).

7 To serve, place 2 potato cakes on each of 4 plates with one cake resting against the other. Place a warm poached egg on top. Delicious served with a spoonful of tomato and chilli sauce (see page 128), spicy tamarind chutney (see page 305) or a good quality mango chutney.

Scrambled eggs

Serves 2–3
6–8 eggs
2–3 tbsp milk
30g butter
Salt and finely ground white pepper

For successful scrambled eggs, you need a gentle heat and a light hand. The aim is to achieve large flakes of tender, soft-cooked egg so take care, as stirring the egg quickly or vigorously will break up the flakes.

1 Break the eggs into a bowl and beat well with a fork to break up the yolk. Add the milk and some seasoning. Melt the butter in a heavy-based saucepan over a low to medium heat. Before it starts to foam, add the beaten egg.

2 Allow the egg to begin to cook on the base of the pan, then carefully drag a spoon through, lifting the cooked egg from the bottom of the pan in large flakes. You may need to adjust the heat a little; the cooking should be very gentle.

3 Continue in this way until all the egg has been lifted. Once most of the egg is cooked, remove the pan from the heat; there should be enough heat in the saucepan to finish cooking the egg.

Note When ready, the scrambled egg should still be soft, with a little slightly underdone egg among the flakes. Taste and adjust the seasoning if necessary. Serve immediately, on toast if you like.

Variations

Scrambled eggs with chilli and coriander Halfway through cooking, add ½ red chilli, deseeded and finely diced, and 2 spring onions, finely sliced on the diagonal. At the end of cooking, stir through 2–3 tbsp coriander leaves, roughly torn, and their finely chopped stalks.

Scrambled eggs with smoked salmon Stir through 2–3 slices of smoked salmon, torn into pieces, at the end of cooking.

Scrambled eggs with chives Add 1–2 tbsp finely chopped chives to the egg mixture before cooking.

Chinese scrambled eggs with prawns and garlic chives Omit the salt and add ½ tsp Shaoxing rice wine, 1 tsp light soy sauce and ½ tsp sesame oil to the beaten eggs. Heat 1 tbsp each of vegetable and sesame oil in a wok, add 150g peeled, deveined raw tiger prawns and stir-fry until just cooked, about 2 minutes. Add 30g Chinese garlic chives, cut into 2cm pieces, then the beaten egg. Allow the egg to set on the base of the wok, then draw a spoon through it, lifting the cooked egg from the bottom of the wok in large flakes. Continue until the egg is all cooked, but still soft and creamy in texture. Spoon onto 2 plates, scatter over some finely shredded spring onion and serve with oyster sauce on the side.

Fried eggs

Always use very fresh eggs for frying and a non-stick or well-seasoned frying pan of an appropriate size for the number of eggs you are frying.

1 To fry 2 eggs, heat a frying pan over a low to medium heat and add ½ tbsp each olive oil and butter. Heat gently for 2 minutes, then crack an egg into a small bowl and carefully pour it into the frying pan. Repeat with the second egg.

2 Allow the egg whites to start to set. You may need to adjust the temperature: if it is sizzling fast and furiously then lower the heat; if there is no sizzle at all, increase the heat a little. The egg should cook, but not brown, on the underside.

3 Once the white has set around the yolk, use a spoon to baste the fat over the yolk.

4 Depending on preference, the yolk can be left very yellow and runny or it can be basted until it has clouded over a little, with the yolk still runny underneath.

5 Carefully insert a fish slice underneath an egg and lift it.

6 Dab some kitchen paper underneath, then slide onto a plate. Repeat with the second egg.

Fried quail eggs with Jersey Royals, asparagus and chorizo

Serves 4 as a starter
3–4 small cooking chorizos
1 tbsp olive oil
400g Jersey Royals or other small
  new potatoes
½ bunch of asparagus
4 quail eggs

For the lemon vinaigrette
½ banana shallot
6 large mint leaves
3 tbsp extra virgin olive oil
½–1 tsp Dijon mustard
1 lemon
Salt and freshly ground black pepper

1 For the vinaigrette, peel and finely dice the shallot and finely chiffonade the mint (see page 89). Put the extra virgin olive oil and mustard in a small bowl, juice the lemon and add 1 tbsp to the bowl. Whisk well, add the shallot and season with salt and pepper. Add the mint.

2 In a small frying pan, fry the chorizos in a little of the olive oil until cooked. Allow to cool a little, then peel and crumble (rather than cut) them into small pieces, about 1cm cubed. Reserve the chorizo oil.

3 Scrub the potatoes and cut any large ones in half. Bring a medium saucepan of salted water to a simmer, add the potatoes and simmer until tender, about 10–15 minutes.

4 Meanwhile, prepare the asparagus by snapping off the woody ends and peeling the lower half of the spears if they are thick (see page 25). Using a swivel peeler, shave the asparagus into long ribbons.

5 When the potatoes are cooked, drain well and very lightly crush them so the skins are broken. Transfer the potatoes to a bowl and, while they are still hot, add the vinaigrette, turning the potatoes to coat them. Add the chorizo and shaved asparagus and turn through gently to coat.

6 Heat a frying pan with the remaining olive oil and fry the quail eggs briefly; they take only 1 minute at most to cook.

7 Divide the warm potato, asparagus and chorizo between individual plates, top with a fried quail egg and drizzle over any remaining vinaigrette and chorizo oil.

Note For a more substantial plate, double the quantities and use hen's eggs.

Variation

Fried quail eggs with Jersey Royals, broad beans and ham hock Omit the chorizo and asparagus and add 100g each blanched, skinned broad beans and shredded ham hock to the potatoes and asparagus.

Chinese crispy duck eggs with oyster sauce

Serves 4
1 red chilli
2 spring onions
½ lime, to taste
4 tbsp oyster sauce
3 tbsp olive oil
4 large duck eggs
Ground Szechuan pepper
4 tsp toasted sesame oil

1 Halve, deseed and finely chop the chilli and finely chop the spring onions, including most of the green part. Juice the ½ lime. Mix the oyster sauce with a little lime juice to taste.

2 Heat a large, heavy-based frying pan over a medium heat and add the olive oil.

3 Break the eggs one at a time into a small bowl, then transfer to the pan. Allow them to bubble, set and become golden and crispy on the edges and underside, then use a spoon to baste the yolks with the oil.

4 When the undersides of the eggs are crisp and the yolks still runny (about 3 minutes), remove to warmed plates. Sprinkle with the chilli and spring onions and season lightly with Szechuan pepper.

5 Drizzle 1 tbsp of the oyster sauce and 1 tsp sesame oil over each egg to serve. These eggs can be eaten as they are for a starter, or served with plain or fried rice dishes and pak choi for a more substantial meal.

Huevos rancheros

Serves 4
Sunflower oil for frying
8 eggs

For the spicy tomato sauce
1 red chilli
1 garlic clove
4 spring onions
2 tbsp sunflower oil
¼ tsp ground cinnamon
¼ tsp ground cumin
¼ tsp ground coriander
Pinch of cayenne pepper
Pinch of paprika
2 x 400g tins chopped tomatoes
½ tsp caster sugar
Salt and freshly ground black pepper

For the corn tortillas
300g instant masa harina
1 tsp salt
300–400ml warm water

For the refried beans
1 onion
1 tbsp sunflower oil
1 tomato
1 garlic clove
1 red chilli
1 tsp ground cumin
400g tin pinto beans
120–150ml water
Small bunch of coriander

1 To make the tomato sauce, halve, deseed and finely chop the chilli. Peel and crush the garlic and finely chop the spring onions. Heat the oil in a saucepan over a medium heat. Add the chilli, garlic and spring onions with the ground spices. Cook, stirring, for 1 minute, then add the tomatoes and sugar and season with salt and pepper. Add a good splash of water and simmer gently for 30 minutes, then adjust the seasoning and add more water if you prefer a thinner sauce.

2 To make the tortilla dough, place the masa harina and salt in a bowl. Pour in two-thirds of the water and mix with a knife to a dough. The quantity of water needed depends on the moisture content of the masa harina; add enough to make a soft, but not sticky, dough. Knead well until smooth, then cover and rest for 15–20 minutes.

3 For the refried beans, halve, peel and finely chop the onion. Heat the oil in a medium saucepan, add the onion and sweat over a low heat until completely soft. Meanwhile, blanch the tomato in boiling water for 10 seconds, then refresh in cold water, dry, peel, quarter, deseed and chop. Peel and crush the garlic, and halve, deseed and finely chop the chilli. Add the tomato, garlic and chilli to the softened onion, with the cumin.

4 Drain the beans, tip into the pan and fry until heated through. Don't worry if they start to break up a little. Add the water and simmer gently until it has nearly all evaporated and the beans are soft. Season with salt and pepper. Chop the coriander leaves and stir half through the beans.

5 Heat the oven to 120°C/gas mark ½. Divide the dough into 12 equal pieces and shape each into a ball. Place each ball between 2 pieces of baking parchment, then, using a rolling pin, flatten the dough into 15–16cm discs. Trim to neaten the edges if preferred.

6 Heat a griddle or frying pan. Cook the tortillas one at a time for about 1 minute on each side until brown spots appear. Keep the cooked tortillas wrapped in a cloth in the low oven.

7 To serve, reheat the tomato sauce and the refried beans. Heat enough sunflower oil to cover the bottom of a frying pan and fry the eggs according to preference (see page 150). Place 2 or 3 tortillas on each plate and spoon the refried beans over them. Top with 2 fried eggs, spoon the tomato sauce over the top and scatter over the remaining coriander. Grind over some pepper and serve at once.

Omelettes

A correctly cooked omelette is pale, with a very small amount of underdone egg through the centre. This is known as 'baveuse'.

Classic omelette

Serves 1
2 eggs
1 tbsp water
10g butter
Salt and finely ground white pepper
Few chives, to finish (optional)

1 Break the eggs into a small bowl and, using a fork, break them up by stirring vigorously. Add the water and some seasoning.

2 Melt the butter in a 15cm non-stick omelette pan or small frying pan (or proved pan, see page 70) over a low heat. When just starting to foam a little, pour in the beaten eggs.

3 Allow the egg to start to set a little, then, using the side of a fork, gently drag the egg from the edges towards the centre of the pan (as shown), allowing the uncooked egg to flood in behind the cooked egg. Repeat this around the pan, creating folds of soft-cooked egg (as shown).

4 When most of the raw egg is cooked and there is only a small amount of slightly undercooked egg on the surface, take the pan off the heat and give it a shake so that the omelette slides up the side of the pan a little.

5 Carefully lift one-third of the omelette over the middle third (as shown), readjust your hold on the pan, then flip the omelette onto a warmed plate. Serve at once, sprinkled with finely chopped chives, if you wish.

Variations

Herb omelette Add 1–2 tsp chopped herbs, such as parsley, chervil or chives, to the beaten eggs.

Cheese omelette Add 1 tsp grated Parmesan cheese to the beaten eggs. Or wrap 1 or 2 slices of soft, melting cheese inside the folded plain omelette.

Mushroom, pepper and onion omelette Spoon 2–3 tbsp fried sliced onions, mushrooms and red pepper over the cooked omelette before folding. You can also wrap 1 or 2 slices of soft, melting cheese inside this omelette.

Spring onion and Parmesan omelette Add 1 tbsp grated Parmesan to the beaten eggs. Finely slice a spring onion, including about half of the green part. Cook gently in the melting butter, then proceed as for the main recipe.

Ham and cheese omelette Finely grate 50g Gruyère or Comté cheese and shred 50g ham. Mix half the grated cheese into the eggs when breaking them up in a bowl. Halfway through cooking the omelette, sprinkle the remaining 25g cheese over the surface, allowing it to melt as the omelette finishes setting. Before folding the omelette, sprinkle the cooked ham over the surface.

Bacon and pea omelette Sauté 2 rashers of smoked streaky bacon, derinded and cut into thin strips, in 10g butter until the fat is rendered and the bacon crisp. Add 30g cooked peas and warm through. Incorporate both into the omelette as you cook it.

Hot-smoked salmon or trout and dill omelette Before folding the omelette, sprinkle over 50–75g flaked hot-smoked salmon or trout and a large pinch of coarsely chopped dill.

Oeufs en cocotte

Serves 4
10g butter
4 large eggs
4 tbsp single cream
Small piece of Parmesan cheese
Salt and ground white pepper

1 Heat the oven to 180°C/gas mark 4. Half-fill a roasting tin with hot water (to make a bain marie). Melt the butter and use to brush the insides of 4 ramekins.

2 Break an egg into each buttered ramekin and season with salt and pepper. Pour 1 tbsp cream over each egg and grate a little Parmesan on top. Carefully place the ramekins in the bain marie and bake in the centre of the oven for 10–15 minutes, or until the whites are set but the yolks are still runny. Serve immediately, as the yolks will continue to cook if left to stand.

Variations

Oeufs en cocotte with spinach Wilt 200g washed spinach, squeeze out any excess liquid, then roughly chop and sauté in a little butter. Season well, stir in 2 tbsp double cream and divide equally between the ramekins before topping with the eggs. Proceed as for the main recipe. (Illustrated)

Oeufs en cocotte with mushrooms and tarragon Sauté 200g cleaned and torn mixed wild mushrooms in 20g butter in a hot frying pan, and season well. Remove and leave to cool. Divide the cooled mushrooms between the buttered ramekins. Top with the eggs as for the main recipe, then sprinkle with a few tarragon leaves before pouring on the cream, grating over the Parmesan and cooking as above.

Frittata with potatoes and thyme

Serves 4
1 large floury potato
1 onion
Few thyme sprigs
3 tbsp olive oil
6 eggs
75ml milk or double cream
75g Parmesan cheese
Salt and freshly ground black pepper

1 Peel and thinly slice the potato. Halve, peel and thinly slice the onion. Finely chop enough thyme leaves to give you 1 tsp. Heat the oven to 170°C/gas mark 3.

2 Heat 2 tbsp of the olive oil in a 22–24cm ovenproof, non-stick frying pan over a low to medium heat. Add the onion and potato and season with salt and pepper. Cover and cook gently until the potato is tender and the onion softening, about 15–20 minutes, stirring occasionally and reducing the heat if necessary. Stir the thyme through, take the pan off the heat and set aside to cool a little.

3 Break the eggs into a large bowl, add the milk or cream and whisk well, using a fork to break them up. Grate the Parmesan, add to the beaten eggs and season well. Add the cooked potato and onion to the egg mixture and stir well.

4 Wipe out the frying pan. Add the remaining 1 tbsp oil and heat gently. Pour in the egg and potato mixture and level the surface. Cook gently for about 5 minutes until set and golden underneath, then place in the oven for 10–15 minutes until just set; it can still be a little soft in the centre. Slide the frittata onto a large plate.

Variations

Asparagus and broad bean frittata Omit the potato and onion. Finely chop enough thyme to give you ½–1 tsp. Sweat 1 finely diced shallot in ½ tbsp olive oil in a non-stick frying pan. Prepare ½ bunch of asparagus spears (see page 25), cut into 2.5cm pieces, blanch and refresh. Blanch, refresh and skin 100g podded broad beans (see page 33). Add these vegetables to the sweated shallot with the thyme. Season well, add to the egg mixture and proceed as for the main recipe.

Smoked salmon and watercress frittata Omit the potato, onion, thyme and Parmesan. Add 150g smoked salmon, cut into strips, and 120–150g watercress, washed, stalks removed and finely chopped, to the beaten egg mixture. Proceed as for the main recipe.

Asparagus custards with creamed morels

Serves 6 as a starter
For the asparagus custard
300g asparagus
250ml vegetable stock (see page 101)
200ml milk
100ml double cream
3 eggs, plus 1 extra yolk
Salt and freshly ground black pepper

For the creamed morels
30g dried morels (or fresh if you can
  get them)
1 shallot
20g butter
¼ bunch of chives
100ml double cream
Few drops of lemon juice

To serve
6 asparagus spears
1–2 tsp lemon oil

1 Heat the oven to 150°C/gas mark 2.

2 If using dried morels, soak them in plenty of boiling water for 30–45 minutes until soft and tender. If fresh, brush or wipe them carefully to remove any grit.

3 For the asparagus custard, snap off the woody ends of the asparagus spears. Put the stock into a saucepan, bring to a simmer and season with salt and pepper. Add the asparagus and cook for 2–3 minutes, or until it is just softened and still retaining its colour. Remove from the pan, reserving the stock, and refresh in cold water to preserve its colour.

4 Transfer the asparagus to a food processor or blender and purée until completely smooth, adding a little of the reserved stock only if necessary to obtain a thick, spoonable consistency.

5 Put the milk and cream in a saucepan and bring to scalding point (see page 133) over a medium heat. Meanwhile, whisk the eggs and extra yolk together in a bowl. Gradually pour the hot milk and cream over the eggs, stirring all the time. Add the asparagus purée, taste and season with salt and pepper. Half-fill 6 ramekins or individual gratin dishes with the mixture.

6 Half-fill a roasting tin with hot water to make a bain marie. Carefully stand the ramekins or gratin dishes in the bain marie and bake in the oven, allowing 20–25 minutes for ramekins or 15–20 minutes for gratin dishes. To check, lightly shake a ramekin or gratin dish; the custard should have a uniform wobble and have formed a skin.

7 While the custards are cooking, prepare the creamed morels. Halve, peel and finely dice the shallot. Melt the butter in a frying pan, add the shallot, cover and sweat until soft and translucent. Finely chop enough chives to give you 1 tsp.

8 When the shallot is soft, drain the morels well, straining and reserving the soaking water. Squeeze the morels to remove excess water. If large, halve or quarter them. Add to the shallots and sauté for 3–4 minutes without allowing the shallots to burn. (Cook fresh morels in the same way.) Add the cream and simmer gently for another 3–4 minutes. Taste and season with salt, pepper and lemon juice, then add the chives. If the cream gets too thick, add a splash of the reserved morel soaking liquor.

9 Use a swivel peeler to shave the 6 asparagus spears into long ribbons. Blanch them in boiling salted water for 10–20 seconds, then refresh in cold water, drain and toss in a bowl with the lemon oil and some salt and pepper.

10 When the custards are cooked, remove the ramekins or gratin dishes from the bain marie and place one on each plate. Spoon a little of the creamed morels on top of the custards and garnish with the asparagus ribbons. Drizzle a little lemon oil over the custards and morels and serve immediately.

Egg whites

Egg whites perfectly display the role that science plays in cooking. Their magical ability to transform into pillows of white foam, adding lightness and volume to savoury dishes and desserts, makes them an essential ingredient. Learning how to use them effectively opens the door to many culinary skills.

Separating eggs

1 To separate an egg, crack the egg on the edge of a table or use a cutlery knife. Avoid too much pressure or you will break the egg in half. You only want to crack the shell. Now carefully ease apart the shell halves over a medium to large bowl. Some of the white will fall into the bowl; it is important that none of the yolk does.

2 Hold the yolk in one half of the shell, if necessary tilting your hands to ensure the yolk is captured in the shell. Now carefully move the yolk between the shell halves, which will encourage the white to fall into the bowl.

3 Once most or all of the white is in the bowl, all that may be left on the yolk is the 'chalaza', or thread. Carefully use the edge of one side of the shell to prise or cut it away from the yolk, allowing it to fall into the bowl. Transfer the yolk to another small bowl.

Storing egg yolks

Unless using immediately, closely cover the egg yolk(s) with cling film to prevent them from drying out and refrigerate; they will keep for up to 3 days.

Whisking egg whites

The constant beating of egg whites is necessary to create a fine, even texture, incorporating as much air as possible. To achieve more stable whisked whites, start whisking slowly to create small bubbles of air, then gradually increase the speed of whisking. As more air is incorporated, the consistency of the egg whites will change. Egg whites are used at different stages of whisking for different purposes, so it helps to be able to recognise the consistency at different stages.

Egg whites should be whisked in scrupulously clean bowls, free from any fat, which can prevent the whites from whisking properly. A copper bowl is ideal, as the metal reacts with egg whites to produce a very stable foam. Otherwise, choose stainless steel or glass, but avoid plastic bowls which tend to trap grease.

As a general rule, unless specified, whisk egg whites to the same consistency as the mixture to which they are being added. Like consistencies will combine more easily and efficiently with minimal loss of volume.

Identifying the different 'peaking' stages of whisking

Egg whites should usually be whisked just before you need to use them; once whisked they should not be left to sit for any length of time or they will separate and begin to collapse.

1 Using a large fine balloon whisk, start to whisk the egg whites in the bowl. Lifting the whisk up and over the whites is more effective and incorporates more air than just a stirring action.

2 As more air is incorporated the whites will become slightly foamy, opaque and very thin. Continue whisking and they will increase in volume, becoming white and foamy. Early on, if you lift the whisk vertically upwards and then turn it upside down, the whites will not hold their shape and will fall from the whisk.

3 Continue whisking and the whites will become a little paler and stiffer.

4 As the whites stiffen a little more, test them again by lifting the balloon whisk vertically, then turning the whisk upside down. If the whites cling to the whisk and start to create a 'peak', but the peak falls over on itself, the egg whites have reached the 'soft peak' stage.

5 If firmer whites are required, whisk for a little longer then test again by lifting the whisk; the whites will definitely cling to the whisk and, as it is pulled up vertically and turned upside down, the clinging whites will start to fall over onto themselves, then stop halfway. This is known as the 'medium peak' stage and is ideal for soufflés and mousses.

6 Continue to whisk again; the whites will become very stiff and when tested the peak will hold its vertical position and not fall over on itself. This is known as the 'stiff peak' stage and is the required consistency for meringues and for sweet soufflés where the egg whites are meringued. At this stage there is still some elasticity in the whites.

A note on over-whisking...

Further whisking would cause the whites to become too stiff and they would 'break' when pulled away on the whisk.

Soufflés

A savoury soufflé is a thick white sauce, enriched with egg yolks, with flavourings added and whisked egg whites folded in to provide lift. Once mastered, soufflés become straightforward to make. For sweet soufflés, made with a crème pâtissière base, see pages 554–5.

Cheese soufflé

Serves 6 as a starter
30g butter, plus 10g to grease
1–2 tbsp dry white breadcrumbs
30g plain flour
Small pinch of mustard
Small pinch of cayenne pepper
300ml milk
85g Cheddar or Gruyère cheese
4 eggs
Salt and finely ground white pepper

1 Heat the oven to 200°C/gas mark 6 and place a baking tray in the oven to heat up. Melt the 10g butter and use to brush the insides of 6 ramekins, then pour the breadcrumbs into the first ramekin. Tilt the ramekin to coat the bottom and sides evenly with the crumbs, then pour the excess into the next ramekin. Repeat until all the ramekins are coated, discarding any excess crumbs.

2 Melt the 30g butter in a saucepan over a low to medium heat, then add the flour, mustard and cayenne pepper. Cook for 1 minute, stirring with a wooden spoon, then remove from the heat and start to add the milk in small amounts, stirring to incorporate each addition. The mixture will be very thick initially, then as more milk is added it will start to loosen. Ensure there are no lumps by beating the mixture well before each addition.

3 When at least half the milk has been incorporated, add the remaining milk in generous amounts. Return the pan to the heat and stir the sauce as it comes to the boil, then lower the heat and leave to simmer for 2 minutes. This thick sauce is called the 'panade'. Remove the pan from the heat. Finely grate the cheese and add it to the panade. The heat of the panade will melt it. Transfer to a large bowl.

4 Separate the eggs (see page 160), putting the whites into another clean large bowl and stirring the yolks into the panade. Taste and season generously with salt and finely ground white pepper. Whisk the egg whites to medium peaks.

5 Fold a large spoonful of the whisked egg whites into the panade to loosen it.

6 Carefully fold in the remaining whites, retaining as much volume as possible.

7 Fill the prepared ramekins three-quarters full with the soufflé mixture.

8 'Top hat' each soufflé by running the tip of a cutlery knife around the inner rim of each ramekin, which helps to create an even rise.

9 Place the ramekins on the hot baking tray (to give them an immediate burst of heat) in the top of the oven and bake for 8–12 minutes until well risen and cooked, but still uniformly wobbly when lightly shaken. Serve immediately. There should be about 1 tsp undercooked soufflé mixture in the centre.

Note To make a large soufflé (to serve 2–3 as a main course), put the mixture into a 15cm soufflé dish instead of individual ones and bake for 25–30 minutes.

Variations

Spinach soufflé Reduce the Cheddar to 30g and add 200g spinach, wilted, seasoned, squeezed dry and finely chopped, to the mixture after the cheese has melted, then proceed as for the main recipe.

Watercress and Gruyère soufflé Use 100g Gruyère and add 150g watercress, picked, washed and finely chopped, to the mixture once the cheese is incorporated.

Stilton soufflé Replace the grated Cheddar with 75g Stilton, crumbled into small pieces.

1 Coating the buttered ramekins with breadcrumbs.

2 Incorporating the milk into the roux base.

3 Adding the grated cheese to the panade.

4 Whisking the egg whites to medium peaks.

5 Folding a large spoonful of the whisked egg whites into the mixture to loosen it.

6 Carefully folding in the rest of the egg whites.

7 Spooning the soufflé mixture into the ramekins.

8 Running a knife around the edge of the mixture to encourage an even rise.

9 Serving the soufflé immediately, before it has time to collapse.

Twice-baked goat's cheese and thyme soufflés with mustard leaves

Serves 6

300ml milk
1 small onion
Few thyme sprigs
2 black peppercorns
50g butter, plus 10g to grease
50g plain flour
3 eggs
100g soft goat's cheese
6 tbsp single cream
3 tbsp freshly grated Parmesan cheese
150g mustard leaves
1 tbsp olive oil
Squeeze of lemon juice
Salt, ground white pepper and freshly
  ground black pepper

1 Heat the oven to 180°C/gas mark 4.

2 Heat the milk gently in a small saucepan. Peel the onion, cut off a large slice and add it to the milk with 1 thyme sprig and the peppercorns. Bring to scalding point, then remove from the heat and allow the flavours to infuse for at least 10 minutes. Strain and reserve the milk.

3 Rinse out the saucepan, then melt the 10g butter and use to brush the insides of 6 ramekins or timbales; set aside to cool and firm up, then re-butter.

4 Melt the 50g butter in the saucepan, stir in the flour and cook for 1 minute, then take off the heat. Gradually add the infused milk, stirring until smooth. Once half the milk has been incorporated, add the rest in generous amounts. Return to a medium heat and bring to the boil, stirring. Reduce the heat and simmer the panade for 2 minutes, stirring occasionally.

5 Remove the pan from the heat, transfer the mixture to a large bowl and leave to cool slightly. Separate the eggs (see page 160), putting the whites into a separate bowl. Stir the yolks into the panade. Chop enough thyme leaves to give you 1 tsp and add to the panade. Coarsely crumble in the goat's cheese, then season to taste with salt and white pepper. Half-fill a roasting tin with hot water, for a bain marie.

6 Whisk the egg whites to medium peaks (see pic 4, page 163). Fold a large spoonful of the whites into the soufflé mixture to loosen it, then carefully fold in the remaining whites. Divide the mixture between the prepared ramekins or timbales; they should be about two-thirds full. Carefully stand them in the bain marie and bake in the middle of the oven until well risen, pale golden brown and set, about 15–20 minutes. Remove from the oven and leave to cool a little; they will sink, but this is fine as they will puff up when they are cooked again.

7 Turn the oven setting up to 220°C/gas mark 7.

8 Remove the soufflés from their dishes while still warm (to avoid them sticking), by inverting them onto your hand, shaking the dish sharply from side to side. You may need to run a small, sharp knife carefully round the sides of the dish to release the soufflé. Place on shallow, individual, ovenproof serving dishes, or arrange them upside down on a larger ovenproof serving dish.

9 Spoon 1 tbsp cream over each soufflé and sprinkle with the Parmesan. Bake for a further 10 minutes, or until golden brown and nicely puffed up.

10 Meanwhile, wash the mustard leaves and toss in enough olive oil and lemon juice to lightly coat the leaves. Season with salt and black pepper.

11 Serve the soufflés as soon as they come out of the oven, as they will lose volume very quickly, with the mustard leaves.

Note Twice-baked soufflés can be prepared to the end of step 6 in advance. Remove from their dishes while still warm, wrap them up closely in cling film and set aside until needed, in the fridge if you're cooking them more than 1 hour later.

Variation

Twice-baked Gruyère soufflé with a red salsa For the salsa, char, skin and dice a red pepper (see page 55); peel, quarter, deseed and dice 2 plum tomatoes (see page 85). Mix with 1 tbsp olive oil, a squeeze each of orange and lemon juice and 1 tbsp chopped basil. Season well. Make the soufflé as above, but using 100g grated Gruyère in place of the goat's cheese. Warm the salsa while the soufflés are baking for the second time. Serve the soufflés with the salsa spooned around.

Arnold Bennett soufflé omelette

Serves 2

150–170ml milk
6 black peppercorns
1 bay leaf
1 small onion
1 carrot
150g piece of smoked haddock, skin on
30g butter
1 tbsp plain flour
3 eggs
3 tbsp single cream
1 tbsp freshly grated Parmesan cheese
Salt (if needed) and freshly ground
  black pepper

1 Heat 150ml of the milk gently in a saucepan with the peppercorns and bay leaf. Peel the onion and carrot, cut off a large slice from each and add to the milk. Bring to a simmer, then remove from the heat and set aside for at least 10 minutes, to cool and allow the flavours to infuse.

2 Add the haddock to the pan skin side down, to protect the flesh from the direct heat. Cover the fish with a piece of damp greaseproof paper and return the pan to the heat. Poach gently for 5 minutes, or until just starting to flake.

3 Remove the fish and strain and reserve the milk, discarding the aromatics. Skin the fish and remove any bones, then flake it into large pieces; set aside. Measure the milk; you need 150ml for the sauce, so top up with more milk as necessary.

4 Melt half the butter in a small saucepan, stir in the flour and cook for 1 minute, then take off the heat. Gradually add the infused milk, stirring until smooth. Once half the milk has been incorporated, add the rest in generous amounts. Return to a medium heat and bring to the boil, stirring. Reduce the heat and simmer the panade for 2 minutes, stirring occasionally. Transfer to a large bowl and set aside to cool slightly.

5 Separate the eggs (see page 160), adding the yolks to the panade and placing the whites in a separate bowl. Beat 2 tbsp of the cream and half the Parmesan into the panade with the yolks. Carefully fold in the cooked fish. Taste and add salt if needed (the fish will probably provide enough) and pepper to taste.

6 Whisk the egg whites to medium peaks (see pic 4, page 163) and fold a large spoonful of them into the sauce to loosen it, followed by the remaining whites.

7 Heat the grill to its highest setting. Melt the remaining butter in a 15cm non-stick omelette pan (suitable for placing under the grill) over a low heat. Tilt the pan so that the butter coats the sides. When the butter begins to foam, pour in the smoked haddock mixture.

8 Gently move the pan over the heat, shaking it slightly to prevent the omelette sticking to the bottom. Cook over a low heat for about 5 minutes until the bottom is set and pale golden and only the upper third of the omelette is still uncooked. Sprinkle over the rest of the Parmesan and pour over the remaining cream.

9 Place on the lowest shelf under the grill for about 3–4 minutes to melt the cheese and brown the top of the omelette. Slide onto a warmed plate and serve.

Variations

Smoked salmon and chive soufflé omelette Omit the smoked haddock and infused milk. Make the sauce with 150ml milk and stir in 150g smoked salmon, cut into thick ribbons, in place of the smoked haddock. Finely chop enough chives to give you 2–3 tbsp and stir half into the mixture before cooking; sprinkle the rest over the finished omelette just before serving.

Breakfast soufflé omelette Omit the smoked haddock and infused milk. Make the sauce with 150ml milk and proceed as for the main recipe, then before grilling, sprinkle shards of grilled bacon, grilled cherry tomatoes and fried mushrooms over the top before the remaining Parmesan and cream.

Red onion and goat's cheese soufflé omelette Omit the smoked haddock and infused milk. Make the sauce with 150ml milk. Finely slice and caramelise 2 red onions (see page 14). Crumble 150g goat's cheese into the egg yolk mixture, with 1 tsp chopped thyme and the cooled onion. Proceed as for the main recipe.

Pasta, Rice, Pulses & Grains

For centuries, different cultures have combined these staples with local ingredients and flavours to create indigenous dishes. Many of these are simple, everyday meals that nourish and sustain, but some have evolved into more refined recipes. A great many have made their mark on other national cuisines and, thanks to the ever wider availability of ingredients, have become popular across the world. Some of the recipes in this chapter, like most of the noodle dishes, are quick and easy accompaniments, while others, including the pasta recipes, are a meal in themselves.

Pasta

There are endless different shapes and sizes of pasta, and all act as an excellent vehicle for sauces and stuffings, from a simple spaghetti with olive oil, garlic and chilli to a complex ravioli.

The recipes in this section specify a pasta shape for a particular sauce or filling. Generally, a shape with tubes, grooves or hollows, such as conchiglie or penne, works best with chunkier sauces, as the sauce gets into the spaces in the pasta, whereas long shapes, such as spaghetti or tagliatelle, work best with smoother sauces or flavoured oils that lightly coat the pasta. Keep this in mind but feel free to vary the pasta shape as you like.

Dried pasta has a firmer texture than fresh, which suits many dishes. It is also of course more convenient, and the ideal option for a quick pasta supper. Making your own pasta, however, is fun and very satisfying, and mastering the basic skills will give you the freedom to create your own flavours and fillings.

The recipes in this section can be made with either fresh or dried, unless a specific shape is required, in which case dried is indicated. As a general rule for substituting dried pasta for fresh, you need to reduce the weight by one-third.

Fresh pasta

Serves 4
400g '00' pasta flour, plus extra to dust
4 large eggs
1 tbsp olive oil

We use whole eggs in our pasta for general purpose use. For a richer flavour, silky smooth texture and more vibrant colour, use only egg yolks or a combination of whole eggs and yolks (2 yolks for 1 whole egg). No salt is added to pasta as it absorbs moisture and can give the pasta a speckled appearance. Salt added to the cooking water will be absorbed by the pasta as it cooks.

1 Sift the flour onto a clean work surface and make a well in the centre.

2 Break the eggs into the well and add the olive oil; the well will hold the eggs and oil.

3 Using the fingers of one hand, combine the eggs and oil, gradually drawing in the flour.

4 Continue until you have a firm, rather than wet and sticky, dough; you will not need to incorporate all the flour. Scrape aside any leftover flour to prevent it from making the dough stiffer.

5 Lightly flour a clean surface. Turn the dough onto it and start to knead it.

6 Continue to knead until the dough is smooth and elastic, about 5 minutes. Wrap the dough well in cling film and leave it to relax in a cool spot in the kitchen (not the fridge) for at least 45 minutes and up to 2 hours.

Note The longer the pasta rests the easier it will be to roll out. It is possible to make a quick pasta that only rests for 15 minutes, but the texture will not be quite as silky. It can be rested overnight in the fridge, but needs to be transferred to a cool room temperature 20 minutes before rolling out.

1 Making a well in the flour.

2 Breaking the eggs into the well.

3 Combining the eggs and oil, and gradually drawing in the flour.

4 Incorporating the flour into the eggs and oil to form the dough.

5 Kneading the pasta dough.

6 The fully kneaded smooth and elastic dough, ready to be rested before rolling out.

A note on '00' pasta flour...

Type '00' pasta flour is a high gluten/high protein flour that is milled to a much finer texture than most flours (the fine milling is indicated by the '00'), resulting in a silky, smooth pasta texture.

Making pasta in a food processor

Put the flour, eggs and olive oil in the food processor bowl and switch the machine on. The ingredients will create a coarse crumb as the flour absorbs the eggs and oil. Switch off, take a little of the crumb between your fingertips and work it into a dough. If the crumb comes together quite easily, is firm and a little tacky, not too dry and stiff and not sticky, then tip it onto a lightly floured surface and knead into a dough.

If the dough is very stiff and dry looking, then add more beaten egg, about a quarter of an egg at a time, pulsing the mixture and checking the consistency after each addition.

If the dough is very soft and sticky, add about 1 tbsp flour at a time until you achieve the correct consistency.

Flavoured pastas

Spinach pasta Blanch 250g spinach, refresh, squeeze to remove as much water as possible, then purée and pass through a sieve to give a fairly dry paste; you might need to add a little egg yolk to achieve this. Follow the fresh pasta recipe (on page 168) but use 3 rather than 4 eggs, adding the spinach to the flour well with the eggs.

Tomato pasta Add about 2 tsp tomato purée to the flour well with the eggs.

Herb pasta Add 1–2 tbsp chopped fresh herbs to taste, such as parsley, thyme or tarragon, with the eggs.

Beetroot pasta Add 1 small cooked, peeled and puréed beetroot with the eggs.

Cracked black pepper pasta Mix 1–1½ tbsp coarsely ground black pepper into the flour before adding the eggs and oil. Best cut into tagliatelle (see right, but not rolled to the thinnest setting as the pepper can make it tear). Drain well after cooking and toss in olive oil. Serve drizzled with a little truffle oil and sprinkled with Parmesan shavings and basil leaves.

Saffron pasta Toast ½ tsp saffron strands in a hot, dry frying pan for 30 seconds, then tip into a small bowl, cover with 2 tsp boiling water and leave to infuse and cool. Add the saffron and soaking water to the eggs and oil when making the pasta. Excellent cut into tagliatelle, well drained after cooking and tossed with flakes of hot-smoked salmon, or finely sliced gravadlax (see page 321), and some crème fraîche and dill sprigs.

Rolling and cutting pasta dough

Pasta can be rolled by hand, or with a pasta rolling machine for speed and ease. When rolling out the dough, roll only a small piece at a time as it dries out quickly and develops a 'skin'. Keep the remaining dough well wrapped in cling film as you work on each piece to prevent it from drying out. Pasta should be rolled extremely thinly; it increases in volume considerably when it cooks, so if it is not rolled thinly enough it can become unpleasantly thick and tough to eat.

Rolling by machine

Attach your pasta machine securely to a work surface. Roll out the dough a little by hand first to make it easier to roll through the machine without putting too much strain on the rollers. Begin with the widest setting and pass the dough through the rollers 3 or 4 times, folding the dough after each pass, and passing the open ends through the rollers first. Try to ensure the pasta is shaped into lengths as wide as the machine (as shown). Now move the gauge to a narrower setting and pass the pasta through, narrowest end first. Repeat this process, narrowing the setting by one notch each time until the second thinnest or thinnest setting is reached.

Rolling by hand

Using a rolling pin, or a pasta rolling pin which is tapered at both ends, roll out the dough as thinly as possible. The work surface can help to anchor the dough, enabling you to stretch it out more, so avoid flouring it. The longer you have rested the dough the easier it will be to roll out, as the gluten will have relaxed and the elasticity will be reduced. Try to roll the dough until it is paper thin.

Cutting by machine

Pasta machines normally come with a set of cutters to cut either linguine or tagliatelle. After rolling pasta into long lasagne sheets, attach the cutters and feed the pasta through the cutters to cut to the required width: 2–3mm for linguine, 5–6mm for tagliatelle (as shown). Unravel each piece of pasta and place over a rack or frame to allow the pasta to dry a little and lose its tackiness, becoming leathery on the outside but staying supple and flexible. This will take about 10 minutes. Leaving the pasta to dry for too long will dry it out completely and it will become brittle and break.

Alternatively, the pasta can be shaped into nests after cutting and placed to dry on a tray lightly dusted with flour or semolina.

Cutting by hand

Very lightly flour the rolled out pasta to prevent it from sticking together, then fold each end towards the middle and keep folding until the pasta is a more manageable size. Trim the ends, then cut the pasta across the folds into the required width; 5–6mm for tagliatelle or fettuccine, 1.5–2cm for pappardelle. For a more rustic look, you can tear rather than cut the pasta. Dry the pasta in the same way as for cutting by machine (see above).

Cooking pasta

Pasta should go into rapidly boiling water, or it will stick together. Add plenty of salt to the boiling water before you add the pasta; there is no need to add oil. Give the pasta a couple of quick stirs as it cooks, to prevent sticking, then leave it to cook, uncovered, at a fairly rapid boil. To test for doneness, taste a piece; it should be al dente, which means tender but still with a little resistance, or bite (literally 'to the tooth'). Drain in a colander.

Crab linguine with chilli and lemon

Serves 4
1 red chilli
2 garlic cloves
4 tbsp olive oil
1 lemon
Small bunch of flat-leaf parsley
1 quantity fresh pasta (see page 168),
 cut into linguine (see page 171) or
 400g dried
200g white crab meat
100g brown crab meat
Salt and freshly ground black pepper

1 Halve, deseed and finely chop the chilli and peel and finely slice the garlic. Put the chilli and garlic into a small saucepan with the olive oil. Heat gently until the garlic sizzles and just starts to turn brown, then remove from the heat and set aside to infuse.

2 Finely grate the zest of half the lemon, then squeeze the juice from the zested half and set aside. Pick the leaves from the parsley and roughly chop.

3 Bring a large saucepan of water to the boil. When it reaches a rolling boil, salt generously and add the linguine. Cook for 1–3 minutes, depending on the thickness of the linguine and how much it has dried out. Test it regularly and drain as soon as it is al dente.

4 While the pasta is draining, add the infused oil with the chilli and garlic to the pan used to cook the pasta. Place over a low heat, add the white and brown crab meat and stir just until heated through. Remove from the heat and add the drained linguine back to the pan (this should all be done quite quickly as the pasta will stick together if left too long in the colander).

5 Stir two-thirds of the chopped parsley through the pasta and add the lemon zest and juice to taste. Season with pepper and very little salt. Serve immediately, sprinkled with the remaining chopped parsley.

Note Use the white and brown meat from a freshly cooked crab (see page 228) or buy good quality pasteurised, prepared crab meat.

Spaghetti with asparagus, broccoli and crab butter

Serves 4
100g fine asparagus spears
100g broccoli
Good handful of tarragon or chervil
 sprigs
350g dried spaghetti
1 tbsp olive oil
Salt and freshly ground black pepper

For the brown crab butter
100g brown crab meat (freshly picked
 or good quality tinned)
50g butter, softened
Pinch of freshly grated nutmeg
Few parsley sprigs

1 To make the brown crab butter, beat together the crab meat and butter and season to taste with pepper and nutmeg. Very finely chop enough parsley leaves to give you 1 tsp, then stir it through the crab butter. Cover and refrigerate for at least 30 minutes.

2 Prepare the asparagus spears by snapping off the woody ends and peeling the lower half of the spears if they are thick. Remove any thick stalk from the broccoli and cut into florets, as small as possible without them falling apart. Pick enough tarragon or chervil leaves to give you about 2 tbsp.

3 Bring a large saucepan of water to the boil. When it reaches a rolling boil, salt generously and add the spaghetti. Cook for 7 minutes, then add the asparagus and broccoli. Cook for a further 3 minutes, then drain; the spaghetti should be al dente at this point.

4 Immediately return the spaghetti and vegetables to the pan and stir through the olive oil to prevent the pasta from sticking together. Fork through the brown crab butter and adjust the seasoning. Stir in half the tarragon or chervil and divide between 4 plates. Sprinkle with the remaining tarragon or chervil and serve.

Macaroni cheese

Serves 2–4
175g dried macaroni
100g cheese (Gruyère, strong Cheddar, Parmesan or a mixture)
20g butter
20g plain flour
Pinch of English mustard powder
Pinch of cayenne pepper
350ml milk
1 tbsp dried white breadcrumbs
Salt and ground white pepper

1 Bring a large saucepan of water to the boil. When it reaches a rolling boil, salt generously, add the macaroni and cook until al dente, 8–10 minutes.

2 Meanwhile, to make the Mornay sauce, grate the cheese and set aside. Melt the butter in a heavy-based saucepan over a gentle heat, then stir in the flour, mustard powder and cayenne pepper, using a wooden spoon. Mix to a smooth paste and continue to cook for 1 minute.

3 Remove from the heat and gradually add the milk, little by little, stirring and incorporating the milk well into the roux as it is added. As more of the milk is added, the sauce will start to loosen and thin. Once a third to half of the milk has been added and incorporated, add the remaining milk in generous additions and return the saucepan to the heat.

4 Increase the heat to medium to high and bring to the boil, stirring constantly. Turn down the heat and simmer, without stirring, for 2 minutes. Remove the sauce from the heat.

5 Drain the macaroni well and heat the grill to its highest setting.

6 Stir all but 2 tbsp of the grated cheese into the sauce, allowing it to melt in the heat of the sauce. Season with salt and white pepper, then add the macaroni and stir well to ensure that the pasta is well coated. Transfer the mixture to an ovenproof dish.

7 Mix together the breadcrumbs and remaining cheese. Sprinkle this over the macaroni cheese. Place the dish under the preheated grill until the topping is golden and bubbling.

Note If you want to make macaroni cheese in advance, once assembled allow it to cool. To serve, bake in an oven preheated to 180°C/gas mark 4 for about 30 minutes, or until piping hot and golden on top.

Variations

Macaroni cheese with bacon and leeks Omit the mustard powder. Cut 100g smoked streaky bacon into thin strips. In a small frying pan, cook until the fat is released, then add 100g sliced, washed leeks and continue to fry until the bacon is starting to brown. Add to the sauce with the macaroni. Stir 1 heaped tsp wholegrain mustard into the finished sauce. Proceed as for the main recipe.

Macaroni cheese with sage and butternut squash Peel and deseed 1 butternut squash, then cut into chunks (you need about 350g prepared weight). Toss in olive oil and season with salt. Roast in an oven preheated to 200°C/gas mark 6 for about 35 minutes until soft and browning. Add 1 tbsp chiffonaded sage (see page 89) for the last 10 minutes of cooking. Add to the sauce with the macaroni and proceed as for the main recipe.

Macaroni cheese with ratatouille Make ½ quantity red ratatouille (see page 56) and spread it across the bottom of an ovenproof dish. Spoon the macaroni cheese over the ratatouille. Proceed as for the main recipe.

Ragout of duck with pappardelle

Serves 4

4 duck legs
1 tbsp olive oil
2 red onions
1 carrot
1 celery stick
1 star anise
1 bay leaf
3 button mushrooms
1 garlic clove
200ml white wine
500ml strong chicken and veal stock
  (see page 96)
75ml double cream
1 quantity fresh pasta (see page 168),
  cut into pappardelle (see page 171)
  or 400g dried
¼ bunch of chervil sprigs
Salt and freshly ground black pepper

1 Heat the oven to 170°C/gas mark 3.

2 Remove the skin from the duck legs. Heat the olive oil in a large frying pan over a medium heat. Add the duck legs and fry until golden brown all over, about 10 minutes. Remove from the heat and transfer the duck to a lidded casserole.

3 Halve, peel and finely chop the onions. Pour off all but 2 tbsp of the fat from the frying pan, add the onions and cook over a low heat until soft. Increase the heat to brown the onions a little, then add them to the duck in the casserole.

4 Peel and halve the carrot, then add it to the casserole along with the celery, star anise, bay leaf and mushrooms. Bash the unpeeled garlic clove with the flat side of a large knife and add it to the casserole. Pour on the wine and stock, then add enough water to completely cover the duck legs.

5 Cover with the lid and cook in the oven for 2–2½ hours, or until the meat is falling from the bones, adding more liquid if necessary to ensure the legs are covered throughout the cooking period.

6 Remove the duck from the casserole, set aside until cool enough to handle, then pull off and shred all the meat. Set the meat aside and discard the skin, sinew and bones, or use the bones for stock.

7 Remove and discard the carrot, celery, garlic, star anise, bay leaf and mushrooms. Skim off all the fat from the cooking liquid, then pour the liquid into a small saucepan. Simmer until reduced to a syrupy concentration, then add the cream and continue to simmer until the sauce is a light coating consistency. Add the duck meat and heat through.

8 Meanwhile, bring a large saucepan of water to the boil. When it reaches a rolling boil, salt generously, add the pappardelle and cook for 1–3 minutes, depending on the thickness of the pasta and how much it has dried out. When the pasta is al dente, drain, then immediately return it to the pan, with some moisture still clinging to it.

9 Adjust the seasoning of the sauce, then toss the sauce through the pasta with some picked sprigs of chervil and serve immediately.

Beef ragù and spinach lasagne

Serves 4–6

¼ bunch of basil

1 quantity ragù sauce, with bacon and red wine (see page 403)

500g spinach

2 tbsp olive oil

Pinch of grated nutmeg

2 x quantity béchamel sauce (see page 104)

½ quantity fresh pasta (see page 168), cut into lasagne sheets (see page 171), or 9 sheets of dried lasagne

1 ball of mozzarella, about 125g

60g Parmesan cheese

2 tbsp dry breadcrumbs

Salt and freshly ground black pepper

1 Tear enough basil leaves to give you about 2 tbsp, then add these to the ragù.

2 Tear out all the coarse stalks and stems from the spinach. Wash in several changes of water until completely free of grit. Heat a large, heavy-based saucepan (that has a lid) until very hot. Add enough of the spinach to loosely fill the pan, then cover with the lid. You may need to do this in batches as the spinach will not wilt properly if there is too much in the pan. Stir every 30 seconds or so until all the spinach has completely wilted. Drain in a sieve, pressing with a spoon to squeeze out as much liquid as possible, then roughly chop.

3 Heat the olive oil in a large frying pan. Add the spinach and sauté quickly with a little nutmeg, salt and pepper. Remove from the heat and set aside to cool.

4 Heat the oven to 190°C/gas mark 5. Have the béchamel sauce ready.

5 Bring a large saucepan of water to the boil. Have a bowl of cold water ready, and a tray lined with a clean tea towel. Once the water reaches a rolling boil, salt generously, add the pasta sheets and cook for 2 minutes, then remove with a slotted spoon and plunge into the cold water to stop them cooking, before transferring to the lined tray to cool.

6 Cut the mozzarella into cubes and stir into the cooled spinach.

7 Spread 2–3 tbsp of the ragù sauce over the bottom of an ovenproof dish, about 27 x 18cm and 5cm deep. Add a layer of lasagne sheets, then one-third of the remaining ragù, one-quarter of the béchamel sauce, a layer of lasagne, half the remaining ragù and another quarter of the béchamel. Spread all the spinach out to create the next layer, then add a layer of lasagne, the remaining ragù, half the remaining béchamel, a layer of lasagne and finally the remaining béchamel.

8 Grate the Parmesan, mix with the breadcrumbs and sprinkle over the top of the lasagne. Bake in the oven for 25–30 minutes, or until golden brown and bubbling.

Note This dish can be assembled up to a day ahead and refrigerated. Increase the baking time to 40–45 minutes if it is fridge-cold when it goes into the oven.

Variations

Tomato and spinach lasagne Replace the ragù sauce with 1 quantity salsa pizzaiola (see page 128). Increase the spinach quantity to 1.25kg and use 3 tbsp olive oil; cook as above. Stir in 100g crumbled ricotta and 75g toasted pine nuts along with the mozzarella. Layer and cook as for the main recipe, sprinkling with the Parmesan crumbs.

Caramelised onion and aubergine lasagne Caramelise 4 large sliced onions, 6 sliced shallots and 2 sliced red onions in 4 tbsp olive oil (see page 14). Add 100ml well-flavoured chicken and veal stock (see page 96) or vegetable stock (see page 101) and simmer for 2 minutes. Cut 2 aubergines lengthways into 7mm thick slices and fry over a medium heat in 2–3 tbsp of olive oil per batch, until golden and no longer spongy. Use 600ml Mornay sauce made with Gruyère (see page 104) in place of the béchamel. Layer up the onions, aubergines, pasta and Mornay sauce, sprinkle with the Parmesan crumbs and cook as for the main recipe.

A note on dried lasagne sheets...

Dried lasagne usually needs to be cooked in boiling salted water and drained before layering, unless it is the sort that can be used without pre-cooking. In this instance, make sure the sauces are a little thinner as the dry sheets will absorb more liquid.

Assembling ravioli

This technique is the same whether you are using a raw or a cooked filling, but if using a filling that requires cooking, avoid being too generous with the filling or the pasta will be overcooked by the time the filling is cooked. Allow the shaped ravioli to dry a little on a lightly floured/semolina sprinkled tray before cooking.

1 Lay a rolled piece of pasta on the work surface. Spoon the filling at intervals along the length, leaving enough pasta around the filling to seal the top layer of pasta. Brush a little water around each spoonful of filling, then carefully lay a second rolled piece of pasta on top.

2 Starting from the middle of the pasta, use the side of your forefingers to seal and shape the ravioli, before moving on to the next little mound of filling. Try to ensure that no air bubbles are left around the filling, within each ravioli.

3 Once all the ravioli are sealed, cut them with a cutter for a clean finish. Using your fingertips, press out the pasta border around the filling to thin it out a little so the pasta cooks evenly; it may be necessary to re-cut the ravioli after this.

Ravioli of Fontina and pumpkin

Serves 6 as a starter
1kg pumpkin (whole or a piece)
4 tbsp olive oil, plus extra to serve
1 onion
1 garlic clove
Pinch of crushed dried chillies
Good handful of basil sprigs
200g Fontina or Taleggio cheese
75g Parmesan cheese, plus extra to serve
Pinch of freshly grated nutmeg
½ quantity fresh pasta (see page 168)
Salt and freshly ground black pepper
30g pumpkin seeds, to serve

1 Heat the oven to 200°C/gas mark 6. Peel the pumpkin and scoop out and discard the seeds. Cut into large chunks and toss in 2 tbsp of the olive oil. Spread out in a roasting tin and bake for 30–40 minutes until soft and starting to brown.

2 Meanwhile, halve, peel and finely chop the onion and peel and crush the garlic. Heat the remaining 2 tbsp olive oil in a medium saucepan and add the onion. Sweat over a low heat until completely soft, then add the garlic and crushed chillies. Increase the heat and cook, stirring, for 1 minute.

3 Add the pumpkin to the pan and cook until sizzling. Allow any juices to evaporate, then remove the pan from the heat and set aside to cool.

4 Roughly chop enough basil leaves to give you 2 tbsp. Cut the Fontina into small cubes, grate the Parmesan and add both cheeses to the cooled pumpkin mixture, with the chopped basil. Beat the ingredients together with a wooden spoon, breaking down the pumpkin. Season well with salt, pepper and nutmeg.

5 Roll out the pasta and assemble the ravioli with the pumpkin mixture (as shown above). Transfer to a lightly floured tray to dry out for 15 minutes.

6 Lightly toast the pumpkin seeds in a hot, dry pan, then tip onto a plate; set aside. Bring a large saucepan of water to a rolling boil. Salt generously, then add the ravioli and cook for 2–3 minutes, or until al dente. Test by cutting one in half.

7 Drain well, toss in a little olive oil and divide between 6 plates. Serve sprinkled with the toasted pumpkin seeds and extra Parmesan, grated over the top.

Chicken and wild mushroom ravioli with morels

Serves 6 as a starter
50g wild mushrooms
20g butter
Handful of tarragon sprigs
½ quantity fresh pasta (see page 168)
Salt and freshly ground black pepper

For the filling
1 skinless chicken breast fillet,
    about 200g
1 egg white
150ml double cream

For the sauce
40g dried morel mushrooms
300ml boiling water
150ml Madeira
300ml chicken and veal stock
    (see page 96)
100–150ml double cream

1 Put the dried morels for the sauce in a bowl, cover with the boiling water and leave to soak for at least 1 hour.

2 For the filling, place a medium bowl in the fridge to chill. Roughly chop the chicken breast and place in a small food processor bowl. Pulse until smooth, then add the egg white, ½ tsp salt and ¼ tsp pepper and pulse again until combined.

3 Pass the chicken through a sieve, pressing it through with a plastic spatula. The finer the mesh the longer this will take, but the smoother the filling will eventually be. Transfer the mixture to the chilled bowl and refrigerate for 15 minutes, or until cool to the touch.

4 Remove the chicken mixture from the fridge and gradually beat in the cream, in several additions, using a spatula and taking care not to overwork or warm the mixture or it will split. Meanwhile, heat a small saucepan of water.

5 Once all the cream is incorporated into the chicken, poach a teaspoonful of the mixture in the simmering water until just firm, so that you can taste it and adjust the seasoning of the rest of the mixture (it is not advisable to taste raw chicken). Add more seasoning to the mixture if necessary, then cover and chill until needed.

6 Brush the wild mushrooms to clean them, then chop. Melt the butter in a frying pan over a medium heat. Add the mushrooms (not the morels) and sauté until softened, then spread them out on a plate to allow them to cool. Chop enough tarragon leaves to give you 1 tbsp and stir this into the cold chicken mixture, along with the cooled sautéed mushrooms, then return the mixture to the fridge.

7 Roll out the pasta and assemble the ravioli with the chicken filling (see page 177). Transfer to a floured tray and set aside to dry for 15 minutes.

8 To make the sauce, drain the morels, reserving any soaking liquid but discarding any grit or sediment at the bottom of the bowl.

9 Put the morels with the reserved soaking liquid and Madeira in a small saucepan and reduce over a high heat until nearly all of the liquid has evaporated. Add the stock and cream and reduce again over a low heat until the sauce has thickened slightly and the flavour has concentrated sufficiently. Season to taste, remove from the heat and set aside.

10 Bring a large saucepan of water to the boil and, when it reaches a rolling boil, salt generously and add the ravioli. Cook for 3–5 minutes, or until al dente and the filling feels just firm when you gently squeeze a ravioli. Test by cutting one in half.

11 Reheat the sauce gently and divide the ravioli between 6 plates. Pour the sauce over the ravioli and garnish with extra tarragon leaves.

Assembling tortelloni

These classic ring-shaped filled pasta are easy to make. Allow the shaped tortelloni to dry a little on a lightly floured/semolina sprinkled tray before cooking.

1 Cut 5–7cm diameter circles from the sheets of pasta. Spoon a little filling into the centre of each circle.

2 Lightly brush the edge of the pasta with water and fold the circle of pasta into a half-moon shape, enclosing the filling.

3 Fold the 'open' edges away from you, bring them together and seal the ends between your fingers.

Note You can make tortelloni squares rather than circles, folding each square in half diagonally to create a triangle.

Tortelloni of mozzarella and prosciutto with sage butter

Serves 4

150g mozzarella cheese
80g prosciutto
30g Parmesan cheese, plus extra to serve
50g ricotta cheese
1 egg
¼ bunch of flat-leaf parsley
½ quantity fresh pasta (see page 168)
50g butter
About 20 sage leaves (as small as possible)
Salt and freshly ground black pepper

1 Roughly chop the mozzarella and prosciutto and grate the Parmesan. Put these ingredients into a food processor with the ricotta, egg and a little salt and pepper. Process until smooth, then transfer to a bowl and adjust the seasoning. Finely chop enough parsley leaves to give you ½ tbsp and stir this into the filling mixture.

2 Roll out the pasta and assemble the tortelloni with the prosciutto and cheese filling (as shown above). Transfer to a lightly floured tray to dry out for 15 minutes.

3 Bring a large saucepan of water to a rolling boil, salt generously, then add the tortelloni and cook for 3–5 minutes, or until al dente.

4 Meanwhile, melt the butter in a small frying pan and fry the sage leaves over a medium heat until they sizzle and start to crisp, then season with salt and pepper.

5 To check that the tortelloni are cooked, cut one in half. Drain the pasta, toss in the sage butter and serve immediately with extra Parmesan shaved over the top.

Variations

Tortelloni of mozzarella and prosciutto with tomato sauce Use fresh tomato sauce (see page 128) in place of the sage butter.

Tortelloni of ricotta and lemon with sage butter Mix 200g ricotta, 1 beaten egg, 50g grated Parmesan and 1–2 tsp finely grated lemon zest, and season very well with salt, pepper and grated nutmeg. Beat well and use to fill the tortelloni. Serve with the sage butter as for the main recipe.

Noodles

A staple food in the Far East, noodles are made from various grains, including wheat, buckwheat and rice. They are most often found in dried form, but some can be bought fresh from Asian supermarkets, or already cooked and vacuum packed.

Wheat-based noodles include pasta, Chinese egg noodles (yellow in colour due to the egg and cooked until slightly chewy in texture) and Japanese udon, a white noodle that contains no egg and is characterised by its thick appearance and soft, chewy texture.

The most common buckwheat noodles are soba noodles. These have a wholesome, nutty flavour, and are delicious eaten cold in salads, or hot in soups and stir-fries. Those made purely from buckwheat are a good option for anyone following a wheat- or gluten-free diet.

Wheat and buckwheat noodles are cooked in water or a broth, then drained and a little oil applied to prevent them from sticking together. Fresh noodles will take about 2–3 minutes to cook, depending on thickness. Dried noodles need longer, often up to 10 minutes.

Rice noodles are generally flat and come either very thin or thick. They are much more delicate than wheat-based noodles, as they lack gluten. Thick noodles for a salad can be boiled quickly for 2–3 minutes, but no longer or they will turn to mush; more often than not you just need to cover them with warm to hot water and leave them to soak and soften, for up to 30 minutes. Add a little oil after draining, to prevent them from sticking together. Rice vermicelli noodles are particularly delicate and only require a brief soaking in warm water to soften, or they can be added dry at the last minute to a dish such as a Vietnamese pho.

While noodles dressed simply with a flavoured oil or soy sauce work well as an accompaniment, the addition of a few fresh ingredients can transform them into interesting and complex dishes to serve alone or alongside others. Substitute seasonally available vegetables to make changes to the suggestions given in these recipes and add meat, poultry or fish to make them into more substantial dishes.

Udon noodles with shiitake mushrooms and spring onions

Serves 4
125g dried udon noodles
1½ tbsp sesame oil
1½ tbsp groundnut oil
200g shiitake mushrooms
6 spring onions
Few coriander sprigs
2½ tbsp nam pla (fish sauce)
2½ tbsp soy sauce
Salt

1 Bring a large saucepan of water to the boil, add salt and the noodles and cook until tender, according to the packet instructions. Drain and refresh under cold running water, then stir through a few drops of both oils to prevent them from sticking together; set aside.

2 Finely slice the mushrooms. Finely slice the spring onions on the diagonal, including most of the green part. Pick a handful of coriander leaves.

3 Heat the oils over a high heat in a wok or frying pan. Add the mushrooms and cook until beginning to soften. Add the spring onions, nam pla, soy sauce and noodles. Heat, stirring, until the noodles are well glazed with the sauce. Serve sprinkled with the coriander leaves.

Singapore noodles

Serves 4

150g vermicelli rice noodles
3 tbsp vegetable oil
3 garlic cloves
2cm piece of fresh root ginger
1 small onion
1 red pepper
2 spring onions
1 red chilli
¼ bunch of coriander
2 eggs
1 tsp curry powder
1–2 tbsp soy sauce
½–1 tbsp oyster sauce
1–2 tbsp mirin (rice wine)
100g bean sprouts

1 Soak the noodles according to the packet instructions. Drain and toss with 2 tsp of the oil to prevent them from sticking together; set aside.

2 Peel and finely slice the garlic and peel and grate the ginger. Halve, peel and cut the onion into thin wedges. Halve the red pepper, remove the core, then cut into thin slices. Thinly slice the spring onions on the diagonal, including most of the green part. Halve, deseed and finely dice or slice the chilli, and pick off the coriander leaves. Beat the eggs well in a bowl to break them up and set aside.

3 Heat a wok over a medium heat, add 2 tbsp oil and fry the garlic and ginger until lightly golden. Add the onion and red pepper and cook for 1–2 minutes until just beginning to soften, then add the curry powder and cook for 1 minute.

4 Add the noodles to the wok and reheat briefly, then add the soy sauce, oyster sauce and mirin, to taste.

5 Draw the noodles to the side. Add the remaining 1 tsp oil to the empty area of the wok and then pour in the beaten eggs. Swirl the pan gently to allow the egg to start setting in a thin layer, then stir the egg into the noodles. Stir in the bean sprouts, chilli and coriander and serve immediately.

Variations

Rice noodles with prawns Before frying the garlic and ginger in step 3, stir-fry 12 prepared prawns (see page 204) until cooked, then remove and set aside. Proceed as above; you may need to add another 1 tbsp oil. Return the prawns to the wok with the noodles in step 4.

Rice noodles with chicken Slice 1–2 skinless chicken breast fillets into thin strips on the diagonal. Before frying the garlic and ginger in step 3, stir-fry the chicken until cooked, then remove and set aside. Proceed as for the main recipe; you may need to add another 1 tbsp oil. Return the chicken to the wok with the noodles in step 4.

Rice noodles with char siu pork Add 250–300g thinly sliced char siu pork (see page 463) with the noodles to reheat in step 4.

Yellow bean and chilli noodles with baby pak choi

Serves 4

2 baby pak choi (no more than 12cm long)
1 garlic clove
1 red chilli
200g medium egg noodles
1 tbsp sesame oil
2 tbsp yellow bean paste
2 tbsp light soy sauce
2 tbsp Shaoxing rice wine
100ml water
1 tbsp groundnut oil
Salt

1 Break the leaves from the pak choi, keeping all the smallest leaves whole but cutting any larger leaves in half. Peel and very finely slice the garlic. Halve, deseed and finely slice the chilli. Set everything aside.

2 Bring a large saucepan of water to the boil, add salt and the noodles and cook, according to the packet instructions, for 2–3 minutes, or until just tender. Drain, then plunge the noodles into cold water and drain again, to cool. Toss the noodles in a little of the sesame oil to stop them sticking together, then set aside.

3 Mix together the yellow bean paste, soy sauce and rice wine. Stir in the water.

4 Heat the remaining sesame oil and the groundnut oil in a wok over a high heat. Add the garlic and chilli and stir-fry until they sizzle. Add the pak choi and stir-fry until it starts to soften, taking care not to burn the garlic.

5 Add the sauce mixture and bring to the boil over the highest heat. Stir in the noodles and continue to cook, stirring, until piping hot. Serve immediately.

Chilli and ginger chicken noodles

Serves 4

300g tenderstem broccoli
6 spring onions
1 red chilli
2cm piece of fresh root ginger
2 garlic cloves
3 boneless, skinless chicken breasts
3 tbsp chilli bean sauce
1½ tbsp Shaoxing rice wine
4 tbsp chicken and veal stock
  (see page 96) or water
1½ tbsp light soy sauce
1½ tsp clear honey
150g dried egg noodles
1 tbsp sesame oil, plus extra to toss
  the noodles
2 tbsp sunflower oil
150g bean sprouts
Salt

1 Cut the broccoli in half or into quarters, depending on the thickness of the stems. Trim off the root end of the spring onions, cut each into 4-finger width pieces, then into julienne. Halve, deseed and finely dice the chilli. Peel and grate the ginger and peel and crush the garlic. Slice the chicken breasts diagonally into slices 5mm thick.

2 In a small bowl, mix together the chilli bean sauce, rice wine, stock, soy sauce and honey and set aside.

3 Bring a large saucepan of water to the boil, add salt and the noodles and cook, according to the packet instructions, for 2–3 minutes, or until just tender. When cooked, drain and toss in a little sesame oil, while still warm.

4 While the noodles are cooking, heat 1 tbsp sunflower oil with the sesame oil in a wok until very hot; it will seem to shimmer slightly. Add the chicken and stir-fry for 1 minute, then take the wok off the heat, remove the chicken with a slotted spoon and set aside while you continue stir-frying.

5 Heat the wok again and add the remaining sunflower oil, the ginger, garlic, chilli and broccoli, and half of the spring onions. Stir-fry for 2 minutes, then add the chicken and the chilli bean mixture. Cook for a further 2 minutes, or until the chicken is cooked.

6 Add the bean sprouts and cook, stirring, for a further 30 seconds.

7 Divide the noodles between 4 plates, place the chicken and vegetables on top of the noodles and scatter with the remaining spring onions.

Soba noodle salad with edamame beans

Serves 4

100g edamame (soy) beans in pods
100g sugar snap peas
4 spring onions
Large handful of coriander sprigs
1 red chilli
1 tbsp sesame seeds
250g soba noodles
2 tbsp toasted sesame oil
2 tbsp light soy sauce
2 tbsp mirin (rice wine)
Salt
Maldon sea salt

1 Pod the edamame beans and de-string the sugar snap peas. Finely slice the spring onions and roughly chop enough coriander leaves to give you 2 tbsp. Halve, deseed and finely chop the chilli.

2 Lightly toast the sesame seeds in a dry frying pan over a medium heat, then tip onto a plate to cool.

3 Bring a large saucepan of water to a rolling boil, add salt and the noodles and cook until tender, according to the packet instructions, usually 5–7 minutes. Skim off any scum that rises to the surface. If the water threatens to bubble over, add a splash of cold water and it will subside.

4 Simmer the edamame beans in another saucepan of boiling salted water for 5 minutes, adding the sugar snaps 2 minutes before the end of the cooking time.

5 Drain the noodles, edamame beans and sugar snaps and rinse with cold water to stop them cooking. Drain well again and transfer to a bowl.

6 Stir through the sesame oil, soy sauce and mirin. Mix in the spring onions, chilli and coriander and season with sea salt. Sprinkle over the toasted sesame seeds to serve.

Note Edamame are young soy beans in pods. Because they are young, they are soft and pliable and the pods can be lightly boiled and eaten whole, or the beans can be podded as in the recipe above. They are available both fresh and frozen.

Rice

Rice is categorised into two types, long grain and short grain. It is highly nutritious and an excellent food to include in a healthy diet.

Long-grain rice includes basmati, which has an aromatic fragrance and is considered to be the prince of rices. The grains are slender and longer than other long-grain rices and retain a delicate, separate fluffiness when cooked. Long-grain Thai rices also have a fragrant aroma and are slightly sticky and glutinous. Long-grain rice is a good accompaniment to stews, curries, pilafs and salads.

Short-grain rice, as the name implies, has short and more rounded grains that absorb much more liquid than long-grain; risotto rice, for instance, can absorb up to five times its volume. Risotto (Arborio, Carnaroli and Vialone Nano) and paella (Calasparra) rices impart a creamy texture while retaining a little bite. Pudding rices lend a similar creaminess, but can break down completely, contributing little in the way of texture. Sticky rices from Asia are also included in this category.

Brown rice is so called because it still has the brown bran layer intact, making it more nutritious than white and giving it a wonderful nutty flavour and chewy texture. Other rices include wild rice (botanically a grass), red Camargue and glutinous black rice, all of which share varying degrees of the nuttiness of brown rice. These rices generally take much longer to cook but provide wonderful colour and texture in dishes.

'Easy cook' rice is widely available. This has been parboiled to ensure the grains remain separate on cooking, but it doesn't necessarily cook more quickly and the flavour and texture are generally inferior.

Particular care must be taken when reheating rice as it can be a source of food poisoning. It must be thoroughly heated throughout, but it is preferable to avoid the need for reheating rice.

Rinsing and soaking

Long-grain rice should be rinsed in cold water to remove any dust or particles, as well as excess starch. Place it in a bowl and cover with water. Give it a few swirls with your hand. The rice will sink to the bottom of the bowl, and you can easily then pour away the water, which will have become a milky colour. Repeat this process 2 or 3 times until the water becomes clearer.

Soaking rice can help to reduce the cooking time. Rinse the rice as above and after the third rinse leave the rice soaking in the water for 10–15 minutes, before draining well and cooking.

Short-grain rice should only be rinsed if really necessary to clean it. The excess starch helps to create the desired creamy texture in risottos etc.

Cooking long-grain rice

There are two main methods of cooking long-grain rice: fast boiling and the absorption method. Use either for white rice; brown, red and wild rices are best cooked using the boiling method. A rice cooker is very efficient, but not essential.

Boiling method

Serves 4
200–250g long-grain white rice
Salt

1 Fill a large saucepan with water, add a good pinch of salt and bring to the boil.

2 Rinse the rice in cold water (see left), then add to the boiling water. Stir and allow the water to return to the boil, then reduce the heat slightly and simmer for 10–12 minutes.

3 The cooked rice should be neither hard nor mushy, but firm to the bite (al dente). If you bite a grain in two, the thread of white through the centre should have almost disappeared.

4 Drain the rice well in a colander or sieve, return to the saucepan and leave to steam for 3–5 minutes before serving.

Absorption method

Serves 4
200–250g long-grain white rice
Salt

1 Tip the rice into a measuring jug and make a note of its volume. Rinse well in cold water (see left), then put into a medium-sized saucepan with a pinch of salt. Add 1½ times the volume of cold water to rice to the pan.

2 Cover and bring to a gentle boil over a medium heat. Once steam escapes from beneath the lid, reduce the heat to low and cook gently for 10 minutes, then take off the heat. Allow the rice to sit for at least 10 minutes without lifting the lid.

3 After 10 minutes, remove the lid and the rice should be perfectly cooked and all the water absorbed.

Cooking times for other rices
Brown rice can take up to 30 minutes to become tender, as does red rice. Wild rice generally takes longer, about 40–50 minutes.

Flavouring rice
You can add spices such as cinnamon sticks, mustard seeds and cardamom pods to the rice when using the absorption method, removing whole spices once the rice is cooked.

Parmesan risotto

Serves 4

1 onion
100g unsalted butter
100g Parmesan cheese, plus extra
  to serve (optional)
300g risotto rice (Arborio, Carnaroli
  or Vialone Nano)
150ml dry white wine
1.5–2 litres chicken and veal stock
  (see page 96) or vegetable stock
  (see page 101)
Salt and freshly ground black pepper

1 Halve, peel and finely dice the onion. Melt half the butter in a large, shallow saucepan, add the onion and sweat over a low heat until completely soft but not coloured, at least 10 minutes. Meanwhile, grate the Parmesan and set aside.

2 Add the rice to the pan and fry gently, stirring until it has had a chance to heat up and every grain is coated in the butter. Add the wine and bring to the boil, then reduce the heat and cook, stirring, until the rice has absorbed all the wine.

3 Meanwhile, put the stock in a separate saucepan and bring to a gentle simmer, then reduce the heat to as low as possible.

4 Once the wine is absorbed, start adding the stock a small ladleful at a time, stirring constantly and gently, making sure each ladleful is absorbed before adding the next. Continue until the rice is just cooked, but still al dente, about 25 minutes. If the stock runs out before the rice is cooked, use a little boiling water.

5 Take the pan off the heat and stir in the remaining butter and the Parmesan. Season to taste with pepper, and salt if required. Allow the risotto to stand, covered, for 5 minutes before serving, with extra grated Parmesan, if you like.

Note A traditional Italian risotto has a loose, almost sloppy texture and should give a little when plated. When left to stand before serving, your risotto will absorb more liquid, so make sure it is fluid otherwise it will become thick and heavy.

Variations

Saffron risotto (risotto Milanese) Add about 15 saffron strands to the hot stock and allow to infuse for 10 minutes before starting the risotto. (Illustrated)

Wild mushroom risotto Add 15–20g dried wild mushrooms to the stock, bring to a simmer, then remove from the heat and leave to infuse for 10–15 minutes. Strain the stock and return to the pan ready for making the risotto. Sauté the soaked mushrooms with 400g mixed wild mushrooms in 50g butter over a medium to high heat for 3–4 minutes, or until lightly browned and the excess water has been driven off. Stir into the risotto with the butter and Parmesan.

Crab risotto Use shellfish or fish stock (see page 100) rather than chicken and veal stock. Omit the Parmesan. Stir in 300g prepared white crab meat once the rice is cooked, then remove from the heat, stir in the unsalted butter, season with salt and pepper and allow to stand as for the main recipe. Before serving, stir in 1–2 tbsp finely chopped chives and a little finely grated lemon zest, and juice, to taste.

Pea risotto Omit the Parmesan. Make a pea purée by sweating 1 finely chopped shallot in 15g butter, then add 200ml chicken and veal stock and 400g defrosted frozen peas. Add a little salt and pepper and simmer gently for 4–5 minutes until the peas are tender. Drain the peas and blend until completely smooth, adding a little of the cooking liquor if it is too thick. Pass through a sieve. The pea purée should be the consistency of Greek yoghurt. Stir this into the risotto, to taste, with 2 tbsp mascarpone and the finely grated zest of ½ lemon. You can also stir in 50g cooked petit pois before serving.

Roast butternut squash risotto Peel and deseed 1 large butternut squash. Grate one-third coarsely and set aside. Cut the rest into 2cm chunks and toss these in enough olive oil to coat. Season well, spread out on a baking sheet and bake in an oven preheated to 200°C/gas mark 6 for 20–30 minutes, turning once, until golden and soft. Proceed as for the main recipe, cooking the grated squash in the butter with the onion. Stir 30g unsalted butter into the finished risotto, followed by the roasted squash. Serve with extra Parmesan and fried sage leaves.

Aubergine pilaf

Serves 4

1 large aubergine
2 tbsp olive oil, plus extra to drizzle
1 onion
2 plum tomatoes
3 tbsp pine nuts
200g long-grain rice
½ tsp ground cinnamon
½ tsp ground allspice
1 tsp soft brown sugar
2 tbsp currants
300ml water
Bunch of flat-leaf parsley
Salt and freshly ground black pepper

1 Heat the oven to 200°C/gas mark 6. Cut the aubergine into 2–3cm cubes and place them in a bowl. Drizzle over enough olive oil to coat the cubes, then sprinkle over a little salt and toss together, using your hands. Spread the aubergine cubes out over a large baking sheet and roast for 20–25 minutes, stirring occasionally, until soft and golden brown at the edges.

2 Halve, peel and dice the onion. Heat the 2 tbsp olive oil in a deep frying pan (that has a lid) and sweat the onion over a low heat until soft. Meanwhile, blanch the tomatoes in boiling water for 10 seconds, then refresh in cold water, dry, peel and dice; set aside.

3 When the onion is soft, increase the heat until it starts to brown, then add the pine nuts and continue to cook until the pine nuts also start to brown. Now add the rice, cinnamon and allspice and stir so that all the grains are coated in the oil. Add the sugar and cook gently for 2 minutes.

4 Add the currants and water to the pan. Season well with salt and pepper and stir briefly to make sure nothing is sticking to the bottom of the pan. Cover with a lid and simmer very gently for 8–10 minutes, or until the rice is just tender. Roughly chop enough parsley leaves to give you about 2–3 tbsp.

5 When the rice is tender, remove the pan from the heat and stir in the aubergine, tomatoes and chopped parsley. Cover the pan again and leave to steam for 10 minutes. Spread the pilaf out on a plate to cool. Serve at room temperature, as an accompaniment to lamb or chicken.

Camargue red and wild rice salad with dried cherries and broad beans

Serves 4–6

200g Camargue red rice
200g wild rice
1 onion
60g shelled pistachio nuts
100g broad beans (freshly podded
    or frozen)
4 spring onions
1 garlic clove
1 orange
1 lemon
125ml olive oil
100g dried sour cherries
Good handful of baby watercress
    or rocket
Salt and freshly ground black pepper

1 Fill 2 medium saucepans with water, add salt and bring to the boil over a medium heat. Simmer the red rice in one pan for about 20 minutes and the wild rice in the second pan for slightly longer, about 25 minutes. Both should be tender but still have some bite. Drain both rices and spread out on trays to cool quickly.

2 Halve, peel and finely slice the onion. Toast the pistachio nuts in a dry frying pan over a medium heat until pale golden, then tip out to cool and coarsely chop. Pod the broad beans, blanch them for 20 seconds, then drain and skin (see page 33). Finely slice the spring onions, including the green part.

3 Peel and crush the garlic, finely grate the zest and squeeze the juice of half the orange. Juice half the lemon, keeping the citrus juices separate.

4 Heat 50ml of the olive oil in a frying pan, add the onion and sauté for 10–12 minutes until an even golden brown, then add the garlic and cook for 1 minute. Transfer to a large bowl and leave to cool completely.

5 Add both rices, the broad beans, pistachios, spring onions and dried cherries.

6 In a small bowl, combine the remaining olive oil, orange zest and juice and 1 tbsp lemon juice. Pour over the salad and toss well to distribute the dressing, then taste and adjust the seasoning as necessary. Stir through the watercress or rocket.

Variations

Petit pois, cooked briefly until just tender, can be used in place of the broad beans. Dried cranberries or large raisins can be substituted for the dried cherries and toasted pecans or walnuts used in place of the pistachios.

Pulses

Dried beans, lentils and dried split peas are excellent storecupboard ingredients. They can be used in place of potatoes or rice, or as additions to stews and salads, and often as a dish in their own right. With a large variety of textures, colours and flavours to choose from, they offer endless potential for creativity.

Dried beans need to be soaked for up to 24 hours to allow them to soften sufficiently. Lentils can require soaking for up to 24 hours, but some, such as Puy lentils, benefit from only 20–30 minutes soaking and can even be cooked with no soaking at all.

Particular care must be taken when cooking certain dried soaked beans, notably kidney beans, which have a toxin in their skins that needs to be removed by correct soaking and cooking. After soaking, these beans must be brought to the boil, the water discarded and replaced with fresh water, then boiled steadily for 10 minutes before lowering the temperature to a simmer.

Tinned cooked beans can be softer than soaked and cooked beans and tend to break up easily, making them ideal for a purée. They should be rinsed under cold water before use.

Beans with tomato and chorizo

Serves 4

200g dried haricot, cannellini or
   flageolet beans
1½ onions
1 bay leaf
Small handful of oregano sprigs
75g cooking chorizo
2 tbsp sherry vinegar
½ x 200g tin chopped tomatoes
200–300ml chicken and veal stock
   (see page 96)
½ tsp caster sugar
1–2 tbsp olive oil
Salt and freshly ground black pepper

You will need to start this the night before, to soak the beans.

1 Place the dried beans in a large bowl, cover with plenty of cold water and leave to soak overnight.

2 The next day, drain the beans and place in a large saucepan with the ½ onion, bay leaf and 1 oregano sprig. Cover with fresh cold water and bring to the boil, then lower the heat. Simmer gently, uncovered, for 1–1½ hours, or until tender but not breaking up. Remove from the heat and leave the beans to cool in the cooking liquid, then drain and set aside.

3 Halve, peel and finely dice the whole onion and finely chop enough oregano leaves to give you ½ tbsp. Remove the skin from the chorizo and cut the sausage into small chunks, about 1cm but not necessarily uniform in shape or size.

4 Once the beans are cooked, heat a large saucepan over a low to medium heat, add the chorizo and cook gently until it releases its oils. Remove the chorizo from the oil with a slotted spoon and set aside.

5 Add the diced onion to the chorizo oil and cook gently until soft and translucent. You may need to add more oil, depending on how much oil the chorizo releases.

6 Deglaze the pan with the sherry vinegar and reduce to a teaspoonful. Add the tomatoes, stock and sugar to the saucepan and simmer for 5–10 minutes until the flavour has developed and the juices have reduced a little. Return the chorizo to the pan along with the beans and oregano. Cook gently for a few minutes, then taste and adjust the seasoning. Drizzle with the olive oil and serve.

Note A tin of cooked beans can be used instead of the dried beans. Drain, rinse and add them directly to the pan at stage 6, along with the chorizo.

Braised beans

Serves 4

250g dried haricot, cannellini
  or flageolet beans
2 shallots
2 garlic cloves
½ anchovy fillet in oil
1 thyme sprig
3 oregano sprigs
2 tomatoes
5 tbsp olive oil, plus extra to drizzle
150ml white wine
300ml chicken and veal stock
  (see page 96)
1 bay leaf
Salt and freshly ground black pepper

You will need to start this the night before, to allow time for the beans to soak.

1 Place the dried beans in a large bowl, cover with plenty of cold water and leave to soak overnight.

2 The next day, drain the beans, put into a saucepan and cover with fresh cold water. Bring to the boil, lower the heat and cook, uncovered, at a gentle simmer for 30 minutes. Remove from the heat and leave the beans to cool in the cooking liquid. Drain and set aside.

3 Meanwhile, halve, peel and finely dice the shallots and peel and crush the garlic. Drain and chop the anchovy. Finely chop enough thyme leaves to give you ½ tsp and enough oregano to give you 1 tsp.

4 Blanch the tomatoes in boiling water for 10 seconds, then refresh in cold water, dry and peel. Quarter, deseed and dice them, then set aside.

5 After draining the beans, return the pan to a low heat and add 3 tbsp of the olive oil. Add the shallots and sweat until soft. Add the garlic and anchovy and cook for 1 minute, allowing the anchovy to soften and break up into the shallots.

6 Add the drained beans and the remaining 2 tbsp olive oil with the wine, stock, bay leaf, thyme and oregano.

7 Bring to the boil, then lower the heat and simmer gently for up to 1 hour until the beans are tender; the liquid should be reduced to a well-flavoured sauce. Check every 15–20 minutes, as you may need to add some water if they are drying out.

8 Remove the bay leaf and, if there is too much liquid, drain the beans in a sieve over a bowl, then taste the sauce. If it seems weak, return the sauce to the pan and reduce until it has developed in flavour, then add back the beans. If the sauce already has a good flavour, use only enough to moisten the beans.

9 Taste and season the beans, add the diced tomatoes and drizzle over a little olive oil. Delicious served with lamb or chicken.

Butter bean mash

Serves 4–6 as an accompaniment

2–3 garlic cloves
1 lemon
Small bunch of flat-leaf parsley
200–250ml olive oil
2 x 400g tins butter beans
Salt and freshly ground black pepper

This can be spooned onto bruschetta or served alongside lamb or fish.

1 Peel and crush the garlic, finely grate the zest of the lemon and coarsely chop the parsley.

2 Warm 150ml of the olive oil in a medium saucepan and add the garlic.

3 Drain the beans and rinse well under cold running water.

4 Add the beans to the pan and warm through. As they are warming, crush them with the back of a spoon or a fork, until smooth or left a little coarse, whichever you prefer.

5 Add enough of the remaining olive oil to thin the bean mash; a little warm water can also be added. Add lemon zest to taste, season with salt and pepper and stir in the parsley.

Minestrone

Serves 4

85g dried haricot beans (or use tinned, see note)

2 rashers of smoked streaky bacon (or 50g piece of pancetta)

1 onion

1 carrot

1 potato

1 celery stick

100g piece of white cabbage

3 tomatoes

50g fine green beans

1 garlic clove

3 tbsp olive oil

1.2 litres vegetable stock (see page 101) or chicken and veal stock (see page 96)

100ml white wine

1 bay leaf

1 tbsp tomato purée

Small bunch of flat-leaf parsley

50g dried spaghetti

Salt and freshly ground black pepper

Parmesan cheese, to serve

If using dried beans, you will need to allow plenty of time to soak them.

1 Soak the dried beans in cold water for at least 3 hours, but ideally overnight.

2 Derind and dice the bacon. Halve, peel and finely slice the onion. Peel and dice the carrot and potato. De-string and dice the celery. Remove and discard the tough core from the cabbage, then shred. Blanch the tomatoes in boiling water for 10 seconds, refresh in cold water and drain, then peel, quarter, deseed and chop. Top and tail the green beans and cut into 1cm lengths. Peel and crush the garlic.

3 Heat the olive oil in a large saucepan over a low heat. Add the bacon, let the fat render a little, then add the onion, carrot and celery and cook for 2 minutes. Add the potato and cook for a further 2 minutes. Add the garlic and cook for 1 minute.

4 Drain the soaked beans and add to the saucepan with the stock, wine, bay leaf, tomato purée and a few parsley stalks. Bring to the boil, then reduce the heat and simmer for about 1 hour. Discard the bay leaf and parsley stalks.

5 Break the spaghetti into short lengths and add to the saucepan. Cook for a further 5 minutes, then add the cabbage, green beans and tomatoes and simmer gently until the spaghetti is cooked.

6 Roughly chop enough parsley leaves to give you 1 tbsp. Season the soup well with salt and pepper and stir in the parsley. Pour into bowls, grate a little Parmesan over each portion and serve.

Note To save time, you can use a 400g tin haricot beans, drained and rinsed. Simmer the soup base without the beans (in step 4) for just 15 minutes. Add the beans and return to a simmer before adding the spaghetti (in step 5).

Variations

If preferred, keep the bacon in one piece; remove at the end of step 4 and discard. For a meat-free version, use vegetable stock and add an end piece of Parmesan (with rind) for extra flavour in place of the bacon; discard after simmering.

Hummus

Serves 6–8

250g dried chickpeas (or use tinned, see note)

2 garlic cloves

1 lemon

2 tsp ground cumin

Pinch of cayenne pepper

4 tbsp olive oil

Few flat-leaf parsley sprigs

Salt and freshly ground black pepper

If using dried chickpeas, you will need to start this the night before, to soak them.

1 Put the chickpeas in a bowl, cover with cold water and leave to soak overnight.

2 The next day, drain the chickpeas and place them in a saucepan. Cover with fresh water and bring to the boil. Lower the heat and simmer for 1–1½ hours, or until soft. Add ½ tsp salt to the water when they are nearly soft, so for the last 15 minutes or so.

3 Peel and crush the garlic and juice the lemon.

4 Drain the chickpeas, reserving the cooking liquor. Allow them to cool a little, then transfer to a food processor with enough of the reserved liquid and process to a smooth paste. Add the crushed garlic, cumin and cayenne to the mixture and blend in the lemon juice and olive oil to taste. Season with salt and pepper.

5 Serve garnished with the parsley. You can also drizzle with a little more olive oil or dust with a little more cayenne or cumin. Serve with hot pitta bread or crisps.

Note If using tinned rather than dried chickpeas, use 2 x 400g tins, drained and rinsed. Use water to achieve the correct consistency when processing to a paste.

Lentil, chickpea and chorizo soup with cavolo nero

Serves 4
100g cooking chorizo
1 onion
2 carrots
2 celery sticks
4 inner cavolo nero leaves
1 tsp smoked paprika
Pinch of crushed dried chillies
400g tin chickpeas
90g red lentils
750ml chicken and veal stock
  (see page 96)
Small handful of flat-leaf parsley sprigs
Salt and freshly ground black pepper

1 Cut the chorizo into roughly 1cm cubes and put into a saucepan over a low heat to start to release the oil.

2 Meanwhile, halve, peel and finely chop the onion. Add to the chorizo, increasing the heat to medium and cook for 5 minutes. In the meantime, peel the carrots, de-string the celery and cut both into 1cm chunks. Remove the central stalk from the cavolo nero leaves and cut the stalk into 1cm chunks. Chiffonade the soft part of the leaves (see page 89) and set aside.

3 Add the chopped cavolo stalks to the pan with the carrots and celery and cook for a further 5 minutes, then add the paprika and crushed chillies and cook for 1 minute, stirring to ensure they do not burn on the bottom of the pan.

4 Drain and rinse the chickpeas and add them to the pan with the lentils and stock. Bring to the boil, lower the heat and simmer for 20 minutes, or until the lentils are tender. Add the cavolo leaves 5 minutes before the end of the cooking time.

5 Roughly chop enough parsley leaves to give you 1 tbsp and stir this through the soup. Season to taste and serve.

Braised lentils

Serves 4
150g Puy lentils
1 tbsp olive oil
50g piece of bacon
1 onion
½ carrot
½ celery stick
½ garlic clove
300ml chicken and veal stock
  (see page 96)
Few thyme sprigs
1 bay leaf
Salt and freshly ground black pepper

1 Rinse the lentils in a bowl of cold water and pick over them to remove any grit. Drain, cover with cold water and leave to soak for 20–30 minutes.

2 Heat the olive oil in a saucepan over a low heat and add the piece of bacon. Allow it to fry gently to render the fat. Halve, peel and very finely dice the onion. Add the onion to the pan, cover with a lid (ideally with a cartouche, see page 13) and sweat until soft and translucent.

3 Meanwhile, peel and very finely dice the carrot and de-string and very finely dice the celery. Peel and crush the garlic. When the onion is soft, add the carrot and celery and fry gently to soften a little, but not take on colour. Add the garlic and cook for 1 minute.

4 Drain the lentils and add them to the pan with the stock, thyme sprigs and bay leaf. Bring to the boil, lower the heat and simmer gently until the lentils are tender, about 20–30 minutes. Drain the lentils in a sieve over a bowl, reserving the cooking liquor and discarding the thyme, bacon and herbs.

5 Return the cooking liquor to the saucepan and reduce until syrupy. Add the lentils and vegetables back to the reduced cooking liquor, which will create a sauce for the lentils and vegetables. Taste and season, then serve. Delicious served with lamb, duck, sausages and meaty fish such as monkfish.

Variation

Braised lentils with chilli and soy Rinse and soak the lentils as for the main recipe. Sweat ½ chopped onion in 1 tbsp olive oil until soft, then add ½ crushed garlic clove, ½ red chilli, deseeded and very finely diced, and a 1cm piece of fresh root ginger, peeled and grated; cook for 1 minute. Drain the lentils and add to the pan with 1 tbsp sherry vinegar. Let this bubble to reduce to down, then add 150ml stock and 150ml water, 1 parsley sprig and 1 bay leaf, and simmer gently until the lentils are tender. Discard the parsley and bay. Add ½–1 tbsp soy sauce, 1–2 tbsp sunflower oil and a few drops of sesame oil, then taste and season as necessary.

Tarka dhal

Serves 4

400g dried yellow split peas
1 litre water
1 tsp ground turmeric
1 tsp ground cumin
1 tsp garam masala
1 tsp asafoetida
2 garlic cloves
3 shallots
½–1 red chilli, to taste
4 plum tomatoes
2 tbsp ghee or sunflower oil
2 tsp nigella seeds
Salt and freshly ground black pepper

This is a mild spiced stew of split peas, traditionally served with a vegetable curry and Indian breads.

1 Place the split peas in a large saucepan with the water, turmeric, cumin, garam masala and asafoetida. Bring to the boil, lower the heat and simmer for 50–60 minutes, or until the peas are tender.

2 Meanwhile, peel and crush the garlic, halve, peel and finely chop the shallots and deseed and chop the chilli. Blanch the tomatoes in boiling water for 10 seconds, then refresh in cold water, dry, peel and roughly chop.

3 Heat the ghee or oil in a small frying pan over a medium heat. Add the shallots and cook until just starting to brown. Add the garlic, chilli and nigella seeds and cook for a further 1 minute.

4 Stir the shallot mixture through the split peas and simmer until it reaches the desired concentration. If the mixture is too watery, simmer to allow it to thicken. If too thick, add more water and bring to a simmer. Stir through the tomatoes, season well with salt and pepper and serve.

Pea and ham soup

Serves 4

1 ham hock, about 1.25kg
1 onion
1 celery stick
1–2 tbsp olive oil
6 black peppercorns
4 thyme sprigs
1 bay leaf
250g dried split peas
1.5–2 litres water
Salt and freshly ground black pepper

Depending on the cure used for the ham, it can be very salty, so you may need to soak it for a few hours or overnight in cold water. Drain off the water before using.

1 Place the ham hock in a large saucepan, add cold water to cover and bring gently to a simmer, then drain.

2 Halve, peel and finely dice the onion. De-string and slice the celery. Heat the olive oil in a large saucepan over a medium heat, add the onion and celery and cook until softened but not browned. Tie the peppercorns, thyme and bay leaf in a little muslin bag.

3 Add the ham hock, split peas and enough water to cover. Add the muslin bag, bring to a simmer, then turn down the heat to a bare simmer and skim off the froth and scum. Simmer gently for 1–1½ hours, or until the split peas have softened and broken up and the ham is falling from the bone. Top up the liquid with water as necessary during cooking.

4 Remove and discard the muslin bag. Remove the ham hock, trim away and discard any fat, then shred the ham into pieces. Set aside.

5 Strain the cooking liquor, reserving the split peas and vegetables in the sieve, and measure out 1 litre. Tip the contents of the sieve into a food processor or blender, add the measured liquor and blitz to a purée.

6 Return the soup to the rinsed-out pan. Adjust the seasoning. Add the ham back to the soup and warm through to serve.

Variation

Green pea and ham soup For a more vibrantly coloured soup, add 50g frozen petit pois to the soup 5 minutes before the end of the cooking time in step 3.

Bulghar wheat, couscous and other grains

These nutritious storecupboard ingredients are excellent flavoured with herbs, spices and other strongly flavoured ingredients. They can be served warm as accompaniments, or cold as salads.

Bulghar wheat (also known as cracked wheat) is a manufactured wheat product from the Middle East. Usually made from durum wheat, it is par-boiled, dried and cracked into a coarse grain to shorten the cooking time. Various sizes of grain are available. Bulghar holds its bite well after cooking and has a nutty flavour and chewy texture.

Couscous is made from durum wheat semolina and was traditionally hand rolled and sieved to create the tiny individual grains. Nowadays the production is mechanised and much of the couscous sold is pre-steamed and requires only a short soak in boiling water, or stock or other flavoured liquid. Giant or jumbo couscous, also called mograbiah, is available in Middle Eastern shops and selected supermarkets.

Quinoa, native to South America, is cooked like a grain although it is technically a seed. It is an excellent source of protein for vegetarians. When cooking, check to see that the grains have turned translucent, with only a small white fleck in the centre.

Polenta is made from dried ground yellow or white maize, or corn. A staple of northern Italy and central and southern Africa, it is also found across the rest of Europe and in North and South America. It is cooked with water to a smoothish paste and takes a long time to yield a soft, tender consistency. A quick polenta is also now available, but is generally considered inferior. Polenta can be eaten soft or it can be cooled to firm it up, then cut and fried or griddled. It can also be flavoured with a variety of ingredients.

Vegetable and barley broth

Serves 4

1.5 litres well-flavoured vegetable stock (see page 101) or chicken and veal stock (see page 96)
4 tbsp pearl barley
2 shallots
1 celery stick
1 parsnip
1 carrot
½ small fennel bulb
1 bay leaf
1 tbsp Marsala or dry sherry
Good handful of parsley sprigs
Salt and freshly ground black pepper

1 Put the stock in a medium saucepan, add the pearl barley and bring to the boil. Reduce the heat and simmer, uncovered, until the barley is nearly cooked through, about 30–35 minutes.

2 Halve, peel and finely chop the shallots. De-string the celery and chop into small dice. Peel and cut the parsnip and carrot into small dice. Discard any tough leaves from the fennel and finely dice.

3 Taste the stock and, if it is too strong, add water to dilute the flavour. If it is too weak, increase the heat and allow it to reduce accordingly. Add the vegetables, bay leaf and Marsala or sherry and simmer for a further 5 minutes, or until the vegetables are soft.

4 Finely chop enough parsley leaves to give you 2 tbsp. Season the broth with salt and pepper, stir in the parsley and serve with crusty bread.

Variation

Chicken, vegetable and barley broth This broth is delicious when prepared with stock made from roast chicken bones, with shreds of the leftover roast chicken heated through in the broth at the end of the cooking time.

Tabbouleh

Serves 4–6

200g bulghar wheat

4 tomatoes

10 spring onions

2 large bunches of flat-leaf parsley

Bunch of mint

2 large lemons

8 tbsp extra virgin olive oil

Salt and freshly ground black pepper

A good tabbouleh needs plenty of parsley: the overall effect should be mainly herbs flecked with bulghar, not the other way around.

1 Put the bulghar wheat in a small saucepan and add enough water to come 3cm above the level of the wheat. Simmer, uncovered, over a low to medium heat until just tender, about 10 minutes. Drain well and spread out on a tray lined with a clean tea towel to cool. Squeeze out any excess moisture, then transfer to a bowl.

2 Blanch the tomatoes in boiling water for 10 seconds, then refresh in cold water, dry and peel. Deseed and concasse (see page 85), then add, with some of their juice, to the bowl. Slice the spring onions very finely, including all but the very coarsest of the green part, and add to the bowl.

3 Pick the parsley and mint leaves and chop them roughly, reserving a few whole mint leaves for the garnish. Add the chopped herbs to the salad and stir through.

4 Juice the lemons. Toss the salad together with the olive oil and lemon juice to taste and season with salt and pepper. Serve topped with the reserved mint leaves.

A note on choosing bulghar/cracked wheat...

These recipes use the coarse bulghar wheat most readily available in this country. However, if you find the fine-ground bulghar available in Middle Eastern shops, you will not need to cook it as the method describes. Instead, just soak in cold water for 10 minutes, then squeeze out excess water before mixing with the other ingredients.

Quinoa, olive and aubergine salad

Serves 4–6

1 aubergine

3 tbsp olive oil

2 red peppers

100g quinoa

300ml chicken and veal stock (see page 96) or vegetable stock (see page 101)

150g cherry tomatoes

30g pitted black olives

Small bunch of basil

Salt and freshly ground black pepper

For the dressing

50ml fresh tomato sauce (see page 128)

1 tbsp olive oil

1 tbsp white wine vinegar

1 tsp caster sugar

1 Heat the oven to 220°C/gas mark 7. Cut the aubergine into large chunks, about 4cm. Put into a bowl with 2 tbsp of the olive oil and stir to coat well.

2 Cut the peppers in half lengthways. Remove the stalk and seeds and rub the skins with the remaining olive oil. Spread out the aubergine chunks on a large baking sheet and add the peppers, skin side up. Roast for about 20 minutes.

3 Remove the peppers when their skins are black, place them in a plastic bag, seal and set aside to allow the steam to loosen the skins. Continue to roast the aubergine until soft and browning, turning the pieces occasionally. When the peppers are cool, peel off the skins and cut the peppers into 4cm pieces.

4 Meanwhile, put the quinoa and stock into a saucepan, bring to the boil, then reduce the heat and simmer, uncovered, for 15–20 minutes, or until tender. Add a little more water if necessary to prevent it from drying out. Drain, then spread the quinoa out on a tray lined with kitchen paper and leave to cool.

5 Cut the cherry tomatoes into halves or quarters, depending on their size. Cut the olives in half lengthways.

6 To make the dressing, mix the tomato sauce with the olive oil and wine vinegar. Season well with the sugar and some salt and pepper.

7 Transfer the cooled quinoa to a bowl and mix in the aubergine, peppers, cherry tomatoes and olives. Stir through the dressing, then tear in the basil, stir well and adjust the seasoning if necessary. This is delicious served with grilled or barbecued chicken, lamb or fish.

Pine nut couscous

Serves 4

1 red onion
1 garlic clove
Bunch of spring onions
50g pine nuts
2 tbsp olive oil
90ml dry white wine
225ml vegetable stock (see page 101)
  or chicken and veal stock (see page 96)
225g couscous
Salt and freshly ground black pepper

1 Halve, peel and finely slice the onion. Peel and crush the garlic. Finely slice the spring onions on the diagonal, including a little of the green part, and set aside.

2 Toast the pine nuts in a large saucepan until golden, then remove and set aside.

3 Add the olive oil to the pan, then the onion. Fry over a low to medium heat until the onion has softened and is starting to caramelise, then add the garlic and cook for a further 1 minute. Add the wine and bring to a simmer, then add the stock, bring back to a simmer and simmer for 2 minutes.

4 Stir in the couscous, remove from the heat and cover the pan with a lid. Leave to stand for 10–15 minutes.

5 Fork through the couscous to separate the grains, stir in the pine nuts and spring onions and season to taste with salt and pepper.

Variations

You can also add sultanas and/or chopped dried apricots to the couscous, or toasted pistachio nuts in place of the pine nuts. Stir through at the end, to taste.

Herbed couscous Use a yellow rather than a red onion and omit the pine nuts. Finely chop 40g herbs, such as flat-leaf parsley, mint, chervil, chives or coriander, or a selection, and stir them through the couscous after forking it through. Use only 2 spring onions and add a little lemon juice when seasoning.

Preserved lemon couscous Replace the red onion with a yellow onion and omit the pine nuts. Stir through ¼ finely chopped preserved lemon and ½ tbsp finely chopped parsley at the end, before seasoning.

Giant couscous with spice-roasted butternut, pine nuts and coriander

Serves 4

1 medium/large butternut squash
2½ tbsp olive oil
1 tsp ground cumin
1 tsp ground coriander
1 tsp paprika
125g giant couscous
15g butter
75g pine nuts
1 red chilli
4 spring onions
Bunch of coriander
Small bunch of flat-leaf parsley
Small bunch of mint
Salt and freshly ground black pepper

For the dressing
½ lemon
50ml olive oil
1 tsp sherry vinegar

1 Heat the oven to 220°C/gas mark 7. Peel and deseed the squash and cut into roughly 1.5cm cubes. Place in a roasting tin, drizzle over 2 tbsp of the olive oil and sprinkle over the spices and a little salt. Toss to coat evenly, then roast in the oven for about 30 minutes until tender and browned. Remove and set aside to cool.

2 To cook the couscous, bring 1 litre water to the boil in a medium saucepan with a pinch of salt. Add the couscous, bring back to a simmer and simmer for 15–18 minutes until tender, but with a notable bite. Drain well, place in a large bowl and stir in the butter and the remaining ½ tbsp oil to coat evenly; set aside to cool.

3 Place the pine nuts on a baking tray and toast in the oven for about 5 minutes until pale golden, then remove and set aside to cool.

4 Halve, deseed and finely dice the chilli. Finely slice the spring onions, including some of the green part. Coarsely chop enough coriander leaves to give you 3 tbsp, and enough parsley and mint to give 1 tbsp each. Juice the lemon for the dressing.

5 Add the roast squash, pine nuts, herbs, chilli and spring onions to the couscous.

6 For the dressing, mix the olive oil, sherry vinegar and 1 tbsp lemon juice together, season with salt and pepper and pour over the couscous mixture. Toss to ensure the dressing is evenly distributed, then taste and adjust the seasoning as necessary.

Variation

Add 150g cubed, griddled halloumi cheese at the end of the main recipe.

Soft polenta

Serves 6

125g Parmesan cheese

About 1.5 litres chicken and veal stock (see page 96)

250g polenta

75g butter

Salt and ground white pepper

1 Grate the Parmesan. Put the stock into a large saucepan and bring to the boil. Reduce the heat to a simmer and stir in the polenta.

2 Stir over a medium heat until the polenta thickens, then reduce the heat to as low as it will go and cover the pan with a lid. Continue to cook for 30–40 minutes, or until the polenta tastes soft and smooth, stirring frequently to prevent the polenta from burning on the bottom of the pan.

3 Beat in the butter and Parmesan, allowing both to melt into the polenta.

4 Add a little more stock or water to loosen the polenta to the desired consistency and season to taste with salt and white pepper. An excellent accompaniment to sausages, braised beef, liver or duck.

A note on quick-cook polenta...

You can use 'quick cook' polenta to speed up the process. Cooking times vary, so be guided by the packet instructions, though they tend to cook in about 5 minutes.

Grilled polenta with Parmesan

Serves 4

1 litre chicken and veal stock (see page 96) or vegetable stock (see pages 101)

200g polenta

150g Parmesan cheese

1 garlic clove

2 tbsp olive oil

Salt and freshly ground black pepper

1 Put the stock into a large saucepan and bring to the boil. Reduce the heat to a simmer and stir in the polenta.

2 Stir over a medium heat until the polenta thickens, season with salt and pepper, then reduce the heat to as low as it will go and cover the pan with a lid. Continue to cook for 30–40 minutes, or until the polenta tastes soft and smooth, stirring frequently to prevent it from burning on the bottom of the pan.

3 Finely grate the Parmesan and line a deep tray, about 20 x 20cm, with cling film. Remove the polenta from the heat and stir in all but 3 tbsp of the Parmesan, then leave to cool slightly.

4 Pour the polenta into the prepared tray and spread it out evenly; it should be about 1cm thick. Leave to cool completely.

5 Heat the grill to its highest setting. Bash the unpeeled garlic clove with the flat side of a large knife, put it into a small saucepan with the olive oil and heat until the garlic sizzles, then remove from the heat and set aside.

6 When the polenta is cool, cut into 4 or 8 even-sized shapes. Brush a baking sheet with some of the garlic oil and arrange the polenta pieces on the sheet. Brush the top of the polenta with the oil and grill until brown and crisp. Turn the slices and grill again until crisp.

7 Remove the tray from the grill and sprinkle with the remaining Parmesan. Grill again until the cheese bubbles and starts to brown.

Note The polenta can be pan-fried or griddled rather than grilled, over a medium to high heat until browned and warm through.

Variations

The polenta can be flavoured with chopped fresh herbs such as basil, flat-leaf parsley or oregano, stirred in with the Parmesan. You can also vary the type of cheese: goat's cheese works well, as does any hard cheese.

Shellfish

Preparing shellfish can seem time-consuming, but the reward is in the eating. Shellfish can be divided into two main categories: crustaceans and molluscs. Crustaceans are all the multi-jointed creatures such as crab, lobster, langoustines and prawns. Molluscs include clams, mussels, scallops, oysters, squid and octopus. It is vital to cook and eat shellfish when they are very fresh, as they deteriorate quickly and can cause food poisoning. Ideally they should be bought live from a reputable supplier and cooked within 24 hours. If you cannot source live shellfish, buy freshly prepared uncooked or cooked shellfish.

Crustaceans

Most of these shellfish are graded and sold according to size, and in certain countries it is illegal to buy very small ones. However, bigger does not necessarily equate to better, so look for medium-sized shellfish where possible. All live shellfish bought from a fishmonger in this country will have health certification so it is best to buy from one if you can. If gathering your own, be aware that shellfish gathered from polluted waters can present a health risk; gather from the sea rather than from estuaries or harbours.

Prawns

Prawns can be purchased raw or cooked, with heads on or off. It is most economical to buy tails only, as more meat is obtained by weight. However, a whole prawn has more flavour, as do the heads and shells of any shellfish. Even if you are buying them pre-cooked, they will be full of flavour and can be used to produce excellent stocks and sauces.

Prawns are generally graded by size for sale and are sold by weight, so the bigger they are the more expensive they will be. As an approximate guide, 20–25 prawns per kg yields prawns of a suitable size for most recipes.

Unless local and fresh, prawns are either cooked as soon as they are caught or are deep frozen because, as in the case of crab and lobster, the meat loses flavour and texture very quickly. So even when a sign in a fishmonger says 'fresh prawns', unless locally caught, they may be frozen and defrosted. Where possible buy prawns still frozen, rather than defrosted, as they deteriorate quickly after defrosting. When checking for freshness, look for tails that are still firm and taut. There should be no obvious discolouration.

Preparing and peeling raw prawns

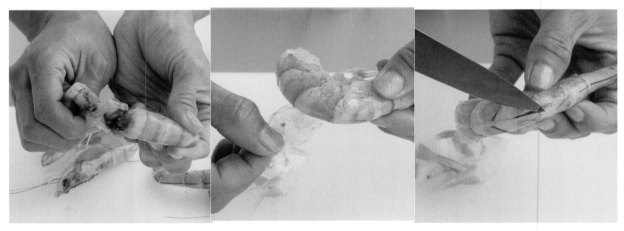

1 Hold the prawn by the tail. Using your other hand, twist the head and pull it away from the tail. Put the heads aside (they can be frozen along with the tail shells and used later to make shellfish stock).

2 The tail shells are soft and hinged and can be removed piece by piece or in several pieces at a time. Start to peel away the shells from the underbelly of the prawn. The tail tip can be kept on or carefully removed.

3 Make a shallow incision, 1–2mm deep, down the length of the back of the tail to expose the intestinal tract. (This is usually dark, but it can be almost translucent.) Carefully pull this away and discard. The prawn tails are now ready to cook.

Butterflying raw prawns shell off

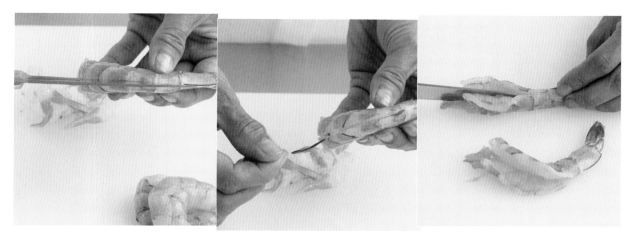

1 Holding the shelled prawn between the fingers and thumb, make a shallow incision, along the length of the back of the tail to expose the intestinal tract.

2 Carefully pull this thread away and discard.

3 Cut deeper along the natural line down the middle of the back, halfway through the prawn, to butterfly it, leaving the tail tip intact.

....

Butterflying prawns shell on

After pulling away the head, turn the prawn over so it is belly side up and pull away the small legs. Cut halfway through the prawn, through the belly, keeping the tail tip intact.

Preparing raw prawns for cooking shell on

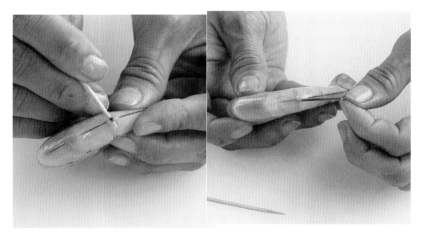

1 To remove the intestinal tract, bend the prawn a little at the point where the head meets the tail. Using a small knife or cocktail stick, isolate and break the intestinal tract. Bend the prawn before the last tail section, to separate the tail sections. Using the point of a small knife or cocktail stick, hook the intestinal tract from underneath and gently tug at it.

2 As it has been released at the head end it should be possible to pull the intestinal tract through the length of the tail and out quite easily. Do not pull too firmly or it will break.

On larger prawns, you can tug and twist at the little triangular shell on top of the tail, which the intestinal tract is attached to, and gently pull out the tract.

Za'atar crusted prawns with a bulghar wheat and herb salad

Serves 4
20 raw prawns
2–3 tbsp olive oil
3–4 tbsp za'atar (see page 32)
½ tbsp plain flour
Salt and freshly ground black pepper

For the salad
100g bulghar wheat
1 red onion
1 tbsp olive oil
1 pomegranate
½ cucumber
½ bunch of dill
Bunch of flat-leaf parsley
¼ bunch of mint

For the dressing
1 lemon
1 orange
5 tbsp olive oil
Pinch of ground sumac
½–1 tsp clear honey

To serve
1 lemon

1 Peel and clean the prawns, leaving the tail tip intact (see page 204), then set aside in the fridge.

2 For the salad, prepare the bulghar wheat (according to the instructions on page 198). When tender, drain well and scatter over a tray lined with kitchen paper, then cover with kitchen paper to absorb the moisture.

3 Meanwhile, halve, peel and finely slice the onion. Heat the olive oil in a frying pan over a low heat and add the onion. Cook gently until the onion is just starting to soften, then increase the heat and allow it to brown a little. Remove from the heat, drain the onion of excess oil and transfer to a large bowl. Heat the oven to 120°C/gas mark ½.

4 Halve the pomegranate and extract the seeds (see page 343). Cut the cucumber in half lengthways, deseed by scraping the length with a teaspoon, then finely dice. Pick the herbs into bite-sized sprigs or very coarsely chop. Add all these ingredients to the onion.

5 Once the bulghar wheat is dry, add it to the bowl. Cut the lemon into wedges and reserve for serving.

6 For the dressing, juice the lemon and orange. Mix 1 tbsp of each with the olive oil, sumac, honey and salt and pepper to taste. Whisk to combine, then set aside.

7 Heat 1 tbsp olive oil in the frying pan over a medium heat. Mix the za'atar and flour with some salt and pepper in a large bowl. Dry the prawns and add them to the bowl. Toss in the za'atar mix to coat.

8 Fry the prawns in batches until pink and the tails have curled, 3–4 minutes. Keep the cooked prawns warm in the low oven while you fry the rest, adding 1 tbsp oil to the pan for each batch.

9 Add the dressing to the salad and toss together. Divide the salad between 4 shallow bowls and arrange the prawns on top. Serve with the lemon wedges.

Variations

Replace the bulghar wheat with couscous or mograbiah.

Za'atar crusted prawns with tabbouleh Substitute tabbouleh (see page 198) for the bulghar wheat, pomegranate and herb salad.

Panko prawns with tamarind dipping sauce

Serves 4 as a starter
12 raw tiger prawns
100g plain flour
2 eggs
200g panko breadcrumbs
Vegetable oil for deep-frying

For the dipping sauce
50g tamarind pulp
100ml boiling water
1 red chilli
2 garlic cloves
3 tsp soft light brown sugar
1 tbsp nam pla (fish sauce)
1 tbsp light soy sauce
1 lime

For the garnish
2 spring onions

Panko breadcrumbs are the favoured Japanese breadcrumbs for frying, and can be used in place of traditional breadcrumbs in most recipes. The bread is processed in such a way that the resulting crumbs are more like flakes. On frying, the result is extra crispness and a less greasy finish.

1 Peel, clean and butterfly the prawns (see pages 204–5), then set aside in the fridge. Heat the oven to 120°C/gas mark ½.

2 To make the dipping sauce, put the tamarind pulp into a small bowl and pour over the boiling water, then leave to soak for at least 10 minutes. Halve, deseed and finely chop the chilli, peel and crush the garlic and mix in a small bowl with the sugar, nam pla and soy sauce. Juice the lime. Stir the tamarind and water well, sieve, discarding the solids, then add the tamarind liquid and lime juice to the chilli dressing, to taste. Set aside.

3 For the garnish, cut the spring onions into 4–5cm lengths, then cut into very fine julienne. Soak in a bowl of iced water (they will curl up).

4 Put the flour on one plate, beat the eggs well, pour onto another plate and put the breadcrumbs on a third plate.

5 One-third fill a deep, heavy saucepan with oil and heat gently to 195°C, or until a small piece of bread browns in 20 seconds (see page 72).

6 Dip the prawns in the flour and tap off any excess. Dip them in the egg and, one by one, coat them in the breadcrumbs, making sure they are well coated.

7 Deep-fry the coated prawns for about 2 minutes, in 2–3 batches, until cooked and golden brown. Transfer the cooked prawns to the low oven to keep warm while you cook the rest.

8 Drain the spring onions. Serve the prawns with the dipping sauce, garnished with the curled spring onions.

Prawns baked with tomato, oregano and olives

Serves 4
24 raw tiger prawns
3 tbsp olive oil
2 garlic cloves
Small bunch of oregano
¼ tsp crushed dried chillies
Pinch of sweet or smoked paprika
8 plum tomatoes
50g black pitted olives
50ml fino sherry
Salt and freshly ground black pepper

1 Heat the oven to 220°C/gas mark 7.

2 Peel, clean and butterfly the prawns (see pages 204–5). Place in a bowl with the olive oil. Peel and finely slice the garlic, roughly chop enough oregano leaves to give you 2 tbsp and add to the prawns with the crushed chillies, garlic and paprika. Leave to marinate in the fridge for at least 30 minutes.

3 Blanch the tomatoes in boiling water, then refresh in cold water, dry, peel, deseed and chop. Halve the olives.

4 Add the tomatoes and olives to the prawns. Stir in the sherry and season with salt and pepper.

5 Transfer to a shallow ovenproof dish and bake in the oven for 10–15 minutes, or until the prawns have turned pink and the mixture is sizzling. Delicious served with crusty bread to soak up the juices.

Stir-fried prawns with baby corn, shiitake and asparagus

Serves 4

24 raw tiger prawns
100g baby corn
100g shiitake mushrooms
300g asparagus
3cm piece of fresh root ginger
3 garlic cloves
3 tbsp vegetable oil
1 tbsp sesame oil
4 tbsp Shaoxing rice wine or dry sherry
2 tbsp Chinese black vinegar or malt
  vinegar
2 tbsp light soy sauce
2 tbsp oyster sauce
4 tbsp caster sugar

1 Peel, clean and butterfly the prawns, leaving the tail tip intact (see pages 204–5); set aside.

2 Cut the baby corn in half lengthways and wipe and slice the mushrooms. Snap off the woody ends of the asparagus spears and peel the lower half of the spears if they are thick, then cut each spear into 4 pieces on the diagonal, keeping the tip intact. Peel and grate the ginger and peel and finely slice the garlic.

3 Heat 2 tbsp of the vegetable oil in a wok until very hot; it will seem to shimmer a little. Add half the prawns and stir-fry for 30 seconds. Remove to a plate with a slotted spoon, then heat the oil again and repeat with the remaining prawns.

4 Discard the wok oil and add the remaining 1 tbsp vegetable oil with the sesame oil. When the oil is hot, add the corn, mushrooms and asparagus and stir-fry for 30 seconds, then add the ginger and garlic and stir-fry for a further 30 seconds.

5 Return the prawns to the wok and add the rice wine, vinegar, soy sauce, oyster sauce and sugar. Stir well to combine, then add a splash of water, so that the sauce lightly coats the prawns and vegetables. Continue to cook for a further minute, or until the prawns are just cooked through. Serve with rice or noodles.

Variations

This basic method can be adapted to a wide variety of stir-fries. Meat or fish can replace the prawns (just add it back to the wok before the vegetables if, like chicken, it needs longer to cook). Flavours such as chopped chilli, coriander and Chinese five-spice powder can be added to the basic sauce, or you can add 1 tbsp hoisin sauce or chilli bean sauce along with the soy and vinegar.

Potted shrimps

Serves 4

200g butter
250g brown peeled shrimps
2 mace blades
Pinch of ground white pepper
Pinch of cayenne pepper
Whole nutmeg
75–100g clarified butter (see page 75)

To serve

Brown toast
Lemon wedges

1 Melt the 200g butter in a large saucepan, then stir in the shrimps, keeping the heat very low.

2 Add the mace, white pepper and cayenne pepper. Grate in a pinch of nutmeg.

3 Cook for 10 minutes, making sure the butter doesn't burn. Taste and add more spices if needed. Tip the shrimps with the butter onto a tray and leave to cool slightly. Remove and discard the mace.

4 Mix the shrimps through again, ensuring that they are fully coated in the spiced butter, then divide between 4 ramekins.

5 Melt the clarified butter, then spoon a thin layer on top of each ramekin to seal. Leave to set in the fridge for at least 4 hours.

6 Serve at room temperature with hot brown toast and a wedge of lemon, or melting over a hot crumpet. Eat within 48 hours.

Prawn laksa with Thai basil and lime

Serves 4

For the spice paste

4cm piece of fresh root ginger

3 shallots

3 garlic cloves

3 lemongrass stalks

4–6 red chillies

1 tsp shrimp paste

4 tbsp peanut or sunflower oil

Handful of coriander leaves

1–1½ tsp ground turmeric

1 tsp caster sugar

3 tbsp tamarind paste

For the laksa

170g rice noodles, 3–4mm wide

2 tbsp groundnut or sunflower oil

16 raw tiger prawns, shell on

600ml chicken and veal stock (see
   page 96) or fish stock (see page 100)

2 tbsp nam pla (fish sauce)

200–300ml coconut milk

1 lime

Handful of coriander

Handful of Thai basil

For the garnishes

½ cucumber

1 lime

Bean sprouts

Thai basil leaves

Chilli oil

Laksa is a Southeast Asian soup made with an aromatic curry paste, to which stock, coconut milk, noodles and garnishes are added.

1 To make the spice paste, peel and finely chop the ginger, shallots and garlic, and finely chop the lemongrass and chillies. Put into a blender or small food processor bowl with the shrimp paste and oil, and blend until smooth. Roughly chop the coriander and add to the mixture with the turmeric, sugar and tamarind paste; blend until combined. The spice paste can be made a few days in advance, but the chilli heat tends to increase with keeping, so take care when using it.

2 Cook the rice noodles according to the packet instructions, or soak in boiling water for 5–10 minutes until tender. Drain and refresh in cold water, drain again and toss a little of the oil through them to prevent them from sticking together.

3 To prepare the garnishes, halve the cucumber lengthways and scoop out the seeds, then cut into julienne. Cut the lime into wedges. Set aside.

4 Prepare the prawns; they can be peeled before or after cooking (see pages 204–5), depending on whether you want everyone to peel their own.

5 Heat the 2 tbsp oil in a large saucepan over a medium heat, add the spice paste and cook for 3–4 minutes, stirring until just beginning to brown, which allows the flavours to develop.

6 Pour in the stock and bring to the boil, then reduce the heat and taste. It can be reduced a little for a stronger flavour, if you like (bearing in mind that the coconut milk will dilute the flavour and make it more rounded). Stir through the nam pla and coconut milk.

7 Just before serving, add the prawns and heat gently. Simmer for 3–4 minutes, or until the prawns are just cooked (they will change from grey to pink and curl up). Meanwhile, juice the lime and coarsely chop the coriander and Thai basil.

8 Season the broth with lime juice and add the chopped herbs. If it needs more saltiness, add a little more nam pla. Divide the noodles between 4 bowls, pour over the hot broth and top with the bean sprouts, Thai basil leaves and cucumber. Serve with a wedge of lime and drizzle over chilli oil for more heat.

Note The quantities of ingredients in the spice paste can be altered according to taste. However, the spice paste and the finished laksa should be a balanced combination of chilli heat, sourness, sweetness and saltiness.

Variations

Meat laksa Substitute lean, tender meat, such as a thinly sliced chicken breast or 225g thinly sliced pork tenderloin, for the prawns and simmer the laksa until the meat is cooked through.

Vegetarian laksa Omit the shrimp paste and fish sauce, seasoning with extra salt. Use vegetable stock. Replace the prawns with vegetables and cook the laksa until they are tender. Try adding 85g each mangetout and green beans a few minutes before the end of the cooking time. Or add ½ small butternut squash, peeled, deseeded, cut into 2cm dice and par-boiled or roasted. Or add 1 small aubergine, cut into 2cm dice and sautéed in sunflower oil until soft.

An easy way to peel ginger....

Scrape the fine papery skin with a teaspoon (as shown); it will come away easily. A teaspoon makes it easier to access awkward bits too, so you don't waste much.

Langoustines

Also known as Dublin Bay prawns or scampi, langoustines are orangey-pink in colour when live. When buying live, select medium-sized langoustines, which have all their legs and pincers intact, and ideally are moving and not limp. They should feel heavy for their size, as this indicates good muscle quality.

If storing before cooking, place the langoustines in a container in the bottom of the fridge covered with a damp tea towel. Do not store for longer than 24 hours.

When buying cooked langoustines, ensure the tail flicks back quickly when opened a little, as this indicates it was in a good condition when cooked.

Cooking langoustines whole

Before cooking live langoustines, place them in the freezer for 15 minutes to sedate them.

1 When ready to cook, bring a large saucepan of well salted water to the boil (use about 25–30g salt per litre of water).

2 Add the langoustines to the pan, cover and bring back to the boil, then lower the heat to a simmer and cook for 2–5 minutes, depending on size. The tails will curl but there will be no change in shell colour. Remove from the water and leave to drain and cool.

Preparing langoustines for grilling

1 Put the langoustine belly side down on a board and cut down through the head and tail to divide in half.

2 Remove the grit or stomach sac from each langoustine half.

3 Remove the intestinal tract from the tail. Any liver in the head area can be left in or spooned out and used in a sauce.

Peeling cooked whole langoustines

Generally only the tail meat of langoustines is used, unless the claws are large, in which case it is well worth the effort of extracting the meat.

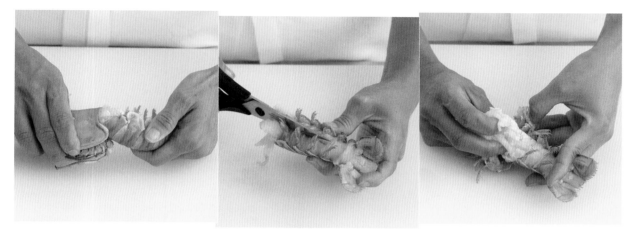

1 Twist the langoustine and pull the head from the tail.

2 To extract the tail meat, turn it belly side up and, with a pair of scissors, cut down on either side of the belly shell.

3 Pull the flap of shell back and lift out the tail meat.

4 Either make a shallow cut across the top of the tail to extract the intestinal tract or cut the tail in half and remove the tract. It depends if the tail is to be served whole or not.

5 If the langoustine claws are a good size, crack them with the back of a knife (as for lobster claws, step 11, page 218) and use a lobster pick to extract the meat.

6 The liver can be removed from the head if you plan to use it.

Grilled langoustines with chilli, garlic and coriander

Serves 4 as a starter
½ garlic clove
1 red chilli
½ bunch of coriander
1 lemon
150ml olive oil
Very small pinch of crushed dried chillies
20 langoustines
Salt and freshly ground black pepper

1 Heat the grill to its highest setting.

2 Peel and crush the garlic and halve, deseed and very finely chop the chilli. Coarsely chop the coriander leaves and juice the lemon.

3 Put half the olive oil in a small saucepan, add the crushed dried chillies and garlic and gently warm over a low heat for 2–3 minutes, then remove from the heat and leave to infuse while you prepare the langoustines for grilling (see page 212).

4 Pour the cool, infused oil into a large bowl, add the langoustines and toss to coat. Place the langoustines shell side down on a lipped baking tray, season with salt and a little pepper and grill for 3–5 minutes, depending on size.

5 Halfway though cooking, baste the langoustines with any remaining infused oil from the bowl.

6 Meanwhile, add 1 tbsp lemon juice to the remaining olive oil with the chopped chilli, coriander and some salt and pepper. Once cooked, the langoustine tail meat will have turned opaque and will be starting to shrink a little from the shell. While still hot, drizzle over the dressing. Serve immediately.

Variation

Grilled langoustines with gremolata Omit the chilli and coriander and turn the raw langoustines through 2 tbsp plain olive oil. Make a gremolata by finely chopping 1–2 peeled garlic cloves with the finely grated zest of 1 lemon and ¼ bunch of flat-leaf parsley. Season with salt and pepper. Season the langoustines and grill as above. Pile onto a platter and scatter the gremolata over the top.

Langoustines with a lemon basil mayonnaise

Serves 4
20 cooked langoustines (see page 212)

For the lemon basil mayonnaise
Small bunch of basil
2 lemons
150ml sunflower oil
1 egg yolk, at room temperature
A little white wine vinegar
Salt and ground white pepper

1 To make the lemon basil mayonnaise, blanch the basil in boiling water for 30 seconds, then refresh in cold water. Drain and dry well. Finely grate the lemon zest of both lemons.

2 Put the oil in a blender with the basil and half to three-quarters of the lemon zest, and blend to a purée. Leave to infuse for 30 minutes, or overnight, then strain through a muslin-lined sieve.

3 Put the egg yolk in a bowl and add a pinch each of salt and pepper. Stir to mix with a wooden spoon, then add the oil gradually (see page 116) until you have a thick emulsion, adding wine vinegar to taste.

4 Serve the langoustines with the lemon basil mayonnaise and warm crusty bread.

Note If you prefer, shell the langoustines before serving.

Langoustine, white bean and artichoke salad with pancetta crumb

Serves 4

For the beans
250g dried cannellini beans
½ onion
1 small carrot
1 celery stick
Few thyme sprigs
Few parsley stalks
1 bay leaf

For the salad
20 medium to large langoustines
8 braised baby artichokes (see page 23)
¾ preserved lemon
½ bunch of basil
Bunch of rocket

For the pancetta crumb
¼ large ciabatta
2–3 tbsp olive oil
4 slices of pancetta

For the dressing
1 lemon
¼ tsp Dijon mustard
3 tbsp extra virgin olive oil
A little clear honey
Salt and freshly ground black pepper

You will need to start this recipe a day in advance.

1 Soak the beans overnight in plenty of cold water.

2 When ready to cook, drain the beans, put into a medium saucepan and cover with fresh cold water. Peel and halve the onion, peel and slice the carrot and slice the celery. Add the vegetables to the beans with the thyme, parsley and bay leaf.

3 Bring to the boil, lower the heat and simmer gently for 30–40 minutes until the beans are tender, but not breaking up. Allow them to cool in the liquor then drain, discarding the vegetables, liquid and aromatics.

4 Meanwhile, cook the langoustines, then peel (see pages 212–3).

5 To make the pancetta crumb, heat the oven to 180°C/gas mark 4. Break the ciabatta into pieces and toss in a bowl with the olive oil. Transfer to a roasting tin with the pancetta and roast in the oven for 10–15 minutes, or until the pancetta has crisped and released its oils and the ciabatta has soaked up the fat, crisped and become golden. Remove and set aside to cool.

6 Transfer both the ciabatta and the pancetta to a food processor and pulse a few times to create very large, coarse crumbs. Set aside.

7 Drain the artichokes, pat them dry and cut into halves or quarters; set aside. Cut out and discard the flesh from the preserved lemons and very thinly slice the rind. Tear the basil leaves.

8 Put the cooked, drained beans in a bowl and add the artichokes, sliced lemon rind, langoustine tails, torn basil and rocket.

9 For the dressing, juice the lemon and put 1 tbsp juice in a bowl with the mustard. Whisk in the olive oil and a drizzle of honey, to taste. Season with salt and pepper to taste.

10 Pour the dressing over the beans, artichokes and langoustines and toss to coat evenly. Divide between 4 plates and sprinkle 1 tbsp or so of the pancetta crumb over each salad.

Note Tinned cannellini beans can be used in place of dried (rinse them well under cold water first). And if fresh baby artichokes are unavailable you could use marinated artichokes instead of braising your own.

Variations

Tiger prawns or freshwater crayfish can be substituted for the langoustines.

Lobster

When buying a lobster, look for a medium-sized one that feels heavy for its size, indicating good muscle quality, with all legs and pincers intact and not hanging limply. The lobster must be alive, show lots of muscular activity, such as tail flapping, and there must be no frothing at the mouth, which can indicate stress.

To store live lobsters before cooking, place in a large container in the bottom of the fridge with a damp tea towel over them. Do not remove the elastic bands from the pincers until after cooking. Only buy cooked lobsters from a trusted source.

You can either cook lobsters whole, then remove the meat, or halve and grill them.

Cooking a lobster whole

Before cooking the live lobster, place in the freezer for 20 minutes to sedate it.

1 Take the lobster from the freezer, place on a board and uncurl the tail and legs. Place a tea towel over the tail and hold on to the tail. To cut through the head, locate the cross on top of the carapace/body shell and place the point of a large, sharp knife in the centre of the cross with the blade towards the head (see step 1, page 221). Push down and then back firmly so the knife penetrates the shell and cuts through the head (see step 2, page 221).

2 Meanwhile, bring a large saucepan of well salted water to the boil (about 25–30g salt per 1 litre of water).

3 Place the lobster head first into the boiling water, ensuring it is completely covered in water, then put the lid on the pan and bring the water back to the boil. Lower the heat to a simmer and cook gently for about 8–10 minutes per 500g, until the lobster turns red and the tail tightens against the body. If cooking more than 2 lobsters, cook in batches. Once cooked, remove the lobster from the water and leave to drain well as it cools, before further preparation.

Note You can use a court bouillon (see page 267) to cook the lobster, or more spicy flavours such as ginger, star anise or lemongrass can be added to the water.

Removing the meat from a cooked whole lobster

1 Twist and pull the head from the tail. Set the head aside.

2 Using a pair of scissors, cut down either side of the belly shell the length of the tail, where the shell is soft and pliable.

3 Peel away the belly shell, then carefully extract the tail meat.

4 Depending on how you want to serve the tail meat, the intestinal tract can be removed by making a shallow cut along the back of the tail and removing the tract (as for prawns, see page 204). Alternatively, cut the tail in half lengthways, then extract and discard the tract.

5 For the head, twist and pull away the large pincers.

6 Pull away the legs and remove and discard the feathery gills (dead man's fingers).

7 Behind the eyes and mouth is the grit, or stomach sac; remove and discard this.

8 Also inside the body will be the liver (tomalley), which will have changed colour from grey to greenish grey when cooked. This is a delicacy and can be kept and eaten, so carefully scoop it out using a teaspoon.

9 Often you will also come across roe (coral) which will be a deep red once cooked. The roe is also a delicacy and can be eaten as is or used to flavour and colour a sauce; spoon this out too.

10 Break the pincers at the joints. Use a crab/lobster pick or skewer to extract the meat from the crevaces below the claws.

11 For the claws, use the back of a large knife or a meat pounder to crack the main claw shell, but try not to crush the claw completely if using a pounder. It is often necessary to crack the shell on both sides.

12 Carefully remove any small bits of shell and discard, then gently pull the shell from the claw meat. If carefully done, the claw meat can be removed whole.

13 Once removed, locate and extract the feather-like internal bone that runs through the centre of the claws.

14 Break the legs at the joints and use a skewer to remove the white meat.

15 The shell, claw and leg pieces can be kept to make a shellfish stock and can be frozen until ready to use. The lobster meat is ready for use.

1 Twisting and pulling the head from the tail.

2 Cutting down either side of the belly shell.

3 Carefully extracting the tail meat.

4 Removing the intestinal tract that runs along the length of the tail meat.

5 Twisting and pulling away the large pincers from the head.

6 Pulling away the legs and removing the feathery gills, which must be discarded.

7 Removing the stomach sac.

8 Scooping out the liver (tomalley) to set aside.

9 Spooning out the coral to save as a delicacy.

(Continued overleaf)

10 Extracting the lobster meat from the crevaces below each pincer.

11 Cracking the main claw shell with the back of a knife.

12 Gently pulling the claw shell from the meat, keeping the claw meat whole.

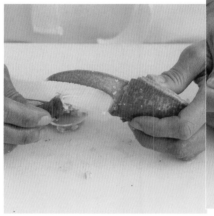

13 Extracting the feather-like bone that runs through the centre of the claw.

14 Extracting the white meat from the leg.

15 The lobster shell, claw and leg pieces set aside, ready to make stock.

Serving simply boiled lobster

Allow ½ lobster per person. Split the cooked lobsters in half lengthways and remove and discard the intestine from the tail and the stomach sac from the head (see page 218). Serve either hot, with hollandaise (see page 120) or beurre blanc (see page 122), or simply with clarified butter (see page 75), or cold, with mayonnaise (see page 116).

Preparing a live lobster for grilling

First place the live lobster in the freezer for about 20 minutes, to sedate it.

1 Remove the lobster from the freezer, place on a board and uncurl the tail and legs. Place a tea towel over the tail. Hold on to the tail.

2 To cut through the head and kill the lobster, locate the cross on top of the carapace/body shell and place the point of a large, very sharp knife in the centre with the blade towards the head. Push down and then back firmly so the knife penetrates the shell and cuts through the head.

3 Lift the tea towel, turn the lobster around and place the tea towel on the head. Repeat the process for the tail, cutting through the shell, as for the head.

4 Put aside the tea towel and turn the lobster halves cut side up. Remove the intestinal tract and discard.

5 Scoop out the grit or stomach sac from behind the mouth and eyes and discard. This will have been cut in two, so both halves will need to be removed.

6 Crack the pincers with the back of a large knife to allow the heat to penetrate through to the meat more quickly.

Grilled lobster with a beurre blanc sauce

Serves 4
3–4 tbsp unsalted butter
2 lobsters, each about 1kg
Pinch of cayenne pepper

For the sauce
1 tsp softened butter (optional)
1 quantity beurre blanc (see page 122)

1 Heat the grill to its highest setting.

2 Put the butter into a small saucepan and melt over a low heat. Remove from the heat and set aside.

3 Prepare the lobsters for grilling (see page 221). If either of the lobsters contain any coral (roe), spoon it into a bowl, mix with the 1 tsp softened butter and set aside for the sauce.

4 Place the lobsters shell side down on a lipped baking tray, brush with a little melted butter and season with a tiny bit of cayenne pepper (it is hot, so take care not to over-season the lobster).

5 Grill the lobsters for 5–10 minutes, basting occasionally with the butter. You may need to turn the lobsters over or reposition the claws a little more directly beneath the grill to allow the heat to properly penetrate the shell. (Cracking the pincer shells first helps this process.) The lobster is cooked when the shell has turned from dark green/blue/black to a bright red and the tail meat is coming away from the shell.

6 Meanwhile, whisk any coral butter into the beurre blanc. As the roe disperses and heats up it should turn the sauce a slightly pinkish colour. Pour any pan juices from the grilled lobster into the sauce for added flavour.

7 Remove the lobster from the grill as soon as it is ready. Arrange on a large platter and serve immediately, with the sauce.

Lobster, avocado and orange salad

Serves 4 as a starter
2 small lobsters
1 orange
1 avocado
Bunch of chervil
Punnet of mustard cress
¼ bunch of chives
1 shallot
3 tbsp extra virgin olive oil
A little Pernod, white wine vinegar
  or lemon juice
Salt and freshly ground black pepper

1 Prepare and cook the lobsters whole and remove the meat from the shell (see pages 217–20).

2 Peel and segment the orange (see page 530), reserving any juice for the dressing. Peel and slice the avocado and drizzle over some of the orange juice to prevent it from discolouring. Pick over the chervil and mustard cress.

3 To make the vinaigrette, finely chop enough chives to give you ½ tbsp. Halve, peel and finely dice the shallot, then mix with 1 tbsp of the reserved orange juice. Whisk in the olive oil and adjust the balance with a little Pernod, wine vinegar or lemon juice. Taste and season with salt and pepper.

4 Put the orange segments, avocado, chervil sprigs, mustard cress and lobster meat into a large bowl, add the vinaigrette and gently turn to coat the salad ingredients with the vinaigrette.

5 Scatter the salad over a large serving dish and drizzle over any remaining vinaigrette from the bowl.

Variation

Lobster, fennel and orange salad Replace the avocado with 1 fennel bulb, shaved very thinly.

Roast lobster with truffled potatoes and tarragon butter sauce

Serves 4

2 lobsters, each about 1kg
1 lemon
4 tbsp olive oil
1 shallot
1 small carrot
½ fennel bulb
½ bunch of tarragon
3 tbsp white wine
1 tbsp Pernod
75ml chicken and veal stock
    (see page 96)
1 quantity mashed potatoes (see page 69,
    using double cream in place of milk)
A few drops of truffle oil
100g unsalted butter
A few shavings of black truffle (optional)
Salt, cayenne pepper and ground
    white pepper

1 Prepare and cook the lobsters (see page 217), but reduce the cooking time to 4 minutes per 500g (to part-cook them, as they will be finished in the oven). Once cooked, plunge the lobsters into a bowl of ice to cool quickly.

2 Once the lobsters are cool, after about 10 minutes, drain them well. Extract the meat from the shells (see pages 218–20), taking care not to break it up, as it will not be fully cooked. Divide the tail meat in half and discard the intestine; discard the stomach sac from the head. Extract the meat from the claws. Put all of the lobster meat to one side. Heat the oven to 230°C/gas mark 8.

3 Juice the lemon and put ½ tbsp juice in a medium to large bowl with 3 tbsp olive oil, a very small pinch of cayenne pepper and a small pinch of salt. Set aside.

4 Halve, peel and finely dice the shallot. Peel the carrot, trim the fennel, and cut both into fine dice, the same size as the shallot (you need about 1 tbsp of each).

5 To make the sauce, heat ½ tbsp olive oil in a small saucepan over a low heat. Add the shallot, carrot, fennel and a few tarragon stalks and cook gently for 1–2 minutes. Add the wine and Pernod and reduce by half, then add the stock, increase the heat and reduce by half again, until you have about 50ml liquid left.

6 Meanwhile, reheat the mash, adding the truffle oil. Keep warm.

7 To finish the sauce, remove and discard the tarragon stalks and cut the butter into small pieces. Reduce the heat to low and whisk the butter into the sauce reduction, a piece at a time, allowing each piece to be dispersed fully into the base before adding the next. The sauce should become creamy in texture and consistency. Don't let it heat too much or it will split; keep warm.

8 Put the remaining ½ tbsp olive oil in a shallow roasting tin and heat in the oven until very hot. Put the large pieces of lobster meat into the bowl with the lemon, oil and cayenne and turn to coat evenly. Transfer to the roasting tin in the oven and roast for 3–4 minutes, or until cooked and the lobster has taken on a little colour and roasted flavour.

9 Add any remaining small pieces of lobster meat to the mash with a few shavings of truffle, if using, and stir through; it should be a soft consistency, not too firm.

10 Chop enough tarragon leaves to give you ½ tbsp, add most of it to the sauce and adjust the seasoning with lemon juice, salt, cayenne and white pepper. Add more tarragon to taste, if necessary. Remove the lobster from the oven.

11 Spoon a little of the truffle and lobster mash onto 4 plates. Divide the lobster between the plates, giving the meat from half a tail and a claw to each person. Spoon a little of the tarragon butter sauce over the lobster. Serve with steamed asparagus spears or some mâche scattered around the plate.

Variation

Roast lobster with truffled potatoes and basil butter sauce Replace the tarragon and fennel with basil and leek.

Lobster bisque with Pernod and tarragon cream

Serves 4

1 cooked lobster, about 650–850g
   (see page 217)
2 shallots
1 carrot
1 celery stick
1 garlic clove
2 tbsp olive oil
1 tsp tomato purée
50ml brandy
100ml white wine
1 bay leaf
Few parsley sprigs
1 mace blade
6 black peppercorns
1 star anise
1 litre fish or shellfish stock
   (see page 100)
1 litre water
50g butter
2 tbsp plain flour
100ml double cream
Salt and ground white pepper

For the tarragon cream
100ml double cream
2 tbsp Pernod
1 shallot
Few tarragon sprigs

1 Cut the lobster in half lengthways and extract all the meat (see pages 218–20), removing and discarding the intestine from the tail and the stomach sac from the head; set aside.

2 Peel and slice the shallots and carrot. Slice the celery and peel and crush the garlic. Chop up the lobster shells with a large knife or cleaver.

3 Heat the olive oil in a large saucepan or stockpot over a medium heat and fry the lobster shells until they start to turn golden brown and begin to smell toasted, then add the shallots, carrot and celery, and cook until the vegetables begin to brown. Add the garlic and tomato purée and continue to cook until the garlic begins to brown.

4 Deglaze the pan with the brandy and wine. Reduce the heat and add the bay leaf, parsley, mace, black peppercorns and star anise to the pan. Add the stock and water and simmer gently for 30 minutes.

5 Remove the softer parts of the lobster shells (the legs, tail and carapace) and whiz in a heavy-duty food processor or bash in a plastic bag with a meat pounder (if using this method, include the claw shells) until they have broken up as much as possible.

6 Add back the broken lobster shells to the stock and scrape all the flavoursome residue from the food processor into the stock. Strain through a fine sieve into a clean saucepan and gently simmer to reduce by half, or until it has become concentrated in flavour.

7 Meanwhile, for the tarragon cream, put the cream in a small saucepan with the Pernod. Halve, peel and slice the shallot and add to the pan with 1 tarragon sprig. Simmer gently until it has reduced by a quarter, then remove from the heat and set aside to infuse.

8 Melt the butter in a medium to large saucepan, stir in the flour and cook for 30 seconds. Pour over the reduced lobster stock and add the 100ml double cream, stirring all the time. Bring to the boil, lower the heat and simmer gently for 5 minutes, then season to taste with salt and white pepper.

9 Cut the reserved lobster flesh into bite-sized pieces, add to the bisque and gently warm it through.

10 Warm through the tarragon cream over a low heat and strain it into a blender. Chop enough tarragon leaves to give you 1 tbsp, add to the cream and blend. Season with salt and white pepper.

11 Divide the bisque between 4 soup bowls, making sure the lobster meat is distributed equally. Spoon a little of the tarragon cream on top of each.

Variations

Crab bisque Use 2 small or 1 large cooked crab in place of the lobster. Remove the crab meat (see page 228) and set it aside. Break up the crab shells with a rolling pin or meat pounder. (Crab shells are generally harder than lobster and will damage your food processor.) Proceed as for the main recipe.

Prawn bisque Use 750g cooked prawns in place of the lobster. Peel and devein the prawns (see page 204), reserving the peeled prawn shells for the stock.

Crab

Buy live crabs where possible, as you can then be sure how fresh they are. Look for medium-sized crabs that are evidently alive with clear signs of muscular activity, such as legs and claws moving. They should have all their pincers and legs intact and feel heavy for their size, which indicates good muscle quality. They are best stored in a container, covered with a damp tea towel in the bottom of the fridge until ready to cook.

Preparing a live crab for cooking

First place the live crab in the freezer for 20 minutes to sedate it.

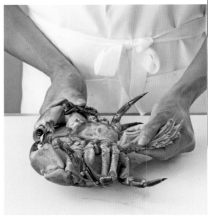

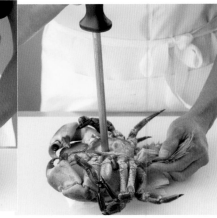

1 Holding the crab at the back to avoid the claws, take it from the freezer and place upside down on a board. Now lift the apron. On a male crab this will be very narrow; on a female crab it will be much wider.

2 Beneath the apron is a hole. Place the point of a steel or thick skewer on the hole.

3 Push the steel down firmly, inserting it into the crab.

4 Move the steel back and forth 2 or 3 times. The claws and legs will become still and limp. Remove the steel.

5 To ensure the crab is dead, turn it over, locate the eyes and insert a skewer between them, about 2cm deep.

6 Move the skewer from side to side, then remove it. The crab is now ready for cooking.

Cooking a crab whole

1 Once you have prepared your sedated crab (as shown left), bring a large saucepan of well salted water to the boil (about 25–30g salt per 1 litre of water).

2 Put the crab into the pan of boiling water, ensuring it is completely covered in water, then cover the saucepan with a lid and bring the water back to the boil. Immediately lower the heat to a simmer and gently cook for about 10–15 minutes per 500g, until the crab turns deep orange. A small to medium crab will take about 15 minutes; a larger one will take 20 minutes or more. A crab over 1kg will take about 25 minutes.

3 Once cooked, remove the crab from the water and place in a bowl. Leave to drain and cool completely before further preparation.

Preparing a cooked crab

1 Twist and pull away the claws and the legs from the body and place in a bowl. Take care to remove the leg knuckles along with the legs.

2 Place the crab upside down on a board, eyes away from you, then lift up and pull off the apron. Place your thumbs at the bottom of the crab on the base of the apron, on either side of the internal body. Push up firmly to release the internal body of the crab and pull away.

3 Pull away and discard the feathery finger-like gills, called 'dead man's fingers'.

4 The internal body contains a little brown meat, but mainly white meat; the claws and legs contain white meat and the main outer crab shell contains brown meat. Turn the internal body over and scrape away the brown meat into a bowl, then put the internal body aside and deal with the main shell.

5 Put the main crab shell, shell side down and eyes towards you, on a board, and locate the little piece of shell immediately behind the eyes. Push down firmly to snap this from the main shell; lift it out and away and discard it (it contains the mouth and stomach).

6 Using a teaspoon, scrape all the brown meat from the shell into a bowl. If the shell is to be used for serving, for a dressed crab for example, remove the inner shell by pressing down firmly along the natural line on both sides of the underside of the shell, then scrub and rinse the shell under cold water to clean completely. Set aside.

7 The internal body is made up of a honeycomb of little compartments divided by very fine shell. It is imperative to avoid getting shell in the crab meat and the best way to reach the white meat is to cut the body in half.

8 Using a crab pick or the tapered handle of a teaspoon or a skewer, carefully pick out the white meat into a separate bowl from the brown meat. It is surprising how much white meat is located in this structure, so make sure you extract all of it. Once all the meat has been removed, the internal body should be hollow and can be discarded.

9 Break the legs at the joints. Use a crab pick or skewer to extract the meat.

10 For the claws, use the back of a large knife or a meat pounder to crack the main claw shell, but try not to crush the claw completely if using a pounder. It is often necessary to crack the shell on both sides.

11 Carefully remove any small bits of shell and discard, then gently pull the shell from the claw meat. If carefully done the claw meat can be removed whole.

12 Once removed, locate and extract the feather-like internal bone that runs through the centre of the claws. For the claw joints, repeat as for the leg joints, using a skewer to remove the white meat.

13 The shell, claw and leg pieces can be kept to make a shellfish stock, and can be frozen until ready to use.

14 Stir through the brown meat to check no shell has been left in.

15 Scatter the white meat, except for any large whole claw pieces, over a large tray and work through it carefully with your fingertips to check for any fragments of shell. It is a good idea to repeat this task. Return the white meat to the bowl. The crab is now ready to use.

1 Twisting and pulling the legs from the body.

2 Pushing the body up to release it from the main crab shell.

3 Removing the feathery gills (dead man's fingers) from the body.

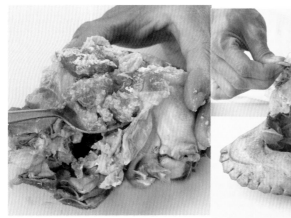

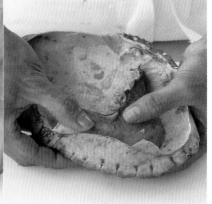

4 Scraping out the brown meat from the body.

5 Removing the piece of shell containing the mouth and stomach sac.

6 Breaking the shell along its natural line to neaten (if using for serving).

7 Cutting the crab body in half to access the white meat.

8 Picking out the white meat from the body.

9 Extracting the meat from the legs.

(Continued overleaf)

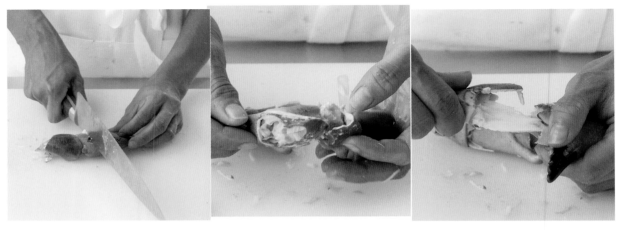

10 Cracking the main claw shell with the back of a knife.

11 Carefully pulling the shell away from the claw meat.

12 Extracting the feather-like internal bone running through the centre of the claw.

13 The shell, claw and leg pieces, reserved for making a shellfish stock.

14 Spooning through the brown meat to check for any pieces of shell.

15 Checking the white meat to feel for any fragments of shell.

To prepare soft shell crabs

1 Cut off the eye and mouth area of the soft shell crabs, taking off about 5–8mm.

2 Hook out the stomach from the opening (this is a small, soft sac).

3 Lift up the sides of the top shell and dig out the feathery finger/gills, then turn the crab over and pull away the apron.

Dressed crab

Serves 2–3
1 crab, about 1kg
1 lemon
2 hard-boiled eggs (see page 144)
½ bunch of flat-leaf parsley
2–3 tbsp fresh white breadcrumbs
¼–½ tsp Dijon mustard, to taste
Salt and freshly ground black pepper

To serve
150ml mayonnaise (see page 116)
Brown bread and butter

1 Prepare and cook the crab, then extract the brown and white meat and place in separate bowls (see pages 226–30). Clean the shell for presentation.

2 Juice the lemon. Scoop out the yolks from the hard-boiled eggs and press them through a sieve to create a fine yellow egg crumb. Finely chop enough parsley leaves to give you 1 tbsp.

3 Add enough breadcrumbs to the brown crab meat to just bind; it should still be soft and spoonable, and predominantly crab rather than breadcrumbs. Taste and season with lemon juice, mustard, salt and pepper. Arrange the brown meat down the centre of the cleaned shell.

4 Season the white crab meat with a little salt and pile it on either side of the brown meat.

5 Garnish with thin lines of egg yolk and chopped parsley. The best way of doing this is to place a little of the yolk or parsley along the edge of a palette knife, neaten it up to create a thin line, then gently tap it into place, holding the palette knife as close to the crab meat as possible.

6 Serve with mayonnaise and brown bread and butter.

Crab and sweetcorn soup

Serves 4
1 litre chicken and veal stock
  (see page 96)
Few coriander sprigs
4 black peppercorns
2 spring onions
4 sweetcorn cobs, about 400g in total
1 onion
50g butter
200g crab meat, half brown and
  half white
50–75ml milk
Salt and freshly ground black pepper

1 Put the stock in a saucepan and add some coriander stalks and the peppercorns. Cut the green ends off the spring onions and add them to the pan. Bring to the boil, then lower the heat and simmer for 20 minutes. Strain the stock through a fine sieve and set aside.

2 Meanwhile, to release the corn kernels from the cobs, hold the cob upright on a board. Use a sharp knife to cut downwards, removing the kernels as you do so. Rotate the cob to cut all the corn away, then set aside. Cut the empty cobs in half and add to the simmering stock.

3 Halve, peel and finely chop the onion. Melt the butter in a saucepan, add the onion and sweat gently until completely soft but not coloured. Add the strained stock and the sweetcorn kernels. Season lightly, then add the brown crab meat and simmer for 10 minutes.

4 Transfer to a blender and blend until smooth, then strain and return it to the pan. Add enough milk to give the soup the consistency of single cream. Taste and add more salt and pepper if needed.

5 Finely slice the spring onion whites on the diagonal and add to the soup with the white crab meat. Gently heat through for 5 minutes.

6 Coarsely chop the coriander leaves and sprinkle over the soup to serve.

Note This soup can be made using a whole crab. Pick out the crab meat (see pages 228–30) and set aside. Add the shell pieces to the stock and simmer gently, as in step 1, to infuse more flavour into the stock, then strain. Continue as above.

Crab and pink grapefruit salad

Serves 4
2 pink grapefruit
2 small cucumbers
2 red Asian shallots
400g white crab meat
1–2 mild red chillies
2 handfuls of baby watercress or rocket
6 tbsp Asian fried shallots (see note)

For the dressing
2–3 limes
40–50g palm sugar
3 tbsp nam pla (fish sauce)

1 Peel and segment the grapefruit (see page 530) and place in a large bowl. Peel the cucumbers, halve lengthways, deseed and finely dice. Halve, peel and finely slice the shallots and add them with the cucumber to the grapefruit, then add the crab meat. Halve, deseed and finely slice the chillies and add to the bowl, then add the watercress or rocket.

2 To make the dressing, juice the limes. Mix the palm sugar, nam pla and 2–3 tbsp lime juice in a small bowl and set aside for the palm sugar to dissolve. Taste and adjust the balance of sweet, salty and sharp; no flavour should dominate. Adjust the balance if necessary.

3 Pour the dressing over the ingredients in the bowl and toss gently to coat evenly.

4 Divide the salad between 4 plates or bowls and sprinkle over some fried shallots.

Note Asian fried shallots are available in jars from Asian food stores; alternatively, you can fry your own sliced shallots until golden and crisp.

Variations
Prawns, langoustines or lobster can be substituted for the crab, and a pomelo used in place of grapefruit.

Tian of crab and avocado with Bloody Mary sauce

Serves 4
400g white crab meat
200g brown crab meat
150ml mayonnaise (see page 116)
4 plum tomatoes
2 ripe (but not soft) avocados
1 lemon
Worcestershire sauce
Tabasco sauce
Salt and ground white pepper
Few chervil sprigs, to serve

For the Bloody Mary sauce
300g ripe plum tomatoes
25ml red wine vinegar
15g tomato purée
10g tomato ketchup
2 tbsp vodka (optional)
½ tsp celery salt
25ml olive oil
Tabasco sauce
Salt and freshly ground black pepper

1 Put the white and brown crab meat into separate bowls. Add 2 tbsp mayonnaise to each bowl, adding a little more if necessary to just bind them together (the brown meat may not need as much). Season both with salt and white pepper, cover and set aside in the fridge.

2 Blanch the tomatoes in boiling water for 10 seconds, then refresh in cold water, dry, peel, deseed and finely dice. Halve and remove the stones from the avocados, then finely dice (the same size as the tomato). Juice half the lemon and sprinkle a little over the avocado to stop it from discolouring. Set aside 1 tsp each of avocado and tomato for a garnish.

3 Mix the remaining tomato and avocado together and season to taste with a little Worcestershire sauce, Tabasco, salt and white pepper. Set aside.

4 To make the sauce, blanch, refresh and peel the tomatoes as above, then chop roughly. Transfer to a blender with the wine vinegar, tomato purée, ketchup, vodka, if using, and celery salt. Blend until smooth, then strain through a fine sieve into a jug. Whisk in the olive oil and season to taste with Tabasco, salt and black pepper.

5 Place a 9cm diameter cutter, 3cm deep, on each plate. Fill it one-third full with the avocado mixture, then add a layer of brown crab meat mixture, then white. Season the remaining mayonnaise with lemon juice, salt and white pepper and spread a thin layer on top of each tian.

6 Carefully remove the cutters. Spoon the sauce around the tians and garnish with sprigs of chervil and the reserved avocado and tomato dice.

Crab and prawn ravioli

Serves 4
300g fresh pasta (see page 168)

For the filling and sauce
175g cooked prawns, shell on
100g white crab meat
½ lemon
1 egg white
¼ bunch of chives
1 small onion
1 garlic clove
2 tomatoes
1 tbsp sunflower oil
1 tsp tomato purée
3 tbsp brandy
1 bay leaf
1 star anise
1 litre shellfish or fish stock
   (see page 100)
150ml double cream
Salt and freshly ground black pepper

1 Once you have made the pasta, wrap it in cling film and set aside to rest at room temperature for 30 minutes.

2 Meanwhile, to make the filling, shell 120g of the prawns, reserving the shells and remaining whole prawns to make the sauce. Put the crab and shelled prawn meat in a food processor. Juice the ½ lemon. Blend the crab and prawn meat until smooth, then add the egg white and 1–2 tsp lemon juice with a little salt and pepper and blend again until well mixed. Taste and adjust the seasoning if necessary. Finely chop enough chives to give you 2 tsp, then add to the mixture. Set aside in the fridge.

3 To make the sauce, halve, peel and roughly chop the onion and peel and crush the garlic. Roughly chop the tomatoes.

4 Heat the oil in a heavy-based saucepan and fry the reserved whole prawns and prawn shells and the onion until beginning to brown. Add the garlic and tomato purée and cook for a further 30 seconds.

5 Flambé the brandy on the prawn shells (see page 382), then add the chopped tomatoes, bay leaf and star anise. Add the stock, bring to the boil, lower the heat and simmer gently for 20 minutes.

6 Roll out the pasta as thinly as possible, through a pasta machine or by hand with a rolling pin, into strips. Lay one strip of pasta on the work surface, covering the other strip(s) with cling film to prevent it from drying out.

7 To assemble the ravioli, place teaspoonfuls of the filling on the pasta strip in even rows at 4cm intervals and brush lightly with water around the filling (as shown on page 177). Lay the other pasta strip over the top. Press around each mound, making sure that all the air is excluded. Cut out the ravioli in squares using a large knife, or in circles using a pastry cutter. Make sure that the edges are sealed.

8 Strain the sauce, return it to the saucepan and reduce over a high heat to about 100ml, or until the flavour is intensely concentrated. Add the cream, return to the heat and reduce to the consistency of single cream. Season to taste with salt and pepper and a few drops of the remaining lemon juice.

9 Bring a large pan of salted water to the boil and cook the ravioli for 3–4 minutes until al dente. Meanwhile, chop a few more chives for the garnish.

10 Drain the ravioli thoroughly. Arrange the ravioli on lipped plates, pour over some of the sauce and top with the chives.

Variations

Crab and ginger ravioli Omit the prawns and chives from the filling (keeping the prawns for the sauce) and increase the crab meat to 200g. In a bowl, mix the crab meat with 1 very finely diced shallot, ½–1 tsp finely grated fresh root ginger, ½ tsp very finely chopped lemongrass and 1–2 tsp chopped coriander to taste (do not blend it). Use this to fill the ravioli. Add 1cm fresh ginger, bashed, 1 lemongrass stalk, bashed, and an extra star anise when making the stock for the sauce.

Lobster and macadamia nut ravioli Omit the crab, prawn and chive filling. Mix 200g cooked finely chopped lobster with 20g toasted chopped macadamia nuts, 4 basil leaves, chiffonaded (see page 89), a small pinch of ground cumin and ¼ garlic clove, crushed. Use this to fill the ravioli and serve with the bisque as in the main recipe. Scatter 2 chiffonaded basil leaves over the finished ravioli.

Molluscs

Molluscs include gastropods, such as limpets and snails, and bivalves, such as clams, mussels and oysters. Once they have been cleaned, they offer huge potential to the cook. Bivalves in particular require careful cleaning and preparation, but are very quick to cook. A scallop, grilled in its shell with a little butter, parsley and garlic, is a real treat yet requires little effort to prepare and is ready in just a few minutes.

Mussels and clams

All mussels and clams must be alive before cooking to ensure they are fresh. Their shells should be closed. Any open shells should close when tapped or squeezed together; if not, discard them as this indicates the mollusc is dead. Throw away any that have broken or damaged shells too. It is also advisable to avoid buying any mussels or clams from a batch where a large number of shells are open, as this indicates that they have been out of the sea for a while and are not fresh.

Store mussels and clams in a dry container in the bottom of the fridge, covered with a damp tea towel. Try not to prepare mussels too far in advance of cooking, as they don't keep well once the 'beard' is removed.

Preparing mussels for cooking

1 First rinse the mussels under cold running water, then scrub the shells with a scourer or scrubbing brush to clean them thoroughly.

2 Pull away the 'beard' (seaweed-like thread) attached to the side of each mussel. Throw away any mussels that are cracked.

3 Tap any open mussels on the side of the bowl or on the work surface; they will close if alive. Any that remain opened should be discarded.

Preparing clams

Clams are cleaned in the same way as mussels, except that they do not have a beard to pull away. It is important to wash them thoroughly in several changes of water to remove sand and grit. As for mussels, before cooking check that they are alive and discard any with damaged shells.

Moules marinière

Serves 4

2kg mussels in shells
1 onion
2 shallots
2 garlic cloves
½ small bunch of parsley
50g butter, chilled
150ml water
150ml dry white wine
Salt and freshly ground black pepper

1 Clean the mussels (see page 235) and set aside.

2 Halve, peel and finely chop the onion and shallots. Peel and crush the garlic. Roughly chop the parsley leaves.

3 Melt half the butter in a large saucepan, add the onion and shallots and sweat for about 10 minutes until soft. Add the garlic and cook for 1 minute, then add the water, wine and half the parsley and simmer gently for 5–10 minutes.

4 Add the mussels, cover the pan quickly with a tight-fitting lid to retain the steam, and cook over a high heat for 5 minutes, shaking the pan occasionally to bring the mussels at the bottom to the top. Remove the lid; if the mussels are all open they are cooked, if most of them are still closed, cover and cook for a further minute or two, or until opened.

5 Tip the mussels into a colander set over a bowl to catch the liquid and discard any mussels that have not opened. Cover the mussels with a pan lid to keep them warm. Pour the mussel liquid from the bowl back into the pan. Taste, then increase the heat and boil to reduce if necessary, until the liquid has a strong enough concentration of flavour. Reduce the heat.

6 Cut up the remaining butter into small pieces, and whisk into the sauce, piece by piece. Taste and season with pepper, and a little salt if needed.

7 Transfer the mussels to serving bowls, pour over the sauce and sprinkle with the remaining parsley. Serve with crusty bread to mop up the juices.

Mussels with spicy tomato sauce

Serves 4

2kg mussels in shells
1 tsp coriander seeds
1 tsp fennel seeds
½–1 tsp cumin seeds
½ tsp crushed dried chillies
½ onion
3 garlic cloves
Small bunch of flat-leaf parsley
3 tbsp olive oil
150ml white wine
400g tin chopped tomatoes
1 tsp tomato purée
1–2 tsp caster sugar
Salt and freshly ground black pepper

1 Clean the mussels (see page 235) and set aside.

2 Toast the spice seeds in a dry frying pan over a low to medium heat. Tip into a mortar to cool, then add the crushed dried chillies and lightly crush with a pestle.

3 Peel and finely dice the onion. Peel and crush the garlic. Coarsely chop enough parsley leaves to give you 2 tbsp.

4 Heat the olive oil in a large saucepan over a low heat. Add the onion and sweat for about 10 minutes until soft and translucent. Increase the heat to medium, add the garlic and cook for 1 minute, then add the crushed spices and cook for a further 1 minute. Add the wine and reduce by half. Add the tomatoes, tomato purée, sugar and some salt and pepper. Simmer gently for 15–20 minutes until the mixture has cooked to a thick tomato sauce.

5 Increase the heat to high, add the mussels, cover quickly with a tight-fitting lid to retain the steam and cook for 5 minutes, shaking the pan occasionally. Remove the lid; if the mussels are all open they are cooked, if most of them are still closed cover and cook for a further minute or two, or until opened.

6 Tip the mussels into a colander set over a bowl to catch the sauce. Return the sauce to the pan and reduce a little to intensify the flavour if required. Meanwhile, discard any mussels that have not opened. Cover with the pan lid to keep warm. Adjust the seasoning of the sauce if necessary, reheat and add half the parsley.

7 Place the mussels in serving bowls and pour the hot sauce over them. Sprinkle with the remaining parsley and serve with crusty white bread.

Clams with beer and sweet paprika

Serves 2, or 4 as a starter

2kg palourde or carpet shell clams
1 shallot
2 garlic cloves
2 tinned Spanish piquillo peppers, drained
½ bunch of flat-leaf parsley
1 lemon
1 tbsp olive oil
¼ tsp sweet paprika
150ml Spanish beer (or similar lager)
50ml water
Salt and freshly ground black pepper

1 Wash and scrub the clams (see page 235).

2 Halve, peel and finely dice the shallot. Peel and finely slice the garlic. Deseed and thinly slice the peppers, coarsely chop the parsley and juice the lemon.

3 Put the olive oil in a large saucepan, add the shallot and cook gently over a low heat until beginning to soften. Add the garlic, peppers and sweet paprika and sauté for 30 seconds, taking care that the garlic doesn't brown.

4 Turn up the heat to high, add the clams, pour in the beer and water and cover the pan quickly with a tight-fitting lid. After 2 minutes, give the saucepan a shake, lower the heat to medium and cook for a further 2 minutes. Remove the lid and check that most of the clams have opened. If they have, put the lid back on, give the pan another shake and take off the heat. If not, replace the lid and continue cooking for another minute, or until they open.

5 Tip the clams into a colander set over a bowl to catch the juices. Return the juices to the pan. Pick over the clams and discard any that have not opened. Cover with the saucepan lid to keep warm.

6 Taste the juices, and if necessary reduce quickly over a high heat until the flavour concentrates a little. If they already taste quite strong, just reheat, then add lemon juice to taste and half the parsley. Add salt and pepper to taste.

7 Tip the clams into serving bowls and pour the juices over them. Sprinkle with the remaining parsley and serve immediately, with warm crusty bread.

Variation

Clams with chilli and garlic Omit the piquillo peppers and paprika. Add another shallot and 1–2 finely diced red chillies. Replace the beer with 100ml white wine.

Spaghetti con le vongole

Serves 4

1kg baby clams in shells
2 garlic cloves
5 tbsp olive oil
6 large tomatoes
250g dried spaghetti
50ml white wine
Few parsley sprigs
Salt and freshly ground black pepper

1 Wash and scrub the clams (see page 235). Peel and finely slice the garlic.

2 Heat 1 tbsp of the olive oil in a large saucepan until very hot. Add the clams, cover quickly with a tight-fitting lid and gently shake the pan over the heat until the shells have opened. Discard any that have not opened, transfer the clams to a bowl and strain the juices into a separate bowl.

3 Blanch the tomatoes in boiling water for 10 seconds, then refresh in cold water, dry, peel, quarter and deseed. Cut the flesh into fine dice (concasse).

4 Cook the spaghetti in plenty of lightly salted boiling water until al dente.

5 Meanwhile, heat the remaining olive oil in the pan, add the garlic and fry until golden brown. Add the strained clam juices, wine and some pepper and cook over a medium to high heat for a few minutes. Add the clams and tomatoes and cook over a low heat for 1–2 minutes.

6 Roughly chop the parsley leaves and stir into the sauce. Adjust the seasoning if needed (the clams can be very salty). Drain the spaghetti, mix through the clam sauce and serve immediately.

Note The tomatoes can be left out of the recipe if preferred.

Grilled razor clams with a garlic parsley butter

Serves 4 as a starter
1 garlic clove
½ bunch of flat-leaf parsley
1 lemon
75g butter
8 razor clams
Salt and freshly ground black pepper

1 Heat the grill to its highest setting.

2 Peel and crush the garlic, coarsely chop enough parsley leaves to give you 1 tbsp and juice the lemon.

3 Melt the butter in a small saucepan and add the garlic, parsley and a little lemon juice. Season with salt and pepper.

4 Wash the razor clams under cold running water to remove any grit, then place on a lipped baking tray and grill for 1 minute, or until they just open.

5 Remove from the grill, set aside to cool, then pull the clams from the shells. Cut off the central dark intestinal tract (as shown), leaving only the firm white cylinder of clam meat. Cut this into 1cm pieces.

6 Break the shells at the hinge, divide the razor clams between 4 half-shells and spoon over a little garlic and parsley butter. Grill again for 2 minutes, then transfer to a platter and spoon over more of the flavoured butter. Serve immediately.

Variation

Grilled razor clams with a ponzu dressing Omit the garlic butter. Mix together 4 tbsp rice wine vinegar, 2 tbsp mirin, 3 tbsp light soy sauce, 1 tbsp lemon juice and ¼ tsp grated fresh ginger. At step 6, when the clams are back in the shell, spoon over a little of the dressing and grill for 2 minutes. Transfer to a platter, add a little more dressing and sprinkle with 1 finely sliced spring onion.

Razor clams Rockefeller

Serves 4 as a starter
350g spinach
Small knob of butter
Small pinch of nutmeg
8 razor clams
⅔ quantity freshly made hollandaise
  (see page 120)
1 tsp Worcestershire sauce
1 tsp anchovy essence
Cayenne pepper, to taste
Salt and freshly ground black pepper

1 Wash the spinach, removing any large stalks. Heat a large, heavy-based saucepan until hot. Add the spinach, with just the water clinging to the leaves after washing, to loosely fill the pan, then cover with a lid. Stir every 30 seconds or so until all the spinach has completely wilted, then transfer to a sieve to drain, pressing out as much liquid as possible with the underside of a ladle.

2 Finely chop the spinach. Heat the butter in a frying pan until foaming. Quickly sauté the spinach for 30 seconds, adding a little nutmeg, salt and pepper. Stir well to ensure the seasoning is well distributed. Preheat the grill to its highest setting.

3 Wash the razor clams under cold running water to remove any grit, then lay on a lipped baking tray. Grill for 1 minute, or until they just open. Set aside to cool, then pull the clams from the shells. Cut off the central dark intestinal tract, leaving only the firm white cylinder of clam meat. Break the shells at the hinge and discard the top half-shell.

4 Spoon the spinach into each of the 4 reserved half-shells, spreading it along the shell, and place 2 clams on top (cutting the clams into pieces first if you prefer).

5 Flavour the hollandaise with the Worcestershire sauce, anchovy essence and cayenne pepper to taste. Spoon 1 tbsp of sauce down the length of each shell. Grill for 1 minute, or until the hollandaise has lightly browned. Remove the clams from the grill and sprinkle with a little more cayenne pepper. Serve immediately.

Variation

Oysters Rockefeller For this classic recipe, use oysters in place of razor clams. Omit step 3. Open the oysters (see page 247) and continue as above.

Scallops

When buying scallops, look for live, closed ones. If they are open, tap the shell or squeeze the shell halves together; the scallop should close. Avoid scallops with broken shells. If many of those on offer are open, avoid buying as this suggests that they are not fresh. You can also buy shelled fresh or frozen scallops, the fresh out-of-shell being superior in flavour and texture to frozen, defrosted scallops. Diver-caught scallops, although expensive, are worth the extra cost as they are more environmentally friendly, and dredged scallops can be gritty and muddy.

Scallops can be kept in a container in the bottom of the fridge, covered with a damp tea towel, and cooked within 24 hours.

Shelling scallops

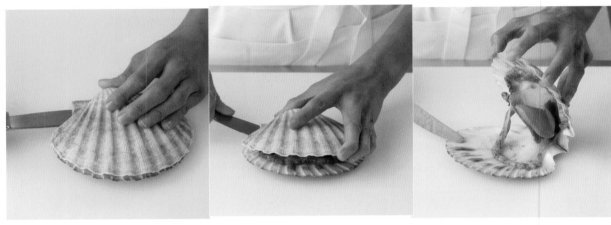

1 Place the scallop rounded side uppermost on a board. Insert the point of a cutlery knife close to the hinge and prise the shell open a little by twisting the knife.

2 Insert the knife a little more. The shells will start to open, but will be held together by the muscle and hinge. Keeping the knife flat against the bottom flat shell, insert it fully and move it from side to side to release the scallop from the shell.

3 Once the scallop is released, the top rounded shell can be easily lifted off, with the scallop still attached, breaking the black rubber-like hinge. Discard the bottom flat shell.

4 With the rounded side of the shell against the board, and the knife against the shell, release the scallop from the rounded shell.

5 Gently pull away the frill and dark stomach sac that surrounds the scallop, and discard. Take care to avoid pulling away the coral.

6 Carefully pull away and discard the small white ligament, attached to the side of the scallop by a thin membrane. Just the white scallop with the coral attached will be left.

Scallops and chorizo with parsley salad

Serves 4
12 large scallops in shells
6–8 small cooking chorizos
4 slices of sourdough bread
1 tsp olive oil
75g butter
1–2 tbsp sherry vinegar
150ml white wine
Salt and freshly ground black pepper

For the parsley and almond salad
Large bunch of flat-leaf parsley
50g Marcona almonds
1–2 garlic cloves
1 lemon
4 tbsp extra virgin olive oil

1 Prepare the scallops (see left) and set aside. Heat the oven to 120°C/gas mark ½.

2 Peel the chorizos and cut on the diagonal into slices 5mm thick.

3 For the salad, pick the parsley leaves from the stalks and put into a large bowl. Cut the almonds into slivers and peel and finely slice the garlic. Finely grate the zest and squeeze the juice from the lemon.

4 Heat 1 tbsp of the extra virgin olive oil in a non-stick frying pan over a low heat, add the almonds and garlic and sauté until just starting to toast, then immediately transfer to a small bowl. Add 1 tbsp lemon juice and a little zest to the almonds and whisk in the remaining 3 tbsp oil. Taste and adjust the seasoning, then pour the dressing over the parsley and toss to coat.

5 Toast the sourdough and keep warm. Meanwhile, put the chorizo slices in a non-stick frying pan over a low to medium heat and cook until the oil is released and the chorizo is cooked through but still tender. Remove and keep warm in the low oven. Pour off and set aside the chorizo oil.

6 Season the scallops with a little salt. Wipe out the frying pan, then add the 1 tsp olive oil and a knob of the butter and place over a medium to high heat. When hot, add the scallops and cook for 1–2 minutes, depending on size, so that they take on some colour and caramelise a little. Turn and repeat on the second side, then remove and keep warm.

7 Deglaze the frying pan with the sherry vinegar and reduce by half, then add the wine and reduce by two-thirds. Add back the reserved chorizo oil and most of the remaining butter. Bring to a simmer, taste and adjust the balance if necessary, adding a little more butter if it is too acidic or lemon juice if too oily. Season with pepper and remove from the heat.

8 Place a piece of sourdough toast on each of 4 plates and pile the scallops and chorizo onto the toasts. Drizzle the sauce from the pan over and around the scallops and chorizo and serve the parsley salad separately.

....

A note on the parsley salad...
Parsley is a robust herb and can sit quite happily dressed as a salad for up to 30 minutes, during which time the flavours will transfer and develop.

Pan-fried scallops with pea purée, pancetta and almond gremolata

Serves 4

12 large scallops in shells
8 thin slices of pancetta
1 tsp olive oil
Knob of butter
Salt and freshly ground black pepper

For the pea purée

250ml chicken and veal stock
  (see page 96)
1–2 rashers of smoked streaky bacon
300g peas
Few chervil sprigs
1 tbsp crème fraîche

For the ciabatta and gremolata crumb

¼ ciabatta
2–3 tbsp olive oil
30g blanched almonds
1 garlic clove
1 lemon
½ bunch of parsley

To finish

Small handful of chervil sprigs

1 Prepare the scallops (see page 242) and set aside. Heat the oven to 180°C/gas mark 4.

2 For the pea purée, put the stock, bacon and peas in a saucepan, add some seasoning and bring to a simmer. Simmer gently until the peas are tender, about 3–5 minutes. Drain, reserving the stock, then remove and discard the bacon. Transfer the peas to a blender, add the chervil and blitz with a little of the reserved stock to a smooth, spoonable consistency. Push through a fine sieve, then taste, add the crème fraîche and adjust the seasoning. Set aside.

3 For the gremolata crumb, tear the ciabatta into pieces and toss in a bowl with the olive oil. Spread the ciabatta pieces out in a shallow roasting tin and toast in the oven for 5–10 minutes until golden and crisp, adding the almonds for the last 5 minutes and making sure that they toast but do not burn. Remove from the oven and set aside to cool.

4 Peel and finely chop the garlic, finely grate the zest from the lemon and finely chop the parsley leaves. Transfer the almonds to a food processor and process to chop coarsely, then add the ciabatta, garlic and lemon zest and pulse to a uniform, coarse crumb. Pulse in a little of the parsley. The mixture should be free flowing and the consistency of couscous. Taste and season if necessary with salt and pepper.

5 Sandwich the pancetta between 2 lightly oiled baking trays and bake in the oven until crisp.

6 Reheat the pea purée over a low heat; it should be soft, not stiff, so add a small splash of reserved stock to loosen if necessary.

7 Heat the 1 tsp olive oil and knob of butter in a large non-stick frying pan over a medium to high heat. Season the scallops and cook for 1–2 minutes, depending on size, so that they take on some colour and caramelise a little. Turn and repeat on the second side. The pan must be hot, or the scallops will stew rather than fry.

8 Spoon the pea purée onto 4 plates and arrange 3 scallops on top. Sprinkle a little gremolata crumb over and around the scallops and place the crisp pancetta across them. Finish with chervil sprigs.

Variations

Scallops with cauliflower purée and black pudding Omit the gremolata crumb and replace the pea purée with cauliflower purée (see page 19). Pan-fry 75g sliced black pudding until cooked, then crumble it onto a baking sheet and dry in an oven preheated to 170°C/gas mark 3 for about 15 minutes. Use the black pudding in place of the gremolata.

Scallops with Jerusalem artichoke purée and crisps Replace the pea purée with a Jerusalem artichoke purée (see page 24). Replace the gremolata with 1 quantity ciabatta and pancetta crumb (see page 216). Finely slice 2 Jerusalem artichokes and deep-fry to make crisps (see page 73); use in place of the pancetta.

Oysters

Buy live oysters, store them covered with a damp tea towel in a container in the bottom of the fridge and use within 24 hours. If you're intending to open them yourself (rather than ask the fishmonger), you will need an oyster knife (shucker). It takes practice, but opening your own oysters means that you retain the juices. Freshly shucked oysters are delicious served raw with a simple dressing (see right).

Opening oysters

1 Wrap the hand that will hold the oyster in a tea towel. Place the oyster rounded side down, flat side up, in the palm of this hand, with the narrower end towards you.

2 Push the point of the oyster knife into the hinge, located at the narrower end of the shell. Just to the left of the 'point' of the narrow end is a good place to insert the knife.

3 Firmly twist the knife back and forth until the hinge is broken.

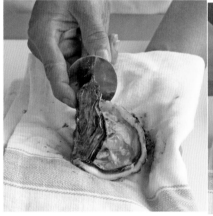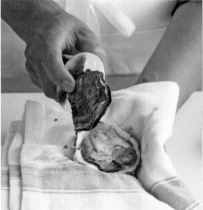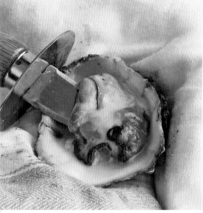

4 Slide the knife between the shells to cut through the ligament and twist one side of the knife upwards to lever up the top shell.

5 Lift off the top shell and discard it.

6 Carefully release the oyster from the bottom shell using the knife, making sure you retain the juices, and pick away any bits of shell.

Dressings to serve with raw oysters

Serve your opened oysters in their half-shell on a platter with a bowl of one of the following sauces. Each serves 4.

Shallot and red wine dressing Peel and very finely dice ½–1 small banana shallot. Mix with 100ml red wine vinegar, a small pinch of sugar and a little salt and pepper.

Cucumber and ginger dressing Peel, deseed and very finely dice ½ cucumber. Halve, peel and very finely dice 1 red Asian shallot or ¼ small red onion. Peel and very finely grate a 1cm piece of fresh root ginger. Put the cucumber and shallot or onion in a bowl with 100ml rice wine vinegar, 1 tsp soy sauce and 1½ tsp palm sugar; stir well, to dissolve the sugar. Add the grated ginger to taste.

Bloody Mary dressing Make one-third of the dressing for tian of crab and avocado (see page 232).

Cephalopods

Cephalopods are characterised by the ring of tentacles around their mouths, and include squid, octopus and cuttlefish. Octopus needs long, slow cooking to tenderise its tough flesh. Squid is more versatile and can be cooked very quickly on a hot grill or frying pan; or slowly, during which time it will become firm, and then tender again.

Squid

Squid comes in a variety of sizes, but you should choose those with bodies about or just bigger than the length of your fingers and hand. When choosing squid, smell it; it should be almost odourless – any hint of ammonia indicates a lack of freshness. Ask the fishmonger to prepare it for you or follow the steps below. Although it is possible to buy frozen squid tubes, the flavour of fresh is better.

Preparing squid

1 Hold the body in one hand and the tentacles in the other and pull them apart; a gentle tug is enough. The intestines will come away with the tentacles. Set aside the body of the squid for further preparation.

2 Cut the tentacles from the head, just above the eyes on the tentacle side.

3 If using the squid ink, look through the intestines for a thin, silvery-pearly tube that is the ink sac. Carefully cut it from the intestines; avoid pressing or cutting into it or you will lose the ink. Set aside the ink sac. Discard the head and intestines.

4 Still working on the tentacles, find the mouth, which is in the centre of the base of the tentacles where they join the head. Squeeze out and discard the mouth, including the beak.

5 Cut off the 2 long tentacles, then cut these into bite-sized pieces. If the rest of the tentacles are very large, cut them into large bite-sized pieces. If small, leave whole. Rinse and set aside.

6 Reach inside the body cavity and feel for something firm against the side of the body, which is the feather-shaped quill. Gently pull it out and discard.

7 Pull away the 2 fins on either side of the body. Pull and peel away the brownish-pink skin covering the body and fins. Rinse the body in cold water and dry it well.

8 Place the body on the board and turn it to find the natural line where the quill was attached. Insert a sharp knife (a fish filleting knife is ideal) into the body and cut the body open along this line. Scrape the inside of the body carefully with the knife blade to remove the membrane and any remaining innards. Rinse and dry well with kitchen paper.

9 Using a sharp knife, score the inside of the body in a diamond pattern. You need to score the flesh about one-third of the way through, so use a light touch. Once scored, cut the body into large bite-sized squares or rectangles (about 4–5cm). Combine the body pieces with the tentacles, ready for cooking.

For squid rings
Choose small to medium squid and follow the above technique to the end of step 7. At this stage pull away any remaining membrane and innards. Ensure you rinse out the inside of the body well and dry it. Cut across the body into pieces about 1cm wide.

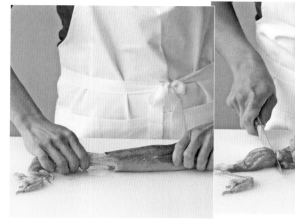

1 Pulling the tentacles and the body free from each other.

2 Cutting the tentacles from the head, just above the eyes.

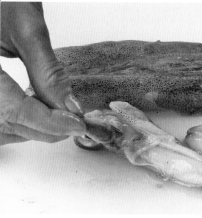

3 Carefully removing the squid ink sac, keeping it intact.

4 Squeezing out the mouth and beak from the base of the tentacles.

5 Cutting off the 2 long tentacles.

6 Pulling out the translucent quill from the body.

7 Pulling away the brownish-pink skin covering the body.

8 Cutting the body pouch open along the natural line (where the quill was attached).

9 Scoring the inside surface of the body in a diamond pattern.

Pan-fried squid with chickpea, tomato, olive and chilli salad

Serves 4
1kg squid
2 tbsp olive oil

For the salad
400g drained cooked or tinned chickpeas
1 red onion
2 red chillies
2 garlic cloves
24 cherry tomatoes
75g rocket or baby spinach leaves
1 lemon
3 tbsp extra virgin olive oil
½ tbsp olive oil
¼–½ tsp crushed dried chillies
75g black olives
Salt and freshly ground black pepper

1 Prepare the squid (see page 248) and set aside.

2 For the salad, rinse the chickpeas and discard any that are discoloured. Halve, peel and finely slice the red onion and halve, deseed and finely chop the chillies. Peel and thinly slice the garlic and halve the cherry tomatoes. Pick over, wash and dry the rocket or spinach. Finely grate the zest and squeeze the juice of the lemon.

3 For the dressing, whisk together 1 tbsp lemon juice, half the zest and the 3 tbsp extra virgin olive oil. Taste and season with salt and pepper, then set aside.

4 Put the ½ tbsp olive oil in a frying pan over a low heat, add the onion and cook gently until just beginning to soften. Add the chopped chillies, garlic and the crushed dried chillies and cook for 1 minute. Add the chickpeas and warm through. Lightly crush them with the back of a wooden spoon until they just to begin to break up.

5 Put the cherry tomatoes and black olives into a large bowl and tip in the warm chickpea mixture.

6 Heat the frying pan over a medium to high heat and add the 2 tbsp olive oil. Dry the squid well and pan-fry until just starting to curl. Turn and cook briefly again, then remove from the pan.

7 Add the rocket or spinach to the chickpeas, pour over the dressing and toss to coat evenly. Add the squid and turn through, then divide between 4 plates and drizzle any remaining dressing from the bowl over the salad.

Variation

Squid with chickpea, chorizo, tomato, olive and chilli salad Add 75g peeled and thinly sliced sautéed cooking chorizo to the salad and use any rendered chorizo oil in the dressing.

A note on cooking squid...
When pan-frying, griddling or deep-frying squid, you need a high temperature to keep the squid tender and to allow for some caramelisation for colour and flavour. Depending on thickness, 2–3 minutes is enough cooking time; any longer and you risk the squid turning tough. Scoring squid helps the heat to penetrate the flesh, so it can cook quickly, and creates sharp edges to catch and caramelise nicely.

An alternative to cooking squid very quickly is to cook it very slowly, as for a stew, which will make it soft and tender. Anything in between can make the squid tough, chewy and unpalatable.

Salt and pepper squid

Serves 4
1kg squid
Oil for deep-frying
Salt

For the batter
¼ tsp Szechuan peppercorns
½ tsp salt
¼ tsp freshly ground black pepper
30g cornflour
1 tbsp sunflower or groundnut oil
2 egg whites

For the relish
1 red chilli
1 garlic clove
2.5cm piece of fresh root ginger
4 spring onions
½ bunch of coriander
1 tbsp sunflower oil
Few drops of sesame oil

To serve
2 limes

1 Prepare the squid (see page 248), scoring it just very lightly in a large diamond pattern so that it doesn't take on too much batter. Cut the squid body into 4–5cm squares or rectangles for a starter size, and slightly larger size for a main course.

2 To prepare the relish, halve, deseed and finely chop the chilli, peel and thinly slice the garlic, peel the ginger and cut into fine julienne, and trim and thinly slice the spring onions on the diagonal. Pick the leaves off the coriander stalks. Cut the limes for serving into wedges. Set everything aside.

3 Toast the Szechuan peppercorns in a frying pan over a low to medium heat until aromatic, taking care not to burn them or they will become bitter. Using a pestle and mortar, pound the salt, pepper and toasted peppercorns together until fine.

4 Put the cornflour and pepper mix in a bowl. Make a well in the centre and add the oil and egg whites. Whisk the egg whites and oil, gradually drawing in the flour until you have a batter. If it is very thick, add extra egg white; it should be the consistency of double cream.

5 One-third fill a deep, heavy saucepan with oil. Heat to 195°C, or until a piece of bread browns in 20 seconds (see page 72). Dry the squid well, dip in the batter to coat well and deep-fry a few at a time for 30 seconds–1 minute, depending on thickness, until golden. Lift out, drain on kitchen paper and sprinkle with salt.

6 Heat the sunflower oil for the relish in a small frying pan, add the chilli, garlic, ginger and spring onions and fry over a high heat for a few seconds until fragrant. Remove from the heat, then add the sesame oil and coriander leaves.

7 Pile the squid onto a serving dish, sprinkle the chilli mixture on top and serve with the lime wedges.

Octopus in red wine with cinnamon

Serves 4
1kg octopus
2 red onions
1 garlic clove
4 tbsp olive oil
400g tin chopped plum tomatoes
200ml water
1 tbsp red wine vinegar
200ml red wine
2 bay leaves
1 tsp soft brown sugar
1 cinnamon stick
Salt and freshly ground black pepper

The octopus needs to be frozen before cooking, in order to tenderise the flesh, so you will need to allow time for this and for defrosting before using it.

1 Clean the octopus; this is similar to cleaning squid (see page 248). Slit the main body of the octopus in half. Remove and discard the ink sac, stomach and eyes. Remove the beak from the middle of the tentacles. Wash well under cold running water. Put the octopus in a large plastic bag and freeze it overnight (or for longer).

2 Defrost the octopus on a tray in the bottom of the fridge for several hours.

3 Bring a large pan of water to the boil. Add the defrosted octopus and simmer for 10 minutes to loosen the outer skin. Remove it from the water and as soon as it is cool enough to handle, pull off the dark membrane. Cut the octopus into 5cm squares and the tentacles into 5cm pieces. Heat the oven to 170°C/gas mark 3.

4 Peel the onions and cut each into wedges about 5mm wide. Peel and crush the garlic. Heat the olive oil in a flameproof casserole, add the onions and octopus and fry until brown, then add the garlic and cook for a further minute.

5 Add the tomatoes, water, wine vinegar, wine, bay leaves, sugar, cinnamon stick and some salt and pepper. Cover and cook in the oven for 1½–2 hours, or until the octopus is tender, checking occasionally; if it seems dry, add some more water.

6 Taste the sauce: add more water or reduce to achieve the desired flavour. Discard the cinnamon, adjust the seasoning and serve, with buttered couscous if you like.

Sea urchins

Sea urchins are hard to come by but worth seeking out. It is the delicate roe that is eaten. In Italy, it forms a topping for bruschetta, whereas in Korea and Japan, it is often served with sushi rice.

Preparing sea urchins

Sea urchins are commonly black, but they are available in a range of colours including purple, deep red and pale beige.

1 Protect the hand that will hold the sea urchin in a tea towel. Place the sea urchin in the palm of this hand with the mouth (soft part in the underside) uppermost.

2 Using sharp scissors, insert the tip into the centre of the mouth and cut through the spiky shell to create a large hole, 4–5cm in diameter.

3 Remove and discard the disc of shell and pour away any juices.

4 Carefully scoop out and discard the black parts inside the sea urchin, leaving the roe intact.

5 The orange roe sits in little clusters. Use a teaspoon to carefully remove each cluster.

Serving sea urchins

Sea urchins can be served as for oysters after preparation, with the same dressings as oysters (see page 247). Alternatively, add the roe to just-cooked and drained pasta that has been tossed in an olive oil, garlic and lemon juice dressing with a little coarsely chopped flat-leaf parsley. The heat of the pasta will gently cook the roe.

Fish

This chapter will give you all the knowledge
you need to select really fresh fish, including some
of the less commonly used species, and to prepare and
cook it using a variety of methods. All you need to do is
master some simple fishmongering skills and techniques.
A basic understanding of the classification of fish is helpful
when it comes to choosing particular fish, and will enable
you to apply appropriate preparation methods. Once you
know how to prepare flat and round varieties of white
fish and large and small round oily fish, as well as
smoked fish and delicate cured fish, you will
find it easy to substitute one species
for another.

Buying fish

It is important to buy fish which has a sustainable supply, and every cook should know how to select a more plentiful variety in place of one that is becoming over-fished. The list of MSC (Marine Stewardship Council) approved fish changes as stocks recover or are overfished, so check their list regularly and make sure that you buy only MSC certified or approved fish. Flavour combinations tend to work well with similar types of fish, so experimenting with new varieties can produce delicious new recipes.

Identifying the freshest fish, whether whole or in fillets, is a useful and important skill.

Choosing whole fish

Smell Fresh fish should smell of the sea, not have an unpleasant 'fishy' odour.

Natural slime Fish should be shiny with a natural moist slime and no dry areas.

Scales These should all be intact, with no dry or scale-free patches.

Eyes These should be clear and prominent, bulging not sunken.

Fins These should all be intact and perky, not dry, limp and broken.

Gills These should be a bright pink or red, not grey or brown or discolouring.

Touch Fish should be firm to the touch, not soft or flabby.

Selecting fish fillets

With fewer indicators than for a whole fish, it is harder to tell if fish fillets are fresh. It is also difficult to examine them properly if they are wrapped. However, there are a few signs to look out for: fillets should be bright and shiny, with a white or pale white or pink colour depending on the type of fish, and no discolouration. The flesh should be firm to the touch, not soft, and your finger should not leave an indentation when you press it. As for whole fish, fillets should smell fresh, of the sea rather than overtly 'fishy'.

Freshwater and farmed fish

Freshwater and farmed fish can be harvested when needed and so can be fresher when purchased than wild sea fish. However, the fish tend to be caught younger and smaller, which does not allow them time to develop the flavour of wild fish. Farmed fish may be reared in small, confined areas, so fins can be stunted and broken; they can also be fattier than wild fish.

Fish classification and identification

There are many ways to classify fish, but the most important distinctions for the cook are whether the fish is flat or round, and white or oily. This determines the best technique to use in preparing the fish, the most appropriate cooking method and which combinations of flavour will work well with the fish.

Flat fish live and feed on or near the sea bed and range from small dabs to the huge turbot. Round fish live both on or near the sea bed, and through the middle and surface levels of the sea, and include cod, salmon, mackerel and herring.

In white fish the oils are concentrated in the liver, whereas in oily fish the oils are spread throughout the fish. These are the beneficial omega-3 oils and oily fish should be eaten at least a couple of times a week as part of a well-balanced diet.

Storing fish

Ideally fish should be used the day you buy it. To store briefly, wrap in cling film and place in a shallow tray in the bottom of the fridge (generally the coldest part).

Try to avoid freezing fish. If you do have to freeze it, wrap it very closely in cling film, excluding any air pockets and use it as soon as you can, as the quality of frozen fish deteriorates over prolonged periods of time. However, fish that is frozen as soon as it is caught can be in a better condition than fresh, depending on how long it has taken to get from the sea to your kitchen. It is best to defrost fish in the fridge, on a tray covered with kitchen paper to absorb any water.

Cooking fish

Fish very rarely needs long, slow cooking as its flesh is made up of short, delicate muscle fibres and connective tissue that break down very quickly on cooking. Fish can be successfully pan-fried, baked, roasted and deep-fried. For more delicate results, it can be poached or steamed.

Assessing whether fish is cooked

While it is feasible to use a thermometer and calculations that involve measuring the thickness of the fillet, it is easier and perfectly possible to use your senses to judge whether fish is cooked; guidance is included in the individual recipes. Great care must be taken to avoid overcooking fish, which causes it to fall apart, lose flavour and become tough and dry.

Flat fish

All flat fish are classified as white fish, because the greatest concentration of their fat is contained in the liver, which ensures they have lean, white flesh. Although similar in appearance, each species has a distinctive flavour. They include plaice, lemon and Dover sole, brill, turbot, flounder and dabs. Skates and rays, with their cartilaginous (soft) frames, are also flat fish, although prepared differently as it is their 'wings' that are prized in cooking.

Filleting a flat fish

This method removes 4 fillets from a flat fish. Fishmongers will often remove a whole side, so 2 double fillets from each flat fish. What is important is that you develop a method of filleting that you are comfortable with, that you use your knife safely and that you waste as little fish as possible. It is essential to use a very sharp knife, preferably with a long flexible blade.

First rinse the fish under cold water and dry with kitchen paper. Fish have a natural slime and rinsing it off makes it easier to handle.

1 Place the fish on a board, tail end towards you and darker side uppermost. Using a fish filleting knife, make an incision along the natural line running down the middle of the fish, from behind the head down to the tail.

2 Make a small cut across the top of the tail.

3 Make a cut from behind the head down to the edge of the fish behind the gill and head on both sides.

4 Release a little of one of the fillets from the back bone, the full length of the fish. Then, using the flexibility and length of a fish filleting knife and long strokes, carefully release the fillet away from the skeleton. Try to keep the knife as flat against the bone as possible. You should hear a rasping sound as the knife blade works its way across the bones.

5 As the knife approaches the edge, lift up the fillet to make it easier to see what you are doing.

6 When you reach the frill, either grip the edge of the skin of the fillet and pull the fillet firmly away from the body, taking care not to damage the flesh, or cut the fillet away from the frill and main body of the fish.

7 Repeat with the remaining top fillet. You need to ensure the knife blade is on the right side of the little vertical back bone before starting to remove the fillet.

8 Turn the fish over and repeat the process on the pale underside. The skin here is a little tougher.

9 Once you have removed all 4 fillets, put them aside ready to skin (see page 260) or cook with the skin on. Remove the head from the frame, bend the frame to break the bone and cut through the breaks, then rinse the bones and use for stock, or freeze for later use.

Note Now scrape the board to get rid of any loose bits of fish and rinse well under cold water, then wash well under hot water and detergent. Dry well.

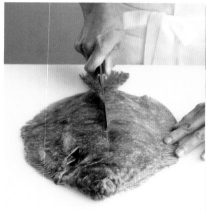

1 Cutting along the natural line down the middle of the fish from below the head to the tail.

2 Cutting across the top of the tail.

3 Cutting beneath the gill and head.

4 Carefully cutting the fillet away from the bone.

5 Lifting the fillet as it is released.

6 Gripping the edge of the skin and pulling the fillet away from the body.

7 Inserting the knife on the right side of the back bone before starting to remove the second fillet.

8 Repeating the filleting process on the pale underside to remove the other 2 fillets.

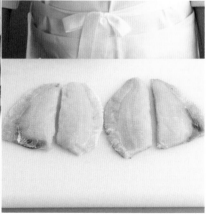

9 The 4 fish fillets removed from the frame, ready to skin if required (see overleaf).

Skinning a flat fish

If necessary, first wipe over the fillets with kitchen paper to ensure they are dry.

1 Place a fillet skin side down on the board with the narrow end towards you. There is a natural break between the fillet and the frill. Use the tip of a finger to identify and open this. Cut down this line to remove the frill on all 4 fillets. As you become more confident with your fish filleting and skinning skills, it may not be necessary to remove the frill first; it will naturally come away as the fillet is skinned.

2 Take a little salt in the fingers of your non-knife hand and hold onto the end of the fillet tightly. Insert the knife between the skin and flesh, just in front of your fingers, at a 30–40° angle.

3 Now, holding firmly onto the skin, move the knife decisively to the left and right using an exaggerated sawing action, while maintaining a firm pressure with the knife on the fish skin, to start to release the flesh from the skin.

4 As you release more flesh adjust the position of the fingers holding the skin closer to the unreleased flesh. It is important to firmly press the knife blade against the skin, which is against the board. Work your way up the fillet like this, releasing the flesh as a whole fillet. Take care not to hold the knife blade too vertically or you will cut through the skin, but too flat against the skin and you will leave flesh on the skin; it takes some practice.

5 Repeat with the remaining 3 fillets. Wipe down the board with kitchen paper and lay the fillets on the board. Once skinned, trim the fillets as necessary, without wasting fish.

6 Feel the fillets all over for bones. Usually this method of filleting leaves the fillets bone free, but it is always good to check. Remove any small bones that you find with kitchen tweezers. The fillets are now ready to use.

Note When skinning, we find it easier to move the knife hand back and forwards, but, as with filleting, if you find it more comfortable to hold your knife hand steady and move the hand holding the skin from side to side, use this technique. You should adopt the method that feels the most comfortable and safest for you, and one that prevents wastage. It is easier to remove the darker skin from the fillets than the paler skin.

Presentation

Generally, when referring to fish, the non-skin side (the bone side) is the best looking side once cooked and will become the presentation side. The skin side generally has a little brown flesh under the skin which is evident after skinning. It also often has a 'V' pattern. You should cook the non-skin presentation side first, as this will almost always end up being the best looking and most appetising side.

When folding fillets, fold them skin side inwards, bone side outwards.

There are always exceptions. When grilling, you should grill the non-skin side last, as the second side of a grilled fillet is generally the better looking.

1 Finding the natural line between the fillet and the frill.

2 Holding the narrow end of the fillet firmly and inserting the knife at an angle between the skin and the fillet.

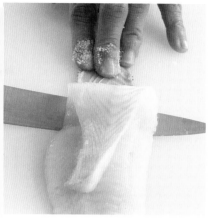

3 Working the fillet away from the skin, using a sawing action, while keeping the knife pressed firmly against the skin.

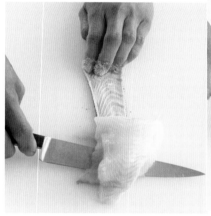

4 Holding the skin closer to the unreleased flesh as you work towards the other end.

5 Trimming the skinned fillets to neaten.

6 The skinned fillets now ready to cook.

Braising and baking

Here the fish is cooked in the oven, covered either with a tight-fitting lid or wrapped in foil, greaseproof paper or baking parchment. A small amount of liquid is added, which helps to retain moisture in the fish, and flavour the cooking liquor, which is more often than not used for a sauce to serve with the fish.

A gentle method of cooking, braising is often used to cook large pieces of meaty fish, such as tuna, or for shellfish such squid or octopus. It is a good alternative to poaching, and in both methods no colour is achieved on the fish.

Sometimes the term baking is used interchangeably with roasting, where fish is cooked in a hot oven and browned in the process.

Sole bonne femme

Serves 4
3 lemon sole, each about 350–450g
2 shallots
150g button mushrooms
40g butter
300ml white wine
450ml fish stock (see page 100)
1 lemon
Salt and ground white pepper

For the sauce
40g butter
20g plain flour
100ml double cream

For the chanterelles
150g small chanterelle mushrooms
30g butter
Freshly ground black pepper

To finish
Small handful of micro salad or small
  salad leaves

1 Heat the oven to 180°C/gas mark 4.

2 Fillet and skin the lemon sole (see pages 258–61). Lightly salt the skin side and fold each fillet loosely into three, skin side inside, to create an even thickness of fish. This is called a delice.

3 Halve, peel and finely dice the shallots. Wipe over and thinly slice the button mushrooms, and the chanterelles to be used later. Melt the 40g butter in a small saucepan over a low heat, add the shallots and sweat until soft and translucent. Once softened, turn up the heat, add the button mushrooms and sauté for 2–3 minutes without allowing the shallots to colour.

4 Add the wine and reduce by one-third, to about 200ml, then add the stock and reduce briskly by half. Meanwhile, juice the lemon. Taste the reduced liquor and very lightly season with salt, white pepper and lemon juice. Avoid adding too much seasoning at this stage as this liquid will be reduced further for the sauce.

5 Transfer the mixture to a shallow ovenproof dish and place the folded fish fillets on top. Cover with a cartouche (see page 13) and a lid and bake in the oven for 15–20 minutes until the fish is cooked; check that the fish is opaque in colour through to the centre. Lift the fillets onto a plate, cover with the cartouche and keep warm in a low oven.

6 Strain the cooking liquor into a saucepan, discarding the mushrooms and shallots. Reduce the liquor to about 300ml, or until the flavour tastes concentrated.

7 For the sauce, melt half the butter in a medium saucepan over a low heat, then add the flour and cook for 2–4 minutes until straw coloured. Remove from the heat and gradually add the reduced cooking liquor, stirring to avoid lumps. Return to the heat and bring to the boil, stirring, then lower the heat and simmer for 2 minutes.

8 Add the cream to create a lightly coating consistency, then beat in the remaining butter, to enrich the sauce and give it a shine. Add salt and white pepper to taste.

9 To cook the chanterelles, heat the butter in a frying pan over a medium to high heat, add the chanterelles and quickly sauté for 1–2 minutes. Season with salt and pepper to taste.

10 Divide the fish between 4 plates, 3 fillets per person, pour a little of the sauce over and around the fish and sprinkle with the chanterelles and micro salad.

Note Turning a fillet into a delice (a skinned fillet of fish folded loosely into three with the skin side innermost) allows the fish to cook more evenly.

Poaching

This is a very gentle method of cooking fish, and ideal for healthier diets as it requires no additional fat. Poaching involves submerging the fish in liquid and cooking either on the hob or in the oven at a very low heat, so there is very little movement of liquid. It is suitable for fish that can easily break up if subjected to a lot of movement. It can help to retain moisture in fish and the poaching liquor is often used to make a sauce to accompany the fish.

Ideally, the poaching liquid should be cool before the fish is added and the heat then increased slowly to ensure even cooking. If placed in a hot liquid, the outside of the fish cooks quickly, and by the time the inside is cooked, the outside can be overcooked. Larger pieces of fish or whole fish are best suited to poaching. To poach a large, whole fish such as a salmon you will need either a fish kettle or a large roasting tin.

The poaching liquid can be stock, milk or a court bouillon (see page 267); adding flavourings to the poaching liquid further benefits the fish.

Halibut with brown shrimp, pea and tomato butter

Serves 4
1 plum tomato
50g petit pois, frozen or fresh
½ bunch of chervil
57g pot of potted shrimps
60g butter
500ml fish stock (see page 100)
50ml white wine
1 bay leaf
Few black peppercorns
4 halibut fillets, each about 170g
Squeeze of lemon juice (optional)
Salt and freshly ground black pepper

1 Blanch the tomato in boiling water for 10 seconds, then refresh in cold water, dry and peel. Quarter and deseed, then cut it into fine dice (concasse).

2 Cook the peas in a small saucepan of simmering, salted water for 1–3 minutes until tender, then drain. Separate the chervil stalks from the leaves, retaining both.

3 Rinse out and dry the saucepan, add the potted shrimps and butter and melt over a low heat.

4 Put the stock, wine, chervil stalks, bay leaf, a few peppercorns and a pinch of salt in a frying pan. Skin the fish fillets (see page 260), place in the poaching liquor and put a dampened cartouche (see page 13) over the fish. Bring just to a simmer, remove from the heat and set aside for 5–7 minutes, for the fish to continue to cook in the residual heat of the liquid. You may need to turn the fish over to finish the cooking.

5 Meanwhile, to make the sauce, add the peas to the shrimps and melted butter. Coarsely chop enough chervil leaves to give you 1–2 tsp, and add to the pan. Taste and adjust the seasoning, adding lemon juice if necessary. Add the diced tomato to warm through.

6 Remove the fish from the poaching liquor and drain well. Place a fish fillet on each of 4 plates, bone side uppermost, and spoon a little of the shrimp, pea and tomato butter over the fish. Serve immediately.

Variations

Poached halibut with tomato and basil infused butter Omit the peas and potted shrimp. Use 2 tomatoes, increase the butter to 100g and replace the chervil with ¼ bunch of basil, adding the stalks to the poaching liquor and the leaves, chiffonaded (see page 89), to the butter sauce as for the main recipe.

Poached halibut with sauce vierge Serve a sauce vierge (see page 291) with the poached fish.

Brill, squid and clam stew

Serves 4
500g brill fillet
250g squid
500g clams
1 onion
1 leek
½ fennel bulb
2 garlic cloves
6 plum tomatoes
3 tbsp olive oil
1 tbsp sun-dried tomato paste
200ml white wine
600ml fish stock (see page 100)
Few thyme sprigs
1 bay leaf
Small bunch of flat-leaf parsley
Sugar, salt and freshly ground black
  pepper

1 Skin the brill fillet (see page 260) and cut into large bite-sized pieces. Prepare the squid (see page 248) and cut the body into thick rings, about 2cm. Scrub the clams and wash them several times in a large bowl of water. Refrigerate everything until needed.

2 Halve, peel and finely slice the onion. Trim and finely slice the leek and fennel. Peel and crush the garlic. Blanch the tomatoes in boiling water for 10 seconds, then refresh in cold water, dry, peel and roughly chop.

3 Heat the olive oil in a large saucepan. Add the onion, leek and fennel and cook over a low to medium heat until soft and just starting to brown. Add the garlic and cook for a further minute. Add the sun-dried tomato paste, chopped tomatoes and wine and bring to the boil.

4 Add the stock, thyme sprigs and bay leaf. Bring to the boil, reduce the heat and simmer for 15 minutes. Meanwhile, roughly chop enough parsley leaves to give you 2 tbsp. Season the sauce with sugar, salt and pepper. Stir in the clams and 1 tbsp chopped parsley and simmer for 3 minutes.

5 Add the fish and squid and simmer for a further 5 minutes, or until the fish is just cooked. When cooked, the brill and squid will have turned opaque and the clams will have opened. Discard any unopened clams. Take care not to overcook the fish.

6 Adjust the seasoning, remove the thyme sprigs and bay leaf and sprinkle the remaining parsley over before serving. This is delicious served with toasted slices of French bread topped with rouille (see page 131).

Variations

Simple bouillabaisse Use a mixture of Mediterranean fish such as gurnard, grey mullet, red mullet, monkfish and mussels in place of the brill and clams. Retain the squid. Add a few saffron strands, a strip of finely pared orange zest and 25–50ml Pernod with the wine.

Quick fish cassoulet Slice 6 derinded rashers of smoked bacon into strips and fry with the onion, leek and fennel. Proceed as for the main recipe and once the stock, thyme and bay leaf have been added, simmer for 20–25 minutes until the liquid has reduced a little. Add the clams and half the parsley and cook for 3 minutes, then add the fish and squid and a drained 400g tin cannellini beans. Simmer until the fish is cooked and the beans are hot. To finish, fry 100g fresh white breadcrumbs in 30g butter until golden brown and crunchy, then sprinkle over the finished cassoulet with the remaining parsley.

Skate with brown butter and capers

Serves 4

4 skate wings, each about 200–250g
150g unsalted butter
½ lemon
½ tbsp water
1 tbsp small capers in brine, drained
   and rinsed
Salt and freshly ground black pepper

For the court bouillon

1 carrot
1 onion
1 celery stick
500ml water
150ml white wine vinegar
10 black peppercorns
2 bay leaves
Good pinch of salt

1 To make the court bouillon, peel and slice the carrot. Halve, peel and slice the onion and slice the celery. Put into a large saucepan with the remaining ingredients and bring to a simmer over a medium to high heat.

2 Simmer for 15–20 minutes, then top up with cold water to make the liquid quantity up to 1 litre. Set aside to cool, then transfer to a shallow pan. The vegetables can be strained out or left in.

3 Wash the skate wings, trim the tapering thin end with a pair of scissors to neaten them, then place in the cold court bouillon. Bring slowly to the boil over a medium heat, then turn down to a bare simmer. Cover and cook very gently for 12–20 minutes, depending on the size and thickness of the skate. It is cooked when the thickest flesh comes away easily from the cartilage. Meanwhile, heat the oven to 120°C/gas mark ½.

4 Remove the skate and drain on kitchen paper, then transfer to a board. You may need to pull away the thick top end of the cartilage. There is a fine membrane and a pale brown flesh that covers the skate flesh; it is best to remove this before serving and it is easier to remove after cooking. Using a fish filleting knife, gently scrape away the membrane, ensuring you aren't wasting too much of the white flesh. Turn the wing over and repeat on the second side. Beneath the membrane will be the long white grain of the skate. Transfer to serving plates and keep warm in the low oven while you make the sauce.

5 Discard the court bouillon and return the pan to the heat. Add the butter and melt. Meanwhile, juice the ½ lemon and mix ½ tbsp lemon juice with the ½ tbsp water. When the butter is foaming, rich golden brown and smells very nutty and biscuity (beurre noisette), remove the pan from the heat and add the lemon juice and water mixture with the capers. Taste and adjust the balance if necessary with a little lemon juice, then add salt and pepper to taste, bearing in mind that the capers are salty.

6 Pour the sauce over the skate wings and serve.

Note It is possible to remove the fillets of skate from the cartilage before serving. Ease it off the cartilage from the thick end, the full length of the thick end. Then, supporting both the fillet and the cartilage, continue to ease the fillet from the cartilage and roll it into a cylinder. Repeat on the second side of the wing.

Variations

You can replace the lemon juice with red wine vinegar, and/or add some finely chopped herbs, such as flat-leaf parsley, chives and chervil, with the capers.

....

Court bouillon

A court bouillon is an acidulated cooking liquor, most often used to poach fish. The acidity in this recipe is white wine vinegar, but white wine or lemon juice can be substituted for the vinegar. The vegetables and bay leaves add flavour and the court bouillon should be lightly seasoned. Parsley stalks and other vegetables may be used to flavour a court bouillon.

Steaming

Steaming is perfect for cooking delicate pieces of fish or small, whole fish. It is a very healthy method, as it uses no fat and there is minimal vitamin and mineral loss, because the fish sits over, not in, the liquid when it is being steamed. The liquid used to steam the fish can be flavoured with spices and aromatics to help flavour the fish.

If you do not have a proper steamer, you can use a large saucepan with a trivet in the bottom, with the fish on a small heatproof plate placed on the trivet. Alternatively, bamboo steamers of various sizes are widely available. When using a bamboo steamer, place the fish on a square of non-stick baking parchment to avoid the bamboo absorbing the fish flavour.

Always ensure the steamer has a tight-fitting lid so little or no steam can escape. The liquid should be kept at a constant generous simmer to ensure enough steam is created to cook the fish quickly.

Plaice with a tomato and sorrel dressing

Serves 4

1 small banana shallot
1 garlic clove
2 ripe plum tomatoes
75ml olive oil
3 plaice, each about 350–450g
½ lemon
1 tbsp red wine vinegar, or to taste
5–6 sorrel leaves
Salt and freshly ground black pepper
1 quantity wilted spinach (see page 60), to serve

1 Halve, peel and very finely dice the shallot. Peel and crush the garlic. Blanch the tomatoes in boiling water for 10 seconds, then refresh in cold water, dry and peel. Quarter and deseed, then cut into fine dice (concasse). Set aside until needed.

2 Heat the olive oil in a small saucepan over a low heat, then add the shallot. Cook very gently until softened, then add the garlic and cook for 1 minute. Remove from the heat and set aside to cool.

3 Fillet and skin the plaice (see pages 258–61), giving 12 fillets (3 per person). Juice the ½ lemon.

4 Season the skin side of each fillet with salt and a few drops of lemon juice and fold loosely into three, skin side inside, so the fish is an even thickness. Place all the folded fillets in a steamer set over a saucepan of simmering water and steam for 3–5 minutes until cooked. The fish is ready when it has turned opaque and firmed a little to the touch. Ensure the inside of the folds are cooked.

5 Meanwhile, to finish the dressing, add the wine vinegar to the shallot and garlic. Finely chiffonade the sorrel (see page 89) and add to the dressing with the diced tomato. Taste and season with salt, pepper and lemon juice or extra wine vinegar.

6 Place 3 mounds of wilted spinach on each of 4 plates, top with 3 fillets of plaice and spoon a little of the dressing over the fish. (Or arrange on 1 or 2 platters.) Serve immediately.

Note The sorrel will discolour very quickly, so only prepare it immediately before you add it to the dressing, ensuring too that the oil is cool before you add it.
If sorrel is not available, basil is a good substitute, or you could use a little finely grated lemon zest.

Skinning and preparing a flat fish before cooking, to be served on the bone

Small flat fish can be skinned prior to cooking whole. Note that flat fish are often sold already gutted, but sometimes the roe is left in the gut area.

First rinse the fish under cold water and dry with kitchen paper.

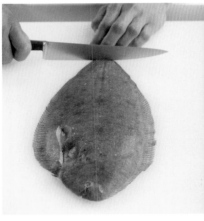

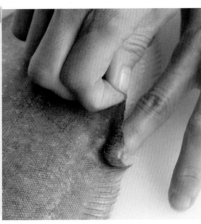

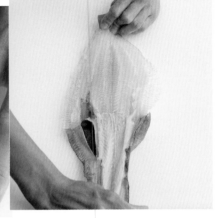

1 Place the fish on a board with the tail end towards you. Using a small knife, make a shallow cut just above the tail.

2 Using the tip of a fingernail, push the skin up from the flesh a little, particularly over the frill. Insert a fingertip between the skin and the frill and release the skin up the entire side of the fish. Repeat on the other side.

3 Salt the fingers to get a good grip on the skin and hold the tail tightly with the fingers of one hand. With the other hand, hold the released skin firmly at the tail end and pull away from you horizontally. Repeat the skinning process on the other side.

4 Check the cavity and gut the fish if necessary; the roe and gut can be pulled out of the belly from behind the gills. Alternatively, release the flesh along the frill line on both sides to open the belly area up. (If serving with the head on, remove the gills at this stage.) Rinse the fish under cold water to clean the belly area, then dry. The fish is now ready to cook.

5 After cooking and while the fish is still on its baking tray, use a small knife to draw the frill bones away from between both fillets on each side of the fish, leaving just the fillets on the bone. Remove the head at this stage (unless you prefer to leave it on).

6 Carefully lift the fish onto a plate to serve.

Grilling

When grilling fish, you need to heat the grill to its hottest setting to achieve colour quickly, while ensuring the fish retains moisture. It can take up to about 10 minutes for a grill to heat properly. Basting the fish as it grills will also help to brown it and keep it moist. Once it is browned, you may need to lower the grill shelf to allow the fish to cook through.

Grilling is best suited to small pieces, or fillets, of fish. Remove the fish from the fridge ahead of grilling to bring it up to room temperature, or the browning can be so quick that the centre remains cold. If the fillets are thin they will probably not need to be turned over, particularly if using a metal baking sheet, as the heat from the grill will be conducted to the underside of the fish.

If the fish is thick (more than 2–3cm), the best option to avoid burning the fish is to grill it until browned, then transfer it to an oven preheated to 180°C/gas mark 4 to finish the cooking. This is particularly useful if you are cooking a large quantity of fish in batches.

When grilling fish with the skin on, score the skin several times with a very sharp knife to prevent it from buckling under the grill.

Slip sole with burnt hollandaise

Serves 2
2 slip soles
½ quantity freshly made hollandaise
  (see page 120)
10g butter, to grease
½ lemon
Salt

To serve (optional)
1 lemon

1 Skin and prepare the slip soles to be cooked on the bone (see left, steps 1–4), then set aside.

2 Keep the hollandaise warm in a bain marie off the heat while you heat the grill to its highest setting.

3 Butter a baking tray and lay the fish on it. Juice the ½ lemon. Season the fish with salt and a little lemon juice, then grill for 4–5 minutes. The heat generated by the tray will cook the underside. Cut the lemon, if serving, into wedges.

4 Once the fish are cooked, remove the frill and head, if desired (see left, step 5).

5 Place the fish on individual serving plates, coat with the hollandaise and briefly grill to brown the hollandaise a little. Take care not to leave the fish under the heat for too long or the hollandaise will split. Serve with lemon wedges.

Note A slip sole is a small Dover sole, generally a perfect size for a single portion.

Lemon wedges
To prepare lemon wedges, cut off the very ends of the lemon. Cut the lemon into quarters, then each quarter in half again lengthways to create 8 wedges. Place each lemon wedge on the board flat side down and trim the inner central membrane away, then remove any pips.

Pan-frying

Pan-frying is a very quick method of cooking small pieces of fish in a minimal quantity of fat (butter and/or oil) and helps to add colour and texture to the dish, creating a good brown crust on the fish. Butter provides flavour but burns easily; adding a little oil helps to raise the temperature at which butter burns, allowing a longer cooking time.

A non-stick pan is ideal for pan-frying, as the skin and fish are not damaged by sticking to the pan. If you don't have a non-stick pan, a pan can be 'proved', or made non-stick (see page 70).

Use a large, shallow pan so that the fish can be easily manoeuvred, and avoid overcrowding the pan by trying to fry too much at a time.

Thin fillets will generally need an equal cooking time on both sides, but if the fillet is thick, most of the cooking can be done on the presentation side, then turned over and briefly cooked presentation side uppermost or transferred to the oven (if using an ovenproof frying pan) to finish the cooking at 180°C/gas mark 4.

The recipe below uses skinned fillets, dusted in seasoned flour to prevent sticking and to encourage a brown crust.

Plaice, cucumber and girolles with rosemary cream sauce

Serves 4

1 cucumber
200g girolles
8 plaice fillets, each about 130–150g
40g butter
150g plain flour, seasoned with a large
 pinch of salt
Salt and freshly ground black pepper

For the sauce

1 shallot
15g butter
150ml dry white wine
200ml fish stock (see page 100)
½ small rosemary sprig, plus extra
 to taste
100ml double cream
A squeeze of lemon juice, to taste

1 To make the sauce, halve, peel and finely dice the shallot. Melt the butter in a small saucepan, add the shallot and sweat over a low heat until soft and translucent. Increase the heat to medium to high and add the wine. Reduce by two-thirds, then lower the heat, add the stock and rosemary, and simmer for 5–10 minutes. Add the cream and simmer gently until just a very light coating consistency. Taste and season, then strain the sauce, discarding the shallot and rosemary. (The sauce can be made in advance and reheated to serve.)

2 Halve and deseed the cucumber and, using a very small melon baller, about 5–7mm in diameter, scoop out little balls of cucumber flesh. Clean the girolles and tear into small bite-sized pieces; set both aside.

3 Skin and trim the plaice fillets, if necessary (see pages 258–61) and heat the oven to 120°C/gas mark ½.

4 Heat through the sauce, adding a pinch of very finely chopped rosemary to revive the flavour if necessary; it should be subtle, not overpowering. Add a few drops of lemon juice to taste, if needed, then keep the sauce warm over a very low heat. If it looks very thick, add a small splash of water to return it to the correct consistency.

5 Heat half the butter in a large frying pan over a medium to high heat. Add the girolles and sauté quickly for 2–3 minutes to soften a little and drive off the excess moisture. Add the cucumber and sauté for a further 1 minute; it should still have a little bite to it. Transfer to a plate lined with kitchen paper and keep warm in the low oven.

6 Wipe out the frying pan and heat half the remaining butter in it. Coat the fish fillets in the seasoned flour, dusting off any excess, and pan-fry in 2 (or 3) batches, transferring the cooked fillets to the low oven to keep warm while you pan-fry the rest, and adding more butter to the pan as necessary.

7 Place 2 plaice fillets on each plate. Spoon the warm sauce around the fish and scatter over the girolles and cucumber. Grind over some pepper and serve.

Sole meunière

Serves 4

¼ bunch of flat-leaf parsley
¼ bunch of chives
¼ bunch of tarragon
¼ bunch of dill
½ lemon
1½ tbsp water
3 lemon sole, each about 350–450g
150g plain flour, seasoned with a large
 pinch of salt
160g slightly salted butter
Flaked sea salt and freshly ground
 black pepper

1 Finely chop enough mixed herb leaves to give you 2 tbsp; set aside. Squeeze 1 tbsp juice from the ½ lemon and mix the lemon juice with the 1½ tbsp water; set aside. Heat the oven to 120°C/gas mark ½.

2 Fillet and skin the lemon sole (see pages 258–61), giving 12 fillets (3 per person).

3 Put the seasoned flour on a tray and dust the sole fillets in the flour, shaking off any excess; you want only a very thin film of flour.

4 Heat 20g of the butter in a large, shallow frying pan over a medium heat and pan-fry 4 fillets, boned side down for 1–2 minutes. Allow the sole to become golden before carefully inserting a palette knife under the full length of the fillet and turning. Cook on the second side for 1–2 minutes, depending on thickness, then remove to a plate and keep warm in the low oven. (This first batch can be slightly underdone as it will continue to cook in the warming oven.)

5 Wipe out the pan with kitchen paper, heat another 20g butter and repeat the process with another 4 fillets, transferring them to the oven. Repeat with the remaining fillets.

6 Working quickly, as the fish is cooked, wipe out the pan again and melt the remaining 100g butter in it. Cook until it starts to foam, is a rich golden brown and smells nutty and biscuity (beurre noisette). Add the lemon juice and water mixture to the pan; it will bubble vigorously. Season, taste and adjust if necessary. Take the pan off the heat, add the chopped herbs and swirl through the sauce.

7 Remove the fish from the oven, divide between 4 plates and pour a little of the sauce over the fillets. Serve immediately.

Brill with a cider mustard sauce and apple and fennel salad

Serves 4

4 skinless brill fillets, each about 170g
½ tbsp olive oil
60g butter
20ml cider
¼ tsp wholegrain mustard, or to taste
Few drops of cider vinegar
Salt and freshly ground black pepper

For the salad

1 fennel bulb, with tops
1 Granny Smith apple
½ tbsp cider vinegar
3 tbsp olive oil
1–2 tbsp mustard cress

1 For the salad, trim the root end off the fennel and the ends off the tops. Shave the fennel into very thin slices with a sharp knife, or use a mandolin, and place in a bowl. Quarter, core and very thinly slice the apple; add to the fennel.

2 Add a pinch each of salt and pepper to the cider vinegar and whisk in the olive oil. Taste and adjust the seasoning for balance, then stir it through the apple and fennel, making sure they are evenly coated. Heat the oven to 120°C/gas mark ½.

3 Season the brill fillets lightly with salt. Heat a non-stick frying pan over a low to medium heat, add the olive oil and 10g of the butter. When hot, add the seasoned fish, boned side down, and cook until caramelised and golden. By this time the fish will be almost cooked through. Lower the heat, turn the fish over and continue to cook until opaque throughout, 2–3 minutes. Remove to a plate and keep warm in the low oven.

4 Pour off any excess fat from the frying pan and wipe out with kitchen paper. Add the remaining 50g butter to the pan and melt over a medium heat. When starting to foam, add the cider and bring back to a simmer. Take off the heat and add the mustard. Taste and adjust the seasoning with salt, pepper and cider vinegar.

5 Add the mustard cress to the salad, toss to coat in the dressing, taste and adjust the seasoning. Place a piece of fish on each of 4 plates, spoon a little of the cider butter sauce over the fish and top with a small handful of the salad.

Roasting

This method of cooking is best for larger pieces of fish or whole fish, particularly when the fish is larger than any of your frying pans. Roasting involves heating the oven to a high heat to achieve colour and to cook the fish through quickly. Fish can be basted while roasting to ensure it stays moist.

For smaller cuts or fillets, fish is often pan-fried first to achieve browning, then roasted in the oven to finish the cooking.

Halibut tronçons with lentils

Serves 4
200g Puy lentils
2 banana shallots
2 garlic cloves
½ carrot
¼ bunch of sage
¼ bunch of thyme
½ bunch of flat-leaf parsley
2 tomatoes
Very small pinch of crushed dried chillies
300ml chicken and veal stock (see page 96)
4 halibut tronçons (cut across the fillet with the bone in), each about 200g
180ml olive oil
½ lemon
1 tsp sherry vinegar
Salt and freshly ground black pepper

1 Rinse the lentils and soak them in cold water for 30 minutes.

2 Halve and peel the shallots, then quarter one and finely dice the second. Bash 1 unpeeled garlic clove with the flat side of a large knife; peel and crush the other clove. Peel the carrot and cut in half lengthways. Finely chop enough sage and thyme leaves to give you 1½ tsp each, and enough parsley to give you 1–2 tbsp.

3 Blanch the tomatoes in boiling water for 10 seconds, then refresh in cold water, dry and peel. Quarter, deseed and cut into fine dice (concasse).

4 Drain the lentils and put into a saucepan with the quartered shallot, bashed garlic, carrot, a sprig each of sage, thyme and parsley, and the crushed dried chillies. Pour in the stock. Bring to a simmer and gently cook, uncovered, until the lentils are tender (not breaking up but not with too much of a bite), about 15–20 minutes. Remove from the heat and set aside for the lentils to cool in the stock.

5 While the lentils are cooking, put the halibut in a bowl and add ½–1 tsp each of the chopped sage and thyme and 2 tbsp olive oil. Finely grate the zest from the lemon over the fish. Rub the halibut steaks in the herbs, zest and oil and leave to marinate for 20 minutes. Heat the oven to 220°C/gas mark 7 and the grill to its highest setting.

6 Meanwhile, for the lentil dressing, heat the remaining olive oil in a medium saucepan over a low heat. Add the diced shallot and cook gently for 5–10 minutes until soft and translucent. Add the crushed garlic and cook for 1 minute to soften. Add ¼ tsp each of the remaining chopped sage and thyme, with the sherry vinegar. Taste and season well (it needs to be boldly flavoured as it will be added to the lentils), then set aside.

7 Season the halibut tronçons and place in a roasting tin. Pour over any marinade and roast in the oven for 10–15 minutes. The fish will change from translucent to opaque and feel firm to the touch. Remove the halibut and place under the grill for 1–2 minutes to colour the skin, then set aside to rest for 2–3 minutes. Pour any juices from the tin into the lentil dressing.

8 Meanwhile, reheat the dressing over a low to medium heat. Drain the lentils, discarding everything but the lentils. Add the drained lentils to the warmed dressing and stir to coat evenly and warm through. Taste and adjust the seasoning, adding sherry vinegar or olive oil if necessary. Finally, stir through the chopped tomatoes and parsley.

9 Divide the lentils between 4 plates and top with a piece of halibut. Drizzle any remaining dressing over the halibut and serve immediately.

Preparing a flat fish to cook whole, skin on and on the bone

1 Rinse the fish under cold water, dry with kitchen paper and place on a board. Remove the gills.

2 Check the cavity for guts and roe. More often than not, flat fish will already have been gutted, but if not, make an incision behind the gills.

3 Pull the guts and roe out of the belly; make an incision along the edge of the fillet on the join with the frill to release them if necessary. Rinse the fish under cold water again and dry.

Roasted whole brill with thyme

Serves 4
Bunch of thyme
5–6 bay leaves
1 large lemon
1 brill, about 1.5–1.75kg
100ml extra virgin olive oil
75ml white wine
Salt and freshly ground black pepper

1 Heat the oven to 220°C/gas mark 7. Sprinkle half the thyme, the bay leaves and some salt and pepper in a shallow roasting tin. Slice the lemon and add half the slices to the tin.

2 Prepare the fish for cooking whole (as shown above). Tuck the remaining thyme and lemon slices in the cavity. Make an incision along the top of the edge of the fillet where it joins the frill. Lay the fish on top of the thyme, bay and lemon and drizzle 2 tbsp olive oil over the skin. Season well with salt and pepper.

3 Roast in the top third of the oven for 15 minutes. Remove the fish and check; the flesh should just be starting to come away from the bone, just behind the head.

4 Drizzle the remaining olive oil and the wine over the fish and return to the oven for 5–10 minutes. The skin should lift away from the flesh and the flesh should be coming away easily from the bone just behind the head. (If preferred, the fish can be placed under a hot grill for this last 5–10 minutes to crisp and brown the skin.)

5 Carefully lift the fish onto a serving platter and pour over the juices from the tin.

6 To serve, cut down the middle of the back to the bone (as shown right), then release the fillets from the bones on both sides. Slide a fish slice under the fillets and lift off (as shown), then pull the bone from the bottom fillets, divide and serve.

Note If you prefer a more natural finish, don't cut along the edge of the fillet by the frill, so allowing the skin to shrink and crack during the cooking.

Variations

Any large flat fish, such as turbot or halibut, can be used and the thyme can be replaced with rosemary or tarragon.

Whole roast brill with tomatoes and capers Place 5–6 vines of small tomatoes around the fish in the roasting tin. Sprinkle over 1–2 tbsp very small rinsed capers and proceed as for the main recipe.

Skate wing with cauliflower purée and hazelnut and parsley butter

Serves 4

4 skate wings, each about 200–250g
150g butter
30g hazelnuts
½ bunch of flat-leaf parsley
1 tbsp red wine vinegar

For the cauliflower purée

1 small cauliflower
1 onion
1 garlic clove
30g butter
Pinch of sweet paprika
750ml milk
75ml double cream (optional)
Salt and ground white pepper

1 For the cauliflower purée, cut the cauliflower into florets and the central core into slices. Halve, peel and finely slice the onion, and peel and crush the garlic.

2 Melt the butter in a heavy-based saucepan, add the onion, cover with a damp cartouche (see page 13) and sweat over a gentle heat until softened. Remove the cartouche, add the cauliflower, garlic and paprika and cook for 2 minutes. Add the milk and season lightly with salt and white pepper. Simmer until the cauliflower is soft, 15–20 minutes.

3 Leave the mixture to cool slightly, then transfer to a blender and blitz until very smooth. This may take quite a long time and you may need to add a little of the cooking liquor to help the process. Pass through a sieve into a clean saucepan, taste and adjust the seasoning. Add the cream to enrich the purée, if you like. Heat the oven to 200°C/gas mark 6.

4 Wash the skate wings, dry with kitchen paper and trim the tapering thin end with a pair of scissors to neaten them. Melt half the butter in a large ovenproof frying pan or roasting tin over a medium to high heat. Season the skate and brown on both sides, about 1–2 minutes per side.

5 Transfer the frying pan or roasting tin to the oven and roast for 8–12 minutes, depending on size and thickness; the skate is cooked when it comes away from the cartilage. Place the hazelnuts on a baking tray and toast in the oven with the skate for 5 minutes, then remove to a board and lightly crush with the flat of a large knife or a rolling pin. Coarsely chop enough parsley leaves to give you 1 tbsp.

6 Transfer the cooked skate to a plate, and keep it warm in a low oven while you make the sauce. Place the frying pan or roasting tin over a medium heat and add the remaining butter to the skate cooking juices. As soon as the butter foams, add the wine vinegar and let bubble for 1 minute. Taste and adjust the balance, adding a little more vinegar if necessary. Add the toasted hazelnuts and parsley, then season to taste.

7 Divide the cauliflower purée between 4 plates, place a skate wing on each plate and spoon over the hazelnut and parsley butter.

Variations

Alternatively, for a similar combination of flavours, serve the skate with roasted cauliflower with beurre noisette, almonds and sherry vinegar (see page 47).

Skate wing with Jerusalem artichoke purée and hazelnut and parsley butter
Replace the cauliflower with Jerusalem artichokes. Peel them and proceed as for the main recipe.

Skate wing with meunière sauce Omit the cauliflower purée and hazelnut and parsley butter. Once the skate wings are cooked, keep them warm in a low oven, wipe out the roasting tin, then melt 150g unsalted butter in it over a low to medium heat. Once coloured to noisette (a deep toffee colour), add 1 tbsp red wine vinegar mixed with ½ tbsp water. Add 1–2 tbsp rinsed, small capers. Taste and adjust the seasoning with salt and pepper and more wine vinegar, if necessary. Stir in 1–2 tbsp coarsely chopped mixed herbs, such as flat-leaf parsley, chives and dill. Pour over the skate wings and serve immediately.

Deep-frying

This quick method of cooking at a very high heat is best for tiny whole fish, such as whitebait, and small pieces or fillets of larger fish. Flavourless oils, such as a vegetable or groundnut oil, are best and should not be re-used, unless for fish frying once or twice more, as the flavour of the fish will transfer to the oil.

Coating fish in a wet batter or dry crumb before deep-frying protects the fish from the high heat of the oil and helps retain its moisture and tenderness, resulting in a pleasing contrast in texture between the crisp coating and the softness of the fish underneath. Dusting the fish in flour before coating in a wet batter ensures the batter adheres to the fish. For a dry crumb, the fish is first dusted in flour, then egg, then crumb to ensure an even coating.

When deep-frying small pieces of coated fish, cook only a few at a time, as the oil temperature drops very quickly once cool food is placed in it, and deep-frying at a low temperature causes the coating to soak up oil, resulting in greasy food.

For more information on the technique of deep-frying, including testing the temperature of the oil if your deep-fat fryer is not thermostatically controlled and safety issues, see page 72.

Goujons of sole

Serves 4 as a starter
4 skinless white fish fillets, such as lemon sole, each about 170g
150g plain flour, mixed with a large pinch of salt
2 large eggs
150g fresh white breadcrumbs
Oil for deep-frying
Salt

To serve
1 lemon
300ml tartare sauce (see page 118)

1 Cut the fish fillets on the diagonal into finger-sized strips.

2 Spread the seasoned flour out on a plate. Crack the eggs into a bowl and beat to loosen. Spread the breadcrumbs out on another plate. Coat the fish pieces first in the flour, dusting off excess, then turn each piece through the beaten egg and finally coat with the breadcrumbs, ensuring they are fully and evenly coated.

3 As you coat each piece of fish with breadcrumbs, twist it in the middle (so it doesn't lie flat) and place on a wire rack set over a tray. Refrigerate, uncovered, for at least 15–20 minutes, for the coating to dry, which will help to keep it crisp. Heat the oven to 120°C/gas mark ½. Cut the lemon, for serving, into wedges.

4 One-third fill a large, deep, heavy saucepan with oil and heat to 190°–193°C, or until a small piece of bread dropped into the oil sizzles and browns in 30–40 seconds (see page 72).

5 Using a slotted spoon, carefully lower the goujons into the oil a few at a time and deep-fry for 2–3 minutes, depending on size, until crisp and golden. To check, break one in half and check the flesh is opaque throughout. Carefully remove the goujons from the oil and place on a tray lined with kitchen paper, to absorb excess oil. Sprinkle lightly with salt and transfer to the low oven, door ajar, to keep warm. Repeat with the remaining pieces of fish.

6 Serve the sole goujons with the tartare sauce and lemon wedges.

Variations

Goujons with dill mayonnaise Replace the tartare sauce with mayonnaise (see page 116) and stir in 1 tbsp finely chopped dill and ¼ tsp finely grated lemon zest.

Coriander goujons with chipotle mayonnaise Add 3 tbsp finely chopped coriander to the beaten eggs. Replace the tartare sauce with mayonnaise (see page 116) and stir in 1–2 tsp chipotle paste, to taste, before serving.

Chilli goujons with lime mayonnaise Add 1 tsp chilli powder to the seasoned flour. Replace the tartare sauce with mayonnaise (see page 116) and stir in the finely grated zest and juice of 1 lime.

Round fish

Round fish are characterised by the back bone running along the length of the body with a single fillet located on either side. The flesh can be oily (see page 300) or white. There are many white-fleshed species, including sea bass, cod, haddock, pollock, bream, John Dory and mullet.

Most white-fleshed round fish can be cooked whole, or filleted for easier serving. The delicate flavour of fish means that it can be prepared with little more than a squeeze of lemon and drizzle of olive oil, as long as it is not overcooked. However, its relatively mild character means that it can also happily take on different flavour combinations, and many round fish pair well with the bold flavours of Mediterranean cooking or the aromatics and spices of Asia.

Descaling and gutting a round fish

1 To descale the fish, put it inside a large plastic bag, head first (to prevent the scales flying everywhere as you remove them). Using a fish filleting knife upside down (the non-sharp side against the fish) and holding onto the fish tail, push backwards towards the head and the scales should flip off. Turn the fish over and repeat on the second side.

2 Once the scales are removed, take the fish out of the plastic bag and rinse under cold running water to remove any loose scales. Pat dry with kitchen paper.

3 Using a pair of kitchen scissors, cut off all the fins except the dorsal fin (in the middle on the back). The tail can be trimmed into a 'V' shape if you like.

4 Remove the gills on both sides, by opening the gill flaps and cutting round the back of the gills towards the body of the fish from the top of the fish down towards the belly.

5 To gut the fish, place one hand on the uppermost side of the fish to help keep the belly skin taut and insert the point of a filleting knife into the vent hole.

6 Cut up the middle of the belly of the fish to just behind the head. Don't push too deep with the knife or the guts will be cut into unnecessarily.

7 Open the belly and pull away the guts, including the heart and liver tucked just behind the head. You might need to snip these out using a pair of scissors.

8 Once the guts are removed, break the blood line with the handle of a teaspoon and scrape out all the blood under the back bone.

9 Rinse the fish and belly area well under cold running water to remove any blood. Wipe the fish out with kitchen paper. It is now ready to cook whole or to fillet.

1 Descaling the fish inside a large plastic bag.

2 Patting the fish dry after rinsing away any loose scales.

3 Cutting off the fins on the side of the head.

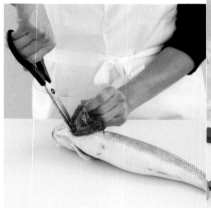

4 Cutting around the back of the gills to remove them.

5 Inserting the point of the knife into the vent hole to make a shallow cut along the belly.

6 Working the knife up towards the head, keeping the cut shallow.

7 Opening out the belly and removing the guts.

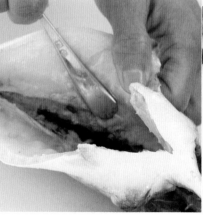

8 Using the handle of a teaspoon to break the blood line.

9 The cleaned whole fish ready to cook.

Baking

Honey baked sea bass with pickled ginger

Serves 4
¾ tsp Szechuan peppercorns
1 sea bass, about 1.5kg
2 tbsp clear honey
1 tbsp sunflower oil
Salt

For the marinade
1 garlic clove
1 lime
2 tbsp sesame oil
2 tbsp sake
½ tbsp pickled ginger (see below)
Salt and freshly ground black pepper

For the lime and ginger sauce
1 tbsp sesame seeds
1 tbsp pickled ginger
2 spring onions
Juice of 1 lime (from the lime zested
   for the marinade)

1 Heat the oven to 220°C/gas mark 7. Place the Szechuan peppercorns on a baking tray and roast in the oven for 5 minutes. Remove, tip onto a plate and set aside to cool.

2 Clean and gut the sea bass (see page 280). Using a sharp knife, cut 3 slashes in both sides of the fish and transfer to a dish. Lightly crush the toasted peppercorns using a pestle and mortar. Transfer to a small bowl and mix in the honey. Rub this mixture over the fish skin on both sides.

3 To make the marinade, peel and crush the garlic. Finely grate the zest of the lime, reserving the lime for the sauce. Put the garlic and lime zest in a small bowl with the remaining marinade ingredients. Mix together, then pour over and inside the fish. Cover and refrigerate for 30 minutes.

4 Place a large piece of foil on a baking tray and brush with the sunflower oil. Place the fish, with its marinade, on the foil. Season with salt and wrap loosely, securing the edges firmly, then bake in the oven for 20–25 minutes. It is cooked when the eyes are opaque and the dorsal fin will pull out easily. Check inside the cavity at the bone; the fish should be opaque.

5 Meanwhile, to make the lime and ginger sauce, scatter the sesame seeds on a baking tray and toast in the oven (with the fish) for 5 minutes, then tip onto a plate to cool. Finely shred the pickled ginger, trim and finely slice the spring onions and put both in a small bowl. Juice the reserved lime. Add the toasted sesame seeds and lime juice to the sauce and mix well.

6 When the fish is cooked, unwrap the foil. Either carefully transfer the fish to a warmed serving dish, pouring over any juice, or leave on the foil. Sprinkle the lime and ginger sauce over the fish to serve.

Variation

Honey baked sea bass with lemongrass and lime Omit the peppercorn rub and the marinade and sauce. Finely chop 3 lemongrass stalks, 2 garlic cloves, 2 red chillies (deseeded if preferred), and a 3cm piece of peeled fresh root ginger. Pound together with a pestle and mortar and add the juice and finely grated zest of 2 limes. Rub half the mixture in the belly of the fish and the rest over both sides of the prepared fish. Wrap and cook as for the main recipe. For the sauce, put the juice and finely grated zest of 1 lime in a bowl with 1 tsp palm (or brown) sugar and leave to dissolve. Add ½ tsp each of soy sauce and nam pla (fish sauce) and stir in 2 spring onions, finely sliced on the diagonal. The sauce should be sweet and sour and salty; adjust the flavourings as necessary. Pour over the cooked fish before serving.

....
To make your own pickled ginger...
Peel and very finely slice a 7.5cm piece of fresh root ginger. Marinate in 2 tbsp rice wine vinegar for 1 hour, or ideally overnight. Drain and use as required.

Filleting a round fish

Although with practice it is possible to fillet a round fish without removing its innards, gutting it first ensures the fillets are not contaminated by guts, should the knife cut through bones into the guts when filleting.

1 Descale and gut the fish (see page 280). Make a cut across the fish at an angle, below the gill flap and fin to the belly.

2 Keeping one hand pressing down firmly on the side of the fish, make a cut from behind the head along the top of the fish down its back, on top of the dorsal fin, to the tail. Use the whole back of the knife to do this, not just the point.

3 Using long strokes of the knife, release the top fillet, making sure the knife blade runs horizontally as closely as possible along the bones. Try to ensure that no fish is left on the bone. Take care coming to and over the back bone; make sure you are on top of the bone rather than under it. Also take care over the belly bones that they are not cut through or fish left on the bone.

4 Once you are over the belly bones, the fillet will come away cleanly. Put the fillet to one side while you work on the second fillet.

5 The second fillet is a little trickier to remove. Start with the exposed bone uppermost, and again make a cut from just behind the head parallel to the cut made for the first fillet, but this time work your knife just beneath the dorsal fin, cleanly cutting along the backbone from head to tail.

6 Now turn the fish over and, if you are able to, hang the fish's head over the side of the board to allow the main body of the fish to be flat against the board. Proceed as for the first fillet. Once the second fillet has been removed the frame can be discarded, or if it is a white fish, you can remove the head, rinse the frame and keep it for stock.

7 Place the fish fillets on a plate while you wash and dry the board. Put the fillets back on the board. Trim any excess fatty skin from the belly side, but keep the fillets as natural a shape as possible.

8 Run the tip of your finger along the middle of the fillet and you will feel the bones running close through the thickest part of the fillet. It is imperative that these are removed before further preparation or cooking.

9 Using a pair of kitchen tweezers, carefully pick out each bone, supporting the fillet as you do, to ensure only the bone and not fish is removed. Repeat with the remaining fillets. The fillets are now ready either for skinning (as for flat fish fillets, see page 260) or for cooking.

1 Making a cut across the fish at an angle, below the gill flap and fin to the belly.

2 Making a shallow cut from behind the head along the top of the dorsal fin to the tail.

3 Skimming the knife over the bones to free the top fillet.

4 Releasing the top fillet from the fish.

5 Cutting just beneath the dorsal fin from head to tail to free the second fillet.

6 With the fish turned onto the other side, releasing the second fillet.

7 Trimming the belly side of the fillet to remove excess fatty skin.

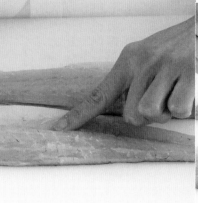

8 Running the tip of a finger along the middle of a fillet to locate the bones there.

9 Carefully pin-boning the fish fillets using kitchen tweezers.

Sea bass en papillote with slow-cooked tomato and fennel

Serves 4

2 tbsp olive oil
6 plum tomatoes
1 fennel bulb
2 garlic cloves
1 tsp caster sugar
Few basil sprigs
100g cherry tomatoes
50g pitted black olives
2 tbsp sherry vinegar
3–4 tbsp Pernod or dry white wine
4 sea bass fillets, skin on, each
   about 140g
Flaked sea salt and freshly ground
   black pepper

Baking fish in a parcel is a great technique. The juices from the fish combine with the flavourings to make a delicious sauce.

1 Heat the oven to 150°C/gas mark 2. Line a large baking sheet with non-stick baking parchment. Use a little olive oil to help stick the parchment to the baking sheet if necessary.

2 Cut the plum tomatoes into quarters. Using a teaspoon, remove and discard the seeds. Press each tomato quarter onto a board, skin side down. Starting at the pointed end, remove the skins using a filleting knife and a zig-zag action, keeping the knife horizontal and pressed closely to the board to waste as little of the flesh as possible.

3 Trim the root end off the fennel and finely slice lengthways, or use a mandolin. Peel and finely slice the garlic. Toss the sliced fennel and tomato quarters in the olive oil with the garlic, sugar and a basil sprig. Season well.

4 Spread the plum tomatoes and fennel out in a single layer on the baking sheet. Roast in the oven for 40–50 minutes, or until the tomatoes have dried out and the fennel has caramelised a little.

5 Cut the cherry tomatoes in half. Add them to the fennel and plum tomatoes 15 minutes before the end of the cooking time. They should just start to soften but keep their shape. Remove from the oven and discard the basil sprig. Increase the oven temperature to 200°C/gas mark 6.

6 Leave the fennel and tomatoes to cool, then gently scoop them into a bowl; try not to break them up too much as it is much more attractive to see whole pieces in the final dish. Chop the olives in half, then stir into the mixture with the sherry vinegar and Pernod or wine. Tear in some basil leaves.

7 Cut out 4 discs of greaseproof paper about 30cm in diameter or at least 5cm wider than the fillet when folded. The discs will be folded in half over the fish, so place them on appropriately sized baking sheets before filling them so there is no need to move them afterwards. You may need 1 or 2 baking sheets, depending on the width of your oven.

8 Place a quarter of the tomato mixture on one half of each paper circle. Season the fillets and place a fillet skin side up on top of each portion of tomato mixture.

9 Fold the paper in half over the fish fillet and fold the two open sides together, trying to make small, crisp folds to seal the parcel. Try to leave a gap all around the fish as the steam will cook the fish quickly as it circulates around the parcel, keeping it moist and allowing all the flavours to permeate its flesh.

10 Transfer the parcels to the oven and cook for 12–18 minutes, depending on the thickness of the fish. To test, gently press the fish through the paper – you should be able to feel the flakes of fish gently separating beneath the pressure from your fingers.

11 Serve immediately, still in the parcels so everyone can fully appreciate the wonderful aroma as they open it up.

Note Vegetables such as mangetout or green beans can be added to the parcel and will all cook in the delicious fish juices.

Fish pie

Serves 4

¼ onion
300ml milk
4 black peppercorns
1 bay leaf
600g haddock, whiting or cod fillet,
  or a mixture
¼ bunch of parsley
3 hard-boiled eggs (see page 144)
25g butter
25g plain flour
2 tbsp double cream
1 quantity mashed potatoes (see page 69)
Salt and freshly ground black pepper

1 Heat the oven to 180°C/gas mark 4.

2 Slice the onion. Put the milk, onion, peppercorns, bay leaf and a pinch of salt in a small saucepan and heat until steaming. Remove from the heat and set aside to infuse and cool.

3 Lay the fish fillet in a small roasting tin, skin side down. Strain the infused milk, discarding the flavourings, and pour the cooled milk over the fish. Place a damp cartouche (see page 13) over the surface.

4 Place the roasting tin over a low heat. As soon as the milk begins to poach (when a bubble or two breaks the surface), remove from the heat. Leave to cool (the fish will continue to cook in the residual heat of the milk). Check that the fish is cooked: it should be opaque, feel firm and begin to flake when pressed.

5 Remove the cartouche and transfer the fish to a bowl. Pull off the skin and discard. Carefully feel for and remove any bones, taking care not to break the fish up, keeping it in large pieces. Put the cartouche back over the fish to prevent it from drying out.

6 Strain the milk, taste and set aside. If it is very strongly flavoured, dilute with a little fresh milk, but you will need to discard some of it as you will only need 300ml. Leave to cool completely.

7 Finely chop enough parsley leaves to give you ½ tbsp. Peel the hard-boiled eggs and quarter lengthways.

8 Melt the butter in a saucepan, stir in the flour and cook for 1 minute. Remove from the heat and begin to add the 300ml reserved milk, a little at a time, stirring to avoid lumps. When at least half the milk has been added, return the pan to the heat, add the remaining milk and bring to the boil, stirring. Reduce the heat and simmer for 2 minutes. Stir in the cream and parsley, taste and season.

9 Pour the sauce over the fish in the bowl and gently combine until the fish is coated evenly. Pile the fish mixture into a pie dish, adding the eggs in as you do so (don't stir them in or they will break up).

10 Spread a layer of mash over the fish, starting from the edges and working towards the centre, and neaten the top with a palette knife. Alternatively, pipe the mash onto the fish in a diagonal pattern. Place the pie on a baking sheet and transfer to the oven for 35–40 minutes until the filling is hot. You can place briefly under a hot grill to give it a little colour if you prefer a crispy top.

Variations

Fish and spinach pie Omit the eggs and parsley. Add 150g wilted spinach, seasoned with salt, pepper and grated nutmeg, to the fish before pouring over the sauce.

Salmon and prawn pie Replace the parsley with 1 tbsp finely chopped dill or chives. Replace the white fish with 400g salmon and 400g peeled, cleaned raw tiger prawns (see page 204).

Cod steaks baked with lemon potatoes and olives

Serves 4

1 garlic clove
100ml olive oil
1 large lemon
4 cod steaks, each about 170g
600g potatoes
2 onions
1–2 rosemary sprigs
70g pitted green olives
Flaked sea salt and freshly ground
  black pepper
1 quantity aioli (see page 117), to serve

1 Bash the unpeeled garlic clove with the flat side of a large knife. Place in a small pan with the olive oil, heat until sizzling, then take off the heat and leave to cool.

2 Finely grate the lemon zest and squeeze the juice. Place half the lemon zest in a dish with the cod steaks. Add enough of the cooled garlic oil to coat the fish, and leave to marinate for 20 minutes. Heat the oven to 200°C/gas mark 6.

3 Wash the potatoes and cut into thick slices or wedges. Halve and peel the onions, remove the root and cut each half into 4 or 5 wedges. Put both into a large bowl with the remaining garlic oil and the lemon juice. Finely chop enough rosemary leaves to give you 1 tsp, then add to the bowl along with a sprinkling of salt and pepper. Stir well, then transfer to a roasting tin or shallow baking dish.

4 Bake for 30–45 minutes, or until the potatoes are soft and beginning to brown, stirring occasionally to prevent them from sticking to the tin.

5 Stir the olives and remaining lemon zest into the potatoes. Place the 4 pieces of cod on top of the potatoes, sprinkle with a little salt and cook in the oven for 15 minutes, or until the fish is cooked; it will have an even colour and firmness. To check, insert a knife into the middle to see if it is opaque.

6 Lift the cod and potatoes onto 4 plates and drizzle any remaining roasting tin juices around the fish. Spoon a little aioli over the cod. Delicious served with cherry tomato and grilled pepper salad (see page 86).

Steaming

Sea bass with garlic, ginger and soy

Serves 4

4 sea bass fillets, each about 170g
2 garlic cloves
4cm piece of fresh root ginger
6 spring onions
1 tbsp sunflower oil
1 tbsp sesame oil
1 tbsp light soy sauce
1 tbsp dark soy sauce
2–3 tbsp coriander leaves
Salt

1 Skin the fish fillets (see page 260) and pat dry with kitchen paper. Sprinkle lightly with salt on both sides and refrigerate for at least 30 minutes. The salt will help to firm the flesh as liquid is drawn out.

2 Peel and finely slice the garlic. Peel the ginger and cut into fine julienne. Trim and finely slice the spring onions on the diagonal, including the green tops; set aside.

3 Put both oils, the garlic and half the ginger into a small pan. Heat gently until the garlic starts to sizzle and turns a pale golden brown. Remove from the heat and set aside to cool and infuse.

4 Set the steamer over a pan of simmering water. Pat the sea bass fillets dry again and place on a heatproof plate in the steamer. Sprinkle with the remaining ginger. Cover and gently steam the fish for 5–10 minutes until just cooked, depending on the thickness of the fillets. To test, press with your fingertips to see if the flakes are moving against one another and if the flesh is opaque.

5 Meanwhile, gently reheat the infused oil. Add both soy sauces together with the spring onions just before serving (these should be heated through in the oil rather than cooked).

6 Place a fillet of sea bass on each plate. Pour over the hot soy and oil mixture, making sure each fillet has an equal amount of the garlic, ginger and spring onions scattered over, and sprinkle with some coriander leaves. This is delicious served with basmati rice and stir-fried Chinese greens.

Grilling

Red mullet with aubergine, caper and pine nut relish

Serves 4
4 medium red mullet, each about
   250–350g
1 large aubergine
2 garlic cloves
5 tbsp olive oil, plus extra to brush
2 small shallots
½ bunch of tarragon
¼ bunch of flat-leaf parsley
1 lemon
1 small red pepper
30g pine nuts
2 tbsp sherry vinegar
50ml brown chicken and veal stock
   (see page 98)
1–2 tsp Pedro Ximenez sherry
1 tbsp small capers, drained and rinsed
Salt and freshly ground black pepper

1 Descale, gut and fillet the red mullet (see pages 280 and 284) and set aside. Heat the oven to 190°C/gas mark 5.

2 Cut very shallow incisions, 1–2mm deep, through the skin of the aubergine, from the stem end to the bottom, every 2–3cm. Place on the gas hob with the heat turned up high (see page 30), or under a hot grill. Turn every few minutes using tongs, until all the skin is black and blistered, then transfer the aubergine to a baking sheet.

3 Brush the garlic cloves with a little olive oil and put them on the baking sheet with the aubergines. Bake in the oven until both are completely soft, about 30 minutes. The garlic may be soft before the aubergine, in which case remove it from the tray and leave the aubergines to cook for longer.

4 Meanwhile, halve, peel and finely dice the shallots and coarsely chop enough tarragon and parsley leaves to give you 1 tbsp each. Finely grate the lemon zest and squeeze the juice.

5 Blacken, peel and deseed the red pepper (see page 55) and cut into small dice. Toast the pine nuts on a baking tray in the oven for 5 minutes, or until light golden brown, then tip onto a plate to cool.

6 Heat 1 tbsp of the olive oil in a small saucepan over a low heat. Add the shallots and sweat gently until very soft. Remove half the shallots and reserve for the relish. Add the tarragon, sherry vinegar and stock to the pan and simmer gently. When the liquid is reduced to about 2 tsp, remove from the heat and set aside to cool a little.

7 Squeeze the roasted garlic cloves to release the soft insides. When the aubergine is cooked, leave to cool a little, then peel off the skin, cut off the stalk and discard. Roughly chop the flesh, put into a sieve and leave to drain for 10–15 minutes.

8 Transfer the shallot mixture to a blender with one-third of the drained aubergine and the squeezed garlic. Blend to a smooth purée; the shallot and tarragon should break down completely.

9 Scoop the mixture into a bowl, taste again and add the remaining aubergine, the sherry and lemon juice, salt and pepper to taste; set aside. Heat the grill to its highest setting.

10 To make the relish, mix together the reserved shallot, capers, remaining 4 tbsp olive oil and the lemon zest, with enough lemon juice to balance the dressing. Add the pine nuts, pepper and parsley, and season. Set aside.

11 Season the red mullet fillets and place them skin side up on a lightly oiled baking tray. Grill for 3–5 minutes, depending on size, until cooked and the skin is bubbling and browning.

12 Divide the aubergine purée between 4 plates. Place 2 red mullet fillets on the purée and spoon a little of the relish over the fillets.

Note The aubergine purée and relish also goes well with grilled lamb cutlets or roasted loin or rump of lamb, or even simple pan-fried chicken breasts.

Sea bream with salmoriglio sauce

Serves 4
4 sea bream fillets, each about 170–200g
1 tbsp olive oil
Salt and freshly ground black pepper

For the salmoriglio sauce
½ shallot
2 garlic cloves
Bunch of flat-leaf parsley
Small bunch of oregano
100ml extra virgin olive oil
1 lemon

1 To make the sauce, peel and finely dice the shallot and peel and crush the garlic. Finely chop enough parsley leaves to give you 2–3 tbsp and enough oregano to give you 1½–2 tbsp. Heat the grill to its highest setting.

2 Heat the extra virgin olive oil in a small saucepan over a low heat, add the shallot and sweat gently until soft, 5–10 minutes. Add the garlic and warm through for 1 minute. Meanwhile, juice the lemon.

3 Remove the pan from the heat and add the chopped herbs with salt, pepper and lemon juice to taste, saving a little lemon juice for the fish.

4 Lightly brush the sea bream fillets with the 1 tbsp olive oil and place on an oiled baking sheet, skin side up. Season the fillets with salt and a little lemon juice and grill for 4–5 minutes, depending on thickness. The heat generated from the baking sheet should be enough to cook the underside.

5 Once the fish is cooked, or opaque with a crisp skin, transfer to a plate and spoon over a little of the sauce to serve.

Note While not traditional, the shallot here adds a sweetness to the sauce to balance the pungency of the oregano.

Noisettes of haddock with sauce vierge

Serves 4
4 haddock cutlets, each about 170g
   and 2cm thick
1 lemon
2 tbsp olive oil
Salt

For the sauce vierge
2 shallots
1 garlic clove
2 plum tomatoes
Large handful of mixed herbs, such as
   flat-leaf parsley, chives and coriander
200ml extra virgin olive oil
1 thyme sprig
1 bay leaf
25ml sherry vinegar
Flaked sea salt and freshly ground
   black pepper

1 Prepare the haddock cutlets as noisettes (see page 312) and juice the lemon.

2 To make the sauce, halve, peel and finely dice the shallots. Peel and lightly bash the garlic with the flat side of a large knife. Blanch the tomatoes in boiling water for 10 seconds, then refresh in cold water, dry and peel. Quarter, deseed and cut the tomatoes into fine dice. Finely chop enough herb leaves to give you 1–2 tbsp.

3 Put the shallots, garlic, extra virgin olive oil, thyme, bay leaf and a good pinch of salt in a saucepan. Place over a very low heat and cook very gently for 15–20 minutes until the shallots are soft but not coloured. Remove from the heat, add the sherry vinegar and set aside to cool. Heat the grill to its highest setting.

4 Put the haddock noisettes in a bowl with the 2 tbsp olive oil and coat carefully with the oil. Drizzle over a little lemon juice. Place the noisettes on a lightly oiled, lipped baking sheet and season lightly with salt. Place under the grill and grill until the haddock is cooked; it will change from translucent to opaque, about 4–6 minutes depending on the thickness.

5 Take the fish noisettes from the grill, remove the string and skin, and leave to rest for 1–2 minutes.

6 Remove and discard the thyme and bay leaf from the sauce and add the diced tomatoes and chopped herbs. Taste and adjust the seasoning with a little salt and generously with pepper.

7 Place a haddock noisette on each of 4 plates and spoon over some of the sauce.

A note on salmoriglio and sauce vierge...
Like salsa verde (see page 126), salmoriglio and sauce vierge are olive oil based sauces. All 3 sauces are good served with any poached, steamed, baked or grilled white fish.

John Dory with sage butter and deep-fried vegetable ribbons

Serves 4

2–3 sage sprigs
1 garlic clove
100g butter
4 John Dory fillets, each about 170g
1 large carrot
1 large courgette
1 leek
Oil for deep-frying
75g plain flour, seasoned with a pinch
  of salt
Salt

1 Finely chop or chiffonade the sage leaves (see page 89). Peel and crush the garlic. Melt the butter in a small saucepan and add the sage and garlic. Heat gently for 1 minute, or until the garlic begins to sizzle. Remove from the heat and leave to infuse for a few minutes.

2 Place the fish skin side up on a baking sheet and brush with a little of the sage butter. Heat the oven to 120°C/gas mark ½ and the grill to its highest setting.

3 Peel the carrot, then, using a swivel peeler, shave the courgette and carrot into very thin, even ribbons. Trim the outer layers and green parts from the leek. Cut into 15cm lengths, then cut each length into ribbons, roughly the same width as the courgette and carrot.

4 Heat the oil in a deep-fat fryer, or one-third fill a deep, heavy saucepan and heat to about 194°C, or until a piece of bread browns in 25 seconds (see page 72). Toss the vegetable ribbons in the seasoned flour. Deep-fry a few vegetable ribbons at a time; do not allow them to become too brown. As they cook, use a slotted spoon to lift them from the oil, and drain on kitchen paper. Sprinkle the ribbons with a little salt and keep warm in the low oven.

5 Brush the fish with the infused butter again. Grill for 4–5 minutes until opaque, indicating it is cooked, basting with the sage butter as it grills.

6 Lift the fish onto 4 plates and spoon over any cooking juices and sage butter. Serve with the deep-fried vegetable ribbons.

Note Any firm white fish can be substituted for the John Dory. If preferred, you can pan-fry the fish, basting it with the sage butter as it cooks.

John Dory with braised peas and lettuce

Serves 4

75g pancetta
3 Little Gem lettuce hearts
½ bunch of flat-leaf parsley
½ tbsp olive oil
200g frozen peas
225ml chicken and veal stock
  (see page 96)
4 John Dory fillets, each about 170g
½ lemon
15g butter
Salt and freshly ground black pepper

1 Derind the pancetta if necessary and cut into lardons. Remove the outer leaves of the lettuce, if coarse. Trim off the root end, leaving the head intact, then quarter lengthways. Coarsely chop enough parsley leaves to give you 1–2 tbsp.

2 Heat the olive oil in a frying pan, add the pancetta and fry over a low to medium heat until the fat has rendered and the pancetta is lightly golden. Remove with a slotted spoon; set aside. Add the lettuce to the pan and lightly brown on all sides.

3 Pour off any excess fat, then add the peas to the pan and lower the heat. Add enough stock to just cover the peas and lettuce, and a little salt and pepper. Cover and simmer gently until the lettuce and peas are tender, 4–5 minutes.

4 Heat the grill to its highest setting. Add the pancetta to the peas and lettuce, taste and adjust the seasoning. Keep warm while you cook the fish.

5 Place the John Dory fillets skin side up on an oiled, lipped baking sheet. Juice the ½ lemon. Season the fish with a little salt and drizzle with lemon juice. Grill the fish until the skin has browned and the flesh is opaque and cooked through, 4–5 minutes. You should not need to turn the fish.

6 Remove the fish from the grill and set aside to rest for 2–3 minutes. Reheat the peas and lettuce, add the parsley and stir through the butter.

7 Divide the lettuce mixture between 4 deep plates. Place a piece of John Dory on top and serve immediately.

Pan-frying

Pollock with skordalia and a pine nut vinaigrette

Serves 4
4 pollock fillets, each about 170g, skin on
1 tbsp olive oil
Salt and freshly ground black pepper

For the skordalia
2 large floury potatoes
1–2 garlic cloves
1 egg yolk
¼ lemon
75–100ml olive oil
1–2 tbsp white wine vinegar
3–4 tbsp warm water (if necessary)

For the vinaigrette
50g pine nuts
½ shallot
½ celery stick
2 green olives
½ bunch of flat-leaf parsley
75ml extra virgin olive oil
2–3 tsp verjuice

1 For the skordalia, peel the potatoes and cut into 2cm dice. Place in a saucepan of cold water, just enough to cover, and heat over a medium to high heat until simmering. Cover and simmer for 8–15 minutes until cooked; a cutlery knife should penetrate the potato easily and be easily released. While the potatoes are cooking, peel and crush the garlic and mix with the egg yolk.

2 Meanwhile, heat the oven to 180°C/gas mark 4. For the vinaigrette, place the pine nuts on a baking tray and toast in the oven for 5–8 minutes until pale golden, then tip onto a plate and set aside to cool.

3 Peel and finely dice the shallot and de-string and very finely dice the celery, the same size as the shallot. Halve, stone and finely chop the olives. Finely chop enough parsley leaves to give you 1–2 tbsp. Put the extra virgin olive oil in a small bowl and add the verjuice. Stir in the pine nuts, shallot, celery, olives and parsley. Taste and adjust the seasoning, then set aside.

4 Once cooled, drain the potatoes well, return them to the empty pan and leave to steam-dry. While still warm, push them through a potato ricer a few at a time, into a clean saucepan. Squeeze the juice from the lemon.

5 Mix the egg yolk and garlic into the potato and then beat in the olive oil, wine vinegar, lemon juice and some seasoning, to taste. Add more olive oil and crushed garlic to taste, if needed. The skordalia should be a soft, spoonable consistency, so stir in 3–4 tbsp warm water to loosen it if necessary.

6 Dry the skin of the pollock well and lightly salt it. Add a drizzle of olive oil to a non-stick frying pan and place over a low to medium heat. Arrange the fillets skin side down in the pan and allow the skin to crisp and brown; it may be necessary to hold the fish down with a fish slice, so the skin is firmly against the pan, to prevent it from curling. Cook without moving until nearly cooked through, then add another drizzle of olive oil, turn the fish over and continue to cook the fish until opaque throughout. (Alternatively, the fish can be finished in an oven preheated to 180°C/gas mark 4 for a few minutes.)

7 To serve, gently warm through the skordalia over a low heat. Place a spoonful on each of 4 plates. Add a piece of pollock and spoon a little of the pine nut vinaigrette over the fish. Serve immediately.

....

A note on skordalia...
Skordalia is a garlic-flavoured purée made using either potato, bread or ground almonds as a base. The egg yolk enriches it, but can be omitted. Skordalia can also be served as a dip for grilled vegetables, or to accompany barbecued lamb.

Sweet and sour snapper curry

Serves 4
4 snapper fillets, each about 170g
Salt

For the marinade
2cm piece of fresh root ginger
1 red chilli
1 tsp ground fennel seed
½ tsp ground turmeric
1 tsp soft light brown sugar
1 lemon

For the curry
50g tamarind pulp
200ml boiling water
2 red onions
2 ripe tomatoes
3 tbsp sunflower oil
1 tsp fennel seeds
1 tsp black onion seeds
½ tsp chilli powder
½ tsp ground fennel seed
1 tbsp soft light brown sugar, plus
   extra if needed
1 star anise
Handful of coriander sprigs

1 For the marinade, peel and grate the ginger into a shallow dish. Halve, deseed and finely chop the chilli, then add it to the ginger with the ground fennel seed, turmeric and sugar. Pare the zest and squeeze the juice of the lemon, then add the zest and half the juice to the dish. Mix well.

2 Cut each snapper fillet into 3 even-sized pieces. Add to the dish, rub the marinade paste all over them, then cover and leave to marinate in the fridge for 20–30 minutes.

3 Meanwhile, put the tamarind pulp in a small bowl, cover with the 200ml boiling water and leave to soak for at least 20 minutes; stir well.

4 While the tamarind is soaking, to make the curry sauce, halve, peel and slice the onions. Blanch the tomatoes in boiling water for 10 seconds, then refresh in cold water, dry, peel and roughly chop.

5 Heat 2 tbsp of the oil in a saucepan and fry the onions over a medium heat until starting to brown, stirring occasionally to prevent them from burning. When they start to brown, add the fennel and onion seeds and cook until they start to pop. Add the chilli powder and ground fennel seed. Reduce the heat and cook, stirring, for 1 minute.

6 Add the sugar, chopped tomatoes and star anise, then strain in the tamarind liquid, discarding the pulp left in the sieve. Season with salt and bring to the boil, then lower the heat and simmer for 5 minutes.

7 Wipe any excess marinade off the fish and season with salt. Heat the remaining 1 tbsp oil in a frying pan. Fry the fish for 1 minute on each side, until lightly browned, then remove from the pan.

8 Taste the sauce, adding the reserved lemon juice to taste, and season with salt, and sugar, if needed. Add the browned fish and simmer gently for 3–5 minutes or until the snapper is just cooked and tender.

9 Roughly chop the leaves from a few coriander sprigs and stir into the curry, reserving some whole leaves. Remove the star anise and lemon zest, sprinkle with the coriander leaves and serve with basmati rice.

Variations

You can substitute any firm, white fish, such as haddock, pollock, sea bass, bream or monkfish.

....
A note on pan-frying or grilling fish with the skin on...
Fish skin will shrink when heated, so scoring it will prevent the fish from buckling in the pan or under the grill. Score it lightly several times, just through the skin and close together, using a very sharp knife for the best effect.

When crisping fish skin, dry it thoroughly, then score and lightly salt it. Place skin side down in a non-stick frying pan. Place the pan over a low to medium heat and allow the skin to slowly crisp. You might need to press down or weight the fish to keep the skin in contact with the pan. Avoid moving it too much as the skin will easily come away from the fish. It is best to do most of the cooking on the skin side, turning it skin side up for just the last few minutes of cooking.

Roasting

Monkfish with sage and Savoy cabbage

Serves 4

4 pieces of monkfish, each about 170g
4 slices of Parma ham
1 banana shallot
½ Savoy cabbage
1 small Granny Smith apple
1 small carrot
¼ bunch of sage
3 tbsp olive oil
150ml white wine
150ml brown chicken and veal stock
  (see page 98)
20–30g unsalted butter
Salt and freshly ground black pepper

1 Prepare the monkfish by carefully removing the outer, opaque membrane. Much of it can be pulled off, then use a very sharp knife to finish. Remove the discoloured brown flesh beneath this membrane, but take care not to cut into the white flesh.

2 Wrap each piece of monkfish in a Parma ham slice, leaving the ends open, and refrigerate. Heat the oven to 150°C/gas mark 2.

3 Halve, peel and finely slice the shallot. Strip out the central hard white core from the cabbage, discard the outer leaves and very finely slice the inner leaves. Peel, core and slice the apple into julienne. Peel and finely dice the carrot, blanch in boiling water for 10 seconds, then refresh in cold water and drain. Chiffonade enough sage leaves (see page 89) to give you ½–1 tbsp.

4 Heat 1 tbsp of the olive oil in a frying pan over a low heat and add the shallot. Sweat for 3–4 minutes until softening, then add the cabbage and apple, turn through to coat with oil and sauté gently for 4–5 minutes until starting to soften. Season with salt and pepper, then tip out into a bowl and keep warm.

5 Wipe out the frying pan and add the remaining 2 tbsp olive oil over a medium heat. Season the monkfish parcels with pepper and place join side down in the hot oil, to seal the join. Fry until the Parma ham is becoming brown and crisp, turning as each side crisps.

6 When the ham is crisp all the way round, transfer the fish parcels to a roasting tin and finish cooking in the oven for 5–8 minutes, depending on the thickness of the fillets.

7 Meanwhile, deglaze the pan with the wine and reduce by half, then add the carrot and simmer gently until the wine has reduced to 2 tsp. Add the stock and simmer for 2–3 minutes until the flavours have developed. Whisk the butter into the sauce. Taste and adjust the seasoning, then remove from the heat.

8 Remove the monkfish from the oven and pour any pan juices into the sauce. Divide the cabbage between 4 plates and spoon a little of the sauce over the cabbage. Place the monkfish on top.

Note If the Parma ham is in danger of unwrapping itself from the monkfish, you can secure it with a cocktail stick, removing the cocktail stick to serve.

Variations

Cod, haddock or any firm white fish can be substituted for the monkfish and you can replace the Savoy cabbage with finely shredded Brussels sprouts.

Whole roasted sea bass with artichokes and tomatoes

Serves 4

1 sea bass, about 1.5kg
2 lemons
¼ bunch of thyme
6 baby artichokes
1 onion
3 garlic cloves
4 plum tomatoes
½ bunch of flat-leaf parsley
6 tbsp olive oil
¼–½ tsp crushed dried chillies
200ml dry white wine
100ml fish stock (see page 100)
3 tbsp pitted black olives
Salt and freshly ground black pepper

1 Descale and gut the sea bass (see page 280). Cut 1 lemon into 6 wedges; squeeze the juice from the other lemon. Season the inside of the belly with salt and pepper and stuff the lemon wedges and the thyme into the belly.

2 Prepare the baby artichokes (see page 23) and halve or quarter unless very tiny. Halve, peel and finely slice the onion. Peel and crush the garlic. Quarter and deseed the tomatoes and coarsely chop enough parsley leaves to give you 2–3 tbsp. Heat the oven to 230°C/gas mark 8.

3 Put 3 tbsp of the olive oil in a large roasting tin or flameproof casserole that will comfortably fit the sea bass, and set over a medium heat. Dry the artichokes on kitchen paper, and sauté in the hot oil for 5–10 minutes until starting to soften and taking on a little colour.

4 Lower the heat, add the onion and sauté until starting to soften, then add the garlic and crushed chillies and cook for 1 minute.

5 Add the wine and reduce by half, then add the stock, tomatoes and olives. Season with salt, pepper and lemon juice.

6 Place the sea bass on top of the artichokes and tomatoes, drizzle with the remaining 3 tbsp olive oil, and season with salt and pepper. Roast in the oven for 20–30 minutes until cooked; the eyes will be opaque and the dorsal fin will pull out easily. Check inside the cavity at the bone; the fish should be opaque.

7 Lift the sea bass onto a serving plate. Stir the parsley through the artichoke and tomato mixture and spoon alongside the fish. Serve immediately.

Deep-frying

Deep-fried fish in a beer batter coating

Serves 4

40g self-raising flour
35g cornflour
½ tsp baking powder
Pinch of paprika
100ml strong ale or beer
Oil for deep-frying
4 pieces of skinless white fish, each
    about 170g
Plain flour, to dust
Salt

1 Heat the oven to 120°C/gas mark ½.

2 Put the flour, cornflour, baking powder, paprika and a pinch of salt in a bowl and make a well in the centre. Pour the ale into the well and, using a wooden spoon, mix it into the dry ingredients to create a smooth batter.

3 One-third fill a large, deep, heavy saucepan with oil (or use a deep-fat fryer) and, over a low heat, heat to 182°C, or until a small piece of bread dropped in the hot oil browns in 60 seconds.

4 Dip a piece of fish in flour to coat, dusting off any excess, then into the batter to coat evenly. Carefully lower into the hot oil and repeat with a second piece of fish. Deep-fry for 5–8 minutes, depending on the thickness of the fish fillets.

5 Drain the fish well on kitchen paper and sprinkle lightly with salt. Transfer to the low oven with the door ajar, to keep warm while you coat and deep-fry the remaining pieces of fish.

Note The cornflour, baking powder and raising agent in the self-raising flour improve the crispness of the batter.

Variation

For the batter, replace the ale or beer with sparkling water.

Brandade fritters with sweet paprika mayonnaise

Makes 25 to serve 4–6
300g salt cod
550g floury potatoes (about 2 large ones)
2 garlic cloves
About 350ml milk
½ small onion
1 bay leaf
4–6 black peppercorns
50ml olive oil
¼ bunch of chives
½ red chilli
Squeeze of lemon juice (optional)
2 eggs
200g fresh white breadcrumbs
Oil for deep-frying
Salt and freshly ground black pepper

For the paprika mayonnaise
1–2 tsp smoked sweet paprika
1 quantity mayonnaise (see page 116)

You need to start this recipe at least 24 hours in advance, to allow sufficient time for soaking the salt cod.

1 Place the salt cod in a bowl, cover with cold water and soak for 24 hours, changing the water 2 or 3 times.

2 When ready to cook, heat the oven to 200°C/gas mark 6.

3 Wash the potatoes and prick with a fork a few times, then place in a roasting tin and bake in the oven for 1–1½ hours until completely tender. Add the unpeeled garlic cloves for the last 15–20 minutes of cooking.

4 When you have added the garlic to the potatoes, remove the salt cod from the water, discarding the water. Place in a sauté pan and add enough milk to cover. Peel and slice the onion and add to the milk with the bay leaf and peppercorns. Bring just to a simmer over a low heat, then turn the heat down and poach gently for 5–10 minutes until the salt cod is cooked; it should flake easily. Leave to cool slightly in the milk.

5 Once the potatoes are soft, remove from the oven, leave to cool for a few minutes, then cut in half and scoop out the flesh. While still hot, push the flesh through a potato ricer into a bowl. Squeeze the garlic cloves from their skins and set aside.

6 Drain the salt cod, reserving the milk, but discarding the onion slices, bay leaves and peppercorns.

7 Place the salt cod and squeezed-out garlic in a food processor and blend until broken down but not completely smooth. You might need to add a little splash of the reserved milk to help, but keep the texture reasonably firm. Add the potato and pulse to combine, then gradually pulse in the olive oil.

8 Finely chop the chives, deseed and finely chop the chilli and add both to the brandade mixture. Taste and season with pepper and lemon juice if necessary. Roll the mixture into walnut-sized balls, using about 1 tbsp for each. Place on a tray lined with baking parchment to firm up until ready to cook.

9 To make the paprika mayonnaise, stir the sweet paprika into the mayonnaise, to taste, making sure the flavour is not overpowering, and transfer to a small bowl ready for serving.

10 Break the eggs into a shallow dish and lightly whisk. Place the breadcrumbs in another dish. Fill a large, deep, heavy saucepan one-third full with oil (or use a deep-fat fryer) and heat over a medium heat to 190°–193°C, or until a piece of bread browns in 30–40 seconds (see page 72).

11 Place a few of the brandade fritters in the egg to coat, then roll them in the breadcrumbs to coat evenly. Gently lower them into the hot oil using a slotted spoon and fry until golden and hot through, about 3–4 minutes.

12 Lift out the fritters, drain well on kitchen paper and very lightly dust with salt. Keep warm in a low oven, with the door ajar, while you coat and deep-fry the remaining fritters. Serve the fritters with the paprika mayonnaise.

....

A note on brandade...
Brandade is a dip made with salt cod and olive oil, and flavoured with garlic. Potato or bread is often added to help firm the mixture a little.

Oily fish

All oily fish are also round fish. As the fat is distributed through the flesh of oily fish, they have a stronger and sometimes more distinctive flavour than white fish. However, this also means that they often work well in bold flavour pairings. The rich flavour of mackerel is complemented by the acidity and sweetness of slow-roasted tomatoes, while the firm texture and robust flavour of tuna makes it an ideal partner for soy, ginger and coriander, or a punchy pesto. Containing essential omega-3 fatty acids, oily fish have the double benefit of being both healthy and delicious.

Baking

Trout en papillote with ginger and galangal

Serves 4
Bunch of spring onions
1cm piece of fresh root ginger
2cm piece of fresh galangal
1 green chilli
3 lemongrass stalks
½ bunch of coriander
2 tbsp nam pla (fish sauce)
2 tbsp mirin (rice wine)
4 trout

1 Heat the oven to 220°C/gas mark 7. Trim off the root end from the spring onions, cut each one across into 4 lengths and then cut into julienne. Peel and very finely julienne the ginger and galangal. Halve, deseed and finely chop the chilli. Trim off the root end from the lemongrass, remove the coarser top part of the leaves and peel away the outer coarse layers, then very finely chop the tender insides. Finely chop enough coriander leaves to give you 1 tbsp.

2 Combine the spring onions, ginger, galangal, chilli and coriander in a small bowl. Add the nam pla and mirin, mix well and set aside. The acidity in the nam pla and mirin will start to soften the ginger, galangal and lemongrass.

3 Fillet and pin-bone the trout (see page 284).

4 Cut out 4 discs of greaseproof paper, about 40cm in diameter. Place the paper discs on 1 or 2 baking sheets, depending on the width of your oven.

5 Place a trout fillet skin side down on one side of each greaseproof paper circle, but not right next to the edge. Spread the spring onion mixture over the fillets. Spoon the nam pla and mirin over each, then place the second fillet skin side up on top of the filling. Fold the free half of the paper over to make a parcel. Fold the edges of the paper over twice together, twisting and pressing firmly to seal.

6 Put the paper cases on a baking sheet, taking care that they are not touching, and bake in the oven for 12–15 minutes, or until the fish starts to flake when pressed gently in the parcel.

7 Serve immediately on large plates, leaving the diners to open their own parcels.

Note This recipe can be adapted for larger fillets of salmon or salmon trout. Double or even triple the stuffing ingredients and sandwich between 2 whole skinned and trimmed salmon fillets from a 1.5kg fish, on a sheet of foil. Wrap the foil well and bake in a preheated oven at 180°C/gas mark 4 for 30–35 minutes until cooked. Use the juices to baste the fish with before serving.

Variation
Trout en papillote with leek, carrot and tarragon Sweat 4 tbsp each of leek and carrot julienne in 20g butter over a low heat, for about 5–10 minutes until just softening. Add 1–2 tsp coarsely chopped tarragon and season to taste with salt and pepper. Sandwich the trout fillets with the leek and carrot mixture, a knob of butter and 1 tbsp white wine per trout, proceeding as for the main recipe.

Salmon fillets with a sweet and hot crust

Serves 4
4 pieces of salmon fillet, each about 170g
3–4 limes
2 tbsp demerara sugar
1 tsp English mustard powder
4 tbsp wholegrain mustard
8 tbsp fresh white breadcrumbs
Pinch of crushed dried chillies

1 Heat the oven to 190°C/gas mark 5. Trim, skin and pin-bone the salmon fillets (see page 284).

2 Finely zest the limes and mix the lime zest with the sugar, mustard powder, wholegrain mustard, breadcrumbs and crushed chillies.

3 Place the salmon skinned side down on a lightly oiled baking tray and press the breadcrumb mixture onto each fillet.

4 Bake in the oven for 10–15 minutes until the salmon is opaque and cooked; it can be left a little rare through the centre. This is delicious served with sweet dill slaw (see page 60), hot raw beetroot with black pepper and lemon (page 40) or fennel salad with blood orange, watercress and black olives (page 52).

Poaching

Salmon quenelles in a lemongrass and ginger broth

Serves 4
For the broth
150g cooked prawns
3 spring onions
2 lemongrass stalks
3cm piece of fresh root ginger
½ red chilli
¼ bunch of coriander
½ bunch of Thai basil
1.5 litres fish stock (see page 100)
1 star anise
1 tsp nam pla (fish sauce)
100ml mirin (rice wine)

For the quenelles
1cm piece of fresh root ginger
1 quantity mousseline, made with salmon
  (see page 367)
500ml fish stock (see page 100)
1 lemongrass stalk
1 tsp nam pla (fish sauce), plus extra
  to taste
Handful of bean sprouts
2 limes

1 Peel the prawns, reserving both the shells and tails. Trim the spring onions, then slice finely. Cut the lemongrass stalks in half lengthways and bash them well. Peel and finely slice the ginger and deseed the chilli. Pick off the coriander leaves, reserving the stalks, and pick some small Thai basil leaves.

2 Put the prawn shells, the 1.5 litres stock, spring onions, lemongrass, ginger, chilli, star anise, nam pla, mirin and coriander stalks into a large saucepan, bring to a gentle simmer and simmer for 20 minutes.

3 Meanwhile, for the quenelles, peel and very finely grate the ginger to extract the juices. Add a little of the ginger juice to the mousseline, to taste; the ginger flavour should not be too strong. Heat the oven to 120°C/gas mark ½.

4 Take the broth off the heat and let cool slightly, then pass through a fine sieve, pushing down on the shells and aromatics to extract as much flavour as possible.

5 Return the broth to the pan (there should be about 1 litre), taste and reduce to concentrate the flavour; it should be fragrant with lemongrass and ginger, but not overpowering. Keep warm.

6 For the salmon quenelles, heat the 500ml fish stock in a sauté pan over a low to medium heat, bash the lemongrass and add to the stock with the nam pla. Cut the bean sprouts into shorter lengths (roughly thirds) and juice the limes; set aside.

7 Quenelle the salmon mousseline (see below), using 2 teaspoons, and poach in the stock for 3–5 minutes. They should be cooked through, but still soft and tender. Remove from the stock and keep warm in the low oven.

8 Reheat the broth, add the prawns, taste and adjust the seasoning with nam pla and lime juice, and divide between 4 bowls. Place the salmon quenelles in the broth, sprinkle with the bean sprouts, coriander and Thai basil leaves and serve.

A note on shaping quenelles...
To obtain a smooth, three-sided oval (ie a quenelle) of mousseline (or mousse, meringue or ice cream), the mixture is passed repeatedly between 2 identical spoons, turning and smoothing each side.

Poached whole salmon with herb mayonnaise

Serves 4–6

1 whole salmon or salmon trout,
  about 2–2.5kg (see note)
Bunch of watercress
1 cucumber
Salt and freshly ground black pepper

For the court bouillon

1 onion
1 carrot
½ bunch of parsley
3 bay leaves
10 black peppercorns
½ tsp salt
4 litres water
600ml white wine vinegar

For the glaze

2 tsp powdered gelatine
300ml cooled court bouillon (from above)

To serve

2 lemons
1 quantity herb mayonnaise
  (see page 117)

1 For the court bouillon, halve, peel and slice the onion. Peel and thinly slice the carrot. Place the vegetables and aromatics in a fish kettle or large heatproof pan in which the fish can lie flat. Pour in the water, add the wine vinegar and bring to a simmer over a low to medium heat. Simmer for 15–20 minutes. Set aside to cool.

2 Descale and gut the fish (see page 280), then place in the cooled court bouillon. A fish kettle will have its own internal tray to help lift the fish in and out but if you do not have a fish kettle, fold 3 long sheets of foil into 5cm wide straps to support the fish when lowering it in to poach and for removing it after poaching. Place over a medium heat and heat until a small bubble breaks the surface occasionally.

3 Poach the fish for about 5 minutes per 500g. Check every 10 minutes from the point at which the liquid comes to a poach. When the dorsal fin pulls away, the fish is cooked. Also check the belly area to ensure the flesh has changed colour from translucent to opaque. Remove from the heat and leave the fish to cool in the liquor, then carefully lift it out onto a tray. It can be kept overnight in the fridge to firm a little before boning. Reserve the court bouillon.

4 To make the glaze, sprinkle the gelatine over the cooled court bouillon in a small saucepan and sponge for 5 minutes (see page 582), then gently dissolve over a low heat. When fully dissolved, set aside to cool, but don't leave until set; it must still be pourable.

5 Peel and very thinly slice the cucumber, using a mandolin or very sharp knife. Blanch the cucumber slices in boiling water for 10 seconds, then refresh in cold water, drain and dry. Set aside. Wash and pick over the watercress and set aside. Cut the lemons for serving into wedges and set aside.

6 Turn the poached fish over on the tray. You need to work with the side that was against the tray first. Carefully and neatly cut away the head and tail and set aside.

7 Pull away the skin covering the fillet. Using a thin bladed knife, scrape away the brown flesh. Divide the fillet along the natural line covering the back bone and gently prise the half fillets away from the bone (as shown). Using a palette knife to support the half fillet, transfer it to a serving platter and turn it upside down, so the boned side is uppermost. Repeat with the second half fillet and match it up with the first half to create a whole fillet (as shown). Scrape away any fat, especially from the belly area. Run your fingers along the flesh and pin-bone it.

8 Remove the fish frame from the second fillet by carefully pulling it away from the fish, while supporting the fish. Discard the frame and scrape away any fat from the belly area. Pin-bone the second fillet. Using a palette knife to support the whole fillet, transfer it to the platter and turn it over onto the prepared bottom fillet, so the skin is now uppermost. Pull away the skin (as shown), carefully scrape away the brown flesh and discard it. Neaten both fillets.

9 Trim the tail and head and place on the platter as if to re-form the fish. Brush a little of the glaze over the fish and arrange the cucumber discs in a scale pattern, starting from the middle of the fish to reveal some of the salmon (or from the tail to cover the whole fish) and overlapping towards the head; the glaze acts as glue. Brush the fish with the glaze again to give it a shine and prevent it from drying out.

10 Place a small bunch of watercress between the tail and fillet and between the head and fillet. Serve with the lemon wedges and herb mayonnaise.

Note To cook a smaller fish, poach as above for 2 minutes, then remove from the heat and leave the fish to finish cooking in the hot court bouillon.

Salmon fillets wrapped in lettuce with a warm fennel citrus dressing

Serves 4
4 large Cos lettuce leaves
¼ bunch of dill
1 quantity mousseline, made with salmon
(see page 367)
4 pieces of salmon fillet, about 3 x 7cm
Salt and ground white pepper

For the fennel citrus dressing
2 shallots
1 lemon
1 orange
½ grapefruit
1 large celery stick
½ fennel bulb
150ml extra virgin olive oil
1 bay leaf
2 tbsp strong brown chicken and veal
stock (see page 98)
½ carrot
2 tbsp sherry vinegar
Salt and freshly ground black pepper

1 To make the fennel citrus dressing, halve, peel and finely dice the shallots. Pare the zest and squeeze the juice from the lemon, orange and grapefruit, keeping the juices separate. De-string, then finely dice the celery. Finely dice the fennel, reserving the fennel tops.

2 Heat 30ml of the olive oil in a medium saucepan over a low heat and sweat the shallots, citrus zests, celery, half the fennel and the bay leaf until softening, then add half the lemon and orange juice, all the grapefruit juice and the stock. Bring to a simmer and let simmer for 3–4 minutes, then strain, discarding the flavourings. Set aside to cool.

3 Blanch the lettuce leaves in simmering water for 10 seconds, or until just wilted. Remove and plunge immediately into cold water, taking care not to damage them. Lay the leaves on kitchen paper and lay more kitchen paper on top to absorb all excess water.

4 Once the leaves are dry, trim each leaf to a rectangle big enough to encase the salmon in a single piece. Try to avoid including the bottom of the stalk end as it will be easier to wrap the fish without the stalk.

5 Finely chop the dill and add to the salmon mousseline. Using a palette knife, spread a thin layer of mousseline, about 3–5mm thick, over the lettuce leaves. Season, lay a piece of salmon on the edge of the mousseline and tightly roll, as for a spring roll.

6 Steam the salmon parcels in a steamer over simmering water for 10–15 minutes, or until the salmon is firm but still fairly rare inside.

7 Meanwhile, peel and finely dice the carrot and mix with the remaining diced fennel. Finely chop the fennel tops. Whisk the sherry vinegar and the remaining olive oil into the dressing, taste and adjust the acidity with the remaining citrus juice. Warm the dressing over a low heat, then remove and add the diced carrot, fennel and fennel tops. Taste and adjust the seasoning.

8 When the salmon parcels are cooked, remove them from the steamer and cut them in half at an angle. Divide between 4 plates and spoon a little of the dressing over the salmon.

Variations

Salmon steamed in lettuce with a warm citrus and marjoram dressing
Replace the dill in the salmon parcels with 1½ tsp finely chopped marjoram. Omit the fennel from the dressing and add ½–1 tbsp finely chopped marjoram in place of the fennel tops.

Salmon steamed in lettuce with a sauce vierge Replace the fennel citrus dressing with a sauce vierge (see page 291).

Grilling

Whole mackerel with gooseberry sauce

Serves 4

350g gooseberries, fresh or frozen
2cm piece of fresh root ginger
30g caster sugar, plus extra to taste
30g butter
4 whole mackerel, each about 250–350g
2 lemons
Salt

1 To make the sauce, top and tail the gooseberries. Peel and finely grate enough ginger to give you ½ tsp.

2 Put the gooseberries in a small saucepan with 1–2 tbsp water and the sugar. Place over a low to medium heat and simmer until tender, about 10 minutes.

3 Pass the gooseberries through a fine sieve into a bowl, add the ginger to taste and beat in the butter, which should melt in the residual heat of the gooseberries. Taste and add more sugar if necessary; the sauce should retain some sharpness to act as a foil for the richness of the mackerel. Set aside; keep warm.

4 Heat the grill to its highest setting.

5 Remove the fins, except for the dorsal fin, and gills from the mackerel, then gut them (see page 280). Rinse well under cold water, then dry with kitchen paper. Juice one of the lemons. Cut the other lemon into wedges; set aside for serving.

6 Using a sharp knife, make 3 slashes in the sides of each mackerel. Season with salt and a drizzle of lemon juice and place on a lipped baking sheet.

7 Grill the fish for 5–8 minutes, allowing the skin to brown and blister. It is cooked when the eyes have turned opaque and the dorsal fin pulls out easily. Carefully open the belly and check that the flesh around the back bone is opaque.

8 Place the fish on a serving platter and arrange the lemon wedges around the fish. Serve the sauce separately.

Note Larger mackerel may need to finish cooking in an oven preheated to 180°C/gas mark 4 for 3–6 minutes, depending on size, after being grilled.

Variations

Mackerel with rhubarb purée Omit the gooseberry sauce. Trim the ends off 2–3 rhubarb sticks and cut into 2–3cm pieces. Put into a roasting tin with 2 tbsp caster sugar, cover with foil and roast in an oven preheated to 180°C/gas mark 4 until tender. Remove and allow to cool. Sieve the rhubarb, pushing through as much of it as possible to create a purée. Taste and season with finely grated fresh ginger, as for the main recipe, and caster sugar, to retain some sharpness.

Mackerel with a spicy tamarind chutney Omit the gooseberry sauce. Heat 1 tbsp olive oil and 1 tsp sesame oil in a saucepan over a low heat. Add 1 shallot, peeled and very finely diced, and sauté for 3–4 minutes until softening. Add 3 crushed garlic cloves and cook for 1 minute; do not allow the garlic to burn. Add a 400g tin chopped tomatoes, increase the heat and simmer vigorously for 4–5 minutes. Add 1 tsp tamarind paste, 20ml rice wine vinegar, 75ml malt vinegar, 1–2 tbsp peeled and finely grated fresh ginger, 1–2 tbsp palm (or brown) sugar, 1 tbsp light soy, a large pinch of crushed dried chillies, 1 tsp ground coriander and ½ tsp ground cumin. Bring to the boil and cook until the sauce has reduced and is thick and pulpy. Taste and season with salt. It should be sour, hot and sweet.

Miso marinated grilled mackerel with soba noodles

Serves 4
120ml white miso
50ml sweet sake
50ml mirin (rice wine)
50g caster sugar
8 mackerel fillets
Sunflower oil, for brushing

For the noodles
2 bundles of soba noodles
1 tbsp sunflower oil
½ tbsp sesame seeds
4 spring onions
1 tbsp pickled ginger
¼ bunch of coriander
30ml light soy sauce
½ tbsp sesame oil
1 tbsp rice wine vinegar
½ tbsp white wine vinegar

1 Put the miso, sake, mirin and sugar in a bowl and stir to encourage the sugar to dissolve, so the paste is smooth.

2 Using kitchen tweezers, pin-bone the mackerel fillets (see page 284). Transfer the marinade to a plastic food bag, add the mackerel and gently work the marinade around the fillets to coat them evenly. Leave to marinate in the fridge for 2–3 hours, or ideally overnight.

3 Bring a large saucepan of water to the boil over a medium to high heat and add the noodles. Return to the boil, lower the heat and simmer for 3–4 minutes until just tender. If the water threatens to bubble over, add a splash of cold water and it will subside. Drain and refresh under cold running water. Drain again thoroughly and place in a bowl, adding 1 tsp oil to prevent them from sticking together.

4 Toast the sesame seeds in a frying pan over a low to medium heat for 2–3 minutes, then tip into the noodles. Trim, peel and finely slice the spring onions on the diagonal and shred the pickled ginger. Pick the leaves off the coriander stalks (you need about 2 tbsp) and set aside.

5 Mix together the soy sauce, sunflower and sesame oils, and both wine vinegars, then add the spring onions and ginger. Taste and adjust the seasoning. Heat the grill to its highest setting.

6 Remove the mackerel fillets from the marinade and place skin side up on an oiled, lipped baking tray. Brush the fillets with oil and grill for 4–6 minutes, depending on thickness, until the fish is cooked and opaque and the skin is blistering and browning. Remove from the grill and set aside to rest for 2 minutes.

7 Stir the dressing and most of the coriander through the noodles. Divide between 4 plates, top with the mackerel fillets and finish with a few coriander leaves.

Note Any oily or white fish fillets can be substituted for the mackerel.

Grilled mackerel with chickpeas and tomatoes

Serves 4
1 garlic clove
4 plum tomatoes
¼ bunch of parsley
400g tin chickpeas
60ml extra virgin olive oil
1 tsp smoked sweet paprika
2 tbsp sherry vinegar
50g pitted black olives
½ lemon
4 mackerel fillets
Salt and freshly ground black pepper

1 Peel and crush the garlic. Blanch the tomatoes in boiling water for 10 seconds, then refresh in cold water, dry, peel and quarter. Coarsely chop enough parsley leaves to give you 1–2 tbsp. Drain and rinse the chickpeas.

2 Heat 50ml of the olive oil in a non-stick sauté pan over a medium heat. Add the garlic, paprika and tomatoes and fry for 2–3 minutes. Deglaze the pan with the sherry vinegar and reduce to 1–2 tsp, then stir in the chickpeas and olives. Reduce the heat and heat through very gently. Meanwhile, juice the ½ lemon.

3 Heat the grill to its highest setting. Using kitchen tweezers, pin-bone the mackerel fillets (see page 284) and place skin side up on a lightly oiled baking sheet. Drizzle with the remaining oil and season with salt and a little lemon juice.

4 Grill the mackerel fillets for 4–6 minutes, depending on thickness, until the skin is caramelised and bubbling slightly and the flesh is opaque, not translucent.

5 Remove from the grill and set aside to rest for 2–3 minutes. Stir the parsley through the chickpea mixture, taste and adjust the seasoning with salt, pepper and lemon juice. Divide the chickpeas between 4 plates. Place a mackerel fillet on top of each and drizzle with a little olive oil.

Pan-frying/griddling

Ginger and sesame glazed tuna

Serves 4

1 tbsp sesame seeds
1 small carrot
½ fennel bulb
1 banana shallot
3cm piece of fresh root ginger
4 tbsp olive oil
1–2 tsp clear honey
75ml white wine
250ml brown chicken and veal stock
  (see page 98)
4 thick-cut tuna steaks, each about 170g
1–2 tsp toasted sesame oil
15g unsalted butter
Salt and freshly ground black pepper
Freshly cooked soba or egg noodles,
  to serve

1 Toast the sesame seeds in a dry frying pan over a low to medium heat for 2–3 minutes, then tip onto a plate and set aside to cool.

2 Peel and finely slice the carrot, finely slice the fennel and halve, peel and finely slice the shallot. Peel the ginger and cut into fine julienne, then set 1 tbsp aside.

3 Heat 2 tbsp of the olive oil in a saucepan over a low heat, add the carrot, fennel, shallot and all but the reserved 1 tbsp ginger. Sweat gently until soft.

4 Add the honey, then the wine, and simmer gently until the wine has reduced to 1–2 tsp. Add the stock and simmer for 10–15 minutes, or until the flavour has developed and the sauce has reduced a little. Strain through a sieve, reserving the sauce and discarding the vegetables.

5 Rub the remaining olive oil all over the tuna steaks. Season them lightly with salt and pepper.

6 Heat a frying pan over a medium to high heat and, when hot, place the tuna steaks in the pan. Cook until the colour changes to halfway up the sides of the tuna, then turn and cook on the other side in the same way. A thick-cut piece should still be rare but warm through the centre.

7 Meanwhile, bring the sauce to a simmer in a pan. Stir in the sesame oil and whisk in the butter. Add the reserved 1 tbsp ginger and the toasted sesame seeds, then taste and adjust the seasoning.

8 Divide the noodles between 4 plates and top with the tuna steaks. Spoon a little of the sauce over the tuna and noodles. Delicious served with wilted greens.

Griddled tuna with a chilli coriander pesto

Serves 4

4 thick-cut tuna steaks, each about 170g
2 tbsp olive oil
Salt and freshly ground black pepper
1 quantity chilli and coriander pesto
  (see page 126), to serve

1 Rub the tuna steaks all over with the olive oil and season with salt and pepper.

2 Heat a griddle pan over a medium to high heat and, when hot, place the tuna steaks on the griddle pan. Cook until the colour changes to halfway up the sides of the tuna, then turn and cook on the other side in the same way. A thick-cut piece should still be rare but warm through the centre.

3 Remove the tuna to 4 serving plates and spoon a little of the pesto onto a corner of the tuna. Serve with roasted red peppers (see page 55) with capers, or a couscous salad.

Note For best results, remove the tuna from the fridge at least 15–20 minutes before cooking, to ensure it is room temperature rather than cold when cooked, so the centre will be warm rather than cold if served very rare.

Salmon and sorrel fishcakes with mustard sauce

Serves 4

For the fishcakes

300g potatoes
400g salmon fillet
5–10 sorrel leaves, depending on size
2 eggs
2 tsp anchovy essence
2 tsp Dijon mustard
Plain flour, to coat
Dried white breadcrumbs, to coat
Oil for shallow-frying
Salt and freshly ground black pepper

For the sauce

300ml strong fish stock (see page 100)
150ml dry vermouth
20g butter
20g plain flour
100ml double cream
½ tsp Dijon mustard
5–10 sorrel leaves

To serve

Wilted spinach (see page 60)

The potatoes and salmon must be cooked in advance to allow them time to cool. Alternatively, you can use leftover mashed potatoes and cooked fish.

1 Peel the potatoes and cut into large, even-sized chunks. Place in a medium saucepan and cover with cold water. Add salt and cook until tender, about 20 minutes. Drain well and mash with a potato masher, or pass through a ricer, or push them through a sieve using a wooden spoon. Set aside to cool.

2 Meanwhile, put the salmon in a frying pan with a large pinch of salt, cover with water and heat gently until barely simmering (a small bubble should break the surface only occasionally). Poach the salmon for 5 minutes, then take off the heat. Leave in the water for a further 5 minutes to finish cooking, then remove the fish from the pan. Set aside to cool.

3 Finely shred the sorrel for the fishcakes and beat the eggs. Put the cooled potato in a bowl and stir in the sorrel, anchovy essence and mustard. Flake one-third of the salmon into the potato mixture and stir well. Add a little of the beaten egg to bind. Season well with salt and pepper, then flake the remaining salmon into the bowl and gently fold it in, trying to keep the flakes as large as possible.

4 Divide the mixture into 4 large or 8 small portions. Flour your hands and shape the portions into cakes. Place some flour on one plate, the remaining beaten egg on another and some breadcrumbs on a third plate. Dust each cake with flour, coat in egg, then cover in breadcrumbs and set aside on a clean plate. They can be made in advance up to this stage and refrigerated until needed.

5 Heat the oven to 190°C/gas mark 5. For the sauce, put the stock and vermouth in a saucepan. Bring to the boil, lower the heat and simmer until reduced by half. Melt the butter in another pan, then stir in the flour and cook for 1 minute. Remove from the heat and add the reduced liquid to the sauce slowly, stirring to avoid lumps. Return to the heat, bring to the boil and simmer for 2 minutes. Stir in the cream and mustard and simmer until the sauce is the required consistency; it should be slightly syrupy. Season and set aside until the fishcakes are cooked.

6 Pour oil into a frying pan to a depth of 1cm and heat over a medium to high heat. When hot, fry the fishcakes until brown on both sides (you may need to do this in batches, depending on the size of the pan). Transfer the browned fishcakes to a baking sheet and bake in the oven for 15 minutes.

7 Meanwhile, heat the sauce, adding a little water if it has thickened too much while it has cooled. Shred the sorrel as finely as possible and stir it into the hot sauce only just before serving, to preserve the colour.

8 Serve the fishcakes with the sauce and wilted spinach (see page 60).

Note Sorrel is not always available to buy, but it is easy to grow, even in a window box. If you can't get it, use a few sprigs of basil, tarragon or dill in its place.

Variations

Salmon fishcakes with dill and lemon sauce Omit the sorrel from the fishcakes and sauce. Finely grate the zest of 1 large lemon; add half to the fish mixture and half to the sauce. Add 1 tbsp lemon juice and 1 tbsp finely chopped dill to the fish mixture. Stir 1 tsp chopped dill and a little lemon juice into the sauce. Serve the fishcakes with lemon wedges.

Haddock and caper fishcakes Replace the salmon with haddock or smoked haddock. Omit the sorrel. Add 1 tbsp chopped parsley and 1 tbsp chopped capers to the mixture. Serve with tartare (rather than sorrel) sauce (see page 118).

Seared tuna with a pickled vegetable salad

Serves 8
8 thick-cut tuna steaks, each about 170g
2 tbsp olive oil
Salt and freshly ground black pepper

For the pickling liquor
100ml rice wine vinegar
100ml water
1 tsp salt
100g palm sugar (or brown sugar)

For the salad
1 green mango
1 carrot
5cm piece of daikon
½ cucumber
50g mangetout
1 small red onion
4cm piece of fresh root ginger
Handful of bean sprouts
Large handful of coriander leaves
Large handful of mint leaves

For the dressing
2 tbsp water
2 tsp palm sugar (or brown sugar)
2 tbsp Chinese plum sauce
2 tbsp lime juice
1 tsp sesame oil

1 To make the pickling liquor, put the vinegar, water, salt and palm sugar in a small saucepan over a low heat. Allow the salt and sugar to dissolve, then remove from the heat and set aside to cool.

2 For the salad, peel, stone and finely shred the mango. Peel the carrot and daikon and cut into julienne. Halve the cucumber lengthways and scoop out the seeds, then cut into julienne. De-string the mangetout and cut into julienne. Halve, peel and finely slice the red onion. Peel the ginger and cut into fine julienne.

3 Place all the prepared vegetables in a bowl or large plastic food bag and pour over the cooled pickling liquor. Marinate for 2 hours, or ideally overnight.

4 Drain the vegetables, discarding the pickling liquor, and put them in a bowl with the bean sprouts. Chop the coriander and mint leaves and add to the bowl.

5 To make the dressing, mix the water and palm sugar together, leave the palm sugar to dissolve, then add the plum sauce, lime juice and sesame oil. Taste and adjust the seasoning as necessary (it should be a balance of sweet, sour and salty), then set aside.

6 Brush the tuna all over with the olive oil and season with salt and pepper.

7 Heat a frying or griddle pan over a medium to high heat and, when hot, place the tuna steaks in the pan. Cook until the colour changes to halfway up the sides of the tuna, then turn and cook on the other side in the same way. A thick-cut piece should still be rare but warm through the centre.

8 Pour the dressing over the pickled vegetables and toss to coat evenly. Divide between 4 serving plates. Cut the tuna steaks in half and arrange next to the salad. Grind over some pepper and serve.

....

A note on the pickled vegetables...
These also go very well with duck breasts with ginger, honey and lime (see page 374) or spiced duck confit (see page 372). Alternatively, try them with char siu pork tenderloin (see page 463).

How to noisette a cutlet of fish

This useful technique is employed to bone a fish cutlet, to create a noisette of fish that is a little easier to cook and looks more attractive.

1 Place the cutlet on a board and carefully release the skin from the ends to halfway up each side, but do not detach completely.

2 Keeping the skin intact at the top of the cutlet, cut down on each side of the bone, then around the circular back bone, continuing down the inside to remove the bone.

3 Using kitchen tweezers, pin-bone the remaining fish; the pin bones are found through the widest section of each half of the cutlet.

4 Take one skinned end and tuck it in the place where the bone was, so it effectively replaces the bone. Wrap the other end around the outside to create a disc of fish.

5 Wrap the loose skin around the noisette to enclose it and tie with string to secure.

6 Place on a large plate or tray and repeat with any remaining cutlets, then weight the cutlets lightly to set their shape. Remove the string after cooking, before serving.

Noisettes of salmon with samphire and asparagus

Serves 4

4 salmon cutlets, each about 170g and 2cm thick

200g samphire

Bunch of thin asparagus spears

1 lemon

20–25g butter

Salt and freshly ground black pepper

1 Prepare the salmon cutlets as noisettes (see left).

2 Pick over the samphire and trim the root ends, if necessary. Trim the coarse ends of the asparagus. Heat the oven to 180°C/gas mark 4.

3 Fill a saucepan with water, place over a medium heat and bring to a simmer. Blanch the samphire in the simmering water for 3 minutes until just tender, then lift out, drain, refresh in cold water and set aside. Blanch the asparagus in the simmering water for 1–2 minutes; drain, refresh and set aside. Juice the lemon.

4 Heat a non-stick ovenproof frying pan over a low to medium heat and add 1–2 tsp butter. Season the noisettes lightly with salt and, when the butter is foaming, add them to the pan. Cook until golden on the underside, then turn over and gently brown the second side.

5 Transfer the frying pan to the oven for 3–4 minutes for the noisettes to cook almost through.

6 Heat another frying pan over a medium heat and add the remaining butter. Allow it to melt before adding the samphire and asparagus, to heat through. Taste and season with pepper.

7 Remove the noisettes from the oven and lift out of the frying pan onto a board; remove the string and the skin. Taste the pan juices and add a few drops of lemon juice and seasoning to taste. Divide the samphire and asparagus between 4 plates and place a salmon noisette on top. Drizzle with the pan juices and serve.

Variations

Noisettes of salmon with crushed new potatoes and peas Replace the samphire and asparagus with 500g new potatoes. Simmer until tender, drain, then lightly crush. While still warm, stir through 50g butter until melted, then 100g cooked, small peas with salt and pepper to taste. Drizzle the pan juices over each plated noisette, as for the main recipe.

Noisettes of salmon with new potatoes and watercress sauce Replace the samphire and asparagus with 500g new potatoes. Blanch the leaves from a bunch of watercress in boiling water for 30 seconds. Drain, refresh in cold water, then drain again. Melt 30g butter in a saucepan, stir in 30g plain flour and cook over a low heat for 1–2 minutes. Stir in 300ml fish stock (see page 100), then 150ml double cream and simmer, stirring, for 2 minutes. Let cool slightly, then blitz with the watercress in a blender or food processor until you have a pale green sauce with dark green flecks. Season with salt and pepper to taste and reheat gently before serving with the noisettes of salmon and new potatoes.

Boning smaller round fish

This technique is suitable for sardines, herring and other small round fish.

First descale and gut the fish to prepare them for cooking whole (see page 280), but trim off the dorsal fin too. Rinse the fish under cold running water and pat dry with kitchen paper.

1 Lay the fish on a board and, at the vent hole, cut towards the tail, opening the 2 fillets completely.

2 Open the belly area and place the fish skin side up, so the fish fillets lie flesh side against the board.

3 Run your thumb from the tail to just behind the head along the back bone of the fish, which will help to release the bone.

4 Turn the fish over so it is skin side down and, using a pair of scissors, snip the bone behind the head and at the tail.

5 Supporting the fish at the head end, carefully pull the bone backwards towards the tail. Do this slowly to avoid pulling fish with the bone.

6 Discard the bone and feel over the fish for any other bones. Pin-bone it, using kitchen tweezers, and trim the belly area to neaten the fish. It is now ready to cook.

Presentation

If you don't want to serve the fish with the head on, cut it off before gutting the fish, which will make it easier to gut and to open and flatten the fillets against the board before releasing the bone with your thumb.

Escabeche of sardines

Serves 4

8 sardines
2 garlic cloves
1 small onion
½ carrot
150ml olive oil
75g plain flour, seasoned with a large
   pinch each of salt and pepper
1 tsp smoked sweet paprika
½ tsp dried oregano
½ tsp dried thyme
1 bay leaf
⅓ cinnamon stick
1 strip of pared orange zest
1 strip of pared lemon zest
150ml dry white wine
50ml sherry vinegar
Salt and freshly ground black pepper

1 Descale and gut the sardines (see page 280), then bone them, removing the heads (see left).

2 Peel and thinly slice the garlic. Halve, peel and thinly slice the onion. Peel and slice the carrot.

3 Heat the olive oil in a deep frying pan over a medium heat. Coat the sardines in the seasoned flour and fry for 1 minute on each side, until lightly cooked. Remove to a shallow dish.

4 Sauté the garlic in the oil left in the pan over a low heat until starting to colour, then add the onion and carrot and cook gently for 5 minutes until softening.

5 Add the paprika, oregano, thyme, bay leaf, cinnamon stick and citrus zest strips. Cook for 1 minute, then add the wine and sherry vinegar and simmer gently for about 10 minutes to allow the flavours to develop and infuse. Season with salt and pepper.

6 Remove from the heat and set aside to cool, then pour the liquor over the sardines. Leave to marinate in the fridge for 12–24 hours before serving.

Note You can use mackerel in place of sardines. Fillet and pin-bone the mackerel and cut the fillets at an angle into 5–6cm pieces.

Fried sardines with a spicy pickled cucumber and red onion salad

Serves 4

8–12 sardines
1 tbsp red or yellow curry paste
½ tbsp water
Oil for deep-frying

For the salad

2 cucumbers
1 tsp salt
150ml rice wine vinegar
30–40g palm sugar (or brown sugar)
1 red onion
1 red chilli
Handful of coriander leaves
Handful of mint leaves

For the garnish

4 spring onions
2cm piece of fresh root ginger

1 To make the salad, peel and halve the cucumbers lengthways. Deseed them, using a teaspoon, and slice them on the diagonal into thin 3–4mm slices. Put the cucumber slices in a colander set over a bowl, add the salt and toss well. Leave for about 1 hour to degorge.

2 Meanwhile, to make the dressing, whisk together the rice wine vinegar and sugar until the sugar is dissolved. Halve, peel and finely slice the red onion. Halve, deseed and finely slice the chilli. Set aside.

3 To make the garnish, trim and finely slice the spring onions on the diagonal; peel the ginger and cut into julienne.

4 Descale and gut the sardines (see page 280), then bone them, removing the heads (see left). In a large bowl, mix the curry paste with the ½ tbsp water. Gently toss the sardines in the curry paste to coat as evenly as possible.

5 Drain the cucumbers and squeeze gently to remove excess moisture, without breaking them up. Place in a large plastic food bag and add the dressing, along with the red onion and half the chilli. Make sure all the vegetables are coated in the dressing. Set aside for up to 1 hour. Heat the oven to 120°C/gas mark ½.

6 To fry the sardines, one-third fill a large, deep, heavy saucepan with oil and heat to 190°C, or until a small piece of bread sizzles and browns in 40 seconds (see page 72). Deep-fry the fish 2 or 3 at a time until cooked, 4–6 minutes, depending on size. Remove with a slotted spoon to a tray lined with kitchen paper, to drain. Keep warm in the low oven, with the door ajar, while you deep-fry the rest.

7 Add the coriander and mint leaves to the cucumber salad. Plate the sardines and sprinkle over the spring onions, ginger and remaining chilli. Serve with the salad.

Pan-fried oated herring with a bacon, pistachio and pomegranate relish

Serves 4
8 medium herring
200g small pin-head oats
100–125g butter, plus a little melted
  to brush

For the relish
75g piece of smoked bacon
1 shallot
¼ bunch of chives
75ml olive oil
1 orange
½ green apple
½ pomegranate
25g pistachio nuts
1–2 tbsp sherry vinegar
Salt and freshly ground black pepper

1 Descale and gut the herring (see page 280), then bone them, removing the heads (see page 314). Wipe with kitchen paper and set aside.

2 To prepare the relish, remove and discard the rind from the bacon and cut the bacon into thin lardons. Halve, peel and finely slice the shallot. Finely chop enough chives to give you 1 tbsp.

3 Place a frying pan over a low to medium heat and add the lardons with 1 tbsp of the olive oil. Sauté until the fat has rendered and the lardons are golden, then remove the lardons to a bowl. Add the shallot to the pan and sauté until starting to soften and caramelise, then add it to the lardons.

4 Finely grate the zest and squeeze the juice from the orange. Core the apple and cut into small dice. Drizzle a little of the orange juice over the apples to prevent them from discolouring. Extract the pomegranate seeds from the fruit (see step 7, page 343). Add the diced apple, pomegranate seeds and pistachios to the lardon and shallot mixture. Heat the oven to 120°C/gas mark ½.

5 You need 5 tbsp fat, made up of oil and rendered bacon fat, in the frying pan, so add extra olive oil if necessary to make it up to this amount. Place over a low heat. Add the sherry vinegar and orange juice to taste. Adjust for balance, then immediately pour it over the relish ingredients. Add the chives and a quarter of the orange zest, then taste and adjust the seasoning with salt and pepper. Set aside.

6 To cook the herring, wipe out the frying pan and place over a low to medium heat. Place the oats on a shallow tray. Brush the herring with the melted butter. Season, then coat the fish on both sides in the oats.

7 Place half the butter in the frying pan and, when foaming, fry the herring a few at a time until the oats are golden and the herring cooked, about 2–3 minutes each side. Keep them warm in the low oven while you repeat with the remaining herring and butter, wiping out the pan between batches.

8 Place 2 herring on each plate and spoon a little of the relish and juices on top.

Note For a more substantial accompaniment, you can double the quantity of bacon, shallot, apple, pomegranate and pistachios, and add some green leaves.

Deep-fried whitebait

Serves 4
400–500g whitebait
1–1½ tsp cayenne pepper
100g plain flour, seasoned with a large
  pinch of salt
Oil for deep-frying
Salt
1 lemon, to serve

1 Pick over the whitebait, discarding any broken fish. Dry well on kitchen paper. Cut the lemon into wedges and reserve for serving.

2 Mix the cayenne pepper with the seasoned flour and sprinkle over the whitebait. Coat the whitebait evenly in the flour, then place handfuls in a sieve, giving the sieve a shake. This will help to remove all excess flour and leave only a very thin layer of flour on the fish.

3 One-third fill a large, heavy saucepan with oil and heat to 195°C, or until a small piece of bread dropped into the oil browns in 20 seconds (see page 72). Deep-fry small handfuls of the whitebait at a time; cooking too many at a time will make them stick together. Fry for no more than 2 minutes, until golden brown, then remove to a tray lined with kitchen paper, to drain. Sprinkle lightly with salt.

4 Repeat with the remaining whitebait and serve with the lemon wedges.

Smoked fish

Smoking is a technique traditionally used to preserve fish, but is now often used to flavour and add texture rather than to preserve.

Fish can be cold- or hot-smoked. Cold smoking is where the fish is smoked over cool smoke so the fish is not actually cooked and may require further cooking. Examples of cold smoked fish include traditional smoked salmon, eaten just cold-smoked, and smoked haddock, which requires further cooking.

Hot-smoked fish is smoked over hot smoke so the fish cooks as it takes on a smoky flavour. Fish smoked this way needs no further cooking and can be eaten straight away. Examples include kippers (hot-smoked herring), eel, and hot-smoked salmon and trout.

Tea-smoked mackerel with horseradish potatoes and chive oil

Serves 4
2 medium mackerel
1 orange
60g light brown sugar
60g white rice
20g jasmine tea leaves

For the chive oil
½ bunch of chives
150ml extra virgin olive oil

For the horseradish potatoes
16–24 new potatoes, depending on size
55g butter
1–2 tbsp creamed horseradish
Salt and freshly ground black pepper

Hot smoking at home is easily done, and you don't need a smoker – a simple smoking apparatus can be put together from a wok or roasting tin, a wire rack or trivet, and foil.

1 Fillet and pin-bone the mackerel (see page 284). Finely pare the zest from half of the orange.

2 To prepare the smoker, line a wok with a double layer of foil. Mix the sugar, rice, tea leaves and pared orange zest together and spread evenly over the bottom of the foil-lined wok. Put a steamer or wire rack inside the wok.

3 To make the chive oil, coarsely chop the chives and place in a blender with the olive oil and a pinch of salt. Blend for 30 seconds until smooth, then pass through a fine sieve and set aside.

4 Bring a saucepan of salted water to the boil. Add the potatoes, bring back to the boil, then lower the heat and simmer until tender. Drain and return to the pan.

5 Place the mackerel on the steamer or wire rack, skin side down. Cover the wok with a double of layer of foil, making sure you seal it tightly around the edges, leaving a small opening to see when the smoking starts. Place over a medium to high heat. Once there is smoke coming out of the opening, seal the hole and leave for 3–5 minutes (depending on the size of the fillets), then remove from the heat. Leave to rest for 2–3 minutes before removing the foil lid.

6 While the mackerel is smoking, add the butter to the potatoes and warm over a low heat. Lightly crush with a fork and mix in the butter with horseradish to taste. Season and keep warm.

7 Place a pastry cutter on each of 4 plates. Divide the potato into 4 portions and press lightly into the cutters.

8 Carefully remove the cutters and drizzle chive oil around the potatoes. Place a mackerel fillet over or on the side of the potato stack on each plate.

Variations
You can replace the horseradish in the potatoes with wholegrain mustard or wasabi. Hot raw beetroot with black pepper and lemon (see page 40) is also an excellent accompaniment to the hot-smoked mackerel.

Hot-smoked trout with roasted beetroot and watercress

Serves 4

500g baby beetroot
1 tbsp olive oil, plus extra for roasting
30g skinned hazelnuts
2 tsp small capers (optional)
Oil for deep-frying (optional)
150g fine green beans
½ lemon
2 tbsp mayonnaise (see page 116)
2 tbsp water
Fresh horseradish root or creamed
  horseradish, to taste
Large bunch of watercress
6 hot-smoked trout fillets
Salt and freshly ground black pepper

1 Heat the oven to 200°C/gas mark 6. Wash the beetroot, cut off the tops, leaving about 1cm still attached, and trim the root. Place in a bowl and toss in enough olive oil to coat and season generously with salt and pepper. Tip into a roasting tin lined with foil and roast in the oven for 45–60 minutes, or until tender (check with the point of a cutlery knife). Leave to cool a little, then slip the skins off with your fingers; they are easier to peel from the root end to the stalk. Cut into halves or even-sized pieces, depending on size. Set aside.

2 While the beetroot are roasting, place the hazelnuts on a baking tray and toast in the oven for 5–10 minutes until golden. Tip onto a board, leave to cool, then coarsely chop. If serving capers, heat a 3cm depth of oil in a small saucepan to 190°C, or until a piece of bread browns in 40 seconds (see page 72). Deep-fry the capers for a minute or two until crisp, then remove and drain on kitchen paper.

3 Top the green beans and blanch them in boiling salted water for 3–5 minutes until tender, then refresh in cold water. Once cool, lift out and set aside.

4 Meanwhile, to make the dressing, finely grate the zest and squeeze the juice from the ½ lemon. Put the mayonnaise in a bowl and stir in the 2 tbsp water and 1 tbsp of the lemon juice. Peel some of the horseradish root and grate finely into the mayonnaise. (Start with ½ tbsp, taste the mixture and add more if required.) Add more lemon juice, some lemon zest, to taste, and season with salt and pepper. Add a little more water or lemon juice if the dressing is too thick, then set aside.

5 Pick the watercress leaves from the stalks; wash and dry, then place in a bowl. Toss with the 1 tbsp oil and a sprinkle of lemon juice. Season with salt and pepper.

6 Divide the dressed watercress between 4 plates. Arrange the warm roast beetroot and the beans over the watercress. Flake the smoked trout into large pieces over the top and sprinkle over the hazelnuts and deep-fried capers, if using. Drizzle with the horseradish sauce and serve at once.

Smoked eel blinis with horseradish cream

Serves 4 as a starter

200g piece of smoked eel, or 1 small
  smoked eel
5 tbsp crème fraîche
5 tbsp Greek yoghurt
2–3 tbsp hot grated horseradish (in a jar)
1 shallot
1 lemon
¼ bunch of parsley
30g raisins
6 tbsp extra virgin olive oil
Salt and freshly ground black pepper
4 blinis (see page 618), to serve

1 Skin and fillet the smoked eel into 4 portions, or remove from the packaging and allow to come to room temperature.

2 For the horseradish cream, mix the crème fraîche with the yoghurt in a small bowl. Add enough horseradish to subtly flavour the mixture; there should be a balance between the heat of the horseradish, the creaminess of the crème fraîche and yoghurt and the acidity in both. Season with salt and set aside.

3 To make the vinaigrette, halve, peel and finely dice the shallot. Juice the lemon and finely chop the parsley. Put the shallot, raisins and olive oil in a small saucepan and warm over a low heat to soften the shallot and plump the raisins. Remove from the heat and leave to cool, then add 1–2 tbsp lemon juice and the parsley, with salt and pepper to taste.

4 Warm the blinis in a low oven and place one on each plate. Top with a piece of smoked eel, spoon a little of the shallot and raisin vinaigrette over and around the eel and blinis and place a dollop of horseradish cream on top.

(Illustrated on page 619)

Smoked haddock chowder

Serves 4

1 onion
50g piece of smoked bacon
100g potato
½ lemon
Small handful of flat-leaf parsley
350g smoked haddock fillet
600ml milk
1 bay leaf
1 small mace blade
30g butter
50–75ml double cream
Salt and freshly ground black pepper

1 Halve and peel the onion, then slice half of it and finely dice the other half, keeping them separate. Remove any rind from the bacon and cut into lardons. Wash, peel and dice the potato. Juice the lemon, finely chop enough parsley leaves to give you 1 tbsp, then set aside.

2 Scrape off any scales from the smoked haddock and place it skin side down in a sauté pan. Pour over the milk and add the sliced onion, bay leaf and mace. If the fish is not completely covered, add a little more milk or tuck a damp cartouche (see page 13) over the fish. Bring the milk to scalding point.

3 Reduce the heat and poach the fish gently for about 5 minutes, depending on the size and thickness of the fillet, then remove from the heat and leave to finish cooking in the cooling milk. The fish is cooked when it has turned opaque and the skin comes away easily.

4 Once cooled, remove the fish from the milk with a fish slice. Remove the skin and any bones and break the fish into large flakes. Set aside.

5 Strain the milk, discarding the onion, bay leaf and mace. Taste it, and if very strongly flavoured, dilute with a little more milk, topping it up to 600ml.

6 Put the lardons in a medium saucepan and sauté over a low to medium heat for 3–4 minutes, or until the fat is beginning to render, then remove the lardons and set aside. Lower the heat, add the butter and the diced onion and cook gently until the onion is softening but still colourless. Add the potato and continue to cook very slowly for a further 10 minutes until the potato begins to soften.

7 Pour in the milk, increase the heat to medium and bring to a simmer. Allow to simmer until the potato is cooked, about 10 minutes, when a cube can be squeezed easily against the side of the pan.

8 Leave the soup to cool a little, then purée in a blender in batches until smooth. Pass the soup through a sieve into the rinsed out saucepan.

9 Reheat the soup gently and add the reserved lardons and smoked haddock. Taste and add some or all of the cream to taste, and season with salt, pepper and a few drops of lemon juice. Stir through the parsley just before serving.

Variations

Smoked haddock chowder with spinach Add 150g spinach, wilted (see page 60), to the finished soup.

Leek and smoked haddock chowder Replace the diced onion with ½ small leek, finely sliced.

Clam chowder Omit the smoked haddock, sliced onion, bay leaf and mace. Steam 400g clams (see page 238) in 20g butter, take out the clams, shell them and set aside, discarding the shells. Strain, taste and reduce the clam liquor if necessary, then add it to the soup when the milk is added to cook the potatoes in step 7. Proceed as for the main recipe, adding the clam meat at the end with the lardons.

Cured fish

This is another method of preserving fish, by drawing out some of the liquid either with a dry cure, as in gravadlax, or an acidic marinade that 'cooks' the flesh as it starts to pickle and preserve it, as in ceviche. Herbs and aromatics can be used to impart flavour during the process.

Ceviche

Serves 4
400g firm white fish fillet such as
    monkfish, halibut or sea bass
1 tbsp extra virgin olive oil
Pinch of cayenne pepper
½ red onion
1 red chilli
4 limes
1 plum tomato
1 ripe avocado
½ bunch of chives or coriander
Salt and freshly ground black pepper

1 Pin-bone the fish, if necessary (see page 284). Using a very sharp knife, cut the fish into very thin slices (without skin if using halibut or sea bass) and put the slices in a bowl with the olive oil and cayenne pepper.

2 Peel and very finely slice the onion. Halve and deseed the chilli, then slice very finely. Finely grate the zest of 1 lime and juice all 4 limes.

3 Add the onion and chilli to the fish with the lime zest and juice. Stir well and leave the fish to 'cook' in the acidic marinade, from 1–6 hours, depending on how thinly sliced the fish is. It is ready when it has an opaque, cooked appearance.

4 Blanch the tomato in boiling water for 10 seconds, then refresh in cold water, dry and peel. Quarter and deseed, then cut the flesh into slivers.

5 When ready to serve, halve, stone and peel the avocado, then cut the flesh into cubes. Roughly chop enough chives or coriander leaves to give you 1 tbsp and stir into the fish mixture with the avocado and tomato. Season to taste with salt and pepper. Spread the ceviche out on a plate and finish with chives or coriander.

Gravadlax with mustard and dill sauce

Serves 15–20
1 whole salmon, 2–2.5kg, wild if possible
Oil to brush
3 tbsp granulated sugar
1½ tbsp flaked sea salt
Bunch of dill
1 tbsp brandy
½ tbsp white peppercorns

For the sauce
1 tbsp Dijon mustard
2 tbsp white wine vinegar
1 tsp caster sugar
6 tbsp sunflower oil
Salt and freshly ground black pepper

1 Fillet and pin-bone the salmon to give 2 sides (see page 284), but do not skin it. Brush lightly all over with oil. Lay one side, skin side down, on a triple layer of cling film, longer than the fish. Mix together the sugar and salt, then pat the mixture all over the flesh side. Chop enough dill leaves to give you about 1 tbsp, enough to cover the fish, and sprinkle it over the salt and sugar layer. Sprinkle the brandy over the dill. Crush the peppercorns with a pestle and mortar and sprinkle over the dill.

2 Place the other side of salmon on top, flesh side down so that it fits closely, sandwiching the dill mixture. Wrap the salmon very tightly in the cling film, leaving the ends open. Place on a lipped tray that will fit in the fridge.

3 Weight the salmon down with another tray topped with some heavy tins or similar weights and refrigerate for 6 hours. Remove the weights, turn the salmon over, weight again and refrigerate for a further 6 hours before removing the weights. The salmon can be kept in the fridge wrapped in cling film for up to 1 week before serving, and should not be served before 12 hours of curing.

4 To make the sauce, put the mustard in a small bowl, stir in the wine vinegar and sugar and gradually whisk in the oil. Chop more dill, enough to give you 1 tbsp, and stir into the sauce. Season with salt and pepper and refrigerate until needed.

5 To serve, scrape and wipe off the marinade. Slice the salmon as thinly as possible (as you would a side of smoked salmon), layering it on individual plates or a platter. Garnish with dill sprigs and serve with the sauce and brown bread and butter.

Poultry & feathered game

While poultry, particularly chicken, dominates our tables, game birds make an excellent alternative. Although often an acquired taste, game has a rewardingly rich flavour and leanness, with the meat ranging in colour from pale guinea fowl to the deep rich pinky-red of grouse. Almost every part of a poultry or game bird can be used, and just a little knowledge of basic butchery skills means you can easily prepare them at home. The broad range of suitable cooking methods for poultry and game, and their ability to take on other flavours, make them incredibly versatile.

Poultry

While duck and game birds can be served pink, chicken and turkey must be cooked through before eating.

Roasting whole birds

The traditional method of roasting a chicken is to cook it for 20 minutes per 450g at a fairly high temperature. However, cooking at a moderate temperature after an initial browning is more popular these days, and generally considered to give excellent results. In this recipe, once the chicken has browned for around 20–30 minutes at a high temperature, you can turn the oven down to 180–190°C/ gas mark 4–5 to roast the chicken a little more gently and slowly. It will take an additional 20–30 minutes to cook, but will potentially be more tender and juicy.

Roast chicken

Serves 4
1 chicken, about 1.35kg
20g butter, softened
8 chipolata sausages
8 rashers of streaky bacon
1–2 tsp plain flour
300ml chicken and veal stock
  (see page 96)
Salt and freshly ground black pepper
Bread sauce (see page 129), to serve

For the stuffing
½ large or 1 small onion
20g butter
½ apple
Large handful of herb sprigs, such as
  sage, parsley, thyme, rosemary, oregano
½–1 lemon
80g coarse fresh white breadcrumbs

1 Heat the oven to 200°C/gas mark 6. Remove the wishbone from the breast, if you wish, to make carving easier (as shown).

2 To make the stuffing, peel and finely dice the onion. Melt the butter in a saucepan over a gentle heat, add the onion, cover and sweat until very soft and translucent. Turn the heat up to medium, remove the lid and allow the excess moisture to evaporate, taking care not to brown the onion. Remove from the heat and set aside to cool. Peel and grate the apple. Finely chop enough mixed herb leaves to give you 2–3 tbsp. Finely grate the zest of the lemon. Add the apple and chopped herbs to the cooled onion with the breadcrumbs and lemon zest. Taste and season with salt and pepper and a little more herbs or lemon zest if necessary.

3 Season the cavity of the chicken with salt and pepper. Loosely tie the legs together with a piece of string (see note on trussing, page 326). Stuff the chicken from the neck end (as shown), carefully using your fingers to release the skin covering the breast for the filling to be spread over the breast beneath the skin and making sure the breast is well plumped. Draw the neck skin flap down to cover the stuffing. Secure with a skewer if necessary and place in a roasting tin.

4 Rub a little softened butter all over the chicken and season with salt and pepper. Place a double piece of buttered foil over the breast to prevent the skin from burning and roast in the oven for about 1¼–1½ hours, occasionally basting with the roasting juices.

5 Meanwhile, make each chipolata into 2 cocktail-sized sausages by twisting it in the middle and cutting in two. Derind each bacon rasher and cut into short lengths, stretch them a little, and loosely roll them up.

6 After the chicken has been roasting for 45 minutes, add the sausages and bacon rolls to the roasting tin, wedging the bacon rolls so they don't unroll.

7 When the calculated roasting time is up, check the chicken is cooked; the legs should be wobbly and the juices should run clear when the thigh is pierced with a skewer. If the breast has not browned, remove the foil for the last 5 minutes of cooking. When the chicken is cooked, lift it out of the roasting tin onto a board set over a tray (to catch the juices) and leave to rest for 10–15 minutes. Remove the sausages and bacon rolls and keep them warm.

(Continued overleaf)

8 To make the gravy, carefully pour off and discard all but 1–2 tsp of the fat from the roasting tin, reserving the juices. Place the roasting tin over a medium heat, add the flour and stir for 1–2 minutes, browning the flour a little until straw coloured. Gradually add the stock, reserved roasting juices and any resting juices, and bring to the boil, stirring. Turn the heat down and simmer for 3–5 minutes until the gravy has developed a good flavour. Season with salt and pepper and strain before serving.

9 Carve the chicken (see right) and transfer the slices to a serving dish with the sausages and bacon rolls. Serve the gravy and warm bread sauce separately.

Variations

Thyme roasted chicken Omit the stuffing, chipolatas, bacon rolls and gravy. Place a small bunch of thyme in the chicken cavity before tying the legs. Spread 15g softened butter over the chicken, season it well with salt and pepper and roast as for the main recipe, for 1 hour. Melt 50g unsalted butter over a low heat and add ½–1 tbsp finely chopped thyme. Remove from the heat and leave to infuse for 15–20 minutes. Strain and reserve the thyme and butter separately. Baste the chicken with the thyme-infused butter at least 3 or 4 times during cooking. When the chicken is cooked, remove it from the oven, add the reserved thyme back to the remaining butter and baste the chicken again.

Five spice, soy and honey roasted chicken Omit the stuffing, chipolatas and bacon rolls. Smear the chicken all over with dark soy sauce and then drizzle with a little oil. Put 1 cinnamon stick and 2 star anise in the cavity and roast for 1 hour. Mix 2 tbsp clear honey with 1 tsp five-spice powder, ½ tsp chilli powder and 1 tbsp sesame oil. Brush the mixture over the chicken and roast for the remaining time. If you want gravy, add 20ml mirin (rice wine) or dry sherry to the tin after pouring off excess fat, and simmer for at least 2 minutes. Serve with stir-fried vegetables.

Provençal roast chicken Omit the stuffing, chipolatas, bacon rolls and gravy. Cut a garlic bulb in half horizontally, rub the surface of one half over the chicken skin, then place inside the cavity with a small handful of mixed herb sprigs such as basil, oregano, thyme, rosemary, tarragon, marjoram, or 1 tbsp dried herbes de Provence. Rub 30g softened butter over the skin, put the other half of the bulb cut side down in the tin and roast for half the calculated time. Pour 200ml red wine into the tin and roast for the remaining time. This gravy can then be strained and left thin.

French roast chicken Omit the stuffing, chipolatas, bacon rolls and gravy. Rub 30g softened butter over the non-breast side of the chicken and season well with salt and pepper. Place breast side down in a roasting tin and add a 2cm depth of water to the roasting tin, along with ½ onion and ½ carrot, both peeled and sliced, and some parsley stalks. Roast at 200°C/gas mark 6 for 30 minutes, then carefully turn the chicken over, rub another 30g softened butter over it and season well. Return to the oven for a further 30–45 minutes. Once cooked, allow the chicken to rest. Strain and taste the cooking juices; they should be savoury and buttery; reduce a little to intensify the flavour if required. Discard the onion, carrot and parsley. Joint rather than carve the chicken (see right) and serve with the sauce and some watercress. Roasting the chicken this way helps to retain the moisture in the breast and creates its own sauce while cooking.

A note on trussing...

Trussing chickens before roasting pushes the legs and thighs close to the body, which prevents hot air from circulating around them and cooking them properly. Instead, we simply tie the legs together loosely to help keep the shape of the chicken. As game birds can be served rare to pink, they can be trussed fully and will keep their shape that way.

Carving a whole roast chicken

It is a good idea to remove the wishbone from any poultry you are going to carve to serve before cooking, as it makes the process easier.

1 Carve slices from the length of the breast, about 3mm thick. Alternatively, carefully remove the whole breast, without the wing attached, and slice across the breast into slices 7–8mm thick. This is often useful for a large chicken or turkey as it gives more manageable pieces.

2 Cut through the thigh joint to remove the thigh and leg and then divide the thigh and leg through the joint (as for jointing a raw chicken, step 3, page 337). The legs/drumsticks can be served as they are or you can carefully carve slices from the thicker end.

3 Finally, carve the meat from both sides of the thigh bone.

Jointing a chicken after cooking

An alternative to carving chicken to serve it is to joint it after cooking. This can be done in almost the same manner as before cooking (see page 336), but it is easier to remove the complete back bone first, by carefully turning the bird onto its breast and cutting down each side of the back bone and removing it (as shown). Then turn the bird breast side up and proceed as for jointing a chicken before cooking. Extra care needs to be taken as the chicken will be hot.

Roast turkey

Serves 12

1 turkey, about 5.35kg, with giblets
1 glass of white wine
150ml water
170g butter
Salt and freshly ground black pepper

For the gravy

½ onion
2 bay leaves
Few parsley stalks
6 black peppercorns
About 500ml chicken and veal stock
  (see page 96)
40g plain flour

For the stuffing

2 onions
60g butter
200g vacuum-packed, cooked, peeled
  chestnuts
3 celery sticks
½ small bunch of parsley
1 turkey liver
100g fresh white breadcrumbs
1 egg, beaten
Freshly grated nutmeg

If possible, buy a fresh turkey within a day or two of cooking. Take the giblets out of the cavity and store the bird and giblets separately in the fridge, removing the bird at least an hour before cooking to bring it to room temperature. Calculate the cooking time, adding the weight of your stuffing to the weight of the bird. The roasting time is affected by various factors, including your oven, the shape of the bird and the temperature it is at when it goes into the oven. Plan the timing so that the bird will be ready 30 minutes before you are eating. This will give you some leeway, and allows time to make the gravy and finish roasting the potatoes while the turkey rests.

1 To prepare the stock for the gravy, remove the wishbone from the turkey (as for chicken, see page 325). Put the giblets, except the liver, into a saucepan with the neck. (The liver is used to flavour the stuffing; it would make the gravy bitter.) Peel and slice the onion and add to the saucepan with the bay leaves, parsley stalks and peppercorns. Add enough water to cover and bring to a simmer over a low to medium heat. Simmer gently, uncovered, for 1 hour, then strain through a fine sieve, discarding the vegetables.

2 To make the stuffing, halve, peel and finely dice the onions. Melt the butter in a small saucepan over a low heat, add the onions, cover and sweat until very soft and translucent. Transfer to a bowl and set aside until cool.

3 Meanwhile, heat the oven to 180°C/gas mark 4. Roughly chop the chestnuts. De-string and finely chop the celery and finely chop enough parsley leaves to give you 1–2 tbsp. Prepare the turkey liver (as for chicken livers, see page 388) and finely chop. Add the chestnuts, celery, parsley and liver to the cooled onions. Add the breadcrumbs and plenty of nutmeg, salt and pepper. Add enough beaten egg to just bind the mixture.

4 Push the stuffing into the neck end of the turkey, making sure the breast is well plumped. Draw the skin flap down to cover the stuffing and secure with a skewer. Season the turkey well with salt and pepper and place it in a large roasting tin. Pour the wine and water into the bottom of the tin.

5 Melt the butter in a small pan and place a muslin cloth, large enough to cover the whole turkey, in the melted butter; soak the muslin until all the butter has been absorbed. Completely cover the turkey with the buttered muslin, tucking the ends down the sides of the turkey inside the tin. Roast the bird for the calculated time (see right). Add a splash of water to the tin if the juices look like they may evaporate and burn during the cooking time.

6 Check the turkey is cooked by piercing the thigh with a skewer to see if the juices are clear; the legs should also be wobbly. If not, return to the oven and roast for a little longer, then test again. Repeat, if necessary, until the bird is cooked. Remove the muslin and carefully transfer the bird to a board over a tray (to catch the juices). Leave to rest somewhere warm for 20–30 minutes before carving.

7 Meanwhile, make the gravy. Pour the juices and fat from the roasting tin into a jug. Skim off the fat, return 2 tbsp of it to the roasting tin and discard the rest. Reserve the juices. Make up 600ml liquid from a mixture of the giblet stock, chicken stock and vegetable cooking water (potato or carrot water works best). Stir the flour into the fat in the roasting tin. Cook over a medium heat until the flour turns straw coloured. Stir in the 600ml liquid with the reserved roasting juices and any resting juices. Bring to the boil, lower the heat and simmer gently for 5 minutes. Taste and adjust the seasoning, then strain into a warmed gravy boat or jug.

8 Carve the turkey and serve, with traditional garnishes and accompaniments.

Roasting times for turkey

The cooking times given below may vary slightly, depending on the initial temperature of your bird, its shape and exact size, and upon the accuracy of your oven. It is essential to cook turkey thoroughly, in order to destroy any bacteria that could otherwise cause food poisoning. Test the bird to check that it is cooked and to allow it to rest for 20–30 minutes before carving.

Oven-ready turkey weight (stuffing included)	Approximate number of servings	Cooking time at 200°C/ gas mark 6	Cooking time at 180°C/ gas mark 4	Internal temperature
4–5kg	8–10	2½–3 hours	–	
5–6kg	10–12	3–3¾ hours	–	
6–7kg	12–14	30 mins, then >	3¼–4 hours	82°C for turkeys of every size
8–9kg	16–18	30 mins, then >	4–4½ hours	
9–11kg	18–20	1 hour, then >	4–4½ hours	

Garnishes

As for the roast chicken recipe on page 324, you can serve chipolata sausages and bacon rolls with the turkey. To serve 12 people, use a minimum of 12 chipolatas and 12 rashers of streaky bacon and roast them in a separate roasting tin in 1–2 tbsp oil, putting them into the oven 15 minutes before the turkey is due to be ready. They can continue cooking while the turkey is resting and you are making the gravy.

A note on stuffing the turkey...

It is important to stuff the neck end of the turkey, not the main cavity. Stuffing the main cavity can impede heat penetration, preventing the temperature in the cavity from becoming high enough to kill any bacteria present, which can cause food poisoning. If preferred, you can cook the stuffing separately in a small roasting tin.

Defrosting a frozen turkey

If you buy a frozen rather than a fresh turkey, it is essential to defrost it thoroughly before cooking and you will need to allow plenty of time for this. The fridge is the safest place to thaw a turkey, to ensure that the outside does not warm up, allowing potentially harmful bacteria to multiply, before the bird is fully thawed. You will need to allow 10–12 hours per kg.

If you do not have room in your fridge (or time for defrosting is limited), it is possible to defrost the bird in a cool room (such as an unheated conservatory), ideally well below 18°C and certainly not above this temperature. Allow at least 3–4 hours per kg at cool room temperature. Do not plunge the turkey into warm water in an attempt to speed up defrosting.

Turkey leftovers

Cooked turkey can happily be used in a whole host of recipes and, of course, is a must for a cold Boxing Day spread. Just don't leave the carved bird sitting around at warm room temperature long after you have eaten. As soon as it is cooled, wrap well and refrigerate. Sound food hygiene applies (see page 660) and if you are reheating the turkey, in a pie or curry for example, make sure it is piping hot before serving.

Pot roasting and braising

Pot roasting involves baking food in an enclosed pot, either in the oven or over a low heat. Usually, the poultry or meat is browned, then cooked in its own juices or in a very small amount of liquid. For a braise the poultry or meat is cooked on a bed of vegetables (a mirepoix) with a little liquid in a covered pan. Vegetables cooked with a pot roast are traditionally served with the meat, and the cooking juices used as a sauce. In the recipe below, the vegetables are discarded for a more elegant dish.

Pot roast chicken with a rosemary and walnut dressing

Serves 4
1 chicken, about 1.35kg
2 tbsp olive oil
1 large onion
1 small carrot
2 celery sticks
4 garlic cloves
2 thyme sprigs
150ml dry white wine
200ml brown chicken and veal stock
  (see page 98)
Salt and freshly ground black pepper

For the rosemary and walnut dressing
30g walnuts
1 shallot
1 rosemary sprig
½ lemon
4 tbsp extra virgin olive oil
½ tsp clear honey
50g pitted black olives

1 Cut off the first 2 wing joints of the chicken and reserve. Tie the legs together loosely (see note on trussing, page 326). Heat the olive oil in a lidded casserole or ovenproof dish big enough to accommodate the chicken. Season the chicken with salt and pepper and brown it all over, taking care when turning it not to tear the skin. This will take about 10 minutes. Remove the browned chicken to a plate and set aside. Pour off the fat from the casserole.

2 Heat the oven to 200°C/gas mark 6. Place the walnuts for the dressing on a baking tray and lightly toast them in the oven for 10 minutes, taking care not to burn them. Tip onto a plate and set aside to cool.

3 Halve, peel and slice the onion; peel and slice the carrot; de-string and slice the celery; peel the garlic. Add the vegetables to the casserole with the thyme and chicken wing tips and sauté over a medium heat until lightly coloured and starting to soften. Add the wine and reduce by half, then add the stock and bring to a simmer. Place the browned chicken on top of the vegetables, cover with a lid and roast in the oven for 50 minutes.

4 To make the dressing, coarsely chop the toasted walnuts. Halve, peel and finely dice the shallot and finely chop enough rosemary leaves to give you ¼ tbsp. Juice the ½ lemon. Combine the shallot, rosemary and extra virgin olive oil in a small saucepan and heat gently to infuse for 2–3 minutes. Whisk in 1 tbsp lemon juice. Taste and adjust the flavour as necessary, adding honey to provide a little sweetness and more lemon juice if required. Season with salt and pepper. Add the walnuts and the olives and set aside.

5 Remove the casserole from the oven and carefully lift out the chicken. To check that it is cooked, place the chicken on a white plate and insert a skewer into the thickest part of the thigh, leave it for 10 seconds, then remove and check it against your inner wrist; it should be hot and the juices should run clear. Return the chicken to the oven if it is not cooked.

6 Once the chicken is cooked, remove to a board and keep warm. Strain the liquid through a fine sieve into a jug, discarding the vegetables. Taste the liquid, return to the pan and reduce over a medium heat until syrupy with a good concentration of flavour. Taste and adjust the seasoning.

7 Carve the chicken or joint it (see page 327). Divide the chicken between 4 plates and pour a little of the sauce around the chicken. Spoon a little of the rosemary and walnut dressing over the chicken.

Braised guinea fowl with smoked paprika and peppers

Serves 4
3 tbsp olive oil
1 large guinea fowl
1 tsp smoked paprika
1 onion
1 red pepper
1 green or yellow pepper
2 garlic cloves
250ml white wine
250ml chicken and veal stock
  (see page 96)
Handful of oregano sprigs
50g pitted black olives
½ lemon
Salt and freshly ground black pepper

1 Heat 1 tbsp of the olive oil in a large, lidded ovenproof casserole or saucepan over a medium heat. Season the guinea fowl with salt, pepper and ½ tsp smoked paprika and brown it all over. This will take at least 10–15 minutes, but it will give the guinea fowl a good colour, which will add flavour to the sauce. Remove the guinea fowl to a plate. Pour off the excess fat and wipe out the casserole with kitchen paper.

2 Halve, peel and finely chop the onion. Halve and core the peppers and cut into strips. Peel and crush the garlic. Add ½ tbsp olive oil to the casserole, then add the onion and cook gently for 5 minutes until starting to soften. Add the peppers and sauté for a further 3–5 minutes. Add the garlic and ½ tsp smoked paprika and cook for 1 minute.

3 Add the wine, stock and 2–3 oregano sprigs, and bring to a simmer. Place the guinea fowl on top of the vegetables and add the olives. Cover with a tight-fitting lid and cook gently over a low heat for 30–40 minutes.

4 To check if the guinea fowl is cooked, remove it to a white plate and insert a skewer into the thickest part of the thigh. Leave it for 10 seconds then remove it and check it against your inner wrist; it should be hot and the juices should run clear. If not, return it to the casserole and cook for a little longer. Once cooked, remove the guinea fowl to a board to rest.

5 Strain the sauce into a jug, discarding the oregano sprigs but reserving the vegetables; keep them warm. Return the sauce to the casserole.

6 If the sauce tastes watery, concentrate the flavour by reducing it a little. Finely chop enough oregano leaves to give you 1–2 tsp. Finely grate the zest from the lemon. When you are happy with the flavour of the sauce, add the oregano and season with salt, pepper and lemon zest.

7 Meanwhile, joint the guinea fowl into 8 pieces (see page 327).

8 Serve the jointed guinea fowl with the reserved vegetables and the sauce.

Note The guinea fowl can be jointed into 8 pieces (as for a chicken, see page 336) before you brown and cook it. Proceed as for the main recipe, but check the guinea fowl after 20 minutes as the joints will cook faster than a whole bird.

Poaching

A poached chicken has a myriad of uses. The shredded meat can be used in salads, curries, soups and sandwiches. Not only is the meat succulent and tender, but the stock that it is cooked in will be delicious and should never be discarded. If you do not want it for a soup within a day or two, reduce the strained skimmed stock by boiling rapidly and freeze it for later use.

It is important to use a good quality flavourful bird and to poach it very gently, with a small bubble only breaking the surface of the liquid occasionally. If it is cooked too rapidly the meat will toughen.

Chicken poached in Chinese stock

Serves 4

50g piece of fresh root ginger
½ bunch of spring onions, white
  part only
1 litre chicken and veal stock
  (see page 96)
500ml Shaoxing rice wine
100g yellow rock sugar or palm sugar
  (or brown sugar)
100ml dark soy sauce
3 pared strips of orange zest
3 star anise
2 garlic cloves
2 cinnamon sticks
1.5 litres water
1 chicken, about 1.35kg

1 Peel and thinly slice the ginger and slice the spring onions. Put all the ingredients, except the chicken, into a large pan. Bring to the boil, skimming as necessary, then reduce the heat and simmer very gently for 1–1½ hours.

2 Remove the pan from the heat and strain the stock through a muslin-lined or a fine sieve. Discard the flavouring ingredients.

3 Return the strained stock to the pan and add the chicken, with more water if necessary so that the bird is nearly covered. Cover with a damp cartouche (see page 13) and bring to a bare simmer. Poach the chicken for 1 hour. Remove from the heat and leave the chicken in the liquor for a further 1 hour, to complete the cooking process and to allow the flavours to permeate the flesh. The chicken is cooked when its legs feel loose and wobbly.

4 Remove the chicken from the stock. The chicken can now be used either at room temperature, skinned in salads, or can be chilled, uncovered, to allow the skin to dry, and then fried to crisp the skin.

Note This aromatic stock can be skimmed of fat, boiled for 5 minutes, cooled and then frozen and used again. Chicken joints can also be poached in this stock.

Chinese poached chicken with chilli and coriander salad

Serves 4

1 chicken poached in Chinese stock
  (see above)
2 garlic cloves
4cm piece of fresh root ginger
50ml groundnut oil
1 lime
1 tsp sesame oil
50ml light soy sauce
1 tsp clear honey
1 large red chilli
2 spring onions
50g roasted, salted peanuts
1 small bunch of coriander

1 Bring the chicken to room temperature. Peel and thinly slice the garlic. Peel the ginger and cut into julienne. Heat the groundnut oil in a small pan, add the garlic and ginger and cook until starting to sizzle (take care as it will burn easily), then remove from the heat and leave to cool.

2 Pull the skin from the poached chicken and discard it. Pull off the flesh in large pieces and arrange the meat on 4 plates, piled in the centre of each.

3 Juice the lime. In a medium bowl, mix together the sesame oil, soy sauce, lime juice to taste and honey. Halve, deseed and finely slice the chilli, finely slice the spring onions, roughly chop the peanuts and add these ingredients to the dressing. Stir in the cooled garlic and ginger in oil.

4 Pick the coriander into sprigs and gently toss them in the dressing. Pile the salad on top of the chicken and drizzle the remaining dressing around the salad.

Crisp-fried poached chicken with spring onion and soy dressing

Serves 4

1 chicken poached in Chinese stock
  (see left), chilled (uncovered)
Oil for deep-frying
1 tbsp sesame oil
1 tbsp chilli oil
1 tbsp peanut oil
1 tbsp Chinese black vinegar
1 tbsp dark soy sauce
1 tbsp kecap manis (sweet soy sauce)
½ green chilli
6 spring onions
½ small bunch of coriander
¼ tsp ground Sichuan pepper

1 Heat the oven to 180°C/gas mark 4.

2 Joint the cold chicken into 8 equal pieces (see page 327).

3 Heat the oil for deep-frying in a wok to 190°C, or until a small piece of bread browns in 40 seconds (see page 72), then gently lower the chicken portions into the oil, skin side down. Deep-fry until the skin is golden brown and crisp; this will take about 5 minutes and may need to be done in batches. Place the browned pieces on a baking tray and transfer to the oven to continue to crisp.

4 Mix the sesame, chilli and peanut oils with the Chinese vinegar, soy sauce and kecap manis.

5 Halve, deseed and finely chop the chilli. Finely slice the spring onions and chop enough coriander leaves to give you about 1 tbsp. Toss the chilli, spring onion and coriander in the dressing with the ground Sichuan pepper.

6 Place 2 pieces of chicken on each plate and pour the dressing around to serve.

Chicken and leek soup

Serves 4

1 chicken, about 1.3kg
150ml white wine
1 carrot
2 celery sticks
2 mushrooms
Bunch of spring onions
1 garlic clove
1 thyme sprig
6 black peppercorns
1–2 leeks, depending on size
¼ bunch of flat-leaf parsley
Salt and freshly ground black pepper

1 Place the chicken in a large saucepan, add the wine and pour on enough cold water to cover. Peel and roughly chop the carrot; roughly chop the celery and mushrooms; cut off and discard the coarse green tops from the spring onions. Bash the unpeeled garlic clove and add to the pan with the thyme and peppercorns.

2 Bring to the boil, then turn down the heat and simmer gently for 1–1¼ hours, skimming off the fat occasionally, as for stock (see page 96). To check whether the chicken is cooked, feel the legs; they should be loose and wobbly. Carefully remove the chicken from the pan and test by inserting a skewer into the thickest part of the thigh; the juices should run clear. Return the chicken to the pan, take off the heat and leave the chicken to cool in the stock.

3 Meanwhile, trim off the root end and most of the green part of the leek, quarter lengthways, then cut across into 1cm pieces. Wash in a colander set in a bowl of cold water; drain well. Coarsely chop enough parsley leaves to give you 1–2 tbsp.

4 When cool, lift the chicken out of the pan onto a board. Strain the liquor, discarding the vegetables and aromatics, and return to the pan. Boil to reduce the liquor down to about 1.2 litres, to concentrate the flavour.

5 Meanwhile, strip the chicken from the bones into bite-sized pieces and set aside. Discard the skin and bones.

6 Skim any fat from the surface of the stock, then strain through a fine sieve into a clean saucepan. Taste and season lightly with salt and pepper, then add the leeks and simmer for 4–5 minutes, or until they are tender. Add the chicken and reheat gently, then taste and adjust the seasoning. Stir through the parsley before serving.

Note The soup can be made with chicken pieces rather than a whole bird. Reduce the simmering time to 15–25 minutes, depending on the size of the pieces.

Variation

Chicken, leek and noodle soup Break 2 nests of fine egg noodles into small pieces, about 2cm long and add to the soup with the leeks in step 6.

Chicken, wild mushroom and chive pie

Serves 4
For the chicken and poaching liquor
1 chicken, about 1.3kg
1 onion
1 carrot
1 celery stick
2 parsley sprigs
6 black peppercorns
2 bay leaves
Salt and freshly ground black pepper

For the pie
250g puff pastry (see page 508,
   or ready-made)
1 small onion
150g wild mushrooms, such as
   chanterelle, blewit or porcini
Small handful of chives
40g butter
30g plain flour
50ml white wine or Marsala
5 tbsp crème fraîche
1 egg, beaten

1 Put the chicken into a large saucepan and cover with cold water. Place over a low to medium heat and slowly bring to the boil. Halve, peel and slice the onion, peel and slice the carrot, de-string and slice the celery and add it all to the pan, along with the parsley, peppercorns, bay leaves and some salt.

2 As the water comes to the boil, turn the heat down and cover with a damp cartouche (see page 13) and a tight-fitting lid. Poach the chicken gently for 1–1¼ hours; it is cooked when the legs feel loose and wobbly and the juices run clear when a skewer is inserted into the thickest part of the thigh.

3 While the chicken is poaching, roll out the pastry until 3–4mm thick and about 5cm larger than the pie dish all round. Cut strips from the edge that together will line the lip of the pie dish. Put all the pastry on a baking sheet, cover and chill.

4 Halve, peel and finely dice the onion. Wipe the mushrooms clean, trimming off the ends if necessary, and break them into halves or quarters, depending on their size. Finely chop enough chives to give you 1 tbsp.

5 When the chicken is cooked, take the pan off the heat. Let the chicken cool a little in the liquor, then remove it and allow to cool completely. Strain the cooking liquor, discarding the vegetables and herbs, and pour it back into the rinsed out saucepan. Carefully skim off the fat, then reduce until it has a concentrated flavour or until 350–400ml remains. Set aside for the sauce.

6 Once the chicken is completely cool, remove any skin, fat, gristle and bone. Break the chicken into large bite-sized pieces and set aside.

7 To make the sauce, melt the butter in a saucepan over a low heat. Add the onion and sweat for 8–10 minutes, or until soft and transparent. Increase the heat, add the mushrooms and sauté for 5–7 minutes. Lower the heat, add the flour and cook for 3–4 minutes. Remove from the heat and gradually stir in the wine, then about half of the reduced liquor. Return the pan to the heat and stir in the remaining liquor in generous additions. Bring to the boil, stirring, then lower the heat and simmer for 2 minutes. Stir in the chives and crème fraîche, taste and season with salt and pepper. Transfer to a bowl and allow to cool.

8 Add the chicken to the cold sauce and turn the pieces to coat evenly. Put the filling into a 1–1.2 litre pie dish, making sure there is enough filling to support the pastry lid (if not, use a pie funnel to do so). Press the pastry strips onto the rim of the dish and brush with a little beaten egg. Carefully position the pastry lid on top and press gently to join the edges. Trim off the excess pastry.

9 Cut out some leaves (or other shapes) from the pastry trimmings. Knock up the pastry with the back of a knife and scallop the edges (as shown on page 517). Make a hole in the centre of the lid to allow steam to escape and arrange any leaves on top of the pie. Brush the pastry with beaten egg. Stand the dish on a baking sheet and chill for 15–20 minutes. Heat the oven to 200°C/gas mark 6.

10 Before baking, brush again with beaten egg. Bake in the top of the oven for 25–30 minutes, or until the pastry is risen and golden and the filling piping hot.

Variations

Chicken and leek pie Omit the mushrooms and add 1 leek, sliced 1cm thick and sweated in the butter with the onion.

Chicken and tarragon pie Omit the mushrooms and add 1–2 tsp coarsely chopped tarragon, to taste, to the sauce.

Jointing chicken and using chicken joints

As whole chickens are often the same price as a couple of breast pieces, it makes sense to know how to joint a chicken yourself and use the portions you don't need in other dishes. Cooking with joints that include bones rather than boneless portions will also result in a much more delicious sauce.

Jointing a chicken into 8 pieces

1 Place the chicken breast side down on a board with the neck end away from you. Make a cut through the skin, down the middle of the carcass, from the neck end to just above the parson's nose. Make a cut on either side of the parson's nose.

2 Identify the oysters, which lie on the carcass at the top of the thigh. Make a cut across the top of the oysters, then release the sinew holding the oysters in place with your knife and release the oysters with your thumb.

3 Now turn the chicken so it is breast side uppermost, still with the neck end away from you. Pull the skin over the breast to ensure it is fully covered. Cut between the drumstick and breast, keeping the knife close to the breast, but on the outside of the carcass bone at the entrance to the cavity, until the joint holding the thigh to the carcass is exposed. Do the same on the other side. Place your fingers under the thigh and your thumb on top of it and push up with your fingers to 'pop' the thigh joint. Repeat on the other side.

4 Tilt the chicken to one side, pulling the thigh/leg backwards towards the carcass, helping to expose the oyster. Release the oyster using a knife and continue to pull back the thigh/leg. You will need to release the tendons holding the thigh bone to the carcass. Once this is done, pull the thigh/leg back towards you to release the joint from the carcass. Repeat on the other side and put the thigh/leg pieces on one side.

5 Now turn the chicken breast side uppermost and stretch the skin over the breast. Cut down one side of the breast bone – either side will do, but not both – until the knife blade comes into contact with bone. Use a pair of kitchen or poultry scissors to cut through the breast bone completely.

6 Put the chicken on its side and from the point of the breast, using the scissors, cut through the ribs following the fat line around the wing and through the wing joint. Repeat on the other side; it might be easier to start at the wing end.

7 Now the 4 pieces need to be divided again. Place the leg/thigh pieces skin side down on the board and, using your knife, cut through the joint, using the fat line covering the joint as a guide. If the knife comes into contact with the bone, move the knife a little to the left or right and try again. It should cut cleanly through the joint. Repeat with the second leg/thigh piece.

8 To divide the breast pieces, tuck the attached wing tips behind them, then take an imaginary line from the bottom of the wing to the 'cleavage'. Cut through the meat with your knife, then through the bone with a pair of scissors to leave a diamond shaped tapering piece of breast and a smaller, but thicker, piece with the wing attached. Trim off the end wing pinion. The chicken should now have been jointed into 8 pieces.

9 The carcass can be trimmed of excess fat and used for making stock.

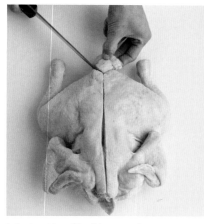

1 Cutting either side of the parson's nose.

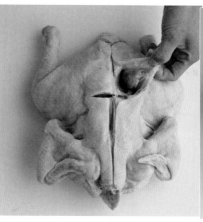

2 Releasing the oysters.

3 Cutting between the drumstick and breast to the joint holding the thigh to the carcass.

4 Pulling the thigh/leg back to release it from the carcass.

5 Cutting through the breast bone.

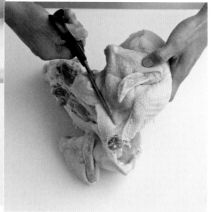

6 Cutting through the ribs.

7 Cutting through the thigh/leg to divide in two.

8 Cutting the breasts pieces in two.

9 Trimming the carcass of excess fat.

Coq au vin

Serves 4

1 chicken, about 1.35kg
½ tbsp sunflower oil
12 button onions
100g piece of bacon
12 button mushrooms
1 garlic clove
Handful of parsley
20g unsalted butter
300ml red wine
300ml chicken and veal stock
 (see page 96)
½ celery stick, tied together with 1 bay
 leaf, 1 thyme sprig and 1 parsley sprig
 (bouquet garni)
2 tsp softened butter mixed with 2 tsp
 flour (beurre manié, see below)
Salt and freshly ground black pepper

1 Joint the chicken into 8 pieces (see page 336). Heat the oil in a large sauté pan over a gentle heat, season the chicken lightly and place it skin side down in the pan in a single layer, to render the fat and brown the skin. This can take up to 10 minutes and may need to be done in batches to avoid overcrowding the pan. Once the skin is brown and crisp, remove the chicken pieces.

2 To peel the onions, bring a saucepan of water to the boil. Plunge the onions into the boiling water for 1 minute, then remove them to a bowl of cold water. Once cool, drain the onions, trim off the hairy root end and peel them, leaving them as natural looking as possible.

3 Derind the bacon and cut into lardons. (If preferred, these can be plunged into boiling water for 30 seconds to remove excess salt.) Wipe over the mushrooms and trim if necessary.

4 Once the chicken is browned, pour off the excess fat and wipe out the sauté pan (or deglaze with a splash of water if you feel the pan is scorched). Add half the butter and brown the lardons, then remove to a plate and put the onions into the pan. Brown the onions, then remove to the plate. Add the remaining butter to the pan, then add the mushrooms and brown evenly. Peel and crush the garlic.

5 Pour off the excess fat from the pan, add the garlic and cook for 1 minute. Add the wine, bring to a simmer and reduce by one-third, then add the stock. Bring back to a simmer and add the bouquet garni, lardons, onions, mushrooms and the chicken, skin side up.

6 Cover and simmer gently for 30–40 minutes, or until the chicken is cooked. To check, remove the pieces to a plate and cut down to the bone on the non-skin side of the chicken; the juices should run clear.

7 Meanwhile, heat the oven to 120°C/gas mark ½. Finely chop enough parsley leaves to give you 1–2 tbsp.

8 Once the chicken is cooked, remove to a board and trim off the knuckles and any exposed bones, then transfer to a serving dish and keep warm in the low oven.

9 Strain the sauce and return it to the sauté pan. Add the lardons, onions and mushrooms to the chicken and keep warm. Discard the bouquet garni. Taste the sauce and reduce if necessary until it has a good concentration of flavour, checking the consistency; it should be lightly syrupy. If not, whisk in beurre manié, ½ tsp at a time, to thicken it. Season with salt and pepper to taste. Pour the sauce over the chicken and sprinkle with the chopped parsley to serve.

A note on marinating...

You can marinate the chicken in the red wine with the bouquet garni for a few hours or even overnight, after which the red wine from the marinade can still be used to make the sauce. This process does make it a little more difficult to render the fat and brown the skin, but it gives the chicken more flavour.

Beurre manié

Beurre manié is equal quantities of softened butter and flour mixed together to form a smooth paste (it is more often than not butter, but any fat could potentially be used). You can then thicken a sauce by whisking a little of this, ½ tsp at a time, into the sauce and bringing it to a simmer. As the butter in the beurre manié melts it releases the flour into the sauce, which in turn thickens it.

Chicken with saffron and preserved lemon

Serves 4

1 chicken, about 1.35kg
2 tbsp sunflower oil
1 onion
3 garlic cloves
Small pinch of ground turmeric
½ tsp ground ginger
1 tsp ground coriander
1 tsp ground cumin
100ml white wine
250ml chicken and veal stock
  (see page 96)
Small pinch of saffron strands, soaked
  in 1 tbsp hot water
2 preserved lemons
Small handful of coriander
Small handful of parsley
½ lemon
12 green olives
Salt and freshly ground black pepper

1 Joint the chicken into 8 pieces (see page 336). Heat 1 tbsp of the oil in a large sauté pan over a gentle heat, season the chicken pieces lightly and place them in the pan skin side down in a single layer to render the fat and brown the skin. This can take up to 10 minutes and may need to be done in batches to avoid overcrowding the pan. Once the skin is brown and crisp, remove the chicken pieces and set aside.

2 Meanwhile, halve, peel and thinly slice the onion and sweat in the remaining oil in a small saucepan over a low heat until soft. Peel and crush the garlic.

3 Drain off the excess oil and add the sweated onion to the sauté pan. Add the garlic and cook for 1 minute, then add the turmeric, ginger, ground coriander and cumin and cook for 1 minute.

4 Pour in the wine and reduce for 2–3 minutes, then add the stock and saffron strands with their soaking liquid and bring to a simmer. Slice the preserved lemons and add them to the pan.

5 Return the chicken pieces to the pan, skin side up. Cover and simmer gently for 30–40 minutes, or until the chicken is cooked. To check, remove the pieces to a plate and cut down to the bone on the non-skin side; the juices should run clear. Heat the oven to 120°C/gas mark ½.

6 Trim off the knuckles and any exposed bones from the chicken and keep warm in the low oven.

7 Taste the sauce and reduce if necessary to concentrate the flavour. Chop enough coriander and parsley leaves to give you 1 tbsp of each. Juice the ½ lemon. Season the sauce with salt, pepper and a little lemon juice and add the olives. Serve the chicken with the sauce spooned over and sprinkled with the chopped herbs.

Preserved lemons

Preserved lemons are available in jars; they are also easy to make: Cut about 2kg lemons vertically almost through into quarters, but leaving the very bottom intact. Spoon ½ tbsp rock salt into each lemon and pack them tightly into a very large sterilised preserving jar. Seal and leave for 10–14 days. After this time, the lemons will have shrunk and released their juice. Remove the lemons from the jar, reserving a little of the juice. Pack the shrunken lemons tightly into a couple of smaller sterilised jars, then add a few star anise, bay leaves, cinnamon sticks and rosemary sprigs to each. Squeeze the juice of 6 fresh lemons and divide the juice between the jars. Add about 75ml per jar of the brined lemon juice and top up with good quality olive oil, ensuring the lemons are completely covered. Seal and allow to mature for at least 3 weeks before using. Store in the fridge and use within 6 months.

Chicken cooked in cider with caramelised onions and apples

Serves 4

300g button onions
1 chicken, about 1.35kg
1 tbsp sunflower oil
400ml cider
1 tbsp clear honey
150ml brown chicken and veal stock
(see page 98)
2 dessert apples
20g butter
1 tsp caster sugar
2 tsp softened butter mixed with 2 tsp
flour (beurre manié), if needed
½–1 tsp white balsamic or sherry vinegar,
to taste
Salt and freshly ground black pepper

1 Peel the button onions (see step 2, page 339). Joint the chicken into 8 pieces (see page 336).

2 Heat half the oil in a large casserole dish. Season the chicken pieces with a little salt and place skin side down in the pan over a medium to low heat to allow the fat beneath the skin to render. Once the skin is golden and crisp, remove from the pan and set aside. The chicken will not be cooked through at this stage.

3 Add the onions to the pan and sauté gently until golden brown. Remove them to a plate and pour off any excess oil from the pan.

4 Deglaze the pan with the cider and boil for 3–4 minutes, then add the honey and stock. Return the chicken to the pan skin side up and add the onions.

5 Cover with a damp cartouche (see page 13) and lid and cook over a gentle heat for about 30–40 minutes until the chicken is cooked and the onions are soft. Heat the oven to 120°C/gas mark ½.

6 Meanwhile, core the apples and cut each into 8 wedges. In a frying pan, melt the butter and when it is foaming, sprinkle over the sugar. Allow to melt a little, then add the apples and fry over a medium heat until golden brown. Keep warm.

7 To check that the chicken is cooked, remove the pieces to a plate and cut down to the bone on the non-skin side; the juices should run clear. Trim off the knuckles and any exposed bones from the chicken, transfer to a warmed dish and keep warm in the low oven.

8 Check the consistency of the sauce and reduce if necessary until syrupy or, if the concentration of flavour is good, thicken with beurre manie (see page 339). Taste and adjust the seasoning, adding the vinegar if needed. Serve the chicken with the sauce, onions and apples.

Chicken in a pomegranate and walnut sauce

Serves 4

½ onion
2 tbsp olive oil
½ garlic clove
1 chicken, about 1.35kg
100g walnuts
200ml brown chicken and veal stock
(see page 98)
1¼ tbsp pomegranate molasses
Squeeze of lemon juice (optional)
1 tsp soft brown sugar (optional)
½ fresh pomegranate
Small bunch of flat-leaf parsley
Salt and freshly ground black pepper

1 Peel and finely dice the onion. Heat 1 tbsp olive oil in a small saucepan over a low heat, add the onion, cover and sweat until soft but colourless. Peel and crush the garlic.

2 Joint the chicken into 8 pieces (see page 336). Heat the remaining oil in a large sauté pan over a gentle heat, season the chicken pieces lightly and place in the pan skin side down in a single layer to render the fat and brown the skin. This can take up to 10 minutes and may need to be done in batches to avoid overcrowding the pan. Once the skin is brown and crisp, remove the chicken pieces and set aside.

3 Grind the walnuts in a food processor until fine, but still a little textured.

4 If necessary, wipe out the sauté pan used to brown the chicken. Transfer the sweated onion to the pan and add the walnuts. Cook over a low to medium heat until the walnuts have darkened in colour and have started to release some of their oils, about 3–4 minutes. Don't do this over a high heat or the onion and walnuts will scorch. Add the garlic and cook for 1 minute.

5 Add the stock and pomegranate molasses with some salt and pepper. Return the chicken pieces to the pan, skin side up, and cook gently for 30–40 minutes, or until the chicken is cooked. Heat the oven to 120°C/gas mark ½.

6 To check that the chicken is cooked, remove the pieces to a plate and cut down to the bone on the non-skin side; the juices should run clear. Trim off the knuckles and any exposed bones from the chicken and keep warm in the low oven.

7 Taste the sauce and reduce if necessary to concentrate the flavour; a little lemon juice and/or brown sugar can be added to adjust the tartness or sweetness accordingly. Add more salt and pepper to taste. Remove the pomegranate seeds from the pomegranate by holding the halved pomegranate cut side down over a bowl and carefully hitting the pomegranate on the skin side with a rolling pin. Coarsely chop enough parsley leaves to give you 2 tbsp.

8 Plate the chicken pieces on a large serving dish and pour the sauce around them. Scatter the pomegranate seeds and parsley over the chicken.

Note The chicken can be served off the bone if preferred. Once cooked, allow the chicken to cool slightly before removing the skin, pulling the chicken from the bones and shredding it into fairly large pieces. Reheat the chicken in the sauce and plate as above.

Mustard baked chicken

Serves 4
30g butter, softened
2 tbsp Dijon mustard
1 tsp caster sugar
1 tsp paprika
½ lemon
1 chicken, about 1.35kg
Salt and freshly ground black pepper
Watercress, to garnish

1 Heat the oven to 200°C/gas mark 6.

2 Put the butter, mustard, sugar and paprika in a small bowl. Juice the ½ lemon, add to the bowl and mix to a smooth paste.

3 Joint the chicken into 8 pieces (see page 336). Arrange the pieces skin side down in a shallow roasting tin.

4 Spread half of the mustard paste over the chicken pieces. Season well with salt and pepper and bake in the oven for 15 minutes.

5 Turn the chicken pieces over to skin side up, spread with the remaining mustard paste and sprinkle with pepper. Bake for 15–20 minutes, or until the chicken is cooked through. To check that the chicken is cooked, remove the pieces to a plate and cut down to the bone on the non-skin side; the juices should run clear. Meanwhile, wash and pick over the watercress.

6 Trim the chicken joints, and if the skin is not dark brown and crisp, heat the grill to its highest setting. Grill until you reach the desired colour; the skin can become quite dark.

7 Arrange the chicken pieces on a serving dish. Pour over any pan juices and garnish with sprigs of watercress.

Variations

Smoked paprika baked chicken Use smoked paprika in place of the sweet paprika, and replace the mustard with ½ finely chopped red chilli.

Spiced baked chicken Replace the mustard, paprika, sugar and lemon juice with 1 tbsp garam masala and 1 crushed garlic clove.

Mustard and herb baked chicken Use English mustard in place of the Dijon. Omit the paprika, replace the sugar with brown sugar or clear honey and add 1 tbsp finely chopped parsley.

Chicken breasts

Chicken breasts can be stuffed, flattened, poached, roasted or griddled. Their convenient one-portion size and the mild flavour of the meat make them a popular and versatile cut. Use the best chicken you can afford and cook the breasts carefully to avoid drying out the lean meat.

Cutting supremes from a chicken

A chicken supreme is a breast with the wing bone attached. The method below can be used to remove the breast and wing from any poultry or game bird.

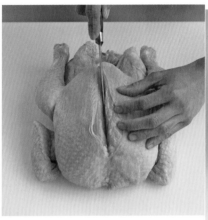

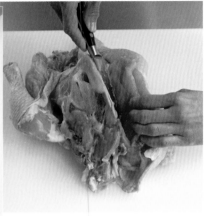

1 Place a chicken, breast side up, on the board and, using a sharp knife, cut down one side of the breast plate until the knife comes into contact with bone.

2 Now angle the knife slightly towards the wing and carefully cut the chicken breast from the bone, keeping the knife blade against the bone to avoid leaving meat on it.

3 As the breast is released, open it out (like a book) away from the breast bone until the wing joint is reached.

4 Cut through the wing joint, leaving it on the breast and trim the breast away from the ribs on the side of the carcass. Repeat with the second breast.

5 Now remove the last 2 wing pinions by cutting through the joints. Use these wing pieces for stocks and sauces.

6 Release the meat close to the breast on the rest of the bone and scrape it away to expose the bone. Finally, cut off the knuckle end of the bone cleanly.

Note The thigh/leg pieces can be removed as for jointing a chicken (see page 336) and used for recipes requiring dark chicken meat. The carcass can be used to make stock.

Chicken breasts with tarragon and crème fraîche sauce

Serves 4

4 chicken supremes (breast with wing
  bone attached, see left)
15g unsalted butter
250ml chicken and veal stock
  (see page 96)
½ lemon
Few tarragon sprigs
4 tbsp crème fraîche
Salt and freshly ground black pepper

1 Season the chicken lightly with salt and pepper. Melt the butter in a frying pan that has a tight-fitting lid, then place the chicken supremes skin side down in the pan and brown over a low to medium heat.

2 Once the fat is rendered and the skin browned, pour off the fat, turn the chicken skin side up and pour in the stock. Cover and cook over a low heat until the chicken is cooked through; this will take about 10 minutes depending on how well browned the breasts were in the first place.

3 Meanwhile, heat the oven to 120°C/gas mark ½. Juice the ½ lemon. Roughly chop enough tarragon leaves to give you ½ tbsp.

4 Check the chicken is cooked by removing the pieces to a white plate and cutting down to the bone on the non-skin side; the juices should run clear. Transfer to the low oven to keep warm.

5 Strain the sauce and return it to the wiped out pan. Taste, then reduce the sauce to concentrate the flavour if it seems weak. Add the crème fraîche and simmer to a light coating consistency (it should just cover the back of a wooden spoon). Add a generous pinch of the tarragon and season to taste with lemon juice, salt and pepper.

6 Carve the chicken breasts into 2 or 3 slices, place on serving plates and pour the tarragon sauce over and around the chicken. Garnish with a few tarragon leaves.

Note The stock can be infused with tarragon to add flavour. Bring it to a simmer, remove from the heat, add a sprig of tarragon and leave the stock to infuse as it cools. Don't be tempted to substitute half-fat crème fraîche in the sauce – it will curdle as the sauce reduces.

Variations

Chicken breasts with thyme and mustard sauce Substitute the tarragon with 1 tsp thyme and add ½–1 tsp wholegrain mustard with the thyme. Omit the lemon juice.

Chicken breasts with vermouth and leek sauce Once the chicken has been transferred to the low oven in step 4, stir-fry 1 finely chopped leek in 1 tbsp melted butter in the wiped out pan, until soft. Add 75ml dry vermouth and cook until nearly evaporated, then proceed as for the main recipe, replacing the tarragon with 1 tsp chopped thyme and omitting the lemon juice.

Chicken breasts with Madeira sauce Omit the crème fraîche and tarragon. Pour off the excess fat from the pan after browning the chicken breasts. Deglaze the pan with 100ml Madeira, reduce by two-thirds to about 2 tbsp, then add 250ml brown chicken and veal stock (see page 98). Once the chicken is cooked, reduce the sauce until lightly syrupy. Taste and add a little double cream or lemon juice depending on taste.

Chicken breasts with Poire William sauce Omit the tarragon and lemon juice. Add 75ml Poire William (pear liqueur) to the browned chicken in step 2 after pouring off the fat and allow to bubble before adding the stock. Proceed as for the main recipe and serve with caramelised slices of pear.

Chicken breasts with rosemary, lemon and pine nuts

Serves 4

4 chicken supremes (breast with wing
  bone attached, see page 344)

1 rosemary sprig

½ lemon

2 tbsp olive oil

30g raisins

75ml dry white wine or verjuice

30g pine nuts

50g butter

Salt and freshly ground black pepper

1 Place the chicken supremes in a large bowl.

2 Strip the rosemary leaves from the stalk and finely chop; you will need about 1 tsp. Finely grate the zest from the lemon. Combine half the rosemary and lemon zest with the olive oil in a small bowl, then pour over the chicken breasts and turn to coat them. Leave to marinate in the fridge for 2–3 hours, or overnight.

3 Soak the raisins in the wine for 2–3 hours, or overnight.

4 Heat the oven to 180°C/gas mark 4. Put the pine nuts on a baking tray and toast in the oven for 10 minutes. Tip onto a plate and set aside. Lower the oven setting to 120°C/gas mark ½.

5 Heat a large, non-stick frying pan over a low to medium heat. Wipe the marinade from the chicken, season with a little salt and place skin side down in the frying pan. Allow the fat beneath the skin to render and the skin to become golden and crisp. This can take up to 10 minutes and must be done over a low heat or the skin will scorch. Season the chicken on the non-skin side as it browns.

6 Once the skin is crisp and golden, turn the chicken over and continue cooking until done. The time will depend on how long it has taken for the fat to render and the skin to become golden. Check the chicken is cooked by removing the pieces to a white plate and cutting down to the bone on the non-skin side; the juices should run clear.

7 Remove the chicken to a plate and keep warm in the low oven. Drain the raisins, reserving the wine.

8 Pour off any excess oil from the pan and wipe with kitchen paper if there is any burnt residue. Add the butter and cook it to the beurre noisette stage (see page 114), then add the reserved wine. Add the raisins, pine nuts and remaining rosemary and lemon zest. Taste, season and adjust the acidity balance with a little lemon juice if necessary.

9 Carve the chicken breasts into 2 or 3 slices, cutting them on the diagonal (as shown), place on serving plates and pour a little of the sauce around the chicken.

Variations

Chicken breasts with marjoram and pine nuts Replace the rosemary and lemon with ½ tbsp coarsely chopped marjoram: use half for marinating the chicken and half for the sauce. Oregano can be used in place of marjoram.

Chicken breasts with basil, olives and cherry tomatoes Omit the pine nuts, rosemary, lemon, raisins, wine and butter. Marinate the chicken in the olive oil with a few bruised basil stalks. For the sauce, once the chicken is cooked, wipe out the pan and add 75ml olive oil and a splash of balsamic vinegar. Season to taste with salt and pepper, adding more vinegar or oil if required to balance the flavour. Add 50g quartered pitted black olives and a handful of quartered cherry or baby plum tomatoes. Warm the sauce through and add a small handful of torn basil leaves.

Pan-fried breast of guinea fowl with morel and bacon risotto

Serves 4

30g dried morels
Few thyme sprigs
4 boneless guinea fowl breasts, with skin
35g unsalted butter
2 tbsp olive oil
75g piece of bacon
1 onion
1 garlic clove
250g mixed wild mushrooms, including
  morels if possible
1 litre chicken and veal stock
  (see page 96)
300g Arborio rice
100ml dry white wine
30g Parmesan cheese
Small bunch of flat-leaf parsley
Salt and freshly ground black pepper

1 Heat the oven to 170°C/gas mark 3.

2 Put the dried morels in a small bowl, cover them in boiling water and leave to soak for 30 minutes.

3 Finely chop enough thyme leaves to give you 1 tbsp, sprinkle all over the guinea fowl breasts and season with salt and pepper. In a large ovenproof frying pan, melt 15g of the butter with 1 tbsp of the olive oil. Over a low to medium heat, fry the breasts skin side down until golden brown, about 5 minutes. Turn the breasts over and transfer the pan to the oven to finish cooking for about 15–20 minutes, while you are making the risotto. Once cooked, the guinea fowl can be set aside to rest while the risotto is finished.

4 To make the risotto, derind the bacon and cut into small dice. Halve, peel and finely chop the onion and peel and crush the garlic. Wipe clean the wild mushrooms and tear into bite-sized pieces. Heat the remaining olive oil in a large saucepan and add the bacon. Cook until lightly browning, then add the onion. Cook over a low heat until the onion is very soft, then add the garlic and fresh mushrooms and cook for a further 2 minutes.

5 Heat the stock in a separate pan. Strain the soaking liquor from the morels into the pan. Roughly chop the soaked morels.

6 Add the rice to the onion and mushrooms and stir until the rice is coated in oil and heated through. Add the wine and simmer until it is absorbed. Add the morels and a ladleful of stock, and stir until it has been absorbed into the rice. Repeat until the stock has all been incorporated. This should take about 25 minutes. The risotto is cooked when the grains are al dente and the mixture is still sloppy, rather than dry or stiff. Add more stock or some hot water if necessary.

7 Adjust the seasoning and then beat in the remaining butter and grate in the Parmesan. Stir well, cover with a lid and leave to stand for 5 minutes. Meanwhile, finely chop enough parsley to give you 3 tbsp.

8 Carve the guinea fowl breasts by cutting into 3 or 4 pieces on the diagonal. Stir the parsley through the risotto and serve a small mound on each plate, topped with a guinea fowl breast. Sautéed morels would be a lovely extravagant garnish.

Variation

Moroccan spiced guinea fowl with hazelnut quinoa Omit the risotto. Mix 1 tbsp ras-al-hanout with 1 tbsp olive oil and ½ tsp sea salt. Rub all over the guinea fowl breasts and leave to stand for 30 minutes. Cook them as for the main recipe. Meanwhile, cook 100g quinoa in 300ml stock for 15–20 minutes until tender, then drain and stir through a handful of toasted, skinned hazelnuts, 1 finely chopped shallot, 1 tbsp roughly chopped flat-leaf parsley and salt and pepper to taste. Serve with the guinea fowl.

Chicken breast stuffed with feta and green peppercorns

Serves 4

4 chicken supremes (breast with wing
  bone attached, see page 344)
½ tbsp olive oil
50ml white wine
75ml chicken and veal stock
  (see page 96)
Salt and freshly ground black pepper

For the stuffing

1 shallot
½ tbsp olive oil
Few thyme sprigs
100g feta
1½–2 tsp green peppercorns
50g fresh white breadcrumbs

To serve (optional)

1 quantity tomato and basil salsa
  (see page 127)

1 Heat the oven to 170°C/gas mark 3.

2 To create a pocket in each chicken breast for the stuffing, place the breast skin side down and carefully pull away the false fillet. Put it to the side. Make a cut two-thirds of the way down through the thickest part of the breast, then, using the knife horizontally in the cut, create a pocket on both sides (as shown).

3 For the stuffing, halve, peel and very finely dice the shallot. Put the olive oil in a small saucepan and sweat the shallot over a low heat until soft and translucent. Finely chop enough thyme to give you 1 tsp. Crumble the feta into a bowl and add the peppercorns, breadcrumbs, thyme and sweated shallot. Divide into 4 portions.

4 Stuff the pocket in each chicken breast with a portion of filling (as shown). To seal the stuffing in, lightly flatten the false fillet and place it back in position on the breast covering the stuffed pocket. Push down gently to help seal the false fillet in place. Season the chicken breasts with salt and pepper.

5 Heat the ½ tbsp olive oil in a frying pan over a low heat and place the chicken breasts skin side down in the pan. Allow the fat beneath the skin to render and the skin to brown and become crisp, about 10 minutes.

6 Turn the breasts skin side up and transfer to a roasting tin. Deglaze the frying pan with the wine and reduce by half. Add the stock, pour over the chicken and roast in the oven for 10–15 minutes until cooked. Check the chicken is cooked by cutting down to the bone on the non-skin side; the juices should run clear.

7 Remove the chicken breasts from the oven and leave to rest for 2–3 minutes before slicing into 2 or 3 pieces. Taste the pan juices and adjust the seasoning. Serve the chicken on a bed of tomato and basil salsa if desired, with the pan juices poured over.

Variations

Feta, olive and tomato stuffed chicken breast Omit the green peppercorns from the stuffing and replace with ½ tbsp black olives, slivered, 2 thinly sliced sun-dried tomatoes, and ¼–½ tsp finely chopped oregano, to taste. Use this to stuff the chicken breasts and proceed as for the main recipe.

Parma ham and lemon mascarpone stuffed chicken breast Cut 2 slices of Parma ham into thin strips and mix with 50g mascarpone, the finely grated zest of ¼ lemon, ¼–½ tsp finely chopped sage, 50g fresh white breadcrumbs and some seasoning. Use this mixture to stuff the chicken breasts and proceed as for the main recipe.

Leek and mushroom stuffed chicken breast Finely slice ½ leek and sweat in 15g butter until very soft and translucent. Increase the heat and add 5–6 finely sliced button mushrooms. Sauté over a medium to high heat until the mushrooms have softened and any liquid has evaporated. Add ¼ tsp finely chopped parsley or tarragon and season. Transfer to a bowl and leave to cool, then add 1–2 tbsp mascarpone and 30–40g fresh white breadcrumbs to bind. Use this mixture to stuff the chicken breasts and proceed as for the main recipe.

Wild mushroom stuffed chicken breast Place 100g chicken breast, trimmed of sinew, in a food processor and pulse until smooth. Transfer to a bowl and beat in 50ml double cream. Sauté 20g wild mushrooms in 10g butter and then coarsely chop. Add to the chicken with ½–1 tsp finely chopped parsley, tarragon or thyme and some seasoning. Use this mixture to stuff the chicken breasts and proceed as for the main recipe.

Jerk chicken salad with corn and black beans

Serves 4
4 boneless, skinless chicken breasts
About 2 tbsp sunflower oil

For the jerk seasoning
3 Scotch bonnets (or milder red chillies)
3cm piece of fresh root ginger
4 garlic cloves
1 tbsp ground cinnamon
1 tbsp ground allspice
1 tsp ground coriander
½ tsp freshly grated nutmeg
1 tbsp soft dark brown sugar
Small bunch of thyme
1 lime
3 tbsp dark rum
2 tbsp olive oil
Salt and freshly ground black pepper

For the salad
200g Cos or other crisp salad leaves
½ bunch of coriander
100g drained, tinned black beans
50g sweetcorn, tinned or cut from
  a boiled or griddled cob
1 quantity avocado sauce (see page 127)

1 Make 3 or 4 diagonal slashes on the skinned side of each chicken breast, about 5mm deep.

2 For the jerk seasoning, deseed and roughly chop the chillies. (Scotch bonnets are particularly hot so wear gloves to avoid getting the fiery oil on your hands.) Peel and grate the ginger; peel and crush the garlic.

3 Put the chillies, ginger and garlic into a small food processor bowl with the dry spices, sugar, ¼ tsp salt and 1 tsp pepper. Strip the thyme leaves from their stalks and add them to the spices. Finely grate the zest from the lime and squeeze the juice, then add both to the mixture. With the motor running, add the rum and enough olive oil to make a smooth, spreadable paste.

4 Spread the chicken breasts all over with the jerk paste and refrigerate for at least 30 minutes, and up to 3 hours.

5 For the salad, roughly tear the salad leaves into a large bowl. Tear the coriander leaves from their stalks, add them to the salad leaves with the rinsed black beans and sweetcorn and mix gently. Add enough avocado sauce to lightly coat the leaves and toss lightly.

6 Heat a large frying pan with enough sunflower oil to lightly cover the bottom. Scrape the excess jerk paste off the chicken breasts and discard it. Add the breasts to the hot pan slashed side down and fry until well browned, then repeat on the other side. Reduce the heat and continue to cook, turning occasionally until the breasts are cooked through; this will take about 10 minutes.

7 Serve the chicken on top of the salad, with any extra avocado sauce in a bowl on the side.

Chinese chicken and mushroom soup

Serves 4
400g boneless, skinless chicken breasts
1 tbsp cornflour
3 tbsp light soy sauce
1 tbsp sesame oil
2 tbsp Shaoxing rice wine
30g Chinese dried mushrooms
1 litre strong chicken and veal stock
  (see page 96)
4cm piece of fresh root ginger
1 red chilli
10 small or 5 large spring onions
3 garlic cloves
2 tsp clear honey
75g fresh shiitake mushrooms
Few coriander sprigs
50g bean sprouts
Salt

1 Cut the chicken breasts into slices 5mm–1cm thick. Transfer to a bowl with the cornflour and 1 tbsp of the soy sauce, the sesame oil and 1 tbsp of the rice wine. Stir to coat, cover and refrigerate until needed. Meanwhile, soak the dried mushrooms in boiling water to cover for 20 minutes.

2 Pour the stock into a saucepan. Peel and grate the ginger, slice the chilli and the spring onions and peel and slice the garlic. Add half the ginger, chilli, spring onions and garlic to the stock and heat until it bubbles, then lower the heat and simmer for 20 minutes. Strain and return the stock to the pan. Add the honey and the remaining soy sauce and rice wine. Season to taste with salt if necessary.

3 Strain and reserve the mushroom liquor and finely slice the soaked mushrooms, discarding any very tough stems. Slice the fresh mushrooms.

4 Heat the strained stock until simmering. Drain the chicken and add to the stock. Add the remaining ginger, chilli and garlic, the fresh and dried mushrooms and the mushroom liquor. Simmer very gently for 2 minutes. Pick the coriander leaves.

5 Add the bean sprouts, the remaining spring onions and a few coriander leaves to the soup and simmer for a further 1 minute. Check the chicken is cooked through, then serve topped with coriander leaves.

Chicken thighs and wings

Often considered the tastiest meat from a chicken, the brown meat from the thighs and wings also has the advantage of being more forgiving in the pan. Whereas chicken breast must be cooked carefully to avoid drying out, the legs and wings can be adapted to slow or quick cooking. Boneless chicken thighs are an excellent alternative to breast meat in recipes, such as curries, where a longer cooking time is desirable to develop the flavours, but can render breast meat dry and stringy.

Sesame and soy glazed wings and drumsticks

Serves 4
1 tbsp sesame seeds
1kg chicken wings and/or drumsticks
1 large garlic clove
½ lemon
2 tbsp dark soy sauce
2 tbsp hoisin sauce
2 tbsp clear honey
1 tsp toasted sesame oil
Pinch of cayenne pepper
1 spring onion

1 Heat the oven to 230°C/gas mark 8. Scatter the sesame seeds in a roasting tin and toast in the oven for 2–3 minutes, then tip them into a small bowl to cool.

2 If using chicken wings, cut off the wing tips and divide the wings at the joint. Place the wings and drumsticks, if using, in the roasting tin in a single layer and roast, allowing 20–25 minutes for wings and 25–30 minutes for drumsticks, to crisp the skin.

3 Meanwhile, peel and crush the garlic and juice the ½ lemon. Mix the garlic, lemon juice, soy and hoisin sauces, honey, sesame oil and cayenne pepper together in a bowl.

4 Lower the oven setting to 220°C/gas mark 7. Spoon the sauce over the chicken and turn the pieces to coat evenly with the sauce. Rearrange the chicken in a single layer again and roast, turning and basting the chicken occasionally until cooked, about 10–15 minutes. To check, use a skewer to pierce the chicken to the bone; the juices should run clear.

5 Take the roasting tin from the oven. The sauce should be coating the chicken. If it is not concentrated and sticky enough, place over a medium to high heat, turning the chicken occasionally so that as the sauce reduces it coats the chicken all over. Meanwhile, finely slice the spring onion on the diagonal.

6 Transfer the chicken to a large serving dish and sprinkle over the toasted sesame seeds and spring onion.

Variations

Hot barbecue wings Use only chicken wings and toss them in flour seasoned with salt, cayenne pepper and paprika. Turn in a little oil and crisp in the oven as for the main recipe. Mix 3 tbsp chilli sauce with 1 tbsp rice wine vinegar, 2 tbsp sunflower oil, 2 crushed garlic cloves, 1 tbsp dark brown sugar and 2 tsp smoked paprika. Use to coat the chicken and return to the oven as for the main recipe, or finish on a barbecue.

Tandoori chicken drumsticks Use 8 chicken drumsticks. Put 300g natural yoghurt, 1 large pinch each of chilli powder, ground cumin and ground coriander, 2 tsp garam masala, 2 tsp tomato purée, 2 crushed garlic cloves, 2 tsp chopped fresh root ginger and the finely grated zest and juice of 1 lemon in a blender with some salt and pepper. Blend until smooth, then transfer to a large bowl. Skin the drumsticks, slash each one 3 times, coat in the tandoori mixture and marinate in the fridge overnight. Scrape off the excess marinade, transfer the drumsticks to a roasting tin and cook in an oven preheated to 220°C/gas mark 7 for 15 minutes on each side until charred. Lower the setting to 190°C/gas mark 5 and cook for a further 15 minutes, or until the juices run clear and the chicken is cooked. Serve with raita (see page 131).

Za'atar chicken with sweet tomato relish

Serves 4

3 tbsp za'atar (see page 32)
1 tbsp ground sumac
8 skinless chicken thighs
2 tbsp plain flour
1–2 tbsp olive oil
Salt and freshly ground black pepper

For the sweet tomato relish

1 red onion
1 tbsp olive oil
100ml white wine vinegar
1 garlic clove
Small handful of coriander
100g soft brown sugar
400g tin chopped tomatoes
Pinch of crushed dried chillies
2 tsp brown mustard seeds
Generous pinch of salt

1 Combine the za'atar and sumac and roll the chicken thighs in this spice mixture, patting it over them to ensure an even coating. Cover and leave in the fridge for 1–2 hours, to allow time for the flavours to penetrate.

2 Meanwhile, to make the relish, halve, peel and finely chop the onion. Heat the olive oil in a medium saucepan, add the onion, cover and sweat for 10 minutes, or until soft. Add the wine vinegar and cook gently for a further 10 minutes. Peel and crush the garlic and roughly chop the coriander.

3 Add the garlic, sugar, tomatoes, chillies, mustard seeds and salt, and simmer gently for 40–45 minutes until thick and syrupy, then set aside to cool.

4 Heat the oven to 190°C/gas mark 5.

5 Place the flour with plenty of salt and pepper in a plastic food bag and toss the chicken thighs in it, making sure they are covered all over with a thin layer of flour.

6 Heat enough olive oil in a wide, heavy-based frying pan to thinly coat the bottom. Add the chicken thighs and fry until lightly golden all over. Transfer to a roasting tin and cook for 10–15 minutes, or until cooked through. Check by cutting to the bone on the underside; the juices should run clear.

7 Stir the coriander into the relish and adjust the seasoning. Serve with the hot chicken. This dish is delicious served with avocado fattoush (see page 32).

Note The relish can be made up to a week in advance, but the coriander must be added just before serving.

Chicken pilau

Serves 4

450g boneless, skinless chicken thighs
2 onions
2 garlic cloves
2cm piece of fresh root ginger
½ tsp ground coriander
½ tsp ground cumin
¼ tsp freshly grated nutmeg
¼ tsp chilli powder
½ tsp ground turmeric
3–4 tbsp oil or ghee for frying
1 cinnamon stick
4 cardamom pods
250g basmati rice
3 curry leaves or 1 bay leaf
400g tin chopped tomatoes
250ml hot water
Salt and freshly ground black pepper
Handful of coriander sprigs, to serve

1 Cut the chicken into 3–4cm pieces and season with salt. Halve, peel and finely slice the onions. Peel and finely chop the garlic and peel and grate the ginger. Measure all the ground spices into a small bowl.

2 Heat 1–2 tbsp oil or ghee in a large frying pan that has a tight-fitting lid. Add the chicken and stir-fry until lightly golden, but not cooked through. Take the pan off the heat, remove the chicken to a plate with a slotted spoon and set aside.

3 Return the pan to the heat, add 1–2 tbsp oil or ghee and sauté the onions until they start to caramelise. Break the cinnamon stick in half and add to the pan. Crush the cardamom pods with the blade of a large knife and add them to the pan with the garlic and ginger. Cook for 1–2 minutes, then add all the ground spices and cook for a further 1 minute.

4 Stir in the rice with the curry leaves or bay leaf, then add the chicken back to the pan with the tomatoes. Add the hot water, season with salt and plenty of pepper, about ½ tsp.

5 Give the mixture a stir, then cover tightly and simmer very gently for about 20 minutes. The rice may still be a little undercooked at this point but the chicken should be cooked.

6 Take off the heat and leave to stand, with the lid on, for 20 minutes; the rice will finish cooking in the residual heat. Remove the lid and stir gently with a fork to fluff up the rice. Serve topped with coriander sprigs.

Spatchcocking poultry

This method of flattening out any poultry or game bird is a useful preparation, as it creates a layer of meat which cooks more evenly, greatly reducing the cooking time. It is an ideal way of preparing birds for grilling or barbecuing.

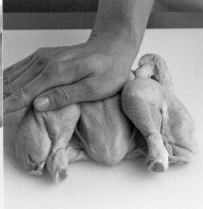

1 Place the bird breast side down on a board and, using a pair of kitchen scissors or poultry shears, remove the back bone.

2 Pull the bird open and turn it skin side uppermost. Press down firmly with the palm of your hand on the thicker end of the breast to flatten. Tuck the legs close to the breast. Remove the wing tips.

3 Insert 2 skewers diagonally through the thigh, leg and breast to keep the bird flat.

To part bone a spatchcock

The breast bone and rib cage can be removed from the chicken before skewering to make it easier to carve: Place the chicken skin side down and, using a small knife, release the meat from the ribs, scraping down to the joint attaching the thigh and leg to the carcass. Cut through this joint, then continue to release the meat from the breast bone. Carefully cut off the breast bone – there is only a thin layer of skin covering the breast plate so take care or you will cut the chicken in half. Skewer the chicken as above to hold its shape.

Poussin with leek, roast pear and goat's cheese

Serves 4

2 poussin
3 firm pears
2 small leeks
4 tbsp olive oil
2 garlic cloves
½ tbsp yellow mustard seeds
1 tsp fennel seeds
Bunch of watercress
¼ lemon
1–2 tbsp white wine or verjuice
100g soft goat's cheese
Salt and freshly ground black pepper

1 Heat the oven to 200°C/gas mark 6. Spatchcock the poussin (see left) and place skin side up in a shallow roasting tin.

2 Quarter and core the pears. Wash and trim the leeks and cut on the diagonal into slices 2cm thick. Place the pears and leeks around the poussin. Drizzle over 3 tbsp olive oil. Peel and finely chop the garlic and scatter it over the poussin with the mustard and fennel seeds. Season lightly with salt and pepper.

3 Roast in the oven for 35–45 minutes, turning the pears and leeks from time to time to ensure even browning, until the poussin are cooked and the pears and leeks are caramelised and tender. Check the poussin are cooked by cutting down to the bone on the non-skin side of the thigh and leg; the juices should run clear.

4 Wash and pick over the watercress and place in a bowl. Squeeze over the juice from the lemon and drizzle over the remaining olive oil. Season with salt and pepper, toss to mix and arrange in a serving dish.

5 Once cooked, transfer the poussin with the pears and leeks to a warmed plate and leave to rest for 5 minutes. Meanwhile, pour off any fat from the juices in the roasting tin and add the wine and some salt and pepper. Bring quickly to the boil.

6 Carve the poussin, place on the watercress with the pears and leeks and dress with the juices. Pull the goat's cheese into pieces and scatter over the pears and leeks to serve.

Poussin with kaffir lime, ginger and lemongrass

Serves 4

2 poussin
20 kaffir lime leaves
3 garlic cloves
4cm piece of fresh root ginger
2 lemongrass stalks
4 shallots
1 long red chilli
1 lime
½ tsp Chinese five-spice powder
½ tsp palm sugar (or brown sugar)
2 tbsp sunflower oil
Salt and freshly ground black pepper
2 limes, cut into wedges, to serve

1 Spatchcock the poussin (see left).

2 Finely chop the lime leaves. Peel the garlic, ginger, lemongrass and shallots and chop roughly. Halve and deseed the chilli and chop roughly. Juice the lime. Place all these ingredients in a small food processor bowl or spice grinder with the five-spice powder, sugar, sunflower oil and some salt and pepper. Blend to a thick paste.

3 Rub the aromatic paste all over the poussin and leave to marinate in the fridge for 3–4 hours, or ideally overnight.

4 Heat the grill to its highest setting and the oven to 180°C/gas mark 4.

5 Place the poussin skin side down on a lightly oiled, lipped baking sheet and grill until the flesh is browning. Turn the poussin over and continue grilling until the skin is brown and crisp. (Unless very small, they will not be cooked at this stage.)

6 Transfer to the oven and cook for 20–30 minutes, or until the juices run clear when you cut down to the bone on the non-skin side of the thigh and leg.

7 Carve the poussin by cutting down the middle of the breast. From the point of the breast, cut between the breast and thigh and leg around the wing, to leave each poussin in 2 breast pieces and 2 thigh and leg pieces. Serve with lime wedges.

Variation

Chilli and coriander poussin Part bone the poussin (see left) and marinate with 3–4 tbsp olive oil, 1 red chilli, deseeded and finely diced, and ¾ tsp coriander seeds, lightly crushed. Season well with salt and pepper before roasting in a shallow roasting tin, skin side up, in a preheated oven at 200°C/gas mark 6 for 30–40 minutes. Leave to rest for 5–10 minutes before carving into pieces.

Poussin with warm fennel, potato and pancetta salad

Serves 4
2 poussin
2 tbsp olive oil
Salt and freshly ground black pepper

For the salad
1 fennel bulb
1 tsp fennel seeds
2 tbsp olive oil
250g new potatoes
100g piece of pancetta
¼ bunch of flat-leaf parsley
1 tbsp sherry vinegar
Bunch of watercress

1 Heat the grill to its highest setting and the oven to 200°C/gas mark 6. Spatchcock the poussin (see page 356).

2 Top and tail the fennel bulb and slice it very thinly through the root end. Scatter it in a lightly oiled shallow roasting tin and sprinkle the fennel seeds over the top.

3 Place the spatchcocked poussin on top of the fennel, skin side up, drizzle with 2 tbsp olive oil and sprinkle with salt and pepper. Place under the grill for about 5 minutes to brown and crisp the skin, then transfer to the oven and roast for 20–30 minutes, or until cooked through. Check by cutting down to the bone on the non-skin side of the thigh and leg; the juices should run clear.

4 Meanwhile, cook the potatoes in a small saucepan of boiling salted water until tender. While the potatoes are cooking, derind the pancetta and cut into lardons. Chop enough parsley leaves to give you ½ tbsp. Heat 2 tbsp olive oil in a small frying pan and sauté the pancetta until golden. Remove from the heat and add the sherry vinegar, parsley and some salt and pepper.

5 When the potatoes are tender, drain and halve or quarter them, depending on their size, then transfer to a large bowl. Pour the pancetta dressing over the potatoes and toss lightly to dress them.

6 Remove the cooked poussin to a board and set aside to rest in a warm place for 5 minutes.

7 Wash and pick over the watercress. Scrape the fennel into the potatoes, taste and adjust the seasoning and stir through a handful of watercress. Serve the poussin with the warm salad.

Note This versatile warm salad is also very good with pan-fried duck breasts and other chicken and guinea fowl dishes.

Variations

Poussin with a warm potato and spring onion salad Omit the potato, fennel and pancetta salad. Place the poussin on a lipped baking tray, drizzle with the 2 tbsp olive oil and cook as for the main recipe. Boil 500g new potatoes and lightly crush while still warm. Add 4 spring onions, finely sliced on the diagonal, 75ml mayonnaise, 75ml crème fraîche thinned with a little water, 1–2 tbsp drained baby capers, 1 tbsp chopped chives and 1 tbsp coarsely chopped flat-leaf parsley. Mix together and season with salt, pepper and lemon juice. Scatter 2 tbsp toasted flaked almonds over the salad and serve with the poussin.

Poussin on a salad of Jersey Royals with radish and mint Omit the potato, fennel and pancetta salad. Place the poussin on a lipped baking tray, drizzle with the 2 tbsp olive oil and cook as for the main recipe. Serve with a salad of Jersey Royals with radish and mint (see page 68). Chives or flat-leaf parsley also work well in this salad, in place of mint.

Boning poultry

Boning out a bird before cooking makes it very suited to stuffing with any number of flavour combinations. Tightly rolled and shaped, boned dishes are simple to carve and highly portable.

Boning a chicken

1 Place the chicken, breast side down, on a board with the neck end away from you. Using a small knife, make a cut through the skin, down the middle of the carcass, from the neck end to just above the parson's nose. Make a cut on either side of the parson's nose.

2 Start to release the skin and meat from the carcass from the neck end, working your way down the length of the chicken. It is important to work your knife on the outside of the shoulder blade near the wing end of the chicken and to release and retain the oyster with the skin. The objective is to remove the skin and chicken meat intact from the carcass. Repeat on the other side of the chicken.

3 As the skin and flesh continue to be released, the thigh and wing joints will be exposed. Cut through the wing joint carefully, without cutting through the skin on the underside. Place your fingers under the thigh and thumb on top of it and pull the thigh backwards to 'pop' the joint, then release the joint with the knife.

4 Continue working down the side of the chicken, releasing the meat. At the top of the ribs the knife must be placed on the outside of a small bone to leave it on the carcass.

5 Scrape the breast meat away from the wishbone at the wing end and continue scraping until the false fillet and main part of the breast is released from the breast plate. Work your knife down the length of the breast bone, scraping away the meat at the point of the breast cartilage. Be careful in this area as there is only a very thin layer of skin covering the breast bone. By now the whole of one side of the chicken should be released from the carcass. Turn the chicken around and repeat on the other side.

6 Once the second side is released, all that should be holding the carcass on to the chicken is the skin under the breast plate. Hold the chicken carcass up and carefully release the skin and meat by carefully cutting along the breast plate. The knife must be kept as close to the bone and cartilage as possible to avoid cutting through the skin. The chicken will fall away. Put the carcass aside.

7 Now tunnel bone the thigh and leg and wing bones. For the wings, hold the last 2 pinions so the exposed joint is uppermost and cut around the exposed joint, then scrape the meat away from the bone. Turn the wing the right way up and cut through the pinion joint closest to the breast. Set aside the last 2 wing pinions that have just been removed. Turn the wing inside out again and pull the wing bone out and set aside. Repeat with the other wing.

8 Hold the thigh, exposing the joint uppermost, and as with the wing, cut just below and around the end of the bone. Scrape the flesh away from the bone until the knee joint is reached.

9 Cut over the 'knee' cartilage, allowing you to hold the thigh bone to release the meat from the leg bone. Cut away the meat from around the joint and scrape away the meat from the bone. Once the leg bone is fully exposed, turn the leg the right way and cut around the leg about 2cm above the ankle to release the skin and tendons fully.

(Continued overleaf)

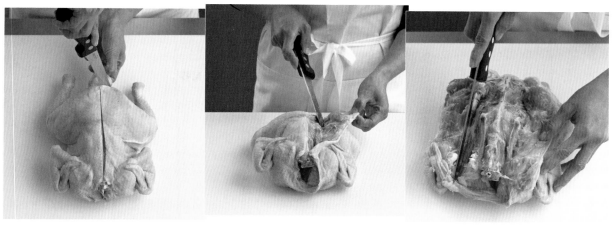

1 Cutting down the back bone and either side of the parson's nose.

2 Releasing the oyster.

3 Releasing the wing joint.

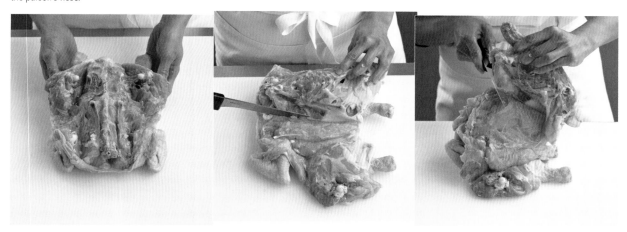

4 The carcass with most of the meat and the thigh and wing joints released from the sides.

5 Gently scraping the meat from the breast bone.

6 Cutting along the breast plate to release the skin and meat.

7 Cutting around the exposed wing joint.

8 Scraping the flesh from the thigh bone.

9 Releasing the meat from the leg bone.

(Continued overleaf)

10 Pulling out the thigh and leg bone.

11 Removing the false fillets to place between the breast, thigh/leg and wing areas.

12 Carefully trimming the skin around the edges of the meat.

10 Turn the leg inside out and the thigh and leg bone should be able to be pulled through, rendering the thigh and leg boneless. Repeat with the other thigh and leg. The chicken carcass and bones can be used for stock.

11 Lay out the chicken skin side down on a board, feel over the meat for any bones or cartilage and remove. Also remove as many of the tendons in the leg and thigh meat as possible. Distribute the meat evenly over the skin to ensure there is an even layer of meat surrounding any stuffing. The wing and thigh/leg areas need to be brought inside out. You may need to cut into the leg meat to help distribute it evenly. Remove the false fillets and place between the breast, leg and wing areas.

12 Scrape the meat off the edge of the chicken skin towards the middle and trim the skin a little to remove excess fat and any overlap. You should be left with a rectangle of chicken skin covered with an even layer of chicken meat, both white and dark. The chicken is now ready for stuffing and rolling.

Part boning a chicken

The chicken can be left with the wings, legs and thighs intact so that after stuffing it can be reshaped. Follow the steps for boning a chicken to the end of step 6, stopping before the tunnel boning.

Preparing a chicken for a ballotine

This technique involves boning out a chicken to leave only the breast meat to be stuffed (see page 364). An extra couple of chicken breasts are required.

1 Bone the chicken as described on pages 360–2 to the end of step 6. Instead of tunnel boning the wings, legs and thighs, they are removed whole, with bones.

2 For the leg/thighs, first cut off the lower knuckle through the joint, then carefully pull the leg/thigh away from the skin. You may need to use a knife to help release them, but take care not to cut through the skin. At the knuckle, keep pulling and the leg/thigh should be released from the skin.

3 For the wings, cut off the last 2 pinions, then pull the pinion closest to the breast away from the skin on the inside. Use a knife if necessary to release the pinion.

4 The wings can be used to make stocks and sauces and the leg and thigh meat used for stuffing the ballotine. The meat will need to be stripped from the leg and thigh bones and tendons trimmed away, leaving only the dark meat.

5 Carefully pull away the chicken breasts from the skin and set aside. Scrape away any other meat and fat from the skin; you should be left with a rectangular piece of skin. Season it lightly. Then replace the breasts with an additional 2 breasts to cover the whole skin with breast meat. Pull the false fillets from the breasts and use these to fill in any gaps. The objective is to create an even layer of chicken breast meat on the skin, about 1.5–2cm thick. You may need to cover the meat with cling film and pound the thicker ends of the breasts. Alternatively, trim a little of this meat off and use to fill in gaps as with the false fillets. Cut off any excess skin. The chicken is now ready for stuffing and rolling.

Carefully pulling the leg away from the skin.

Releasing the leg and thigh.

The chicken with an even layer of breast meat on the skin, ready for stuffing and rolling.

Ballotine of chicken with wild mushrooms

Serves 4
1 chicken, about 1.35kg
2 boneless, skinless chicken breasts
50ml sunflower oil
Salt and freshly ground black pepper

For the stuffing
15g dried porcini mushrooms
1 shallot
1 garlic clove
Few tarragon sprigs
30g pancetta
1 tsp vegetable oil
30g fine fresh white breadcrumbs

For the sauce
75g wild mushrooms
15g butter
75ml port
75ml red wine
Reserved mushroom juices, about 125ml
125ml brown chicken and veal stock
  (see page 98)
1 tsp arrowroot

1 Place the dried porcini for the stuffing in a small bowl, cover with boiling water and leave to soak for 30 minutes.

2 Bone out the chicken for use as a ballotine, using the extra 2 chicken breasts (see page 363) and remove the brown meat (reserve for the stuffing). Fold the boned chicken over in half, cover and refrigerate until ready to stuff. Trim the tendons from the leg and thigh meat, then put the meat in a food processor with a pinch of salt and pulse until breaking up but not turning smooth. Transfer the minced leg and thigh meat to a bowl and set aside.

3 To make the stuffing, drain the porcini, straining and reserving the soaking liquor for the sauce, and chop finely. Halve, peel and finely dice the shallot and peel and crush the garlic. Chop enough tarragon leaves to give you ½–1 tsp. Derind the pancetta and cut into 5mm dice; set aside. Heat the 1 tsp oil in a small saucepan over a low heat and sweat the shallot until soft but not coloured. Add the garlic and cook for 1 minute, then remove from the heat and leave to cool.

4 Add the porcini, sweated shallot and garlic, tarragon, pancetta and breadcrumbs to the minced leg and thigh meat. Season with salt and pepper and mix well. To check the seasoning, fry a teaspoonful and taste.

5 Place a piece of muslin, 25 x 35cm, in a bowl and pour over boiling water. Once cool enough to handle, wring out all the water, put the muslin back into the drained bowl, and pour over the sunflower oil, so that the muslin soaks it up.

6 Lay the oiled muslin out on a board and sprinkle with salt. Lay the boned chicken skin side down on the muslin and, if necessary, rearrange the breast meat as evenly as possible over the skin. Season with salt and pepper.

7 Shape the stuffing into a sausage and lay it lengthways down the centre of the chicken. Carefully bring the chicken, supported by the muslin, around the stuffing, ensuring it is tightly rolled without too much of an overlap. Wrap in the muslin and secure the ends with string. The ballotine should be about 6cm in diameter. Chill for 30 minutes to set the shape.

8 Heat the oven to 200°C/gas mark 6. Meanwhile, prepare the wild mushrooms by brushing off excess grit and tearing them into bite-sized pieces.

9 Place the chilled chicken ballotine on a wire rack set over a baking tray and cook in the oven for 45 minutes–1 hour, or until a skewer pushed into the centre of the stuffing and left for 10 seconds feels very hot when held briefly against your inner wrist. Once cooked, remove the muslin immediately to prevent it from sticking to the skin. Keep the ballotine warm.

10 Make the sauce while the chicken is cooking. Heat the butter in a frying pan over a medium to high heat and sauté the mushrooms quickly for 2–3 minutes. Remove to a bowl and set aside. Deglaze the pan with the port and wine and simmer until reduced by half. Add the reserved mushroom liquor (leaving 1–2 tbsp in the bowl in which there might be grit). Pour in the stock and bring back to the boil. Turn down to a simmer and reduce the liquid again by half. Slake the arrowroot with a little water (see page 111) and whisk into the sauce. Bring back to a simmer and cook, stirring, for 1 minute. Season to taste with salt and pepper and return the mushrooms to the sauce.

11 Carve the ballotine on a slight diagonal into slices 1–1.5cm thick. Place 2 or 3 slices on each plate and pour a little of the sauce around the chicken. Serve with a green vegetable, such as asparagus.

Ricotta and herb stuffed chicken

Serves 4

1 chicken, about 1.8kg
170g ricotta cheese
½ beaten egg
85g fresh white breadcrumbs
6 anchovy fillets in oil
Few sprigs each of marjoram, thyme,
 basil and rosemary
30g pitted black olives
50ml sunflower oil
Salt and freshly ground black pepper

1 Bone the chicken completely, including the legs and wings (see page 360).

2 Heat the oven to 200°C/gas mark 6.

3 To make the stuffing, put the ricotta into a large bowl and beat to loosen it, then beat in the egg and breadcrumbs. Drain and chop the anchovies and roughly chop enough herb leaves to give you 1–1½ tbsp. Halve the olives if they are large. Stir the anchovies, herbs and olives into the ricotta and season to taste with salt and pepper.

4 Place a rectangle of muslin, 25 x 35cm, in a bowl and pour over boiling water. Once it is cool enough to handle, wring out all the water, put back into the drained bowl and pour over the oil, so that the muslin soaks it up.

5 Lay the oiled muslin out on a board and sprinkle with salt. Lay the boned chicken skin side down on the muslin and, if necessary, rearrange the meat as evenly as possible over the skin. Season with salt and pepper.

6 Shape the stuffing into a thick sausage and place it widthways across the middle of the boned chicken. Carefully bring the chicken, supported by the muslin, around the stuffing, ensuring it is tightly rolled without too much of an overlap. Wrap in the muslin and secure the ends with string.

7 Place the chicken breast side up, with the muslin join underneath, on a wire rack set over a roasting tin, and cook in the oven for 1–1½ hours, or until a skewer pushed into the centre of the stuffing and left for 10 seconds feels very hot when held briefly against your inner wrist.

8 Remove the chicken from the oven and unwrap the muslin (do this straight away or it will stick). If serving hot, cut the chicken into slices and serve. If serving cold, leave it to cool completely before slicing. It is delicious served either way, but it is easier to cut tidy slices once it has cooled.

Variations

Sun-blushed tomato and caper stuffed chicken Replace the anchovies with 75g sun-blushed or sun-dried tomatoes, cut into slivers, and replace the olives with 2 tbsp drained baby capers. Use basil sprigs in place of the mixed herbs.

Feta and lemon stuffed chicken Reduce the ricotta to 100g and add 60g crumbled feta. Omit the anchovies and use green rather than black olives. Use 1 tbsp chopped parsley in place of the mixed herbs and add the finely grated zest of 1 lemon.

Chicken mousseline

Makes 400g

200g boneless, skinless chicken breasts
½ egg white
175ml double cream, chilled
Salt and ground white pepper

A mousseline can be poached as it is and served with a sauce, or used as a base to which other flavourings are added, in which case it often becomes a stuffing.

1 Trim any sinew from the chicken breasts and cut them into chunks. Place in a food processor and blend until broken down and smooth. Try not to blend for too long or the chicken will become warm. Add the egg white and a pinch of salt and blend again to mix.

2 Pass the chicken through a very fine drum sieve into a bowl, a little at a time, using a scraper to push it through the mesh. Work in small batches, as trying to sieve too much at once will overwork and warm up the chicken. Once it is all sieved, weigh it. You will need three-quarters of this weight in cream. Cover the chicken and chill for about 30 minutes until cold.

3 Now add 1–2 tbsp chilled cream at a time to the chicken, beating it in quickly after each addition, using a plastic spatula. It must be added gradually or the mousseline will be too thin to hold its shape. Once all the cream has been added, poach a little of the mousseline in simmering water to test for seasoning, then taste and add salt and white pepper as necessary.

4 Chill the mixture until ready to use.

Variation

Fish mousseline Replace the chicken breast with skinless salmon fillet or a white fish fillet.

A note on preparing mousselines...

A mousseline is generally chicken or fish, blended to a paste and with an equal quantity of cream added before it is seasoned.

All ingredients and ideally all equipment (particularly if making larger quantities) must be kept chilled at all times, or the cream can curdle as it is added and cause the mousseline to separate, or make it very thin and unable to hold its shape.

Enough cream needs to be added to lighten the mousseline, or it will be heavy and dense. Conversely, if too much cream is added, it dilutes the flavour of the chicken or fish and prevents the mousseline from binding. As a guide, use between three-quarters and equal parts of cream to chicken or fish.

Mousselines must be cooked carefully to ensure they remain very soft and tender. Overcooking will toughen them, making them rubbery, and if very overcooked and overheated they can split and become grainy and watery.

Recipes using mousselines

Chicken and wild mushroom ravioli (see page 179)

Salmon quenelles in a lemongrass and ginger broth (see page 301)

Salmon fillets wrapped in lettuce with a warm fennel citrus dressing (see page 304)

Duck

Duck, with its dark, flavoursome flesh, works well when paired with bold flavours, particularly those with some sweetness or acidity, from the classic combination of duck with orange, to Asian pairings with tamarind, plum and star anise. It is best served pink.

Aylesbury and Gressingham duck are generally plump and well flavoured and perfect for roasting or for when you are looking for crisp skin. Wild duck, usually mallard, has a stronger flavour and tends to be better suited to braised dishes.

Roast duck with bitter orange sauce

Serves 3–4

1 oven-ready duck, about 1.8kg
2 Seville oranges
60g granulated sugar
75ml water
1 tbsp white wine vinegar
150ml strong chicken and veal stock
   (see page 96)
1 tbsp brandy
2–3 tsp arrowroot (if needed)
Salt and freshly ground black pepper

1 Heat the oven to 200°C/gas mark 6.

2 Wipe the duck clean inside and out with kitchen paper. Season inside the cavity with salt and pepper. Quarter one of the oranges and stuff into the cavity. Prick the duck all over with a fork, pushing the prongs in wherever you can feel a fat deposit around the legs. Sprinkle lightly with salt and place breast side down on a wire rack set over a roasting tin. Roast in the oven for 30 minutes, then turn it breast side up and roast for a further 30 minutes.

3 Meanwhile, remove the zest from the remaining orange using a swivel peeler, and cut it into fine strips or julienne (see page 531). Juice the orange and set aside. Place 30g of the sugar in a small saucepan with the water. Dissolve the sugar over a low heat, then increase the heat to a simmer and add the orange zest. Simmer for 3–4 minutes, then remove from the heat and set aside to cool. Once cool, remove the zest with a slotted spoon and set aside, reserving the syrup in the pan.

4 Remove the duck from the oven and set it aside to rest in a warm place for 10 minutes before transferring to a board and jointing it into 6 pieces (as shown overleaf). Put the leg/thigh pieces skin side up into a clean roasting tin, saving the roasting juices for the sauce.

5 Return the duck to the oven and continue to roast until cooked through and the skin is crisp, up to 20 minutes. The breast pieces should be pink.

6 Put the remaining sugar and the wine vinegar into a clean saucepan and dissolve the sugar over a low heat. Increase the heat and boil until the vinegar sugar syrup caramelises and turns a deep mahogany colour; tilt the pan gently to encourage even browning. Remove from the heat and immediately add the stock, taking care as it will spit. Stir to melt the caramel, then stir in the orange juice to taste, the zest julienne and the brandy. Skim any fat off the reserved roasting juices and add the juices to the sauce. Simmer until reduced to the required concentration of flavour, adding more juice or reserved orange syrup for tartness or sweetness as required. If necessary thicken the sauce by slaking in a little arrowroot (see page 111).

7 Serve the duck with the orange sauce.

Note When preparing the duck for roasting, the parson's nose can be removed if required; this encourages more fat from the bird to be released during roasting.

Variation

This recipe also works well with ordinary oranges when Seville oranges are not available, with the finished dish tasting a little sweeter.

Jointing a duck after cooking

1 Place the duck on a board breast side down and, using a pair of poultry shears or kitchen scissors, remove the back bone.

2 Turn the duck over and cut down the middle of each breast to remove the middle section of the breast completely.

3 Use a knife to cut through the meat, then use scissors to cut through the bone.

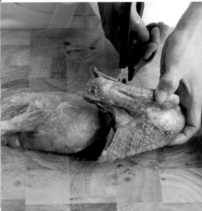

4 The breast piece tapers slightly. Divide it into one-third and two-thirds, the smaller piece being the thicker end of the breast.

5 Divide the leg and thigh from the remaining breast and wing. Trim off the outer wing pinions.

6 Repeat on the other duck half to give 6 pieces of duck. The leg and thigh pieces can be divided at the joint to give 8 pieces.

Gastrique

A gastrique is a sugar and vinegar/acid reduction, in which the sugar is sometimes caramelised. The vinegar is added to halt the caramelisation and to add an acidic or sour note. This combination of sweet and sour flavours, added judiciously to a sauce, helps to round out, balance and enhance the underlying base flavours in a sauce as well as imparting a dark colour. It works particularly well in savoury fruit-based and tomato sauces.

Braised duck with herbs, chestnuts and gremolata

Serves 4

1 duck, about 1.5kg
2 fennel sprigs
1 rosemary sprig
2 flat-leaf parsley sprigs
2 oregano sprigs
2 thyme sprigs
3 garlic cloves
1 tsp fennel seeds
100ml olive oil
120ml Vin Santo
100g piece of pancetta
6 shallots
120ml brown chicken and veal stock
  (see page 98)
50g dried cherries
4 cloves
1 cinnamon stick
12 vacuum-packed, cooked, peeled
  chestnuts
Salt and freshly ground black pepper

For the gremolata
Small handful of parsley sprigs
½ orange
½ lemon

1 Joint the duck into 8 pieces (as for jointing after cooking, see left). Trim off any excess skin and fat. Working in 2 batches, place the duck pieces skin side down in a large, lidded sauté pan or flameproof casserole, and place over a low heat to render the fat beneath the skin, about 10 minutes.

2 Meanwhile, strip the herb leaves from the stalks and finely chop. Peel and crush the garlic. Place the herbs, garlic and fennel seeds in a bowl and add all but 1 tbsp of the olive oil, with some salt and pepper.

3 Remove the browned duck pieces to a plate and allow to cool, then rub the herb mixture into the meat side of each piece. Pour off the rendered fat from the sauté pan, then deglaze the pan with half of the Vin Santo. Pour this déglaçage into a small bowl and set aside.

4 Wipe out the pan with kitchen paper. Derind the pancetta and cut into lardons. Halve, peel and finely dice the shallots.

5 Heat the remaining olive oil in the pan and fry the pancetta until golden, then remove and set aside. Add the shallots to the pan and sauté until starting to soften and colour. Deglaze with the remaining Vin Santo and the reserved déglaçage (if not bitter or burnt-tasting). Add the stock and bring to a simmer, then add the lardons, dried cherries, cloves, cinnamon stick and some salt and pepper. Add all the duck pieces except for the breast portions, ensuring the meat is skin side up. There should be enough liquid to come one-third of the way up the duck, leaving the skin exposed.

6 Cover and cook over a low heat until the duck is tender, about 1¼–1½ hours. Add a little water, about 75ml, if the sauce is becoming dry. About 10–15 minutes before the end of the cooking time, add the chestnuts and the breast pieces.

7 To make the gremolata, finely chop enough parsley leaves to give you 1 tbsp and finely grate the zest from the orange and lemon. Mix together in a bowl. Heat the oven to 120°C/gas mark ½.

8 Once the duck is cooked and tender (the meat should come away from the leg bone easily), remove to a serving dish, trimming any exposed bones, and keep warm in the low oven. Taste the sauce and reduce if necessary to intensify the flavour. Remove and discard the cinnamon stick and adjust the seasoning.

9 Pour the sauce around the duck and sprinkle the gremolata over to serve.

Duck confit

Serves 4

3 juniper berries
3 coriander seeds
40g sea salt
1 tsp black peppercorns
2 rosemary sprigs
8 thyme sprigs
4 bay leaves
1 garlic bulb, plus 3 extra cloves
4 duck legs
1.5–2 litres duck fat

1 Lightly crush the juniper berries and coriander seeds using a pestle and mortar. Add the salt, peppercorns, rosemary sprigs, 4 thyme sprigs and 2 bay leaves and pound until bruised and starting to break up. Bash the 3 unpeeled garlic cloves with the flat side of a large knife.

2 Place the duck legs in a large, heavy plastic bag and add the crushed aromatics. Massage the aromatics into the duck and leave to marinate in the fridge overnight.

3 Heat the oven to 150°C/gas mark 2. Put the duck fat into a deep roasting tin that will hold the duck legs in a single layer and put in the oven to melt. Cut the garlic bulb in half horizontally and add with the remaining thyme and bay leaves to the roasting tin.

4 Remove the duck legs from the bag, wipe off the marinade and submerge the legs in the duck fat. Place back in the oven and cook gently for 3–4 hours, until the meat has slightly shrunk away from the bones and is tender.

5 Carefully lift out the duck legs and trim off the knuckles. Place the legs in a stainless steel or ceramic container.

6 Strain the duck fat into a large saucepan, leaving behind the juices in the bottom of the roasting tin and discarding the garlic and herbs. Bring the fat to a simmer and cook for 5–10 minutes to evaporate any water. Allow the fat to cool to room temperature, then pour it over the duck legs to submerge them completely. The duck can be kept like this for 2–3 weeks.

7 When ready to use, allow the duck fat to come to room temperature and carefully remove the legs. To reheat, either place the duck legs in a roasting tin in an oven preheated to 190°C/gas mark 5 for 20 minutes, or place them skin side down in an ovenproof frying pan set over a low to medium heat, to allow the skin to crisp, about 10 minutes, before transferring to the oven to heat through.

Variation

Spiced duck confit Omit the aromatics. Dry-roast 2 tsp coriander seeds, 1 tsp cumin seeds, 4 star anise and 1 large cinnamon stick in a frying pan set over a medium heat, until they release their aromas, about 3–4 minutes. Allow the spices to cool, then grind using a pestle and mortar with 1 tbsp sea salt, 2 peeled garlic cloves and the washed stems (and roots if you have them) from 4 coriander sprigs to a fairly smooth paste. Place the duck legs in a large plastic bag, add half the spice paste, rub into the legs and leave to marinate in the fridge overnight. Reserve the remaining half of the paste to add to the duck fat when cooking the duck. Proceed as for the main recipe.

Warm duck confit salad

Serves 4 as a starter
2 duck confit legs (see left)
100g fine green beans
50g walnuts
50g semi-dried cherries
1 frisée
75g smoked bacon
2½ tbsp olive oil
½ shallot
½ garlic clove
1½ tbsp sherry vinegar
Salt and freshly ground black pepper

1 Heat the oven to 190°C/gas mark 5.

2 Heat a sauté pan, put the duck confit legs in skin side down and cook until the skin is crisp. Transfer to a roasting tin skin side up and place in the oven for 20 minutes, or until the duck is hot through and the skin crisp.

3 Top the green beans and blanch in a pan of boiling salted water for 4–5 minutes, drain and plunge into cold water, to refresh. Once cool, drain and dry the beans and transfer to a large bowl.

4 Halve the walnuts and add them with the cherries to the bowl. Pick out the central pale green leaves of the frisée, wash well, dry, break into bite-sized pieces and add to the bowl.

5 Derind the bacon and cut into lardons. Heat ½ tbsp of the olive oil in a frying pan and fry the lardons over a medium heat until golden, then remove to a plate. Peel and very finely dice the shallot, and peel and crush the garlic.

6 Once the duck confit is hot, strip the duck from the bones into large pieces and keep warm.

7 Add the remaining olive oil, the shallot, garlic and sherry vinegar to the oil in the frying pan, with salt and pepper to taste, and warm it through. Stir through the lardons to warm them.

8 Pour the warm dressing and lardons over the salad and toss lightly. Add the duck, toss lightly again and serve.

Spiced duck confit in a ginger broth

Serves 4
4 spiced duck confit legs (see left)
Small bunch of Thai basil
Small bunch of coriander
1 long red chilli
Small handful of bean sprouts
4 pak choi

For the broth
750ml chicken and veal stock
  (see page 96)
2cm piece of fresh root ginger
1 long red chilli
2 spring onions
3 star anise
1 cinnamon stick
½ lime
1 tbsp oyster sauce
1 tbsp nam pla (fish sauce)
¼ tsp palm sugar
Dash of kecap manis (sweet soy sauce)

1 Heat the oven to 190°C/gas mark 5. Put the duck confit into a roasting tin and cook in the oven for 20 minutes, or until it is hot through and the skin crisp.

2 To make the broth, put the stock into a saucepan. Peel and slice the ginger. Halve, deseed and coarsely chop the chilli. Slice the white of the spring onions, reserving the green tops. Add the ginger, chilli, white spring onion, star anise and cinnamon to the stock and bring to a simmer over a medium heat. Gently simmer for 10–15 minutes, until the aromatic flavours have infused into the stock.

3 Pick off 2 tbsp each of Thai basil and coriander leaves. Halve the chilli, deseed and cut into julienne (see page 54). Slice the reserved green spring onions tops on the diagonal. Put these ingredients in a bowl with the bean sprouts and set aside.

4 Meanwhile, juice the ½ lime. Season the broth with the oyster sauce, nam pla, sugar and lime juice. Adjust the seasoning to taste, adding a little kecap manis for an intense, salty sweetness.

5 Strain the broth, discarding the aromatics, and return it to the saucepan over a medium heat. Split the pak choi in half through the root, add to the stock and simmer for 2 minutes until wilted.

6 Divide the broth between 4 shallow bowls and add half a pak choi to each. Place a duck leg on top and scatter over a small handful of the bean sprout mixture.

Note Instead of serving the duck legs whole, you can if you like, after reheating, remove the skin and cut it into strips, and strip the duck from the bones to serve in the broth, on rice noodles (soaked/cooked according to packet instructions).

Duck breasts with thyme and cherries

Serves 4
4 duck breasts
2 small shallots
Few thyme sprigs
150g fresh cherries
1 tbsp red wine vinegar
200ml brown chicken and veal stock
  (see page 98)
1–2 tbsp redcurrant jelly, to taste
Salt and freshly ground black pepper

To serve
Wilted spinach (see page 60)
Rosti (see page 71)

1 Trim the sinew off the underside of the duck breasts, and trim the skin, bearing in mind that the skin will shrink when cooking. Score the skin in diagonal lines about 3mm apart, cutting only through the skin, not the flesh.

2 Heat the oven to 150°C/gas mark 2.

3 Rub a little salt into the duck skin and place the duck breasts skin side down in a frying pan set over a low heat to render the fat beneath the skin. This can take up to 10 minutes and should be done over a low heat or the skin will burn. From time to time, pour off the rendered fat to prevent too much spitting. Season the meat side of the breasts with salt and pepper.

4 Halve, peel and finely dice the shallots. Finely chop enough thyme leaves to give you ¼ tsp. Halve the cherries and remove the stones.

5 Once the skin is brown and crisp and the fat beneath the skin rendered, turn the duck breasts over, transfer to a roasting tin and place in the oven for 7–10 minutes, depending on the size of the breasts. Ideally they will still be pink in the centre, but the fibres will be set.

6 Pour off any excess fat from the frying pan, place over a low to medium heat and sauté the shallots until softening, about 4–5 minutes. Deglaze with the wine vinegar, add the stock and reduce by one-third, then add the redcurrant jelly to taste and bring to a simmer, allowing the jelly to melt into the sauce.

7 Add the thyme and cherries to the sauce and bring back to a simmer. Taste and season with salt and pepper. If the sauce is ready before the duck, remove from the heat so that it doesn't over-reduce.

8 When cooked, remove the duck breasts from the oven and pour any juices into the sauce. Leave the duck to rest for 3–4 minutes to allow the juices to redistribute before carving each breast into 5 or 6 slices. Spoon the wilted spinach into the middle of each serving plate and top with a rosti. Arrange the sliced duck breast on top and pour the sauce around.

Variations

Duck breasts with ginger, honey and lime Cook the duck breasts as for the main recipe, but before they go in the oven brush the browned skin with warm honey. Omit the cherry sauce. Pour off any excess fat from the pan and deglaze with 200ml white wine. Reduce to 1 tbsp, then add 300ml brown chicken and veal stock (see page 98) and ¼ tbsp fresh ginger cut into julienne. Reduce until lightly syrupy. Flavour the sauce with ½–1 tsp clear honey and ½–1 tbsp lime juice and season with salt and pepper to taste. You can also add some lime segments to the sauce. Serve the duck breasts with the sauce and noodles tossed in a little sesame oil.

Duck breasts with cranberry and almond relish Cook the duck breasts as for the main recipe. Omit the sauce and serve with a cranberry and almond relish. To make this, put 100g dried cranberries, 25g raisins, 75g soft light brown sugar, 250ml cider vinegar, a pinch of ground cloves and ¼ cinnamon stick in a heavy-based pan. Cook gently for about 20 minutes until the cranberries are soft and the sauce is syrupy. Remove and discard the cinnamon stick. Scatter 25g toasted flaked almonds over the duck breasts before serving, with the relish.

Tamarind and sesame duck salad

Serves 4
4 duck breasts
2 tbsp tamarind paste
1 tsp clear honey
1 tbsp dark soy sauce
4cm piece of fresh root ginger
1 garlic clove
2 tbsp sesame seeds
1 tbsp toasted sesame oil
2 tbsp sunflower oil
1 tsp nam pla (fish sauce)
1 tbsp light soy sauce
1 tsp soft light brown sugar
1 lime
1 red chilli
½ cucumber
1 mango
6 spring onions
½ bunch of coriander
½ bunch of mint
150g mixed salad, including pea shoots
  if available

1 Remove the skin from the duck breasts. Mix 1 tbsp of the tamarind paste with the honey and dark soy sauce. Peel and grate the ginger, peel and crush the garlic and add both to the soy mixture. Spread this over the duck breasts and set aside for at least 20 minutes, ideally overnight in the fridge, to absorb the flavours.

2 Lightly toast the sesame seeds in a hot frying pan, then tip onto a plate to cool.

3 For the salad dressing, whisk together the sesame oil, 1 tbsp of the sunflower oil, the nam pla, light soy sauce, sugar and the remaining tamarind paste. Finely grate the zest and juice the lime. Add the lime zest to the dressing with juice to taste. Halve, deseed and finely slice the chilli, then add it to the dressing.

4 Heat a large frying pan with the remaining sunflower oil. Remove the duck breasts from the marinade and fry them over a medium heat until the first side caramelises, then turn over and repeat on the other side. Turn down the heat and cook the breasts for a further 2 minutes on each side (it should still be pink inside), then remove them to a board to rest for 5 minutes.

5 Meanwhile, to make the salad, cut the cucumber into fine dice. Peel the mango and cut the flesh from the stone, then dice it. Finely slice the spring onions and roughly chop or tear the coriander and mint leaves. Put everything into a bowl with the sesame seeds, salad leaves and enough of the dressing to coat the leaves, being careful not to crush the mango as you toss the salad.

6 Slice the duck breasts and put on serving plates with a pile of salad and any juices or extra dressing drizzled around.

Variation

For a more substantial salad, cook 200g soba noodles and toss with the salad.

Duck and spinach curry

Serves 4
Sunflower oil for frying
4 boneless, skinless duck thighs
1 cinnamon stick
4 cardamom pods
2 bay leaves
2 onions
4cm piece of fresh root ginger
4 garlic cloves
½ tsp ground cinnamon
½ tsp ground turmeric
2 tsp ground cumin
2 tsp ground coriander
½ tsp crushed dried chillies
2 tsp garam masala
400g tin chopped tomatoes
500ml water
300g spinach
Salt and freshly ground black pepper

1 Heat just enough oil to cover the bottom of a large, lidded frying pan. Add the duck thighs and fry on all sides until golden brown. Remove and set aside.

2 Break the cinnamon stick in half and add to the pan with the cardamom pods and bay leaves. Leave over a very low heat while you prepare the onions.

3 Halve, peel and finely slice the onions and add them to the pan. You may need to add another 1–2 tbsp oil. Cook gently until very soft, then increase the heat slightly and allow them to brown. Meanwhile, peel and grate the ginger and peel and crush the garlic. Put all the dry spices into a small bowl.

4 Once the onions are brown, discard the cardamom and cinnamon. Add the garlic and ginger, stir well for a minute, then add all the dry spices. Cook, stirring, for 2 minutes. Add the tomatoes and water, bring to the boil and season with salt and plenty of pepper. Add the duck, then lower the heat, cover and simmer until tender, about 2 hours. If the sauce becomes very thick, add 4–5 tbsp water.

5 Wash the spinach well, put into a large saucepan with just the water clinging to the leaves, and cook for 2 minutes, or until just wilted. Drain and cool in a sieve under cold running water, then press out excess water. Roughly chop the spinach.

6 Take out the duck and reduce the sauce if necessary, to get a rich flavour. Adjust the seasoning, then add the spinach and duck to heat through. Serve with rice.

Feathered game

Game birds are very lean compared with farmed poultry and so need to be cooked carefully to ensure they do not dry out. Most benefit from being served slightly pink, as more moisture is retained in their very lean flesh. Also the meat is often marinated and stewed, or covered in bacon before roasting to keep it moist.

Game is hung to develop the flavour of the meat, but also to tenderise the flesh as the enzymes start to break it down. The length of time game birds are hung for varies according to personal taste. While some people like their game well hung and 'high', many prefer a less gamey flavoured bird and therefore do not hang it for long.

Feathered game should be hung by the neck in a cool, dry, dark place. There must be room for good circulation of air around the birds and they should be hung away from other food to avoid cross-contamination.

Game bird seasons and classic serving suggestions

Most game birds are only available during a certain part of the year or 'season', to ensure breeding stocks are high enough to guarantee an annual supply. Some birds, such as quail, are farmed, which provides a continual supply.

Pheasant	1st October – 1st February	1 pheasant serves 3 or 4 people	Serve with a thin gravy, bread sauce, fried crumbs and game chips
Grouse	12th August – 10th December	1 grouse per person, or a very plump grouse could feed 2 people	Serve on a croûte with thin gravy, fruit jelly, fried crumbs and game chips
Partridge	1st September – 1st February	1 partridge per person	Serve with a thin gravy and game chips
Snipe	August – January	1 or 2 per person	Roast on a croûte to absorb the juices, and serve pink
Woodcock	1st September – 31st January	1 per person	Split in half and serve on a croûte
Pigeon	Farmed – all year	1 pigeon per person or 3 breasts	Serve breasts pink
Quail	Farmed – all year	2 quail per person when served plain roasted	Mild flavour, can be served pink

Plucking and drawing a pheasant

1 Cut a large bin bag down one side and across the bottom and open it out on your work surface. If you have a drawer under your work surface, open a second bin bag and tuck it in the drawer, then close the drawer, leaving the bag open. If you don't have a drawer, then place a chopping board over one top side of the second open bin bag. Squirt a thin line of washing up liquid around the inside of the bag; this will help to keep feathers in the bin bag. Lay the pheasant on the opened-out bag on your surface, breast side down.

2 Now begin to pluck the pheasant. On the non-breast side, legs and thighs, you can pull out the feathers in the opposite direction to the way they lie, but on the breast side, where the skin is delicate, you need to pull them out in the same direction to avoid tearing the skin. Support the skin with one hand, take a few feathers in the other and pull firmly to pluck, dropping the feathers into the bag.

3 Either pluck the wings up to the first joint, then cut through the joint to remove the outer 2 wing parts, or cut off the outer 2 wing joints before starting to pluck the bird. Continue to pluck the bird on the non-breast side until the back is fully cleaned of feathers up to the head. Turn the pheasant over and start on the legs and thighs, then finally the breast. There will be a few small soft feathers still on the bird but these can be scorched off later.

4 Turn the pheasant breast side down again and cut through the neck as close to the head as possible, discarding the head. Now make a cut down the length of the neck and pull the skin from the neck. As close to the body as possible, cut off the neck and reserve. Take care not to puncture or break the crop, which is found at the base of the neck in the body of the pheasant at the top of the breasts, and can be carefully released away from the pheasant and removed whole. If you don't manage this, don't worry, as the crop is only filled with undigested grain, which can be wiped away with kitchen paper. Trim the neck skin.

5 To remove the feet, make a shallow incision around the knee joint to release the skin, then place the pheasant on the surface with the feet hanging over the edge. Bend the feet over the edge, twisting and pulling as you do to help pull the strong tendons from the legs. The feet should pull away with the tendons attached. Discard the bin bag covering the work surface and clear all feathers from the area.

6 To draw (gut) the pheasant, locate the vent. Insert the point of a knife into the vent and cut down to extend the opening.

7 Then, for a two-fingered draw, place your middle and forefingers in the cavity, keeping them as close as possible against the breast bone. Push your fingers as deep as possible, as close to the neck end of the pheasant as you can get them. Then move them left and right, down to the back bone to release the entrails. Once released, use your fingers to pull the entrails towards the entrance of the cavity and out. Make sure you remove all the entrails and wipe out the cavity with kitchen paper to clean it.

8 Place the entrails on the board and pull away the gizzard, liver, kidneys and heart. Discard all other entrails. Pull away any extraneous bits from the heart, liver and kidneys; set aside. Take the gizzard and, using a knife, make a shallow incision halfway around it. Open the gizzard and rinse out the ground grain.

9 Carefully pull away the inner membrane from the gizzard and rinse again. Set the entrails aside until ready to use. Hold the pheasant over an open gas flame to scorch off any remaining feathers. If you do not have a gas burner use a blowtorch, but don't get so close to the pheasant as to scorch the skin. Wipe over the pheasant with kitchen paper to remove the remains of any scorched feathers. The pheasant is now ready to cook.

1 The pheasant, ready to pluck.

2 Pulling the feathers out firmly from the breast.

3 Cutting through the joint to remove the outer wing parts.

4 Cutting off the neck close to the body.

5 Bending the feet over the edge of the worktop and twisting to pull the tendons from the legs.

6 Opening up the vent to allow you to draw the pheasant.

7 Releasing the entrails, using the middle and forefingers.

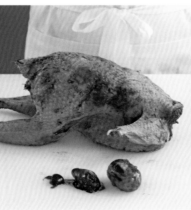

8 The heart, kidneys and gizzard separated from the other entrails.

9 Pulling away the inner membrane from the gizzard.

Roast pheasant

Serves 4
2 oven-ready pheasants
1 apple
4 tsp softened butter
4 rashers of streaky bacon for barding
1 tbsp port
1 tsp redcurrant jelly
2 tsp plain flour
Bunch of watercress
Salt and freshly ground black pepper

To serve
Fried crumbs (see right)
Game chips (see page 73)
Glazed baby vegetables (see page 88)

This is pheasant roasted and served the traditional way, with fried crumbs, game chips and watercress.

1 Heat the oven to 200°C/gas mark 6.

2 Wipe over the pheasants and remove any remaining feathers. Season inside the cavities, halve the apple and insert half an apple in each cavity, which helps keep the flesh moist.

3 Tie the legs loosely together. Rub 1 tsp of butter over each bird and season well with salt and pepper. Lay 2 rashers of streaky bacon over the breasts of each bird, to help keep the meat moist. Tie the bacon on if the birds do not sit straight.

4 Place the pheasants side by side in a roasting tin and pour in water to a depth of about 5mm. Roast in the oven for about 40–50 minutes, basting the pheasants frequently and removing the bacon after about 20 minutes to allow the breasts to brown. Game birds can be served pink, so the juices will be pink when the thickest part of the thigh is pierced with a skewer.

5 When the pheasants are cooked, lift them out of the roasting tin onto a warmed serving dish and set aside in a warm place while you make the gravy.

6 Put the roasting tin on the hob. Taste the roasting juices and, if necessary, reduce over a medium heat to concentrate the flavour. Add the port and redcurrant jelly with any resting juices from the pheasants and bring to a simmer. Thicken the gravy if necessary with a little beurre manié (see page 339) made with the remaining 2 tsp of butter and the flour. The gravy should be lightly syrupy but not too thick. Taste and adjust the seasoning.

7 Arrange the watercress between the pheasants, which are now ready to be carved. Serve the gravy and accompaniments separately.

....

Fried crumbs
Melt 50g butter in a frying pan over a low heat. Add 5–6 tbsp dry white breadcrumbs and fry them very slowly until they are evenly golden in colour, crisp and have absorbed all the butter. Quickly remove from the pan, as they will continue to colour. Serve warm.

If preferred you can use fresh white breadcrumbs, but you will need more butter, as fresh crumbs are much more absorbent than dry ones. They also require even more care when frying as they need to become crisp before they take on too much colour.

....

A note on barding game birds...
Rashers of bacon or pancetta are often laid over the breast of game birds before they are cooked to bard them and help to keep the breast meat moist. The rashers can be removed towards the end of roasting to allow the breasts to brown. On small birds the rashers are usually tied in place with kitchen string.

Pheasant with whisky

Serves 4

2 small onions
100g butter
2 oven-ready pheasants
150ml whisky
150ml chicken and veal stock
  (see page 96)
300ml double cream
1–2 tbsp Dijon mustard
Squeeze of lemon juice
Salt and freshly ground black pepper

1 Heat the oven to 190°C/gas mark 5.

2 Halve, peel and finely dice the onions. Melt the butter in a flameproof casserole over a low to medium heat and gently fry the onions until golden. Remove the onions and set aside. Season the pheasants and brown them all over, one at a time, in the casserole, about 10–15 minutes per pheasant.

3 Return the onions and both pheasants to the casserole and flambé (see below) with 120ml of the whisky, shaking the pan gently until the flames subside. Add the stock, cover tightly and cook in the oven for 20–30 minutes until the birds are just cooked and tender. Pheasant can be served pink, so don't overcook them.

4 Remove the birds to a board and set aside in a warm place to rest.

5 Strain the cooking liquid, discarding the onions, return the liquid to the casserole and place over a high heat. Boil to reduce to about 4–5 tbsp, taking care not to let the juices boil dry. Add the cream and reduce again until the sauce lightly coats the back of a wooden spoon. If the sauce over-reduces and becomes too thick, add a splash of water.

6 Joint the pheasants (as for chicken, see page 327), transfer the pieces to a warmed serving dish and set aside in a warm place.

7 Remove the casserole from the heat, add the mustard and remaining 30ml whisky, or to taste, and season with salt and pepper. Add a little lemon juice to balance the cream, then pour the sauce around the pheasant. The whisky should give a subtle and not overpowering flavour.

Variations

Any poultry can be used in place of pheasant; guinea fowl is particularly good. If you prefer, you can joint the pheasants before browning and cooking them (see page 336), or just use pheasant breasts. The cooking time, once browned, would need to be reduced to 10–20 minutes, depending on the size of the joints.

Flambé

This technique is used to burn off alcohol quickly and to caramelise the essence of a spirit or wine around meat or poultry. You need to make sure the pan and food in it are hot, so keep the pan over a low to medium heat.

Pour in the measured amount of alcohol, strike a long match and light the alcohol. Or, if you are using a gas hob, put the alcohol in a ladle and warm over a direct flame, then tip the ladle a little to allow the alcohol to catch alight. Immediately pour the flaming alcohol over the food in the pan, tilting the ladle away from you.

Take care to ensure your arms are covered with long sleeves and you are not standing directly over the pan. Sometimes the alcohol will not light, but the alcohol in it will be evaporated off through simmering and the flavour will remain. Always have a pan lid or baking sheet close by to smother any excessive flame.

Pheasant breast with prunes in Armagnac

Serves 4

2 oven-ready pheasants
4 tbsp olive oil
2 thyme sprigs
12 pitted prunes
150ml Armagnac
1 onion
4 garlic cloves
750ml chicken and veal stock
  (see page 96)
Few parsley sprigs
1 bay leaf
½ tsp black peppercorns
20g butter
2 tbsp crème fraîche
Salt and freshly ground black pepper

To serve
Rosti (see page 71)
Savoy cabbage with pancetta
  (see page 57)

1 Carefully remove the pheasant breasts from the pheasants (see page 344 for supremes) and place them in a plastic bag with 1 tbsp of the olive oil, the thyme and 2 or 3 turns of pepper. Leave to marinate in the fridge for 2–3 hours.

2 Remove the legs and thighs from the carcass and cut in half. Break the carcass in two. Put the remaining olive oil in a deep saucepan and place over a medium to high heat. Brown the legs, thighs, wings and carcasses well, turning them to colour evenly, about 15–20 minutes.

3 Meanwhile, soak the prunes in the Armagnac. Halve, peel and chop the onion and bash the unpeeled garlic cloves with the flat side of a large knife. Remove the pheasant bones from the saucepan; set aside. Add the onion and garlic to the pan and sauté quickly for 3–4 minutes. Pour off any excess fat and discard.

4 Drain the prunes, reserving the Armagnac.

5 Deglaze the saucepan with the Armagnac and reduce by at least one-third. Add the stock, parsley sprigs, bay leaf and peppercorns, the browned bones and enough water to just cover the bones, then bring to the boil. Turn down to a simmer and cook gently for 45 minutes, skimming occasionally. Strain the sauce through a fine sieve and set aside.

6 To cook the pheasant breasts, remove them from the marinade and season with salt. Heat a frying pan over a low to medium heat and place the breasts skin side down in the pan to render the fat beneath the skin and gently brown the skin, about 4–6 minutes. When the skin is golden and crisp, turn the breasts over and cook for a further 4 minutes. Pour off the excess fat and add the butter. Allow the butter to melt before basting it over the breasts. When the breasts are cooked (feel for a firmness on the sides), remove from the frying pan and set aside to rest.

7 Pour off the butter from the frying pan, add the sauce to the pan and reduce until the flavour is concentrated and the consistency is lightly syrupy. Add the crème fraîche, taste and season. Finally, add the prunes to heat through.

8 Transfer the pheasant breasts to plates and pour the sauce and prunes around them. Serve with the rosti potatoes and Savoy cabbage.

Variations

This is a very useful way of cooking any game bird. The smaller the bird the less cooking time the breasts will require. The Armagnac can be substituted with brandy or a fortified wine such as Madeira, and the vegetable accompaniments can be varied.

Pheasant breast with red cabbage and chestnuts Omit the prunes. Serve the pheasant with red cabbage with chestnuts and bacon (see page 59) rather than Savoy cabbage and pancetta.

Pheasant breast with Marsala and wilted spinach Use Marsala in place of Armagnac in the sauce. Serve the pheasant with wilted spinach (see page 60) and celeriac purée (see page 19) instead of the cabbage.

Partridge with pancetta and lentils

Serves 4
200g Puy lentils
1 onion
100g piece of pancetta, plus 4 thin slices
  for barding
2 garlic cloves
Small bunch of thyme
4 tbsp olive oil
4 oven-ready partridges
600ml chicken and veal stock
  (see page 96)
150ml Marsala
Salt and freshly ground black pepper

1 Soak the lentils in cold water for 30–45 minutes, then drain.

2 Halve, peel and finely chop the onion. Derind the piece of pancetta and cut into small dice. Peel and crush the garlic. Finely chop enough thyme leaves to give you 1–1½ tbsp and set aside 2 whole sprigs.

3 Heat the olive oil in a large flameproof casserole. Sprinkle the partridges with salt and fry over a medium heat until golden brown all over. Remove from the casserole and set aside to cool a little, then wrap the slices of pancetta over the breasts and secure with string if necessary.

4 Add the pancetta dice and onion to the casserole and cook gently until the onion is soft. Increase the heat and allow the pancetta and onion to turn golden. Add the garlic and cook for a further 1 minute. Add the drained lentils with the thyme sprigs and stock and simmer for 5 minutes.

5 Return the partridges to the casserole, cover with a lid and simmer gently over a low heat until the partridges are cooked and their legs will wobble when pulled, about 10–15 minutes for very small partridges. The partridges are likely to be cooked before the lentils are tender, so remove them from the casserole and keep them warm while the lentils finish cooking.

6 When the lentils are tender, drain and set aside, reserving any liquid; discard the thyme sprigs. Add the Marsala to the casserole and reduce by half, then add the reserved liquid and simmer until syrupy. Add back the lentils with half of the chopped thyme, heat through and season with salt and pepper.

7 Carve or joint the partridges (as for chicken, see page 327). Place the lentils in a deep serving dish, arrange the partridge joints on top and sprinkle with the remaining chopped thyme.

Variations

Pheasant breast with pancetta and lentils Replace the partridge with 4 large pheasant breasts and omit the pancetta slices used for barding. The breasts may take less time to cook than the whole partridge, so prepare the lentils as for the main recipe and in the meantime season the breasts and fry until brown and the skin is crisp. Place the breasts on top of the lentils as for the main recipe, cover and cook for 10 minutes, or until the meat is just cooked through. Remove the breasts and keep warm while you finish the lentils, then serve as above.

Partridge with pesto and lentils Omit the diced pancetta and replace the Marsala with white wine. Proceed as for the main recipe, stirring in 1 large tbsp pesto (see page 126) in place of the chopped thyme in step 6. Finish with a sprinkling of torn basil rather than chopped thyme.

Wood pigeon with morcilla and sage salad

Serves 4 as a starter

30g raisins

2 tbsp sherry

½ shallot

100g mixed salad leaves, including lamb's lettuce

Few sage sprigs

2 wood pigeons

100g morcilla sausage

100g piece of pancetta

3–4 tbsp olive oil

1 tbsp sherry vinegar

1 quantity sage croûtons (see page 613)

Salt and freshly ground black pepper

1 Soak the raisins in the sherry. Peel and finely dice the shallot. Wash, dry and pick over the salad leaves and place in a bowl. Chiffonade enough sage leaves (see page 89) to give you 1 tbsp and set aside. Heat the oven to 120°C/gas mark ½.

2 Remove the breasts from the pigeons, keeping the skin intact (see page 344). Cut the morcilla into thick slices. Derind the pancetta and cut into lardons.

3 Heat ½ tbsp olive oil in a frying pan over a low to medium heat and fry the morcilla for 5–8 minutes, turning them, until cooked. Remove to a plate and keep warm in the low oven. Wipe out the pan, add another ½ tbsp olive oil and fry the lardons until golden. Transfer to a plate; keep warm in the oven.

4 Season the pigeon breasts, add to the frying pan skin side down and cook for 3–4 minutes, then turn and cook for 2–3 minutes on the other side; the meat should be pink and the fibres set. Remove and set aside to rest.

5 Sauté the shallot in the frying pan for a few minutes to soften, then add the remaining 2–3 tbsp olive oil to the pan with the sherry vinegar, raisins and sherry, sage and lardons. Warm through, then taste and season with salt and pepper.

6 Pour enough warmed dressing over the salad leaves to coat the leaves evenly, tossing to mix. Add the croûtons and divide the salad between 4 plates. Slice each pigeon breast into 3 or 4 slices and divide between the plates. Crumble the morcilla over the salad and drizzle over any remaining dressing.

Wood pigeon with a grape and clementine relish

Serves 4

4 wood pigeons

1–2 tbsp olive oil

Salt and freshly ground black pepper

For the sauce

1 tbsp olive oil

2 shallots

1–2 thyme sprigs

½ tsp black peppercorns

2 tbsp verjuice

50ml Marsala

400ml brown chicken and veal stock (see page 98)

For the relish

75g seedless red grapes

2 clementines

50g candied pecans (see page 38)

1 rosemary sprig

½ tbsp clear honey

1 tbsp verjuice or white wine

3 tbsp olive oil

1 Remove the breasts from the pigeons and set aside in the fridge, then cut the thigh and leg pieces from the carcasses.

2 To make the sauce, heat the olive oil in a saucepan, add the legs, thighs and carcasses and brown all over. Halve, peel and finely dice the shallots. Once the bones are browned, remove and set aside. Pour off the excess fat and add the shallots, thyme sprigs and peppercorns to the pan. Sauté for 5–6 minutes until starting to soften. Deglaze the pan with the verjuice and reduce to ½ tbsp, then add the Marsala and reduce again to 1 tbsp. Add the stock and bring to a simmer. Add back the bones and simmer gently for 30–40 minutes, skimming occasionally.

3 Meanwhile, for the relish, peel and halve the grapes; place in a bowl. Segment the clementines, removing all skin and pith (see page 530) and add to the bowl with the candied pecans; set aside. Finely chop enough rosemary leaves to give you ½–1 tsp.

4 To finish the sauce, strain and reduce to about 150ml, until the flavour is concentrated, skimming often. Taste, adjust the seasoning; keep warm.

5 Heat the olive oil in a frying pan over a medium to high heat, season the pigeon breasts and cook them skin side down until well browned and the skin is crisp, about 3–4 minutes. Turn them over, reduce the heat and cook for 1–2 minutes for medium rare. Remove from the pan and leave to rest for 3–4 minutes.

6 To finish the relish, whisk together the honey, verjuice, olive oil and rosemary to taste. Pour this dressing over the fruit and pecans. Season with salt and pepper.

7 To serve, reheat the sauce. Slice the pigeon breasts and arrange on plates. Spoon a little of the relish to the side and finish with the sauce.

Quail with honey, thyme and figs

Serves 4 as a starter
4 quail
Few thyme sprigs
40g butter, softened
2–3 drops of anchovy essence
4 figs
2 tsp clear honey
50ml Pedro Ximenez sherry or port
50ml brown chicken and veal stock
  (see page 98)
Salt and freshly ground black pepper
Watercress, to garnish

1 Heat the grill to its highest setting and the oven to 200°C/gas mark 6.

2 Spatchcock and skewer the quail (see page 356). Finely chop enough thyme leaves to give you ½ tsp, mix into 30g of the butter with a few drops of anchovy essence and season with salt and pepper. Carefully release the skin over each quail breast by inserting a finger from the neck end between the breast and skin. Spread a quarter of the flavoured butter over each quail breast, under the skin.

3 Place the quail, skin side up, on a lipped baking tray or shallow roasting tin and rub the remaining softened butter over them. Season with salt and pepper and grill for 3–5 minutes until the skin is browned and crisp.

4 Cut a deep cross into the figs through the stem end to come three-quarters of the way down. Squeeze the base of each fig a little to open out the quarters.

5 Once the quail are brown, add the figs to the roasting tin and scatter the leaves of 2 thyme sprigs over them. Drizzle the honey, sherry and stock over the quail and figs. Cook in the oven for 10–15 minutes, taking care that neither the quail nor the figs burn. To check that the quail are cooked, cut down to the base on the non-skin side; the meat can be served pink. Remove the skewers.

6 Serve the quail and figs, drizzled with the pan juices, with a watercress garnish.

Quail with pomegranate molasses, watercress and feta salad

Serves 4
4 quail

For the marinade
1 garlic clove
1 shallot
2 tbsp pomegranate molasses
Pinch of ground cinnamon

For the salad
75g pine nuts
200g watercress
Few oregano sprigs
1 pomegranate
200g feta

For the dressing
1 garlic clove
Pinch of ground cumin
2 tbsp pomegranate molasses
½ tbsp orange juice
½ tsp clear honey
4 tbsp olive oil
Sea salt and freshly ground black pepper

1 Spatchcock and part bone the quail (see page 356).

2 For the marinade, peel and crush the garlic and halve, peel and roughly chop the shallot. Place all the marinade ingredients in a small food processor bowl and blend until smooth. Rub well all over the quail and leave to marinate for at least 2 hours, or in the fridge overnight.

3 Heat the grill to high and the oven to 180°C/gas mark 4. Toast the pine nuts on a baking tray in the oven for 5 minutes until lightly coloured. Tip onto a plate to cool.

4 Wash, dry and pick over the watercress, tear into sprigs and place in a bowl. Finely chop enough oregano leaves to give you 1 tsp; add to the bowl. Extract the seeds from the pomegranate by holding the halved fruit cut side down over a bowl and carefully hitting it on the skin side with a rolling pin. Add the pomegranate seeds to the salad with the toasted pine nuts. Break the feta into chunks; set aside.

5 Place the quail breast side down on a lightly oiled lipped baking sheet and grill until caramelised. Turn the quail over and repeat on the other side. Once the skin is brown and crisp, transfer to the oven to cook through, about 10–15 minutes.

6 To make the dressing, peel and crush the garlic, put into a small bowl and mix in the cumin and pomegranate molasses, then add the orange juice and honey and whisk in the olive oil; the dressing should emulsify. Taste and season with salt and pepper, adding more honey if the dressing is too sharp.

7 Check the quail are cooked by cutting down to the bone on the non-skin side; it can be served pink. When cooked, baste the quail with the pan juices, then cut each bird in half through the middle of the breast. Trim any exposed bones.

8 Dress the salad and gently mix through the feta, taking care that it doesn't break up. Serve 2 quail halves per person, with the salad.

Poultry offal

Poultry offal is still undervalued but chicken, duck and goose livers, in particular, lend themselves to tasty, nutritious and economical dishes, especially pâtés and salads. Freshness is of the essence with offal, so choose carefully, keep refrigerated and use within a day or two.

Chicken liver pâté

Serves 6
500g chicken livers
1 onion
200g butter, softened
1–1½ garlic cloves
1½ tbsp brandy
Salt and freshly ground black pepper

For sealing the pâté (optional)
75–100g clarified butter (see page 75)

1 Prepare the chicken livers by trimming away any discolouration or green areas and any tubes and fat, leaving the livers as whole as possible to help prevent them from overcooking.

2 Halve, peel and finely dice the onion. Melt half the butter in a frying pan, add the onion and sweat until very soft and translucent. Peel and crush the garlic, add to the sweated onion and cook for 1 minute. Transfer the onion and garlic to a plate using a slotted spoon, leaving the butter in the frying pan.

3 Reheat the frying pan over a low to medium heat. Season the trimmed livers with salt and pepper and fry gently, turning to lightly brown on all sides; they should be pink in the middle but must not be rare or raw. Remove to a sieve to drain off any bitter juices.

4 Return the livers to the pan over a low to medium heat and flambé with the brandy (see page 382), then take the pan off the heat. Leave to cool slightly.

5 Blend the livers and onion in a food processor with the remaining butter until smooth, ensuring no ingredient is too cold or it will split the mixture. The pâté should be pale pink. Season to taste, then sieve it as quickly as possible through a fine sieve into a bowl to prevent discolouring. Divide the pâté between small ramekins or spoon into an earthenware dish and smooth the surface.

6 If you plan to keep the pâté for more than 3 days, pour the clarified butter over the top of the pâté to create a 2–3mm layer. This will harden and seal the pâté, excluding all the air and so preserving it and preventing it from discolouring. Once sealed, it can be kept in the fridge for up to a week.

Variations

Champagne and chicken liver pâté Omit the brandy and add 100ml warm Champagne to the food processor when blending the livers.

Chicken liver pâté with thyme Add 1–1½ tsp finely chopped thyme when blending the livers.

Soaking livers for a milder flavour
Soaking livers in milk, or a mixture of milk and water, for 30–60 minutes before cooking can help remove to some of the strong, bitter flavours and mellow the taste.

A note on oxidisation...
A pink pâté will quickly oxidise and turn brown once it comes into contact with air. Sieving the pâté as quickly as possible after blending helps prevent this.

Salade tiède

Serves 4
100g piece of bacon
200g chicken livers
5 spring onions
1 small frisée
Bunch of watercress
1 radicchio
Bunch of chervil
2 tbsp olive oil
1½ tbsp tarragon vinegar
1 quantity French dressing (see page 125)
1 quantity croûtons (see page 613)
Salt and freshly ground black pepper

1 Derind the bacon and cut into lardons. Prepare the chicken livers by trimming away any discolouration or green areas and any tubes and fat, leaving the livers as whole as possible to help prevent them from overcooking.

2 Slice the spring onions thinly on the diagonal. Wash, dry and tear the frisée, watercress, radicchio and chervil into small bite-sized pieces.

3 Heat 1 tbsp of the olive oil in a frying pan over a medium heat and fry the bacon lardons until lightly browned all over. Remove from the frying pan and set aside.

4 Season the trimmed chicken livers. Return the frying pan to a medium to high heat, add the livers and sauté until brown on the outside but still very pink in the centre, about 2–3 minutes (they will continue to cook as they cool). Place the livers in a sieve set over a bowl to drain.

5 Wipe out the pan with kitchen paper. Heat the remaining olive oil in the frying pan, add the spring onions and sauté for 30 seconds. Add the tarragon vinegar and return the bacon and livers to the pan to heat through. Taste and add a little more olive oil, vinegar or salt and pepper as needed, and to create a generous amount of pan juices.

6 Dress the salad leaves and chervil with the French dressing and divide between 4 plates. Scatter the croûtons, bacon, liver and spring onions and the pan juices over the leaves and serve immediately.

Variations

Chicken livers with olives and cherry tomatoes Cook the chicken livers as for the main recipe then, after removing them from the pan, add 100g pitted halved black olives and 200g halved cherry tomatoes and stir until hot. Use sherry vinegar in place of the tarragon vinegar. Omit the bacon, spring onions and croûtons and use whatever leaves you prefer.

Chicken livers with baby spinach, warm apple, raisin and bacon dressing Substitute baby spinach for the salad leaves and omit the spring onions, French dressing and croûtons. Follow the main recipe to the end of step 4, but cook the livers until set yet still pink inside; keep warm. Heat 2–3 tbsp olive oil in the pan. Add 30g raisins (soaked in 50ml boiling water for 30 minutes and drained), and ½ Granny Smith apple, peeled, cored and cut into 5mm dice, with the browned bacon. Sauté for 15–20 seconds to warm through. Add the tarragon vinegar and 2–3 chiffonaded sage leaves (see page 89). Taste and season, then pour over the spinach leaves so they wilt slightly. Divide between 4 plates and top with the livers.

Meat

The choice of meat available to the home cook today, including rare breeds, which are being reintroduced, is vast, so it really helps to know about the different cuts and the best ways to cook them. Simple butchery skills are also useful. The tenderness and flavour of meat are influenced by various things, including the breed, the age of the animal, the amount it has exercised, the state of the animal prior to slaughter and how long the carcass has hung for – factors that are all beyond the cook's control. However, it is important to know what to look for when you are buying meat, and how to decide which cut to buy for a particular dish.

Beef and Veal

From the robust flavour of aged beef to the subtle nature of tender veal, there are endless opportunities for creative cooking with both meats. Once the technique has been mastered, a perfectly cooked steak offers the ultimate in fast, convenient cooking. Served with a simple salad and perhaps some fried potatoes, it is the ideal, elegant quick meal. At the other end of the spectrum, the tougher cuts, with their gelatinous nature, offer the cook the opportunity to develop slow, intense flavour combinations, from spicy curries to classic red wine and herb-infused braises and casseroles.

Well hung beef will have the best developed flavour, and some fat is desirable in a joint or minced beef. Any marbling of fat running through the fibres and muscles will melt during the cooking process and help to keep the meat tender and succulent.

Veal is the meat of young cows. Rose veal, while not as tender as milk-fed calves who have restricted movement, is guaranteed to be from calves raised on farms in association with the RSPCA's Freedom Food programme. It will still have a subtler, sweeter flavour and lighter colour than beef.

Roasting

Roasting involves cooking meat at a high temperature for a fairly short amount of time. Meat is normally dry roasted, without the addition of any liquid to the roasting tin. This way of roasting works well and produces a good gravy, although there can be a lot of moisture loss and shrinkage when cooking at such high temperatures. To reduce this effect, we often prefer to brown the joint quickly at a high temperature for colour and flavour (this can be done either in the oven or over direct heat), then roast the meat at a much lower temperature for longer, resulting in more tender, succulent meat. This method therefore employs both roasting and slow cooking techniques.

When choosing a piece of beef for roasting, look for a cut from the centre area of the animal, near the back bone, as this is the least exercised part of an animal and so is naturally more tender. Such cuts include fore and wing rib, sirloin and fillet. Avoid using topside and silverside as these cuts are very lean and much tougher, and are best suited to pot roasting or braising.

Beef should be deep red in colour with some marbling of fat through the fibres and muscles. If there is surface fat it should be creamy in colour and dry. Good beef is hung to intensify the flavour and tenderise it; the longer the meat has been hanging, the darker red it will be.

The shape of the joint

Most cooking times are for a piece of meat that is uniform (almost square) and compact. Long, narrow pieces of meat, such as a fillet, do not need as long a cooking time when calculated by weight, as the heat will take less time to penetrate to the centre of the joint. When cooking such pieces, you may need to reduce the cooking time by 5 minutes per 450g or by 15–20 minutes overall.

The temperature of the meat

Remove the meat from the fridge at least 1–2 hours in advance of roasting, depending on size, to let it come to room temperature. This will result in a more even cooking.

Cooking on the bone

Bone is a very good conductor of heat, and so meat on the bone cooks a little more quickly than boneless joints. This means you need to check it a little earlier than the suggested time.

Small roasts

A very small joint will overcook and toughen while it roasts at a high temperature to brown it, so it is often best to brown smaller joints on the hob and then roast them in the oven at the lower temperature for the calculated cooking time. To do this, heat 1 tbsp oil in a frying pan over a medium to high heat. Season the joint with salt and brown evenly all over in the pan before seasoning with pepper and transferring it to a roasting tin in the oven. Deglaze the frying pan with a little water after the browning process and reserve these juices for the gravy; it all adds flavour.

Roast beef

Serves 10
1 rib of beef, about 2.5kg
1–2 tsp English mustard powder
1–2 tbsp plain flour
500ml brown chicken and veal stock
  (see page 98)
Salt and freshly ground black pepper

To serve
Yorkshire puddings (see page 397)
Horseradish sauce (see page 130)

1 Heat the oven to 220°C/gas mark 7.

2 Weigh the joint of beef to calculate the cooking time. Allow 20 minutes per 450g for medium, 15 minutes per 450g for medium-rare and 10–15 minutes per 450g for rare.

3 Rub the mustard powder over the meat and season well with salt and plenty of pepper. Place in a roasting tin just big enough to fit the meat comfortably, and roast for 20 minutes. Now lower the oven setting to 170°C/gas mark 3 and time the cooking from this point.

4 Check to see if the meat is already cooked to your liking 30 minutes before the end of the cooking time. Depending on the shape, it can sometimes be cooked a little sooner than the calculated time. To check, insert a skewer through the thickest part and leave it there for 10 seconds. Remove and touch it to your inner wrist; it should be just warm for rare, warm for medium-rare and hot for medium.

5 Once the beef is cooked, place it on a board over a tray to catch the juices and rest for at least 15–20 minutes while you make the gravy (and cook the Yorkshire puddings). Resting the meat will make it easier to carve and the beef will retain more of its juices.

6 To make the gravy, pour the fat and juices from the roasting tin into a bowl and allow them to separate. Adding a splash of cold water helps this. Skim off the fat and return 2 tbsp of it to the roasting tin. Add the flour and stir over a medium heat until the flour has browned a little and any sediment from the bottom of the pan is loosened.

7 Add back the roasting juices and pour in up to 500ml stock. Stir over the heat until simmering, then simmer for 2–3 minutes. Taste and continue to simmer until the gravy has developed a good strong, meaty flavour, then season with salt and pepper. The juices released from the meat while it is resting can also be added to the gravy or poured over the carved meat. Strain the gravy through a fine sieve into a warmed jug or sauceboat.

8 Carve the beef very thinly (as shown overleaf). Serve with the gravy, Yorkshire puddings, horseradish sauce, roast potatoes and seasonal vegetables.

Variations

Roast sirloin Weigh and calculate the cooking time and proceed as for the recipe for roast rib above.

Roast peppered fillet of beef Weigh and calculate the cooking time. Fillet roasts are long and narrow and the cooking time may need to be reduced a little, by 15 minutes or so. Season the fillet with salt and brown in ½–1 tbsp oil in a frying pan over a medium to high heat. Brush the fillet with melted butter and roll it in finely crushed black peppercorns so the peppercorns form a crust around the fillet. Roast the fillet for the required cooking time before resting and carving.

A note on gravy...
Adding 100ml red wine before the stock will enhance the flavour of the gravy. If you don't want to serve the beef with a flour-thickened gravy, then jus de viande – simply the roasting and resting juices – can be poured over instead.

Carving a roast rib of beef

This method of carving a rib of beef can be used for all types of roast on the rib/bone, such as a roast pork loin. This is the technique for a chined joint with the chine (back) bone already removed.

1 Once the meat is cooked and rested, stand the joint so the ribs are pointing upwards; if it doesn't balance well like this then lie the meat so the ribs are uppermost.

2 Position a sharp carving knife or large knife between the ribs and the meat.

3 Keeping the knife pushing against the ribs, gradually release the meat from the ribs.

4 Continue until the ribs are released. The ribs can be divided into individual ribs and added to the gravy while you carve the meat, to lend extra flavour.

5 Identify which way the grain, or fibres, of the meat lie and slice the meat very thinly across the grain.

6 Continue to carve the meat into slices of even thickness.

Carving a joint that has not been chined

Sometimes a roast comes with the chine (back) bone attached, as well as the ribs. If the back bone is still on, it should have at least been cut through close to the ribs (ie chined) to be able to remove it separately from the ribs. Once the ribs have been removed, stand the meat so the chine is to your left, then remove the chine by keeping the knife firmly against the bone and cutting the meat off the chine bone.

If the meat has not been chined, so the chine is still attached to the ribs, then once the ribs are released you will need to angle the knife to continue cutting the meat from the chine bone. In this case the ribs cannot be divided individually; discard or use for stock.

Single-bone rib roast or steak

The carving technique (shown left) assumes more than one rib. Where the joint is smaller and only one rib is attached, then the removal of the rib is much more straightforward. The meat can be carved with rather than against the grain, as the largest flatter side can be against the board, for example for a bone-in rib eye.

Sirloin or fillet

Sirloin or fillet roasts are not on the bone, so to carve either, simply identify the grain of the meat and slice across the grain into thin slices. For a sirloin roast, have the surface fat uppermost.

Yorkshire puddings

Makes 8 (to serve 4)
100g plain flour
Pinch of salt
2 eggs
275ml milk, or a mixture of milk and water
60g goose or duck fat, or 60ml vegetable oil

The traditional accompaniment to roast beef, these are best baked while the joint is resting. Prepare the batter in advance.

1 Sift the flour and salt into a bowl and make a well in the centre. Beat the eggs in a bowl to loosen, then add them to the well.

2 Stir the eggs with a wooden spoon, concentrating your stirring only in the eggs, gradually drawing in flour from around the edge. Don't force flour in; it will be incorporated automatically as you stir the eggs.

3 As the egg mixture becomes thicker, add a little milk to loosen it, then keep stirring. Continue in this way until all the flour has been incorporated. Beat to ensure the thick mixture is smooth before adding the remaining milk. Chill the batter in the fridge for at least 30 minutes.

4 Heat the oven to 220°C/gas mark 7.

5 Spoon a little fat into 8 moulds of a deep muffin tin; there should only be about 2mm fat in the bottom of each mould. Place the tin on a baking tray in the oven to heat.

6 When the fat is very hot, test a few drops of batter in one well; the oil should sizzle, so if it doesn't, return the tin to the oven to heat. Quickly fill the muffin moulds about half to two-thirds full with the batter and return to the oven immediately. Cook for 20–25 minutes until well risen, a deep golden colour and crisp on the outside. Do not open the oven door during baking, or the puddings may collapse.

7 Remove from the oven, unmould each pudding and drain on a tray lined with kitchen paper, then serve at once.

Fillet of beef en croûte

Serves 6–8

1 piece of fillet of beef, from the thick end, about 1.3kg
Worcestershire sauce (optional)
1 tbsp olive oil
350g puff pastry (see page 508, or use ready-made)
100g button or chestnut mushrooms
1 garlic clove
¼ bunch of thyme
30g butter
100g chicken liver pâté (see page 388)
1 egg, to glaze
Salt and freshly ground black pepper

1 Heat the oven to 230°C/gas mark 8.

2 Trim the fillet and season well with salt, pepper and Worcestershire sauce, if using. Tie with string at 2–3cm intervals to help hold its shape. Heat the olive oil in a roasting tin over a medium to high heat and brown the meat evenly on all sides.

3 Transfer the meat to the oven and roast for 15 minutes. This will give you rare beef once the fillet is baked within the pastry; for medium allow a further 10 minutes at this early stage; for well-done meat allow a further 15 minutes. Remove the fillet from the roasting tin, leave to cool and remove all the string.

4 Roll out one-third of the pastry on a floured board until it is a little more than the length and width of the fillet. Place on a baking sheet, prick all over with a fork and bake for about 20 minutes until golden. Transfer to a wire rack and leave to cool.

5 Wipe and finely chop the mushrooms, peel and crush the garlic and finely chop enough thyme leaves to give 1 tsp. Heat the butter in a frying pan over a medium to high heat and fry the mushrooms quickly to release and evaporate their liquid. Add the garlic and thyme and cook for 1 minute; the mixture should be dry. Allow the mushrooms to cool, then mix with the pâté. Taste and adjust the seasoning.

6 Spread the mushroom and pâté mixture over the cooled fillet and place it on the cooked pastry sheet. Cut away any pastry not covered by the fillet.

7 Roll the remaining pastry on a floured board until large enough to cover the fillet easily. Lay it gently over the fillet. Lightly press the pastry to the fillet and seal the corners. Cut off any excess pastry at the corners; reserve the trimmings.

8 With a palette knife, lift the cooked pastry base and tuck the uncooked pastry edge neatly underneath it. Repeat with the other 3 sides. The pastry trimmings can be used to cut strips or leaves to decorate the top. Lightly beat the egg with a small pinch of salt, then pass through a sieve. Brush the pastry with the beaten egg, stick any decorations on the pastry, then brush again with egg. If the pastry is very soft, chill the parcel in the fridge for 15 minutes before baking.

9 Bake in the middle of the oven for 20–30 minutes, or until the pastry is dark brown and shiny. Remove and leave to rest for 15–20 minutes before carving.

Note You can prepare this in advance up to the final baking stage, prior to glazing. Loosely cover with cling film and place in the fridge until ready to cook.

Variation

Steak Wellington Use 4 fillet steaks, each 170g, seasoned, browned and cooled. Make half the quantity of mushroom pâté mixture, divide it into 4 portions and spread on top of each steak. Roll out the pastry to a 3mm thickness and cut into 4 squares. Lay the steaks, mushroom mix down, on the pastry and bring the pastry around the beef to envelop it completely. Avoid too much overlap as it will create a thick layer of pastry that won't cook through completely. Trim off any excess pastry. Turn the parcels over and glaze them with beaten egg. Chill for 30 minutes, then glaze again before baking in an oven preheated to 230°C/gas 8 for 15 minutes or until the pastry is a deep golden colour. Rest for 10 minutes before serving.

Using crêpes

Traditionally, crêpes are wrapped around the beef fillet and pâté before encasing in pastry to help to keep the pastry crisp. If you do this, wrap in a single layer of crêpes, trimming as necessary to ensure minimal overlap.

Stewing and braising meat

Gently cooking cuts of meat that are suitable for stewing and braising over a long period of time, either fully or partly submerged in liquid, produces tender, flavourful results. Browning the meat first to caramelise the surface sugars adds an element of richness and colour.

The most suitable cuts of meat for these slow, moist treatments are those that have been heavily exercised, such as chuck, flank, cheek and shin; ie tougher cuts with a good development of connective tissue in the meat. This breaks down during the long, slow cooking process to provide added succulence. Look for a good marbling of fat running between the fibres and muscles, as this will add moisture and flavour.

Surface fat can generally be removed, but keeping a little does provide extra flavour. The silvery, shiny sinew on the surface needs to be removed, as this will not break down during cooking and will stay tough.

Preparing meat for stewing

1 Place the meat on a board and, using a sharp knife, trim away most of the surface fat. Trim away the larger pieces of sinew too, but avoid cutting the meat into small pieces to extract the sinew between the fibres and muscles, as this risks the meat falling apart.

2 Cut the meat across the grain (ie across the fibres) into thickish steaks, about 2–3cm, so when the meat is eaten the short fibres will give the perception of tenderness.

3 Then cut the steaks into large chunks, about 2–3cm square (without aiming for perfect squares; they should look natural).

Browning meat

Browning meat quickly over a high heat before long, slow cooking is in most cases recommended. The caramelisation of the surface sugars adds colour and flavour to the meat, some of which also transfers to the liquid, giving richer results. The meat is browned only briefly, and left raw in the middle to cook slowly at a gentle temperature.

Brown the meat in small batches so you don't overcrowd the pan and cause the temperature to drop, which will impede the browning.

1 Heat a heavy-based pan over a medium to high heat. It shouldn't be smoking. Season the meat lightly with salt to aid the browning process, but only just before browning or it will draw moisture out of the meat.

2 Add a little oil to the pan, only thinly coating the bottom of the pan, then add the first batch of meat. The meat should sizzle vigorously as it comes into contact with the pan. If it doesn't, the oil is not hot enough.

3 Allow the meat to brown before moving it. Once browned underneath, it will release easily and can be turned to brown the next side.

4 Brown the meat evenly on all sides, but take care not to cook it any longer than necessary to colour, or it will toughen.

5 Remove the meat from the pan and repeat the process until all the meat has been browned. Deglazing can be done in between the batches (see right).

6 Pour off any excess oil from the pan, then deglaze by adding a little water and allowing it to come to the boil, stirring to lift any sediment from the bottom of the pan with a wooden spoon. This liquid, called the déglaçage, can be added to the dish for additional flavour. However, if it tastes burnt, you should discard it.

Browning mince

When browning mince, much the same technique applies as for pieces of meat, but without adding any salt. Once you have added the mince to the frying pan it will need to be broken down into very small pieces, using either the back of a fork or a wooden spoon (as shown). It will not turn as dark as larger pieces of meat, and would turn overly hard if it did. Again, unless you are only browning a small amount, you will need to work in batches to avoid overcrowding the pan.

Stewing

Generally this involves small pieces of meat, which are covered in liquid and cooked gently for a long period of time. Browning both the meat and any vegetables before cooking adds richness, colour and flavour to the sauce and the resultant dishes are called brown stews. White stews, conversely, have no initial browning. In both cases, the meat is served in the liquid it is cooked in, thickened to a syrupy consistency.

Braising

In its truest form, braising is cooking food on a bed of vegetables, often referred to as a mirepoix, in a very small amount of liquid, generally stock, so the liquid comes only about one-third of the way up the food. The pan is covered with a tight-fitting lid, so introducing an element of steaming. As for stewing, browning the meat before braising provides colour and additional flavour, while the long period of cooking time over a low to moderate heat that follows produces tender, flavourful results. The bed of vegetables is usually strained from the sauce and the sauce reduced before serving.

A note on larding and barding...

Some cuts of meat, poultry and game can be very lean, with minimal marbling of fat running through the muscle structure. To help keep the meat succulent when cooking, you can apply a technique called larding to lean meat cuts, and barding to poultry and game birds.

For larding, pork fat is generally used, cut into a thin strip and threaded through the meat using a larding needle. Several strips larded through the joint will melt as the meat cooks, with the melted fat working its way through the fibres and adding succulence.

For barding, rashers of bacon or pancetta, or strips of fat, are used. These are laid over the breast of game and poultry birds before they are cooked to help retain moisture in the lean meat. On small birds, the rashers are usually tied in place with kitchen string.

Ragù sauce for pasta

Serves 4

1 onion
1 carrot
1 celery stick
50g smoked bacon (optional)
2 garlic cloves
Small bunch of basil
About 2 tbsp olive oil
700g beef mince
½ tbsp tomato purée
200ml red wine (optional)
500ml brown beef or chicken and veal
  stock (see page 98)
500g passata
1 bay leaf
1 tsp caster sugar
Salt and freshly ground black pepper

1 Halve, peel and finely chop the onion. Peel the carrot and de-string the celery, then finely dice both. Derind and finely dice the bacon, if using. Peel and crush the garlic and pick the basil leaves from the stalks.

2 Heat a heavy-based frying pan, add enough of the olive oil to barely cover the bottom of the pan and fry the mince in batches over a medium to high heat. Don't overcrowd the pan or it will stew rather than brown. Use a fork if necessary to break up the mince in the pan so it doesn't cook in large lumps. If the mince produces a lot of fat, drain the fat from each batch by placing the mince in a sieve over a bowl for a few minutes, then transfer the browned mince to a saucepan. The fat that has drained into the bowl can be discarded.

3 Deglaze the frying pan with a little water, stirring well to lift the sediment on the bottom of the pan. Taste this liquid and if it is not bitter, add it to the mince (if bitter, discard it).

4 Heat enough olive oil in the frying pan to just cover the base again and fry the carrot and celery over a medium heat until beginning to brown. Add the onion and bacon, if using, and continue to cook until the vegetables are evenly browned. You may need to do this in batches, depending on the size of the pan. Add the garlic and cook for 1 minute.

5 Return all the vegetables to the frying pan and stir in the tomato purée. Add the wine, if using, and reduce by two-thirds.

6 Add the stock and passata, stir well and pour the vegetable mixture over the mince in the saucepan. Add the bay leaf, basil stalks, a little seasoning and enough water to ensure the meat is just covered. Bring to the boil, then lower the heat, cover and simmer gently for 1½–2 hours, or until tender. Halfway through the cooking, remove the lid to allow the sauce to reduce and thicken.

7 When the meat is tender, skim and discard any fat from the surface. (If the sauce is too thin, tip the mince into a sieve over a bowl. Return the liquid to the pan and reduce by boiling to the desired concentration and consistency, then stir the mince back in.) Add the sugar, with salt and pepper to taste. Chop or tear enough basil leaves to give you 2 tbsp, then stir them through the ragù just before serving.

Variations

Omit the optional bacon and red wine from the recipe for these variations.

Smoky chilli with black beans Omit the carrot, celery and basil. Fry 1 chopped red pepper with the onion. Add 1 tsp Worcestershire sauce, 1–1½ tsp crushed dried chillies, depending on taste, 1 tbsp ground cumin, 1 heaped tsp smoked paprika and 1 tsp dried oregano with the tomato purée. Substitute the passata with a 400g tin chopped tomatoes and, 20 minutes before the end of the cooking time, add a drained 400g tin black beans and 1 tbsp light soft brown sugar in place of the sugar. Serve with rice and soured cream.

Cottage pie Follow the ragù recipe, but omit the garlic, passata, basil and sugar, and add 1 tsp Worcestershire sauce. Boil and mash 3 large floury potatoes, beat in 100ml warmed milk, 60g melted butter and salt and pepper to taste. Put the mince into a pie dish, allow to cool a little, then spread or pipe the potato on top. Bake in an oven preheated to 200°C/gas mark 6 for 20 minutes until browned. The dish can be assembled ahead and chilled, in which case bake for an extra 20 minutes.

Shepherds pie Prepare in the same way as cottage pie, but using minced lamb instead of beef.

Beef with caramelised baby onions and rosemary

Serves 4

1kg chuck or feather blade steak
3–4 tbsp olive oil
250g button onions or shallots
3 carrots
¼ celeriac
2–3 rosemary sprigs
½ bunch of parsley
1 garlic clove
500ml brown chicken and veal stock
  (see page 98)
1 bay leaf
2 tsp softened butter mixed with 2 tsp
  flour (beurre manié), if needed
Salt and freshly ground black pepper

To serve

Mashed potatoes (see page 69)

1 Heat the oven to 150°C/gas mark 2.

2 Trim the meat of any surface fat and sinew and cut into large chunks, about 2.5–3cm. Heat 1 tbsp of the olive oil in a flameproof casserole over a medium to high heat. Season the meat with salt and, working in batches, brown it evenly all over. Deglaze the casserole with water after each batch and start each batch with clean oil. If these juices (the déglaçage) don't taste bitter, reserve them to add to the sauce later. As each batch browns, transfer the meat to a bowl.

3 Blanch the button onions in boiling water for 1 minute. Remove and leave until cool enough to handle, then trim off the hairy end and peel, leaving them as natural looking as possible. Peel the carrots and celeriac, cut the carrots into thick slices and the celeriac into 1.5cm cubes. Finely chop enough rosemary and parsley leaves to give you ½ tbsp of each and peel and crush the garlic.

4 Heat 1 tbsp olive oil in the casserole and brown the onions, transferring them to a clean bowl once they have browned. Brown the carrots and celeriac and transfer them to a separate bowl once they have browned. Add the stock and déglaçage, if using, to the casserole and bring to a simmer.

5 Add the bay leaf, garlic, chopped rosemary and half of the chopped parsley to the casserole, with salt and pepper to taste. Add the meat, cover and cook in the oven for 2½–3½ hours. Check from time to time to ensure the stew is not boiling vigorously; it should be very gently simmering.

6 After 2 hours, check to see if the meat is becoming tender. If it is, add the browned baby onions and continue to cook for another 30 minutes. If the meat still seems tough, leave it for another 20–30 minutes before adding the onions. After another 30 minutes, add the carrots and celeriac.

7 When the meat is tender and can be cut easily with the side of a fork or spoon, and the vegetables are soft, remove from the oven and strain, reserving the sauce.

8 Return the sauce to the casserole, taste and reduce over a medium heat if necessary to concentrate the flavour, or thicken with beurre manié (see page 111), then taste again and adjust the seasoning. Discard the bay leaf.

9 Return the meat and vegetables to the sauce and reheat gently. Serve the beef stew sprinkled with the chopped parsley on a bed of mashed potatoes. Delicious with steamed kale or other greens.

Variations

Beef with root vegetables and thyme Use thyme instead of rosemary. Peel and cut 2 small turnips into 1.5cm chunks and brown with the carrots and celeriac. Any root vegetable can be used in place of the carrots, celeriac and turnips.

Beef with red wine and thyme Replace the rosemary with thyme and omit the parsley. Replace 200ml of the stock with red wine and add before the stock in step 4, allowing the wine to come to a simmer before you add the stock.

....
A note on slow-cooked dishes...

It is important for the pan to be well sealed to minimise evaporation. If the lid is not tight-fitting, or the casserole is rather large for the quantity of ingredients, place a dry cartouche (see page 13) over the surface, in direct contact with the ingredients, before putting the lid on.

Carbonnade of beef

Serves 4

1kg chuck steak
3–4 tbsp olive oil
3 onions
1 garlic clove
1–2 thyme sprigs
2 tsp soft dark brown sugar
2 tsp plain flour
300ml Guinness or other stout,
  or dark ale
300ml brown chicken and veal stock
  (see page 98)
1 tsp wine vinegar
1 bay leaf
Pinch of freshly grated nutmeg
2 tsp softened butter mixed with 2 tsp
  flour (beurre manié), if needed
Salt and freshly ground black pepper

1 Trim any excess fat and sinew from the meat. Cut the meat into small, thick steaks, about 5–6cm long and 2.5cm thick.

2 Heat 1 tbsp of the olive oil in a frying pan over a medium to high heat. Season the meat with salt and pepper and brown in batches, evenly all over; deglaze the pan with water between batches and start each batch with clean oil. Taste and keep the juices (déglaçage) if they don't taste bitter. Transfer the browned meat to a flameproof casserole.

3 Halve, peel and thinly slice the onions. Peel and crush the garlic and chop enough thyme leaves to give you a good pinch. Heat 1 tbsp olive oil in a saucepan over a low heat and sweat the onions slowly until starting to soften, about 5 minutes. Increase the heat to medium and allow the onions to caramelise until golden brown. Add the garlic and sugar and cook for 1 minute, then add the flour and cook for a further 1 minute.

4 Heat the oven to 150°C/gas mark 2.

5 Slowly add the ale to the pan, stirring to ensure no lumps are created. Add the stock, wine vinegar and déglaçage, if using, and bring to a simmer. Season with salt and pepper, add the thyme, bay leaf and nutmeg. Pour this over the browned beef in the casserole, cover and cook gently in the oven for 2½–3½ hours. Check from time to time to ensure the stew is not boiling too vigorously; it should be very gently simmering.

6 When the meat is tender and can easily be cut with the side of a fork or spoon, remove from the oven and check the flavour and consistency of the sauce. If the flavour is a good concentration and the sauce is syrupy, then simply season to taste. If it is watery and thin, strain and return the sauce to the casserole, then reduce over a medium heat until it has a good concentration of flavour. If it has a good flavour but is too thin, thicken it with a little beurre manié (see page 111), then season.

7 Remove the bay leaf and return the meat and onions to the sauce, if necessary. Reheat gently before serving, with mashed potatoes and a green vegetable such as sprouting broccoli.

Note The bitterness of the Guinness works particularly well with the sweetness of the onions.

Variation

Beef braised in red wine Replace the chuck steak with 4 thick slices of braising steak or flank of beef. Marinate overnight in 500ml red wine, then strain, reserve the wine and use in place of the 300ml ale or Guinness. Only use a pinch of sugar to taste and omit the nutmeg.

Beef rendang

Serves 4

For the spice paste

4–6 dried red chillies

4 shallots

4 garlic cloves

3cm piece of fresh root ginger

3cm piece of fresh galangal

3 lemongrass stalks

For the rendang

75g fresh coconut

900g chuck steak

½ tbsp olive oil

1 piece of cassia bark or 1 cinnamon stick

3 star anise

3 cloves

6 green cardamom pods

300ml coconut milk

2 lemongrass stalks

3 tsp tamarind paste (or 2 tbsp pulp
   soaked in 100ml water and strained)

2 tsp palm sugar (or brown sugar)

6 lime leaves

Salt

1 For the spice paste, soak the dried chillies in boiling water for 15–20 minutes. Halve, peel and coarsely chop the shallots and peel and chop the garlic. Peel and coarsely chop the ginger and galangal. Cut off and discard the green tops and root end from the lemongrass and coarsely chop the tender inner part. Drain the chillies and chop them coarsely.

2 Using a pestle and mortar or food processor, pound or blend all the paste ingredients together to a smoothish paste, adding a little water if necessary.

3 For the rendang, grate the coconut finely and, in a dry frying pan over a medium heat, toast until golden. Remove to a bowl and cool.

4 Trim the excess fat and sinew from the steak, then cut it into 2.5–3cm chunks.

5 Heat the olive oil in a large saucepan over a low to medium heat. Add the cassia bark, star anise, cloves and cardamom pods and cook for 2 minutes, then add the spice paste and cook for a further 2–3 minutes, taking care it doesn't burn.

6 Add the beef, stir to coat in the spice paste and cook for 1 minute, then add the coconut milk. Cut off the green tops and root end from the lemongrass. Bruise with the flat side of a large knife to release the flavour and add to the pan with the meat. Add the tamarind paste, sugar, lime leaves and toasted coconut.

7 Lower the heat, cover and simmer very gently for 2–2½ hours until the meat is tender. Halfway through cooking, remove the lid and reduce a little to a thick sauce that coats the meat. If the sauce becomes too thick, add a splash of water.

8 Taste and adjust the seasoning with salt or sugar. Remove and discard the star anise, cassia and lemongrass. Serve with steamed rice.

Szechuan beef short ribs

Serves 6

3 tbsp olive oil

1½ tsp Szechuan peppercorns

2cm piece of fresh root ginger

½ orange

1.5kg beef short ribs, cut into
   individual ribs

150ml Shaoxing rice wine

500ml chicken and veal stock
   (see page 96)

50ml dark soy sauce

50g palm or brown sugar

1 tbsp chilli bean sauce

3–4 star anise

1 cinnamon stick

3 tbsp rice wine vinegar

1–2 tsp cornflour (if needed)

1 Heat the oven to 150°C/gas mark 2.

2 Heat the olive oil in a flameproof casserole over a low heat, add the peppercorns and cook gently for 5–8 minutes until darkened in colour. Remove from the heat and leave to cool. Strain, reserving the oil. Using a pestle and mortar, grind the cooled peppercorns to a fine powder and set aside. Peel the ginger and cut into julienne. Finely pare the zest from the ½ orange.

3 Heat the infused oil in the casserole over a medium to high heat and brown the ribs evenly all over, in batches. When the ribs are all browned, deglaze with the rice wine and add all the other the ingredients (except cornflour), including the browned meat, pepper, ginger and orange zest. Pour over enough water to cover the ribs. Bring to a simmer, then transfer to the oven and cook gently until the meat is very tender and comes away from the bone easily, 2½–3½ hours. Check from time to time to ensure it is not boiling; it should be very gently simmering.

4 Taste the sauce. It may need to be reduced a little to intensify the flavour, in which case take out the meat and aromatics, discarding the star anise, cinnamon and orange zest. If the sauce already has a strong flavour, then thicken it by slaking a little cornflour into the sauce (see page 111).

5 Carefully strip the meat off the bones, keeping it in big pieces and removing any sinew, then gently reheat in the sauce. Serve with steamed Chinese greens and rice.

Ox cheek daube with star anise, hazelnut and orange

Serves 4
750g–1kg ox cheeks
2 carrots
1 celery stick
2 onions
½ orange
4–5 tbsp olive oil
200ml red wine
400ml brown chicken and veal stock
  (see page 98)
2 bay leaves
3 thyme sprigs
1 cinnamon stick
2 star anise
2 tsp softened butter mixed with 2 tsp
  flour (beurre manié), if needed
Salt and freshly ground black pepper

For the gremolata
25g hazelnuts
Large bunch of flat-leaf parsley
1 garlic clove
½ orange
½ lemon
1–2 tbsp olive oil

To serve
Soft polenta (see page 201)

1 Heat the oven to 150°C/gas mark 2.

2 Prepare the ox cheeks by trimming off any surface sinew and cutting the cheeks into small steaks, about 5–6cm long and 3–4cm thick. Peel the carrots, de-string the celery and cut both into thick slices. Halve, peel and cut the onions into wedges through the root. Finely pare the zest from the ½ orange.

3 Heat 2 tbsp of the olive oil in a flameproof casserole over a medium to high heat. Season the ox cheeks with salt and brown them in batches, evenly all over, deglazing with water after each batch. If these juices (déglaçage) don't taste bitter, reserve them for the sauce. Place the browned cheeks in a bowl.

4 Heat the remaining olive oil in the casserole, add the vegetables and brown evenly, then add the wine, stock, bay leaves, thyme, cinnamon, star anise, orange zest, and some salt and pepper. Bring to the boil, then return the ox cheeks to the casserole, with the déglaçage, if using. Cover and cook in the oven for 3–4 hours until the ox cheeks are tender but not falling apart. Check from time to time to ensure the stew is not boiling too vigorously; it should be very gently simmering.

5 Just before the meat is cooked, make the gremolata. Toast the nuts on a baking sheet in the oven for 15–20 minutes until pale golden, then coarsely chop and place in a bowl. Chop enough parsley leaves to give 4–5 tbsp. Peel and finely chop the garlic. Finely grate the zest from the ½ orange and ½ lemon and add to the nuts with the parsley and garlic. Add the olive oil and season with salt and pepper.

6 When the meat is tender, drain in a sieve over a bowl, discarding the vegetables, herbs and spices, and reserving the sauce. Return the sauce to the wiped-out casserole. Taste and reduce over a medium heat until it has a good concentration of flavour, thickening it with a little beurre manié (see page 111), if necessary, to achieve a syrupy consistency. Taste again and adjust the seasoning.

7 Return the ox cheeks to the reduced sauce and reheat gently. Serve with a little gremolata sprinkled over the top and the soft polenta.

Oxtail stew

Serves 4
1–2 oxtails, 1.5–1.7kg in total
Plain flour, to coat
2 tbsp sunflower oil
200g carrots
200g onions
Few thyme sprigs
1 garlic clove
300ml red wine
400ml brown chicken and veal stock
  (see page 98)
1 bay leaf
½ tsp sugar
200g tin chopped tomatoes
Salt and freshly ground black pepper

1 Heat the oven to 150°C/gas mark 2.

2 Wash and dry the oxtails. Trim off any excess fat and cut into 2.5cm lengths, if not already cut. Season the flour with salt and pepper and toss the oxtail pieces in the seasoned flour; this will help to thicken the sauce.

3 Heat the oil in a large flameproof casserole over a medium heat and brown the oxtail, a few pieces at a time, evenly on all sides. Remove to a plate as they are browned. Deglaze the pan in between batches (see step 6, page 401).

4 Peel and cut the carrots into thick slices. Halve, peel and cut the onions into wedges through the root. Heat a little more oil in the casserole and brown the carrots and onions evenly. Finely chop enough thyme leaves to give you 1 tsp, and peel and crush the garlic.

5 Pour the wine and stock over the browned vegetables and add the thyme, garlic, bay leaf, sugar, and some salt and pepper. Add the tomatoes and bring to the boil, then turn down to a simmer.

6 Return the oxtail to the casserole, cover and cook in the oven for 3–4 hours until very tender and coming away from the bones easily. Check from time to time to ensure the stew is not boiling too vigorously; it should be very gently simmering.

7 Remove the oxtail and vegetables from the sauce and leave the sauce to sit for 30–40 minutes, for the fat to rise to the surface. Skim off the fat using a spoon or ladle, taste the sauce and reduce if necessary, to concentrate the flavour.

8 Remove and discard the carrots, onions and bay leaf. Either leave the oxtail on the bone or strip it from the bone into large pieces.

9 Taste and adjust the seasoning, add the oxtail back to the sauce and reheat gently to serve.

Note If you want to serve vegetables in the stew (such as carrots or caramelised shallots), then add them to the finished sauce and cook gently until almost done, before adding the oxtail and reheating. If the sauce becomes too strong at this point, add a splash of water.

Braised veal shank with white wine and gremolata

Serves 4
3 tbsp olive oil
2 veal shanks, each about 1–1.2kg
1 large onion
1 carrot
2 celery sticks
3 garlic cloves
20g butter
300ml white wine
300ml chicken and veal stock
  (see page 96)
1 bay leaf
3 thyme sprigs
1 sage sprig
2 tsp softened butter mixed with 2 tsp
  flour (beurre manié), if needed
Salt and freshly ground black pepper

For the gremolata
1 garlic clove
Small bunch of flat-leaf parsley
½ lemon

To serve
Soft polenta (see page 201) or saffron
  risotto (see page 188)

1 Heat 2 tbsp of the olive oil in a large flameproof casserole over a medium to high heat. Season the veal shanks with salt and pepper, add to the pan and brown them evenly all over. Remove and set aside.

2 Halve, peel and dice the onion. Peel the carrot, de-string the celery and thinly slice both. Peel and crush the garlic.

3 Heat the remaining oil and the butter in the casserole over a low to medium heat, add the onion, carrot and celery and cook gently for 8–10 minutes until softening. Add the garlic and cook for 1 minute.

4 Add the wine, stock and herbs and bring to a simmer. Season, then add the veal shanks. Cover and cook over a very gentle heat for 3–4 hours until the veal is tender and coming away from the bone easily. Check from time to time to ensure the stew is not boiling too vigorously; it should be very gently simmering.

5 For the gremolata, peel and finely chop the garlic and chop enough parsley leaves to give you 2–3 tbsp. Grate the zest from the lemon and place in a small bowl with the garlic and parsley. Mix together and season with salt and pepper to taste; set aside.

6 Carefully remove the veal shanks and strain the sauce, discarding the vegetables. Return the sauce to the casserole and reduce until it has a good concentration of flavour. Check the consistency and thicken if necessary with a little beurre manié (see page 111).

7 Remove the veal from the bone in large chunks, then add back to the sauce and reheat gently.

8 Sprinkle with the gremolata and serve with soft polenta or saffron risotto.

Pan-frying

Pan-frying is the quickest method of cooking small, very tender cuts of meat such as steaks. Browning the meat on both sides requires a very high heat, which then needs to be slightly lowered to cook the meat to the point desired. Provided it is good quality produce, it is quite safe to eat beef raw, blue, rare, medium-rare and medium, so the end result is a matter of personal preference.

The cuts most suited to this rapid method of cooking are those that are less exercised, and are therefore the most naturally tender. As with roasts, these are found in the area between the shoulder and back legs near the back bone, and include fillet, sirloin, rump and rib eye.

Thicker cut steaks, with a deep red colour and marbling of fat through the fibres and muscles, are ideal, as it is easier to cook them to your preferred point without overcooking. Fillet steaks, for example, can be up to 6cm thick. If tenderness is a priority, then fillet is the cut of choice, followed by sirloin and rump. If flavour is more important, choose rump, then sirloin and fillet. Sirloin, strip loin or rib eye offer a good combination of both tenderness and flavour. T-bones are on the bone, with the sirloin on one side and fillet on the other and porterhouse is a double-sized T-bone.

It is best to treat a very thick cut steak, such as a fillet, chateaubriand (thick end of the fillet to serve two), côte de boeuf, or rib eye on the bone, almost like a roast. Brown it over direct heat all over, then finish cooking it in the oven.

Tougher cuts of meat, such as hanger steaks, can be cooked very quickly to retain their tenderness, but must be cooked rare to medium-rare. The more they are cooked the tougher they become. Small, tender cuts of meat are also useful for stir-fries and salads.

Pan-fried steak

Serves 4
4 sirloin steaks, cut 2cm thick, or
   fillet steaks, cut 2.5cm thick
Sunflower oil for frying
Salt and freshly ground black pepper

1 If the steaks have been chilled, remove them from the fridge and bring to room temperature about 30–45 minutes before cooking. Sprinkle lightly with pepper and salt on both sides, just before cooking.

2 Heat a very little oil in a frying pan (it should just barely cover the surface of the pan) until hot and almost smoking.

3 Brown the steaks quickly on one side, then turn the heat down to medium and cook for the required length of time, determined by how you like your steak cooked (see right). Turn the steak over and cook the second side for roughly the same amount of time. (The pan will still be hot enough to brown the second side.)

4 With experience, it is possible to tell from the feel of a steak how well cooked it is. When blue, it feels very soft. It will become firmer as it cooks, feeling very firm when medium cooked. If you want to be certain, make a tiny cut in the fattest part of the meat and take a look, but not until you are fairly sure that the steak is ready, as too many cuts will mean loss of juices.

5 Remove the steaks from the frying pan to a warmed plate and leave to rest in a warm place for 3–5 minutes. This is important as it allows the juices to be re-absorbed back into the meat. The steak will hold its heat for this length of time, so resting does not affect the final eating temperature.

A guide to steak cooking times

The times given are guidelines only, as the length of cooking time varies according to how many steaks are being cooked, the type of steak, the degree of heat and the weight of the frying pan. For a blue or rare steak, keep the heat reasonably fierce for the whole cooking time. For medium-rare or medium steaks, lower the temperature to medium after the initial browning.

Sirloin	Blue	1–1½ minutes per side
	Rare	1½–2 minutes per side
	Medium-rare	2–3 minutes per side
	Medium	3–4 minutes per side
Fillet	Blue	1½–2 minutes per side
	Rare	2½–3½ minutes per side
	Medium-rare	3½–4½ minutes per side
	Medium	4½–5½ minutes per side

Degrees of cooking

All cooked steaks should be well browned on the surface, but the varying degrees of 'doneness' are defined as follows.

Blue The inside is raw, but warm. The fibres of the meat are not set.

Rare The fibres of the meat are not set through the central 75% of the steak (as shown, top left).

Medium-rare As for rare but a slightly paler colour and only 50% of the fibres are not set through the centre of the steak (as shown, left).

Medium Pink in the centre with juices and fibres set (as shown, bottom left).

Well done The centre is beige but the flesh is still juicy.

A note on cooking the fat layer...

Steaks such as rump and sirloin have a fat layer around one side which adds flavour and moisture, although it can be trimmed away before cooking if preferred. If it is left on, hold the steak fat side down in the hot pan with tongs, to render and brown the fat before cooking the steak.

Pan-frying

This very quick cooking method is suitable for small, not too thick, tender pieces of meat and uses fat, some of which is served with the meat. Choose a fat that is either flavourless, so it does not detract from the flavour of the meat, or that has a flavour that complements the meat. Because the fat needs to reach a high temperature, oils or clarified butter are most suitable; ordinary butter would burn. It is also important to choose the right pan. A wide, shallow, uncovered pan is preferable as it prevents any steam from being trapped, which would steam rather than fry the meat. The fat should be heated properly before you add the meat or it won't brown, and you need to fry in small batches so as not to lower the heat of the pan and prevent browning. Fry quickly to achieve colour, after which you may need to reduce the heat to allow the meat to cook through. Always serve fried food as soon as possible after resting for best results.

Côte de boeuf with béarnaise sauce

Serves 1–2
1 côte de boeuf/single rib eye, thick cut
  on the bone, 500–600g
1 tbsp olive oil
Salt and freshly ground black pepper

To serve
Béarnaise sauce (see page 120)
Chips (see page 72)

1 Remove the beef from the fridge at least 30 minutes before you intend to cook it. If the beef is not tied, tie it with string to keep it compact (as shown). Heat the oven to 150°C/gas mark 2.

2 Heat a frying pan over a medium to high heat until very hot. Season the beef with salt and pepper. Add the olive oil to the pan, then the beef, and brown well on all sides; this can take up to 5–8 minutes. Remove the beef from the frying pan and transfer it to a roasting tin or, if your frying pan is ovenproof, leave it in the pan.

3 Roast in the oven for 15–20 minutes, depending on your preference. (Cooking the beef at this low temperature helps to prevent shrinkage and moisture loss.)

4 Once cooked, remove the beef from the oven and set aside to rest in a warm place for about 10 minutes before carving and serving with the béarnaise sauce and chips.

Note The beef can be browned well in advance of roasting it in the oven and allowed to cool. If using a marinade after browning (as in the variation below), the beef will benefit as there will be more time for the flavours of the marinade to be absorbed into the meat.

Variation

Côte de boeuf with thyme, garlic and a red wine sauce Finely chop the leaves of ½ bunch of thyme and peel and crush 2–3 garlic cloves. Mix with 2 tbsp olive oil and season generously with salt and pepper. Once the beef is browned, remove it from the pan and set aside. Rub this mixture all over the beef, then roast in the oven for the allotted time while you make the sauce. Deglaze the pan with 250ml red wine and reduce to about 100ml, then add 300ml brown chicken and veal stock (see page 98), 1 sliced shallot, 2 bashed garlic cloves, 1 bay leaf, 1 or 2 thyme sprigs, a pared piece of orange zest and 1 star anise. Gently simmer for 10–15 minutes until the flavours have developed. Taste, strain and thicken with a little beurre manié (see page 111) or cornflour, only if necessary, and adjust the seasoning. Serve with the beef once it has rested.

Roast veal chop with a caper, pancetta and shallot sauce

Serves 4
50g piece of pancetta
1 shallot
½ garlic clove
1 rosemary sprig
3 tbsp olive oil
15g butter
4 veal chops, each about 225g
1–2 tbsp sherry vinegar
½ tbsp small capers, rinsed and drained
Salt and freshly ground black pepper

1 Derind the pancetta, then cut into lardons. Halve, peel and finely dice the shallot, crush the garlic and finely chop enough rosemary leaves to give you ½ tsp.

2 Heat 1 tbsp of the olive oil with the butter in a large frying pan over a medium to high heat. Season the veal chops and pan-fry them for 3–4 minutes on each side, depending on thickness and according to taste. Once they have browned, turn the heat down to cook the chops through. Ideally, they should be cooked to medium (see page 411).

3 Remove the chops from the frying pan and set aside to rest for 3–5 minutes.

4 Wipe out the pan with kitchen paper, add 1 tbsp olive oil and place over a medium heat. Sauté the lardons until golden brown, then remove from the pan.

5 You should have about 3 tbsp oil in the pan. If not, add the remaining olive oil. Add the shallot and sauté briefly for 2 minutes until starting to soften, then add the garlic. Add back the lardons with the sherry vinegar and capers. Add salt and pepper to taste, then add the rosemary and any juices from the resting veal chops.

6 Place a veal chop on each plate and pour the sauce over the top to serve.

Veal in Marsala sauce

Serves 4
4 veal escalopes, each about 200g
1 tbsp olive oil
15g butter
75ml Marsala
25ml water
50–60ml double cream, to taste
Salt and freshly ground black pepper

1 Heat the oven to 120°C/gas mark ½.

2 Trim the veal of any sinew and place between 2 sheets of cling film or baking parchment. Beat lightly with a meat mallet or rolling pin until about 1.5cm thick.

3 Heat a large frying pan over a medium to high heat and add half the olive oil and half the butter, just enough to cover the bottom of the pan (too much fat can prevent browning). Season 2 veal escalopes with salt and pepper and fry for 1–2 minutes on each side until brown but still slightly underdone through the centre (they will continue to cook while you make the sauce). Remove to a plate and keep warm in the low oven while you fry the remaining escalopes.

4 Wipe out the pan lightly with kitchen paper. Heat the remaining oil and butter in the frying pan and brown the remaining escalopes. (If your pan is not large enough you may need to cook them in more than 2 batches.)

5 Pour off the excess fat from the pan and deglaze with the Marsala and water, then reduce to about 60ml. Add the cream to taste and bring to a simmer. Season with salt and pepper to taste.

6 Place a veal escalope on each plate and pour the sauce over to serve.

Note You can also use pork fillet in place of the veal.

A note on tenderising meat...

Cuts of meat can be made more tender. Pounding, as for the veal escalopes, grinding or cutting, all break down the structure of the muscle bundles. Marinating meat in wine or citrus juices allows the acid to break down muscle fibres and connective tissue, making the meat more tender.

Miso-marinated rump steak

Serves 4
4 garlic cloves
6 spring onions
200ml mirin (rice wine)
2 tbsp soft light brown sugar
6 tbsp miso
4 rump steaks, each about 225g
1–2 tbsp olive oil
Freshly ground black pepper

You will need to start this the night before, or at least 12 hours ahead, to allow time for the meat to marinate.

1 Peel and coarsely chop the garlic and coarsely chop the spring onions. Place in a blender with the mirin, sugar, miso and some pepper, and blend until smooth.

2 Put the steaks in a plastic sealable food bag or bowl, add the marinade, turn the steaks to coat and leave to marinate in the fridge for 12 hours, or overnight.

3 Remove the steaks from the marinade and pat dry, reserving the marinade. Heat enough olive oil to just cover the bottom of a large frying pan over a medium to high heat and brown the steaks on both sides, 1–2 minutes per side.

4 Pour the marinade into the pan and bring to a simmer. Continue to cook the steaks to your preferred doneness, turning them to coat evenly in the marinade.

5 Remove the steaks from the pan and leave to rest in a warm place for 5 minutes before slicing thinly to serve. Pour over any remaining pan juices.

Sesame beef salad

Serves 4–6
450g sirloin steak, in 2 thick-cut slices
5 tbsp mirin (rice wine) or dry sherry
5 tbsp light soy sauce
3 tbsp sesame oil
2 onions
250g button mushrooms
250g mangetout
2–3 tbsp sunflower oil
Salt and freshly ground black pepper

For the dressing
1 tsp clear honey
1 tbsp Dijon mustard
3 tbsp white wine vinegar
6 tbsp sunflower oil

You will need to start this the night before, or at least 6 hours ahead, to allow time for the meat to marinate.

1 Remove any fat and sinew from the steak. In a bowl, mix together the rice wine, soy sauce and sesame oil. Halve, peel and finely slice the onions and add them to the mixture with the steak, making sure the steak is completely covered. Cover and leave to marinate in the fridge for at least 6 hours, or overnight, turning the steak in the marinade occasionally.

2 Wipe over and finely slice the mushrooms. Bring a large pan of salted water to the boil. Trim the mangetout, then blanch in the boiling water for 10 seconds. Drain them and plunge into cold water to refresh; drain well. Set aside.

3 To make the dressing, put the honey, mustard and wine vinegar into a large bowl and whisk together. Season with salt and pepper, then whisk in the oil.

4 Remove the steak and onions from the marinade and pat the steak dry, reserving the marinade. Heat a heavy-based frying pan over a medium to high heat with enough oil to just cover the bottom of the pan. Brown the steak on both sides, then lower the heat to medium and continue to cook to your preferred doneness. Remove from the pan and leave to cool completely.

5 Heat 1 tbsp oil in the frying pan, add the onions from the marinade and cook over a medium heat until soft and starting to brown. Transfer the onions to the dressing. Sauté the mushrooms in the pan, adding a little more oil if necessary, until golden brown. Add the reserved marinade to the pan and simmer until reduced to a syrupy consistency. Add the mushrooms and reduced marinade to the onions and dressing.

6 Slice the steak thinly, then add to the dressing with the mangetout and toss to combine. This works well as a buffet lunch, served with Asian style noodles and a leafy salad.

Thai beef salad

Serves 4

1–2 tbsp sunflower oil
500g beef sirloin or rump, in
    2 thick-cut slices

For the dressing

2 garlic cloves
1cm piece of fresh root ginger
1 lemongrass stalk
1 red chilli
2 limes
3 tbsp nam pla (fish sauce)
2 tbsp caster sugar

For the salad

3 shallots
Large handful of Thai basil
Large handful of coriander
Large handful of mint

To serve

5 tbsp roasted unsalted peanuts
    (see right)
3 tbsp fried shallots (see below)

1 To make the dressing, peel and crush the garlic and peel and finely grate the ginger, reserving any juice. Remove the outer leaf of the lemongrass stalk and trim away the root end and the coarser green end, leaving the tender middle section; very finely chop this. Halve, deseed and finely dice the chilli. Squeeze the juice from the limes; you need 4 tbsp.

2 Put the lime juice, nam pla and sugar in a large bowl and stir until the sugar dissolves. Add the garlic, ginger (with any reserved juices), lemongrass and chilli and stir again. The dressing should have a balanced flavour of sour, hot, sweet and salty. Adjust the flavour as necessary.

3 For the salad, halve, peel and very thinly slice the shallots. Pick the herb leaves from their stalks and leave whole unless very big, in which case roughly tear them.

4 Over a medium to high heat, heat enough oil to just cover the bottom of a heavy-based frying pan. Add the steak and cook for 1–2 minutes each side, or to your liking (see page 411). Remove and set aside to rest for 3–5 minutes.

5 Put the raw shallots and herbs into a large bowl. Finely slice the steak across the grain and add it to the salad. Add half the dressing and turn everything through it to ensure that the salad and steak are evenly coated. Place on a serving dish or divide between 4 plates or bowls and scatter with the peanuts and fried shallots. Serve the remaining dressing in a bowl on the side.

Note Roasted unsalted peanuts and fried shallots are used extensively in Southeast Asian cooking and can be bought in Asian supermarkets. Alternatively, they can be prepared very easily.

Roasted unsalted peanuts Place the peanuts on a lipped baking tray and roast in an oven preheated to 190°C/gas mark 5 for 8–10 minutes until evenly golden. Remove from the oven and tip into a bowl to cool.

Fried shallots Halve, peel and very finely slice 4–6 shallots. Heat 5mm–1cm of oil in a frying pan or wok over a medium heat and shallow-fry the shallots until golden. Using a slotted spoon, transfer the shallots from the oil to kitchen paper and leave to cool. As they cool they will crisp.

Stir-fried beef with green peppercorns

Serves 4

3 garlic cloves
2 red chillies
1 shallot
450g beef sirloin, fillet or rump
2 tbsp sunflower oil
½ tbsp nam pla (fish sauce)
½ tbsp dark soy sauce
½ tbsp palm sugar
½ tbsp kecap manis (sweet soy sauce)
½ tbsp fresh green peppercorns, or
    bottled, drained
Handful of coriander leaves

1 Peel and finely slice the garlic. Halve, deseed and finely slice the chillies. Halve, peel and finely slice the shallot. Trim the beef of any fat and sinew and slice very thinly across the grain.

2 Heat the oil in a wok or large frying pan over a medium to high heat. Add the garlic, chillies and shallot and stir-fry quickly, then add the beef slices and cook for 2 minutes.

3 Add the nam pla, soy sauce, sugar, kecap manis and green peppercorns and heat through.

4 Remove from the heat, add the coriander leaves and pile onto a serving dish. Serve with rice and steamed greens.

Beef carpaccio with horseradish dressing

Serves 4
350g fillet steak, in one piece
2 large handfuls of rocket leaves
½ tbsp olive oil
Squeeze of lemon juice
Small piece of Parmesan cheese
Salt and freshly ground black pepper

For the dressing
¼ horseradish root
100ml crème fraîche
½–1 tsp red wine vinegar

1 Wrap the beef fillet well in cling film and place in the freezer for 1 hour, or until the outside is beginning to firm up. (This will make it easier to cut thin slices.)

2 Meanwhile, to make the dressing, peel and finely grate into a bowl enough horseradish to give you 1 tbsp, or more if you prefer a hotter dressing. Add the crème fraîche with the wine vinegar and salt and pepper to taste. Stir to combine and leave to infuse for 30 minutes. Add a little water to make the dressing liquid enough to drizzle, then taste and adjust the seasoning.

3 Wash and dry the rocket leaves.

4 Cut the beef into the thinnest slices you can, across the grain. Place them in a single layer with space between each slice on a sheet of non-stick baking parchment. Cover with another sheet of baking parchment and flatten the slices with a rolling pin or mallet until as thin as possible.

5 Arrange the slices of beef, spread out, on each plate. Lay a sheet of baking parchment on top and press down on the beef to make a flat layer.

6 Put the rocket in a bowl and dress with the olive oil, lemon juice and some salt and pepper. Strew the rocket leaves over the beef, shave slices of Parmesan over and drizzle with the horseradish dressing.

Note This is also delicious without the horseradish dressing.

Steak tartare

Serves 4 as a starter
2 shallots
2–3 tbsp capers, rinsed and drained
¼ bunch of flat-leaf parsley
450g fillet or rump steak
1–2 tsp Dijon mustard
Dash of Worcestershire sauce
Dash of Tabasco sauce
½–1 tbsp extra virgin olive oil
4 egg yolks
Salt and freshly ground black pepper
Sourdough bread, to serve

1 Halve, peel and very finely dice the shallots. Very finely chop the capers and finely chop enough parsley leaves to give you 1–2 tbsp.

2 Use a very sharp knife to finely dice the steak. Start by slicing it thinly, then cut the slices across the grain into fine dice, about 2–3mm.

3 Place the steak in a bowl with the shallots, capers and parsley. Add the mustard, Worcestershire sauce, Tabasco and extra virgin olive oil and mix thoroughly. Taste and adjust the flavour, adding more of any one ingredient to suit your taste. Season with plenty of salt and pepper.

4 Divide the mixture into 4 portions. Place a 6–7cm round pastry cutter on an individual plate and shape a quarter of the mixture into the cutter. Create a little dip in the centre and gently sit an egg yolk in the dip. Carefully remove the cutter and repeat with the remaining steak mixture and egg yolks.

5 Serve the steak tartare with thinly sliced, toasted sourdough bread and extra flavouring ingredients if you wish.

Note Although best chopped by hand, the beef can be minced through a fairly large gauge mincer, but should not result in a paste; some texture is ideal.

Veal and beef offal

Offal has been enjoying something of a revival in the past few years, as people have started to appreciate the flavour and diversity of these once thrift-associated cuts. The new surge of interest in these non-muscular parts of the animal shows that it is not just the prized tender cuts of beef that have something to offer. The cuts we tend to use most are calf's liver, veal sweetbreads, ox kidney and the milder veal (or calf's) kidneys.

All offal must be very fresh when you buy it and used within a day or two of purchase as it is more perishable than other meats.

Preparing calf's liver

Calf's liver needs careful preparation and cooking as it can spoil easily. It requires quick cooking and is best eaten pink. You generally buy calf's liver as a slice. Look for firm slices with a moist, shiny appearance, avoiding those with too many tubes, which make preparation harder. Ideally keep the slice whole for cooking, but if it is too large to cook in one piece, cut it into no more than 2 or 3 pieces.

1 Look for a milky white, very fine film on the non-cut edges of the liver; this needs to be removed as it shrinks on cooking. Use your fingernail to release this film from the edge of the liver (it can be difficult to separate, but is well worth the effort). Once released, carefully pull it away and discard.

2 The larger, grey, sinewy tubes also need to be removed. Take care when removing the sinew as what looks like a small area on one side of the liver expands and extends further on the other side. Use the point of a small knife or scissors to get between the sinew and liver and release the sinew, then remove and discard it.

3 Continue in this way with the remaining sinew. If there is too much sinew on the liver to remove without risk of the liver falling apart, cut through the sinew at intervals to prevent if from shrinking too much during cooking. The liver is now ready to cook.

Calf's liver with a ginger, pecan and thyme sauce

Serves 4

4 pieces of calf's liver, each about 170g
2cm piece of fresh root ginger
50g pecan nuts
½ bunch of thyme
Plain flour, to dust
30g butter
2 tbsp hazelnut oil
1 tbsp dark brown sugar
3 tbsp orange juice
3 tbsp Madeira
2 tbsp balsamic vinegar
300ml brown chicken and veal stock
  (see page 98)
1 tsp cornflour
Salt and freshly ground black pepper
Parsnip crisps (see page 73), to serve

1 Heat the oven to 120°C/gas mark ½.

2 Trim the liver, removing the fine outer membrane and any large tubes (see left). Peel and grate the ginger, roughly chop the pecans and finely chop enough thyme leaves to give you ½–1 tbsp.

3 Season the flour with salt and pepper, add the liver pieces and shake off any excess; there should be only a very fine coating.

4 Heat the butter with 1 tbsp of the hazelnut oil in a large frying pan over a medium to high heat until foaming. Add the liver to the pan and fry for about 1–2 minutes on each side, depending on thickness, until well browned on the outside but pale pink in the middle. Drain well and keep warm in the low oven.

5 Pour off the excess fat and deglaze the pan with a little water, tipping out and reserving these pan juices if they are not bitter.

6 Heat the remaining oil in the frying pan over a low to medium heat and add the ginger, pecans, thyme and sugar. Cook for 1 minute, then add the orange juice, Madeira, balsamic vinegar and stock, together with any reserved pan juices, and simmer for 2–4 minutes. Taste the sauce and adjust the flavours and seasoning if necessary. Slake the cornflour with a little water into the sauce (see page 111) and bring the sauce to a simmer, stirring to thicken it to a lightly syrupy consistency.

7 Serve the liver with the sauce and parsnip crisps.

Preparing ox kidney

Kidneys are nutritious and simple to cook, once you become confident with their preparation. Ox kidney has a strong flavour and is traditionally included in steak and kidney pudding and steak pie, but it can also be sliced and fried, with onions for example. Veal and lamb's kidneys are smaller, milder in flavour and most often cooked quickly and served with a simple pan sauce.

1 Ox kidneys are lobulated, meaning that they have the appearance of bunches of large grapes. Holding the lobes together is a system of tubes and fat, which are not suitable to eat.

2 The easiest way to prepare ox kidneys is to trim away individual lobes or groups of lobes from the central core.

3 Check the cut end of the lobes for any pieces of core, tubes or fat that still need removing; use a knife or scissors to cut these away.

Veal kidneys with wild mushrooms and brioche croûtes

Serves 4
350g veal kidneys
2 thick slices of brioche
40g unsalted butter, plus an extra
   20g, melted, for brushing
Few parsley sprigs
150ml dry white wine
150g mixed wild mushrooms (ceps,
   small chanterelles, small morels),
   or flavourful cultivated mushrooms
   (chestnut, field, oyster)
2 tsp Dijon mustard
6 tbsp double cream
Salt and freshly ground black pepper

1 Heat the oven to 200°C/gas mark 6. Remove the membranes and cores from the kidneys (see page 421) and cut into chunks or slices. Set aside.

2 Remove the brioche crusts and cut each slice into 2 triangles. Brush both sides with melted butter, place on a baking sheet and bake in the oven for 5 minutes, then turn over and cook for a further 5 minutes, or until golden brown; remove the croûtes and set aside. Finely chop enough parsley leaves to give you 1 tbsp.

3 Bring the wine to the boil in a small saucepan and let bubble to reduce by half.

4 Clean the mushrooms and cut or tear into bite-sized pieces. Heat half the butter in a large frying pan and sauté the mushrooms for 3 minutes, or until softened and just starting to brown, then remove from the pan and set aside.

5 Melt the remaining butter in the frying pan and, when hot, add the kidneys and cook over a medium heat until lightly browned all over. If the kidneys don't fit in the pan with space around them, then fry in batches to avoid overcrowding the pan. Transfer the kidneys to a sieve set over a bowl to drain off the bitter juices.

6 Add the reduced wine to the frying pan, stir in the mustard and cream and bring to the boil. Reduce until the sauce is just syrupy, then season with salt and pepper. Stir in the kidneys and mushrooms with half the parsley and heat through until piping hot. Divide between 4 warmed plates, sprinkle with the remaining parsley and top with a croûte to serve.

Preparing veal sweetbreads

Sweetbreads are the thymus (throat, gut or neck) or pancreatic (stomach or heart) glands, usually of a calf or lamb. Creamy white in colour, they have a soft texture that firms slightly on cooking, and a delicate flavour. Their outer membrane needs to be removed and this is easily done by poaching the sweetbreads briefly, which firms the membrane. The most commonly used sweetbreads are from the pancreas. First, sweetbreads are soaked in water in the fridge overnight to remove any blood.

1 Drain the sweetbreads after soaking and place in a saucepan of clean cold water. Bring gently to a simmer and poach, uncovered, for 2 minutes. Drain and refresh in cold water. As soon as they are cool, remove and pat dry with kitchen paper.

2 Pull away the membrane and sinew, trying to keep the sweetbreads as whole as possible.

3 The sweetbreads can be weighted to firm them for a few hours or overnight before portioning as appropriate before cooking. Put a tray over them, with a board on top of the tray, and refrigerate to firm them up.

Deep-fried spiced sweetbreads with sauce gribiche

Serves 4 as a starter
350g veal sweetbreads
200ml buttermilk
½ tsp cayenne pepper
½ tsp paprika
100g plain flour, to dust
2 eggs, beaten
150g panko or fresh white breadcrumbs
Vegetable oil for deep-frying
Salt and freshly ground black pepper
Gribiche sauce (see page 117), to serve

1 Prepare the sweetbreads (see left) and cut them into 2.5cm chunks. Place in a bowl, add the buttermilk and leave to soak for 1 hour.

2 Drain the sweetbreads well and pat dry with kitchen paper, discarding the buttermilk. Heat the oven to 120°C/gas mark ½.

3 Add the cayenne and paprika with some salt and pepper to the flour. Dust the sweetbreads in the seasoned flour, gently shaking off the excess, then dip them in the beaten egg and then in the breadcrumbs, to give an even coating. Place them on a wire rack set over a tray and place in the fridge as the oil heats.

4 Fill a deep, heavy saucepan one-third full with oil and heat gently to 190°C, or until a small piece of bread browns in about 40 seconds (see page 72). Deep-fry the sweatbreads in batches, 3 or 4 pieces at a time for 3–5 minutes, depending on size, until golden and crisp. Test one to ensure it is cooked and hot through the centre to give you a guide as to the cooking time.

5 Remove the sweetbreads and drain on a tray lined with kitchen paper. Sprinkle very lightly with salt. Keep them warm in the low oven with the door ajar while you fry the remaining batches.

6 Divide the fried sweetbreads between 4 plates and serve with a spoonful of gribiche sauce.

Variation

Sweatbreads with celeriac and apple rémoulade This piquant salad (see page 18) makes a good alternative to gribiche sauce.

Pan-fried sweetbreads with baby spring vegetables and Madeira sauce

Serves 4
500g veal sweetbreads
12 baby carrots
100g podded broad beans
100g podded peas
1 quantity Madeira jus (see page 110)
70g butter
Plain flour, to dust
Salt and freshly ground black pepper

1 Prepare the sweetbreads (see left) and cut them into 4–5cm pieces. Set aside in the fridge.

2 Scrub and top the baby carrots, leaving a little of the green stalks on, blanch in boiling water for 2–3 minutes, then refresh in cold water. Blanch the broad beans for 1–2 minutes, then refresh and skin them. Blanch the peas for 2–3 minutes, then refresh.

3 Reheat the Madeira jus, taste and adjust the seasoning and keep warm.

4 Heat a frying pan over a medium heat and add 20g of the butter. Season the flour with salt and pepper, toss the sweetbreads in the seasoned flour and shake off the excess. Pan-fry the sweetbreads for 1–2 minutes on each side until they have taken on some colour. Add a further 30g of the butter to the pan and fry for a further 2–3 minutes on each side, basting with the butter, until browned and slightly firm to the touch; they should be just cooked through the centre. Remove from the pan and set aside to rest for 2–3 minutes.

5 Wipe out the frying pan with kitchen paper and melt the remaining 20g butter in it over a low to medium heat. Add the prepared vegetables and sauté briefly to reheat and finish the cooking. Add 1–2 tbsp Madeira jus to glaze.

6 Divide the vegetables and sweetbreads between 4 plates and spoon a little of the sauce around.

Lamb

This is a naturally tender meat, so many cuts of lamb can take both slow and quick cooking. It has a distinctive, almost sweet flavour and is often paired with bold flavours like rosemary, garlic and anchovy. When choosing lamb, look for a deep pink colour and dry, white fat.

Roasting

As lamb is a young animal the muscles have not been overworked so almost any cut can be roasted. The most common cuts for roasting are the leg, shoulder, best end of neck and, considered to be the best and most expensive, saddle of lamb.

Roast lamb is most often served pink or medium, at its most succulent. However, very slow roasting gives intensely flavoured, very tender results. For further information on roasting, see page 392.

Roast leg of lamb with rosemary

Serves 4–6
1 leg of lamb, about 1.5kg
3 large rosemary sprigs
200ml red wine
2 tsp plain flour
300ml brown chicken and veal stock
  (see page 98)
1 tsp redcurrant jelly
Salt and freshly ground black pepper

1 Heat the oven to 220°C/gas mark 7.

2 Weigh the lamb and calculate the cooking time as 20 minutes per 450g plus 20 minutes (for pink in the middle), allowing for more or less time according to how you like your lamb cooked.

3 Season the lamb well with salt and pepper. Place in a roasting tin, just big enough to accommodate the meat, tuck the rosemary sprigs underneath and roast in the oven for 20 minutes, then lower the oven setting to 190°C/gas mark 5. After 45 minutes' roasting, pour the wine over the lamb.

4 Check the meat 30 minutes before the end of the cooking time; depending on the joint, the lamb may be done a little earlier than the calculated time (see page 392). Insert a skewer through the thickest part for 10 seconds. Remove the skewer and check the heat against your inner wrist; it should be warm.

5 Once the lamb is cooked, transfer it to a board over a tray to catch the juices and leave to rest for at least 15–20 minutes while you make the gravy.

6 Pour off the fat and juices from the roasting tin into a bowl and allow them to separate; adding a splash of cold water helps this. Skim off the fat and return 2 tsp of it to the roasting tin. Add the flour and stir over a medium heat until it has browned a little and any sediment from the bottom of the tin is loosened.

7 Skim off any remaining fat from the roasting juices and add the juices to the tin, with the stock (you may not need it all). Add the redcurrant jelly and bring to a simmer. Simmer for 2–3 minutes, then season to taste with salt and pepper. Add any juices released from the meat while it is resting to the gravy.

8 Carve the lamb and serve the gravy separately.

Note You can roast shoulder of lamb in the same way.

Variation
Roast lamb with rosemary and garlic Make small incisions all over the meat before roasting and insert little rosemary sprigs and 2 garlic cloves, cut into slivers, into the incisions, to give an intense rosemary and garlic flavour.

Garlic and rosemary scented slow-roasted shoulder of lamb

Serves 4–6
1 shoulder of lamb, about 1.8kg
2 tbsp olive oil
6 banana shallots
1 carrot
5 garlic cloves
3–4 rosemary sprigs
350ml red wine
Salt and freshly ground black pepper

To serve
Aioli (see page 117)
Marinated Mediterranean vegetables
  (see page 84)

1 Heat the oven to 120°C/gas mark ½.

2 Remove any bark (paper-like skin covering the fat) from the lamb (see step 1, page 435) and trim away any excess fat. Heat the olive oil in a roasting tin, just large enough to accommodate the meat, over a medium to high heat. Season the lamb well with salt and pepper and brown it all over, or as well as you can given its uneven shape.

3 Remove the lamb from the roasting tin and set aside.

4 Halve and peel the shallots and peel and cut the carrot into slices 1cm thick. Bash the unpeeled garlic cloves with the flat side of a large knife. Brown the shallots and carrot in the roasting tin over a medium heat. Remove from the heat, add the garlic and rosemary and sit the lamb shoulder, skin side down, on top of the vegetables.

5 Pour in enough water to come halfway up the vegetables (about 2cm deep). Cover with foil and roast in the oven for 3 hours. The meat at this stage should be starting to shrink away from the bone a little.

6 Remove the foil and turn the lamb over, cover again and continue to roast for a further 1 hour.

7 Turn the oven setting up to 150°C/gas mark 2, uncover the lamb, pour the wine over it and continue to roast for a further 2 hours, or until the lamb is very tender and comes away from the bone very easily; it should be easy to shred using 2 forks. Check every 30 minutes to ensure the liquid has not all evaporated, adding more water if necessary.

8 Remove the lamb from the roasting tin and set aside to rest. Strain the sauce, reserving the shallots and garlic, but discarding the carrots, rosemary and garlic skins. Taste the roasting juices and reduce over a medium heat on the hob to concentrate the flavour if necessary. Adjust the seasoning and keep warm.

9 Using 2 forks, shred the lamb from the bones into large chunks, and transfer to a large, warmed serving dish. Pour some of the juices over the lamb and serve the remainder separately. The shallots and garlic can also be served separately.

10 Serve the lamb with the aioli and marinated vegetables.

Variation

Moroccan slow-roasted shoulder of lamb Omit the shallots, carrot, all but 2 garlic cloves and the rosemary. Follow the main recipe to the end of step 3. Mix 5 tbsp pomegranate molasses with 1 tbsp ras-al-hanout, 2 crushed garlic cloves and the finely grated zest and juice of 1 orange. Spread this mixture all over the lamb. Place in a roasting tin and add 2cm water (as above). Cover with foil and proceed as for the main recipe. Delicious served with giant couscous with spice-roasted butternut, pine nuts and coriander (see page 200).

Boning legs and shoulders of lamb

Boning meat is easier than most people imagine. A knowledge of where the bones lie within a joint of meat makes it easier to understand how to go about it. A short, sharp knife with a rigid blade is ideal, the sharper the better.

Open or butterfly boning involves cutting along the bone and opening the joint out to be cooked open or butterflied, or stuffed, rolled, tied and cooked. Tunnel boning is a more difficult technique that involves removing the bones to leave the joint intact, thereby creating a cavity, which can then be stuffed. Your butcher should be happy to tunnel bone a leg or shoulder of lamb for you, or butterfly a joint if you would prefer it done for you.

Ideally the joint should be removed from the fridge well in advance of boning to allow it to come up to room temperature. Work slowly and carefully, holding the knife in a dagger-like hold with the point of the knife always pointing downwards to prevent you from pulling the knife directly towards your body. Always keep the blade of the knife against bone and scrape, rather than cut the meat away.

With tunnel boning it is best to work from both ends, starting from the body end and working the bone free for a short while, before starting from the hoof end. By alternating ends you are not trying to tunnel bone the full length of the joint, which is difficult and can be less safe.

Open boning or butterflying a leg of lamb

The even thickness of butterflied boned lamb makes it ideal for the barbecue.

1 Cut through the flesh closest to the bone, along the length of the bone.

2 Carefully scrape the meat away from the bone, working out the bone along its full length. Remove the bone.

3 If you intend to cook the meat flat, open it out a little more to create a flat rectangle of even thickness. If you are going to stuff the opened out leg, you don't need to do this. Trim away excess fat and tendons.

Butterflied leg of lamb with a caper and anchovy relish

Serves 6–8
1 leg of lamb, about 2–3kg
Salt and freshly ground black pepper

For the relish
2 shallots
1 garlic clove
75g anchovy fillets in oil
2 tbsp olive oil
½ lemon
Large bunch of parsley
¼ bunch of thyme
¼ bunch of oregano
3–4 tbsp small capers, rinsed and drained
180ml extra virgin olive oil

1 Bone and butterfly the lamb (see page 427).

2 Heat the oven to 220°C/gas mark 7. Weigh the lamb and calculate the cooking time, allowing 6–8 minutes per 450g, plus 20 minutes.

3 Open out the lamb, season it on the underside and lay it skin side up in an oiled roasting tin. Sprinkle the skin with salt and roast in the oven for 20 minutes, then lower the oven setting to 190°C/gas mark 5 and continue to roast for the remainder of the calculated cooking time.

4 Meanwhile, to make the relish, halve, peel and finely dice the shallots, peel and crush the garlic and drain and coarsely chop the anchovies. Heat the 2 tbsp olive oil in a small saucepan, add the shallots and sweat for 5 minutes until just starting to soften. Add the garlic and anchovies and sauté over a medium heat for 2–3 minutes until the anchovies start to melt. Remove from the heat and leave to cool.

5 Juice the ½ lemon. Finely chop enough of the parsley, thyme and oregano leaves to give you 4–5 tbsp in total.

6 Add the capers, herbs and extra virgin olive oil to the cooled relish mixture and stir in enough lemon juice to balance the oil. Taste and season with pepper (the anchovies and capers add enough salt).

7 Once the lamb is cooked, remove it from the oven and leave to rest for 15–20 minutes. To serve, slice the meat across the grain and arrange on a large serving platter. Spoon a little of the relish over the lamb and serve the rest in a bowl.

Butterflied leg of lamb with star anise

Serves 6–8
1 leg of lamb, about 2–3kg
Salt and freshly ground black pepper

For the marinade
1 small onion
2 garlic cloves
2 star anise
2 bay leaves
½ tsp Chinese five-spice powder
4 tbsp dark soy sauce, plus extra
  for the sauce
2 tbsp vegetable oil

For the sauce
300ml brown chicken and veal stock
  (see page 98)
100ml red wine
2 tsp softened butter mixed with
  2 tsp flour (beurre manié), to thicken,
  if needed

You will need to start this the night before, to allow time for the meat to marinate.

1 Bone and butterfly the lamb (see page 427). Weigh the lamb and calculate the cooking time, allowing 6–8 minutes per 450g, plus 20 minutes.

2 Peel and roughly chop the onion and garlic. Grind the star anise in a spice grinder. Put the onion, garlic, star anise, bay leaves and five-spice powder in a blender or food processor and blend until smooth, then add the soy sauce and oil.

3 Open out the lamb and press half the marinade onto the meat, then fold the lamb to enclose it. Coat the skin side with the remaining marinade. Place the lamb in a large plastic food bag and leave to marinate overnight in the fridge.

4 Heat the oven to 220°C/gas mark 7. Remove the lamb from the bag, open it out and lay it skin side up in a roasting tin. Sprinkle with salt and roast in the oven for 20 minutes, then lower the oven setting to 190°C/gas mark 5 and continue to roast for the remainder of the calculated cooking time.

5 Remove the lamb from the oven, transfer it to a carving board and leave to rest in a warm place while you make the sauce.

6 Skim as much fat as possible from the juices in the roasting tin. Add the stock and wine to the tin and bring to the boil. Reduce to the desired concentration of flavour, then add salt and pepper to taste, and more soy sauce too if required. If you prefer a thicker sauce, thicken with some beurre manié (see page 111).

7 Carve the lamb and serve with the sauce and vegetables of your choice.

Sage and fig stuffed lamb

Serves 6–8

3 onions
3 tbsp olive oil
3 garlic cloves
100g pine nuts
100g dried figs
1 shoulder of lamb, about 1.75kg,
   tunnel boned (see page 427)
1–2 sage sprigs
300ml brown chicken and veal stock
   (see page 98)
2 tbsp clear honey
75ml white wine
75ml Marsala
Salt and freshly ground black pepper

1 Halve, peel and slice the onions. Heat the olive oil in a medium saucepan and sweat the onions until completely soft, then increase the heat and continue to cook until golden brown. Meanwhile, peel and crush the garlic and toast the pine nuts in a small frying pan.

2 Cut the figs into slices, place in a small bowl and pour boiling water over to soften them. Add the garlic to the browned onions and cook for 1 minute. Remove from the heat and leave to cool.

3 Add the toasted pine nuts and drained figs to the onions, reserving the fig soaking liquor for the sauce.

4 Heat the oven to 220°C/gas mark 7.

5 Place the tunnel-boned lamb shoulder on a board. Add salt and pepper to the onion mixture, and tear in a few leaves from the sage sprigs, taking care not to add too many or the flavour can become medicinal. Push this mixture into the lamb, trying to spread it out well.

6 Tie the shoulder at regular intervals with 3 pieces of string, then from end to end with a long piece of string, so that it is divided into 8 equal 'segments'. Weigh the lamb and calculate the cooking time as 20 minutes per 450g, plus 20 minutes. Season the outside of the lamb with salt and pepper and transfer to a roasting tin, tucking a couple of sage leaves underneath it. Pour the stock into the tin.

7 Roast the lamb in the oven for 20 minutes, then lower the oven setting to 190°C/gas mark 5 and cook for the remainder of the calculated cooking time. About 30 minutes before the end of the cooking time, take the roasting tin from the oven, brush the lamb with the honey and return it to the oven.

8 Remove the cooked lamb from the oven, transfer it to a serving dish and keep it warm while you make the sauce.

9 Skim the fat from the juices in the roasting tin. Add the wine, Marsala and reserved fig liquor to the tin and bring to the boil over a high heat. Boil until reduced to a syrupy consistency, then adjust the seasoning and strain the sauce. Cut the lamb into rustic slices and serve with the sauce, mashed potatoes and a leafy salad or seasonal green vegetable.

Sewing up whole joints after stuffing

After stuffing either a tunnel- or open-boned joint you may need to sew up the open ends so the stuffing doesn't fall out, and to ensure the joint keeps its shape as it cooks. You can follow the method of tying a shoulder as outlined in the recipe above, or alternatively use the following method:

Use a larding needle; if it's slightly curved, all the better. Use thin, old-fashioned white string or butcher's string, but not nylon, which will melt at high temperatures. Leave a good length of string at the beginning and end and avoid elaborate knots as they are difficult to undo once the joint is cooked and you're ready to carve. Simple, large loose stitches are best so the full length of string can be pulled out in one movement once the joint is cooked.

Cooking prime cuts from the leg, loin and best end

Small cuts from a leg of lamb, such as a leg steak or rump of lamb, should be cooked in much the same way as beef steaks (see page 411). As an individual portion, the cut requires browning and quick cooking, either over a direct heat or in a hot oven.

Rump of lamb with braised beans and tomatoes

Serves 4

For the braised beans
250g dried haricot, cannellini or white
   flageleot beans
2 shallots
2 garlic cloves
½ anchovy fillet in oil
1 bay leaf
1 thyme sprig
3 oregano sprigs
2 tomatoes
5 tbsp olive oil
150ml white wine
300ml chicken and veal stock
   (see page 96)

For the lamb
½ tbsp olive oil, plus extra to drizzle
4 lamb rumps, each about 225g
¼ bunch of parsley
Salt and freshly ground black pepper

You will need to start this the night before, to allow time for the beans to soak.

1 For the braised beans, place the beans in a large bowl, cover with plenty of water and leave them to soak overnight.

2 Drain the beans, place in a saucepan and cover them with fresh water. Cook at a gentle simmer for 30 minutes.

3 Meanwhile, halve, peel and finely dice the shallots. Peel and crush the garlic. Drain and chop the anchovy. Finely chop enough thyme to give ½ tsp and enough oregano to give 1 tsp. Blanch, refresh, peel, quarter, deseed and dice the tomatoes.

4 Drain the beans and set aside in the sieve. In the saucepan, heat 3 tbsp of the olive oil and sweat the shallots until soft. Add the garlic and anchovy and cook for 1 minute, allowing the anchovy to soften and melt into the shallots.

5 Add the beans to the saucepan with the shallots, the remaining 2 tbsp olive oil, the wine, stock, bay leaf, thyme and oregano. Bring to the boil, then lower the heat and simmer gently for about 1 hour until the beans are tender, checking every 15–20 minutes, as you may need to add some water.

6 When the beans are cooked, the liquid should have reduced to a well flavoured sauce. Remove and discard the bay leaf. If the sauce is too thin, drain the beans, return the sauce to the pan and reduce to concentrate the flavour, then add back the beans. Set aside.

7 To cook the lamb, heat the oven to 170°C/gas mark 3.

8 Heat the olive oil in an ovenproof frying pan over a low heat. Score the fat side of the lamb rumps (as shown) and season with salt and pepper. Place fat side down in the frying pan to render the fat. Keep the heat low to prevent the fat from burning. Once the fat is rendered and golden, pour off the excess from the pan and brown the rumps evenly all over, before transferring to the oven and roasting for 10–12 minutes until medium.

9 While the lamb is cooking, reheat the beans, taste and adjust the seasoning. Coarsely chop enough parsley leaves to give you ½–1 tbsp and stir through the beans with the tomatoes.

10 Once the lamb is cooked, remove it from the oven and leave to rest for 3–4 minutes before carving, against the grain. Pour any roasting juices into the beans. Serve the lamb on the braised beans, drizzled with a little olive oil.

Variations

Rump of lamb with broad beans, peas and mint Replace the braised beans with 1 quantity broad bean, pea and mint salad (see page 36, omitting the feta). Warm through before serving with the lamb.

Rump of lamb with braised summer vegetables Serve the lamb rumps with braised summer vegetables (see page 440).

Preparation of a rack of lamb (or best end of neck)

Rack of lamb is an expensive but elegant cut, ideal for entertaining. It can be sliced into cutlets for presentation or cut into 3-bone portions (see page 437). This is the classic way of preparing a rack of lamb. A French-style rack is trimmed still further for a more attractive presentation (see page 436).

1 Take the rack from the fridge and, while cold, remove the bark (paper-like skin covering the fat). It is easier to pull it away from the chine/backbone end towards the ribs. Lift the bark at one corner of the chine end with your fingertips or a small, sharp knife. Once you have enough to hold on to, slowly pull it back towards the ribs. If it is not pulling away easily, then use the knife to release a little of it first, then try pulling it away. You do not want to pull away the fat, just the skin.

2 If there is a thick layer of fat beneath the bark, carefully shave it off using a sharp knife, leaving no more than 1–2mm fat covering the eye/loin of lamb. The rack doesn't take long to cook and a thick layer of fat will not render, leaving underdone lamb fat. If there are alternate layers of fat and meat covering the eye, you will need to judge whether the layers of fat within the layers of meat will have time to render. If not, then remove the first layer of fat and meat, then shave the inner layer of fat to a 1–2mm thickness. Do not remove all the fat to reveal the sinew covering the eye. Use any trimmings of meat for stocks and sauces. Feel for and remove any shoulder blade by cutting the half-moon shaped cartilage out.

3 Now trim and 'battlement' the ribs. To begin with, it is easier to do this with the chine bone still on. The length of the ribs should be about one and a half times the width of the eye, so measure the ribs from the eye end and trim the ribs if necessary with scissors or a cleaver (take care if using a cleaver). Now measure 2–3cm from the non-eye end of the ribs, score through the fat across the rack at this point and cut it away.

4 With the rack standing on the chine, cut down on both sides of each rib, just to the scored line, then cut across to release the meat between the ribs. Remove and use for stocks and sauces.

5 Remove the chine bone by having the underside of the rack uppermost. Use a small knife to angle beneath the end of the ribs against the chine bone and, keeping the knife firmly against the chine bone, cut down carefully a little at a time to release the eye of meat and ribs from the chine. Avoid making a deep incision as if the knife is not angled correctly you will cut into the eye of the meat.

6 When the bottom of the chine is reached release it and set it aside to use for stocks and sauces.

7 Remove the gristle, which lies close to the eye just beneath the fat covering the eye at the chine end of the rack; it is a thick creamy elastic tendon that does not soften on cooking, so needs to be removed.

8 The last task is to clean the bones, made easier after removing the chine as the rack can be 'bent' and angled as required. Place the rack on the board, rib side down and, using a small knife positioned vertically on the first rib (not with the blade horizontally flat on the rib) and held firmly, scrape the thin film of sinew off the rib and away from you. You will need to bend the rack to reach the inside of the ribs and turn the rack over to scrape the underside of the ribs.

9 While the rack is turned over, also remove any excess fat from the outside of the rib area covering the eye. The ribs should be completely clean of sinew, or it discolours and burns in the heat of the oven. Tidy up the areas between the ribs and the rack is now ready to use.

1 Pulling the bark (thin skin) away from the fat.

2 Cutting away excess fat, leaving an even 1–2mm layer on the eye/loin.

3 Scoring through the fat across the rack 2–3cm from the end of the ribs, then cutting it away.

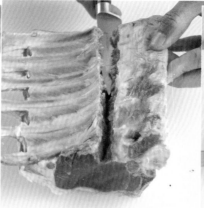

4 Cutting down both sides of the ribs to the scored line.

5 Cutting the eye of the meat and ribs from the chine.

6 Releasing the chine.

7 Removing the gristle at the chine end of the rack.　8 Cleaning the rib bones.

9 Trimming away excess fat from the outside.

Rack of lamb with a mustard and herb crust

Serves 4
2 x 6-bone racks of lamb

For the crust
80g unsalted butter, softened
4 tbsp Dijon mustard
6 tbsp fresh white breadcrumbs
½ tsp salt
1 tsp freshly ground black pepper
Large handful of mixed herbs, such as
    mint, chives, parsley and thyme

1 For the crust, mix the softened butter, mustard, breadcrumbs and salt and pepper together in a bowl. Finely chop enough mixed herb leaves to give you about 3 tbsp and incorporate them into the crust mixture.

2 Trim the racks of lamb according to preference (see below or page 434–5).

3 Press a thin layer of the mixture over the rounded, skinned side of the racks. Place them in a small, shallow roasting tin and chill in the fridge for 20–30 minutes, or until the crust has firmed up. Heat the oven to 220°C/gas mark 7.

4 Roast in the oven for 20–25 minutes for pink lamb, or about 5 minutes longer if you prefer it well done. A 4–5 bone rack will take only 20 minutes to cook. Leave to rest for 10 minutes before serving.

Variations

Rack of lamb with a hazelnut and herb crust Omit the crust. Put 80g toasted hazelnuts in a food processor with 1½ tbsp chopped parsley, ¼ tbsp chopped rosemary, 50g fresh white breadcrumbs and 80g unsalted butter and mix to a smoothish paste. Season with salt and pepper and spread evenly and neatly over 2 prepared 6-bone racks of lamb, proceeding as for the main recipe.

Rack of lamb with a pistachio crust Omit the crust. Put 80g pistachio nuts in a food processor with ½ tbsp chopped thyme, 50g fresh white breadcrumbs and 80g unsalted butter and blend until the nuts are broken down and the mixture is a smoothish paste. Season with salt and pepper before spreading it evenly and neatly over 2 prepared 6-bone racks of lamb, proceeding as for the main recipe.

To prepare a French trimmed rack of lamb

1 Follow steps 1 and 2 on page 434, but remove all of the layers of fat and meat covering the eye of the meat and ribs, to reveal the sinew on the eye. Scrape the rib bones clean up to the eye. To prevent the eye falling away from the ribs, cut only up to the little triangular-shaped fat, which helps hold the eye to the ribs.

2 Follow steps 4–7 on page 434 to clean the rib bones and remove the chine bone and gristle.

3 Trim away the layer of sinew covering the eye.

To cut a prepared rack of lamb into cutlets

Once you have prepared your rack, take a good look at it before you start to cut it into cutlets – the bones may be placed in such a way that cutting exactly between the bones might result in 'losing' a cutlet or having the first cutlet very thick and the last very thin. Your aim is to cut the rack into cutlets that are an even thickness to ensure they cook evenly. It might be necessary to cut against each bone, rather than right down the middle of two bones.

1 Prepare the rack following the instructions on page 434.

2 Once the rack is prepared, cut between the bones into individual cutlets.

3 Take care to follow the natural curve of the bone and the knife will cut cleanly through the meat.

Lamb cutlets with herbs

Serves 4
60g butter
2–3 large handfuls of mixed herbs such as thyme, basil, mint, parsley, oregano and rosemary
12 trimmed lamb cutlets (see above)
Salt and freshly ground black pepper

1 Heat the grill to its highest setting.

2 Melt the butter and finely chop enough herb leaves to give you at least 4 tbsp. Put the cutlets on a board and brush with the butter. Season with salt and pepper and sprinkle with half the herbs.

3 Place the cutlets on a lipped baking sheet and grill, about 3cm under the heat source, for 2–3 minutes.

4 Turn the cutlets over, baste with the melted butter from the baking sheet and sprinkle over the remaining herbs and a little seasoning. Grill for a further 2–3 minutes, or according to your preference.

5 Serve the cutlets on warmed plates with the pan juices poured over them.

Variations

Lamb cutlets with harissa Omit the herbs. Rub the cutlets with 1–2 tbsp harissa paste before brushing with melted butter and grilling as for the main recipe. Serve with preserved lemon couscous (see page 200).

Tandoori lamb cutlets Omit the herbs. In a blender, blitz 300g natural yoghurt with a large pinch each of chilli powder, ground cumin and coriander, 2 tsp garam masala, 2 tsp tomato purée, 2 crushed garlic cloves, 2 tsp chopped fresh ginger and the finely grated zest and juice of 1 lemon in a blender with some salt and pepper until smooth. Transfer to a large bowl. Add the cutlets, turn to coat and marinate overnight in the fridge. Scrape off the excess, then cook as for the main recipe.

To remove the eye/loin of lamb from a rack of lamb

If you only want the eye, or loin, of lamb you do not need to prepare the whole rack. Take the unprepared rack of lamb and remove the chine bone, gristle and any shoulder blade (see steps 5, 6 and 7, page 434). You can often buy just the eye/loin, in which case only the sinew needs removing.

1 After removing the chine, with the bones uppermost, carefully cut and release the bones from the eye/loin only to the edge of the eye.

2 The eye can now gently be pulled from the rack whole.

3 Clean the eye of the grey silvery sinew and fat. Try to leave the little false fillet in place.

Note The bones can be stripped of fat and used, along with the chine, for lamb stock.

Loin of lamb with broad beans, peas and mint

Serves 4

1 tbsp olive oil
2 pieces of lamb loin, each about 350g
100ml red wine
200ml brown chicken and veal stock (see page 98)
1 quantity broad bean, pea and mint salad (see page 36, omitting the feta)
Salt and freshly ground black pepper

1 Heat the oven to 180°C/gas mark 4.

2 Heat the olive oil in a frying pan over a low to medium heat. Season the lamb with salt and pepper, add to the pan and brown evenly all over.

3 Transfer the lamb loins to a roasting tin and roast in the oven for 6–10 minutes until pink.

4 Deglaze the frying pan with the wine and reduce to ½ tbsp, then add the stock and simmer for 4–5 minutes until reduced and syrupy. Taste and season with salt and pepper.

5 Remove the lamb from the oven and set aside to rest for 3–4 minutes before slicing. Warm through the broad bean and pea mixture and serve with the slices of lamb, with a little sauce drizzled around the lamb.

Variations

Loin of lamb with ratatouille Replace the bean and pea salad with 1 quantity red ratatouille (see page 56) and serve with grilled polenta with Parmesan flavoured with basil (see page 201).

Loin of lamb with soubise sauce Omit the bean and pea salad and serve the lamb with buttered leeks (see page 49) and soubise sauce (see page 105).

Loin of lamb with braised summer vegetables

Serves 4
1½ tbsp olive oil
2 loins of lamb (from a 6–7 bone rack)
Salt and freshly ground black pepper

For the braised summer vegetables
1 shallot
6–8 medium-thick asparagus spears
1 baby gem lettuce
2 tomatoes
100g peas
100ml chicken and veal stock
  (see page 96)
Few mint or basil sprigs
15g butter

1 Heat the oven to 180°C/gas mark 4.

2 Heat 1 tbsp of the olive oil in a frying pan over a low to medium heat. Season the lamb with salt and pepper, transfer to the pan and brown quickly all over.

3 Transfer the lamb to a roasting tin and roast in the oven for 6–10 minutes until pink. Remove from the oven and set aside to rest for 3–4 minutes.

4 Meanwhile, for the braised summer vegetables, halve, peel and finely slice the shallot. Snap the asparagus near the root end and cut into pieces 1–1.5cm in length. Cut out the white stem of the lettuce and finely shred the leaves. Blanch the tomatoes in boiling water for 10 seconds, then refresh in cold water. Peel, quarter and deseed, then cut the flesh into fine dice (concasse).

5 Wipe out the frying pan with kitchen paper and add the remaining olive oil and the shallot. Cook over a low to medium heat until starting to soften, about 3–4 minutes.

6 Add the peas and asparagus and cook for 1 minute, then add the stock and bring to a simmer. Simmer for 2–3 minutes, or until the peas are just tender. Chiffonade 4–6 mint or basil leaves (see page 89).

7 Remove the pan from the heat and vigorously stir in the butter to thicken the sauce a little. Add the shredded lettuce, tomato concasse and the mint or basil. Taste and adjust the seasoning.

8 Divide the braised summer vegetables between 4 plates. Carve the lamb into slices and place on top of the vegetables.

Variations

Loin of lamb with braised peas and baby onions Replace the braised summer vegetables with 1 quantity braised peas and baby onions (see page 36). Proceed as above.

Loin of lamb with crushed Jersey Royals and tomato mint salsa Omit the braised summer vegetables. Boil or steam 500g Jersey Royals or small new potatoes until tender, then drain and crush with a fork while still warm, adding 20g butter and some salt and pepper. Cook the lamb as for the main recipe and serve with the potatoes and a tomato and mint salsa (see page 127, substituting mint for the basil).

Loin of lamb with beans and artichokes Omit the peas, asparagus and lettuce and add 1 crushed garlic clove to the shallot at the beginning of step 5. After adding the stock, add 400g tin drained and rinsed small white beans, such as cannellini, and 1 quantity braised artichokes (see page 23), cut in half, or a 300g jar drained roasted artichoke hearts, halved or quartered. Simmer for 3–4 minutes to heat through the beans and artichokes, then taste, season and stir though the butter to thicken the sauce a little. Finally, add the tomato concasse and 1–2 tbsp coarsely chopped parsley in place of the mint or basil. Serve with the lamb, cooked as for the main recipe.

Harissa lamb with spinach and chickpeas

Serves 4

2 tbsp harissa paste

6 tbsp Greek yoghurt

2 loins of lamb (from a 6–7 bone rack)

2 red onions

4 garlic cloves

2 red chillies

3 tbsp olive oil

1½ tsp ground cumin

1½ tsp ground cinnamon

1½ tsp ground coriander

400g tinned (or cooked) chickpeas,
   drained weight

2 tsp caster sugar

2 x 400g tins chopped tomatoes

200g baby spinach

¼ bunch of coriander

Salt and freshly ground black pepper

For the tzatziki

¼ cucumber

½ garlic clove

½ lemon

Few mint sprigs

150g Greek yoghurt

If possible, start this recipe the night before, to allow plenty of time for the meat to marinate.

1 Mix the harissa paste with the Greek yoghurt and spread all over the lamb to coat evenly. Place in a large plastic food bag and leave to marinate for at least 30 minutes, but ideally overnight in the fridge.

2 Heat the oven to 180°C/gas mark 4.

3 Halve, peel and finely dice the red onions, peel and crush the garlic and halve, deseed and finely dice the chillies. Heat 2 tbsp of the olive oil in a large saucepan over a low heat, add the onions and sweat until translucent and soft. Add the garlic and chillies and cook for 1 minute. Add the ground spices and cook for a further 1 minute.

4 Increase the heat to medium and add the chickpeas, sugar and tomatoes. Allow to simmer for 20–30 minutes until syrupy. If the liquor appears too thin, boil it vigorously for 2–3 minutes; if too thick, add a little water.

5 To make the tzatziki, peel, halve and deseed the cucumber, then cut into fine dice or grate. Put the cucumber into a sieve, sprinkle with ½ tsp salt and leave to drain for 20 minutes. Crush the garlic, juice the ½ lemon and finely chiffonade enough mint leaves (see page 89) to give you 2 tsp. Squeeze out as much liquid as possible from the cucumber and put in a small bowl with the yoghurt, garlic and mint; stir well to combine. Taste and season with lemon juice, salt and pepper, then cover and refrigerate until needed.

6 Heat the remaining 1 tbsp olive oil in a heavy-based frying pan over a medium to high heat, until hot. Wipe off the marinade from the lamb, season with salt and pepper and brown the fillets evenly all over. Transfer to a roasting tin and cook in the oven for 6–10 minutes, according to your preference; the lamb should ideally be served pink/medium.

7 Wash the spinach well, add it to the chickpea mixture and stir until just wilted. Taste and adjust the seasoning and keep warm.

8 Remove the lamb from the oven and leave to rest for 3–4 minutes. Pick the leaves from the coriander stalks.

9 Carve the lamb into even slices. Divide the chickpea mixture between 4 plates, top with slices of the lamb and scatter the coriander leaves over the top. Serve with the tzatziki.

Preparing racks of lamb for noisettes

Noisettes are the boneless eye meat of a rack of lamb, wrapped in a thin layer of lamb fat and sliced into medallions. The meat can be cut into noisettes before or after cooking. You will need two 6-bone racks of lamb to serve 4.

First you need to remove the bark (paper-like skin covering the fat) and the chine bone and gristle as for preparing a rack of lamb (see steps 5, 6 and 7, page 434).

1 Place the rack rib side uppermost on the board, with a sharp knife positioned between the ribs and the eye of the meat. Keeping the knife firmly against the ribs, cut between the ribs and eye to remove the rib bones. Reserve the ribs for stocks and sauces.

2 Carefully start to release the eye of the meat from the sheet of fat to which it is still attached. Once a corner of the fat is released you should be able to pull it away.

3 Trim off any excess fat and the silvery grey sinew covering the eye meat.

4 Try to leave the little false fillet on and avoid removing the sinew between it and the eye as this holds it in place. Set the cleaned meat aside and work on the rectangle of fat.

5 From what was the inside of the fat layer, which is what should be uppermost to you after removing the eye, carefully shave off all the meat and fat so all that is left is a 1–2mm thick rectangular sheet of lamb fat, which will wrap around the eye completely. You may need to cover the fat with a sheet of baking parchment or cling film and bash it out a little with a rolling pin or small saucepan to get it thin enough. Take care as too much force will break the fat.

6 Season the sheet of fat with salt and black pepper. At this stage, a stuffing could be spread on the fat before rolling the eye in it.

7 Place the cleaned, trimmed eye on the fat and roll it up in the fat fairly tightly, leaving a small overlap of fat of about 5–7mm, to allow for shrinkage of the fat as it cooks. If the fat does not overlap, use some of the trimmings to place on the inside of the sheet of fat.

8 Tie the rolled lamb fairly tightly in the middle with kitchen string, then at each end to hold it in place.

9 Now tie the meat in between at 2–3cm intervals to keep it intact. To create noisettes, slice the lamb evenly between the string so that each noisette is held together by a piece of string, to keep it intact while cooking. Alternatively, cook the lamb whole, then cut it into noisettes after browning.

Replacing the layer of fat with pancetta or bacon

The fat used to cover the eye can be replaced with pancetta or very thinly cut streaky bacon, in which case the preparation is much simpler. Remove the chine bone and then carefully pull out the eye (as in step 2 above). Trim and clean off any sinew.

Lay a sheet of cling film on a work surface and lay rashers of either pancetta or thin streaky bacon on the cling film, with all the rashers lying in the same direction and almost touching each other. Cover the rashers with another sheet of cling film and, using a rolling pin, roll on top of the cling film and bacon rasher sandwich. This will help to thin out the bacon and creates a sheet of bacon in which to roll up the lamb.

Remove the top layer of cling film and season the bacon with black pepper (the bacon will add sufficient salt). Place the eye of lamb on the bacon and roll up, using the cling film to support the bacon, taking care not to roll the film between the bacon and lamb. Again you need a small overlap of bacon to prevent shrinkage, and there only needs to be a single layer of bacon covering the lamb. Use the cling film to tightly wrap the eye and bacon to hold it together. Twist the ends to seal and refrigerate until needed.

1 Cutting between the ribs and eye of the meat.

2 Pulling the fat away from the eye of the meat.

3 Starting to cut away the silvery grey sinew.

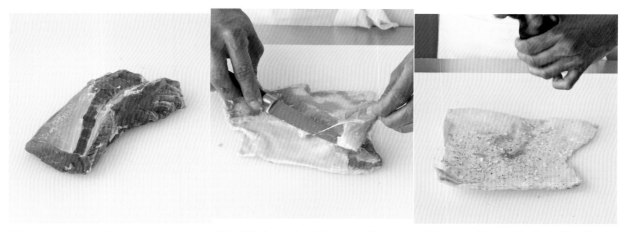

4 Continuing to remove the sinew in strips, but retaining it between the false fillet and the eye.

5 Carefully shaving the thicker pieces of fat to give an even layer.

6 Seasoning the even, thin sheet of fat with salt and black pepper.

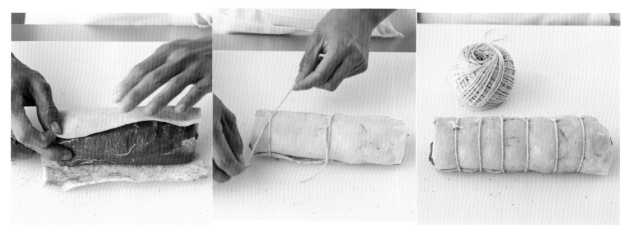

7 Rolling the sheet of fat around the meat.

8 Securing the fat in place with string.

9 The meat ready for cutting into noisettes, before or after cooking.

Noisettes of lamb with ratatouille

Serves 4
2 best end necks of lamb, 6–7 bone racks
1 tbsp olive oil
Salt and freshly ground black pepper

For the ratatouille
½ quantity sauce pizzaiola (see page 128, omitting the dried herbs)
Small handful of basil, plus 4 sprigs to finish
½ red onion
½ red pepper
1 courgette
½ small aubergine
3–4 tbsp olive oil
1 plum tomato
¼ tsp ground coriander

1 Prepare the lamb for noisettes (see page 444), keeping the rolled lamb whole.

2 Heat the olive oil in a frying pan over a low to medium heat, sprinkle the lamb with salt and place in the frying pan. Brown and crisp the fat, turning every so often to ensure it is evenly brown all round the noisettes, about 5–10 minutes. Transfer to a roasting tin and set aside until ready.

3 For the ratatouille, put the sauce in a saucepan. Pick the basil leaves off their stems and reserve. Bash the stems with a rolling pin to bruise them, then add to the sauce and heat until simmering. Take off the heat and set aside to infuse.

4 Peel and very finely chop the onion. Peel the red pepper with a swivel vegetable peeler and cut into very fine dice. Trim the ends off the courgette and aubergine and cut both into dice the same size as the pepper. Keep the vegetables separate.

5 Heat enough olive oil to just cover the bottom of a large frying pan. Add the onion and fry over a low heat until softening, then increase the heat to colour a little. Tip into a bowl and set aside. Wipe out the pan and, over a medium heat, add more oil and fry the red pepper, then the courgette, leaving them slightly firm. As each vegetable is cooked, add it to the bowl with the onion. Add more oil and repeat with the aubergine, covering the pan initially. Remove the lid when there is a little liquid in the bottom of the pan. Cook until soft.

6 Blanch the tomato in boiling water for 10 seconds, then refresh in cold water. Peel, deseed and cut into fine dice (concasse). Heat the oven to 170°C/gas mark 3.

7 Transfer the sauce pizzaiola to a food processor, discarding the basil stalks. Blend until smooth and return to the pan. Add all the vegetables and tomato concasse, tear in the basil leaves and heat through, stirring gently. Taste and adjust the seasoning, add the ground coriander and keep warm.

8 Roast the lamb in the oven for 4–8 minutes until pink, then leave to rest for 4–5 minutes before removing the string. To carve the lamb, trim off the end pieces and cut each piece of meat into 6 equal-sized noisettes.

9 Spoon the ratatouille onto 4 plates and place 3 slices of lamb on each portion. Finish with basil sprigs.

Thyme-wrapped noisettes of lamb with lentils

Serves 4
2 best end necks of lamb, 6–7 bone racks
¼ bunch of thyme
1 tbsp olive oil
1 quantity lamb and thyme jus (substituting thyme for the rosemary, see page 108)
1 quantity braised lentils (see page 195)
Salt and freshly ground black pepper

1 Prepare the lamb for noisettes (see page 444). Finely chop enough thyme leaves to give you 1 tbsp. Roll the prepared loins in the thyme and season with salt and pepper, then roll them in the prepared layer of fat and tie them as for noisettes. Heat the oven to 170°C/gas mark 3.

2 Heat the olive oil in a frying pan over a low to medium heat, sprinkle the lamb with salt and place in the pan. Brown and crisp the fat, turning to ensure it is evenly brown all round, 5–10 minutes. Transfer the noisettes to a roasting tin and roast in the oven for 4–8 minutes until pink. Meanwhile, heat the lamb jus and lentils in separate pans.

3 Remove the lamb from the oven and set aside to rest for 4–5 minutes. Once rested, remove the string, trim the ends and slice each roll into 6 noisettes. Spoon the braised lentils onto 4 plates, pour a little of the sauce over them, then top with 3 pieces of lamb per person. Delicious served with wilted spinach or other greens.

Stewing and braising lamb

The slow cooking of a stew or braise is best suited to leg, shoulder (although it is fattier), neck fillets and the knuckle/shank. See page 400 for preparing large pieces of meat to stew, and page 401 for browning meat.

Lamb daube

Serves 4
900g boneless lamb (ideally shoulder)

For the marinade
1 onion
1 garlic clove
4 allspice berries
300ml red wine
½ celery stick, tied together with 1 bay leaf and 1 sprig each of thyme and parsley (bouquet garni, make 2, one for the daube, see below)

For the daube
100g piece of streaky bacon
1 onion
3 tbsp vegetable oil
250ml brown chicken and veal stock (see page 98)
1 bouquet garni (see above)
100g plain flour (for the luting paste)
8 rashers of pancetta
2 tsp softened butter mixed with 2 tsp flour (beurre manié), if needed
Salt and freshly ground black pepper

You will need to start this the night before, to allow time for the meat to marinate.

1 For the marinade, halve and peel the onion and cut each half into 3 or 4 wedges. Bruise the garlic and lightly crush the allspice berries. Mix all the marinade ingredients together and place in a large bowl or plastic food bag.

2 Trim the lamb of excess fat and remove any sinew, then cut into 3–4cm cubes. Place the pieces of meat in the marinade, cover or seal the bag and leave to marinate overnight in the fridge.

3 Preheat the oven to 150°C/gas mark 2.

4 Derind the bacon and cut into lardons or dice. Halve, peel and dice the onion.

5 Drain the lamb from the marinade, reserving the marinade. Heat 1 tbsp of the oil in a flameproof casserole over a medium to high heat and, working in 2 batches, brown the lamb. If the marinade appears to be preventing the pieces from browning, wipe them dry with kitchen paper. Deglaze the pan after each batch with a little water; taste the deglazing juices and if they are not bitter, reserve them. Add more oil to the pan to brown the second batch.

6 Set the browned lamb aside and heat about 1 tbsp oil in the casserole. Lower the heat to low to medium and brown the bacon and onion.

7 Strain the marinade, discarding the onion and bouquet garni, then pour it over the bacon and onion. Return the lamb to the pan, add the stock and deglazing juices, if using, and bring to a simmer. Season with salt and pepper, add the fresh bouquet garni and top up with water if necessary to ensure the meat is covered.

8 Put half the flour in a small bowl and add enough water to make a stiff dough, or luting paste. Put the lid on the casserole and press a band of the dough around the join of the lid to seal (as shown).

9 Transfer the casserole to the oven and cook gently for 1½–2 hours. Check after 30 minutes; the daube should be bubbling only gently. If it is cooking too quickly, turn the heat down slightly. (Break away the flour paste seal to check the daube and re-seal with fresh luting paste made with the rest of the flour.)

10 Once cooked, check the meat is tender; it should break easily against the side of a fork. Drain the meat, bacon and onion from the sauce, discard the bouquet garni and return the sauce to the casserole. Taste and reduce to concentrate the flavour.

11 Meanwhile, turn the oven setting up to 180°C/gas mark 4. Place the pancetta between 2 baking sheets and bake in the oven until crisp, about 10 minutes.

12 Add a little beurre manié (see page 111) to thicken the sauce to a lightly syrupy consistency if necessary. Return the lamb, bacon and onions to the pan and reheat gently. Serve topped with the crisped pancetta. Delicious with a root vegetable mash, such as parsnip and crème fraîche, or potato and celeriac.

Note You can use leg or neck in place of shoulder; neck should only take about 45–60 minutes to cook.

Lamb shanks braised in Pineau and fennel

Serves 4

375ml full-bodied red wine

375ml Pineau (if not available, use
   medium sweet white wine)

2 garlic cloves

2 red onions

3 bay leaves

4 lamb shanks

3 tbsp sunflower oil

2 tbsp plain flour

1 tsp tomato purée

1 tbsp fennel seeds

750ml brown chicken and veal stock
   (see page 98)

Bunch of flat-leaf parsley

Salt and freshly ground black pepper

1 Pour the red wine and Pineau into a non-metallic bowl. Peel and bash the garlic cloves with the flat side of a large knife, leaving the cloves whole. Halve, peel and slice the onions. Add the garlic, onions and bay leaves to the bowl with the lamb shanks, turn to coat and set aside for at least 2 hours, or preferably overnight in the fridge.

2 Heat the oven to 150°C/gas mark 2.

3 Remove the lamb shanks from the wine. Pat dry with kitchen paper and sprinkle lightly with salt. Heat the oil in a large frying pan over a medium heat and brown the lamb shanks all over, then transfer them to a casserole.

4 Drain the onions and garlic, reserving the wine and bay leaves as well. Add the onions and garlic to the frying pan and cook over a medium heat until golden brown. Add the flour and tomato purée and cook for 1 minute. Add the reserved wine and bay leaves and bring to the boil, scraping the bottom of the pan to lift any sediment.

5 Tip the onions and wine over the shanks in the casserole, then add the fennel seeds and stock. Cover and cook in the oven for 3–4 hours, or until the meat is completely tender and coming away from the bone, checking from time to time to ensure it is gently simmering, not boiling vigorously.

6 Once cooked, carefully remove the lamb shanks from the sauce and keep warm. Remove and discard the bay leaves. Skim any fat from the sauce and reduce by boiling if the flavour needs to be concentrated. Taste and season.

7 Pour the sauce over the shanks. Roughly chop enough parsley leaves to give you about 3 tbsp and sprinkle some over each shank. Delicious served with a root vegetable mash or red cabbage.

Variations

Lamb shanks braised in red wine Omit the fennel seeds and use yellow onions in place of red. Omit the Pineau, marinating the shanks as above with just the red wine and aromatics. Braise the shanks in the red wine and 400ml brown chicken and veal stock (see page 98), adding a few thyme and marjoram sprigs, 1 star anise and a pared strip of orange zest to the casserole. Serve with soft polenta (see page 201) and buttered kale.

Lamb shanks braised in ale with leek and mustard mash Omit the fennel seeds and tomato purée and use yellow onions in place of red. Omit the Pineau, red wine and marinating stage. Braise the shanks in a mixture of 500ml ale and 250ml brown chicken and veal stock (see page 98), adding a small handful of thyme sprigs to the casserole. Serve with leek and wholegrain mustard mash; to the basic mashed potato recipe on page 69, add 1 medium leek, thinly sliced and sweated in 30g butter until very soft and 1–2 tbsp wholegrain mustard to taste.

Lamb and lentil curry

Serves 4–6

1kg lamb neck fillets (or boneless leg or shoulder, see note)

About 3 tbsp olive oil

2 onions

5 garlic cloves

2cm piece of fresh root ginger

200g brown lentils

6 green cardamom pods

½ tsp coriander seeds

½ tsp cumin seeds

1 cinnamon stick

½ tsp crushed dried chillies

1 tsp ground turmeric

200g tin chopped tomatoes

500ml brown chicken and veal stock (see page 98)

2 potatoes

Salt and freshly ground black pepper

Coriander leaves, to serve

1 Cut the lamb into 2.5cm pieces. Heat 1 tbsp of the olive oil in a flameproof casserole or heavy-based saucepan over a medium to high heat. Season the lamb with salt and brown evenly in batches, deglazing the pan after each batch with a little water and adding a little more oil to the casserole to brown each batch. Transfer the browned lamb to a bowl.

2 Halve, peel and finely dice the onions. Peel and crush the garlic. Peel and finely grate the ginger. Pick over the lentils and rinse in cold water.

3 Add 1 tbsp olive oil to the casserole and heat gently. Add the onions and sauté over a low heat until starting to soften, then add the garlic and cook for 1 minute.

4 Add the cardamom, coriander, cumin and cinnamon and cook for 1 minute, taking care that they don't burn.

5 Add the ginger, dried chillies and turmeric and stir well. Add the tomatoes and lentils and stir to combine. Pour over the stock and bring to a simmer. Season with salt and pepper.

6 Add back the lamb, cover and cook very gently for 50–60 minutes until the meat is tender. Meanwhile, peel and dice the potatoes into 1.5cm cubes. After 30 minutes' cooking, add the potatoes.

7 When the lamb is cooked the sauce should have been naturally thickened by the potatoes and lentils. Taste and adjust the seasoning. Pile into serving bowls and sprinkle with coriander leaves. Serve with flatbreads and raita (see page 131).

Note Leg or shoulder will take slightly longer to cook. Check after 1–1½ hours; only add the lentils after 30 minutes of cooking, and the potatoes after 1 hour.

Moroccan lamb tagine

Serves 6

1.5kg lamb neck fillets

¼ tsp smoked paprika

1 tsp ground coriander

1 tsp ground cumin

½ tsp cayenne pepper

1 tsp ground turmeric

1 tsp ground ginger

1 tsp salt

1 tsp ground black pepper

2 onions

2 tbsp olive oil

3 garlic cloves

225g ripe tomatoes

100g dates

100g dried apricots

1 heaped tsp plain flour

About 1 litre chicken and veal stock (see page 96)

Coriander leaves, to serve

1 Trim the meat and cut into 2–2.5cm pieces. Put all the spices with the salt and pepper into a large bowl, add the meat and toss to coat.

2 Halve, peel and finely dice the onions. Heat the olive oil in a large sauté pan and sweat the onions over a low heat for 10–15 minutes.

3 Meanwhile, peel and finely chop the garlic. Blanch the tomatoes in boiling water for 10 seconds, then refresh in cold water and drain. Peel, quarter, deseed and roughly chop the tomatoes. To soften the dates and apricots, chop them, put into a small bowl, add boiling water to cover and leave to soak.

4 Once the onions are soft and translucent, add the garlic and cook for 1 minute. Increase the heat to medium, add the meat and cook for 5 minutes. The meat does not need to be browned. Add the flour and cook for a further 1 minute.

5 Add enough stock to cover the meat, then the tomatoes, and bring slowly to the boil. Reduce the heat to low, cover and simmer for 30 minutes.

6 Drain the apricots and dates and add to the casserole, then simmer for a further 15–20 minutes until the lamb is tender. You may need to add a splash of water if the sauce becomes too thick; taste and adjust the seasoning.

7 Sprinkle the tagine with the coriander leaves, whole or roughly torn, and serve with couscous.

Lamb offal

Kidneys, liver and sweetbreads are the most commonly used offal from lamb. Lamb's liver is a good alternative to calf's liver and often a little cheaper. It is considered to have slightly less flavour than calf's liver, but can be easily substituted in calf's liver recipes. The preparation is much the same as for calf's liver (see page 420) and it requires a quick cooking so as to retain its tenderness, pinkness and juiciness.

Preparing lamb's kidneys

1 Lamb's kidneys are covered in a milky white film that needs to be removed before further preparation. It comes away easily and can be discarded. Cut the kidneys in half to expose the system of finger-like creamy white tubes.

2 Using a pair of scissors or a small knife, work under the main section towards the natural dip in the kidney shape, then work either the point of the scissors or knife under and down each little tube that works its way into the kidney, and snip at the bottom end.

3 After doing this to all the veins, the system can be removed and discarded as one piece. There is only one system of tubes, so depending on how you have halved the kidney the second half may be clear. Try to keep the kidneys as intact as possible, retaining their natural shape.

Lamb's kidneys with mushrooms in a mustard sauce

Serves 4
6 lamb's kidneys
3–4 large flat mushrooms
¼ bunch of flat-leaf parsley
50g clarified butter (see page 75)
100ml double cream
30ml crème fraîche
3–4 tsp Dijon mustard
Salt and freshly ground black pepper

1 Prepare the kidneys (see above). Wipe and slice the mushrooms. Coarsely chop enough parsley leaves to give you 1 tbsp.

2 Melt half the clarified butter in a frying pan over a medium to high heat. Season the lamb's kidneys and brown them on both sides. Transfer to a sieve to drain the bitter juices.

3 While the kidneys are draining, wipe out the frying pan with kitchen paper and melt the remaining butter in it over a high heat. Sauté the mushrooms quickly, driving off any water they release and trying to achieve a little colour.

4 Once drained, return the kidneys to the pan, reduce the heat and stir in the cream and crème fraîche with mustard, salt and pepper to taste. If the sauce becomes too thick, add a little water; it should be slightly syrupy and lightly coat the back of a spoon.

5 Serve immediately, sprinkled with the chopped parsley.

Pan-fried lamb's kidneys bourguignon

Serves 4

6 lamb's kidneys
300ml red wine (ideally Burgundy)
12 button onions
30g butter
1 garlic clove
60g fatty bacon
100g button mushrooms
¼ bunch of flat-leaf parsley
300ml brown chicken and veal stock (see page 98)
½ celery stick, tied together with 1 bay leaf and 1 sprig each of thyme and parsley (bouquet garni)
2 tsp softened butter mixed with 2 tsp flour (beurre manié), if needed
20g clarified butter (see page 75)
4 slices of sourdough bread
Salt and freshly ground black pepper

1 Prepare the kidneys (see left). Pour the wine into a saucepan and reduce by at least two-thirds over a medium heat.

2 Meanwhile, to peel the onions, blanch them in boiling water for 30 seconds, then remove, cool and peel off the skins. Dry them well.

3 Heat half the butter in a lidded frying pan until foaming and brown the onions well all over. Turn the heat to low, cover and cook gently until tender and soft.

4 Peel and crush the garlic; derind the bacon and cut into lardons; wipe the mushrooms; halve or quarter these if large. Coarsely chop enough parsley leaves to give you 1 tbsp.

5 Once the onions are soft, add the garlic and cook for 1 minute. Add the reduced wine, the stock and bouquet garni, and bring to the boil. Transfer to the saucepan (used to reduce the wine) and simmer gently over a low heat for 15 minutes.

6 Meanwhile, wipe out the frying pan with kitchen paper, add the remaining butter and place over a medium heat. Fry the lardons and mushrooms until golden, then remove from the pan and set aside. Wipe out the pan again.

7 Check the concentration of the sauce and thicken to a syrupy consistency, if necessary, with a little beurre manié (see page 111).

8 Add the clarified butter to the frying pan over a medium heat, season the kidneys and pan-fry them for 2–3 minutes on each side, leaving them still rare in the centre. Remove them to a sieve to drain off the bitter juices, then return them to the frying pan, add the sauce, lardons and mushrooms and heat through. Remove the bouquet garni. Taste and adjust the seasoning.

9 Meanwhile, lightly toast the bread and place a slice on each of 4 plates. Divide the kidneys, lardons and mushrooms between the plates and pour over the sauce. Sprinkle over some parsley and serve.

Lamb's liver with bacon and Amontillado

Serves 4

4 slices of lamb's liver, each about 170g
1 onion
½ tsp plain flour, plus extra to dust
50g butter
8 rashers of bacon
2 tbsp Amontillado sherry
300ml brown chicken and veal stock (see page 98)
Salt and freshly ground black pepper
Small bunch of watercress, to garnish

1 Prepare the liver as for calf's liver (see page 420). Halve, peel and finely slice the onion. Season some flour with plenty of salt and pepper. Heat the grill to its highest setting and the oven to 120°C/gas mark ½.

2 Melt half the butter in a frying pan, add the onion and fry slowly over a low heat until soft and golden, then remove to a plate and set aside. Wipe out the pan.

3 Meanwhile, derind the bacon and grill the rashers on each side under the hot grill until crisp but not brittle, then transfer to the low oven to keep warm.

4 Dip the liver in the seasoned flour and shake off any excess. Heat the remaining butter in the frying pan and fry the liver for 2–3 minutes on each side, depending on thickness, until well browned but still pink inside. Add to the bacon in the oven.

5 Put the onion back in the frying pan (used for the liver), stir in the flour and cook over a medium heat for 1 minute. Add the sherry and bring to the boil. Add the stock and reduce to a syrupy consistency, then taste and adjust the seasoning.

6 Place a slice of liver on each serving plate, with 2 bacon rashers. Spoon over the sauce and garnish with a few watercress sprigs.

Pork

Because of its thick layer of fat, pork is often thought of as a rich meat, more suited to roasting, but it has an excellent affinity with many flavours, including fruit, spices and Asian aromatics. Some tender cuts can be used for both quick and slow cooking.

Roasting

The ideal cuts to use for roasting are from the loin, tenderloin, leg, shoulder and belly. Look for pink meat with a good layer of fat on the surface, and dry skin. Generally, the aim is to produce a crisp crackling and juicy, succulent meat, which is achieved by roasting at a high temperature to start with, to crisp the skin, and lowering the temperature for the rest of the cooking time to keep the meat moist.

Pork may now be served pink as the health risks that were once associated with undercooked pork no longer apply. As long as the meat reaches 63°C in the centre and is allowed to rest for 3 minutes, it is considered safe to eat, even if pink. However, we tend to roast pork until cooked through, but still succulent and juicy.

Roast pork

Serves 4

1.5–1.8kg loin of pork (with or without bone), skin on
1 tbsp olive oil
2 tsp plain flour
About 300ml brown chicken and veal stock (see page 98)
Salt and freshly ground black pepper
Apple sauce (see page 129), to serve

1 Heat the oven to 220°C/gas mark 7. Weigh the pork and calculate the cooking time as 25 minutes per 450g, plus 20 minutes.

2 Using a very sharp knife, score the pork skin in cuts about 5mm apart, taking care to cut only through the skin and not the fat. Brush the skin with the olive oil and sprinkle with salt. Rub the salt into the scoring, which will help to create good crackling. Season the non-skin sides with salt and pepper.

3 Put the meat skin side up in a roasting tin, just big enough to hold it comfortably, and roast in the oven for 20 minutes. Lower the oven setting to 190°C/gas mark 5.

4 Check to see if the meat is cooked 30 minutes before the end of the cooking time. Insert a skewer through to its thickest part and hold it in for 10 seconds. Remove the skewer and place against your inner wrist; it should feel hot. Check the crackling too. If the skin has not crackled properly, lift the meat onto a board and, using a large knife, carefully cut off the skin with a 3mm layer of fat beneath it. Return the meat to the roasting tin and transfer to the middle shelf of the oven for further cooking, if necessary. Lightly salt the fat side of the skin and place on a lipped baking sheet on the top shelf of the oven to allow the skin to crackle more. The salt helps to render the fat more quickly and encourages it to crisp up.

5 Transfer the cooked pork to a board over a tray to catch the juices and leave to rest in a warm place for 15–20 minutes while you make the gravy.

6 To make the gravy, pour the fat and juices from the roasting tin into a bowl and let them separate; adding a splash of cold water helps this. Skim off the fat and return 2 tsp of it to the roasting tin. Add the flour and stir over the heat until the flour has browned a little, loosening any sediment on the bottom of the pan. Add the roasting juices and up to 300ml stock, and stir over the heat until simmering. Simmer for 2–3 minutes, then taste. If it seems too weak, simmer to reduce it still further and season to taste with salt and pepper. The juices released from the meat while it is resting can also be added, or poured over the carved meat.

7 Carve the pork into slices 3–4mm thick and serve with the gravy and apple sauce.

Spiced pork loin roast with butternut squash and sage

Serves 4

1 large butternut squash
50g butter
1kg boneless, skinless pork loin
½ tsp Chinese five-spice powder
½ tsp ground star anise
½ tsp ground cumin
Few sage sprigs
150ml cider
250ml chicken and veal stock
  (see page 96)
2 tsp softened butter mixed with 2 tsp
  flour (beurre manié), if needed
Salt and freshly ground black pepper

Although pork crackling is lovely, pork loins are often sold without the skin, or with not enough fat beneath the skin for the skin to crackle. This recipe uses a skinless pork loin.

1 Heat the oven to 200°C/gas mark 6.

2 Peel, halve and deseed the butternut squash, cut into 3cm chunks and place in a bowl. Melt 10g of the butter, pour it over the squash and season with salt and pepper. Transfer to a lipped baking sheet and roast in the oven for 45–50 minutes, or until tender; a knife inserted through the flesh should pass through very easily.

3 Meanwhile, weigh the pork loin and calculate the cooking time as 25 minutes per 450g, plus 20 minutes.

4 Use a sharp knife to score the fat of the loin, in lines to create a diamond pattern, and taking care to cut only through the fat. Mix the spices together, with some salt and pepper, and rub the mixture all over the scored fat. Place in a small roasting tin and roast in the oven for the calculated time, alongside the butternut, lowering the oven setting to 170°C/gas mark 3 after 20 minutes.

5 When the squash is cooked, remove it from the oven and leave to cool. Once cool, blend in a food processor until completely smooth.

6 Meanwhile, heat the remaining butter in a small saucepan and cook to a beurre noisette (see page 114). Chiffonade 4–5 sage leaves (see page 89). Add the puréed squash and the sage to the beurre noisette, taste, adjust the seasoning and keep warm.

7 Check the pork: a skewer inserted into the thickest part for 10 seconds and held against your inner wrist should feel hot. Transfer the pork to a board and leave to rest in a warm place for 10 minutes.

8 Meanwhile, place the roasting tin over a medium heat, deglaze with the cider, and reduce to 2–3 tbsp, then add the stock and simmer for about 5 minutes to develop the flavour. Taste and adjust the seasoning. Pour in any resting juices from the pork. If necessary, thicken with a little beurre manié (see page 111).

9 Carve the pork into thin slices and serve with the sauce and puréed squash. Braised greens or tenderstem broccoli would be an ideal accompaniment.

Variation

Pork loin roast with za'atar and thyme sweet potato Omit the five-spice powder, star anise and cumin. Replace the spice rub with 2 tsp pomegranate molasses, spreading it thinly on the pork skin, and dust with 2–3 tsp za'atar (see page 32). Replace the butternut squash with 3 large sweet potatoes, roasted whole in their skins until tender (omitting the butter), then cooled and the flesh scooped out and puréed. Omit the sage. Strip the leaves of a small handful of thyme sprigs, finely chop and add to the beurre noisette with the sweet potato.

Slow-roasted pork shoulder in a barbecue sauce

Serves 4–6

2 onions
3 red chillies
5 garlic cloves
5 tbsp olive oil
250ml tomato ketchup
1 tsp celery salt
250ml smoked barbecue sauce
125ml clear honey or maple syrup
125ml white wine vinegar
1–2 tsp Tabasco or other hot sauce
1 pork shoulder roast, about 1.5kg
Salt and freshly ground black pepper
Sweet dill slaw (see page 60) or soft
  white rolls, to serve

1 Halve, peel and finely dice the onions. Halve, deseed and finely dice the chillies. Peel and crush the garlic.

2 Heat 3 tbsp of the olive oil in a saucepan over a low heat, add the onions, cover and sweat until soft and translucent. Add the chillies and garlic and cook for 1–2 minutes, then add the ketchup, celery salt, barbecue sauce, honey, wine vinegar, Tabasco and ½ tsp ground black pepper, and simmer for 10–15 minutes.

3 Meanwhile, heat the oven to 150°C/gas mark 2.

4 Remove the skin and fat from the pork. Heat the remaining 2 tbsp olive oil in a large frying pan over a medium heat, season the pork, add to the pan and brown it evenly all over.

5 Place the pork in a large roasting tin and pour over the sauce. Cover the pork and tin with foil and roast in the oven for 5–6 hours until the meat is very tender and can be easily shredded. Baste the pork occasionally and turn it halfway through cooking.

6 Remove the pork to a board. Strain the sauce into a bowl and skim off any fat, then transfer to a saucepan. Taste and reduce to intensify the flavour and develop a syrupy consistency.

7 Shred the pork, using 2 forks, and place back in the sauce to reheat gently and for the sauce to coat it evenly. Serve with sweet dill slaw or in soft white rolls.

Note The pork shoulder can be marinated in the sauce before roasting. Put the pork into a large bowl. Prepare the sauce, allow to cool, then pour over the meat and turn to coat. Cover and leave to marinate in the fridge for up to 24 hours. When ready to cook, simply transfer the meat and sauce to a roasting tin and roast as above. (There is no need to brown the meat first.)

Variations

Slow-roasted pork with citrus and coriander Juice 3 oranges and 2 limes and put the juice in a blender. Peel and chop 5 garlic cloves and add to the blender with the leaves of ½ bunch of oregano and ½ bunch of coriander. Add 1 tsp smoked paprika, ½ tsp dried oregano, ½ tsp ground cumin, ½ tsp ground black pepper and ½ tsp salt. Add 20ml cider vinegar and 50ml olive oil. Blend until smooth. Put the skinned pork roast in a bowl, pour over the marinade and leave to marinate in the fridge for at least 2–3 hours, or preferably overnight. Transfer the pork and marinade to a roasting tin, cover with foil and roast in an oven preheated to 150°C/gas mark 2 for 5–6 hours until very tender. Rest the pork and reduce the tin juices and marinade until the flavour has intensified a little. Pull the pork apart with 2 forks and pour over the reduced pan juices and marinade. Garnish with coriander sprigs and lime wedges. Also good with sweet dill slaw.

Barbecue roast pork tenderloin To serve 2, use a 350g pork tenderloin rather than pork shoulder, and about a quarter of the barbecue sauce ingredients. Quickly brown the tenderloin, then wrap in foil with the sauce and bake in the oven for 60–75 minutes. Serve as above.

Fennel and black pepper roasted pork belly

Serves 4

1.2kg boneless pork belly
½ tbsp olive oil
1 tbsp fennel seeds
¾–1 tsp black peppercorns
1 tsp yellow mustard seeds
1 tsp coriander seeds
200ml white wine
200ml chicken and veal stock
  (see page 96)
2 tsp softened butter mixed with 2 tsp
  flour (beurre manié), if needed
Salt and freshly ground black pepper

1 Check the pork belly for any small bones and remove. Score the skin, rub all over with the olive oil and sprinkle with ½ tsp salt, rubbing the salt into the scoring, which will help with the crackling.

2 Heat a frying pan over a medium heat and dry-fry the spices together until the mustard seeds begin to pop. Remove from the heat and allow the spices to cool, then grind them to a coarse powder using a pestle and mortar or small bowl of a food processor.

3 Heat the oven to 250°C/gas mark 10.

4 Rub the spices over the non-skin sides of the pork belly and place, skin side up, in a roasting tin just big enough to fit the meat.

5 Roast in the oven for 60–75 minutes to allow the skin to start to crackle, taking care that the crackling does not burn; if it appears to be over-darkening, turn down the oven (sooner than suggested in the following step).

6 Lower the oven setting to 150°C/gas mark 2, pour the wine and stock into the tin and roast for 1 hour. Finally, turn the heat down to 120°C/gas mark ½ and continue to cook until the pork is tender and the skin has crackled, about another 1 hour. Don't let the liquid in the roasting tin dry out; if necessary, add a little water during the cooking.

7 When the pork is cooked, a fork will slide easily in and out of it. Remove the pork to a board and leave to rest in a warm place for 10–15 minutes before carving into thick slices.

8 If you want to make a sauce, while the meat is resting pour the roasting tin juices into a bowl and allow to separate. Skim off the fat and taste the juices. Strain the juices and, if necessary, pour them back into the roasting tin and reduce a little to concentrate the flavour. The sauce can be thickened with a little beurre manié (see page 111) if required. Taste and adjust the seasoning. Delicious served with roasted leeks with lemon and pine nuts (see page 49).

Variation

Salt and spice roasted pork belly Omit the fennel and mustard seeds. Using a pestle and mortar or spice grinder, pound ½ tsp black peppercorns, 2 tsp coriander seeds, 1 star anise, 2 bay leaves and 1 tsp rock salt to a coarse powder. Use this spice mix to rub into the pork and proceed as for the main recipe.

Cider roasted pork belly

Serves 4

1.2kg boneless pork belly
½ tbsp olive oil
½ bunch of parsley
½ bunch of sage
½ bunch of thyme
1 lemon
1 tsp fennel seeds
1 Granny Smith apple
450ml dry cider
2 tsp plain flour
250ml chicken and veal stock
  (see page 96)
2 tsp softened butter mixed with 2 tsp
  flour (beurre manié), if needed
Salt and freshly ground black pepper

1 Check the pork belly for any small bones and remove. Score the skin. Rub the olive oil over the skin and sprinkle with ½ tsp salt, rubbing the salt into the scoring, which will help with the crackling.

2 Heat the oven to 250°C/gas mark 10.

3 Finely chop the parsley, sage and thyme, and finely zest the lemon. Mix the herbs and zest with the fennel seeds, season well with salt and pepper and pat onto the non-skin sides of the belly.

4 Place the pork belly in a roasting tin and roast for 60–75 minutes to allow the skin to start to crackle, taking care that it doesn't burn; if it appears to be over-darkening, turn down the oven (sooner than suggested in the following step). Meanwhile, peel, quarter and core the apple.

5 When the pork skin has started to crackle, lower the oven setting to 150°C/ gas mark 2. Carefully remove the pork belly, pour off any fat and place the apple pieces in the tin. Put the pork belly on top of the apple. Pour half the cider into the roasting tin and return to the oven for a further 1 hour.

6 Lower the oven setting to 120°C/gas mark ½, add the remaining cider and cook for a final 1 hour, or until the pork is tender and the skin has turned to crisp crackling. Don't let the liquid in the roasting tin dry out; if necessary, add a little water during the cooking.

7 When the pork is cooked, a fork will slide easily in and out of it. Transfer the pork to a board over a tray and set aside to rest in a warm place for 10 minutes.

8 To make the gravy, strain the contents of the roasting tin into a bowl, reserving the apple to serve with the pork, and skim off the fat. Return 2 tsp of the fat to the roasting tin, add the flour and cook over a medium heat until it has browned a little and the sediment in the tin has lifted.

9 Add the stock slowly, stirring to prevent lumps, then add the roasting juices and bring to a simmer. Simmer for 4–5 minutes to develop the flavour. Taste and adjust the seasoning, and thicken with a little beurre manié (see page 111) if necessary. Carve the pork into thick slices and serve with the apple and gravy.

Pork tenderloin

Pork tenderloin, also known simply as pork fillet, is the cut from the eye of the loin. The meat is very lean and tender, and it cooks quickly. Because it readily takes on a variety of flavours, it is also very versatile. For even quicker cooking, it can also be sliced into escalopes.

Preparing pork tenderloin

1 Covering the pork tenderloin will be a thin membrane, a little fat and silvery sinew. The membrane pulls away easily, as does the small amount of fat. Use a knife if the fat is not coming away easily.

2 To remove the sinew, insert the point of a small knife midway along it and slide the knife along the tenderloin to the end to release a 4–5mm wide strip of sinew from the meat. Continue to do this until half the sinew has been released.

3 Turn the tenderloin around and repeat, holding on to the already released sinew. This should clean the tenderloin of sinew without damaging the meat. Tenderloins are long so it may be easier to cut them in half before marinating and cooking.

Herb roasted pork tenderloin

Serves 4
2 pork tenderloins, each about 250–350g
1 tbsp fennel seeds
1 tbsp dried oregano
1 tsp dried thyme
½ tsp crushed dried chillies
½–1 tbsp olive oil
Salt and freshly ground black pepper
Warm fennel, potato and pancetta salad
   (see page 359), to serve

1 Prepare the pork tenderloins by removing the silvery sinew (see above).

2 Using the small bowl of a food processor or a pestle and mortar, grind the fennel seeds, oregano, thyme and chillies with some salt and pepper to a coarse powder.

3 Rub this marinade over the pork tenderloins, place them in a bowl and leave to marinate for at least 30 minutes, or in the fridge for up to 2–3 hours.

4 Heat the oven to 170°C/gas mark 3.

5 Heat the olive oil in a frying pan over a medium heat and brown the tenderloins evenly all over, taking care not to burn the marinade rub, or it will taste bitter.

6 Transfer the tenderloins to a roasting tin and roast in the oven for 20–25 minutes, or until cooked through but still juicy. Test by inserting a skewer into the thickest part of the meat for 10 seconds, then remove and rest it on your inner wrist; it should feel hot. Remove the meat from the oven and set aside to rest for 3–4 minutes before carving into slices 7–8mm thick.

7 Arrange the salad on 4 plates and place the pork slices alongside.

Note Fennel salad with blood orange, watercress and black olives (see page 52) and lemon and olive oil mash (see page 69) are also very good with this pork.

Chipotle roasted pork

Serves 4
2 pork tenderloins, each about 250–350g
1 tsp coarse sea salt
1 tsp chipotle paste
½ tsp olive oil
Freshly ground black pepper
Avocado and black bean salsa
  (see page 127), to serve

1 Prepare the pork tenderloins by removing the sinew from the surface of the meat (see page 461). Cut each tenderloin across in half, to make 4 shorter pieces.

2 In a small bowl, mix together the salt, chipotle paste, olive oil and some pepper. Rub the marinade all over the pork tenderloins, ensuring they are fully coated. Place in a bowl and leave to marinate for at least 30 minutes, or up to a few hours in the fridge.

3 Heat the oven to 170°C/gas mark 3.

4 In a non-stick frying pan over a medium heat, brown the pork tenderloins evenly all over. Transfer to a roasting tin and roast in the oven for 20–25 minutes until they are cooked through but still juicy. Test by inserting a skewer into the thickest part of the meat for 10 seconds, then remove and rest it on your inner wrist; it should feel hot.

5 Remove from the oven and leave to rest for 3–5 minutes before carving the tenderloins on the diagonal into slices 7–8mm thick. Spoon the avocado and bean salsa onto a platter and top with the pork slices.

Char siu pork

Serves 4
2 pork tenderloins, each about 250–350g

For the marinade
2 garlic cloves
4 tbsp clear honey
4 tbsp hoisin sauce
4 tbsp kecap manis (sweet soy sauce)
4 tbsp Shaoxing rice wine
1 tsp sesame oil
1 tsp Chinese five-spice powder

To serve
Chilli, coriander and mint salad
  (see page 56)

1 For the marinade, peel and crush the garlic. Place in a small saucepan with the rest of the ingredients and bring to a simmer over a low heat. Simmer for 4–5 minutes, remove from the heat and allow to cool.

2 Trim the tenderloins of fat and sinew (see page 461) and place them in a large plastic food bag with half of the cooled marinade, reserving the remainder for cooking the pork. Massage the marinade into the pork and leave for at least 2–3 hours, or ideally overnight, in the fridge.

3 Heat the oven to 230°C/gas mark 8.

4 When ready to cook, lift the tenderloins out of the marinade, reserving the marinade, and place on a wire rack set over a roasting tin lined with foil.

5 Roast in the oven for 10 minutes, then lower the oven setting to 190°C/gas mark 5 and continue to roast for 10–15 minutes, turning and basting the pork with the reserved marinade every 5 minutes, until cooked. For a more barbecued flavour, place the pork under a hot grill for the last 5 minutes of cooking, basting and turning to develop an even colour.

6 Remove the pork to a board and leave to rest for 5 minutes, before cutting it into slices 3–5mm thick. Serve with the chilli, coriander and mint salad.

Note You can use 1.2kg pork belly in place of tenderloin. Remove the skin from the pork and cut the belly into 5cm thick slices to marinate. Pork belly requires a longer, slower cooking, so reduce the oven setting to 140°C/gas mark 1 and roast for 2 hours, or until tender. Turn and baste the pork with the reserved marinade frequently, to ensure an even, sticky coating.

Stir-fried pork with lemongrass

Serves 4
2 pork tenderloins, each about 250–350g

For the marinade
5 garlic cloves
1cm piece of fresh root ginger
½ orange
1 tbsp nam pla (fish sauce)
2 tsp palm sugar (or brown sugar)
1 tsp cornflour

For the stir-fry
1 shallot
1 green chilli
1 garlic clove
4 lemongrass stalks
2 spring onions
1 tsp sesame seeds
2 tbsp sunflower oil
75ml chicken and veal stock
  (see page 96)
1–2 tbsp nam pla (fish sauce)
3 tsp palm sugar (or brown sugar)

1 Trim the pork tenderloins of fat and sinew (see page 461), cut them in half lengthways, then into 1.5–2cm cubes. Place in a bowl.

2 For the marinade, peel and crush the garlic, peel and grate the ginger and juice the ½ orange. Put into a small bowl with the rest of the marinade ingredients. Pour evenly over the pork and leave to marinate for at least 30 minutes or, ideally, in the fridge for 2–3 hours.

3 Halve, peel and finely slice the shallot. Deseed and finely dice the green chilli. Peel and crush the garlic. Remove the outer leaves of the lemongrass, trim off the coarse green tops and very finely chop the tender inner stem. Finely slice the spring onions on the diagonal, including the green tops.

4 Toast the sesame seeds in a dry frying pan over a low heat for 2–3 minutes until just starting to brown. Tip immediately onto a plate to cool.

5 Heat the oil in a large frying pan or wok over a medium to high heat. Add the shallot, chilli, garlic and lemongrass and sauté for 1 minute. Add the pork with its marinade and stir-fry for 4–5 minutes.

6 Add the stock, nam pla and sugar and continue to stir-fry until the pork is cooked. The pieces of pork will have firmed up; cut a piece in half to check that the fibres have set if you are uncertain.

7 Pile the cooked pork into a serving dish and sprinkle with the spring onions and sesame seeds.

Char siu noodle soup

Serves 4
1.2 litres strong chicken and veal stock
  (see page 96)
4 spring onions
1 pak choi or choi sum
2–3 tbsp soy sauce
2 tbsp oyster sauce
2 tsp nam pla (fish sauce)
1 tsp palm sugar (or brown sugar)
150g rice noodles, 4mm wide
½ quantity char siu pork (see page 463),
  warm or hot

To serve
1 red chilli
Handful of bean sprouts
Handful of coriander leaves
Lime wedges

1 Pour the stock into a large saucepan and bring to a simmer over a medium heat.

2 Meanwhile, trim and thinly slice the spring onions and slice the pak choi. Put both aside. Halve and deseed the chilli for serving, then slice thinly and set aside.

3 Add the soy sauce, oyster sauce and nam pla to the simmering stock with the sugar. Return to a simmer, add the noodles and cook them in the stock until tender. Using a slotted spoon, remove the noodles and divide between 4 bowls.

4 Add the spring onions and pak choi to the stock and bring to a simmer. Taste and adjust the seasoning. Ladle the hot soup over the noodles. Thinly slice the char siu tenderloin and place on top of the noodles.

5 Serve the chilli, bean sprouts, coriander and lime wedges separately, squeezing over the juice to taste.

Pork loin chops

Pork loin chops, either on the bone or boneless, are suited to quick browning and cooking either on the hob or in the oven.

Pork loin chops with potatoes and red onions

Serves 4

600g potatoes
1 red onion
4–5 tbsp olive oil
4 bone-in pork loin chops, each
    about 200g
¼ bunch of rosemary
½ bunch of parsley
2 bay leaves (soft-textured, young ones)
½ tsp sea salt
150ml dry cider
200ml brown chicken and veal stock
    (see page 98)
2 tsp softened butter mixed with 2 tsp
    flour (beurre manié)
Salt and freshly ground black pepper

1 Heat the oven to 200°C/gas mark 6.

2 Peel the potatoes and cut into large chunks. Place in a saucepan of cold, salted water, cover and bring to the boil over a medium to high heat. Reduce to a simmer and cook for 5 minutes, or until the surface of the potatoes is beginning to soften, then drain and transfer to a colander to steam-dry for 2–3 minutes.

3 Meanwhile, halve, peel and cut the onion into 8 wedges.

4 Heat 3–4 tbsp of the olive oil in a large roasting tin over a medium to high heat. Add the par-cooked potatoes and onion and turn the vegetables through the hot oil, allowing them to start to take on colour. Season well with salt and pepper, then transfer to the oven and roast for 40–50 minutes.

5 Meanwhile, trim the skin off the pork chops and cut through the fat at 1–2cm intervals. Finely chop the herbs and mix with the sea salt to create a dry rub.

6 Heat a frying pan over a medium to high heat, add the remaining 1 tbsp olive oil and quickly brown the chops all over. Spread half the herb rub on a tray, place the browned chops on the herbs, then sprinkle the remaining rub over the top of the chops, pressing the rub in well.

7 Turn the potatoes and onion 10–15 minutes before they are ready, sit the herbed pork chops on top and roast in the oven until the pork is cooked.

8 While the chops are cooking, place the browning pan over the heat and deglaze with the cider. Reduce to 2–3 tbsp, then add the stock and simmer for 3–4 minutes to develop the flavour. Taste and adjust the seasoning and thicken with a little beurre manié (see page 111) if required.

9 Remove the chops from the oven. Divide the potatoes and onion between 4 plates, top each serving with a pork chop and pour the sauce over.

Variation

Pork loin chops with mustard Add 1 tsp yellow mustard seeds to the potatoes and onion as they go into the roasting tin. Omit the herb rub. Use non-brown stock in the sauce, and stir in 2 tbsp crème fraîche and 1–2 tsp wholegrain mustard. Taste and adjust the seasoning. Just before serving, stir ½ tbsp coarsely chopped parsley through the potatoes and onion.

Pork loin chops with braised greens and mustard aioli

Serves 4

1 Savoy or green cabbage, or greens
4 bone-in pork loin chops, each
   about 200g
½–1 tbsp wholegrain mustard
1 quantity aioli (see page 117)
1 tbsp olive oil
30g butter
75ml chicken and veal stock
   (see page 96)
Salt and freshly ground black pepper

1 To prepare the cabbage, pull away and discard the outermost leaves, retaining as many of the darker green leaves as possible. Quarter the cabbage, cut out the thick white stem, then cut the cabbage into pieces 5mm wide.

2 Trim the skin off the chops, cut though the fat at 1–2cm intervals and set aside.

3 Mix the mustard, to taste, into the aioli, and set aside.

4 Heat a frying pan over a medium heat and add the olive oil. Season the pork chops with salt and pepper and brown well on both sides. Turn down the heat to low and continue to cook for a further 6–10 minutes, depending on the thickness of the chops, until they are cooked through. Check by inserting a skewer into the thickest part for 10 seconds; it should feel very hot.

5 Meanwhile, heat the butter in a large saucepan over a medium heat, add the cabbage and sauté for 3–4 minutes. Lower the heat and add the stock and some seasoning. Cover and cook until the cabbage is tender but still retaining its colour, about 3–4 minutes.

6 Divide the cabbage between 4 plates, place a pork chop on each serving and add a spoonful of mustard aioli. This is delicious with sauté potatoes.

Spare ribs with garlic, honey and soy

Serves 4

1.25kg pork spare ribs

For the marinade

5 garlic cloves
1 lemon
5 tbsp clear honey
2½ tbsp soy sauce
Salt and freshly ground black pepper

If possible, start this the night before to allow plenty of time for the spare ribs to marinate.

1 For the marinade, peel and crush the garlic and juice the lemon. Put into a large plastic food bag with the rest of the marinade ingredients.

2 If the ribs are in a rack, cut them into individual ribs. Put the ribs into the bag and leave to marinate for at least 1 hour, or preferably overnight in the fridge. The longer they marinate, the more flavour the ribs absorb.

3 Heat the oven to 180°C/gas mark 4.

4 Tip the ribs, with the marinade, into a roasting tin, cover with foil and bake for 2–2½ hours, or until the meat is tender and comes away from the bones easily.

5 Turn the oven setting up to 200°C/gas mark 6. Remove the foil and cook, basting and turning the ribs occasionally, for 30–45 minutes, or until glazed and sticky. You may need to adjust either the honey or soy or lemon juice to taste as you are basting the ribs.

Note Once the ribs are tender, you can reduce the sauce and glaze the ribs on the hob instead of in the oven. If there is a lot of sauce, remove the ribs and reduce the sauce until syrupy, then add back the ribs, turning them in the sauce until it is clinging to the ribs and is sticky.

Stewing and braising

Pork cuts suitable for stewing and braising include leg, shoulder, cheek and belly. See page 400 for preparation of cuts for stewing and page 401 for browning meat.

Hoisin-braised pig cheeks

Serves 4
4–8 pig cheeks, depending on size
1–2 tbsp vegetable oil
150ml orange juice
Small bunch of spring onions

For the marinade
100ml hoisin sauce
50ml dark soy sauce
1 tbsp clear honey
1 tbsp sesame oil
1 tbsp Chinese black rice vinegar
2cm piece of fresh root ginger
1 garlic clove
1 red chilli
2 tsp Chinese five-spice powder
1 tsp ground Szechuan pepper

You will need to start this the night before, or at least 6 hours ahead, to allow time for the meat to marinate.

1 Combine the liquid marinade ingredients in a bowl. Peel and grate the ginger, peel and crush the garlic, and halve, deseed and finely chop the chilli. Add these ingredients to the mixture and stir in the five-spice powder and Szechuan pepper.

2 Trim the pig cheeks of fat and sinew, then add them to the marinade. Turn to coat and leave to marinate in the fridge for at least 6 hours and, ideally, overnight.

3 Heat the oven to 150°C/gas mark 2. Remove the pig cheeks from the marinade, scraping off and reserving any excess marinade.

4 Place a flameproof casserole over a medium heat and add enough oil to lightly cover the bottom. Add the pig cheeks and brown them swiftly; the marinade will make them colour quickly, so take care that they don't burn. To halt the browning, pour in the orange juice, then the reserved marinade. Add enough water to cover, put on a tight-fitting lid and cook in the oven for 2–2½ hours until really tender.

5 Remove the casserole from the oven, carefully lift out the pig cheeks and simmer the sauce, uncovered, over a medium heat until it turns syrupy and sticky. Return the pig cheeks to the casserole to glaze them in the intensely flavoured sauce.

6 Finely slice the spring onions, including most of the green part, and sprinkle over the pig cheeks to serve. Serve with basmati rice and steamed Chinese vegetables.

Braised pig cheeks in red wine

Serves 4
4–8 pig cheeks, depending on size
1 onion
1 carrot
2 tbsp olive oil
500ml red wine
300ml brown chicken and veal stock
 (see page 98)
½ celery stick, tied together with 1 bay
 leaf and 1 sprig each of thyme and
 parsley (bouquet garni)
Salt and freshly ground black pepper

1 Heat the oven to 150°C/gas mark 2. Trim the fat and sinew from the pig cheeks. Halve and peel the onion, then cut into wedges. Peel and thickly slice the carrot.

2 Heat 1 tbsp of the olive oil in a frying pan over a medium to high heat. Brown the pig cheeks lightly, then remove and set aside. Deglaze the pan with a little water, then pour the liquid into a bowl and reserve.

3 Heat the remaining olive oil in the pan and brown the onion and carrot; remove and set aside. Deglaze with the wine and reduce by one-third to about 200ml, then add the stock, bouquet garni, pig cheeks, onion and carrot. Add the deglazing liquid, if it doesn't taste bitter. Bring to a simmer and season lightly.

4 Transfer to a flameproof casserole, cover and cook in the oven for 2–2½ hours until the pig cheeks are tender, but not falling apart.

5 Remove the pig cheeks from the sauce; set aside. Strain the liquor, discarding the vegetables and aromatics. Return the liquor to the casserole and reduce over a medium heat to concentrate the flavour and obtain a slightly syrupy consistency.

6 Add the pig cheeks back to the sauce and reheat, basting to coat them in the sauce. Delicious with butter bean mash (see page 192) or beans with tomato and chorizo (see page 191), with a little of the sauce stirred through the beans.

Gammon and ham

A ham is particularly versatile, being as delicious to eat cold as it is hot. Although the terms gammon and ham are used almost interchangeably, a butcher would understand a gammon to be pork leg meat that has been cured and is ready to be cooked. A ham is cured and already cooked.

Served cold, a joint of ham makes the ideal centrepiece for a buffet or informal gathering. Pairing it with interesting salads, such as broad bean, pea, feta and mint salad (see page 36), sweet dill slaw (see page 60) or avocado fattoush with za'atar crisps (see page 32) turns a simple lunch into something quite special.

Glazed ham with cider and mustard sauce

Serves 4

1 unsmoked gammon or ham joint, about 1.4kg

1 onion

1 carrot

2 thyme sprigs

5 black peppercorns

440ml dry cider

2 tbsp clear honey

2 tbsp English mustard

Small handful of cloves

50g butter

50g plain flour

300ml milk

1 heaped tbsp wholegrain mustard, or to taste

Freshly ground black pepper

Ham and gammon joints can be salty. To remove excess salt you can soak the joint in cold water overnight. Alternatively, place the joint in a large saucepan of cold water, bring very slowly to a simmer, then discard the water.

1 Place the ham in a large saucepan. Halve, peel and slice the onion and peel and slice the carrot, then add both to the pan with the thyme, peppercorns and cider. Top up with cold water to cover the ham, then bring to the boil. Reduce the heat, cover and simmer very gently for 25 minutes per 450g, keeping the water level topped up during cooking so the ham is covered. To check that it is ready, insert a fork into the ham; it should push through easily. Once cooked, take off the heat and allow the ham to cool slightly in the liquor.

2 Lift the ham out of the liquid onto a board. Strain the cooking liquor, discarding the aromatics. Bring to the boil and boil steadily over a high heat to reduce until the flavour is strong but not too salty; set aside. Heat the oven to 200°C/gas mark 6.

3 Using a sharp knife, remove the skin from the ham (wearing gloves if it is still too hot), leaving the layer of fat underneath. Place the ham on a baking tray and cut a diamond shaped lattice pattern into the fat, avoiding cutting into the meat itself. Mix together the honey and English mustard and spread over the ham, then stud the centre of each diamond with a clove. Bake in the oven for 20 minutes, or until browned and caramelised.

4 Meanwhile, melt the butter in a small saucepan, stir in the flour and cook, stirring, for 1 minute. Remove from the heat and gradually stir in the milk. Strain the ham cooking liquor and gradually add 500ml to the sauce, stirring as you do so. Return to the heat, bring to the boil, stirring, then lower the heat and simmer for 2–3 minutes. Stir in the wholegrain mustard to taste and season with pepper.

5 Slice the ham and serve with the sauce. This is also delicious served with baked leeks with cheese (see page 45) in place of the sauce.

Variation

Glazed ham with Cumberland sauce Omit the cider and mustard sauce. Cut the finely pared zest of 1 orange and 1 lemon into fine julienne strips. Place in a saucepan with the juice of 1 lemon and 2 oranges. Add 200g redcurrant jelly, 1 finely chopped shallot, 150ml port, ½ tsp Dijon mustard and a pinch each of cayenne pepper and ground ginger. Simmer for 10 minutes. Leave to cool before serving with the glazed roast ham.

Furred game

Game meat often has a characteristically strong flavour. Coming as it does from animals surviving in the wild, it is lean by nature but can be cooked using similar methods to other types of meat, if care is taken so that it doesn't dry out. As such, it is often marinated when slow cooked or, when cooked quickly, is usually served pink to avoid the meat becoming dry and tough. Many beef recipes can be easily adapted to use venison, and rabbit can be substituted for chicken in most instances.

Roast rack of venison with a cherry and thyme crust

Serves 4

Few thyme sprigs
Few parsley sprigs
30g fresh white breadcrumbs
75g dried cherries
30g butter, softened
8-bone rack of venison
1 shallot
3 juniper berries
1 tbsp olive oil
150ml red wine
50ml ruby port
Pared strip of orange zest
500ml brown chicken and veal stock
  (see page 98)
2 tsp softened butter mixed with 2 tsp
  flour (beurre manié), if needed
15g plain chocolate, ideally about
  70% cocoa solids
Salt and freshly ground black pepper

To serve

Parsnip or celeriac purée (see page 19)
Savoy cabbage (see page 57, omitting
  the pancetta)

1 To make the crust, finely chop enough thyme and parsley leaves to give you 1 tsp of each. Place in a small food processor bowl with the breadcrumbs, dried cherries, butter and some salt and pepper, and blend to a coarse paste.

2 Trim the venison bones and meat, if necessary. The bones should extend no more than 5–6cm above the meat and any sinew should be removed from the meat. Reserve any venison trimmings. Spread the paste over the rounded presentation side of the venison rack; you want just a thin, complete layer. Chill in the fridge for at least 30 minutes before cooking.

3 Heat the oven to 200°C/gas mark 6.

4 For the sauce, halve, peel and finely chop the shallot. Crush the juniper berries using a pestle and mortar or with the end of a rolling pin.

5 Heat the olive oil in a saucepan over a medium heat and sauté the shallot and any venison trimmings for 2–3 minutes. Deglaze with the wine and port and reduce to 2–3 tbsp. Add the juniper berries, orange zest, 1 thyme sprig and the stock. Bring to a simmer and simmer for 10–15 minutes to reduce a little and for the flavours to develop. Skim any scum off the surface.

6 Taste the sauce and, when you are happy with the strength of flavour, season with salt and pepper and strain through a fine sieve. Discard the aromatics and return the sauce to the wiped out saucepan; it should be lightly syrupy and can be thickened with a little beurre manié if necessary (see page 111). Set the sauce aside. Finely chop the chocolate.

7 Season the non-crust side of the venison carefully and place the joint crust side up in a roasting tin. Transfer to the oven and roast for 20–30 minutes until medium rare. Remove from the oven, place the venison on a board and leave to rest in a warm place for 10–15 minutes.

8 Add the chocolate to the sauce and very gently reheat, whisking to encourage the chocolate to melt into the sauce; do not let the sauce simmer.

9 Carve the venison rack into individual bones and put onto plates with the parsnip or celeriac purée and Savoy cabbage. Spoon a little of the sauce around the venison.

Venison casserole with caramelised quince

Serves 4

For the marinade

1 onion
1 garlic clove
5 tbsp sunflower oil
6 juniper berries
1 slice of lemon
1 bay leaf
250ml red wine
2 tbsp red wine vinegar
6 black peppercorns

For the casserole

650g venison
2–3 tbsp olive oil
1 onion
100g button mushrooms
1 garlic clove
30g butter
2 tsp plain flour
250ml brown chicken and veal stock
   (see page 98)
1 tbsp redcurrant jelly
¼ bunch of parsley
Salt and freshly ground black pepper

For the caramelised quince

100g caster sugar
100ml cider vinegar
200ml water
1 cinnamon stick
2 whole star anise
2 quinces
50g butter

You will need to start this the night before to allow time for the meat to marinate.

1 Cut the venison into large cubes, trimming away any tough membrane or sinew. For the marinade, halve, peel and thickly slice the onion and put into a bowl with the venison. Peel and crush the garlic.

2 Mix the rest of the marinade ingredients together and add to the venison bowl. Mix well, cover and leave to marinate in the fridge overnight.

3 Heat the oven to 150°C/gas mark 2.

4 Lift the venison from the marinade and pat dry with kitchen paper. Strain the marinade, reserving the liquid but discarding the aromatics.

5 You will need to brown the venison in batches. Heat 1 tbsp of the olive oil in a flameproof casserole, add about one-third of the venison cubes and brown over a medium heat, then transfer to a bowl using a slotted spoon and deglaze the pan with a little water; pour the juices over the browned venison pieces. Repeat to brown the rest of the meat, in batches, in the same way.

6 Halve, peel and finely dice the onion. Slice the mushrooms and peel and crush the garlic. Melt the butter in the casserole and cook the onion over a gentle heat until soft, then increase the heat and brown the onion. Add the mushrooms and garlic and continue to cook for 2 minutes.

7 Stir in the flour and cook for 1 minute. Remove from the heat and gradually add the strained marinade and stock, stirring to keep the mixture smooth. Return to the heat and stir until boiling, again scraping the bottom of the pan. Return the browned venison to the casserole with any juices and add the redcurrant jelly. Season with salt and pepper, cover and cook in the oven for 2 hours, or until the venison is very tender. Check from time to time to ensure it is not boiling too vigorously; it should be very gently simmering.

8 Meanwhile, for the caramelised quince, put the sugar in a small saucepan with the cider vinegar and water and dissolve over a low heat. Break the cinnamon stick in half and add to the pan with the star anise. Bring to the boil, reduce the heat and simmer for 5 minutes. Peel and core the quinces and cut into quarters or thick slices, depending on their size. Add to the pan and poach until just tender, about 10 minutes. Drain the quinces and pat dry with kitchen paper. Melt the butter in a frying pan over a medium heat and fry the quinces until golden.

9 Using a slotted spoon, lift the cooked venison, mushrooms and onion into a serving dish, cover and keep warm. Boil the sauce rapidly until reduced to a shiny, almost syrupy consistency and a good concentration of flavour.

10 In the meantime, finely chop enough parsley leaves to give you 1 tbsp. Adjust the seasoning of the sauce, then pour over the venison, mushrooms and onion and top with the caramelised quinces and chopped parsley to serve.

Venison steaks with blackcurrant sauce

Serves 4

4 venison fillet steaks, each about 140g
100g blackcurrants
150ml well-flavoured brown chicken and
  veal or beef stock (see page 98)
50ml crème de cassis
50ml red wine
50ml ruby port
2 tbsp olive oil
1–2 tsp redcurrant jelly
30g unsalted butter
Salt and freshly ground black pepper

1 Trim any gristle and fat from the steaks, then season with pepper and set aside. Pick over the blackcurrants and put to one side.

2 Put the stock, crème de cassis, wine and port into a small saucepan, bring to the boil and reduce by about half. Remove from the heat and set aside.

3 Heat the olive oil in a heavy-based frying pan over a medium to high heat. Season the steaks with salt and fry for 3 minutes on each side until well browned but rare. (Or, fry for longer if you prefer. For well-cooked venison, allow an extra 2 minutes on each side, depending on the thickness of the steaks.) Remove the venison from the pan and rest in a warm place while you finish the sauce.

4 Pour off any oil from the frying pan. Add the reduced stock mixture and stir over a low heat to incorporate the meat juices. Add the blackcurrants and simmer until softened. Taste the sauce and season with salt and pepper. Add redcurrant jelly to taste, to balance the acidity of the blackcurrants if required. Beat in the butter using a small whisk; the blackcurrants will start to break up into the sauce a little.

5 Serve the venison steaks with the blackcurrant sauce. Delicious with roasted root vegetables or a watercress salad.

Note The venison can be marinated overnight in equal quantities of red wine and olive oil with onion slices and juniper berries. Drain and pat dry before cooking.

Braised rabbit in Dijon and tarragon sauce

Serves 4

1 farmed rabbit, jointed into 6 pieces
Small handful of tarragon sprigs
30g Dijon mustard
50g unsalted butter
1 onion
85g piece of bacon
1 garlic clove
1 tsp plain flour
600ml chicken and veal stock
  (see page 96)
30–60ml crème fraîche
Salt and freshly ground black pepper

We use farmed rather than wild rabbit as it is more tender and has a better flavour. It is cooked in the same way as its wild counterpart, albeit for not as long. Wild rabbit can be soaked in cold salted water for 3 hours to whiten the flesh. You will need to start this the day before to allow time for the meat to marinate.

1 Trim the rabbit joints if necessary. Chop enough tarragon leaves to give you 1 tsp and mix with all but 1 tsp of the mustard, spread over the rabbit joints, cover and refrigerate overnight. Save the rest of the tarragon sprigs.

2 Heat the oven to 170°C/gas mark 3. Heat the butter in a heavy-based frying pan over a medium heat. Scrape the mustard off the rabbit pieces, then brown them all over. Transfer all but the loin pieces to a casserole.

3 Halve, peel and finely chop the onion, add to the frying pan with the bacon piece and cook over a gentle heat until the onion has softened. Peel and crush the garlic. Increase the heat to brown the onion, then add the garlic and cook for 1 minute. Stir in the flour and cook for a further 1 minute.

4 Take the pan off the heat and stir in the stock. Return to the heat, bring to the boil, then lower the heat and simmer for 2 minutes. Season with salt and pepper, then pour the sauce over the rabbit pieces in the casserole, adding a tarragon sprig.

5 Cover and cook in the oven for 1–1½ hours, adding the loin after 30–45 minutes. The rabbit is cooked when it is tender and coming away from the bones easily.

6 Trim any exposed bones from the rabbit and transfer to a warmed serving dish; keep warm. Discard the bacon and reduce the sauce over a medium heat to concentrate the flavour a little. Stir in the remaining 1 tsp mustard with crème fraîche to taste, and heat through gently. Adjust the seasoning, then pour the sauce over the rabbit, garnish with tarragon and serve with green beans.

Pastry

What makes this subject so fascinating is that all pastries use the same basic ingredients: flour, fat, salt and liquid. It is the different proportions of these ingredients and the techniques employed that create such an impressive array of pastries for use in so many different ways, both savoury and sweet. Inexperienced cooks often shy away from pastry making, opting for ready-made products instead, but the skills required are not that difficult to master. A basic knowledge of the techniques and an understanding of the simple rules will give you the confidence to make excellent pastry.

Understanding pastry

Pastry quantities

For easy reference, the recipes in this chapter call for a quantity (or half quantity) of the specific pastry. If you are using a smaller flan ring, you will need less pastry. Don't throw away excess pastry as it freezes well. Trimmings come in useful for patching and repairing pastry cases after baking blind.

Note that traditionally where a weight of pastry is given in a recipe this refers to the flour quantity rather than the total weight of the pastry. So if a recipe calls for 250g shortcrust pastry, it means pastry made using 250g flour. However, if you are buying ready-made pastry, the weight of pastry stated on the packet is the total weight, not just the amount of flour.

Gluten

Wheat flour, which is most commonly used for pastry, contains gluten, which begins to develop as soon as flour comes into contact with liquid. When making shortcrust pastry you need to restrict the development of gluten, in order to keep the pastry short and tender. This is in contrast to making bread, where the aim is to develop the gluten to create an elastic texture and tough crust, achieved by adding plenty of water and vigorous kneading. Layered pastry requires some gluten development to strengthen the layers.

There will always be some gluten development in pastry, just by adding liquid to flour, but the extent can be controlled if you have an understanding of the process, employ the correct pastry-making technique and remember to rest the pastry to prevent shrinkage. The most important point to remember about gluten and pastry making is that overworking (or kneading) the pastry will continue to develop the gluten and result in tough pastry, as will adding too much liquid.

Fat

Although there are some types of pastry that are made using oil, the fat used in traditional pastry is one that is solid at room temperature. These include:

Lard An excellent fat for creating shortness, such a prized quality in pastry. However, it is relatively tasteless, so a combination of lard and butter is often used in shortcrust pastry. White vegetable shortening is a suitable vegetarian substitute for lard.

Butter The perfect fat, as it provides both shortness and flavour. Many chefs prefer unsalted butter, as it has a fresher, purer flavour, but salted butter can be used in all recipes. You will need to adjust the amount of salt added to the pastry according to the type of butter used.

Margarine This will produce a short pastry. However, it softens very quickly and doesn't provide the same rich flavour that butter does.

Making pastry in a food processor

The rubbing in can be done in the large bowl of a food processor. It is important to make sure the butter is fully rubbed in, so look for a uniform coloured crumb with no lumps of butter within the flour. It is best to then transfer the crumb to a bowl and add the liquid by hand, to avoid overworking and adding too much liquid.

Chilling pastry

Fat softens as it is incorporated into flour, so pastry needs to be chilled to let the butter firm up and prevent the pastry from becoming greasy. Chilling also relaxes the gluten, slowing continued gluten development that can make pastry tough.

For layered pastry, the fat must be kept cool to avoid it melting into the layering dough, which would seal the layers together and prevent the pastry from rising. For hot water crust pastry, which use melted fats, the chilling is essential in order to be able to mould the pastry into shape.

However, the most important time to chill pastry is once it is shaped and before it is baked. This firming of the butter sets the pastry case into the desired shape so that when it is baked, the butter melds with the flour immediately to create a bond. If not sufficiently chilled, the butter will melt and the result will be greasy, misshapen pastry.

To chill pastry, wrap closely in cling film or a plastic bag to prevent the surface from drying out. Most pastries need at least 30 minutes in the fridge to chill until firm to the touch. Some, such as pâte sucrée and hot water crust that use soft or melted butter, will need to chill for longer. If you are short of time, you can chill pastry in the freezer.

Shortcrust pastry

As the name implies, shortcrust has a short, tender crumb, and it is used in sweet and savoury recipes. The most important element of the technique is rubbing the fat into the flour, which coats the flour with fat and creates a fine crumb. The fat acts as a protector around the grains of flour and hinders the development of gluten, which would make the pastry tough. You should need only a small amount of liquid to bring the crumb together and make the pastry manageable. Using as little liquid as possible to bind the dough also helps to achieve a tender crumb.

Rich shortcrust pastry

Makes enough to line a 24cm flan ring
250g plain flour
Pinch of salt
140g chilled butter
2 egg yolks
3–4 tbsp chilled water

Shortcrust is traditionally made with a combination of lard and butter. Lard lends a superior shortness but lacks the flavour of butter, so we generally use all butter.

1 Sift the flour and salt into a medium bowl.

2 Cut the butter into small pieces and add to the flour. Using 2 cutlery knives and working in a scissor action, cut the butter into the flour, keeping the 2 knives in contact. Using knives rather than fingers helps to keep the butter and flour cool.

3 Once the butter has been broken down to small pea-sized pieces, use your fingertips to gently rub the little pieces of flour and butter together.

4 Give the bowl an occasional shake to lift larger lumps of butter to the surface. The mixture should become a uniform fine, pale crumb with no visible lumps of butter. If the mixture begins to turn yellow, the butter is softening too quickly and you need to put the bowl in the fridge for 5–10 minutes to chill the butter.

5 Mix the egg yolks and water together in a small bowl with a fork until evenly combined. Add 2–2½ tbsp of the yolk mixture to the crumb and, using a cutlery knife, distribute the liquid as quickly as possible (this will create flakes of pastry).

6 Pull some of the flakes to the side and feel them; if they are very dry, add a little more of the liquid to any dry areas of crumb and use the knife again. Don't be tempted to add too much liquid, as it can make the pastry tough. Once you think the flakes will come together, stop adding liquid.

7 Use the flat of the knife to bring a few of the flakes and dry crumb together, to create larger lumps. At this stage the pastry should be uniform in colour, not streaky. Continue like this until there are no dry crumbs in the bottom of the bowl.

8 Pull the pastry together with your hands, shaping it into a flat disc, about 10cm in diameter and 1.5cm thick. Do this as quickly as possible, without overworking the pastry, which also makes it tough.

9 Wrap the pastry in cling film and chill for 20–30 minutes before rolling out. This will relax it and prevent too much shrinkage, as well as firm up the butter.

Variations

Herb rich shortcrust pastry Add ½–1 tbsp chopped herbs such as thyme, rosemary, oregano or sage to the crumb mixture before the liquid.

Cheese rich shortcrust pastry Reduce the butter to 110g and add 30g finely grated hard cheese, such as Cheddar or Parmesan, before the liquid.

Wholemeal shortcrust pastry Use wholemeal flour in place of plain, omit the egg yolk and use 80g butter and 45g lard. You will need a little extra water too.

Plain shortcrust pastry For a less rich pastry, use 80g butter and 45g lard and omit the egg yolks. It may be necessary to add up to 1 tbsp extra water.

Sweet rich shortcrust pastry Add 2–3 tsp caster sugar before the liquid.

1 Sifting the flour and salt into the bowl.

2 Cutting the butter into the flour.

3 Gently rubbing the fat and flour together with the fingertips.

4 Checking the evenness of the crumb.

5 Adding the beaten egg yolks and water.

6 Using a cutlery knife to mix in the liquid.

7 Drawing the pastry together with the knife.

8 Bringing the pastry together into a ball.

9 Wrapping the disc of pastry in cling film.

Rolling pastry

An efficient rolling technique helps to ensure pastry is not stretched or overworked (which can cause excessive shrinkage during baking). It also helps to prevent the pastry from warming up during the shaping and lining process, which makes it difficult to handle and can result in greasy pastry.

After chilling the pastry in the fridge, remove it when it is cold and firm to the touch, not completely hard or it will crack when rolled; it should be just pliable. If it has been chilled for more than 2–3 hours, remove from the fridge and leave at room temperature for 5 minutes before rolling, to soften it slightly.

Use only as much flour on the work surface as you need to prevent the pastry from sticking, and no more (although a little more is useful when rolling out layered pastries). Flour the rolling pin too, but avoid sprinkling flour over the pastry itself, or it can result in grey, floury patches.

1 First 'ridge' the pastry disc: hold the rolling pin in both hands loosely and tap it lightly over the entire surface of the pastry once or twice. Turn the pastry 90° and ridge again. Repeat until the circle has at least doubled in size. Don't turn the pastry over; it is unnecessary and can result in overworking.

2 Once the circle has at least doubled in size, start to roll it. Use 3 short, sharp strokes of the rolling pin, rather than one long roll. Turn the pastry 90° after every few rolls.

3 Once the pastry is rolled to the required thickness (usually about 3mm), the pastry should be an even thickness and circular in shape with no excessive cracking at the edges.

A note on ridging...

Ridging is much gentler on the pastry than rolling, so try to continue as long as possible before starting to roll. Ridging layered pastry helps to preserve the layers, and is also a useful technique when you are trying to roll out fridge-cold pastry. More often than not pastry has to be rolled into a disc, so turning the pastry 90° every few ridges and rolls will help to keep the pastry in a circle. Avoid twisting and turning the rolling pin as this will stretch the pastry unevenly. If the pastry starts to crack a little at the edges, stop ridging and seal the crack with your fingertips.

A note on rolling...

Always turn the pastry rather than the rolling pin. Use a loose grip on the rolling pin and avoid applying too much pressure when the rolling pin comes into contact with the pastry; you just need a light pressure to encourage the pastry gently to expand, not stretch. Also be aware that your dominant hand will be stronger and may push down a little more firmly than your other hand; even pressure is important for the end result.

Lining a flan tin or ring

When making a pastry case, for ease of unmoulding we generally use a loose-based metal flan tin or flan ring (without a base) placed on a baking sheet. If you do not have either of these, use a solid metal tin, or if none of these is available, a ceramic flan dish is the next best thing. Most of the recipes in this chapter were made using a 24cm diameter flan ring, 2.5–2.8cm deep.

1 Roll the pastry to a circle large enough to line the bottom and sides of the flan tin or ring. You can work out the diameter of pastry needed by measuring the tin or ring from side to side with a piece of string and checking this against the rolled out pastry. However, with practice it is easy to measure by eye.

2 Carefully wrap the pastry once over the rolling pin to support it and place it over the flan tin or ring, set on a baking sheet, with the side of the pastry that was uppermost when rolling now against the baking sheet.

3 Gently lift the overhanging pastry up a little, encouraging the pastry inside the tin or ring to fit snugly, right down to the corners. Now start to lift the edges of the pastry out and over the edge of the tin or ring.

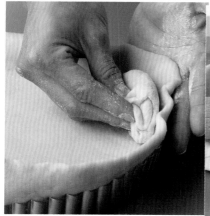

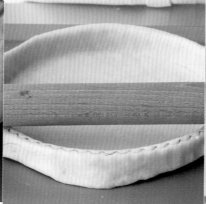

4 Tear a small piece from the excess and use it to push the pastry well into the corners. (You could use the side of your knuckle instead.) Ensure the pastry is smoothed up the sides of the flan tin or ring and folded over the edge.

5 Using a rolling pin and starting from the middle of the flan tin or ring, roll away from you and cut through the pastry, removing the excess. Turn the baking sheet around and repeat.

6 Working your way around the edge with your thumbnail, release the pastry a little from the flan tin or ring, then neaten and smooth the top rim of pastry. Cover the pastry closely with cling film and chill until ready to use.

A note on lining...

Avoid stretching and pulling the pastry as you line the flan tin or ring. Note that it is important to get the pastry well into the corners, or it will fall into them as it bakes and cause uneven shrinkage around the top edge.

Baking pastry blind

When a pastry case is filled with a custard or liquid filling, it is difficult to get the pastry cooked through by the time the filling is set. Pre-baking or 'baking blind' ensures that the pastry is cooked properly. Most, but not all, tarts call for this.

Before baking blind, chill the pastry case for at least 30 minutes, to firm the butter so that the pastry will hold its shape. Heat the oven to 200°C/gas mark 6.

1 Make a cartouche of greaseproof paper, 8–10cm bigger than the tart tin (see page 13). Scrunch it up, then unfold it and use to line the pastry case. Add a layer of dried beans or ceramic baking beans and fold the edge of the paper over the edge of the flan ring.

2 Bake for 15–20 minutes in the upper third of the oven until the sides are set. To check, remove from the oven and carefully pull the cartouche away from the pastry. If the pastry is holding up and looking less translucent and grey, remove the beans and gently tweak out the cartouche.

3 Return the pastry to a lower shelf of the oven for about 5 minutes, or until the base of the pastry looks dry and feels sandy to touch, but has not taken on any colour. Remove from the oven and allow to cool slightly before using.

A note on baking blind...

The dried (or special-purpose ceramic) beans help to support the sides and edges of the flan case and weigh down the base to prevent it from rising in the oven. Scrunching up the cartouche first, before unfolding it, helps to get it into the edges of the pastry case, ensuring the sides are well supported by the beans. If you are blind baking individual tart cases, use small dried beans or rice.

Repairing holes or cracks

If you are adding a liquid filling to a pastry case it must be watertight. After baking blind, check the pastry carefully for little holes at the edges or cracks up the sides, which can cause leakages. To repair these, soften a little of the leftover pastry in your fingers and plug the holes (as shown), or lay a strip of raw pastry over a crack, being very gentle with the pastry case. Return the repaired pastry to a lower shelf of the oven for 5–10 minutes to cook the raw pastry.

Using egg white

To provide a protective seal between the blind baked pastry and a wet filling, so the pastry won't turn soggy, you can brush the pastry with lightly beaten egg white and return it to the oven for 3–4 minutes. This will also seal any very small holes.

Pea, asparagus and goat's cheese tart with thyme pastry

Serves 6

1 quantity herb rich shortcrust pastry
  (see page 478), made using thyme
Extra flour, to dust

For the filling

150g fresh podded or frozen peas
150g asparagus spears
100g soft goat's cheese
3 eggs
300ml double cream
Salt and ground white pepper

1 Roll out the chilled pastry on a lightly floured surface to a 3mm thickness and use to line a 24cm loose-based flan tin or flan ring set on a baking sheet (see page 481). Cover with cling film and chill in the fridge until firm to the touch. Wrap and chill any leftover pastry to use for repairs. Heat the oven to 200°C/gas mark 6.

2 Meanwhile, cook the peas in boiling salted water until tender, 3–4 minutes, then refresh in cold water. Snap off the woody ends of the asparagus, cut the spears into 7–8mm pieces, leaving the tips a little longer, then cook in boiling water for 2–3 minutes, depending on thickness, and refresh. Break the goat's cheese into small pieces.

3 Blind bake the pastry (see page 482) for 15–20 minutes, then remove the cartouche and beans and bake for a further 5 minutes, or until the pastry looks dry and feels sandy to the touch. Remove from the oven and reduce the oven temperature to 150°C/gas mark 2.

4 Put the eggs and cream into a small bowl and mix well with a fork. Pass this mixture through a sieve into a clean medium bowl.

5 Add the peas, asparagus and cheese to the egg and cream mixture. Taste and season with salt and white pepper.

6 Using a slotted spoon, spoon the peas, asparagus and cheese into the pastry case; they should half-fill the case. Pour the egg and cream mixture over the filling, making sure the pastry case is as full as possible.

7 Carefully transfer to a shelf in the lower third of the oven and bake the tart for 40–50 minutes until the custard is set. To check, give it a little shake; there should be no violent wobble in the centre and the filling should be a pale yellow colour and just a little soft in the centre. (An overcooked filling will feel springy to the touch and will rise up.)

8 Allow to cool slightly on the baking sheet, then remove the side of the tin, if using, and slide the tart onto a wire rack, or lift off the flan ring after transferring.

Variation

For a lighter version, replace half the double cream with half-fat crème fraîche.

....

A note on seasoning with pepper...

We use ground white pepper in egg custards as freshly ground black pepper can look unsightly if not ground fine enough, but if you prefer the flavour of black and don't mind the visual effect, feel free to use that instead.

Leek and Gruyère tart

Serves 6
1 quantity rich shortcrust pastry
(see page 478)
Extra flour, to dust

For the filling
2 small leeks, white part only
30g butter
100g Gruyère cheese
3 eggs
350ml double cream
Salt and ground white pepper

1 Roll out the chilled pastry on a lightly floured surface to a 3mm thickness and use to line a 24cm loose-based flan tin or flan ring set on a baking sheet (see page 481). Cover with cling film and chill in the fridge until firm to the touch. Wrap and chill any leftover pastry to use for repairs. Heat the oven to 200°C/gas mark 6.

2 Meanwhile, slice the leeks lengthways in half with the root still intact (holding the leek together), then thinly slice into half-rings and discard the root end. Wash well in cold water to remove any grit, then drain well.

3 Melt the butter in a small saucepan, add the leeks, cover with a damp cartouche (see page 13) and lid and sweat over a low heat until soft and slightly translucent (do not let them take on any colour). Drain the leeks or remove the lid and cartouche and allow the liquid to evaporate.

4 Blind bake the pastry (see page 482) for 15–20 minutes, then remove the cartouche and beans and bake for a further 5 minutes, or until the pastry looks dry and feels sandy to the touch. Remove from the oven and reduce the oven temperature to 150°C/gas mark 2.

5 Put the eggs and cream into a small bowl and mix well with a fork. Pass this mixture through a sieve into a clean medium bowl. Grate the cheese.

6 Add the sweated leeks and 85g of the grated cheese to the egg and cream mixture. Taste and season with salt and white pepper.

7 Using a slotted spoon, spoon the leeks and cheese into the pastry; they should half-fill the case. Pour the egg and cream mixture over the filling, making sure the case is as full as possible. Sprinkle over the remaining cheese.

8 Carefully transfer to a shelf in the lower third of the oven and bake the tart for 40–50 minutes until the custard is pale yellow colour and just a little soft in the centre. To check, give the tart a little shake; there should be no violent wobble in the centre. (An overcooked filling will rise up and feel springy to the touch.)

9 Allow to cool slightly on the baking sheet, then remove the side of the tin, if using, and slide the tart onto a wire rack, or lift off the flan ring after transferring. Serve slightly warm or at room temperature.

Variations

For a lighter filling, replace half the cream with half-fat crème fraîche or milk.

Quiche Lorraine Replace the leeks with 1 onion, diced and sweated as for the leeks, and add 75g streaky bacon, diced and sautéed until golden, to the egg and cream mixture.

Mustard and leek tart Spread 1–1½ tbsp wholegrain mustard over the base of the baked pastry case before adding the filling. Use Gruyère instead of Cheddar.

Crab and chive tart Omit the leeks and Gruyère and add 150g white crab meat and ½–1 tbsp chopped chives to the egg and cream mixture. Replace 100ml of the double cream with crème fraîche and use 2 whole eggs and 1 yolk in place of the 3 eggs.

Smoked haddock and watercress tart Omit the leeks and Gruyère and add 200g poached, pin-boned and flaked smoked haddock to the egg and cream mixture, with a large handful of blanched and refreshed baby watercress sprigs and 75g grated Cheddar. Before cooking, lift some sprigs of watercress to the surface, for colour.

Double crust apple pie

Serves 6–8
2 x quantity sweet rich shortcrust pastry
  (see page 478)
Extra flour, to dust

For the filling
1 Bramley apple
6 Golden Delicious apples
75–100g caster sugar
½–1 tsp ground cinnamon
¼ tsp ground cloves
50g raisins
2 tbsp plain flour

1 Cut the chilled pastry in half and reshape into 2 discs. Wrap one disc closely in cling film and place in the fridge. Roll the remaining disc on a lightly floured surface to a large circle, 2–3mm thick. Use to line a 24cm pie dish and carefully trim off the excess using a sharp knife. Save any trimmings for decorating the top of the pie. Cover with cling film and place in the fridge to chill.

2 Roll out the second disc into a large circle, big enough to cover the pie, about 2–3mm thick, and place on a baking sheet. Cover with cling film and place in the fridge to chill.

3 To make the filling, peel, quarter and core all the apples and cut into 5mm thick slices. Place in a large bowl and sprinkle with the sugar, cinnamon and cloves. Stir through the raisins, sprinkle in the flour and toss together to mix.

4 Heat the oven to 200°C/gas mark 6. Place a flat baking sheet on a lower shelf in the oven to provide 'bottom heat'.

5 Remove the pie case from the fridge and fill with the apple mixture, ensuring the pie case is generously filled.

6 Remove the pastry lid from the fridge. Brush the rim of the pie case with a little water and place the pastry lid on top of the apples, pressing down a little on the edge of the pie dish to seal the pastry.

7 Trim the pastry edges to neaten, then crimp the edge (as shown on page 636). Make a steam hole in the centre of the pie and decorate with pastry trimmings, if desired. The trimmings should be rolled very thinly, to about 1–2mm, and stuck to the top of the pie with a little water.

8 Stand the pie dish on the hot baking sheet in the oven and bake for 30 minutes to cook the bottom pastry before the top browns too much. Lower the oven setting to 180°C/gas mark 4, transfer the pie on its baking sheet to the top third of the oven and continue to cook until the pastry is golden and the filling hot (test with a skewer through the steam hole). Remove from the oven. Allow to cool slightly before serving, with custard, ice cream or pouring cream.

Variations

Cherry pie Replace the apple filling with 1kg pitted red cherries mixed with 2½ tbsp cornflour and 100–125g caster sugar.

Apple pie (top crust only) Make 1 quantity sweet rich shortcrust pastry only. Roll out to a disc at least 2–3cm bigger than the top of the pie dish and about 3mm thick. Cut a strip of pastry from the edge of the disc, the same width as the lip of the pie dish. Chill all the pastry on a baking sheet. Put the filling straight into the unlined dish. Press the strip of pastry onto the rim of the pie dish and lightly dampen with water. Lay the pastry disc over the apples, pressing the edge down a little on the rim of the pie dish to seal. Continue with step 7 of the main recipe. Bake the pie in the top of the oven preheated to 180°C/gas mark 4 for 35–45 minutes until the apples are hot and the pastry is cooked and golden in colour.

....
A note on using a pie funnel...
If making a large single crust pie, to ensure the pastry is held up over the filling, it may be necessary to stand a pie funnel in the middle of the dish. This will support the pastry, holding it above the filling and helping to keep it crisp.

Lemon meringue pie

Serves 6

1 quantity sweetened rich shortcrust
  pastry (see page 478)
Extra flour, to dust

For the filling

4 tbsp cornflour
200g caster sugar
300ml water
4 egg yolks
2 large lemons

For the meringue

4 egg whites
200g caster sugar, plus a little extra
  to sprinkle

1 Roll out the chilled pastry on a lightly floured surface to a 3mm thickness and use to line a 24cm flan ring (see page 481) set on a baking sheet. (You can use a loose-based flan tin, but a ring works better here.) Cover with cling film and chill in the fridge until firm to the touch. Heat the oven to 200°C/gas mark 6.

2 Blind bake the pastry (see page 482) for 15–20 minutes, then remove the beans and cartouche and bake for a further 5 minutes, or until the pastry looks dry and feels sandy to the touch. Remove from the oven and reduce the oven temperature to 180°C/gas mark 4.

3 Meanwhile, to make the filling, put the cornflour and sugar in a saucepan and stir in the water to create a smooth paste, then place over a medium heat and bring to the boil, stirring constantly; it will become thick and translucent. Take off the heat, cool slightly, then beat in the egg yolks. Pass through a sieve into a bowl.

4 Finely grate the zest of the lemons, squeeze the juice and add three-quarters of each to the egg mixture. Taste and adjust with more lemon zest, juice or sugar.

5 Pour the still-warm filling into the warm pastry case and place on a shelf in the middle of the oven for about 10 minutes until a skin has formed on the surface.

6 Meanwhile, to make the meringue topping, whisk the egg whites to stiff peaks (see page 161) in a large bowl, then add 4 tbsp of the sugar, 1 tbsp at a time, whisking after each addition to return the meringue to stiff peaks. Gradually whisk in the remaining sugar until the meringue becomes very stiff and shiny.

7 Remove the flan ring, if using. Pile the meringue onto the lemon filling, working from the edge towards the centre and mounding the filling slightly in the middle. Sprinkle with a little sugar and bake for 10–15 minutes until lightly browned.

8 Let the tart cool slightly, then carefully remove from the flan tin, if using. Slide it onto a wire rack and allow to cool a little before serving, for the filling to set.

Treacle tart

Serves 6

1 quantity sweetened rich shortcrust
  pastry (see page 478)
Extra flour, to dust

For the filling

3 eggs
100g fresh white breadcrumbs
1 lemon
1cm piece of fresh root ginger
450g golden syrup

1 Roll out the chilled pastry on a lightly floured surface to a 3mm thickness and use to line a 24cm loose-based flan tin or flan ring set on a baking sheet (see page 481). Cover with cling film and chill until firm to the touch.

2 Heat the oven to 190°C/gas mark 5 and put a baking sheet in the top third of the oven (this will provide some 'bottom heat', as the pastry is not baked blind).

3 Beat the eggs and pass through a sieve into a bowl. Put the breadcrumbs through a coarse sieve to remove any lumps. Finely grate the zest of the lemon and squeeze the juice. Peel and finely grate the ginger. Add the golden syrup and breadcrumbs to the eggs with ¼–½ tsp lemon zest, ½–1 tsp juice and ¼–½ tsp ginger, to taste.

4 Slowly ladle the mixture into the pastry case, then carefully slide the flan tin or baking sheet onto the hot baking sheet in the oven. Bake for 20–25 minutes; if the filling starts to rise up, lower the oven setting to 150°C/gas mark 2.

5 If the oven hasn't been turned down, do so now and move the tart on its baking sheet to the bottom third of the oven. Bake for a further 20–30 minutes until set.

6 Allow the tart to cool slightly on the baking sheet, then remove the side of the tin, if using, and slide the tart onto a wire rack, or lift off the ring after transferring.

Pear and almond tart

Serves 6

1 quantity sweetened rich shortcrust
  pastry (see page 478)
Extra flour, to dust
2 firm, ripe large pears
½ quantity warm apricot glaze
  (see page 642)

For the frangipane

150g blanched almonds
1 egg, plus 2 extra yolks
150g butter, softened
150g caster sugar
3 tbsp Poire William liqueur, or brandy
45g plain flour

1 Roll out the chilled pastry on a lightly floured surface to a 3mm thickness and use to line a 24cm loose-based flan tin or flan ring set on a baking sheet (see page 481). Cover with cling film and chill in the fridge until firm to the touch. Heat the oven to 200°C/gas mark 6.

2 Meanwhile, to make the frangipane, blend the almonds in a food processor to a very fine crumb (if too coarse they will not bind the frangipane). Beat the egg and extra yolks in a bowl.

3 Beat the butter in a separate bowl until softened, then gradually beat in the sugar, in 4 or 5 additions, until fully incorporated. Gradually add the eggs, beating well after each addition. Stir in the Poire William, add the almonds and flour and stir well to combine evenly.

4 Blind bake the pastry (see page 482) for 15–20 minutes, then remove the cartouche and beans and bake for a further 5 minutes, or until the pastry looks dry and feels sandy to the touch. Remove from the oven and leave to cool. Reduce the oven temperature to 180°C/gas mark 4.

5 Spread the frangipane evenly over the base of the cooled pastry case. Quarter and core the pears and thinly slice across the width of the pear quarters (not with the length) into small slices, keeping the slices together.

6 Take a sliced quarter of pear, fan it out a little and place it on the frangipane so the top end of the pear is at the middle of the tart and the pear extends to the edge of the tin in fanned out slices, radiating from the centre like the spokes of a wheel. Arrange the remaining pear quarters in the same way to make 6 or 8 spokes. (You may not need all of the second pear or you may need to add extra slices from the remaining 2 pear quarters if you have 6 spokes.)

7 Press the pears down gently into the frangipane a little. Bake in the middle of the oven for 30–40 minutes until the frangipane has risen a little, is pale golden and has set. To check, insert a skewer into the middle; it should come out clean. Leave to cool slightly on the baking sheet, then remove the side of the tin, if using, and slide the tart onto a wire rack, or lift off the flan ring after transferring.

8 While the tart is still warm, brush only the pears with the warm apricot glaze. The tart is best served between warm and room temperature on the day it is made, but it will still be delicious the following day.

Note This frangipane can be used for a variety of recipes. Grinding whole almonds yourself gives the best flavour, but you can use ground almonds if necessary.

Variations

You can leave the cored pears in quarters, or even halves, instead of thinly slicing them. Very firm pears can be poached first (see page 540).

Apricot and almond tart Replace the Poire William in the frangipane with Amaretto. Replace the pears with 1 quantity poached apricots (see page 539, omitting the spices), halved and placed cut side down over the frangipane.

Plum and almond tart Replace the Poire William with rum and the pears with 4–6 plums, depending on size. Halve and stone the plums and place cut side down in the frangipane.

Tarte tatin

Serves 6–8
For the pastry
170g plain flour, plus extra to dust
55g ground rice
Pinch of salt
140g butter
50g caster sugar
1 egg

For the filling
1.5kg dessert apples
1 lemon
100g butter
100g granulated sugar

This version of a classic tarte tatin adds ground rice to a basic shortcrust pastry, which produces a delicious texture, although puff pastry is more traditional (see page 508). You will need a tatin mould or a heavy-based ovenproof frying pan, about 24cm in diameter, that will fit in your oven.

1 To make the pastry, sift the flour, ground rice and salt into a large bowl. Cut the butter into small pieces and add to the bowl. Using 2 cutlery knives and working in a scissor action, cut the butter into the flour, then rub it in with your fingertips until the mixture resembles fine breadcrumbs (see steps 2–4, page 478). Stir in the sugar. Beat the egg with a fork, then using a cutlery knife, add enough to bind the dough together.

2 Shape the pastry into a flat disc, place between 2 sheets of baking parchment and roll gently to a circle the size of your ovenproof frying pan, no thinner than 5mm. Chill in the fridge until firm.

3 Peel, quarter and core the apples and finely grate the lemon zest. Heat the oven to 190°C/gas mark 5.

4 Melt the butter in the frying pan over a low heat. Add the sugar and continue to cook gently until the sugar has started to melt and turn a toffee colour.

5 Arrange the first layer of apple quarters, rounded side down, on top of the melted butter and sugar. Sprinkle over the lemon zest and continue to layer on the apples, with the next layer rounded side up and fitting neatly in the spaces in the bottom layer.

6 Continue to cook over a low to medium heat. Initially the apples will release juice and prevent the butter and sugar from caramelising, but as the juice mixes with the butter and sugar it will become a homogeneous sauce. Then as the juice evaporates, the butter and sugar will begin to caramelise again. Continue cooking until deep golden, and the apples have taken on the same colour, about 15–20 minutes; you will be able to smell the change as the apples and sugar caramelise. You may need to move the frying pan around over the heat to ensure even caramelisation. Carefully lift up the apples from time to time, using a palette knife, to check the underside (as shown).

7 Remove from the heat and place the frying pan on a lipped baking tray.

8 Remove the pastry from the fridge and peel away one layer of parchment. Lay the pastry on top of the apples and peel off the other layer of parchment. Press down lightly, particularly over the edge of the frying pan (as shown) so that the heat of the frying pan cuts through the pastry. Remove any excess pastry. Transfer to the oven and bake for 25–30 minutes until the pastry is golden.

9 Remove from the oven and allow to cool slightly for a few minutes. Now carefully invert a plate over the frying pan (as shown) and turn both the frying pan and plate over, so the frying pan is uppermost. Ideally, cover your forearms as you do this to protect them from any hot caramel that may be released. Lower the plate and frying pan to the work surface and carefully lift off the frying pan to reveal the golden apples and caramel sauce. Best served warm, with ice cream, pouring cream or crème fraîche.

Note If you do not have a suitable ovenproof frying pan, caramelise the butter and sugar in a frying pan, then tip into an ovenproof dish. Lay the apples in as for the main recipe, cover with the pastry and bake in the oven, inverting it in the same way once cooked. The apples may not be as well caramelised, though.

Pâte sucrée

This is an enriched version of shortcrust pastry, with extra butter and egg yolks replacing the water. We use a traditional method of making pâte sucrée by hand, although it can be made in a food processor. It tends to be cooked at a slightly lower temperature than shortcrust because of its high fat and sugar content, as fats and sugars both encourage browning. It should be thoroughly cooked but only to a very pale biscuit colour. Once cooked, it needs to be released from tins or baking trays while still warm, or the pastry will stick.

Pâte sucrée

Makes enough to line a 24cm flan ring
250g plain flour
Pinch of salt
125g unsalted butter, softened
125g caster sugar
4 small egg yolks
2–3 drops of vanilla extract

1 Sift the flour and salt onto a clean work surface and, using the side of your hand, spread the flour out into a large ring.

2 Place the softened butter, in one piece, in the middle and, using the fingertips of one hand, push down ('peck') on the butter to soften it a little more, but without it becoming greasy; it should be soft, but still cold. It is important that the butter is uniformly soft, as if there are still small lumps of cold, hard butter in the mixture they can cause greasiness and holes in the finished pastry.

3 Sprinkle over the sugar and 'peck' until the sugar is just fully incorporated.

4 Add the egg yolks and vanilla extract and continue to 'peck' until the egg yolk is fully incorporated and there is no colour streakiness.

5 Using a palette knife, flick all the flour onto the butter, sugar and egg yolks and, using the edge of the palette knife, 'chop' the flour into the butter and sugar mixture. This technique helps to keep the flour from being overworked. Use the palette knife to lift any flour left on the work surface to the top occasionally.

6 As you continue to do this, you will create large flakes of pastry. Continue until there are no obvious dry floury bits among the pastry; it should be a fairly uniform colour. Floury patches at this stage will mean having to overwork the pastry at the next stage to incorporate them.

7 Now shape the pastry into a long sausage and, using the palette knife on its side, scrape a little of the large flakes together at a time. This will finally bring the pastry together and is called 'fraisering'. As more pastry sticks to the palette knife, scrape it off using a cutlery knife to avoid overworking it. Continue in this manner until all the pastry is fraisered: one or two more fraiserings are possible, but the more you fraiser the more the pastry will be overworked.

8 Bring the pastry together with your hands to form a ball.

9 Now shape the pastry into a flat disc. Wrap well in cling film and chill to allow the butter to firm up before rolling out.

Variation

Almond pastry (pâte frollée) Replace 100g of the flour with ground almonds. Increase the butter to 150g, reduce the sugar to 100g and use 3 egg yolks (not 4).

Making pâte sucrée in a food processor...

Place the softened butter and sugar in the bowl of a food processor and pulse until fully combined. Add the egg yolks and vanilla and pulse again until fully incorporated. Add the flour and salt and pulse quickly until all the flour has been incorporated into the butter, sugar and egg yolk mixture and it has a uniform colour and texture. Remove from the food processor and bring the pastry together in your hands before chilling.

1 Spreading the sifted flour into a large ring.

2 'Pecking' the butter to soften it.

3 'Pecking' the sugar and butter together.

4 Incorporating the egg yolks and vanilla.

5 'Chopping' the flour into the mixture.

6 Creating large flakes of pastry by 'chopping'.

7 'Fraisering' the pastry with the palette knife to bring it together.

8 Bringing the pastry together to form a ball.

9 Shaping the pastry into a flat disc.

Lemon tart

Serves 6
1 quantity pâte sucrée (see page 492)
Extra flour, to dust

For the filling
3 lemons
6 eggs, plus 1 extra yolk
150–170g caster sugar
225ml double cream
Icing sugar, to dust

1 To make the filling, finely grate the zest of the lemons and squeeze the juice; you will need about 100–125ml juice. Put the eggs and extra yolk into a large bowl, add 150g of the sugar and, using a balloon whisk, mix well. Add the cream, zest and juice, and stir until combined. Cover and chill in the fridge for 2–3 hours, preferably overnight, to allow the flavours to develop.

2 Roll out the pâte sucrée on a lightly floured surface into a disc about 30cm in diameter and about 3mm thick. Use to line a 24cm loose-based flan tin or flan ring set on a baking sheet (see page 481). Cover with cling film and chill until very firm to the touch. Meanwhile, heat the oven to 190°C/gas mark 5.

3 Once firm, blind bake the pastry (see page 482) for 15–20 minutes, ensuring the paper cartouche is pushed well into the corners of the pastry and the excess paper is folded over the edge of the pastry case, to help prevent the pastry from browning. Remove the beans and cartouche, taking care as the pastry is still very soft, and bake for a further 5 minutes. Remove from the oven and reduce the oven temperature to 150°C/gas mark 2.

4 Taste the filling. If it seems too sharp, add some or all of the remaining sugar, to taste. Strain into a jug and pour the filling into the pastry case, filling it about half full. Transfer the tart to the oven and pour in more filling until the tart is as full as possible. Bake for 40–50 minutes until almost set, with a very soft wobble across the surface. A violent ripple across the middle of the filling indicates it is not set.

5 Take the tart out of the oven as soon as the filling is set, allow it to cool a little, then carefully remove the sides of the tin or flan ring. Leave to cool completely, then dust with icing sugar. You can glaze the icing sugar dusting using a kitchen blowtorch if you wish, but take care not to burn the pastry.

French apple flan

Serves 6
1 quantity pâte sucrée (see page 492)
Extra flour, to dust

For the filling
1–1.25kg large dessert apples
1–2 tbsp caster sugar
1 quantity warm apricot glaze
  (see page 642)

1 Roll out the pâte sucrée on a lightly floured surface into a disc about 30cm in diameter and about 3mm thick. Use to line a 24cm loose-based flan tin or flan ring set on a baking sheet (see page 481). Cover with cling film and chill in the fridge until very firm to the touch. Meanwhile, heat the oven to 190°C/gas mark 5.

2 Once firm, blind bake the pastry (see page 482) for 15–20 minutes, ensuring the paper cartouche is pushed well into the corners of the pastry and the excess paper is folded over the edge of the pastry case, to help prevent the pastry from browning. Remove the beans and cartouche, taking care as the pastry is still very soft, and bake for a further 5 minutes. Remove from the oven and reduce the oven temperature to 180°C/gas mark 4.

3 Peel, quarter, core and slice the apples as thinly as possible. Layer them in the pastry case, packing them in tightly and layering so they come above the level of the pastry (they will shrink). Arrange the last layer in a neat, overlapping circle.

4 Sprinkle the apples with the sugar. Bake the tart in the oven for 25–30 minutes, or until the apples are soft and the pastry is a deep golden. Use the tip of a cutlery knife to check the apples; it should pass through easily.

5 Remove the flan from the oven and allow to cool a little, then remove the side of the tin, if using, and slide the tart onto a wire rack, or lift off the flan ring after transferring. Brush the warm apricot glaze over the apples and serve.

Chocolate tart

Serves 8
1 quantity pâte sucrée (see page 492)
Extra flour, to dust

For the filling
300ml double cream
50g caster sugar
275g good quality dark chocolate,
  minimum 60% cocoa solids
60g unsalted butter
3 eggs, plus 2 extra yolks

1 Roll out the pâte sucrée on a lightly floured surface into a disc about 30cm in diameter and about 3mm thick. Use to line a 24cm loose-based flan tin or flan ring set on a baking sheet (see page 481). Cover with cling film and chill in the fridge until very firm to the touch. Meanwhile, heat the oven to 190°C/gas mark 5.

2 Once firm, blind bake the pastry (see page 482) for 15–20 minutes, ensuring the paper cartouche is pushed well into the corners of the pastry and the excess is folded over the edge of the pastry case, to help prevent it from browning. Remove the beans and cartouche, taking care as the pastry is still very soft, and bake for a further 5 minutes. Remove from the oven and reduce the oven temperature to 150°C/gas mark 2.

3 To make the filling, put the cream and sugar into a medium saucepan and bring to a simmer over a medium heat. Break the chocolate into pieces, cut the butter into cubes and put both into a bowl. Pour the hot cream over the chocolate and butter and stir until melted, then keep stirring until the mixture is shiny and glossy.

4 Beat the eggs and yolks well with a fork in a separate bowl. Add to the chocolate and cream mixture, stir well, then pass the mixture through a sieve into a jug.

5 Carefully pour the filling into the pastry case and transfer to a shelf in the middle to lower part of the oven. Bake for 25–30 minutes until softly set. Remove from the oven and leave to cool completely. Serve the tart at room temperature.

Individual fruit tarts

Makes 8
1 quantity pâte sucrée (see page 492)
Extra flour, to dust

For the filling
1 quantity crème pâtissière with
  100–150ml whipped cream folded in
  (see page 134)
Selection of summer berries or plums,
  peaches, apricots or oranges
1 quantity redcurrant glaze for red fruits
  or apricot glaze for lighter coloured
  fruits (see page 642)

1 Divide the pastry into 8 equal pieces and reshape into flat discs. Cover all but one of the discs with cling film and put in the fridge. On a lightly floured surface, roll out the disc to a circle about 13cm in diameter and 2mm thick. Use to line a 10cm loose-based flan tin (see page 481).

2 Cover with cling film, transfer to the fridge and repeat with the remaining discs of pastry.

3 Chill all the pastry cases until completely firm to the touch. Meanwhile, heat the oven to 190°C/gas mark 5.

4 Once firm, blind bake the individual pastry cases in the oven (see page 482) for 10–15 minutes, ensuring the paper cartouches are pushed well into the corners of the pastry and the excess paper is folded over the edge of the cases, to help prevent the pastry from browning. Remove the beans and cartouches, taking care as the pastry is still very soft and thin, and bake for a further 5 minutes, still not allowing the pastry to colour. Remove the cooked tart cases from the oven.

5 Leave the tart cases to cool for a minute, then release them from the tins while still warm (or they will stick as they cool down), being very gentle as they are delicate. Transfer to a wire rack and leave to cool completely.

6 Put the crème pâtissière into a piping bag fitted with a 7mm–1cm nozzle and pipe into the pastry cases as neatly as possible. It should come just below the rim of the pastry.

7 Hull, stone and slice or segment the fruit as necessary. Arrange the fruit carefully on each tart, covering the cream and overlapping any sliced or segmented fruit. Glaze the fruit, not the pastry, with the redcurrant or apricot glaze.

Pâte sablée

Like pâte sucrée, this is an enriched pastry, but made with icing sugar (not caster), which gives it a much finer, shorter and more tender crumb. In the same way as pâte sucrée, it can be made in a food processor (see page 476), though we prefer to make it by hand. It must be cooked through, but only to a very pale biscuit colour and it needs to be released from tins or trays while still warm to avoid sticking.

Pâte sablée

Makes '1 quantity'
250g plain flour
Pinch of salt
200g unsalted butter, softened
100g icing sugar
2 egg yolks
2–3 drops of vanilla extract

1 Sift the flour and salt onto a clean work surface and, using the side of your hand, spread the flour out into a large ring.

2 Place the softened butter, in one piece, in the middle of the ring and, using the fingertips of one hand, push down, or 'peck' on the butter to soften it a little more, but without it becoming shiny and greasy; it should be uniformly soft, but still cold (see step 2, page 492). It is important that there are no small lumps of cold, hard butter as these can cause greasiness and holes in the pastry.

3 Sprinkle over the icing sugar and continue to 'peck' until the sugar is just fully incorporated; it should be quickly absorbed.

4 Add the egg yolks and vanilla extract to the butter and sugar mix and continue to 'peck' until the egg yolk is fully incorporated and there is no colour streakiness.

5 Using a palette knife, flick all the flour onto the butter, sugar and egg yolks and, using the edge of the palette knife, 'chop' the flour into the butter and sugar mix (see step 5, page 492). This technique helps to keep the flour from being overworked. As you continue to do this, you will create large flakes of pastry. Continue until there are no obvious dry floury bits in the pastry; it should be a fairly uniform colour. Often sablée pastry does not require fraisering (see step 7, page 492), as it will have come together though the chopping process.

6 Finally, bring the pastry together with your hands and shape into a flat disc. Wrap well in cling film and chill to allow the butter to firm up. Before chilling, the pastry is too soft to roll out and shape.

Sablées aux fraises

Serves 4
1 quantity pâte sablée (see above)
Extra flour, to dust
2 small punnets of wild, or small cultivated, strawberries
1 quantity raspberry coulis (see page 136)

1 Roll out the pâte sablée on a lightly floured surface to about a 2mm thickness (the finished biscuits should be thin and crisp). Be quick and efficient when rolling as the pâte sablée softens very quickly. Using a 10cm plain pastry cutter, cut out 12 discs and lay them on a baking tray. Cover with cling film and chill in the fridge until firm to the touch. Meanwhile, heat the oven to 190°C/gas mark 5.

2 Bake the pastry discs for 6–8 minutes until evenly cooked and very pale, with just the barest hint of a biscuit colour; take care as they colour and brown quickly. Remove from the oven and leave to cool on the tray for a minute, then transfer them to a wire rack to cool completely.

3 Hull the strawberries and, if not very small, cut them in half. Fold them through about half of the raspberry coulis, to coat lightly and evenly.

4 To assemble the sablées, place a pastry disc on each of 4 plates and spoon a few strawberries on top; they need to be level for the next biscuit to be laid on top.

5 Add another pastry disc to each, then more strawberries and finally another pastry disc. Drizzle the remaining coulis around the plate and serve.

Layered pastries: rough puff, flaky and puff

Layered pastry consists of layer upon layer of very fine leaves of pastry created through a rolling and folding technique. It starts off by using the same method as shortcrust, but with less butter and more water to make the base, known as the détrempe, which is softer, stickier and less short than shortcrust. This is because some gluten development is needed to strengthen the layers. This base is then rolled out, fat incorporated, depending on the method, and the pastry folded and turned, with the process repeated to create layering. The aim is to create layers without allowing the incorporated fat to soften too much, and to trap as much air in the layering as possible. As the pastry bakes, the water turns to steam, helping the layers to separate and rise. The butter melts and is absorbed into the pastry layers.

You need to begin with cold or chilled ingredients and equipment. An efficient rolling and folding technique with short, quick strokes helps to keep the butter cool between the layers, which is crucial for a good, even rise. Maintaining shape and a uniform thickness is also important for even rising. If the pastry feels as though it is warming up and becoming elastic through overworking, chill it in the fridge. This will help to keep the butter firm. By resting it for a while, you are also helping to relax the gluten that has developed, making the pastry easier to roll.

Layered pastry needs to be cooked at a high temperature, to encourage rapid expansion of the air trapped between layers, to quickly separate and raise the layers, and to seal the butter into the pastry.

The layering technique

The objective is to incorporate the butter into the layers of détrempe (the pastry base) as thinly as possible, without allowing the butter to become greasy or melt.

Once the layering technique is mastered, you can make puff, rough puff or flaky pastry. The difference between these classic pastries is the quantity of fat used and at what stage the fat is incorporated, which helps to determine how high the pastry rises. The layered pastries are generally interchangeable between recipes, with puff the richest with the highest rise, followed by flaky, then rough puff.

The gluten development needed to strengthen the layers, protect the butter and help keep the layers separate does need to be limited and controlled, to ensure the pastry remains light, tender and does not shrink excessively.

Guidelines for making layered pastry

• Keep the ingredients cold at all times, particularly the butter and pastry, which should remain cold but pliable, when rolling and folding, and shaping. If the pastry warms too much, the fat will begin to melt and stick the layers together.

• Work efficiently, keeping an awareness of the temperature of the pastry at all times. Two sets of roll and folds should take no longer than 5 minutes.

• The détrempe should be soft rather than dry, and should be worked sufficiently to make it smooth and uniform in colour. Excess working will require a longer relaxing time for the dough.

• Develop an efficient ridging and rolling technique. Keep checking for straight sides and square corners and avoid creating ridges at the ends of the pastry. Also avoid rolling over the edges. Uniformity will ensure an even rise.

• Relaxing of the détrempe, and the pastry between roll and folds, will prevent overworking, stretching and shrinkage. Relaxing in the fridge will help to maintain the cold but pliable quality of the pastry, but if the pastry is left in the fridge too long then the butter will firm up too much and may break through the layers when rolled again.

• When relaxing pastry in the fridge, wrap it closely in cling film to ensure it doesn't dry out, and always make a note of the number of roll and folds that you have done, as it's easy to lose track.

• Avoid rolling the pastry too wide or long – it will become too large to manage easily and will become too thin, which will destroy layering. Conversely, avoid leaving it too thick – in this instance, the butter will not thin out enough so the pastry will be too heavy to rise properly and will bake to a greasy mass.

Rough puff

Here, all the butter is added to the détrempe, in large cubes. When the pastry is rolled and folded, the butter thins into large patches between layers, which helps to create a flakiness in the pastry but no defined, complete layers. Rough puff generally has 4 roll and folds, and rises about as much again as the thickness it is rolled. See page 498 for guidance on making layered pastry. Like puff pastry, rough puff can be prepared in advance; the same guidelines apply (see page 510).

Rough puff pastry

Makes about 500g
250g plain flour, plus extra to dust
Scant ½ tsp salt
150g cold but pliable unsalted butter
90–120ml (6–8 tbsp) chilled water

1 Sift the flour and salt into a medium bowl. Cut the butter into 1.5cm cubes and add to the bowl. Add 90ml cold water and, using a cutlery knife, mix together quickly and efficiently for about 15–20 seconds, turning the bowl as you stir.

2 The flour and water will form large flakes, some of them attaching themselves to the cubes of butter. Drag the large flakes to the side of the bowl and add more water, ½ tbsp at a time, to the dry flour and butter in the bottom of the bowl. Quickly stir again with the knife, to create large flakes, adding a little more water if necessary. You should not ideally add any more than about 8 tbsp water, or the pastry may start to toughen.

3 Feel the large flakes and, if there seems to be a good amount of moisture within them and the water is evenly distributed, pull the large flakes together with the butter and mould the pastry in your hands a little to bring the détrempe together.

4 Gather the détrempe into a ball; it should now be a homogeneous dough, with no dry, floury patches. The butter cubes will be dotted throughout the détrempe; try to cover any exposed butter with flour and water. Overworking with your hands will cause the butter to soften too much and become greasy. Shape the détrempe into a block about 12 x 17cm and 2–3cm thick, wrap closely in cling film and place in the fridge to relax for about 20 minutes.

5 Remove the détrempe from the fridge, unwrap and place on a floured surface, with a short end facing you. Ridge gently, patting up and down on the détrempe, keeping the rolling pin parallel to your body. Try to keep the sides straight and the corners of the pastry square, using a palette knife or your hands, but keep hand contact to a minimum to prevent the pastry warming up. Keep ridging as much as possible, as it is better for the pastry than rolling.

6 Now roll with quick, short sharp rolls, gently encouraging the pastry to lengthen rather than applying too much pressure and stretching it. Avoid creating thick ends at the top and bottom of the pastry. Roll back a little if necessary and avoid rolling over the top and bottom edge, as you will stretch the top layer and create uneven numbers of layers, which will result in uneven rising.

7 When the pastry is about 3 times as long as it is wide, re-check the sides are straight and corners square, then fold the bottom third of the pastry up over the middle third and the top third down and over the bottom and middle third. Turn the pastry so the folded side is to your left. This is known as a 'roll and fold'.

8 Repeat the roll and fold, making sure the pastry is cold to the touch and the butter is not becoming greasy. If some butter breaks through on the surface, then scatter some flour over it, dust off with a pastry brush and continue. Two roll and folds should take no longer than about 5 minutes. Wrap closely, making a note of how many roll and folds you have done, and place in the fridge again to relax.

9 Repeat the 2 roll and folds again, wrap and chill again. If after 4 roll and folds the butter is still evident and streaky, you will need to do one more, but generally rough puff pastry has 4 roll and folds. Keep wrapped in the fridge until needed.

1 Quickly mixing the butter cubes and water into the flour with a knife.

2 Stirring a little more water into the dry flour and butter to create large flakes.

3 Feeling the large flakes to check the amount of moisture within.

4 Bringing the dough together with the hands to form a homogeneous pastry.

5 Ridging the rested pastry gently with the rolling pin.

6 Rolling out the pastry, using short, sharp strokes, to lengthen it.

7 Folding and turning the pastry to complete one 'roll and fold'.

8 Dusting off excess flour (sprinkled onto any exposed butter).

9 Wrapping the pastry in cling film after 4 roll and folds, ready for a final chilling before use.

Lebanese cheese parcels

Makes 8–9
1 quantity rough puff pastry
(see page 500)
Extra flour, to dust
1 egg
Salt

For the filling
100g full-fat cottage cheese
100g feta
100g mozzarella
1 lemon
Small handful of dill or flat-leaf
parsley sprigs
Freshly ground black pepper

1 To make the filling, put the cottage cheese in a sieve set over a bowl, to drain. Discard the liquid and put the cheese in a bowl. Crumble in the feta and chop and add the mozzarella. Mash all the cheeses together with the back of a fork.

2 Finely grate enough lemon zest to give ½ tsp and add to the cheeses. Roughly chop enough dill or parsley leaves to give ½–1 tbsp and add to the mixture with a good grinding of pepper. Adjust the seasoning, herbs and lemon zest to taste.

3 Roll out the chilled pastry on a lightly floured surface to a 3mm thickness. Using a 10cm plain or fluted pastry cutter, cut out 8 or 9 circles. Divide the filling between the circles, placing it on one half of the circle and leaving a border around the edge.

4 Using a fork, lightly beat the egg with a pinch of salt, then pass through a sieve. Brush a little beaten egg around the edge of each pastry circle. Fold each circle in half, encasing the filling, seal carefully to make half-moon shaped parcels and brush with a little more of the beaten egg to glaze. Transfer to a baking sheet and chill until firm. Meanwhile, heat the oven to 200°C/gas mark 6.

5 Glaze the parcels again and bake in the oven until puffed up and lightly golden. Delicious served with a leafy salad and a caramelised onion marmalade.

Eccles cakes

Makes 6–8
1 quantity rough puff pastry
(see page 500)
Extra flour, to dust

For the filling
1 lemon
20g butter
50g soft light brown sugar
100g currants
30g chopped mixed peel
½ tsp ground cinnamon
¼ tsp freshly grated nutmeg
¼ tsp ground ginger

To finish
1 egg white
Caster sugar, to sprinkle

1 Roll out the chilled pastry on a lightly floured surface to a 3mm thickness. Using a saucer or template, cut out 6–8 discs about 12.5cm in diameter. Place on a baking sheet, cover with cling film and chill in the fridge while you make the filling.

2 Finely grate the zest of the lemon and squeeze the juice. Melt the butter in a small pan over a low heat, then take off the heat and add half the zest and 1 tsp juice with the sugar, currants, mixed peel and spices. Set aside to cool completely.

3 Remove the chilled pastry from the fridge and place 2 teaspoonfuls of the filling on the middle of each pastry disc. Dampen the edges of the pastry lightly with a little water, then bring the edges of the pastry up and around the filling and squeeze into a money bag shape around the filling, making sure the filling is completely sealed in. Trim away the excess pastry with a pair of scissors, making sure the cut is made as close to the filling as possible without exposing it.

4 Turn the Eccles cakes over and flatten a little with your fingers, or lightly with a rolling pin, just until the fruit filling is evident beneath the pastry.

5 Cover with cling film and chill on the baking sheet in the fridge until firm to the touch, about 20 minutes. Meanwhile, heat the oven to 220°C/gas mark 7.

6 When the Eccles cakes are firm, whisk the egg white until frothy, then use a pastry brush to brush the tops with the egg white foam and sprinkle with sugar.

7 With a small, sharp knife make 3 parallel shallow cuts in the middle of the pastry, about 2mm deep, with the middle slightly longer than the others.

8 Bake near the top of the oven for 20–25 minutes, or until golden brown and the pastry is cooked through, particularly on the underside; there should be no grey patches. The baking sheet can be moved to a lower shelf in the oven once the pastry has set, to prevent over-browning. Transfer the Eccles cakes to a wire rack to cool and eat while still slightly warm, or at room temperature.

Flaky pastry

Flaky pastry has small cubes of butter added in stages to the détrempe as well as during the rolling and folding process. These small cubes flatten out in the layers, separating the layers and creating a flakiness in the finished baked pastry. Flaky pastry has 5 roll and folds and can rise double its thickness when cooked. See page 498 for guidance on making layered pastry. Like puff pastry, flaky pastry can be prepared in advance; the same guidelines apply (see page 510).

Flaky pastry

Makes about 500g

250g plain flour, plus extra to dust
Scant ½ tsp salt
170g cold but pliable unsalted butter
90–120ml (6–8 tbsp) chilled water

1 Sift the flour and salt into a medium bowl. Cut the butter into small cubes (about 5–7mm) and divide into 4 piles; add one pile, so a quarter of the butter, to the bowl. Using your fingertips, rub the butter into the flour until it resembles fine breadcrumbs (see step 3, page 478). Add 90ml chilled water and, using a cutlery knife, mix everything together quickly and efficiently for about 15–20 seconds, turning the bowl as you stir.

2 The flour, butter and water will form large flakes. Drag the large flakes to the side of the bowl and add more water, ½ tbsp at a time, to the dry flour and crumb in the bottom of the bowl. Quickly stir again with the knife, to create large flakes, adding a little more water if necessary. You should ideally not add any more than about 8 tbsp water, or the pastry may start to toughen.

3 Feel the large flakes, and if there seems to be a good amount of moisture within them and the water is evenly distributed, pull the large flakes together in your hands and work the pastry a little to bring it together into a homogeneous pastry that is fairly smooth with a uniform colour.

4 Shape the détrempe into a block about 12 x 17cm and 2–3cm thick, wrap closely in cling film and place in the fridge to relax for about 20 minutes.

5 Remove the détrempe from the fridge, unwrap and place on a floured surface, with a side end facing you. Ridge the détrempe gently, patting up and down on it and keeping the rolling pin parallel to your body (see step 5, page 500).

6 Try to keep the sides straight and the corners of the pastry square, using a palette knife or your hands, but keep your hand contact with the pastry minimal to prevent the pastry warming up. Keep ridging as much as possible, as it is better for the pastry than rolling, then roll with quick, short sharp rolls, gently encouraging the pastry to lengthen rather than applying too much pressure and stretching it. Avoid creating thick ends at the top and bottom. Roll back a little if necessary and avoid rolling over the top and bottom edge, as you will stretch the top layer and create uneven numbers of layers, which will result in uneven rising.

7 When the pastry is about 3 times as long as it is wide, re-check that the sides are straight and corners square, then, using a cutlery knife, dab another quarter of the cold, pliable butter over the top two-thirds of the pastry, leaving a 1cm border around the edge without butter. Fold the bottom third of the pastry up over the middle third and the top third down and over the bottom and middle third, so the butter is interwoven in the layers. Turn the pastry so the folded side is to your left. This is known as a roll and fold.

8 Now commence the second roll and fold, making sure the pastry is cold to the touch and the butter is not breaking through the détrempe and becoming greasy. If it appears to be, then scatter some flour over the butter, dust it off with a pastry brush and continue. Once the pastry is 3 times as long as it is wide again, fold the pastry into three as before, this time without butter. This is known as a blind roll and fold.

9 Wrap the flaky pastry closely in cling film, making a note of how many roll and folds you have done, and place in the fridge again to relax and keep the fat cool.

10 Repeat the 2 roll and folds again, adding the third pile of butter in the third roll and fold and the remaining butter in the fourth. Wrap closely in cling film and chill again for about 20 minutes, making sure the butter does not firm up too much.

11 Repeat a blind roll and fold (without butter), to make a total of 5 roll and folds. If the pastry is streaky, you will need a sixth, but generally flaky pastry has 5 roll and folds. Keep wrapped in the fridge until needed.

Note Traditionally flaky pastry was made using half butter and half lard.

Red onion and goat's cheese tarts

Makes 6
1 quantity flaky pastry (see left)
Extra flour, to dust
1 egg

For the filling
1 quantity caramelised onion confit
  (see page 14, made using red onions)
6 slices of goat's cheese, 1cm thick,
  from a crottin or log about 3cm
  in diameter
¼ bunch of thyme
About 3 tbsp olive oil
Salt and freshly ground black pepper

1 Roll out the chilled pastry on a lightly floured surface to a rectangle, about 3–4mm thick. Using a round pastry cutter or template about 12.5cm in diameter, cut out 6 discs of pastry as cleanly as possible. Transfer the discs to a large baking sheet, cover with cling film and chill until firm to the touch. Meanwhile, heat the oven to 200°C/gas mark 6.

2 Cut up the sides of the pastry (as shown on page 517).

3 To create a border, use a small, sharp knife to cut a circle about 1cm in from the edge of the case; take care to cut only halfway through the pastry. Using a fork and avoiding the border, prick the circle of pastry very well, to stop the middle rising as it cooks.

4 Divide the caramelised onion confit between the tarts and spread it over the middle of the pastry, but not on the border. Top with a disc of goat's cheese.

5 Lightly beat the egg with a very small pinch of salt, using a fork, then pass through a sieve into a bowl. Brush the border of each disc with the egg glaze, making sure it doesn't drip down the sides of the pastry, which could seal the layering together.

6 Decorate the glazed borders with patterns; these should be indentations rather than cuts, and they will help control the top layers from shattering too much as they cook.

7 Bake in the oven for 15–20 minutes, or until the pastry has risen around the filling and is golden brown, the onions are hot and the cheese is starting to melt. Meanwhile, pick off ½ tsp thyme leaves.

8 If the cheese has not browned at all, a kitchen blowtorch can be used to colour it, taking care to avoid burning the pastry. Scatter the thyme leaves over the tarts and drizzle with a little olive oil, about ½ tbsp per tart. Serve hot with a dressed green salad.

Steak and Guinness pie

Serves 4
½ quantity flaky pastry (see page 504)
Extra flour, to dust
1 egg

For the filling
1 onion
3 tbsp olive oil
Handful of mixed herbs, such as parsley, thyme, rosemary and oregano
1kg beef chuck steak
450ml Guinness
½ x 400g tin chopped tomatoes
1 bay leaf
2 tsp softened butter mixed with 2 tsp flour (beurre manié), if needed
Salt and freshly ground black pepper

Although this recipe uses only a half quantity of pastry, it is much easier to make a whole batch, so use half and freeze the leftover.

1 For the filling, halve and peel the onion and cut each half into 4 wedges. Place in a medium flameproof casserole or ovenproof pan with 1 tbsp of the olive oil, cover, ideally with a cartouche (see page 13), and sweat over a low heat until soft and translucent but not taking on any colour.

2 Meanwhile, finely chop enough herb leaves to give you 1–2 tbsp and set aside. Trim off any excess fat and sinew from the beef and cut it into 2–3cm cubes.

3 Heat the oven to 150°C/gas mark 2.

4 Once the onion is soft, remove it from the pan and set aside. Brown the meat in batches in the pan (see page 401), using as much of the remaining oil as necessary and deglazing with a little water after each batch.

5 Return the onion to the pan and add the Guinness, tomatoes, chopped mixed herbs, bay leaf and some salt and pepper, and bring to a simmer. Return all the meat to the pan and add a little water if the meat is not covered.

6 Cover, transfer to the oven and cook gently for 2–2½ hours, or until the beef is tender. To check, remove a piece of beef; you should be able to cut through it with the side of a fork or spoon.

7 Remove from the oven and drain the cooking liquid into a small pan. Discard the bay leaf, then taste and reduce the sauce, if necessary, to a consistency that lightly clings to the meat and a good concentration of flavour. If the sauce needs thickening, use a little beurre manié (see page 111).

8 Add the beef back to the sauce and transfer to a lipped pie dish, ensuring the filling fills the dish generously. Use a pie funnel (see page 486) if necessary. Leave to cool completely.

9 Roll out the chilled pastry on a lightly floured surface to a rectangle about 3mm thick and 3cm bigger all round than the pie dish. Cut off strips that together will line the lip of the pie dish. Lightly beat the egg with a very small pinch of salt, using a fork, then pass through a sieve into a bowl.

10 Press the pastry strips onto the dish lip and brush with a little beaten egg. Carefully lift the pastry rectangle on top and press gently over the lip, to join the edges. Trim off the excess pastry and cut up the sides (as shown on page 517). Place 2 fingers lightly on the edge of the pastry and draw the back of a cutlery knife between your fingers and upwards, to create a scalloped effect (as shown on page 517). Make a hole in the centre of the lid to allow steam to escape. Cut out leaves or decorations from the pastry trimmings, if desired, and stick to the pie lid with beaten egg. Glaze the pastry with the beaten egg. Chill in the fridge for 30 minutes to firm the pastry. Meanwhile, heat the oven to 200°C/gas mark 6.

11 Brush the pastry with the beaten egg again. Bake the pie in the top of the oven for 25–30 minutes, or until the pastry is well risen and golden and the filling is piping hot when tested with a skewer.

Variation

Steak and mushroom pie Add 200g halved button mushrooms to the sweated onion and sauté for 3–4 minutes to soften. Replace the Guinness and tomatoes with 500ml brown beef or chicken and veal stock (see page 98). Add ½ tbsp chopped thyme in place of the mixed herbs and proceed as for the main recipe.

Puff pastry

The lightest and flakiest pastry, puff is also considered to be the trickiest to make. However, it is far superior to bought puff pastry, so well worth the effort. If you do need to resort to the bought version, buy a good quality, all-butter puff pastry.

Only a very small amount of butter is added to the détrempe when making puff pastry, with the remaining butter all added in one block in the first roll and fold, which creates the most defined, complete layers of all the layered types of pastry. Puff also has 6 roll and folds, which equates to 729 layers, and rises to at least 3 times the depth rolled. See page 498 for guidance on making layered pastry.

Puff pastry

Makes about 500g
250g plain flour
Scant ½ tsp salt
180–200g cold but pliable unsalted butter (see note, overleaf)
90–120ml (6–8 tbsp) chilled water

1 Sift the flour and salt into a medium bowl. Cut a 30g piece from the butter, then cut this into small cubes and add to the flour and salt. Rub into the flour with your fingertips until it resembles fine breadcrumbs (see step 3, page 478). Add 90ml chilled water and, using a cutlery knife, mix everything together quickly and efficiently for about 15–20 seconds, turning the bowl as you stir.

2 The crumb and water will form large flakes. Drag the large flakes to the side of the bowl and add more water, ½ tbsp at a time, to the dry crumb in the bottom of the bowl. Stir again quickly to create large flakes and add a little more water if necessary. You should ideally not add more than about 8 tbsp water, or the pastry may start to toughen.

3 Feel the large flakes, and if there seems to be a good amount of moisture within them and the water is evenly distributed, pull the large flakes together in your hands and work the pastry a little to bring the détrempe together into a homogeneous pastry that is fairly smooth and a uniform colour. Shape into a block about 12 x 17cm and 2–3cm thick, wrap closely in cling film and place in the fridge for 20 minutes.

4 Unwrap the pastry and place on a floured surface, with a short end facing you. Ridge gently, patting up and down on the pastry, keeping the rolling pin parallel to you. Try to keep the sides straight and the corners of the pastry square, using a palette knife or your hands, but keep hand contact to a minimum to prevent the pastry from warming up. Keep ridging as much as possible before you roll, then roll with quick, short, sharp rolls, gently encouraging the pastry to lengthen rather than applying too much pressure and stretching it. When the pastry is about twice as long as it is wide, re-check the sides are straight and corners square.

5 Place the remaining butter between 2 sheets of greaseproof paper. Bash with a rolling pin to flatten, then shape into a rectangle half the size of the rolled détrempe. If the butter gets too big, fold it. At this stage it should still be cold and, if it folds without breaking, it is pliable enough. Neaten it quickly to a rectangle and check it for size.

6 Place the butter on the bottom half of the détrempe, press the border lightly to flatten it, then bring the edges of the détrempe up the sides of the butter and press them over the edge of the butter. Bring the top half down over the exposed butter. Press the edges down against the sides of the butter, ensuring a good seal; the butter must not be able to escape.

7 With the folded side away from you, ridge and then roll the pastry to 3 times as long as it is wide, keeping the sides straight and the corners square. Avoid creating thick ends at the top and bottom; roll back a little if necessary and avoid rolling over the top and bottom edge as you will stretch the top layer and create uneven layers, which will result in uneven rising.

(Continued overleaf)

1 Mixing the ingredients together quickly, using a cutlery knife.

2 Dragging the flakes to the side and adding more water to the dry crumb.

3 Pulling the large flakes together in your hands to start to bring the dough together.

4 Gently ridging the rested détrempe with the rolling pin.

5 Flattening the butter between 2 sheets of greaseproof paper.

6 Bringing the edges of the détrempe up the sides of the butter.

7 Rolling the butter-enclosed détrempe out until it is 3 times as long as it is wide.

8 Folding the bottom third of the pastry up over the middle third.

9 After folding the top third down, the pastry is turned 90° so the fold is at the left.

8 Fold the bottom third of the pastry over the middle third (as shown on page 509), then the top third down over the bottom and middle third.

9 Now turn the pastry 90° so the fold is at your left (as shown on page 509). This is the first roll and fold.

10 Now repeat the roll and fold, making sure the pastry is always cold to the touch and the butter is not breaking through the détrempe and becoming greasy. If it is, then scatter some flour over the butter, dust it off with a pastry brush and continue. When making puff, all the roll and folds are 'blind', as all the butter has already been incorporated. Wrap closely, making a note of how many roll and folds you have done, and place in the fridge again to relax and keep the butter cool and firm, for about 20 minutes. The butter must be cool but pliable, so don't let it firm up too much in the fridge.

11 Repeat the 2 roll and folds again twice, covering the pastry closely and chilling for about 20 minutes after each 2 roll and folds, and making a note of how many roll and folds you have done. Once the pastry has had 6 roll and folds, it can be kept in the fridge until needed. If very streaky, you may need to do one more roll and fold.

A note on butter content...

This recipe gives a range of butter quantity. If making puff for the first time, use the smaller amount. When you are confident with the method and the pastry works for you, increase the amount of butter for a richer flavour.

Making puff pastry in advance...

If making puff pastry either the day before use or for freezing, don't complete the last roll and fold. Wrap the pastry closely in cling film, mark the number of roll and folds on the cling film and chill or freeze. Defrost frozen pastry in the fridge over 24 hours; it must be kept chilled when defrosting or the butter within the layers may melt.

If you have chilled the pastry for more than 2–3 hours, leave it at room temperature for 5 minutes before rolling out, to let it soften very slightly. When ready to use, perform the last roll and fold which will help to 'refresh' the pastry and release the layers.

Individual shallot tatins

Makes 4
½ quantity puff pastry (see page 508)
Extra flour, to dust

For the filling
6–8 banana shallots
50g butter
2 thyme sprigs
1½ tbsp balsamic vinegar
1½ tbsp brown sugar
Salt and freshly ground black pepper

1 Heat the oven to 200°C/gas mark 6.

2 Roll out the chilled pastry on a lightly floured surface to a 3mm thickness and, using an 12.5cm plain pastry cutter, cut out 4 discs. Place the pastry discs on a baking tray, cover with cling film and place in the fridge to rest while you prepare the shallots.

3 Blanch the shallots in boiling water for 2 minutes, then remove to a bowl and leave to cool. Peel and cut into round slices, 1.5cm thick, keeping the layers intact.

4 Melt the butter in a large non-stick frying pan over a low to medium heat, add the shallots and cook gently until starting to brown. Turn them over carefully, keeping the slices intact, and cook gently over a low heat on the other side until tender, about 10–15 minutes.

5 Pick the thyme leaves from the sprigs and add to the shallots with the balsamic vinegar and sugar. Increase the heat to medium and cook for 5–6 minutes until the sugar has melted, taking care it doesn't burn. Season with salt and pepper.

6 Remove from the heat and divide the shallots and juices between 4 individual tatin tins or 10cm flan tins (not loose-based).

7 Place a disc of chilled pastry over each tin, tucking the sides down around the shallots. Place the tatins on a baking sheet and bake on the top shelf of the oven for about 15 minutes until the pastry is risen, golden and cooked.

8 Remove from the oven and set aside for 1–2 minutes, then invert a plate over each and carefully turn them out, protecting your hands from any hot syrup. Serve hot with a salad. These also go well with duck breasts (see page 374).

Tomato tart

Serves 4–6
1 quantity puff pastry (see page 508)
Extra flour, to dust
1 egg

For the filling
1 tsp dried oregano
1 tsp dried thyme
100g mascarpone cheese
6–8 tomatoes, depending on size
2 tbsp extra virgin olive oil
½ bunch of basil
Salt and freshly ground black pepper

1 Roll out the chilled pastry on a lightly floured surface to a rectangle, roughly the size of an A4 sheet of paper, 4mm thick, and trim the edges. Lift the pastry onto a baking sheet, cover with cling film and chill until firm to the touch. Meanwhile, heat the oven to 200°C/gas mark 6.

2 Once chilled and firm, cut up the sides of the pastry (as shown on page 517). To create a border, use a small, very sharp knife to cut about halfway through the pastry about 2.5cm in from the edge of the case. Using a fork and avoiding the border, prick the pastry well, to prevent it from rising as it cooks.

3 Using a fork, lightly beat the egg with a very small pinch of salt, then pass through a sieve into a bowl. Brush the pastry border with beaten egg, avoiding dripping any glaze down the sides of the pastry (which might seal the layering together). Lightly score a pattern on the glazed borders; the indentations will help control the top layers from shattering too much as they cook.

4 Bake in the top third of the oven until golden, with a risen border. If the middle has risen, gently press it down while still warm using the back of a tablespoon. Carefully transfer to a wire rack to cool; it may be a little fragile, so take care and, if necessary, leave it on the baking sheet. Reduce the oven temperature to 150°C/gas mark 2.

5 For the filling, mix the dried herbs with the mascarpone and season with salt and pepper. Return the cooled pastry case to the baking sheet and spread the seasoned mascarpone in the case, up to the border on all sides.

6 Thinly slice the tomatoes, placing them on a tray lined with kitchen paper as you slice them to remove excess juices. Lay them on top of the mascarpone, overlapping the slices closely together. Season generously with salt and pepper.

7 Bake in the oven for 1½–2 hours, or until the tomatoes have dried out and any excess water has evaporated. Remove the tart from the oven, drizzle with the olive oil and sprinkle with basil leaves before serving.

Note Because the pastry is already cooked, the tomatoes can be cooked at this low temperature for a long time, so they dry out.

Seafood feuilletée with spinach and beurre blanc

Serves 4
1 quantity puff pastry (see page 508)
Extra flour, to dust
1 egg

For the filling
225g spinach
150g salmon fillet
2–3 plaice fillets, depending on size
8 raw tiger prawns
4 scallops
30g butter
Pinch of freshly grated nutmeg
300ml fish stock (see page 100) or
   court bouillon (see page 267)
1 quantity warm beurre blanc
   (see page 122)
Few chervil sprigs
Salt and ground white pepper

1 To make a template for the pastry, fold a piece of A4 paper in half, then in half again, and measure 5cm along one side from the folded point and 6cm along the other side. From the point along one side draw a line across the paper to the other point, then cut along this line. Unfold the paper to a diamond shape.

2 Roll out the chilled pastry on a lightly floured surface to a square, 1cm thick. Trim the edges with a large, sharp knife. Use the template to cut out 4 diamonds neatly (as shown). Cut up the sides of the pastry (as shown on page 517).

3 Lightly beat the egg with a small pinch of salt, using a fork, then pass through a sieve. Brush each pastry diamond with the egg glaze, without letting it drip down the sides. Using a small, sharp knife, cut 1cm in from the edge of the case (as shown), about 3mm deep, to create a border. Transfer to a baking sheet and chill until firm. Meanwhile, heat the oven to 200°C/gas mark 6.

4 Brush more egg glaze over each pastry diamond and bake for 20–30 minutes, or until well risen, deep golden on top and the sides are firm to the touch. Remove from the oven and, using a sharp knife, cut out the lid within the border and set aside. Carefully scoop out all the undercooked pastry in the middle (as shown). Return to a lower oven shelf for 5–10 minutes to allow the insides to dry out. The feuilletée cases are then ready to use. Lower the oven setting to 150°C/gas mark 2.

5 For the filling, pick over the spinach, remove the stalks and wash well. Heat a large, heavy-based saucepan until hot. Add enough of the spinach, with just the water clinging to the leaves, to loosely fill the pan, then cover with a lid. Stir every 30 seconds or so until all the spinach has completely wilted, then tip it into a sieve to drain, pressing out as much liquid as possible with the underside of a ladle.

6 Skin and pin-bone the salmon and divide into 4 pieces. Skin the plaice and cut on the diagonal into 2cm wide pieces. Prepare the prawns (see page 204, deveining and leaving the very end tail shell on). Prepare the scallops (see page 242).

7 Heat a frying pan over a low to medium heat, melt half the butter and sauté the spinach, seasoning it with salt, white pepper and nutmeg. Transfer to the low oven to keep warm. Wipe out the frying pan.

8 Place the feuilletée cases in the oven to warm through. Pour the stock into a small saucepan, season lightly with salt and set over a low heat. Add the salmon and prawns and poach for 2 minutes, then add the plaice and poach until just cooked through, about 1 minute. Remove all the fish with a slotted spoon to a warmed plate and transfer to the oven to keep warm.

9 Heat the frying pan over a medium heat and add the rest of the butter. Season the scallops with salt, add to the hot butter and fry until caramelised, then turn over and caramelise the second side until just cooked through (see page 243).

10 Remove the warm feuilletée cases from the oven and place on a board. Divide the spinach between the cases and add a spoonful of beurre blanc. Divide the fish between the cases and place the filled cases on 4 plates, arranging any remaining fish to the side of the cases and spooning the remaining beurre blanc around the pastry and fish. Put each pastry lid on top and garnish with the chervil sprigs.

....

A note on feuilletée...
Known generically as feuilletée cases (feuille meaning leaf – a reference to the layers of pastry), these have other names, depending on their size. Bouchées, used for canapés, are smaller than vol-au-vents. Feuilletée cases can be filled with savoury or sweet fillings.

Pork and fennel sausage rolls

Makes 10 large or 20 small rolls
1 quantity puff pastry (see page 508)
Extra flour, to dust
1 egg
1 tsp fennel seeds

For the filling
1 onion
1 celery stick
2 tbsp olive oil
2 garlic cloves
2 tbsp fennel seeds
1kg pork mince
Salt and freshly ground black pepper

1 For the filling, halve, peel and very finely dice the onion and de-string and very finely dice the celery. Heat the olive oil in a small saucepan, add the onion and celery, cover (ideally with a cartouche, see page 13) and sweat over a low heat until soft and translucent. Meanwhile, peel and crush the garlic and crush the fennel seeds in a pestle and mortar.

2 When the onion and celery are very soft, add the garlic and cook for 1 minute, then add the crushed fennel seeds and cook for a further 1 minute. Transfer the mixture to a bowl and leave to cool.

3 Once cool, add the pork mince and mix thoroughly. Season with salt and pepper, then heat a frying pan over a medium heat and fry 1 tbsp of the mixture in a splash of oil until cooked. Taste and adjust the seasoning as necessary.

4 Roll out the chilled pastry on a lightly floured surface to a large rectangle, 30 x 34cm and about 3mm thick. Trim off the edges using a large knife, then cut the rectangle in half, each piece measuring 17 x 30cm.

5 Take about half the filling and shape it between the palms of your hands into a sausage shape, about 2–3cm in diameter. Lay it along the length of the pastry. Lightly dampening your hands with water before shaping will help prevent the filling from sticking to your hands.

6 Lightly beat the egg with a very small pinch of salt, using a fork, then pass through a sieve into a bowl. Brush a little down one long side of the pastry. Roll the pastry closely over the filling and seal over the egg washed side, ensuring a good seal.

7 Repeat with the remaining pastry and filling, then cut into 6cm lengths, or shorter pieces for smaller sausage rolls. Place on a baking tray, sealed sides down and glaze with beaten egg. Chill in the fridge for 20–30 minutes. Meanwhile, heat the oven to 190°C/gas mark 5.

8 When the pastry is firm to the touch, brush each sausage roll with the beaten egg again, scatter with fennel seeds, then bake in the top of the oven for about 30 minutes until the pastry is a deep golden colour. Check the filling is cooked by inserting a skewer into the middle of a sausage roll. Leave it for 10 seconds, then remove it and check the heat of the skewer against the inside of your wrist; it should be hot. If not, return to the oven for a further 5–10 minutes. If they are browning too much, place them on a lower shelf.

9 Remove from the oven and leave to cool a little before serving.

Variation
Pork and herb sausage rolls Omit the fennel seeds and add 2 tbsp very finely chopped mixed fresh herbs, such as parsley, sage, thyme and chives to the filling.

Cheese straws

Makes about 20
60g Parmesan cheese
60g Gruyère cheese
1 quantity puff pastry (see page 508)
Extra flour, to dust
1 egg
Cayenne pepper
Salt

1 Finely grate both the cheeses.

2 Roll out the pastry on a lightly floured surface to a rectangle 3mm thick, then cut in half lengthways.

3 Lightly beat the egg with a very small pinch of salt, using a fork, then pass through a sieve into a bowl. Brush one half of the pastry with beaten egg, then sprinkle over half the grated cheeses and a large pinch of cayenne.

4 Place the other half of the pastry on top and, using a rolling pin, roll the pastry lightly to about a 2–3mm thickness, to stick the 2 layers of pastry together and make it a little thinner. Chill if the pastry becomes too soft to handle.

5 Brush the surface of the pastry with more beaten egg and sprinkle over the remaining cheeses.

6 Cut the pastry into long strips, about 1–1.5cm wide, then hold each end of one strip and twist lightly in opposite directions, to create a spiral. Repeat with the remaining strips of pastry and place on a baking sheet lined with baking parchment, spacing them well apart as they will expand. Cover with cling film and chill well until firm to the touch, about 30 minutes. Meanwhile, heat the oven to 200°C/gas mark 6.

7 Bake in the oven for 15–20 minutes until the pastry is golden and cooked through, then transfer the cheese straws to a wire rack and leave to cool a little before serving warm.

Note Cheese straws can also be made with any leftover layered pastry.

Palmiers

Makes about 20
About 250g puff pastry trimmings and leftovers (see below)
100g caster sugar

1 Lay the puff pastry trimming pieces flat on top of each other (rather than squidge them together), folding them if necessary.

2 Use about half of the caster sugar to dust the work surface and roll the pastry out into a rectangle 5mm thick. Sprinkle well with 2–3 tbsp caster sugar. Roll the long ends of the pastry into the middle, where they will meet (as shown).

3 Cut the roll across into 1cm wide slices. Lay the slices flat on a damp baking sheet, set well apart, and flatten well using a rolling pin or your fingers.

4 Cover with cling film and chill in the fridge for 15 minutes until firm. Meanwhile, heat the oven to 200°C/gas mark 6.

5 Sprinkle with a little more caster sugar and bake in the oven for 10 minutes, or until pale golden and cooked through, with the underside caramelised. Turn them over and bake for a further 10 minutes. Remove from the oven, transfer to a wire rack and leave to cool.

Note These palmiers are an excellent way of using up trimmings and off-cuts from other recipes. When saving the trimmings, don't roll them into a ball, or it will spoil the carefully created layering in the pastry.

Gâteau Pithivier

Serves 6–8
1 quantity puff pastry (see page 508)
Extra flour, to dust
1 quantity frangipane (see page 542, made using rum)
1 egg
Icing sugar, to dust
Salt

1 Cut the chilled pastry into 2 pieces, with one slightly bigger than the other. Roll out the smaller piece on a lightly floured surface to a large square, about 3mm thick. Using an appropriate size of saucepan lid or plate as a template, cut out a disc of pastry, about 25cm in diameter. Use a large, sharp knife to do this, making as few cuts as possible to avoid dragging through the pastry as you cut it. Place the disc of pastry on a baking tray, cover with cling film and chill in the fridge while you roll out the top.

2 Roll out the larger piece of puff pastry to about 26–27cm square, ideally slightly thicker than 3mm.

3 Remove the chilled pastry from the fridge and spoon the frangipane filling onto the pastry, leaving a 2.5cm border around the edge. Flatten the frangipane into a disc, 2.5cm thick.

4 Lightly beat the egg with a very small pinch of salt, using a fork, then pass through a sieve into a bowl. Brush the pastry border with egg glaze. Carefully place the second, larger piece of pastry over the filling, smoothing it out from the middle of the filling to remove any air bubbles. Press the edges together firmly to seal.

5 Cut the top pastry layer into a round to fit the bottom layer, then cut up the sides of the pastry (as shown). Place 2 fingers lightly on the edge of the pastry and draw the back of a cutlery knife between your fingers (as shown) and upwards, to create a scalloped effect.

6 Brush all over with beaten egg, then score the top of the pastry from the centre, curving the scoring like the petals of a flower, without cutting right through the pastry. Chill until very cold and firm to the touch. Meanwhile, heat the oven to 220°C/gas mark 7.

7 Brush the top of the Pithivier again with beaten egg, making sure the glaze does not drip down the scalloped edges. Bake in the oven for 30–40 minutes, or until the pastry has risen, is a deep golden colour and firm to the touch at the sides.

8 Heat the grill to its highest setting. Sift the icing sugar liberally over the surface of the Pithivier. Place under the grill briefly to melt the icing sugar, to give it a high gloss sugar glaze, taking care that the sugar does not burn. Serve warm or at room temperature.

Cutting up the sides of the pastry

This helps the layers of pastry to separate and rise. To 'cut up', use a knife or palette knife to carefully tap the cut sides of the pastry horizontally (as shown). These taps should not cut into the pastry, but should be shallow indentations into the sides. The thinner the pastry, the more difficult this is to do.

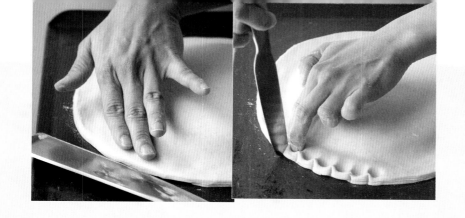

Choux pastry

The timeless popularity of classics such as chocolate éclairs and profiteroles makes this simple pastry well worth mastering. It is extremely versatile and can be used for both savoury and sweet recipes. Steam, created from the water and eggs, puffs up the pastry and creates a hollow pastry case, which can be up to 3 times its original uncooked size. The crisp container this produces is ideal for a variety of delicious fillings, sweet and savoury.

While choux pastry is straightforward and quick to make, the ingredients need to be measured accurately and the method followed carefully for successful results.

Choux pastry

Makes '1 quantity'
220ml water
85g butter
105g plain flour
Pinch of salt
3 eggs, at room temperature

1 Measure the water into a small saucepan. Cut the butter into 1cm cubes and add to the water. Place over a low heat and allow the butter to melt, without letting the water simmer or boil (which would result in less liquid, through evaporation, and a stiff mixture that won't rise as well).

2 Meanwhile, sift the flour and salt 2 or 3 times to aerate and remove any lumps. Do the last sifting onto a sheet of greaseproof paper. Fold the paper in half and fold up the bottom edge a couple of times to create a pocket for the flour to sit. (This will make it easier to add it all at once to the water and butter.)

3 Once the butter has melted, increase the heat to medium high and have the flour and a wooden spoon close by. As the water begins to simmer, watch it carefully and, as it boils and rises up the sides of the pan, with the melted butter collecting in the middle, shoot the flour in all at once and turn off the heat.

4 Beat the flour in vigorously for just 20–30 seconds, getting into the corners of the saucepan, until the flour is fully incorporated, there are no lumps and the mixture is thick and a uniform colour. Spread this panade onto a plate and let it cool to about 38°C, or blood temperature. (Cooling the panade will allow the incorporation of more egg, to ensure a greater rise.)

5 Meanwhile, break the eggs into a bowl and whisk lightly with a fork. Once the panade is cool to the touch, return it to the saucepan (there's no need to wash it), add about 1 tbsp of the beaten egg and beat it into the panade with a wooden spoon (off the heat). Once the egg is fully incorporated, add a little more egg and beat again, adding about three-quarters of the remaining egg in additions and beating well to incorporate each addition fully before the next. Initially, the panade will thicken, but as more egg is beaten in it will start to loosen and become smooth and shiny.

6 Once about three-quarters of the egg has been added, check the consistency; you need a silky smooth pastry with a reluctant dropping consistency, which means that when you fill the wooden spoon with pastry and lift it up over the saucepan the pastry should fall back from the spoon into the saucepan to the slow count of six. Continue adding egg a little at a time until the correct consistency is achieved. The pastry can now be used, or covered and either stored in the fridge overnight or frozen.

1 Adding the butter to the water to melt.

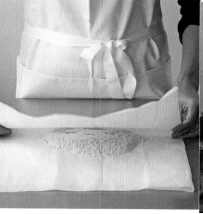

2 Folding the paper to enclose the flour and contain it in a pocket.

3 Shooting the flour into the boiling water and melted butter mixture.

4 Spreading the panade out on a plate to cool.

5 Incorporating the beaten egg into the panade a little at a time (off the heat).

6 Checking the consistency: it should be a silky smooth paste, reluctant to drop from the spoon.

A note on beating in the flour...

Beating the flour in for just 20–30 seconds is very important, as any longer and the panade may become greasy and look split, creating slightly greasy cooked pastry and an unattractive cracked surface.

A note on adding the egg...

If too little egg is added, the choux pastry will not rise successfully. If too much egg is added, the choux will be too thin to hold its shape and it may struggle to rise. So 3 eggs in the recipe is a guide only; you need to add just enough to achieve a reluctant dropping consistency.

The egg can be incorporated using a hand-held electric whisk if preferred, still in several additions and taking care not to add too much.

Leek and mushroom gougère

Serves 4

75g Gruyère cheese

1 quantity choux pastry (see page 518, adding a pinch each of English mustard powder and cayenne to the flour)

For the filling

2 large leeks

75g button mushrooms

¼ bunch of thyme

2 tbsp olive oil

75ml white wine

150ml crème fraîche

1 tbsp white breadcrumbs

Salt and freshly ground black pepper

A gougère is cheese-flavoured choux pastry with a savoury filling.

1 Cut 50g of the Gruyère into small dice, grate the remaining 25g and set aside. Heat the oven to 200°C/gas mark 6.

2 Stir the diced Gruyère into the choux pastry mixture.

3 Spoon or pipe the choux around the edges of a shallow, greased ovenproof dish, about 30 x 30cm and 4–5cm deep (about 1 litre in volume), leaving a space for the filling in the centre. Bake for 35–45 minutes, or until well risen, a deep golden colour and very firm to the touch at the sides. Lower the oven temperature to 180°C/gas mark 4.

4 Meanwhile, to make the filling, trim the root end and most of the green from the leeks and thinly slice, then soak in a large bowl of cold water to remove grit. Wipe over and slice the mushrooms. Pick over and finely chop enough thyme leaves to give you 1–2 tsp.

5 Drain the leeks well. Heat the olive oil in a large saucepan, then add the leeks and cover with a cartouche (see page 13) and lid. Sweat over a low heat until the leeks are soft and translucent. Remove the lid and cartouche and increase the heat a little to evaporate off the excess water. Add the mushrooms and thyme, and sauté until soft.

6 Add the wine, bring to the boil and let bubble for 2–3 minutes to drive off the alcohol. Remove from the heat, stir in the crème fraîche and season to taste with salt and pepper.

7 When the choux pastry is cooked, remove from the oven. If it has risen towards the middle of the dish, push this aside a little to allow room for the filling.

8 Spoon the filling into the centre of the choux and return to the oven to warm through. If the filling is warm, this will take 10–15 minutes and if it has cooled, 20–25 minutes. Mix the breadcrumbs with the reserved grated Gruyère. About 5–10 minutes before it is due to come out of the oven, turn the oven setting up to 200°C/gas mark 6 and sprinkle the cheese and breadcrumbs over the filling. Cook until golden and the crumb topping is lightly browned. Serve hot or warm.

Variation

Aubergine and prosciutto gougère Omit the leek and mushroom filling. Cut 1 large aubergine into small dice. Fry in 2 tbsp olive oil over a medium heat in a large frying pan until tender and beginning to brown a little. Mix with 100g shredded prosciutto, 1–2 tbsp basil leaves, chiffonaded (see page 89), 75ml double cream and salt and black pepper to taste. Use to fill the gougère and bake as for the main recipe.

Individual gougères

Gougères can be made in individual ramekins. The quantity of choux in the main recipe will make 8 individual gougères, using standard 7.5–8cm diameter ramekins. Follow the above method but cut and shred the filling ingredients into smaller pieces. You don't need to pre-bake the gougère before filling. They will take about 30–35 minutes to cook; the choux will rise around the filling and give a softer result.

Chocolate profiteroles

Makes 20

1 quantity choux pastry (see page 518)
250g good quality dark chocolate,
  minimum 60% cocoa solids
2 tbsp water
15g butter
600ml double cream
2 tbsp icing sugar

1 Heat the oven to 200°C/gas mark 6. Very lightly oil a non-stick baking sheet.

2 Put teaspoonfuls of the choux pastry onto the prepared baking sheet, spacing them about 4–5cm apart. (They need plenty of room to rise as if 2 buns join while rising they can make each other collapse.) Use a dampened, clean finger to smooth out any spikes or peaks on the choux buns.

3 Bake in the top third of the oven for 20–30 minutes, until well risen and puffed, and a deep golden brown all over, checking after 20 minutes (no earlier or they may collapse). The choux buns should also be very firm to the touch on the base where they sit on the baking tray. If they are soft and pale golden, cook for longer.

4 Remove from the oven and lower the oven setting to 170°C/gas mark 3. While hot, turn each choux bun over and use a skewer to make a hole in the base, about 5mm in diameter or the size of your smallest piping nozzle, to allow the steam to escape. Place the buns, base up, on the baking sheet and return to the oven for 5–6 minutes to dry the insides. Transfer to a wire rack to cool completely.

5 While the choux buns are cooling, put the chocolate, water and butter into a small heatproof bowl set over a saucepan of just-boiled water, ensuring the bowl is not touching the water. Give it an occasional stir to encourage melting.

6 Put the cream and icing sugar into a large bowl. Whisk to a pipeable consistency (see page 568), then place in a piping bag fitted with a nozzle the size of the hole in the base of the profiteroles.

7 When the profiteroles are completely cold, take one in the palm of a clean hand and pipe the cream into the hole. Once filled, scrape away any escaping cream and return to the wire rack. Repeat with all the profiteroles.

8 Hold one profiterole upside down at its base, using your fingertips, and turn the top of the profiterole through the melted chocolate (as shown), keeping your fingers clear of the chocolate. Carefully turn the profiterole over and place on a serving plate. Repeat with the remaining profiteroles.

Variations

You can fill the profiteroles with crème pâtissière (see page 134) instead of cream.

Coffee éclairs Omit the chocolate icing. Follow the main recipe but use a piping bag fitted with a 7–8mm nozzle to pipe the choux pastry into flat 'S' shapes, 7–8cm long, making 12–15 in total. Make the hole for the steam to escape in the side rather than base of each éclair. Pipe the sweetened cream into the middle as for the profiteroles. Beat 250g icing sugar with 2–3 tbsp hot double espresso or 1–2 tsp instant coffee powder dissolved in 2 tbsp hot water. Dip each éclair top into the icing, turn over and place on a plate. Alternatively, you can spoon the icing onto the éclairs to coat them evenly (ie napper).

Chocolate éclairs Follow the coffee éclair variation above and fill with crème pâtissière (see page 134) instead of cream. Coat with chocolate as for the chocolate profiteroles, rather than the coffee icing.

A note on freezing...

Choux buns, profiteroles and éclairs can be frozen in an airtight container once they are cooked and before they are filled. Store for up to a few months, defrosting them overnight in the fridge. Warm through on a baking sheet in an oven preheated to 190°C/gas mark 5 for 5–10 minutes to crisp them up again.

Hot water crust

Hot water crust pastry is traditionally used for raised pies. It is an unusual pastry, similar to choux although it doesn't rise when baked, and can be said to be twice cooked. Ideally, making the pastry and shaping the case should be done a day ahead to allow the pastry time to firm up before filling and baking.

Hot water crust pastry

Makes enough for a raised pie to serve 6–8
150ml water
60g butter
60g lard
350g plain flour
¾ tsp salt
1 large egg

1 Put the water in a medium saucepan. Cut the butter and lard into 1cm cubes and add to the pan. Place over a low heat and melt the fats; the water must not boil before they have melted.

2 Meanwhile, sift the flour and salt into a large bowl and make a well in the middle. Break the egg into a small bowl, beat lightly with a fork and pour into the well. Carefully flick flour over the egg to protect it from the hot water and fats.

3 Once the fats have melted, increase the heat and bring to the boil. As it comes to a rolling boil, take off the heat, pour over the flour in the bowl and immediately mix everything together well with a cutlery knife, until you can no longer see any dry flour. The pastry should be warm and greasy to the touch. Bring it together in your hands until smooth, then divide into 2 pieces, one twice the size of the other.

4 Shape the smaller piece of pastry into a disc, 10–12cm in diameter, and the larger piece into a disc, 15–18cm in diameter. The discs should be smooth, with no cracks or pleats. Wrap both individually in cling film and chill for 45–60 minutes for the fats to firm up.

Shaping hot water crust for a raised pie

While the pastry is chilling, prepare the mould for the raised pie. Traditionally, a wooden mould is used. A large 400ml soufflé dish, 12.5cm in diameter, works well. (Individual pies can be raised without moulds.)

1 Cut a disc of greaseproof paper for the outside base of the dish and a band to go around the outside walls of the dish. Stick the greaseproof paper to the outside of the dish using sticky tape. Now place the dish on a large sheet of cling film and bring the cling film up the sides of the dish and down into it, pulling the cling film so it is taut. The soufflé dish is now ready for the pastry.

2 Remove the larger disc of pastry from the fridge; it should be firm, but pliable. Turn the soufflé dish upside down and lay the pastry across the upturned base. Gently ease the pastry down the sides of the dish. The warmth from your hands will help to soften the pastry a little and make it easier to mould. Avoid pushing too firmly or the pastry will crack. Roll a rolling pin lightly across the top of the dish or use your hands flat against the top, to encourage the pastry to expand and ease down the sides of the dish.

3 With your fingers flat against the side of the dish, gently ease the pastry down (as shown). You need to work on the top and sides alternately to coat the dish all over in an even layer of pastry. Avoid using your fingers over the corners of the dish as this can easily create a thin layer of pastry. Place uncovered on a tray in the fridge for 5–6 hours, or ideally overnight, for it to firm even more and dry out.

Note The aim here is to make a watertight container in which meat is cooked in the oven with just a band of baking parchment around the sides as support. The pastry must be thick enough to withstand the weight of the meat, but not so thick that it is unpleasant to eat. It must not have any weak points, or be too thin, or the pie will collapse. It is therefore important that the original shaping of the warm pastry into a disc creates no pleats, and that when shaping round the dish it is not forced or pushed too hard, which could cause it to crack or break.

Veal and ham raised pie

Serves 4

1 quantity hot water crust pastry
  (see left)
1 egg

For the filling

1 small onion
Bunch of flat-leaf parsley
550g boned shoulder of veal
100g piece of gammon
150–200ml aspic (see overleaf)
Salt and freshly ground black pepper

1 Prepare and shape the pastry around a 400ml soufflé dish (see left).

2 The next day, or when ready to cook, heat the oven 190°C/gas mark 5.

3 For the filling, halve, peel and finely dice the onion. Finely chop enough parsley leaves to give you 3 tbsp. Remove any surface gristle and sinew from the veal, trim any excess fat off the gammon and veal and cut both meats into 1.5cm cubes.

4 Mix the onion, meats and half the parsley together in a large bowl and season well with salt and pepper. Reserve the rest of the parsley for the aspic.

5 Remove the shaped pastry and the smaller disc from the fridge. Turn the shaped pastry the right way up and peel the cling film away from inside the dish. Ease the cling film a little from the dish and lift the dish out of the pastry (as shown overleaf) without damaging the pastry. Peel away the cling film and greaseproof paper from the inside of the pastry case.

6 Carefully lift the pastry case up to the light and check the corners; if you can see light through them you will need to reinforce them using a thin band cut from around the edge of the pastry for the lid, by gently pushing it into the area needed.

7 Wrap a double layer of baking parchment around the outside of the pie case to support it and secure with paper clips or string (don't tie string too tightly or it will create a waist in the pie once cooked). Make sure the rim of pastry is not covered by paper, so you can seal it with the lid.

8 Place the pie case on a lipped baking sheet and add the filling, packing it into the corners, to help support the pastry, and doming it on the top (as shown overleaf).

9 Check the pastry lid is the right size to fit over the top. Lightly beat the egg with a very small pinch of salt, using a fork, then pass through a sieve into a bowl. Brush beaten egg on the inside of the pastry lid. Lay the lid on top of the pie, fold the edges of the lid up against the inside of the pie and press together to seal. Using a pair of scissors, trim off only the top edge, not too deep or you will break the seal.

10 Using your thumb and forefinger, crimp the pastry edge. Now make a steam hole in the middle of the top and insert the tip of a 5mm piping nozzle (this will prevent the hole closing). If you have any pastry left, roll it out thinly and cut out decorations, if desired; stick them to the top of the pie with the beaten egg.

11 Brush the top of the pie with beaten egg to glaze. Bake for 15 minutes, then lower the oven setting to 170°C/gas mark 3 and bake the pie for a further 30 minutes. Remove from the oven and take off the paper collar. If the pie suddenly begins to slump and lose shape, tie the paper round the pie again and continue to cook for a further 15 minutes. If the pie holds its shape, brush the sides and the top again with beaten egg and return to the oven for a further 30 minutes, or until cooked.

12 To check that the pie is cooked, insert a skewer into the middle through the steam hole, leave it for 10 seconds, then remove and immediately touch it to your inner wrist; it should be hot. If not, cook the pie for a further 15 minutes.

13 Once the pie is cooked, remove it from the oven and set aside to cool to room temperature.

14 Follow the instructions on the aspic packet to dissolve and sponge it. When the aspic begins to thicken and set a little (still pourable but thick enough to hold the parsley in suspension), add the reserved parsley.

(Continued overleaf)

15 Carefully pour the aspic through the piping nozzle into the pie (as shown), allowing it to seep into the air holes and between the meat and the pastry. You might need to lift the pastry around the steam hole first to allow the aspic to feed through, taking care not to break the pastry. Allow the aspic to set for 3–4 hours before cutting the pie.

Variations

Duck, sour cherry and pistachio raised pie Omit the ham and parsley. Reduce the veal to 150g and add 400g duck leg meat (about 3–4 duck legs, meat only, sinews removed) and toss in 1½ tbsp cornflour. Add 75g dried sour cherries and 50g skinned whole pistachios, with the onion. Season generously and proceed as for the main recipe.

Duck and green peppercorn raised pie Omit the ham and parsley. Reduce the veal to 150g and add 400g duck leg meat (about 3–4 duck legs, meat only, sinews removed) and toss in 1½ tbsp cornflour. Add ½–1 tbsp green peppercorns with the onion.

Pork, apple and sage raised pie Replace the filling for the main recipe with 650g cubed shoulder of pork, 1 small finely diced onion, 1 peeled, cored and finely diced dessert apple, 30g raisins and 1 tsp dried sage or 5–6 fresh sage leaves, chiffonaded (see page 89) or finely chopped. Season well with salt and plenty of pepper.

Raised game pie Replace the filling in the main recipe with 350g mixed game, cut into 1.5cm dice (venison, rabbit, partridge, pheasant or pigeon would be good), 250g minced pork belly, 3 rashers of streaky bacon, cut into strips, 1 small finely diced onion, 5–6 finely chopped sage leaves and ¼ tsp allspice. Season well.

Individual raised pies Shape the pastry crust around ramekins and proceed as for the main recipe, or shape the pie cases by hand.

A note on leakage...

Raised pies can sometimes leak, if the pastry is a little thin or has a weak spot. If after cooking the pie is leaking, allow it to cool, then use soft butter to plug any holes. Allow the butter to firm completely by putting the pie in the fridge for 30–45 minutes. After the aspic has been added to the pie and set, the butter can be scraped away before serving.

A note on aspic...

Aspic is added to raised pies because as the meat cooks it shrinks and releases juices, and as it cools the meat re-absorbs the juice but leaves a gap between the meat and the pastry walls of the pie. Aspic fills all the air holes and holds the pie together when cut. It also helps to preserve the pie, so it can be kept for a few days.

Traditionally, the bones from the meat would be simmered in water and flavourings, strained and cooled to produce a savoury jelly. But these days you can buy aspic powder and use it in the same way as gelatine.

Alternatively, you can use gelatine: 1 tsp powdered gelatine is enough to soft-set 150–200ml lightly flavoured chicken stock. Add a little tarragon or sherry vinegar (about 1 tsp or to taste), 1 tsp finely chopped parsley and salt and pepper.

Suet crust

Suet pastry is most often used for steamed puddings. The raising agent in the flour helps to give the pastry a lighter texture.

Suet pastry

Makes enough for a pudding to serve 4–6
350g self-raising flour
Large pinch of salt
175g shredded beef or vegetarian suet
100–150ml very cold water

Unlike most other pastries, suet pastry should not be rested before use because the raising agent starts working as soon as the liquid is added.

1 Sift the flour and salt into a large bowl. Stir in the suet and rub it into the flour a little with your fingertips, to help break it down.

2 Add 100ml very cold water and, using a cutlery knife, mix everything together. Once you have large flakes, feel them to see if you need more liquid, drawing them to the side and adding more water to the dry flour as necessary.

3 Use your hand to bring the pastry together, feeling the large flakes to ensure there is enough water in the pastry to bring it together comfortably. It should be soft, but not sticky or tacky. Work it in your hands until smooth.

Lining a pudding basin with suet pastry

1 Divide the pastry into 2 unequal pieces, two-thirds and one-third. On a floured surface, pat out the larger piece into a circle about 2cm thick and 15cm in diameter. Flour one half of the pastry circle (to stop it sticking together) and fold the pastry over to form a half-moon shape.

2 Place the pastry fold side towards you and ridge it lightly with the side of your hand so that the straight side becomes curved and the whole rounded again. You will need to use your hands to encourage the open sides away from you.

3 Open the pastry out like a purse, roughly the shape of the pudding basin. Use it to line the basin, easing the pastry where necessary to fit, and trimming off the top to leave a 1cm ridge that sits proud of the top.

Steak and kidney pudding

Serves 4–6
½ small onion
Handful of flat-leaf parsley
400g beef chuck steak
150g ox kidney
2–3 tbsp plain flour, plus extra to dust
1 quantity suet pastry (see left)
Salt and freshly ground black pepper

1 Prepare the greaseproof paper, foil and string for steaming, following the instructions on page 546.

2 Peel and very finely dice the onion; you need about 2 tsp. Finely chop enough parsley leaves to give you 2 tsp. Put both in a large bowl.

3 Trim the beef of excess surface fat and sinew and cut into cubes about 2.5cm square. Prepare the kidneys by removing the large lobes from the central fat and tubes (see page 421). Unless the lobes are very large, leave them whole.

4 Put the beef and kidney into a large sieve. Sprinkle over the 2 tbsp flour and shake until the meat is lightly coated. Add the meat to the onion and parsley. Mix together and season well with salt and pepper.

5 Generously butter a 1 litre pudding basin. Divide the pastry into 2 unequal pieces, two-thirds and one-third. On a floured surface, pat out the larger piece into a circle about 2cm thick and 15cm in diameter, using a rolling pin or your hands, then use to line the pudding basin (see left).

6 Fill with the meat mixture, without packing it too tightly, to leave room for water. Add water to come just below the top pieces of meat.

7 Roll the remaining piece of pastry to a circle 5mm thick, big enough to just cover the pudding filling. Place it on top, wet the edges and press them together securely so that the lid is sealed to the inside of the pastry lining the pudding basin, not around the outside.

8 Cover with the greaseproof paper and foil, and make a string handle, following the instructions on page 546.

9 Stand the covered basin on a trivet, or 3 pieces of cutlery placed in a triangle, in a saucepan of boiling water to come halfway up the sides of the pudding basin. Cover with a tight-fitting lid. Alternatively, use a steamer. Steam the pudding for 5–6 hours, taking care to top up the boiling water occasionally so it doesn't boil dry. It is important to keep the water at a generous boil for the first 30–45 minutes, to ensure the suet in the pastry starts to melt and set with the flour and to achieve a good golden colour.

10 After steaming, carefully remove the pudding basin from the saucepan, using the string handle, and remove the string, paper and foil. Run a knife around the top rim of the basin to release the pudding, invert a plate over the pudding and turn it the right way up so the pudding basin is upside down. Using oven gloves, carefully lift off the pudding basin. Serve immediately, with seasonal vegetables.

Variations

Steak and mushroom pudding Omit the kidneys and replace with 6–8 small chestnut mushrooms, halved or quartered, depending on size.

Steak, kidney and oyster pudding Add a small can of smoked oysters to the meat filling – a delicious and traditional addition.

....

A note on part-steaming a pudding...
You can steam the pudding for at least 3 hours one day, then remove it from the steamer, allow to cool, and chill overnight. The pudding can be finished in the steamer the next day. When heating the following day, just ensure that the first 30 minutes to 1 hour is at a generous boil, to get the inside of the pudding hot as quickly as possible.

Fruit & Puddings

A pudding can be a simple arrangement of seasonal fruit or a baked crumble, or an elaborate and complex combination of flavours and textures. This chapter teaches the skills and techniques needed to create recipes that can be served as stand-alone puddings, or be used as a component of a more intricate dessert. Flavourings are classic, well known and loved, with some interesting contemporary twists. This allows the cook to create the popular classic puddings and, having mastered the techniques, to experiment with and explore more unusual flavour combinations.

Citrus fruit

Citrus fruit, whether playing a dominant or minor role, is an essential ingredient in many puddings and plays an important part in savoury dishes too. The aromatic zest adds depth and contrast, particularly to rich dishes, and can transform creams, chocolate or even crumble toppings from the ordinary to the sublime. The juice can be used to make jellies, and the segmented flesh is easily transformed into the much loved classic pudding: caramel oranges (see overleaf for an exotic version).

Segmenting citrus fruit

Removing the segments cleanly from citrus fruit, leaving behind the core and membrane, makes the segments more attractive and more palatable. To catch any juice as you segment the fruit, you can place the board over a lipped tray.

1 Top and tail the fruit, to remove just the ends and no more.

2 Stand the fruit on its end. Using a small, serrated knife, cut off the remaining zest and pith, following the natural curve of the fruit.

3 Trim away any pith left on the fruit, but don't over-trim, which wastes fruit and makes the segments misshapen.

4 Put the fruit on its side on a board and carefully cut on either side of the membrane, dividing the segments.

5 Use the knife to ease each segment out and place in a bowl.

6 Once all the segments have been removed, squeeze the remaining core and membrane over a bowl, to extract all the juice. Tip any juice caught on the tray beneath the board into the bowl as well.

Zesting citrus fruit

The zest is the very thin outer skin of citrus fruit and does not include the thick, white, soft pith lying beneath, which is very bitter. The zest is made up of tiny little cells filled with the natural oils of the particular citrus fruit, which provide a wonderful, concentrated flavour. Buy unwaxed fruit if you are using the zest.

The best way to remove the zest is to use a very fine, very sharp grater or fine zesting Microplane, and to grate only the outer skin (as shown). Avoid digging too deep with the grater or some of the white pith will be removed with the zest, giving a bitter flavour.

Sometimes a strip of finely pared zest (see below) is used to lend flavour to a savoury or sweet recipe, then discarded before serving. Again, use unwaxed fruit.

Where a recipe calls for the zest of ½ lemon, lime or orange, you will find it easier to zest this quantity from a whole fruit. If the juice is not required for the recipe, wrap the fruit in cling film and keep in the fridge to use another time.

Paring citrus zest

1 Using a swivel peeler, start from the top of the fruit and, as you draw the peeler down towards the bottom, wiggle it a little to remove a wide, fine strip of zest, avoiding the bitter pith.

2 If some pith is removed with the zest, place the pared zest on a board, pith side uppermost, and use a serrated knife to carefully shave the pith off the zest.

Citrus zest julienne

To obtain needle-like shreds of zest, to use as a garnish, trim off any uneven edges from zest strips, then layer on the board and, using a large knife, slice through the zest into fine julienne.

To soften citrus zest julienne

To use the julienne in a savoury dish, simmer them in water for 3–5 minutes to soften before adding them.

If you are using them in a sweet dish, they must be softened in a sugar syrup first: Pare and julienne the zest from one or more oranges, lemons and/or limes. Put 1 quantity of stock sugar syrup (see page 138) in a saucepan and add the citrus zest julienne. Place over a medium heat and simmer gently for 3–5 minutes, or until the zest is starting to soften. Remove the julienne with a slotted spoon and place on baking parchment, spreading them out to cool and dry.

To crystallise citrus zest julienne

Dredge a sheet of baking parchment with caster sugar. Once the julienne have softened in the sugar syrup, remove them with a slotted spoon to the parchment, separating and coating each julienne with the sugar. Once cool, transfer to an airtight container.

Citrus fruit salad in spiced caramel

Serves 4

¼ quantity spiced caramel sauce (see
   page 141, using 125g sugar)
2 large oranges
1 yellow or pink grapefruit
4 kumquats
½ small pineapple

1 Leave the caramel sauce to cool, then cover and refrigerate overnight to allow the flavours to infuse.

2 Prepare the fruit. On a board set over a lipped tray, to catch the juice, peel and segment the oranges and grapefruit, taking care to remove all the pith (see page 530). Slice the kumquats as finely as possible, discarding any seeds. Peel the pineapple, cut out the core and cut the flesh into even chunks, about 2cm. Reserve any juice. Put all the prepared fruit in a serving dish.

3 Stir the reserved fruit juice into the caramel sauce to loosen it. If it has thickened a lot overnight, add a little extra water.

4 Strain the caramel sauce over the fruit, stir in any reserved fruit juice and chill before serving.

Variation

Pineapple and mango in a lime caramel Use the lime caramel sauce variation (on page 141) and add 4–6 dried lime leaves, ½ small pineapple, peeled and cut into wedges, and a mango, peeled and sliced off the stone. Leave to macerate in the fridge for 24 hours before serving.

Orange and Medjool date salad

Serves 4–6

2 large oranges
2 clementines
1 pomegranate
5 ripe apricots
200g Medjool dates
1 tbsp orange flower water
Pinch of ground cinnamon
Caster sugar, to taste
Small mint leaves, to finish

1 Segment the oranges (see page 530), retaining any juice that is released. Put the orange segments and juice in a glass bowl. Peel the clementines, remove as much pith as possible and slice, across the segments, into rounds. Add to the oranges, with any juice.

2 Cut the pomegranate in half and, holding each half over the bowl, bash the skin side with a wooden spoon to release the seeds. Halve or quarter the apricots, discarding the stones, and add to the bowl.

3 Halve or quarter the dates lengthways, discarding the stones, and stir them into the rest of the fruit, with the orange flower water and cinnamon. Sweeten with sugar to taste, depending on the ripeness of the fruit: start with a scant teaspoonful and taste before adding more.

4 Transfer to the fridge for at least 30 minutes, ideally 2 hours, to allow the flavours to mingle. Sprinkle with the mint leaves and serve.

Compotes

Any seasonal fruits can be used to make compotes, which are delicious served with yoghurt, ice creams, bavarois, plain baked cheesecakes or in soufflé omelettes. Spooned over pancakes or waffles, a compote can transform breakfast. They can be successfully frozen too, providing summer flavour for the darkest winter days. Any kind of dried fruit can also be soaked and then used to make a tangy compote when soft fruits are unavailable or out of season.

Apple and blackberry compote

Makes about 600ml
Serves 4
1kg Bramley apples
25ml Somerset cider brandy or
    apple juice
60–75g caster sugar, to taste
100g blackberries

1 Peel, core and cut the apples into 3cm chunks. Place in a heavy-based pan with the cider brandy or apple juice and the sugar.

2 Cover and simmer over a gentle heat for 10–15 minutes, or until the apple is soft. Add the blackberries and cook, uncovered, for a further 3–5 minutes, or until they are starting to soften.

3 Taste and add more sugar if the compote is too sharp. Serve hot or cold with Greek yoghurt or ice cream.

Variations

Apple and date compote Omit the blackberries. Replace the cider brandy with water and add a pinch of cinnamon. Add 200–250g chopped dried dates 10 minutes before the end of the cooking time. Makes about 800ml/Serves 4–6

Pear and apple compote Omit the blackberries. Replace the 1kg apples with 500g apples and 500g pears, peeled, cored and chopped, and cook with cider brandy, Poire William (pear liqueur) or water. Add 1 tbsp chopped preserved stem ginger (drained of its syrup) at the end of cooking, if desired. The cooking time will vary depending on the ripeness of the pears; choose fruit that are ripe but not soft. Makes about 850ml/Serves 4–6

Apple and orange compote Omit the blackberries. Add the finely grated zest of 1 orange to the apples and replace the cider brandy with orange juice or half water and half Cointreau. Peel and segment the orange (see page 530) and chop roughly. Stir into the apple mixture when it is completely soft and remove from the heat immediately. Depending on the sweetness of the fruit, this compote may need a little more sugar, about 20–30g. Makes about 650ml/Serves 4

Blueberry and lemon compote

Makes about 500ml
Serves 4
500g blueberries
5–6 tbsp caster sugar, to taste
1 lemon

1 Put the blueberries and sugar into a small saucepan. Pare the zest from the lemon in strips and add to the pan. Halve the lemon and squeeze the juice from one half; set aside.

2 Cook over a low heat until the blueberries release their juices and just begin to pop, then reduce the heat and simmer very gently for 5 minutes, or until the syrup has thickened enough to coat the back of a spoon.

3 Leave the compote to cool, then remove the lemon zest and add lemon juice to taste. Serve at room temperature or chilled, with vanilla ice cream (see page 592) or vanilla bavarois (see page 586).

Rhubarb and vanilla compote

Makes about 550ml
Serves 4
500g rhubarb (about 2–3 thick or 4–5
   thin sticks)
100ml apple juice or sweet dessert wine
100–150g caster sugar, to taste
¼–½ vanilla pod

1 Heat the oven to 200°C/gas mark 6.

2 Trim the ends off the rhubarb, cut into 2cm pieces and place in a baking dish, in a single or double layer.

3 Put the apple juice or wine in a small saucepan, add the sugar and vanilla pod and place over a low heat to dissolve the sugar. Occasional gentle stirring will help this process, but avoid splashing the syrup up the sides of the pan. Once dissolved, bring to a simmer for 1 minute, then pour it over the rhubarb.

4 Bake in the oven for 15–20 minutes, then gently stir the mixture without breaking up the rhubarb. Taste the rhubarb and syrup and sprinkle over a little more sugar if it tastes too sharp. Return to the oven until the rhubarb is tender, but still holding its shape.

5 Remove from the oven and leave the rhubarb to cool in the dish, then discard the vanilla pod. Serve the compote cold or warm with pannacotta (see page 584) or vanilla ice cream (see page 592).

Raspberry and passion fruit compote

Makes about 750ml
Serves 4–6
500g fresh or frozen raspberries
2 passion fruit
300ml hot sugar syrup (see page 138)
1 lime

1 Place the fresh or frozen raspberries in a heatproof bowl. Cut the passion fruit in half and scoop out the seeds over the raspberries.

2 Pour over the hot sugar syrup, stir and leave to cool.

3 Finely grate the lime zest and squeeze the juice, then add both to the fruit, to taste. Cover and set aside for the fruit to macerate. Serve cold with sorbet, ice cream or meringues and cream, or with yoghurt and granola for breakfast.

Note If using frozen raspberries, they must be individually frozen rather than in a block. Pouring on the hot sugar syrup will defrost them and the individual berries will retain their shape.

Earl Grey infused dried fruit compote

350g mixed dried fruits, such as apricots,
   pears, apples, prunes and mango
Pot of strong Earl Grey tea
1 lemon
1 cinnamon stick
1 star anise
½ tsp ground mixed spice

This compote is best made a day in advance, to allow plenty of time for the fruit to soften and absorb the flavours.

1 Put the dried fruit into a bowl. Pour enough of the Earl Grey tea over the fruit to cover by about 2cm. Leave to soak for at least 4 hours, or ideally overnight.

2 Transfer the fruit and tea to a saucepan. Finely grate the zest from the lemon and squeeze the juice from half of it. Add both to the pan with the cinnamon, star anise and mixed spice. Bring to a simmer and cook very gently for 15 minutes, or until all the fruit is very soft, then remove from the heat and set aside to cool.

3 Once cool, strain through a sieve, reserving the tea and discarding the cinnamon and star anise. Return the tea to the saucepan and reduce it a little until it thickens slightly and becomes syrupy, then add back the fruit to the syrup. Serve warm.

Summer pudding

Serves 6

1kg mixture of fresh redcurrants,
blackcurrants, blackberries, raspberries
and strawberries
150ml water
170g caster sugar, or to taste
10 medium-thick slices of white bread,
ideally 1–2 days old

You need to start this pudding a day in advance.

1 Put the fruit, except the strawberries, in a medium saucepan with the water and sugar and cook gently over a low heat for about 5 minutes until the fruit is softening but still has a vibrant colour. Add the strawberries and continue to cook for 2 minutes until the strawberries are just softening. Taste and adjust the sweetness, if necessary.

2 Transfer the fruit to a colander set over a bowl and set aside until most of the juice has drained into the bowl. Press the fruit a little to extract more juice, but avoid crushing it to a pulp.

3 Cut the crusts off all but 2 slices of the bread, and cut in half slightly on the diagonal, but not in triangles. Cut 2 discs from the remaining 2 slices of bread, one to fit in the bottom of a 1 litre pudding basin and the larger one to cover the top of the basin once filled with fruit. (This top layer will not be seen so you can fill any gaps with bread off-cuts.)

4 Dip the smaller disc of bread in the juice and place in the bottom of the pudding basin. Dip the diagonal pieces of bread in the juice and use them to line the basin, overlapping each piece of bread a little and pressing them together to ensure a good seal.

5 While the fruit is still just warm, spoon it into the bread-lined basin, ensuring the fruit is well packed in to give the pudding a good shape. Dip the larger bread disc in the juice and use to cover the fruit. Stand the pudding basin on a lipped tray, then press a saucer or plate on top of the pudding and put a heavy weight, about 500g, on top. Leave in a cool place overnight to allow the pudding to set in shape.

6 Pour any remaining fruit juice into a saucepan and boil to reduce to a syrupy consistency. Taste and add more sugar if necessary, then leave to cool.

7 When ready to serve, remove the weight and the saucer. Invert a serving dish over the bowl and turn both over together. Give the pudding basin a sharp shake, which should release the pudding, and carefully remove the pudding basin. Spoon the reduced juice over the pudding. Serve with double cream lightly whipped with a little caster sugar to sweeten.

Note You can use frozen fruit, but reduce the water quantity to 50ml, as it will release more water as it is heated.

A note on unmoulding...

To ensure an easy release, you can line the pudding basin with several layers of cling film before lining it with the bread. After inverting the pudding, carefully peel away the cling film.

Roasting, poaching and pan-frying fruit

For a light, seasonal pudding, fruit can be roasted, poached or pan-fried. The recipes below use cooking techniques that can be adapted to many fruits. They can be accompanied by ice cream, bavarois, Greek yoghurt, crème fraîche and even rice puddings.

Honey roasted figs with Greek yoghurt

Serves 4

12 small, ripe figs
4 tbsp clear honey
½ orange
Greek yoghurt, to serve

1 Heat the oven to 220°C/gas mark 7.

2 Cut a cross into the figs through the stem end to come three-quarters of the way down, so that they are still held together at the base. Squeeze the base of each fig a little to open the quarters out and reveal the inside of the fruit. Arrange the figs in 4 small ovenproof serving dishes, three per dish, so they are close together but not squashed.

3 Drizzle 1 tbsp of the honey over each trio of figs. Squeeze the juice from the ½ orange and drizzle 1 tsp over each dish.

4 Bake in the oven for 10–15 minutes, or until the figs are hot, softening and browning on top. Serve warm with yoghurt.

Variation

Honey and thyme roasted figs Scatter the leaves of 1 thyme sprig over the figs with the honey. Omit the orange juice and sprinkle 50ml Pedro Ximenez sherry or Marsala over the figs.

Roasted Marsala peaches

Serves 4

4 peaches
15g butter
2 tbsp soft brown sugar
2 tbsp clear honey
100ml Marsala

1 Heat the oven to 200°C/gas mark 6 and the grill to its highest setting.

2 Cut the peaches in half vertically and remove the stones. Place them cut side up in an ovenproof dish. Cut the butter into tiny pieces and dot all over the peaches.

3 Sprinkle the sugar evenly over the fruit and place under the grill for 5–8 minutes to caramelise a little.

4 Drizzle the honey over the peaches, add the Marsala to the dish and roast in the oven for about 10 minutes until tender. Serve hot or at room temperature; they are delicious with cinnamon ice cream (see page 592) or Greek yoghurt sweetened with honey.

Poached spiced plums

Serves 4
200g granulated sugar
250ml water
1 cinnamon stick
1 vanilla pod
1 star anise
500g plums

1 Put the sugar into a medium saucepan with the water and heat gently until the sugar has dissolved, stirring occasionally, then add the cinnamon stick. Split the vanilla pod lengthways and add to the pan with the star anise.

2 Cut the plums in half and remove the stones. Add the plums to the sugar syrup and cook over a gentle heat for 10 minutes, or until they are soft but not falling apart. If the plums are very ripe, take the pan off the heat as soon as the sugar syrup starts steaming.

3 Remove from the heat and set aside to cool. Remove the spices and serve the plums at room temperature with some of the syrup spooned over. They are lovely with ice cream, crème fraîche or Greek yoghurt.

Variations

Greengages with ginger Use greengages instead of plums. Replace the vanilla, cinnamon and star anise with a 4cm piece of fresh root ginger, peeled and sliced. Remove the ginger slices when the greengages have cooled and stir in 2 pieces of preserved stem ginger, chopped.

Cardamom poached apricots Use apricots instead of plums, reduce the sugar to 100g and replace 150ml of the water with sweet dessert wine. Omit the vanilla pod and star anise and add the pared zest and juice of 1 orange and 6–8 cracked cardamom pods. Poach gently for 5 minutes, or until the apricots are tender but still keeping their shape. Leave to cool in the syrup and, once cool, remove the zest and spices.

....
The poaching technique
Once you've mastered the technique of poaching, any firm fruits can be poached in the same way, such as peaches, nectarines, greengages or quince (allowing a considerably longer poaching time for the latter, as they are very hard).

Poaching means cooking very gently, ensuring the ingredients do not break up during the cooking process and allowing for a transfer of flavour from the ingredient being poached to the poaching liquor. We define the terms of poaching, simmering or boiling as follows:

Poaching is when a small bubble occasionally breaks the surface

Simmering is when small bubbles consistently break the surface

Boiling is the dynamic movement of large bubbles breaking the surface.

Poached pears

Serves 6
1 lemon
1 litre water
500g caster sugar
6 pears

Select firm pears to poach. Conference or Packham are the best varieties to use, as they will hold their shape when cooked

1 Finely pare the zest from the lemon in a long strip and squeeze the juice. Put the water, sugar and lemon zest into a saucepan, just large enough for the pears to stand upright. Place over a low heat and dissolve the sugar; occasional gentle stirring will help this process, but avoid splashing the syrup up the sides of the pan.

2 Meanwhile, core the pears using a melon baller; the smaller the melon baller the less pear will be wasted. Start by carefully inserting the melon baller at the base of the pear and removing a little of the pear. Continue to tunnel through, removing a little at a time until the core has been removed, leaving the stalk intact (as shown).

3 Peel the pears using a swivel peeler. Leave the stalk attached and start peeling the pear from the base of the stalk, drawing the peeler down and following the natural curve of the pear (as shown). Take care not to dig too deeply into the flesh. Trim the base of each pear, if necessary, so it can stand upright. If you don't plan to cook the pears immediately, keep them immersed in cold water with the lemon juice added to prevent them from discolouring (see oxidisation and discolouration page 18).

4 To cook, stand the pears upright in the saucepan, ensuring they are covered by the sugar syrup; add a little more water if necessary. If the pears start to float, place a dampened cartouche (see page 13) on top of them, in contact with the sugar syrup (as shown).

5 Increase the heat until an occasional bubble rises to the surface. Maintain this gentle heat and poach the pears until tender, about 20–30 minutes, depending on the variety and ripeness. When cooked, their colour will have changed from opaque to slightly translucent. To check, carefully remove a pear from the liquid and insert a cutlery knife a little way in, where you have removed the core; it should meet minimal resistance.

6 Once the pears are tender, carefully transfer them to the container in which they will be stored or served. Bring the syrup to the boil and reduce to intensify the flavour. Keep tasting the syrup as it reduces and, when you are happy with the flavour and sweetness, leave to cool before pouring over the pears.

7 The pears will keep in the fridge for up to a week. They can be used whole or cut up for use in various recipes.

Variations

Aromatic poached pears Use the following ingredients individually or in any combination to flavour the poaching syrup: the pared zest of ½ orange; 1 vanilla pod, split lengthways; 1–2 cinnamon sticks; 2 star anise; 8–10 cloves.

Pears poached in red wine For the poaching liquid, use 1 bottle of good quality red wine, 300g caster sugar and 1–2 cinnamon sticks (or other spices from the suggestions in the variation above).

Muscat poached pears Substitute half the water with Muscat or Sauternes dessert wine and reduce the sugar by half.

Honey poached pears Substitute clear honey for half the sugar.

Baked apples with frangipane

Serves 4
4 small Bramley apples
1 tbsp flaked almonds
1 tbsp soft light brown sugar, plus
  extra to sprinkle
100ml Amaretto liqueur

For the frangipane
125g butter, softened
125g caster sugar
1 egg, plus 1 extra yolk
125g blanched almonds
1 tbsp plain flour
2 tbsp dark rum or ½ tsp vanilla extract

1 Heat the oven to 190°C/gas mark 5.

2 Remove the apple cores using an apple corer or a small, sharp knife, making sure you remove all the seeds and the sharp pieces of core. You need to create a generous cavity, about 1.5cm in diameter.

3 Using a sharp knife, score the apples all the way around, about two-thirds of the way up each apple. Place the apples in an ovenproof dish.

4 To make the frangipane, cream together the butter and all but 2 tbsp of the caster sugar until pale, then beat in the egg and the extra yolk. Put the blanched almonds and the reserved caster sugar in a blender or the small bowl of a food processor and process until fine. Stir into the creamed mixture with the flour, then stir in the rum or vanilla extract and mix to a smooth paste.

5 Spoon or pipe the frangipane into the apple cavities, to come not quite to the top. Sprinkle a few flaked almonds and 1 tsp light brown sugar on the top of each apple.

6 Pour the Amaretto into the dish and top up with water so the liquid is about 1.5–2cm deep. Stir the 1 tbsp light brown sugar into the liquid.

7 Bake in the oven for 50–70 minutes, depending on the size of the apples, or until they are completely soft when pierced with a skewer or sharp knife and the frangipane is well risen and brown. Serve with custard or cream.

Note If your blender has a large goblet, you may need to grind more nuts than you need for this recipe, or they will not grind easily. Adding a little sugar helps to get a finer result. Ready ground almonds are available, but they do not have quite the same flavour and texture.

Caramelised bananas with rum butter

Serves 4
4 bananas
50g unsalted butter
50g soft dark brown sugar
6 tbsp light rum

1 Peel the bananas, cut them in half lengthways, then cut each half into 2 or 3 pieces, depending on size.

2 Melt the butter in a frying pan and, when foaming, sprinkle in the sugar and add the bananas. Fry quickly over a medium heat until the bananas are a deep golden brown and the sugar has caramelised. Remove from the heat, transfer the bananas to a plate and set aside.

3 Return the pan to the heat. Add the rum and simmer, stirring to melt the caramelised sugar. Reduce until sticky, then return the bananas to the pan, stirring gently to coat them in the sauce and taking care not to break them up.

4 Divide the bananas between 4 plates and serve with a scoop of ice cream.

Variation

Caramelised rum and coconut bananas Heat a frying pan over a medium heat and add 3–4 tbsp shredded fresh coconut. Gently toast until light brown, then immediately tip onto a plate and set aside to cool. Proceed as for the main recipe, using dark rather than light rum and adding 150ml coconut milk to the pan with the rum. Sprinkle the toasted coconut over the bananas before serving.

Crumbles

Crumbles make a warming and satisfying pudding and are always popular. Varying the flavour means that you can make the most of fruit gluts in season, but fresh, frozen or even good quality tinned fruit can be used to delicious effect when fresh fruit is scarce. You can replace some of the flour with oats or granola to add interesting flavour and texture, or add chopped nuts and spices. The method for a crumble topping uses the rubbing in technique used for shortcrust pastry making (see page 478). Taste the fruit filling before topping with the crumble; you may need to add more sugar if the fruit is less ripe and therefore less sweet.

Rhubarb and ginger crumble

Serves 4

500g rhubarb (about 2–3 thick or
  4–5 thin sticks)
10g butter, to grease
1 small piece of preserved stem ginger in
  syrup, plus 2–3 tbsp syrup from the jar
3–5 tbsp soft light brown sugar, to taste

For the crumble

200g plain flour
Pinch of salt
½–1 tsp ground ginger
125g butter
60g caster sugar

1 Heat the oven to 200°C/gas mark 6.

2 Trim the ends off the rhubarb and cut into 3cm pieces. Use the butter to grease an ovenproof dish and place the rhubarb in it.

3 Roughly chop the stem ginger and stir it into the rhubarb with the sugar and the ginger syrup. Set aside.

4 For the crumble, sift the flour, salt and ground ginger into a large bowl. Cut the butter into small cubes and rub it into the flour with your fingertips until it resembles coarse breadcrumbs. Stir in the caster sugar and sprinkle the crumble mixture over the rhubarb.

5 Cook in the oven for 40–50 minutes, or until the rhubarb is soft when prodded with a sharp knife and the crumble is lightly browned. Serve hot or warm with ice cream, custard or pouring cream.

Variations

Pear and mincemeat crumble Omit the rhubarb, stem ginger and soft brown sugar. Peel, core and chop 1kg pears into large pieces. Add 3–4 tbsp mincemeat. Proceed as for the main recipe.

Raspberry and nectarine crumble Omit the rhubarb, ginger and sugar. Remove the stones from 4 nectarines and cut the fruit into large chunks. Mix with 200g fresh raspberries, adding 1 tbsp caster sugar if the raspberries taste a little sour. Omit the ground ginger from the crumble and use either vanilla sugar instead of the caster sugar, or stir ½ tsp vanilla extract thoroughly through the caster sugar before adding it to the crumble mixture.

Rosemary and red fruit crumble Replace the rhubarb and ginger with 500g red fruit, such as raspberries, blueberries, blackcurrants, strawberries and blackberries, adding only 1–2 tbsp caster sugar, depending on tartness. Alternatively, add some chopped peaches to make up the weight or use a bag of frozen forest fruits supplemented with available fresh fruit. Make the crumble as for the main recipe, omitting the ground ginger and stirring 1–2 tsp very finely chopped rosemary into the crumble with the sugar.

Plum and orange crumble

Serves 4
500g plums (about 10–12 plums)
10g butter, to grease
3–5 tbsp light muscovado sugar, to taste
2 oranges

For the crumble
200g plain flour
Pinch of salt
125g butter
60g light muscovado sugar

1 Heat the oven to 200°C/gas mark 6.

2 Halve the plums and remove the stones. Use the butter to grease an ovenproof baking dish. Spread the plums out in the dish and sprinkle with the sugar.

3 Finely grate the zest of one of the oranges, then peel and segment both fruit (see page 530), reserving the segments and catching any juice. Sprinkle the juice over the plums with half of the zest, reserving the rest.

4 Very ripe plums don't need to be pre-baked. If your plums are quite firm, bake them in the oven for 10 minutes, or until they are starting to soften.

5 Meanwhile, to make the crumble, sift the flour and salt into a large bowl. Cut the butter into small cubes and rub it into the flour with your fingertips until the mixture resembles coarse breadcrumbs. Stir in the sugar and the remaining orange zest, rubbing it in gently to ensure it is evenly distributed through the crumble.

6 Remove the plums from the oven and stir in the orange segments, turning the top layer of plums cut side down. Sprinkle the crumble mixture over the top. Cook in the oven for 30–40 minutes, or until the crumble is lightly browned and the fruit juices are bubbling. Serve hot or warm with ice cream, custard or pouring cream.

Variation

Individual apricot and almond crumbles Cut 12 ripe apricots in half vertically and remove the stones. Divide the apricot halves between 4 ramekins, sprinkle with about ½ tbsp brown sugar and 1 tbsp apple or peach juice and bake for 15–20 minutes, as above. Make the crumble using 75g flour, a pinch of salt, 30g ground almonds, 60g butter and 30g caster sugar. Grind 5 amaretti biscuits to a coarse powder in a food processor and stir into the crumble. Top each ramekin with the crumble and bake for 25–30 minutes, or until the crumble topping is brown and the fruit juices are bubbling. Any leftover crumble mix can be frozen.

Apple, oat and raisin crumble

Serves 4
750g Bramley apples
100g raisins
60–90g soft light brown sugar
1 lemon
10g butter, to grease

For the crumble
100g plain flour
½–1 tsp ground cinnamon
Pinch of salt
100g oats
125g butter
90g soft light brown sugar

1 Heat the oven to 200°C/gas mark 6.

2 Peel and core the apples and cut them into 2–3cm chunks. Place in a bowl with the raisins and sugar (the amount depending on the sweetness of the apples). Finely grate the zest of half the lemon into the apple mixture, and stir it through.

3 Use the butter to grease a shallow ovenproof dish, about 20 x 15cm and 5cm deep. Tip in the apple mixture.

4 For the crumble, sift the flour, cinnamon and salt into a bowl and stir in the oats. Cut the butter into small chunks and rub it into the dry ingredients with your fingertips until the mixture resembles coarse breadcrumbs. Stir in the sugar and sprinkle the crumble over the fruit.

5 Cook in the oven for 30–40 minutes, or until the apple is soft when prodded with a sharp knife and the crumble is lightly browned. Serve with custard.

Variation

Classic apple crumble Omit the raisins and top the apple filling with the more classic crumble topping (see plum and orange crumble, above).

Steamed puddings

Steamed puddings are simple to make, although this gentle method of indirect steaming does take longer than baking in a conventional oven. The basic recipe, which is a creamed sponge, can be adapted to include fruits or spices, and offers the creative cook the opportunity to experiment. Assembled well in advance to cook slowly, this is the ideal comfort pudding to round off a leisurely dinner in cold weather, when you want to avoid last minute preparation. Just don't allow the pan to boil dry!

Preparing a pudding for steaming

1 Put a trivet into a large saucepan (big enough to easily contain the pudding basin) that has a tight-fitting lid. Alternatively, use a folded piece of thick cardboard or a cardboard egg carton (trimmed to fit). This will keep the base of the pudding basin off the bottom of the saucepan, which is its hottest part.

2 Cut out one sheet of foil and 2 sheets of greaseproof paper, at least twice the diameter of the top of the pudding basin. Make a small pleat, about 3cm wide, in the middle of the foil.

3 Put one sheet of greaseproof paper on top of the other and make a similar pleat. Lightly butter one side of the double greaseproof paper. Cut a piece of string, the length of your open arms.

4 Spoon the mixture into the pudding basin and level it out. Place the greaseproof paper buttered side down on top of the pudding basin.

5 Cover with the sheet of foil and push it down and around the top rim of the pudding basin.

6 Fold the string in half and place the doubled string around the pudding basin under the lip, over the foil. Feed the cut ends between the folded end and tighten the string. Separate the 2 cut ends and bring each string around the pudding basin, still under the lip, then tie tightly in a knot.

7 Put the 2 strings together, take them over the pudding basin to the other side and tuck through the string on the other side, leaving the ends loose to create a handle. Tie the string securely.

8 Lift up the foil around the string to expose the greaseproof paper and trim the paper fairly close to the string. Trim the foil to leave a 3–4cm border.

9 Tuck the foil around the greaseproof paper towards the lip of the pudding basin, ensuring all the greaseproof paper is enclosed in the foil. Your pudding is now ready for steaming.

1 A makeshift trivet in place (to keep the base of the basin off the bottom of the saucepan).

2 Pleating the foil that will cover the pudding.

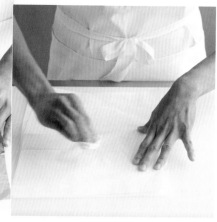

3 Buttering the doubled greaseproof paper.

4 Covering the pudding with the buttered greaseproof paper.

5 Covering the top of the pudding basin with the sheet of foil.

6 Tying the string under the rim of the basin to hold the foil cover firmly in place.

7 Creating a handle from the excess string to make it easier to lift the pudding from the pan.

8 Trimming away the excess greaseproof paper.

9 Tucking the foil border up over the paper.

Treacle sponge

Serves 4–6

120g butter, softened, plus extra
   to grease
75g golden syrup
3 tsp fresh white breadcrumbs
120g caster sugar
½ lemon
2 large eggs, at room temperature
120g self-raising flour
1 tsp ground ginger

1 Grease an 850ml pudding basin well with butter. Prepare the saucepan for steaming and the cover for the pudding (see page 546). Weigh the syrup into the bowl (see page 623) and sprinkle over the breadcrumbs.

2 Cream the butter and sugar in a large bowl until pale and fluffy. Finely zest the ½ lemon and stir into the mixture.

3 Beat the eggs lightly in a separate bowl to loosen and gradually add to the creamed butter and sugar, beating well after each addition.

4 Sift the flour and ginger together and carefully fold into the mixture with a large metal spoon.

5 Spoon the mixture into the pudding basin and level the surface. Cover with the greaseproof paper and foil and secure under the rim (see page 546).

6 Place the pudding basin on the trivet in the steamer and pour in enough boiling water to come at least halfway up the sides of the basin (not touching the foil). Place the pan over a medium heat and ensure the water is bubbling gently, but still not coming into contact with the foil.

7 Put the lid on the pan and steam the pudding for 1¼–1½ hours, checking the water level in the saucepan frequently and topping up with hot water to ensure it doesn't burn dry and no heat is lost.

8 Lift the pudding out of the steamer and remove the string, foil and greaseproof paper. Wearing oven gloves, invert a serving dish over the bowl and turn both over together. Give the pudding basin a sharp shake, which should release the pudding, then carefully remove the basin. Serve with cream or custard.

Variations

Individual sponges Butter 6 individual pudding basins or dariole moulds and put 1 tbsp golden syrup and 1 tsp breadcrumbs in the bottom of each. Divide the mixture between them and proceed as for the main recipe, covering them individually with foil and greaseproof paper. (As this is time-consuming, you might prefer to use heatproof plastic pudding basins with snap-on lids.) Reduce the cooking time to 25 minutes.

Lemon sponge pudding Omit the syrup, breadcrumbs and ground ginger. Add the finely grated zest of 2 lemons to the mixture and proceed as for the main recipe, cooking the pudding for 1½ hours. Warm 150g lemon curd (see page 591) to a thick coating consistency and pour over the pudding before serving.

Medjool date and cardamom pudding Replace half the golden syrup with date syrup. Use ½ tsp ground cardamom in place of the ground ginger and replace the caster sugar with soft dark brown sugar. Remove the stones from 8 Medjool dates and coarsely chop. Stir the chopped dates into the mixture, then proceed as for the main recipe, cooking the pudding for 2½ hours. Serve with Greek yoghurt, sweetened with a little sugar.

Christmas pudding

Serves 8

60g mixed dried apricots and dried figs
1 lemon
50g raisins
30g currants
50g sultanas
20g chopped mixed peel
75ml brown ale
½ tbsp rum
1 teabag
30g prunes
60g butter, softened, plus extra to grease
½ small dessert apple
20g blanched almonds
85g soft dark brown sugar
½ tbsp treacle
1 small egg, at room temperature
30g self-raising flour
¼ tsp ground mixed spice
Pinch of ground cinnamon
Small pinch of freshly grated nutmeg
Small pinch of ground ginger
Small pinch of salt
60g fresh white breadcrumbs

The fruit for this pudding needs to be prepared a day ahead of steaming.

1 Roughly chop the apricots and figs. Finely grate the zest from the lemon, then squeeze the juice from half the lemon. Put the raisins, currants, sultanas and mixed peel into a bowl and add the ale, rum and lemon zest and juice. Cover and leave to soak overnight. Make a pot of tea with the teabag and leave to cool. Put the prunes in a separate bowl, pour over the cold tea and leave to soak overnight.

2 When ready to steam the pudding, grease a 1 litre pudding basin with butter. Prepare the saucepan for steaming and the cover for the pudding (see page 546).

3 Drain the prunes, discarding the tea, then coarsely chop them and add to the fruit and beer. Grate the unpeeled apple and finely chop the almonds.

4 Put the butter and sugar into a large bowl and cream together until pale and fluffy. Stir in the treacle.

5 Beat the egg and gradually add to the creamed butter and sugar, beating well after each addition.

6 Sift the flour, spices and salt together over the mixture. Add the breadcrumbs and fold in with a large spoon. Stir in the nuts, dried fruit and soaking liquor.

7 Spoon the mixture into the buttered pudding basin and level the surface. Cover with the greaseproof paper and foil and secure under the rim, leaving a string handle to make it easier to lift the pudding (see page 546).

8 Place the pudding basin on the trivet in the steamer and pour in enough boiling water to come at least halfway up the sides of the basin (not touching the foil). Place the pan over a medium heat and ensure the water is bubbling gently, but still not coming into contact with the foil.

9 Put the lid on the pan and steam the pudding for 8 hours, checking the water level in the saucepan frequently and topping up with hot water to ensure it doesn't burn dry.

10 After 8 hours, lift the pudding carefully out of the steamer and remove the string and greaseproof paper cover. Wearing oven gloves, invert a serving dish over the bowl and turn both over together. Give the pudding basin a sharp shake, which should release the pudding, and carefully remove the basin. Serve the Christmas pudding with brandy butter or custard.

....

A note on steaming and reheating...

The first few hours of steaming are the most important, so make sure it maintains a good, steady boil. Once the pudding is cooked it can be cooled intact, with the foil still on, and kept in a cool place for a few months. To reheat the pudding, steam it as above for 2–2½ hours.

....

To make your own brandy butter...

Beat 75g butter until well softened. Sift in 75g icing sugar (or use caster sugar if you prefer a slightly granular texture) and beat again until light and fluffy. Gradually beat in 3 tbsp brandy and scoop into a serving bowl.

For an orange flavoured version, use Cointreau in place of the brandy and add the grated zest of ½ orange as you beat the butter to soften it.

Baked sponge puddings

The lovely self-saucing lemon sponge below and the slightly more temperamental chocolate fondant (overleaf) are two of the most tempting baked puddings. The lemon pudding separates invitingly on baking into a light sponge over a zesty sauce. The beauty of the fondants is that the batter can be made well in advance, transferred to the tins and kept in the fridge until required. As long as you keep a careful eye on the clock when they are in the oven, the centre should remain rich and saucy. Few puddings can boast this level of indulgence, or are more popular.

Self-saucing lemon pudding

Serves 4
30g plain flour
125–140g caster sugar, or to taste
15g butter
1 lemon
2 eggs
220ml milk

1 Heat the oven to 180°C/gas mark 4.

2 Put the flour and all but 2 tbsp of the sugar in a medium bowl. Rub in the butter until the mixture resembles fine breadcrumbs.

3 Finely zest and juice the lemon and separate the eggs (see page 160). Stir the lemon zest and juice into the flour and sugar mixture with the egg yolks. Add the milk and stir to combine well.

4 In a separate bowl, whisk the egg whites to medium peaks (see page 161), then add the remaining 2 tbsp sugar and whisk back to medium peaks.

5 Stir one spoonful of whisked egg white into the sponge mixture to loosen it, then carefully fold in the rest.

6 Spoon the mixture into a 1 litre ovenproof dish, 4–5cm deep. Half-fill a roasting tin with boiling water to make a bain marie and place the dish in the tin, making sure the water comes about half to three-quarters up the sides of the dish.

7 Bake in the middle of the oven for 20–30 minutes, or until the sponge has risen a little and turned pale golden; a skewer inserted through just the first 2cm of sponge (no deeper or it will reach the sauce) should come out clean.

8 Remove from the oven and leave to rest for 4–5 minutes before serving.

Variation

Self-saucing lime pudding Replace the lemon with 1–2 limes.

Chocolate fondants

Serves 4 (makes one extra as a test)
For the moulds
20g unsalted butter, to grease
Cocoa powder, to dust

For the fondants
100g butter
200g good quality dark chocolate,
    about 70% cocoa solids
3 eggs, plus 2 extra yolks
100g caster sugar
50g plain flour

These can be prepared up to 24 hours in advance. They are delicious served with vanilla ice cream, as the molten centre acts as a hot chocolate sauce.

1 Melt the 20g butter and use to brush the insides of five 150ml dariole moulds. Sift some cocoa powder into each and shake it around so the insides of the moulds are lightly dusted. Tap out any excess and place the moulds in the freezer.

2 Cut the butter into cubes and put it with the chocolate into a medium heatproof bowl. Bring a pan of water to the boil, then take it off the heat. Place the bowl over the steaming pan, making sure the bottom of the bowl is not in contact with the water. Set aside for the butter and chocolate to melt, stirring occasionally.

3 Put the eggs, extra yolks and sugar in a large bowl and whisk using a hand-held electric whisk until thick and mousse-like. This can be done over a steaming pan to speed up the process, but must then be whisked off the heat until cool again.

4 Using a large metal spoon, fold the melted chocolate mix into the egg mixture, then sift and carefully fold in the flour. Divide between the chilled moulds, filling them to 1cm from the top. Refrigerate for at least 30 minutes, or up to 24 hours.

5 Heat the oven to 200°C/gas mark 6.

6 Place the fondants on a baking tray and transfer to the oven to cook for 12–15 minutes, depending on the oven (an electric oven will be quicker than a gas oven). Remove the spare 'tester' fondant after 12 minutes to test. It should be well risen and set on the outside but still molten in the centre when you cut into it. When they are ready, take the remaining puddings out of the oven. Leave to stand for a minute or two, then remove the fondants from the moulds, inverting them onto plates. Serve immediately.

Sweet soufflé omelette

Serves 2
2 eggs
2½–3 tbsp caster sugar, to taste
20g butter
75–100g fruit compote (see pages
    534–5) or good quality jam
Icing sugar, to dust

1 Heat the oven to 180°C/gas mark 4.

2 Separate the eggs (see page 160), placing the yolks and whites in separate mixing bowls. Add the sugar to the yolks and whisk until pale. With clean beaters, whisk the whites to medium-stiff peaks (see page 161).

3 Heat the butter in a 15cm non-stick frying pan until just starting to foam. Meanwhile, take a large spoonful of whisked whites and stir it into the egg yolk and sugar mixture to loosen it, then carefully fold through the remaining whites.

4 Pour the mixture into the foaming butter, spread out in the pan and cook for 1–2 minutes, or until the base has set and become golden, then transfer the pan to the oven and cook for 5 minutes, or until a skin has just formed over the top.

5 Gently warm through the compote or jam in a small pan. Thick jam may need a little water added to make it a spoonable consistency.

6 Meanwhile, heat 2 long skewers on the hob until red hot.

7 Remove the omelette from the oven; it will still be a little soft inside. Spread the warm compote or jam over half of the omelette and fold it in half using a palette knife. Slide the omelette onto a serving dish and sift icing sugar over the top.

8 Wearing sturdy oven gloves, brand a criss-cross pattern over the top of the omelette with the hot skewers and serve immediately.

Sweet soufflés

Considered the most luxurious and (some would say) most challenging dessert, soufflés display the magical science of cookery at its best, yet they are actually relatively straightforward to prepare. A crème pâtissière base (or a variation of one) is flavoured, then lightened by folding in a simple meringue (whisked egg whites and sugar). On baking the mixture rises impressively in the oven.

Vanilla soufflé

Serves 4–6
10g unsalted butter, to grease
50g caster sugar, plus 1–2 tbsp to coat
  the ramekins
300ml whole milk
1 vanilla pod
3 eggs
15g plain flour
15g cornflour
2–3 tbsp icing sugar

1 Heat the oven to 200°C/gas mark 6 and put a baking tray in to heat. (The hot baking tray will provide 'bottom heat', giving the soufflés an immediate burst of heat from the base to encourage a quick and even rise.)

2 Melt the butter and use to brush 4–6 ramekin dishes, then pour the 1–2 tbsp caster sugar into the first ramekin. Tilt the ramekin to coat the bottom and sides evenly with the sugar, then pour the excess into the next ramekin. Repeat until all the ramekins are coated in sugar.

3 To make the vanilla crème pâtissière, put the milk into a medium saucepan and bring to scalding point (see page 133) over a medium heat. Meanwhile, split the vanilla pod lengthways and scrape out the seeds. Add the pod and the seeds to the milk to infuse. Separate the eggs (see page 160), putting the whites into a large bowl and the yolks into a separate, medium bowl.

4 When the milk has been scalded, take off the heat, skim off any skin that may have formed and remove the vanilla pod. Mix the egg yolks with all but 1 tbsp of the 50g caster sugar, add a splash of the milk, then both flours, and combine well to ensure there are no lumps. Add the remaining milk and stir. Rinse out the milk pan to remove the milk solids.

5 Return the mixture to the rinsed out pan and place over a low to medium heat. Bring to the boil, stirring continuously with a wooden spoon. It will go lumpy, but stir vigorously and it will become smooth. Lower the heat and simmer for 2 minutes. Remove from the heat, transfer to a bowl and leave to cool slightly.

6 Whisk the egg whites to medium-stiff peaks (see page 161), then whisk in the remaining 1 tbsp caster sugar, to stabilise. Take a large spoonful of the whites and fold it into the vanilla crème pâtissière, to loosen it, then gently fold in the remaining whites.

7 Fill the prepared ramekins with the soufflé mixture and use a palette knife to level the tops, scraping away any excess mixture. Clean the outside of the ramekin if necessary and 'top hat' the soufflé by running the tip of a cutlery knife around the top inner rim of the ramekin, which will help to create an even rise.

8 Place the ramekins on the hot baking sheet in the top third of the oven and bake for 8–12 minutes, until cooked but still uniformly wobbly when shaken.

9 Remove the soufflés from the oven, sift the icing sugar over the tops through a fine sieve and serve immediately. There should be about 1 tsp undercooked soufflé mixture in the centre of each.

Baking a large soufflé
To make one large soufflé (to serve 4) instead of individual ones, cook in a 15cm soufflé dish and increase the cooking time to 25–30 minutes.

Variations

Raspberry soufflé Omit the vanilla pod and add 100ml raspberry purée (from about 200g frozen, defrosted and sieved raspberries) to the crème pâtissière. Taste and adjust the sweetness by adding a little more sugar, up to 1 tbsp, then proceed as for the main recipe.

Seville orange soufflé Stir the finely grated zest of 1–2 Seville oranges and 3–4 tbsp of their juice into the crème pâtissière and proceed as for the main recipe. Taste and adjust the sweetness with a little more caster sugar. If Seville oranges are not in season, stir in 2–3 tbsp good quality Seville orange marmalade (ideally thin-cut) instead.

Pistachio soufflé Omit the vanilla pod, stir 2 tbsp pistachio paste into the crème pâtissière, then proceed as for the main recipe.

Caramel soufflé Omit the vanilla pod and reduce the sugar to 25g. Make a dry caramel using 100g caster sugar (see page 141). When the caramel is a deep golden colour, stir it quickly into the still warm crème pâtissière, then proceed as for the main recipe.

Prune and Armagnac soufflé Gently simmer 75g prunes in 75ml Armagnac and 75ml water until soft and at least one-third of the liquid has evaporated. Leave to cool, then purée to a smooth paste. Proceed as for the main recipe, using a few drops of vanilla extract instead of the vanilla pod in the thickened crème pâtissière. Spoon 1 tsp of the prune purée into the prepared ramekins, then stir the remaining purée into the crème pâtissière and proceed as for the main recipe.

Hazelnut nougatine soufflé Omit the vanilla pod. Make ½ quantity of hazelnut nougatine (see page 648) and grind to a fine powder in a food processor. Use 2 tbsp of this to coat the ramekins in place of the sugar. Stir the remaining nougatine into the crème pâtissière and proceed as for the main recipe.

A note on the crème pâtissière...

Try to avoid the crème pâtissière from cooling down completely before folding through the egg whites, or it will stiffen up too much. If this does happen, either warm the crème pâtissière over a low heat to soften it or pulse in a food processor until smooth, then transfer to a bowl and proceed as for the recipe.

A note on stabilising egg whites...

In many recipes where caster sugar is added to whisked egg whites, they can be 'meringued', or stabilised, by whisking a spoonful of the measured sugar into the egg whites once they have reached their desired peak. The mixture is then whisked until stiff again (about 30 seconds with an electric whisk) and will last much longer before it collapses. In this way, whisked egg whites for sweet soufflés can be stabilised and left for up to an hour before they are needed. This is very useful if you don't want to leave everything to the last minute.

Alternative ramekin preparation

Take ¼ tsp softened unsalted butter and spread a very thin layer of it, about 1mm thick, around the inner top rim of the ramekin, to a depth of about 1cm. For a large soufflé dish, use about 1 tsp softened butter; this can give a cleaner rise, but you lose the sweet crust.

Custards and crèmes

Eggs are the common factor in all the recipes in this section, primarily used for their ability to thicken, set, lighten and enrich a mixture. When whole eggs are used, the set of a dish is firmer than when only the yolks are used, so a baked custard set using whole eggs will be firmer than a crème brûlée, where yolks alone are used. Where eggs are the main component in a recipe, it is often necessary to use a bain marie (see step 3, page 120) to ensure gentle cooking, and success here is dependent on knowing how to cook eggs gently.

Bear in mind that the oven temperatures given are a guide. They will differ depending on the size of the ramekin or dish, the heat of the water in the bain marie and the oven.

Baked egg custard

Serves 4
3 eggs, plus 1 extra yolk
3 drops of vanilla extract
60g caster sugar
325ml milk
100ml double cream
1 large bay leaf
Freshly grated nutmeg

1 Heat the oven to 150°C/gas mark 2.

2 Put the eggs, extra yolk, vanilla and sugar in a mixing bowl. Using a wooden spoon, mix until smooth. Take care not to beat in air bubbles as these will adversely affect the texture of the final custard. Stir in the milk and cream.

3 Strain the custard into a fairly shallow 1 litre ovenproof dish. Place the bay leaf on top and sprinkle over some nutmeg.

4 Half-fill a roasting tin with boiling water to make a bain marie. Carefully place the dish in the tin, making sure the water reaches about half to three-quarters up the sides of the dish.

5 Transfer to the lower third of the oven and cook for 55–75 minutes, or until there is a skin on top and the centre is just set and no longer liquid. The custard should still wobble a little when gently jiggled, but there should be no violent wobble. Serve hot, warm or chilled.

Variations

Baked orange custard Omit the bay leaf and nutmeg. Replace 2–3 tbsp of the milk with Cointreau and add the finely grated zest of ½ orange. Leave to infuse for a few minutes before straining into the dish.

Rosewater custard Omit the bay leaf and nutmeg. Reduce the milk quantity by 2–3 tbsp and add 2–3 tbsp rosewater to the custard mixture. If you can find edible rose petals to buy (that have not been sprayed), sprinkle a few on the top of the custard before serving.

Individual baked egg custards
Baked custards can be made in individual ramekins. The quantity above will fill about 6 ramekins, depending on size. Instead of 1 large bay leaf, select 6 small bay leaves to place on the custards before cooking. Individual custards will generally take less time to cook, about 40–50 minutes.

Crème caramel

Serves 6
100g granulated sugar
4 tbsp water
600ml milk
Few drops of vanilla extract
4 eggs
2 tbsp caster sugar

You need to prepare this dish a day in advance, to allow time for it to set properly.

1 Heat the oven to 150°C/gas mark 2 and place a 1 litre ovenproof dish, 4–5cm deep, in the oven to warm up.

2 Put the granulated sugar and water into a heavy-based saucepan and heat gently until the sugar has dissolved. Using a pastry brush dipped in water, brush down the sides of the pan (see page 138) and bring the syrup to a gentle simmer. Simmer until it caramelises and reaches a rich golden colour, then immediately remove from the heat.

3 Working quickly and wearing oven gloves to protect your hands, remove the dish from the oven and pour in the caramel. Immediately tip and rotate the dish so that the caramel coats the insides evenly. Set aside.

4 Pour the milk into a saucepan, place over a low to medium heat and bring to scalding point (see page 133), then remove from the heat and stir in the vanilla extract.

5 Mix the eggs and caster sugar in a large bowl until well combined, but avoid introducing too many air bubbles. Gradually pour the milk into the egg mixture, stirring well, then strain the custard into the prepared dish. Cover with foil to prevent a thick skin from forming when cooking.

6 Half-fill a roasting tin with boiling water to make a bain marie. Place the dish in the tin, making sure the water comes about half to three-quarters up the sides of the dish.

7 Carefully transfer the tin to the bottom third of the oven and cook for 60–75 minutes, or until the centre is just set. There will be a uniform (but not violent) wobble to the custard when it is jiggled gently, but it will no longer be liquid. (The custard will firm up once it is cool.)

8 Leave to cool, then chill overnight in the fridge.

9 To serve, remove the crème caramel from the fridge at least 30 minutes before serving, to bring it to room temperature, as the flavour will be better. Ease the top edge of the custard away from the dish using only the very tip of a small knife. Invert a plate over the dish then, holding on to the dish and the plate, turn the plate the right way up with the dish now upside down. The crème caramel should drop down onto the plate. Carefully lift away the dish.

Variation

Rum and raisin crème caramel Put 50g raisins in a saucepan with 4 tbsp dark rum and 4 tbsp water. Bring to the boil, remove from the heat and set aside for 20 minutes to plump up. Drain the raisins, reserving the liquor. Make the liquor up to 4 tbsp (it doesn't matter if it is a little more) with more rum, and use in place of the water to make the caramel. Replace 50ml of the milk in the custard with 50ml dark rum. Once the dish has been lined with the caramel, sprinkle over the soaked raisins before you strain over the custard. Proceed as for the main recipe.

Individual crème caramels

If using individual ramekins, this quantity will serve about 6, and will take less time to cook, about 40–50 minutes. You will need to work very quickly when dividing the caramel between the ramekins.

Crème brûlée

Serves 4
300ml double cream
1 vanilla pod
4 egg yolks
1–2 tbsp caster sugar, to taste, plus extra
   for the topping

You need to start preparing this dish a day in advance to allow time for chilling.

1 Heat the oven to 150°C/gas mark 2.

2 Put the cream into a saucepan. Split the vanilla pod in half lengthways, scrape out the seeds and add them to the cream along with the pod. Bring to scalding point (see page 133) over a low to medium heat. Remove from the heat and leave the vanilla to infuse for at least 10 minutes, then remove and discard the pod.

3 Mix the egg yolks with the sugar in a medium bowl, then pour the warm cream into the bowl and stir until combined.

4 Strain the custard into 4 ramekins. Stand them in a roasting tin. Pour in enough boiling water to come half to three-quarters up the sides of the dishes. Transfer to the oven and cook for 30–40 minutes, or until just set and a skin has formed. Leave to cool and then chill in the fridge overnight, to allow them to set further.

5 For the topping, use either a kitchen blowtorch or the grill heated to its highest setting. Sprinkle an even 2–3mm layer of caster sugar over each custard (as shown). Wipe the rim of the dish to remove any excess sugar, to avoid it burning. Spraying the sugar very lightly with water, using a spray bottle, can speed up the caramelising process, helping the sugar to dissolve. If using a blowtorch to caramelise the sugar (as shown), avoid holding the torch too close to the sugar and keep it moving to avoid burnt patches. If placing the ramekins under the grill, move the dishes as necessary to achieve an even colour.

6 Leave the caramel to cool and serve within 1 hour. Do not chill or the caramel will liquefy.

Variations

White chocolate and Earl Grey tea crème brûlée Omit the vanilla pod and infuse the cream when scalding with 1 tsp Earl Grey tea leaves, or to taste; it shouldn't be too strong. Strain the cream and discard the tea. Reheat the cream, adding 30g white chocolate, in pieces. Allow the chocolate to melt fully in the cream, then proceed as above.

Coffee crème brûlée Omit the vanilla pod. Add 1–2 tsp instant coffee granules to the cream when scalding, allowing it to melt into the cream. Proceed as above.

Stem ginger crème brûlée Omit the vanilla pod. Cut a ball of preserved stem ginger into julienne and add to the cream when scalding. In place of the 1–2 tbsp sugar, use syrup from the jar of preserved ginger to taste.

Kahlua crème brûlée Omit the vanilla pod and add 2½–3½ tbsp Kahlua to the custard before straining into ramekins.

Orange crème brûlée Omit the vanilla pod and infuse the scalding cream with the zest of 1 orange, then strain and proceed as above. A few drops of orange flower water or Grand Marnier can be added to the custard, before straining, to taste. It might also be necessary to add an extra 1–2 tsp caster sugar, to taste.

Cinnamon crème brûlée Omit the vanilla pod and infuse the scalded cream with 2–3 cinnamon sticks for 30 minutes. Remove the cinnamon and proceed as above.

Using classic crème brûlée dishes
Use the traditional shallow 'ear dishes' (125ml capacity) if you have them; the custard will probably cook more quickly, so check after 20–30 minutes.

Bread and milk puddings

Owing their existence to thrifty times, when a filling but inexpensive pudding was required, these have been both nursery and grown-up favourites through history. Appealing in their simplicity, they tend to be comforting rather than elegant. However, replace the bread in a bread and butter pudding with leftover panettone and a humble classic becomes something rather more sophisticated. Similarly, a rice pudding can be infused with spices, or adorned with a fruit compote to take it to a different level.

Bread and butter pudding

Serves 4

50g butter, at room temperature
4–5 slices of white bread, cut
   7–8mm thick
2 tbsp sultanas or raisins
2 eggs, plus 1 extra yolk
40–50g caster sugar, to taste
Few drops of vanilla extract
600ml milk
1–2 tbsp demerara sugar, to sprinkle
Freshly grated nutmeg or ground
   cinnamon

1 Heat the oven to 150°C/gas mark 2. Use a little of the butter to grease a 1 litre ovenproof dish, 4–5cm deep.

2 Remove the crusts from the bread, butter the slices generously and cut them diagonally into triangular quarters. Starting with the dried fruit, layer the bread and dried fruit in the buttered dish, finishing with a layer of bread. Try to avoid a flat piece of bread as the last layer, so fan the bread out across the dish, if necessary. This will help the edges of the bread to crisp and colour.

3 Mix the eggs, extra yolk, sugar and vanilla extract together in a jug, then pour in the milk, stirring well. Strain this custard mixture over the bread, gently pushing the bread down into the custard to ensure it is fully coated. (The bread does not have to be completely covered with custard, but the top layer should have soaked some up.) Set aside to soak for up to 30 minutes.

4 Sprinkle the demerara sugar and a pinch of nutmeg or cinnamon over the surface of the pudding.

5 Half-fill a roasting tin with hot water to make a bain marie and stand the dish in the tin. Transfer to the middle of the oven and cook for about 1¼–1½ hours, or until the custard is just set but still slightly runny in the middle and the top is brown and crusty. If it has not taken on colour, place under a hot grill for a very short time, less than a minute, to brown a little.

Variation

Panettone pudding Replace the bread with slices of panettone and use good quality chopped candied peel in place of the sultanas or raisins. Replace 30ml of the milk with 2 tbsp Amaretto liqueur.

....

For a crisp top...

Bread and butter pudding can be cooked without a bain marie for a brown and crunchy crust, but the custard itself will not be as smooth. Sliced white bread can be used for bread and butter puddings, but slicing a loaf yourself produces better results.

Pain perdu with cardamom and grilled apricots

Serves 4
2 eggs
150ml milk
1 tsp vanilla extract
1–2 tbsp soft light brown sugar, to taste
½ tsp ground cardamom
4 thick slices of stale bread
½ quantity (6 apricots) cardamom
  poached apricots (see page 539)
1–2 tbsp icing sugar, to dust
50g unsalted butter

1 Whisk the eggs and milk in a bowl with the vanilla, brown sugar and cardamom. Strain the mixture onto a wide plate with a lip.

2 Cut the bread slices into triangular halves or quarters, depending on their size, removing the crusts if you like. Dip them into the egg mixture on both sides and then leave in the mixture for at least 10 minutes to soak up the remainder.

3 Heat the grill to its highest setting. Remove the poached apricots from the syrup with a slotted spoon and place them on a baking sheet, cut side up. Strain the syrup and reserve.

4 Pat the cut surface of the apricots dry with kitchen paper, sift over a heavy layer of icing sugar, then grill until the sugar caramelises (or use a kitchen blowtorch).

5 Heat half of the butter in a frying pan and, when it foams, add half of the soaked bread slices and fry until golden brown, then turn them over and fry the other side. Remove to a plate and keep warm while you fry the rest of the bread slices in the remaining butter.

6 Serve the pain perdu with the grilled apricots, spooning over some of the syrup. Greek yoghurt is a delicious accompaniment.

Variation

Pain perdu with fruit compote Omit the cardamom and serve a fruit compote (see pages 534–5) with the pain perdu instead of the apricots.

Baked rice pudding with nutmeg

Serves 4
10g butter, to grease
400ml milk
200ml double cream
100g pudding (short-grain) rice
1–2 tbsp caster sugar, to taste
Nutmeg, to grate

1 Heat the oven to 170°C/gas mark 3.

2 Use the butter to grease a fairly shallow 750ml ovenproof dish, about 4cm deep. Add the milk, cream, rice and sugar to the dish and stir to mix.

3 Bake in the oven for 2½ hours, stirring gently every 30 minutes. Turn the oven setting up to 180°C/gas mark 4 and finely grate a light coating of nutmeg over the top of the pudding. Bake for a further 30 minutes, or until the rice is soft and a golden brown skin has formed. Serve on its own, or with a fruit compote (see pages 534–5) or homemade jam.

Variations

Black rice pudding with coconut Omit the nutmeg. Replace the pudding rice with 200g Chinese black rice, the milk and cream with coconut milk, and the caster sugar with 2 tbsp soft light brown sugar.

Stovetop vanilla rice pudding Omit the nutmeg. Put all the ingredients into a saucepan, add a vanilla pod and simmer, stirring occasionally, for 40 minutes or until the rice is soft. Serve with poached fruit (see page 539).

Batters

Batters form the basis of so many simple and delicious dishes, from pancakes to Yorkshire puddings. The trick is knowing how much liquid to add, so that the perfect consistency is achieved, particularly when mastering the art of the French crêpe. Resting a crêpe batter before use also makes the end result lighter and more delicate. Clafoutis, a classic French dessert traditionally made with black cherries, is easy to prepare, and transforms a simple batter into an informal pudding which can be adapted to accommodate the soft and stone fruits of the season.

Cherry clafoutis

Serves 4
350–400g sweet black cherries
4 tbsp Kirsch
½ vanilla pod
150ml milk
100ml double cream
4 eggs
120–140g caster sugar, to taste, plus
  extra to sprinkle
20g plain flour
Pinch of salt
10g butter, to grease

1 Heat the oven to 180°C/gas mark 4.

2 Remove the stones from the cherries using a cherry or olive stoner (as shown). Place the cherries in a bowl and sprinkle over the Kirsch.

3 Split the half vanilla pod lengthways and put it into a small saucepan with the milk and cream. Bring to scalding point (see page 133), then remove the pan from the heat and set aside to infuse for at least 10 minutes.

4 Put the eggs and sugar into a medium bowl and whisk until light and creamy. Add the flour and salt and whisk again until smooth.

5 Remove the vanilla pod from the milk and scrape the seeds back into the milk. Strain the infused milk onto the egg mixture and whisk well.

6 Use the butter to grease a 1–1.25 litre ovenproof dish, 3–4cm deep, and sprinkle it with caster sugar. Scatter the cherries over the bottom of the dish, discarding the remaining Kirsch, then pour over the batter.

7 Cook in the middle of the oven for 50–60 minutes. It should be slightly risen and browning round the edges, but although set, the mixture will still be a little softer in the centre. Sprinkle with caster sugar and serve with a cherry compote or with clotted cream, or both.

Note To make individual clafoutis, use four 15cm gratin dishes and bake for 20–25 minutes.

Variations

Apricot clafoutis Replace the Kirsch with 2 tbsp Amaretto liqueur. Halve 8 small, ripe apricots, remove the stones and place, cut side down, in the dish, instead of the cherries. Alternatively, use 1 quantity poached apricots (see page 539, omitting the cardamom).

Blueberry clafoutis Replace the cherries with 300–350g blueberries and the Kirsch with 2 tbsp Amaretto liqueur. Add the finely grated zest of ½ lemon to the batter, if you like.

Blackberry clafoutis Replace the cherries and Kirsch with 300g blackberries and 4 tbsp crème de mûres. If the blackberries are very sharp, add a little more sugar.

Plum clafoutis Halve 8 small, ripe plums, remove the stones and place, cut side down, in the dish, instead of the cherries. Add a good pinch of ground cinnamon or a very finely diced ball of preserved stem ginger to the batter, if you like.

Prune clafoutis Soak 200g prunes overnight in a mixture of 50ml brandy and 150ml apple juice and use in place of the cherries, discarding any remaining soaking juices.

Crêpes

Makes about 12
100g plain flour
Pinch of salt
1 egg, plus 1 extra yolk
300ml milk
1 tbsp sunflower or light olive oil
30g unsalted butter, for frying

1 Sift the flour and salt into a mixing bowl. Make a well in the centre. Beat the egg and extra yolk in a small bowl with a fork and add them to the well.

2 Stir the eggs, concentrating your stirring only in the eggs, gradually drawing in flour from around the edge. Don't force the flour in, it will be incorporated automatically as you stir the eggs.

3 As the egg mixture becomes thicker, add a little milk to loosen it, then keep stirring. Continue like this until all the flour has been incorporated. Beat to ensure the thick mixture is smooth, then add the remaining milk and oil. Chill the batter in the fridge for at least 30 minutes, which allows the starch cells in the flour to swell (so lightening the batter).

4 When ready to use, check the consistency of the batter; it should be a thin cream consistency. Pour it into a jug.

5 Melt the butter and set aside in a small bowl. Prove a small 16cm diameter frying pan (see page 70) or use a non-stick pan. Place the pan over a low to medium heat. Wipe out the pan with kitchen paper dipped in the melted butter.

6 Pour a little of the batter into the frying pan, just enough to thinly coat the bottom of the pan, about 1–2mm thick. As you pour the batter in, swirl the pan to encourage the batter to cover the bottom completely, then pour off any excess, back into the jug. Return the pan to the heat and use a palette knife to trim away any batter left up the side of the pan from pouring excess batter back into the jug.

7 After 1–2 minutes, use the palette knife to release and lift the edge of the crêpe to check the colour on the underside.

8 When golden brown, use the palette knife and your fingertips to turn the crêpe over. Cook the second side until golden, 1–2 minutes, then carefully remove it from the pan to a plate.

9 As the pancakes are cooked, stack them interleaved with strips of greaseproof paper (about 3cm wide). This will help to keep the crêpes separate as they are piled up. Repeat with the remaining batter, wiping out the pan with kitchen paper dipped in the melted butter for each crêpe.

A note on cooking crêpes...

Often the first couple of crêpes will either be too thick, or thin and will break. Check the consistency of the batter and add a little milk if too thick. As you become more familiar with pouring the batter into the pan and swirling it, the crêpes will improve.

Avoid overcooking the crêpes or they will toughen; they need only 1–2 minutes each side. They should be very thin, with no crisp edges. Adjust the heat a little if necessary.

Storing and serving

Crêpes can be kept warm wrapped in a clean tea towel. Place one under the first crêpe and wrap the crêpes while making the next one.

Crêpes can be kept in the fridge for 1 or 2 days or frozen in a stack, wrapped in foil and defrosted before use. To warm them through, place the wrapped crêpes in a low oven for 5–10 minutes.

Crêpes can be filled with a variety of fillings, both savoury (such as the gougère fillings on page 520) and sweet, such as flavoured crème pâtissière (see page 134) or fruit compotes (see pages 534–5).

1 Pouring the beaten egg into the flour well.

2 Gradually incorporating the flour into the egg.

3 Stirring a little of the milk into the mixture to loosen it.

4 Checking that the crêpe batter is the correct 'thin cream' consistency.

5 Lightly greasing the pan using kitchen paper dipped in melted butter.

6 Swirling the pan to cover the bottom with a thin layer of batter.

7 Lifting the edge of the crêpe to check the colour on the underside.

8 Turning the crêpe over in the pan.

9 Stacking the cooked crêpes, interleaved with greaseproof paper.

Crêpes with sugar and lemon

Serves 4
1 lemon
12 crêpes (see page 564)
3–4 tbsp caster sugar, to taste

1 Juice the lemon.

2 To serve, place a crêpe on each serving plate and sprinkle over a little sugar. Drizzle over a little lemon juice and roll the crêpe up loosely. Repeat with the other crêpes, pile them up and sprinkle with a little more lemon juice and sugar.

Note A pinch of cinnamon can be added to the sugar.

Crêpes Suzette

Serves 4
12 crepes (see page 564)

For the orange butter
1 orange
150g unsalted butter
50–60g caster sugar, to taste
4–5 tbsp Grand Marnier

To flambé
1–2 tsp caster sugar
2 tbsp Grand Marnier
1 tbsp brandy

1 For the orange butter, finely grate the zest and squeeze the juice from the fruit. Put the butter, sugar, orange zest, 4–5 tbsp orange juice and the Grand Marnier in a large frying pan and simmer gently for 2 minutes over a low to medium heat.

2 Lower the heat and lay a crêpe in the frying pan, with the side that was cooked first downwards. Baste it in the orange syrup and, using a spoon and a fork, fold it in half and then in half again to make a triangle. Push the pancake to the side of the pan, add a second pancake and repeat the basting and folding, then repeat with the remaining pancakes. Add a little water if the pan becomes dry.

3 Once all the pancakes are folded, sprinkle them with the 1–2 tsp caster sugar and increase the heat to medium.

4 Heat the Grand Marnier and brandy in a ladle directly over a flame and set alight. Pour the lit alcohol over the pancakes, tipping the ladle away from you as you do so, and shake the pan until the flames subside. Serve immediately.

Variation
Segment a second orange (see page 530) and add to the sauce to heat through before serving.

American pancakes

Serves 4
100g plain flour
1½ tsp baking powder
Pinch of salt
Generous pinch of caster sugar
15g butter
1 egg
150ml milk
Butter or oil, for frying

To serve
1 quantity Earl Grey infused dried fruit compote (see page 535)
Crème fraîche

Also known as drop scones, these pancakes are often served with butter at teatime.

1 Sift the flour and baking powder into a large bowl and add the salt and sugar. Make a well in the centre.

2 Melt the butter and leave to cool a little. Beat the egg and add to the well with the milk and the cooled melted butter. Beat into the flour using the batter method (see step 2, page 564). Leave to stand in the fridge for 20 minutes before using. Heat the oven to its lowest setting.

3 Heat a knob of butter or 1 tbsp oil in a frying pan until hot, then add small ladlefuls of the mixture. Cook over a medium high heat for 30–45 seconds, or until the pancakes puff up and brown, then turn and cook the second side. Keep warm in the low oven or wrapped in a tea towel while you cook the rest of the pancakes. You will need to cook 1 large or 2 smaller pancakes per person.

4 Serve the pancakes with a spoonful each of compote and crème fraîche.

Note These pancakes are also ideal to serve for breakfast or brunch, as above or with fresh berries and a sifting of icing sugar, or maple syrup and crispy bacon.

Rich and creamy puddings

Many of these desserts are conveniently prepared well ahead and kept in the fridge ready to serve. For an effortless creamy pudding that doesn't require a recipe, fold broken meringues and lightly crushed raspberries or strawberries through whipped cream to make an irresistible Eton Mess.

Lemon syllabub

Serves 4
75g granulated sugar
150ml water
2 lemons
300ml double cream
2–2½ tbsp sweet white wine
Icing sugar, to taste

1 Put the sugar and water into a small saucepan. Place over a low heat and stir very gently without splashing up the sides of the pan, until the sugar has dissolved.

2 Once the sugar has dissolved, dip a pastry brush in water and brush down the sides of the pan. Turn up the heat and boil the sugar syrup, without stirring, for 4 minutes.

3 Finely pare the zest from half of 1 lemon using a swivel peeler, then cut into very fine julienne (see page 531). Put the zest julienne into the syrup and simmer for 4 minutes. Remove from the syrup with a slotted spoon and set aside.

4 Put the cream into a medium bowl and finely grate in the zest of half the second lemon. Juice both lemons. Start whisking the cream, adding the lemon juice and wine and sifting in icing sugar to taste, little by little as you whisk. The cream will thicken up on adding the lemon juice, but will be thinned out by adding the wine. The aim is to add all the liquid without letting the syllabub get too thin.

5 Adjust the sweetness with sifted icing sugar, spoon the syllabub into individual glasses and chill for at least 20 minutes. Scatter a few lemon zest julienne on the top of each glass before serving.

Variation

Blackcurrant syllabub Omit the sugar syrup and lemons. Put 150g blackcurrants and 30ml water into a saucepan and simmer over a low to medium heat until the blackcurrants are soft and the water has reduced to about 1–2 tsp. Add 2 tbsp crème de cassis and push the blackcurrants through a sieve to make a purée. Whisk the purée into the cream as for the main recipe, replacing the sweet wine with crème de cassis. Save a few berries for decoration and dust with caster sugar.

Zabaglione

Serves 4
4 egg yolks
75–85g caster sugar, to taste
75ml Marsala

1 Put the egg yolks, sugar and half the Marsala into a heatproof bowl. Whisk well and set the bowl over a saucepan of simmering water, taking care that the bowl is not touching the water (or the eggs will overheat and scramble).

2 Continue to whisk for up to 10 minutes over the heat until the mixture is frothy, pale and very thick.

3 Remove the bowl from the heat and continue whisking for a couple of minutes until the bowl feels cool. Gradually fold in the remaining Marsala using a large metal spoon or spatula.

4 Pour the zabaglione into glasses and serve immediately.

Note Make sure you stop whisking the mixture over the heat as soon as it has reached a thick consistency, as continuing for too long after this point can cause the foam to collapse.

Whisking cream

When cream is whisked, air bubbles are trapped as the cream thickens, enabling whipped cream to lighten and enrich mixtures, even helping them to set.

Whipping cream, which generally has a fat content of 35%, creates a good volume when whisked. Double cream (45% fat) can be relatively easily whisked, but produces a heavier result than whipping cream. Single cream has too low a fat content (22%) to be successfully whisked.

It is very easy to over-whisk cream; many a roulade has been ruined by the grainy, fatty texture of over-whipped cream. To help avoid this, make sure the cream is cold before you whisk it. On a hot day, it is a good idea to whisk cream slowly, by machine or with a balloon whisk, as it can suddenly thicken.

If you are adding sweetness and flavourings to cream, such as icing or caster sugar, vanilla seeds or grated orange zest, add them before you start whisking. If added at the end of whisking, too often the cream becomes over-whisked, because as you adjust the seasoning, the cream thickens up more and more. If you add acid or alcohol to cream, it will thicken much faster than usual.

If you are folding whipped cream into a sweet mixture, taste it when the other ingredients have been added, then adjust the sweetness accordingly. If you are eating the whipped cream with no added flavourings, you need to sweeten it with sugar or it will taste bland. If the cream is to go with something very sweet, such as meringue, it must be sweetened more, rather than less, than cream served with something less sweet. This is because the extreme contrast in sweetness gives the cream a slightly savoury flavour.

Whipping cream to different consistencies

Soft peak When whisked to this stage, cream is thick enough to form soft peaks that hold briefly as you lift the whisk, then dissipate back into the cream. If cream is to be folded into another mixture, such as crème pâtissière, it should be of a similar consistency, usually soft peak.

Medium peak To use for sandwiching cakes together or for piping, cream needs to be whisked to a slightly firmer peak, so it is just holding its shape but not splitting or looking ragged and textured if piped.

Piping consistency When piping whisked cream, it may overheat in a piping bag held by warm hands, and the last of the cream may curdle before it is piped. To avoid this, slightly under-whisk the cream, or only half-fill the piping bag.

Rescuing over-whipped cream...

If cream is a little over-whipped, you can rescue it by folding a little milk into it. It may first appear to thicken lumpily, but then it should smooth out and soften a little. Take care, as too much milk will loosen the cream too much, and it will be too runny to use.

Rhubarb fool

Serves 4

300g rhubarb (about 2–3 thin sticks)
150ml water
100g caster sugar
½ vanilla pod
300ml milk
3 egg yolks
1 tbsp cornflour
150ml double cream
A little icing sugar, to taste

1 Trim the ends off the rhubarb, cut into 3cm pieces and put into a saucepan with the water. Cover and cook over a low heat for about 20 minutes until the rhubarb has completely softened. Stir in half of the sugar and simmer, uncovered, until all but about 2 tbsp of the liquid has evaporated. Take off the heat and leave to cool.

2 Meanwhile, make the custard. Split the half vanilla pod lengthways, put into a saucepan with the milk and bring to scalding point (see page 133). Beat the yolks and cornflour with the remaining sugar in a bowl until smooth. Gradually stir in the hot milk, reserving the vanilla pod, then pour the custard back into the rinsed out pan and return to a medium heat. Stir with a wooden spoon until the custard comes to the boil. Remove from the heat and scrape the seeds out of the vanilla pod into the custard. Strain into a bowl and cover the surface with a piece of cling film while it cools, to prevent a skin from forming.

3 When the rhubarb and custard are both cool, lightly whisk the cream to the soft peak stage (see left).

4 Stir the rhubarb into the custard, then fold in the cream. Taste and add icing sugar if needed. Spoon into tall glasses to serve.

Variations

Gooseberry and elderflower fool Replace the rhubarb with 300g gooseberries, adding 75ml elderflower cordial in place of the sugar once the gooseberries are soft. Push the fruit through a sieve to make a purée before cooling and adding to the custard and cream. Add more cordial or icing sugar to sweeten if desired.

Quick summer berry fool Omit the rhubarb. Mash 300g mixed summer berries with 50g sugar and mix with the custard and cream.

Raspberry and Amaretto trifle

Serves 6

For the sponge base

1 x 20cm Victoria sandwich layer,
  (see page 624, ½ quantity)
4 tbsp good quality raspberry jam
90–120ml (6–9 tbsp) Amaretto liqueur

For the custard

150ml milk
150ml double cream
1 vanilla pod
6 egg yolks
2–3 tbsp caster sugar, to taste

For the fruit and topping

200g fresh raspberries
300ml double cream
1–2 tbsp icing sugar, to taste
4 small ratafia biscuits

For best results, make the Victoria sandwich a day ahead and leave it unwrapped overnight to dry.

1 For the custard, place the milk and cream in a small saucepan. Split the vanilla pod lengthways and add it to the pan. Slowly bring up to scalding point (see page 133) over a low heat, then remove from the heat and leave to stand for 15 minutes to allow the vanilla to infuse into the milk.

2 Cut the cake into thick slices. Sandwich the slices together in pairs with the raspberry jam and arrange in the bottom of a glass serving dish. Sprinkle with the liqueur and set aside to soak while you make the custard.

3 To make the custard, lightly beat the egg yolks and sugar together in a bowl. Bring the milk back to scalding point and pour over the yolks, stirring. Rinse out the pan and pour the custard back in. Heat over a low to medium heat, stirring with a wooden spoon, until the custard is thick enough to coat the back of the spoon (see step 5, page 132). Remove from the heat, strain into a bowl and leave to cool down slightly, for 5 minutes.

4 Pour the custard over the cake and set aside until cold.

5 Sprinkle the raspberries over the cold custard layer. Whip the cream with the icing sugar to a little firmer than soft peaks and spoon decoratively over the trifle. Crumble the ratafia biscuits over the cream to serve.

Folding-in technique

Developing an effective and efficient folding in technique will help to maintain volume in egg whites, mousses and foams and prevent lumps of flour or other dry ingredients from being suspended in the mixture. When folding in, choose a very large bowl and spoon (with a fine edge, so ideally metal; a wooden spoon is not ideal for folding). A large rubber spatula is also effective for folding in.

Recipes will often ask for you to stir one spoonful of egg white into the mixture first. This 'sacrificial' spoonful can be stirred in more vigorously than the rest (as shown), as it helps to loosen the mixture, making it more accepting of the remaining egg white. It is then easier to fold through the remaining egg white, creating minimal loss of volume.

When folding, use the spoon to cut through the centre of the mixture down to the bottom of the bowl (as shown), then draw the spoon diagonally through the mixture to the opposite side of the bowl closest to you (as shown). Turn the bowl about 90° and repeat the folding action, and keep repeating it until almost all the egg white has been incorporated. The mixture will be further folded as it is poured into moulds; it is important that the mixture is not over-mixed or it will lose volume.

Flour and butter are folded into egg and sugar foams when making cakes. When folding in flour to a mixture, wiggling the spoon a little as it is drawn diagonally through the mixture is often effective in breaking up small pockets of flour.

Chocolate mousse

Serves 4
100g good quality dark chocolate,
  about 60% cocoa solids
4 eggs

1 Chop the chocolate up into small pieces and place in a heatproof bowl. Bring a small pan of water up to boiling point, then remove it from the heat and place the bowl of chocolate on top, making sure the bowl isn't in direct contact with the water. Allow the chocolate to melt, stirring occasionally, then remove the bowl from the pan and set aside to cool a little.

2 Separate the eggs into two medium bowls (see page 160). Whisk the whites to medium-stiff peaks (see page 161).

3 Stir the melted chocolate into the egg yolks until evenly combined.

4 Using a large metal spoon or rubber spatula, stir a large spoonful of the egg whites into the mixture to loosen it, then carefully fold in the remainder of the egg whites (as shown).

5 Divide between 4 individual dishes or glasses and wipe away any drips.

6 Chill for at least 4 hours before serving. The mousse can be served as it is, or decorated with chocolate curls or fresh raspberries.

Variations

You can flavour the chocolate with a little liqueur: Amaretto, Kahlua, Irish cream, brandy, Cointreau and crème de menthe work particularly well: add ½ tsp of the liqueur to the chocolate after it has melted. Alternatively, flavour the chocolate with 8–10 drops of flavoured oil, such as mint, bitter orange or basil, adding the oil to the chocolate before melting.

Chocolate roulade

Serves 4–6
250g good quality dark chocolate, about 60% cocoa solids
90ml water
1 tsp instant coffee granules
5 eggs
150g caster sugar
2 tbsp icing sugar, plus extra to dust
200ml double cream

1 Heat the oven to 200°C/gas mark 6. Line a shallow roasting tin or deep baking tray, 25 x 30cm, with a piece of non-stick baking parchment, 3–4cm bigger on all sides than the tin. Fold the parchment in half and cut diagonally through the corners, about 4–5cm deep. Press into the roasting tin; the cuts in the corners allow it to sit neatly in the tin.

2 Put the chocolate, water and coffee in a small saucepan and melt over a low heat. Once melted, remove from the heat and set aside to cool a little.

3 Separate the eggs into 2 medium bowls (see page 160). Using an electric whisk, beat the yolks with all but 1 tbsp of the caster sugar until pale and mousse-like.

4 With clean beaters, whisk the whites to medium-stiff peaks (see page 161), then whisk in the remaining 1 tbsp of caster sugar quickly, to stabilise the whites.

5 Stir the melted, cooled chocolate mixture into the yolk and sugar mixture, just until the mixture is marbled. Stir in one large spoonful of the whites to loosen the mixture, then add the remaining whites and carefully fold in (as shown on page 570).

6 Spread the mixture into the lined tin and bake in the upper half of the oven for about 15–20 minutes, or until a crust has formed and it is set in the middle. It will still be spongy when pressed with your fingertips.

7 Remove from the oven, carefully slide the sponge on its baking parchment onto a wire rack and immediately cover with lightly dampened kitchen paper or a damp tea towel to prevent it from drying out. Leave it to cool completely.

8 Place a piece of greaseproof paper, just bigger than the sponge, on the work surface and sift a fine layer of icing sugar onto it. Turn the sponge onto the icing sugar, using the wire rack and baking parchment to support the sponge (as shown), then peel off the parchment.

9 In a large bowl, lightly whisk the cream with the icing sugar, to taste, until it is just holding its shape; it should not be too stiff. Spread it over the cooled sponge, leaving a 1–2cm border around the edge (as shown).

10 Make an indentation across the width of the sponge 1cm in from the edge, using a palette knife, then using the greaseproof paper to support the sponge, roll it up like a Swiss roll, removing the greaseproof paper as you do so (as shown).

11 Wrap the roulade in the greaseproof paper and chill in the fridge for about 15–20 minutes to firm up slightly.

12 When ready to serve, carefully unwrap the roulade on a board, removing the greaseproof paper. Trim the ends with a large knife, then carefully place the roulade on a large rectangular or oval plate. Sift over a little additional icing sugar and serve with orange segments, fresh raspberries or a fruit compote.

Variations

You can flavour the cream in the roulade with cooled coffee or melted chocolate, or you can fold through fresh berries, pitted cherries, orange segments or finely chopped preserved stem ginger. You can also add 1–2 tbsp liqueur, to taste, such as Cointreau, Amaretto or Kahlua, before whisking the cream.

Tiramisu

Serves 4
2 eggs
100g caster sugar
150ml Marsala
100g mascarpone
150ml double cream
24 Savoy or 'ladies fingers' biscuits
8 tbsp strong espresso coffee
Cocoa powder, to dust

1 Separate the eggs (see page 160), setting the whites aside in a medium bowl. In a large bowl, beat the egg yolks with half of the sugar and 1 tbsp of the Marsala, using a hand-held electric whisk. Continue to whisk until the mixture is pale and mousse-like. Beat the mascarpone in a separate bowl to make sure it is smooth, then stir it into the yolk mixture.

2 In another bowl, whisk the cream until it holds soft peaks; set aside. Whisk the egg whites to medium peaks (see page 161), then gradually whisk in the remaining sugar to stabilise the foam, forming a meringue mixture.

3 Whisk the egg yolk mixture, whipped cream and meringue together, using a free-standing mixer if possible, until well combined and the mixture has a light, mousse-like consistency.

4 Mix the espresso with the remaining Marsala in a shallow dish. Dip the biscuits into the coffee mixture but only briefly or they will be too soggy to handle. Layer up the cream mixture and soaked biscuits in a glass serving dish, starting and ending with a layer of the cream mixture. Refrigerate until ready to serve.

5 Dust the surface of the tiramisu with a little cocoa powder just before serving.

Baked cheesecake

Serves 9–10
For the base
75g butter
150g digestive biscuits
1½–2 tbsp caster sugar, to taste

For the topping
6 tbsp caster sugar
20g cornflour
500g cream cheese
2 tsp vanilla extract
4 eggs
200ml double cream

1 Heat the oven to 200°C/gas mark 6.

2 For the base, melt the butter. Put the biscuits into a strong plastic bag and crush with a rolling pin, or whiz briefly in a food processor. Tip into a bowl and stir in the melted butter and the sugar. Press this mixture over the bottom of a 23cm springform cake tin and bake in the oven for 10–15 minutes, then remove and leave to cool. Lower the oven temperature to 150°C/gas mark 2.

3 For the topping, put 4 tbsp of the sugar with the cornflour in a large bowl and beat in the cream cheese and vanilla, using a wooden spoon.

4 Separate the eggs (see page 160) and beat the yolks into the cream cheese mixture, with the cream.

5 In a clean large bowl, whisk the egg whites to medium peaks (see page 161). Whisk in the remaining 2 tbsp sugar, to stabilise. Using a large metal spoon, fold the whisked whites into the cream cheese mixture.

6 Pour the mixture over the biscuit base and bake in the lower half of the oven for 45–60 minutes, or until the topping has just set; there should be a slight uniform wobble.

7 Leave the cheesecake to cool in the tin, then chill in the fridge before carefully unmoulding to serve.

Variation

Lemon and raspberry cheesecake Add the finely grated zest of 1 lemon and the juice of ½ lemon to the cheesecake mixture. When ready to serve, arrange 250g fresh raspberries on the top and sift a little icing sugar over to finish.

Meringues

Meringues are universally popular and they form the basis of many desserts, from pavlova to Îles flottantes (poached meringues floating on a pool of custard). There are three basic types of meringue:

Swiss meringue This is the most straightforward, widely used meringue, made by incorporating caster sugar into whisked egg whites. It is also the least stable and should be cooked as soon it is made. The resulting meringues should be crisp and dry all the way through. The addition of acidity such as white wine vinegar or lemon juice, as well as a little cornflour, helps to keep the meringue mallowy inside if required, for example for a pavlova. Using an electric whisk, the sugar can be added, little by little, once the whites have reached the stiff peak stage. The method (overleaf) adds just a tablespoonful of sugar per egg white to begin with, before the remainder is folded or whisked in. This method is less likely to lead to a loss of volume or softening due to over-whisking.

Meringue cuite This is most often used to create baskets and structures, because the mixture is so stable and the resulting meringue is very dense, chalky and dry throughout. It is made using icing sugar, added to egg whites which have been whisked to a foam. The meringue is then whisked over heat, which helps to stabilise the egg whites. Meringue cuite's stability means that the uncooked mixture can be kept for 24 hours before using.

Italian meringue For this meringue a sugar syrup, made with granulated sugar, is whisked into egg whites that have been whisked to the stiff peak stage, which helps to stabilise the meringue. It should be dry throughout when cooked.

Meringues

Makes about 20
4 egg whites
200g caster sugar
350ml double cream
2 tbsp icing sugar

This recipe uses the Swiss method.

1 Heat the oven to 120°C/gas mark ½. Line 2 baking sheets with non-stick baking parchment. In a medium to large bowl, whisk the egg whites to stiff peaks (see page 161), using an electric whisk.

2 With the beaters still running, whisk in 4 tbsp of the caster sugar, sprinkling 1 tbsp in at a time and whisking the meringue back to stiff peaks again between each addition.

3 Fold in the remaining sugar using a large metal spoon, until just incorporated. Once you are confident with the method, the remaining sugar can be whisked in gradually.

4 Fill a piping bag with the mixture. Use a little of the mixture to anchor the corners of the baking parchment to the tray.

5 Make beehive-shaped meringues by piping 3 squeezes of the piping bag on top of each other, each layer smaller than the one before.

6 Bake in the oven for 1½–2 hours, or until the meringues will lift off the parchment cleanly and have completely dried out. Remove from the oven and leave to cool completely.

7 In a large bowl, combine the cream with 1 tbsp of the icing sugar and whip using a balloon whisk or a hand-held electric whisk until it just holds its shape. It is very easy to over-whip cream, so take care. Use the cream to sandwich the meringues together. Serve piled on a plate, dusted with the remaining icing sugar.

Variations

Individual vacherins with chestnut filling Pipe the meringue mixture into tight 10cm diameter coils (as shown). Cook as above and sandwich together with sweetened cream mixed with 1–2 tbsp sweetened chestnut purée.

Îles flottantes Whisk 2 tsp cornflour into the meringue mixture after all the sugar has been added, then poach quenelles (see page 301) of the mixture in a mixture of milk and water for about 2 minutes each side. Serve on a pool of crème anglaise made with half milk and half double cream (see page 132). This can be served drizzled with hot caramel (see page 140).

1 Whisking the egg whites to stiff peaks.

2 Gradually whisking 4 tbsp of the sugar into the whisked egg whites.

3 Carefully folding in the remaining sugar.

4 Fixing the corners of the baking parchment to the baking sheet with little blobs of meringue.

5 Piping beehive-shaped meringues.

Individual vacherins Piping tight coils to form the meringue layers.

To ensure successful meringues...

For the most accurate measurements, separate the eggs and then weigh the whites. You should then use twice this weight in sugar. Quantities have been given in the recipes using medium eggs.

It is important to use non-stick baking parchment for all meringues, as they can then be left to cool on the parchment without sticking. Generally, you can tell meringues are cooked when the parchment can easily be released from the meringue (as shown). Do not use greaseproof paper, as meringues stick fast to it and have to be chipped off.

Although meringues are very sweet, cream served with meringues is best sweetened with icing sugar, as the contrast if it is plain can make the cream taste almost savoury.

Summer berry pavlova

Serves 6

4 egg whites
200g caster sugar
1 tsp cornflour
1 tsp vanilla extract
1 tsp white wine vinegar or lemon juice
300ml double cream
1–2 tbsp icing sugar, to taste
400g mixed berries, such as strawberries, raspberries, blueberries, blackberries and redcurrants

1 Heat the oven to 140°C/gas mark 1. Line a large baking sheet with non-stick baking parchment.

2 Put the egg whites in a bowl and whisk, using an electric whisk, to stiff peaks (see page 161).

3 Whisk in 4 tbsp of the caster sugar, 1 tbsp at a time, making sure the mixture re-stiffens again after each addition, then fold in the remaining sugar using a large metal spoon. Alternatively, continue whisking while pouring in the remaining sugar in a steady stream.

4 Add the cornflour, vanilla and wine vinegar or lemon juice and whisk briefly, just until incorporated.

5 Pile the meringue in a mound onto the prepared baking sheet and spread out into a circle. (You can draw an 18–20cm diameter circle on the baking parchment to help you, but turn the parchment over before adding the meringue.) Make a shallow dip with the back of a metal spoon in the centre of the meringue mixture to accommodate the cream and fruit.

6 Bake for about 1 hour, or until the shell is firm to the touch and can be peeled off the parchment. Remove from the oven and leave to cool completely.

7 Whisk the cream with the icing sugar in a large bowl until it is just holding its shape. Wash and dry the berries; cut strawberries into halves or quarters if necessary, depending on their size. Pile the cream into the middle of the pavlova and decorate with the fruit.

Variations

Golden fruit pavlova Top the cream with a mixture of ripe apricot and peach slices, orange segments and even physalis.

Mango and passion fruit pavlova Top the cream with slices cut from 2 or 3 ripe mangoes and the pulp of 4 ripe passion fruit.

Individual pavlovas Make 4–6 individual pavlovas and top with sweetened cream and your choice of fruit, as for the main recipe.

Another serving option...

The pavlova can be inverted before adding the cream and fruit, so the crust stays crisp underneath and the cream sits on the mallowy centre.

Hazelnut meringue cake

Serves 6

150g skinned hazelnuts

300g caster sugar

6 egg whites

2–3 drops of vanilla extract

¾ tsp white wine vinegar

300ml double cream

1–2 tbsp icing sugar, to taste, plus extra to dust

Melba sauce (see page 136), to serve

1 Heat the oven to 190°C/gas mark 5. Line two 20cm round cake tins with non-stick baking parchment to cover the bottom and sides.

2 Place the hazelnuts on a baking sheet and roast in the oven for 10–15 minutes, or until lightly browned. Tip onto a plate and set aside to cool.

3 Put the cooled nuts in a blender or food processor with 1 tbsp of the sugar and process until the texture of coarse breadcrumbs. Do not over-process them, or process them while still warm, or they will become greasy.

4 Using an electric whisk, whisk the egg whites in a medium bowl to stiff peaks (see page 161). With the beaters still running, add 4 tbsp caster sugar, sprinkling it in 1 tbsp at a time and making sure the mixture re-stiffens after each addition.

5 Stir the remaining sugar into the ground nuts. Fold the vanilla and wine vinegar into the meringue, then fold in the nuts very carefully, until just combined. Divide the mixture between the tins and smooth the tops with a palette knife. Bake for about 40 minutes, or until risen a little and light brown.

6 Remove from the oven to a wire rack and leave the meringue rounds to cool completely in the tins. Once cold, carefully remove from the tins, then peel away the baking parchment.

7 Put the cream and icing sugar in a large bowl and whisk until just holding its shape. Sandwich the meringue rounds together with the cream (bottom to bottom) and sift icing sugar over the top. Serve in slices, with the Melba sauce.

Variations

Walnut meringue cake Replace the hazelnuts with walnuts (the skins are difficult to remove, so leave them on) and proceed as for the main recipe. Stir ½ quantity of lemon curd (see page 591) through the cream to create a marbled effect, before sandwiching the halves together.

Macadamia meringue cake Replace the hazelnuts with macadamia nuts and proceed as for the main recipe.

Toasted almond meringue grissini

Makes about 20

75g small nibbed almonds

4 egg whites

250g icing sugar

3 drops of vanilla or almond extract

These are made using the meringue cuite method. (The grissini are illustrated on page 575.)

1 Heat the oven to 180°C/gas mark 4. Place the almonds on a baking sheet and bake for 10 minutes, or until lightly browned. Tip onto a plate and leave to cool.

2 Reduce the oven temperature to 140°C/gas mark 1 (leave the door open for a while if necessary to cool the oven). Line 2 large baking sheets with non-stick baking parchment.

3 Select a large heatproof bowl that will fit over the top of a saucepan. Fill the saucepan one-third full with water and bring to the boil. Remove the pan from the heat and put the bowl on top, checking that the base of the bowl is not touching the water.

4 Put the egg whites into the bowl and, using an electric whisk, whisk until foamy. Remove the bowl from the saucepan and whisk in the icing sugar a little at a time.

5 Return the bowl to the pan and continue to whisk to stiff peaks (see page 161), then remove from the heat and continue whisking until the bowl is hand-cool. Whisk in the vanilla or almond extract.

6 Fit a piping bag with a 5mm–1cm plain nozzle and spoon in the meringue mixture. Pipe long, straight lines of meringue, about 15–20cm in length, leaving a 2cm gap between them. Sprinkle with the toasted almonds, pressing them lightly into the meringue if necessary. Bake in the oven for 45–60 minutes, or until they are completely dry and lift off the baking parchment easily.

7 Serve the meringue grissini in a tall glass or vase, as petits fours with coffee.

Variations

Flavour the meringue with instant coffee granules, cocoa powder or freeze-dried crushed fruits, such as strawberries or rhubarb, in place of the toasted almonds. Pipe shorter lengths and different shapes for meringues to serve with ice cream or mousses.

Coffee meringue petits fours

Makes 70–80
200g granulated sugar
100ml water
2 tsp strong espresso or coffee essence
4 egg whites
Cocoa powder, to dust

These are made using the Italian meringue method. (The meringue petits fours are illustrated on page 575.)

1 Heat the oven to 140°C/gas mark 1. Line 2 baking sheets with non-stick baking parchment.

2 Put the sugar, water and coffee in a small, heavy-based pan. Dissolve over a very low heat, stirring gently without splashing up the sides of the pan.

3 When the sugar has dissolved, brush down the sides of the pan with a pastry brush dipped in water, then increase the heat and stop stirring. Boil the syrup until it reaches 120°C. Use a sugar thermometer to check the temperature or test to see if the syrup has reached firm ball stage (see page 139).

4 Meanwhile, using an electric whisk, whisk the egg whites in a medium bowl to stiff peaks (see page 161). As soon as the sugar syrup has reached the correct stage, pour it steadily onto the egg whites with the beaters still running. Try not to pour it onto the beaters themselves as the syrup can sometimes solidify on the metal and is then lost. Continue whisking until the mixture is cool and stiff.

5 Fill a piping bag with the mixture, reserving about 5 tbsp for the filling. Use a little of the mixture to anchor the 4 corners of the baking parchment to the tray, then pipe cherry-sized mounds onto the prepared baking sheets. Bake in the oven for 1½–2 hours, or until they will lift off the paper cleanly. They may still feel a little sticky, but they will dry out as they cool.

6 Leave the meringues to cool, then use the reserved mixture to sandwich them together. You need only very little of the mixture, to act as glue. Serve either piled on a plate and dusted with sifted cocoa powder, or place each meringue in a petits fours case.

Gelatine-set desserts

A well-flavoured fruit jelly, creamy pannacotta or softly set cold soufflé can provide a light and elegant end to dinner. Understanding how to use gelatine is a valuable addition to your culinary skills.

A guide to using gelatine

Gelatine is a natural setting agent, refined commercially from animal bone and skin. It has a fairly low setting and melting point, so dishes set with gelatine are always served cold. Agar agar, a vegetarian alternative, can be used to set dishes that are served hot.

Gelatine has a better mouthfeel than agar agar and can literally be soft and melting when served at the right temperature. Agar agar has a different structure and retains this even when warm, providing a much firmer texture than gelatine.

Gelatine is available in both powdered and leaf form. A guide for use is that 3 tsp powdered gelatine is equivalent to 3 sheets of bronze leaf gelatine, which will set 570–600ml liquid. If the liquid is a purée, a little less gelatine is required.

Gelatine is affected by alcohol and acidity and you may need to add extra gelatine when using a high proportion of these ingredients. For agar agar, follow the packet instructions, as different brands can vary. Gelatine is also sensitive to certain enzymes in fruit and will not set kiwi, papaya or pineapple, although pineapple jelly will set if you add a little chilli to it.

When serving gelatine-set mixtures such as jellies, mousses and cold soufflés, always remove them from the fridge at least 20–30 minutes before serving to allow the mixture to come to room temperature, which softens the gelatine and makes it more palatable.

Using powdered gelatine

Powdered gelatine needs to be rehydrated with water, a technique called 'sponging'. The gelatine is then dissolved gently over a low heat before use.

1 Sprinkle the powdered gelatine evenly over a minimum of 3 tbsp cold water in a small saucepan.

2 Leave this to 'sponge' (absorb water) for 5–10 minutes. The gelatine will become jelly-like and translucent. The sponged gelatine can happily sit like this for a while.

3 When ready to use, put the saucepan over a very low heat and leave the gelatine to dissolve gently, until no grains are visible. Avoid stirring or splashing up the sides of the pan.

A note on powdered gelatine...

Don't dissolve gelatine over a high heat. If gelatine gets too hot, it can lose some of its setting properties.

Once the powdered gelatine is fully dissolved and has the appearance of a clear, smooth liquid, it is ready to use.

Make sure the liquid or mixture you are adding dissolved gelatine to is not fridge cold, or the gelatine will cool very quickly into strings and lumps as it is added, resulting in an uneven set and unsatisfactory texture.

Using leaf gelatine

Leaf gelatine is much easier to use than powdered, but because it needs a warm to hot liquid or mixture to dissolve, it can't be used universally, as powdered gelatine can.

1 Place the leaf gelatine in a bowl of cold water, ensuring the leaves are covered and leave for 5–10 minutes to soften.

2 Once the leaf gelatine is soft to the touch, pick out the individual leaves. Count the sheets in and out to ensure they are all removed and used (as the leaf gelatine absorbs water it turns translucent and is difficult to see in the water).

3 Give the sheets a squeeze to remove excess water, then add them to a warm to hot liquid or mixture, to dissolve them completely. Strain the mixture, if possible, to ensure all the gelatine is completely dissolved, checking the sieve for any undissolved gelatine.

A note on leaf gelatine...

You need to be aware that different brands of commercial leaf gelatine vary in strength. The gelatine recipes in this book have been tested with bronze leaf gelatine. If you are using a different variety, follow the recommended quantity on the packet per 570–600ml liquid.

Don't use warm or hot water to sponge leaf gelatine, or it will melt and dissolve in the water, leaving nothing to lift out.

Orange and passion fruit jelly

Serves 4
3 tbsp water
3½ tsp powdered gelatine
10–12 ripe passion fruit (or 200ml
  passion fruit juice)
2–3 tbsp caster sugar, to taste
400ml orange juice (from about
  4–5 large oranges)

To serve
2 oranges
2 passion fruit

1 Put the water into a small saucepan, sprinkle over the gelatine and leave for 5 minutes to absorb the water and become spongy (see page 582). Place over the lowest heat and leave to dissolve, without stirring.

2 Halve the passion fruit, scoop out the seeds and juice into a sieve over a bowl and press with the back of a wooden spoon to extract the juice. In a second pan over a low heat, dissolve the sugar in half of the orange juice, stirring.

3 Pour the warm orange juice into the melted gelatine and stir well. Stir in the passion fruit juice and remaining orange juice. Taste and add sugar if necessary.

4 Rinse out a jelly mould or 4 dariole moulds with cold water, and pour in the mixture. Refrigerate for at least 4 hours, or until the jellies are completely set.

5 Half an hour before serving, take the jellies out of the fridge. Segment the oranges (see page 530) and scoop out the pulp from the passion fruit; mix together. To turn out the jellies, loosen the top with a finger. Dip each mould into a dish of boiling water (just to the rim), then invert over a damp serving plate. Give a sharp sideways shake side to release the jelly. Serve with the oranges and passion fruit.

Variations

Use good quality fruit juice (from a carton), such as raspberry and pomegranate.

Pannacotta

Serves 4
1 tsp oil, to grease
400ml double cream
¼–½ vanilla pod
1 pared strip of lemon zest
60–75g caster sugar
2½ sheets of leaf gelatine
200ml whole milk, at room temperature

To serve
Fruit compote such as rhubarb and vanilla
  (see page 535), or roasted fruit such
  as honey roasted figs (see page 538),
  or fresh berries

1 Brush 4 x 150ml moulds very lightly with oil; invert on a wire rack to drain.

2 Put the cream into a saucepan with the vanilla pod and lemon zest, then bring to scalding point over a medium heat (see page 133). Remove from the heat, add 60g sugar and stir to dissolve. Set aside to infuse for 15–20 minutes.

3 Soak the gelatine in cold water until soft, about 5 minutes (see page 583).

4 Remove the vanilla and lemon zest from the infused cream and gently reheat over a low to medium heat. Squeeze the excess water out of the gelatine, then add the gelatine sheets to the warmed cream, stirring to dissolve. Strain the mixture into a bowl and add the milk. Taste and add a little more sugar if needed (there should still be enough heat in the mixture to dissolve it).

5 Pour into the moulds and chill in the fridge for a few hours, or ideally overnight.

6 Half an hour before serving, take the pannacottas out of the fridge. To turn out, dip the moulds (to the rim), in warm water for 5 seconds, then remove and gently release the pannacotta from the mould using the tip of a finger. (Don't leave them in the water any longer than necessary or the pannacotta will melt.) Invert onto a plate and, while holding the mould and the plate, give a good sideways shake to release the pannacotta. Serve with a fruit compote, roasted fruit or berries.

Variations

For an even richer flavour, omit the milk and use 600ml double cream.

Cardamom pannacotta Replace the vanilla with ½–1 tsp crushed cardamom seeds. Proceed as for the main recipe.

Rosewater pannacotta Omit the vanilla and add ½ tsp rosewater to the pannacotta with the milk.

Bavarois

A bavarois is a flavoured custard, or crème anglaise, lightened with cream and set with gelatine. It is unmoulded to serve and often presented with a fruit compote.

Vanilla bavarois

Serves 4

1 tsp sunflower oil, to grease
300ml double cream
300ml milk
1 vanilla pod
1½ sheets of leaf gelatine
4 egg yolks
60–75g caster sugar

To serve

Fruit compote such as blueberry and lemon (see page 534), or roasted fruit such as honey roasted figs (see page 538), or fresh berries

1 Very lightly oil 4 dariole moulds. Lightly whisk the cream in a bowl and set aside in the fridge until needed. Pour the milk into a saucepan. Split the vanilla pod in half lengthways, scrape the seeds out into the milk and add the pod. Bring the milk slowly to scalding point over a low to medium heat (see page 133), then remove from the heat and leave to infuse for about 15 minutes.

2 Meanwhile, put the gelatine sheets in a bowl, cover with cold water and leave to soften for 5–10 minutes.

3 In a separate bowl, mix the egg yolks and sugar together, using just 60g to start with; more can be added to taste later. Pour the flavoured milk onto the egg yolks, stirring steadily, and return the mixture to the rinsed out saucepan. Discard the vanilla pod.

4 Stir the mixture continuously with a wooden spoon over a low to medium heat, until it thickens enough to evenly coat the back of the spoon (see page 132) and becomes a thin custard. Remove from the heat.

5 Remove the gelatine from the water, squeeze out any excess water and add the gelatine leaves to the warm custard. Stir gently to dissolve the gelatine, then pass the mixture through a fine sieve into a bowl.

6 Place the bowl over an ice bath and bring the mixture to setting point (see page 589). The custard must come to setting point to hold the vanilla seeds in suspension. Remove the bowl from the ice bath and gently fold the lightly whipped cream into the mixture.

7 Pour the bavarois mixture into the prepared moulds and chill in the fridge for a few hours until set, or overnight.

8 To unmould the bavarois, suspend the darioles in warm water just to the rim for 5 seconds (as shown); this is just enough time to melt the surface of the bavarois. Remove and gently release the bavarois using the tip of your finger or thumb (as shown). Invert onto a serving plate and, while holding the dariole and the plate, give everything a good sideways shake (as shown); this should release the bavarois from the mould. Wipe away any melted bavarois as cleanly as possible, using dampened kitchen paper. Serve with a fruit compote, roasted fruit or berries.

Variations

Chocolate bavarois Omit the vanilla and add 100g good quality dark chocolate, chopped into small pieces, to the cold milk. Stir over a low heat until melted, then proceed as for the main recipe. Adding chocolate gives a firmer set.

Mocha bavarois Omit the vanilla and add 1½ tbsp instant coffee granules and 40g good quality dark chocolate, chopped into small pieces, to the cold milk. Stir over a low heat until melted, then proceed as for the main recipe.

....

A note on unmoulding...
A disc of non-stick baking parchment can be placed in the bottom of each dariole to ensure an easy release when unmoulding.

Cold soufflés

Cold soufflés are really very light flavoured mousses set with gelatine, using the technique of setting point described (see right); they are not made at all in the same way as hot ones. Traditionally, they are set in soufflé dishes, within a paper collar, so the sides are raised, giving a soufflé-like appearance (see right). Alternatively, they can be served in glasses or a large bowl, just like a mousse.

Cold lemon soufflé

Serves 4
2 large lemons
1½ tbsp water
1½ tsp powdered gelatine
3 eggs
150g caster sugar
150ml double cream
2–3 tsp icing sugar (optional)
Citrus zest julienne softened in
    sugar syrup (see page 531),
    to finish (optional)

1 Pour about 5cm water into a large saucepan, bring to the boil over a medium heat, then remove from the heat.

2 Finely grate the zest from the lemons, then juice them. Put 1½ tbsp water and 1½ tbsp lemon juice in a small saucepan and sprinkle the gelatine evenly over the surface. Leave for 5 minutes until the gelatine has absorbed the water and become spongy.

3 Separate the eggs (see page 160), putting the yolks in a medium heatproof bowl with the caster sugar and 1–1½ tbsp lemon juice; put the whites in another bowl.

4 Lightly whip the cream and set aside in the fridge.

5 Sit the bowl with the yolks and sugar over the hot water pan, making sure the bottom of the bowl is not touching the water. Using a hand-held electric whisk, whisk until the mixture becomes paler in colour and increases in volume a little. Remove from the heat, continue whisking until cool, then whisk in any remaining lemon juice (about 1½–2 tbsp) and the zest.

6 Put the saucepan containing the gelatine over a very low heat and dissolve the gelatine without stirring. An occasional swirl of the mixture helps to see if it has dissolved. Pour the dissolved gelatine into the lemon mousse mixture, stirring as you do so. Place the bowl over an ice bath, stirring gently until it reaches setting point (see right). At this stage it will have thickened slightly and the bottom of the bowl will be exposed for several seconds when a spatula is drawn through before the mixture floods back.

7 Remove the bowl from the ice bath and, working efficiently, fold the whipped cream into the lemon mixture.

8 Using an electric whisk, whisk the egg whites to medium peaks (see page 161) and stir one spoonful into the mixture, to loosen it, then fold the remaining whites in carefully, using a large metal spoon. Taste and add a little icing sugar if the mixture seems too tart.

9 Spoon the mixture into a prepared 1–1.2 litre soufflé dish (see right), or into a serving bowl or individual glasses, and chill in the fridge for 2–3 hours before serving. You can decorate the soufflé with citrus zest julienne (see page 531), if you wish.

Variations

Cold raspberry soufflé Omit the lemon zest and juice. Make a purée using 350g raspberries, heated, sieved and cooled. Dissolve the gelatine in 3 tbsp water and proceed as for the main recipe, adding the raspberry purée at the end of step 5.

Cold blood orange soufflé Use 1 blood orange and ½ lemon in place of the 2 lemons, using the lemon juice to dissolve the gelatine and adding the blood orange juice to the egg and sugar mixture at the end of step 5.

Cold passion fruit soufflé Scoop the pulp from 8–10 passion fruit and sieve to remove the seeds. Dissolve the gelatine in half the lemon juice. Reduce the quantity of sugar to 120g. Add the sieved passion fruit pulp to the mixture at the end of step 5, with the remaining lemon juice and zest to taste.

Cold lime soufflé Replace the lemons with 4 limes.

Using a soufflé dish for a cold soufflé

Tie a double band of lightly oiled greaseproof paper around the top of the dish, to extend about 3cm above the rim with the non-folded edge uppermost. When the soufflé mixture is poured in, it should come about 2.5cm above the rim of the dish.

Once the soufflé is set, heat a palette knife in hot water, dry it and run it between the double sheets of greaseproof paper against the side of the set soufflé. The heat will very slightly melt just enough of the gelatine to enable the paper collar to be removed cleanly. The exposed raised side of the soufflé can be spread with a thin layer of lightly whipped cream and coated with nibbed toasted almonds to finish.

Setting point for cold soufflés, mousses etc.

A liquid or mixture with gelatine in it must be brought to 'setting point' (over an ice bath for speed), so it can combine with a foamy mixture without separating. Whipped cream, whisked egg whites or a mousse of yolks may be added to a gelatine mixture, to create volume and lightness in the finished dish. The gelatine also prevents other ingredients sinking to the bottom, such as the vanilla seeds in a cold vanilla soufflé.

1 Once you have added the gelatine (either dissolved powdered or sponged leaf) to the mixture, place it over an ice bath (a larger bowl half-filled with ice cubes and cold water) and begin stirring gently.

2 Stir continuously and gently to ensure an even cooling and setting, until there is a visible thickening, and when a spatula drawn through the middle of the mixture creates a 'parting of the waves' (when the mixture parts briefly, for 3–5 seconds before flooding back together).

3 At setting point, remove the dish from the ice bath and gently fold in the lighter mixture, such as lightly whipped cream or soft/medium peak whisked egg whites.

Ice creams, sorbets and granitas

These can be served on their own or to complement another pudding and have the advantage that they can be made well ahead. There are 4 main methods of making ice creams. Some of these use techniques covered in other chapters; you may find it useful to refer to these.

Ice creams

All-in-one method The easiest and quickest method, often used for a yoghurt-based ice cream with added flavouring, such as a fruit purée. The ice cream usually needs churning to develop a smooth texture, which is difficult to achieve otherwise as the fat content is low. These ice creams are crystalline and hard when frozen, but melt very quickly and are therefore difficult to blend in a food processor.

Custard method This uses crème anglaise as a base, so the ice cream can be very rich. Flavourings are added by infusing the milk or cream before making the crème anglaise, or by adding flavourings, such as fruit purées, once the custard is made. Solid ingredients such as chocolate chips or chopped nuts need to be added after churning or breaking down the ice crystals in a food processor.

Meringue method For this method a sugar syrup is whisked into stiffly whisked egg whites. Air is incorporated during this process, which gives the ice cream a smooth, creamy texture and makes churning unnecessary. Cream is folded into the meringue base to lend richness. Flavouring, often in the form of a fruit purée, is added at this stage too; intensely flavoured fruits with a high acidity work particularly well with meringue-based ice creams.

Mousse method Here a sugar syrup is whisked into egg yolks to create a light foam or mousse. The ice cream is enriched with lightly whipped cream folded into the yolk and sugar syrup base. Air incorporated during the whisking process gives the ice cream a rich, smooth texture, which makes churning unnecessary; the ice cream can be frozen immediately. Small quantities of flavourings can be added to the yolks in powder or purée form before the syrup is incorporated. Alternatively, they can be folded into the mousse base, before the whipped cream is added. An ice cream made by this method is often referred to as a parfait.

Churning

Using an ice-cream machine is the best method of churning an ice cream, to break down ice crystals and incorporate air for smoothness and creaminess. If you don't have an ice-cream machine, the ice cream can be blended in a food processor. It must be frozen in a shallow tray, cut into cubes when frozen and quickly blended to a purée before it melts. Returning the ice cream to the freezer immediately is essential, as if it becomes liquid again the churning is rendered ineffective. If using a food processor, the ice cream ideally should be blended at least twice.

Freezing

Freshly made ice creams are best eaten within 24 hours. They can be frozen for 2 months or more, but their flavour and texture will deteriorate after 2 or 3 days.

Serving

Unless the ice cream is very soft, you should transfer it from the freezer to the fridge 20–30 minutes before serving to allow it to soften a little, making it easier to scoop and serve.

Lemon curd yoghurt ice cream

Serves 4

For the lemon curd

2 small lemons

120g caster sugar

50g unsalted butter

2 eggs

For the ice cream

400g Greek yoghurt

This ice cream is made using the all-in-one method.

1 To make the lemon curd, finely grate the zest of the lemons and squeeze the juice. Put the juice into a saucepan with the sugar and butter. Beat the eggs to break them up and add them to the pan.

2 Stir the mixture over a low to medium heat with a wooden spoon until the sugar and butter have melted, then increase the heat. Bring the curd just to the boil, stirring continuously, then remove from the heat. Strain through a sieve into a bowl and stir in the lemon zest. Set the lemon curd aside to cool completely; it will thicken as it cools.

3 Once cool, stir the lemon curd into the yoghurt. Churn the ice cream for a smooth creamy texture. Alternatively, simply cover and freeze, either in individual moulds lined with cling film for easy removal, in a lined loaf tin, or in a plastic container if you want to scoop it to serve. Allow at least 5 hours for it to freeze.

4 If you want to scoop the ice cream, transfer the plastic container to the fridge an hour before serving. Individual portions should be unmoulded when the ice cream is still frozen solid. If it has been set in a loaf tin, slice it with a hot knife when it has just come out of the freezer, or it will be too difficult to handle.

Variation

Lime curd ice cream Replace the lemons with 3 limes, and proceed as for the main recipe.

A note on the fat content of ice cream...

Some fat is needed in an ice cream to give it a creamy, rich texture. If there is too much fat, the texture will be quite chalky and the ice cream will not scoop properly. Whipping cream is ideal for making ice cream, or double cream and milk combined. For a lighter ice cream, more milk and less cream can be used, or Greek yoghurt (as above) but don't alter the quantities too far, or the finished ice cream will have rocky ice crystals and be difficult to scoop.

Vanilla ice cream

Serves 4
200ml milk
200ml double cream
1 vanilla pod
4 egg yolks
75g caster sugar
Pinch of salt

This ice cream uses the custard method.

1 Put the milk and cream into a saucepan. Split the vanilla pod in half lengthways and add it to the pan. Bring to scalding point (see page 133), then remove from the heat and set aside for 20 minutes to allow the vanilla flavour to infuse.

2 Put the yolks in a bowl with the sugar and salt, and mix well. Pour in the cream mixture and stir well. Return the mixture to the rinsed out pan and cook over a low to medium heat, stirring constantly, until the custard coats the back of the wooden spoon; do not allow it to boil (see page 133).

3 Strain the custard into a bowl. Scrape the seeds from the vanilla pod into the custard. Leave to cool completely.

4 Churn the mixture in an ice-cream machine, then transfer to a plastic container and put into the freezer until needed. Alternatively, freeze the mixture in a shallow tray. When it is just frozen, cut into chunks and briefly whiz it in a food processor, then immediately return to the freezer. Repeat this process when it has just re-frozen to create a smooth-textured ice cream. After the second whizzing, transfer the ice cream to a plastic container.

5 Transfer the ice cream from the freezer to the fridge 20–30 minutes before serving to soften slightly before serving, scooped into glass bowls.

Variations

Coffee ice cream Omit the vanilla and add 5 tsp instant coffee granules to the milk and cream before scalding; this gives a good intense flavour. Alternatively, you can also replace some of the liquid measurement with coffee essence or 6 shots of espresso.

Cinnamon ice cream Omit the vanilla, break a cinnamon stick into 3 pieces and add to the milk and cream before scalding. Leave to infuse for at least 30 minutes then proceed as for the main recipe.

Chocolate malt ice cream Omit the vanilla and add 100g good quality dark chocolate, cut into pieces, 2 tbsp malt extract and ½ tsp vanilla extract to the milk and cream. Bring to scalding point, stirring to melt the chocolate. Proceed as for the main recipe.

Coconut ice cream Use 300ml coconut milk and 100ml double cream or coconut cream. Omit the vanilla and proceed as for the main recipe.

Salted caramel ice cream Omit the vanilla and add ¼ tsp Maldon salt flakes to the milk and cream before scalding. Make a dry caramel with the sugar (see page 141), taking it to a deep golden colour. Slowly and carefully (it will splutter) pour the scalded milk and cream onto the caramel to stop it cooking, and reheat gently to ensure all the caramel is dissolved. Add this to the egg yolks and stir well, then proceed as for the main recipe.

Cream cheese ice cream Omit the vanilla and substitute 150ml soured cream for the double cream. Whisk 200g cream cheese into the custard once it has cooled slightly and add ½ tsp vanilla extract. Strain and allow to cool completely, then proceed as for the main recipe.

Blackcurrant ripple ice cream

Serves 6
350g blackcurrants
250g caster sugar
100ml water
4 egg whites
200ml double cream

This ice cream uses the meringue method.

1 Wash the blackcurrants and put them in a pan with 100g of the sugar. Cover and gently cook over a low heat until they are very soft, stirring occasionally.

2 Push the blackcurrants through a sieve, trying to push as much of the pulp through as possible; you should have about 250g blackcurrant purée. Set aside.

3 Put the remaining 150g sugar in another pan with the water. Dissolve over a low heat, agitating the sugar only gently. Once the sugar has dissolved, brush down the sides of the pan with a pastry brush dipped in water, then increase the heat and boil until the syrup registers 120°C on a sugar thermometer or test to see if the syrup has reached the firm ball stage (see page 139).

4 Meanwhile, once the syrup has reached 110°C, whisk the egg whites to stiff peaks (see page 161), using an electric whisk. As soon as the syrup has reached 120°C, pour it onto the egg whites, with the beaters still running, taking care not to pour the syrup onto the beaters or it may set hard on the metal.

5 Continue to whisk until the mixture becomes a stiff meringue. Lightly whip the cream and fold it into the meringue with 200g of the blackcurrant purée. Add the remaining 50g purée and marble it into the ice cream with as few stirs as possible.

6 Freeze the ice cream in a mould or loaf tin lined with cling film. Transfer the ice cream from the freezer to the fridge 20–30 minutes before serving to soften slightly. It can be sliced or scooped to serve.

Variations
Any strong flavoured acidic fruit purée can be used in place of the blackcurrants.

Ginger ice cream

Serves 4
85g granulated sugar
150ml water
600ml double cream
4 pieces of preserved stem ginger
  in syrup, drained
4 egg yolks
2 tsp ground ginger

This ice cream is made with a mousse base.

1 Put the sugar and water into a small heavy-based saucepan over a low heat and carefully dissolve the sugar (see page 138). Lightly whisk the double cream and cut the ginger into julienne.

2 When the sugar has dissolved, bring the syrup to a simmer for about 4–5 minutes, until it registers 104°C on a sugar thermometer and a little of the syrup rubbed between your thumb and finger has a 'vaseline' feel (see page 139).

3 Put the egg yolks and ground ginger in a large bowl and whisk lightly until just frothy. Pour the warm sugar syrup onto the egg yolks, whisking constantly and avoiding the syrup from touching the whisk, as the syrup will cool fast against the cold metal and can harden and stick. Continue whisking until the mixture is foamy and mousse-like and just at the ribbon stage (just starting to leave a trail on the surface when the whisks are lifted, see page 630).

4 Gently fold in the cream and ginger julienne and pour into a container. Cover and transfer to the freezer. (If you are churning the ice cream, stir the ginger in after churning and before freezing.)

5 Remove from the freezer 30 minutes before serving to allow the ice cream to soften a little, before scooping.

Sorbets and granitas

Sorbets are frozen flavoured syrups or purées. The ratio of sugar in the syrup or purée is important: too much and the sorbet will be too sweet and will freeze to only a soft mush; too little and the sorbet will be icy and hard with large ice crystals. Generally a sorbet made with 1 part sugar to 2 parts other ingredients (such as fruit purée and lemon juice) will achieve a good texture.

Churning gives the smoothest sorbets, but if you don't have an ice-cream machine, blending in a food processor once the sorbet is semi-frozen will break down the large ice crystals into smaller ones and incorporate air to give a more even texture. In the recipes that follow this is done once, but it can be done twice for an even smoother result. Adding a little egg white also helps to achieve a smoother texture, in part by restricting the formation of large ice crystals.

Granitas are made with slightly less sugar and are not churned or blended. They have an even texture of coarse crystals which are created by forking or breaking up the granita several times during the freezing process.

Pear sorbet

Serves 4
4 ripe pears
2 lemons
160g caster sugar
1 egg white

1 Peel, quarter and core the pears. Juice the lemons.

2 Half-fill a medium saucepan with water, add the sugar and dissolve over a low to medium heat. Add the pears, with a little more water if there is not enough liquid to cover them. Cover with a damp cartouche (see page 13) and poach gently for 15–20 minutes, or until translucent.

3 Transfer the pears to a food processor with a slotted spoon. Reduce the poaching liquid by boiling rapidly to the short thread stage (see page 139). When ready, remove from the heat immediately. Leave to cool slightly.

4 Add the sugar syrup to the pears in the food processor with the lemon juice and blend until completely smooth. Pour the mixture into a bowl (or a freezer container if you are not using an ice-cream machine) and leave to cool.

5 Beat the egg white until lightly frothy. Once the pear purée is cool, churn in an ice-cream machine, adding the egg white as the sorbet thickens. (Or place in the freezer until firm, then remove and cut the sorbet into chunks. Blend in the food processor to break down the ice crystals, but don't let it melt completely. Add the egg white and blend for 30 seconds, then return to the container and freeze again.)

6 Transfer the sorbet to the fridge 20–30 minutes before serving to soften slightly.

Variations

Apple sorbet Replace the pears with 4 Granny Smith apples and proceed as for the main recipe. As apples are more acidic than pears, you may need to add an extra 40–50g sugar, to taste, and use less lemon juice.

Raspberry sorbet Replace the pears with 350g frozen raspberries. You don't need to poach them. Dissolve the sugar in 450ml water and bring to the short thread stage before cooling briefly and adding to the raspberries in a food processor, with the juice of ½–1 lemon. Blend for 1 minute, then strain through a fine sieve, cool and proceed as for the main recipe.

Passion fruit sorbet Replace the pears with 450g passion fruit pulp (this is about 32 passion fruit, but you can buy passion fruit pulp, fresh or tinned). Dissolve the sugar in 450ml water and bring to the short thread stage. Stir into the pulp with the juice of 1 lemon, and strain through a fine sieve. Chill and proceed as above.

Strawberry and black pepper granita

Serves 4

½–1 tsp coarsely ground black pepper
150g granulated sugar
600ml water
1 lemon
350g fresh strawberries

Strong or sharp flavours work best with the large icy crystals of the granita.

1 Put the pepper, sugar and water in a heavy-based saucepan over a low to medium heat to dissolve the sugar. Once the sugar has dissolved, increase the heat and simmer for 4–5 minutes, or until the syrup registers 104°C on a sugar thermometer and has a 'vaseline' feel (see page 139).

2 Remove from the heat and set aside to cool. Juice the lemon.

3 Blend the strawberries until smooth in a food processor or mash them to a purée, then push them through a sieve to remove the seeds.

4 Once the syrup is cool, strain it into the purée, add the lemon juice to taste and stir well. Place the mixture in a shallow container and freeze for about 1–2 hours, or until beginning to solidify at the edges.

5 Remove from the freezer and stir with a fork to mix the ice crystals evenly. Return it to the freezer until the granita is again beginning to solidify at the edges.

6 Repeat this stirring process 2 or 3 times, or until the granita has an even texture of small ice crystals; it should be grainy but not mushy. Serve immediately.

Note If you want to prepare the granita a day in advance, remove it from the freezer 2 hours before serving and leave to soften for 30 minutes. Stir thoroughly with a fork, then return to the freezer. After a further 30 minutes, stir once more and refreeze until ready to serve.

Coffee granita

Serves 4

6 shots of strong espresso, made up to
  600ml with water
120–130g granulated sugar, to taste

1 Put the coffee in a saucepan with the sugar and dissolve the sugar over a low to medium heat.

2 Once the sugar has dissolved, leave to cool before pouring into a shallow container, then freeze for about 1–2 hours, or until the granita is beginning to solidify at the edges.

3 Remove from the freezer and stir with a fork to mix the ice crystals evenly. Return to the freezer until the granita is again beginning to solidify at the edges.

4 Repeat this stirring process 2 or 3 times, or until the granita has an even texture of small ice crystals; it should be grainy but not mushy. Serve as soon as possible.

Variation

Coffee granita Add 1–2 tbsp Kahlua, Tia Maria or other coffee liqueur to the coffee before freezing.

A note on alcohol in granitas and sorbets...

A small amount of alcohol can be added to the mixture, but too much will prevent the sorbet or granita freezing and will result in a very soft texture, similar to the effect of adding too much sugar.

Bread, Biscuits & Cakes

With enticing aromas and delicious end products, baking is one of the most satisfying experiences for the cook. Here we focus on sweet and savoury breads, cakes, traybakes and biscuits, as well as icings and glazes used to finish them. All the basic skills you need are covered. Once the techniques are mastered, there are endless opportunities for you to develop your own variations. For consistent success, it is important to understand the techniques and to follow the recipe carefully, measuring ingredients accurately, and to use the correct tin size and oven temperature.

Bread

Learning to bake even the simplest loaf can give huge satisfaction. The most basic bread is made with flour, water, salt and yeast. Strong flour gives structure and texture to the loaf, water binds and develops the gluten in the flour, salt flavours the dough and controls the action of the yeast, and yeast leavens the bread. The recipes in this chapter use fresh or dried yeast, and do not include sourdoughs or other breads made with a starter.

Bread is fairly simple to make and you will find the texture of the finished loaf will improve the more you practise the basic skills. It is important in all bread making, whether making basic or heavily enriched loaves, that the consistency or 'feel' of the dough is correct. The quantity of liquid added to the dry ingredients will always vary slightly depending on the moisture content of the flour and how you incorporate and distribute the liquid. Being familiar with the ideal consistency of the dough is therefore very important, and is something that comes with practice. As a starting point, it is worth remembering that a softer, slightly stickier dough is preferable to a firmer, drier dough, so add as much of the liquid indicated as you can without it becoming too sticky to knead or handle.

Don't be put off by the lengthy rising and proving time in recipes; the actual hands-on work is often less than 15 minutes. Other timings are guides only, and a bread will not suffer particularly for being left at any stage for a while longer than outlined, if that fits your schedule.

The stages of bread making

Mixing combines the ingredients evenly.

Kneading distributes the yeast evenly and develops the gluten.

Rising allows the yeast to grow and multiply, producing carbon dioxide bubbles which cause the bread to rise.

Knocking back is kneading the dough again after it has risen, to create a more even texture, by breaking down the larger bubbles produced by the yeast.

Shaping gives the bread form and an even crust.

Proving is the second rising. This allows the yeast to work and rise the dough again. The proving process usually only takes half the time of the rising stage.

Baking the bread at a high temperature kills the yeast and sets the shape, and gives the bread colour and flavour.

Fresh or dried yeast?

The recipes in this section use fresh yeast, but this can sometimes be difficult to obtain. If using fast-action dried yeast, use a quarter of the fresh weight, adding it directly to the flour before the liquid. If using ordinary dried yeast, use half the weight of fresh yeast, dissolving it in a little of the warm water or milk to help it rehydrate before use. If in doubt as to whether your dried, or indeed fresh, yeast will work, leave the dissolved yeast mixture in a warm place for 10–15 minutes and it should start to grow and become foamy. This indicates that the yeast is alive and well.

The importance of gluten

For bread, unlike pastry, it is essential to develop the gluten in the flour, to give structure and texture to the finished loaf. This development starts when the flour comes into contact with liquid, and continues throughout the kneading process. As the gluten develops, the dough becomes elastic and smooth.

Flour used in bread making is generally strong flour, which has a higher gluten content. As gluten is a protein, this means the higher the gluten content in flour the higher the protein content. For the effect on gluten of using added ingredients to enrich bread see page 606.

Salt

Salt improves the flavour of bread and helps the gluten to develop, creating the characteristic chewy bread texture. It also contributes to the formation of a good brown crust. About 2 scant tsp salt is enough for every 500g of flour; any more and the salt will inhibit yeast growth and the dough will rise very slowly.

Water

The liquid most often used in bread, this should be just warm to the touch, or just above blood temperature, so about 37–38°C, when it is added. At this warmth, the yeast will start to work at once, so speeding the process and showing that the yeast is working. A high temperature will kill yeast, so the water must not be too hot. A lower temperature slows the yeast action down but does not kill it, so cooler water is fine to use; the dough will just take longer to rise.

Using milk, scalded and cooled to the correct temperature (see page 133), in place of water, will result in a softer, more cake-like crumb.

Making bread in a mixer

Most free-standing electric mixers come with a kneading paddle attachment. Using a mixer is faster because the mixer is much more efficient at kneading than your hands. To make dough in a mixer, place all the dry ingredients in the bowl. Start the mixer on the slowest speed to ensure the dry ingredients are mixed within the bowl. Now add the wet ingredients, three-quarters to start with, then more as necessary. Once the ingredients have come together as a dough, you can increase the speed a little. It should take a further 5 minutes at about the same speed or slightly faster (the next speed up) to knead the dough. Test the dough in the same way as if kneaded by hand.

Kneading the dough

A thorough, vigorous kneading after mixing helps develop the gluten and will result in the necessary 'chew' in a well textured loaf. It also distributes the yeast throughout the dough, ensuring an even rise. It should take 10 minutes by hand or 5 minutes using a mixer with a dough hook attachment.

Rising the dough

The optimum ambient temperature for rising a bread dough is 22°C, ie warm room temperature, away from draughts and intense direct heat (for example on the top of the stove). Airing cupboards, if they are not too hot, are ideal. The dough should double in size in approximately 1 hour for most recipes; much faster than this, and the flavour will be impaired. Bread will happily rise in much colder conditions, even overnight in the fridge, but the colder it is, the longer it will take. Bread dough can also be frozen, and will rise once it has defrosted.

White bread

Makes a 500g loaf
250g strong plain flour, plus extra
　to dust
1 tsp salt
10g fresh yeast
150–175ml warm water

1 Put the flour and salt into a large bowl. Put the yeast in a small bowl, add 2 tbsp of the water and mix with a teaspoon to a loose paste. Add the yeast mixture to the flour, swirl a little more of the water into the yeast bowl, to ensure no yeast is lost, and pour it into the flour. Add three-quarters of the remaining water and mix with a cutlery knife to distribute the water.

2 Feel the dough with your hands and add the remaining water, if necessary. The dough should be tacky, but not too sticky to work with. If not enough water is added, the dough will be dry and firm, difficult to knead and will make a dry, heavy loaf.

3 Turn the dough out onto a very lightly floured surface and knead it well for 5–8 minutes, using the bottom of the palm of one hand to push the dough away from you diagonally across you, and rolling it back with the fingertips of the same hand. Repeat with the other hand and continue kneading in this way, alternating between hands. Avoid adding flour even if the dough sticks to the table a little. As you knead and the water becomes fully distributed, the dough will become a little drier and less tacky.

4 After about 5 minutes of kneading, shape the dough into a ball, pulling it around itself to create a taut surface. Press the dough with your finger. If it bounces at least three-quarters of the way back and shows some elasticity, it is kneaded sufficiently. If the dough doesn't bounce back, or only a very little, you should continue kneading.

5 Once the dough is sufficiently kneaded, place it in a large, very lightly oiled bowl, cover with lightly oiled cling film or a damp tea towel and put in a warm place to rise until doubled in size, about 1 hour.

6 Remove the risen dough from the bowl and knock it back on your work surface, kneading for 2–3 minutes, to break down and distribute all the large bubbles created by the yeast during rising, giving a more even texture to the dough.

7 Shape the dough by pulling it around itself to create a smooth, taut surface. Roll it a little, smooth side down, on the work surface, then place neatly, smooth side up, in a lightly oiled 500g loaf tin, cover with lightly oiled cling film and leave to prove (rise again) in a warm place to at least half its size again. Meanwhile, heat the oven to 200°C/gas mark 6.

8 After about 30 minutes, check the dough by lightly pressing it in one corner with your finger; if it leaves a little indentation, it is ready. If it springs back fully, prove the loaf for longer. The dough should have almost reached the top of the tin (it will rise further in the oven).

9 Dust the top of the risen loaf with flour and bake in the oven for 25–30 minutes until golden. To check it is done, remove it from the oven and, using oven gloves, invert the tin to remove the loaf; it should feel light and sound hollow when tapped on the underside. If not, return the loaf to the tin and oven and cook for a little longer. Once cooked, leave the unmoulded loaf to cool on a wire rack.

1 Mixing the water into the dough, using a cutlery knife.

2 Checking the consistency of the dough; it should feel tacky but not too wet.

3 Kneading the dough until it feels smooth and elastic.

4 Shaping the dough into a ball with a smooth, taut surface.

5 The dough in the process of rising.

6 Kneading the dough vigorously to knock it back and produce a more even texture.

7 Placing the dough in the lightly oiled loaf tin, ready to prove.

8 Checking the dough by pressing lightly with a finger; it is ready if it leaves a little indentation.

9 Dusting the surface of the loaf with flour before baking.

Rolls and baps

All the recipes in the bread section can be made into rolls. Allow 35–45g dough for a dinner roll and 50–55g for a bap. Allow to prove on the baking sheet and bake for 10–15 minutes. For softer rolls, cover with a clean tea towel as they cool.

Shaping plain rolls

1 Divide the knocked back dough into equal pieces and shape into balls. Take a ball and gently stretch and pull the dough towards the top, creating a smooth surface underneath.

2 Turn the roll over so the smooth side is uppermost, and neaten the roll with the sides of your hands. Shape the other rolls, working quickly to ensure the first ones do not over-prove.

3 Place the rolls on a lightly greased baking sheet, spacing them apart. Lightly pat down the tops to flatten a little. Leave to prove until at least half their size again, then bake (see above).

Variations

Crown Shape as for plain rolls and cut a cross in the top before proving.

Pawnbroker Divide the small ball of dough into 3 equal pieces. Form each piece into a ball and place next to each other on the baking sheet to make a triangle.

Catherine wheel Shape the small ball of dough into a sausage about 15cm long. Coil the dough round from the centre, forming a catherine wheel.

Knot Shape the small ball of dough into a sausage about 10cm long. Carefully, without stretching, tie the dough into a knot. Try to hide the ends under the knot.

Pointed Carefully roll opposite ends of the small ball between your hand and the table into tapered points. The points of dough can be gently twisted.

Baps Shape as for dinner rolls, but flatten the tops of the rolls even more.

Bread finishes and glazes

There are a various ways to enhance the appearance of the crust, the simplest being a dusting of flour before baking, which gives a rustic, natural and soft finish. For shine and a rich colour, you can brush the top of the loaf with sieved beaten egg before baking and sprinkle with seeds too if you like. A milk glaze will give a softer crust and matt finish. Liquid glazes should be applied very thinly, using a pastry brush, avoiding any dripping, as this can cause the bread to stick to the tin.

You can also slash the top of the bread to give a rustic appearance, either before the bread proves (the slashes open and expand while proving and even more when baking), or 10–15 minutes before baking so they open up a little. Use a very sharp knife or single sided razor blade to make shallow cuts in the dough.

For a very soft crust, cover the bread with a tea towel as it cools.

Enriched white bread

Makes two 500g loaves

300–350ml milk

30g butter

20g fresh yeast

1 tsp caster sugar

500g strong plain flour, plus extra
  to dust

2 tsp salt

2 eggs

1 Put the milk in a small saucepan and bring to scalding point (see page 133) over a medium heat. Remove from the heat, transfer 2 tbsp to a small bowl and set aside to cool to blood temperature, about 38°C. Cut the butter into small dice and add to the remaining milk in the pan. Leave to melt and cool to blood temperature.

2 Add the yeast and sugar to the cooled milk in the bowl and stir until dissolved.

3 Put the flour and salt into a large bowl.

4 Break an egg into a small bowl, beat lightly and add to the flour, along with the dissolved yeast and at least three-quarters of the milk and butter mixture (using some of it to swill out any remaining yeast in its bowl). Use a cutlery knife to distribute the liquid evenly and bring the ingredients together into a dough. Add more milk and butter if necessary to create a soft, slightly tacky dough.

5 When the dough is beginning to form, use your hands to bring it together. Transfer to a very lightly floured surface and knead for 5–8 minutes (see step 3, page 602) until smooth and elastic.

6 Put the dough into a large, very lightly oiled bowl, cover with lightly oiled cling film and leave to rise in a warm place until doubled in size, about 1 hour.

7 Transfer the risen dough back to the work surface and knock it back, kneading it for 2–3 minutes.

8 Divide the dough in half and shape into 2 loaves (see step 7, page 602). Place in 2 lightly oiled 500g loaf tins, cover with oiled cling film and leave to prove in a warm place until risen by at least half their size again. Meanwhile, heat the oven to 200°C/gas mark 6.

9 To check the dough has proved enough, lightly press it in one corner with your finger; it should leave only a little indentation. Whisk the other egg with a fork, sieve it and use to brush the risen loaves. Bake in the top third of the oven for 25–30 minutes until golden. Turn the bread onto a wire rack; it should feel light and sound hollow when tapped on the underside. If not, return the bread to the oven to cook for a further 5 minutes. Leave to cool on a wire rack.

A note on enriching doughs...

Adding fats in the form of butter, oil or egg yolk, or adding sugar, alcohol or spices to a bread dough affects the way the yeast and the gluten work. The gluten strands won't be as strong, so the bread will have a softer, more cake-like texture. The yeast will also work more slowly, so the process will take longer. Often enriched dough bread recipes use a little more yeast to counterbalance these effects. If the liquid used is milk rather than water, it is heated to scalding point to destroy an enzyme that interferes with gluten, then cooled to the right temperature before mixing.

Wholemeal bread

Makes two 500g loaves

300–350ml milk

20g fresh yeast

1 tsp caster sugar

50g butter

250g wholemeal flour

250g strong plain white flour, plus extra
  to dust

2 tsp salt

1 Pour the milk into a small saucepan and bring to scalding point (see page 133) over a medium heat. Remove from the heat and set aside to allow the milk to cool to blood temperature, about 38°C.

2 Put the yeast and sugar into a small bowl, add 2 tbsp of the warm milk and stir to dissolve.

3 Cut the butter into small dice, add to the remaining warm milk and leave to melt.

4 Put the flours and salt in a large bowl. Add the yeast mixture and about three-quarters of the milk and butter mixture, trying to ensure all the butter is added. Using a cutlery knife, distribute the liquid evenly and bring together into a soft dough, adding the remaining milk and butter as needed. When the dough is beginning to form, use your hands to bring it together.

5 Transfer to a very lightly floured work surface and knead for 5–8 minutes (see step 3, page 602) until smooth and elastic.

6 Put the dough in a large, lightly oiled bowl and cover lightly with oiled cling film. Leave to rise in a warm place for about 1 hour until doubled in size.

7 Transfer the dough back to the work surface and knock it back, kneading it for 2–3 minutes.

8 Divide the dough in half, shape into 2 loaves (see step 7, page 602) and place in 2 lightly oiled 500g loaf tins. Cover with lightly oiled cling film and leave to prove in a warm, but not too hot, place. Meanwhile, heat the oven to 200°C/ gas mark 6.

9 To check the dough has proved enough, lightly press it in one corner with your finger; it should leave only a little indentation. Sprinkle flour over the tops of the loaves and bake in the oven for 25–30 minutes until browned. Turn a loaf onto a wire rack; it should feel light and sound hollow when tapped on the underside. If not, return to the oven to cook for a further 5 minutes. Remove from the tins and leave to cool on a wire rack.

Variation

Wholemeal seeded loaf Knead in 5 tbsp mixed seeds such as poppy, sesame, sunflower or millet seeds when you knock back the dough in step 7.

A note on using wholemeal flour...

You can use all wholemeal flour for this bread, but be aware that the greater the proportion of wholemeal to white flour, the heavier and denser the loaf will be. We don't use strong wholemeal flour, as ordinary wholemeal gives a softer loaf, but use strong wholemeal if you prefer.

Rosemary focaccia

Makes 1 focaccia
4½ tbsp olive oil
2 rosemary sprigs
10g fresh yeast
150–160ml warm water
250g strong plain flour, plus extra
   to dust
1 tsp salt
1 tsp Maldon sea salt

Focaccia is quick and easy to prepare as it has just one rise, unlike other breads. This produces a characteristic uneven, more open texture with bigger holes. It can be flavoured with various herbs, garlic or grated cheese.

1 Put 2 tbsp of the olive oil in a small bowl, add the rosemary sprigs and set aside.

2 Put the yeast in a small bowl, add 2 tbsp of the water and stir to dissolve.

3 Put the flour and the 1 tsp salt in a large bowl. Pour in the dissolved yeast, remaining 2½ tbsp oil and at least three-quarters of the remaining water, using some to swill out any yeast stuck in the small bowl. Stir quickly, adding the remaining water if the dough feels a little dry or firm, bearing in mind that a wetter dough is better than a drier one.

4 When all the ingredients are well mixed, remove the dough to a very lightly floured work surface and knead for a couple of minutes (see step 3, page 602). The dough might be a little soft and wet, but don't be tempted to add more flour. A scraper is useful for this.

5 Remove a rosemary sprig from the oil and place it on an oiled baking sheet. Pat out or roll the dough with a rolling pin into an oval about 2cm thick, and place on top of the rosemary.

6 Cover with a piece of oiled cling film and leave to rise in a warm place for about 1 hour, until it has nearly doubled in size and is soft and pillowy. To check the dough has risen enough, lightly press it in one corner with your finger; it should leave a little indentation. Meanwhile, heat the oven to 200°C/gas mark 6.

7 Remove the cling film and, using the lightly oiled fingers of one hand, make dimples at regular intervals in the dough, taking care not to push too hard and collapse the dough.

8 Remove the second rosemary sprig from the oil, reserving the oil, then tear off small sprigs and push these into the dimples in the dough. Drizzle the infused oil over the dough and sprinkle with the sea salt.

9 Bake for 20–30 minutes until golden. Transfer the bread to a wire rack and leave to cool, covering it with a tea towel to soften the crust, or leaving it uncovered if you prefer a hard crust.

Variations

Red onion focaccia Omit the rosemary. As the dough is rising, halve and peel 2 red onions. Cut each half through the root end into 3 wedges, keeping the wedges intact. Place on an oiled baking tray and toss in 2 tbsp olive oil. Roast in a hot oven for 20 minutes, adding 3 unpeeled garlic cloves after 10 minutes. Remove from the oven, allow to cool a little, then squeeze the garlic from their papery skins and break into smaller pieces. Scatter the onions and garlic over the risen dough and press them in lightly. Drizzle with olive oil, sprinkle with sea salt and bake as for the main recipe.

Sage and Gorgonzola focaccia Omit the rosemary and make a double quantity of dough. Divide the dough in half and pat or roll out into 2 discs, about 1.5cm thick. Place one on a lightly oiled baking sheet and scatter over 150g Gorgonzola, broken into small pieces, and 6–8 torn sage leaves. Carefully lay over the second dough disc, pressing down the edges to seal and encase the flavourings. Dimple the risen dough as above, drizzle with olive oil, sprinkle with salt (but sparingly as the cheese is salty) and bake for 10–15 minutes more than the main recipe.

Beer bread

Makes a 500g loaf

30g butter
1 tsp soft light brown sugar
175ml brown ale
10g fresh yeast
1 tbsp warm water
125g wholemeal flour
125g strong plain white flour, plus extra
  to dust
1 tsp salt
1 small egg

1 Use a little of the butter to grease a 500g loaf tin, then put the remainder in a small saucepan with the sugar and ale. Place over a medium to high heat, stir to melt the sugar and butter into the liquid, then bring to the boil. Remove from the heat and leave to cool to lukewarm.

2 Put the yeast in a bowl, add the water and mix to a loose paste.

3 Sift the flours and salt into a large bowl. Reserve 1 tsp of the bran from the sieve for the top of the loaf and tip the rest into the bowl with the flours.

4 Break the egg into a small bowl and beat lightly, then add it to the flours. Add the yeast mixture and three-quarters of the ale and butter mixture. Mix first with a cutlery knife and then with your fingers, adding enough of the reserved ale mixture to make a soft but not sticky dough.

5 Turn out onto a very lightly floured surface and knead for about 5–8 minutes (see step 3, page 602) until smooth and elastic, using as little extra flour as possible on the work surface to stop the dough sticking.

6 Place the dough in a very lightly oiled bowl and cover with lightly oiled cling film or a damp tea towel. Leave in a warm place until doubled in size, about 1 hour.

7 Transfer the risen dough to the work surface and knock it back, kneading it for 2–3 minutes.

8 Shape the dough into a loaf (see step 7, page 602) and place smooth side up in the greased loaf tin. Cover with lightly oiled cling film and leave to prove until risen by at least half its size again. Meanwhile, heat the oven to 200°C/gas mark 6.

9 Sprinkle the reserved bran over the top of the loaf and bake in the oven for 30–40 minutes, or until golden brown and it feels light and sounds hollow when tapped on the bottom. Remove from the tin and leave to cool on a wire rack.

Note Beer lends a unique, slightly sour taste to bread. The darker beer you use, the darker the bread and the heavier the flavour of the bread will be.

Variations

Walnut and raisin bread Replace the wholemeal flour with malted brown flour and the ale with 300ml milk, brought to scalding point (see page 133) and cooled to lukewarm before using. Knead 100g raisins and 100g roughly chopped walnuts into the dough when knocking it back, then proceed as for the main recipe.

Rosemary and fig bread Replace the ale with 175ml milk, brought to scalding point (see page 133) and cooled to lukewarm before using. Knead 200g sliced dried figs and 1 tbsp roughly chopped rosemary into the dough when knocking it back, then shape the dough as a flat round or oval loaf on an oiled baking sheet. Place olive oil soaked sprigs of rosemary on top before baking (as for focaccia, see page 608) and drizzle with a little honey when it first comes out of the oven.

....

A note on adding solid ingredients to bread doughs...

It is better to add ingredients like nuts, seeds, herbs or dried fruit to the basic dough after it has risen, as if incorporated earlier such additions can slow the rise and break up into the dough. Either knead them in while knocking back the dough or roll the dough out after it has had its first rise, scatter the ingredient(s) over the surface, roll it up like a Swiss roll and then continue to knead. This achieves a good even distribution throughout the final loaf.

Soda bread

Makes an 800–850g loaf
250g plain flour, plus extra
   to dust
250g wholemeal flour
1½ tsp salt
2 tsp bicarbonate of soda
1 tbsp caster sugar
50g butter
300–350ml buttermilk

Leavened with chemical raising agents rather than yeast, this is a quick bread.

1 Heat the oven to 190°C/gas mark 5. Lightly flour a baking sheet.

2 Sift the flours, salt, bicarbonate of soda and sugar into a large bowl and add back any bran still left in the sieve.

3 Cut the butter into 1cm pieces and rub into the flour mixture with your fingertips, then briskly stir in just enough buttermilk to make a soft dough.

4 Transfer to the floured baking sheet and shape, with a minimum of handling, into a large disc about 4–5cm thick. With the floured handle of a wooden spoon, make a dent 2cm deep in the shape of a cross on top, then lightly dust with flour.

5 Bake in the oven for 35–45 minutes, until the soda bread is risen, golden brown and with no greyness evident in the cross. Remove to a wire rack to cool.

Note If you can't find buttermilk, use milk and add 2 tsp cream of tartar to the dry ingredients. Alternatively, add 2–3 tbsp lemon juice to ordinary milk and leave in a warm place for 10–15 minutes to sour the milk, which will provide enough acidity.

Variation

Fruited white soda bread Use all white flour and add an extra 6 tbsp sugar to the flour, with 175g raisins or sultanas.

English buttermilk muffins

Makes 10
150ml milk
15g fresh yeast
2 tbsp warm water
½ tsp caster sugar
1 egg
500g strong plain flour, plus extra
   to dust
1 tsp salt
100ml buttermilk (see note, recipe above)
Rice flour, to dust

1 Pour the milk into a small pan and bring to scalding point (see page 133) over a medium heat. Remove from the heat and leave to cool to lukewarm. In a small bowl, cream together the yeast, water and sugar. Beat the egg in another bowl.

2 Put the flour and salt in a large bowl and make a well in the middle. Pour in the egg and buttermilk and add the yeast mixture, taking care to scrape all the yeast in. Add two-thirds of the milk. Stir with a cutlery knife, then with your hands, adding enough of the reserved milk to make a soft but not sticky dough.

3 Turn the dough out onto a very lightly floured surface and knead for about 8–10 minutes (see step 3, page 602), until soft and elastic. Place the ball of dough in a lightly oiled bowl, turning to coat it lightly. Cover with lightly oiled cling film and leave to rise in a warm place for about 1 hour until doubled in size.

4 Roll the dough out until 2cm thick, without kneading again. Sprinkle the work surface with a fine layer of rice flour, then lift the dough onto it and sprinkle with another fine layer of rice flour. Cut out 10 muffins using an 8cm floured cutter.

5 Place on a large, oiled baking sheet, leaving plenty of space for them to expand as they rise. Gently cover with lightly oiled cling film and leave to rise to 1½ times their original thickness, about 1 hour. Heat the oven to 180°C/gas mark 4.

6 Heat a large non-stick frying pan over a medium heat and cook the muffins in batches for 3–5 minutes each side. You may need to turn the heat down to prevent them from scorching. Transfer the muffins to another baking sheet.

7 When all the muffins have been fried, bake in the oven for 10–15 minutes until cooked through. Transfer the cooked muffins to a wire rack to cool, loosely wrapped in a clean tea towel to keep the crusts soft. Serve split in half with butter.

Crostini

Makes 20–30
1 small baguette
75–100ml olive oil

These are little crisp bread rounds onto which you can place a variety of toppings (see below).

1 Heat the oven to 180°C/gas mark 4.

2 Slice the baguette on the diagonal into very thin slices, about 2mm thick.

3 Spread the slices over 2 baking sheets, if they won't fit on a large one.

4 Brush the slices on both sides with olive oil and bake for 10–15 minutes, or until golden and crisp. Transfer to a wire rack to cool.

Bruschetta

Makes about 20
75ml olive oil
2 garlic cloves
1 ciabatta loaf

Similar to crostini, bruschetta are lightly toasted slices of bread brushed with a garlic-infused olive oil.

1 Put the olive oil into a small saucepan and place over a low heat. Bash the unpeeled garlic cloves with the flat side of a large knife, remove the skin and add the garlic to the oil. Warm gently for 5 minutes, then remove from the heat and set aside to infuse for 10–15 minutes.

2 Meanwhile, heat the grill to its highest setting and slice the ciabatta on the diagonal into slices about 5mm thick.

3 Scatter the slices of ciabatta over 2 baking sheets, if they do not fit on a large one, and grill until toasted and golden on both sides, turning as necessary. Remove from the grill.

4 Strain the infused olive oil and either drizzle or brush over the bruschetta.

Topping suggestions for crostini and bruschetta

Butter bean mash

Seared tuna and guacamole

Pear and Gorgonzola

Manchego and membrillo (quince paste)

Diced deseeded tomato with mozzarella and basil

Broad bean mash with Parmesan

Griddled vegetables and mozzarella

Goat's cheese, caramelised red onion and sage

Sautéed chicken livers with oven-roast cherry tomatoes

Croûtons

Makes enough to fill a large storage jar
1 small loaf of white bread (unsliced)
500–750ml sunflower oil
Salt

1 Cut the crusts off the loaf of bread and slice it 1.5cm thick, then cut the slices into 1.5cm cubes.

2 Pour a 2cm depth of oil into a saucepan or sauté pan and heat slowly over a medium heat until a piece of bread dropped into the oil browns in about 20–30 seconds. Shallow-fry a few croûtons at a time, keeping them on the move so they colour evenly.

3 Once the croûtons have achieved a pale golden colour all over, remove them with a slotted spoon to a tray lined with kitchen paper to drain. Sprinkle with a little salt before serving. If not using straight away, transfer to a wire rack to cool, then store in an airtight container in a cool place for up to 1 month.

Oven baked croûtons

Makes enough to fill a large storage jar
1 small loaf of bread (unsliced)
60g butter
Salt and freshly ground black pepper

1 Heat the oven to 180°C/gas mark 4.

2 Cut the crusts off the loaf. Slice the bread into 1.5cm thick slices, then cut the slices into 1.5cm cubes. Place in a bowl.

3 Melt the butter in a small saucepan and pour over the bread cubes. Toss to coat as evenly as possible and season with salt and pepper.

4 Tip into a shallow roasting tin and bake in the oven for 15–20 minutes until evenly golden, turning the croûtons occasionally to encourage even browning.

5 Remove from the oven and leave to cool a little before using.

Variations

Sourdough croûtons Remove the crusts, tear the sourdough into largish pieces and proceed as for the main recipe.

Herbed croûtons Add 1–2 tbsp coarsely chopped herbs, such as rosemary, sage or thyme to the butter when melting, then strain before pouring over the bread.

Smoked paprika croûtons Add ½ tsp smoked paprika to the butter before pouring it on the bread.

Croûtons baked in olive oil Brush the cubes of bread with olive oil instead of butter, using a flavoured oil if you prefer.

A note on making breadcrumbs…

Leftover bread can be made into breadcrumbs and, if you don't need them immediately, frozen successfully. Cut off and discard the crusts from a 1–2 day old loaf. Cut the bread into large cubes and blend in batches in a food processor, until broken up into fine crumbs. Transfer to a plastic bag to store or freeze.

If you need a fine crumb, you can pass them through a sieve. You can also make breadcrumbs without removing the crusts, to produce a pale golden crumb.

Brioche

Makes 2 loaves
85ml milk
20g fresh yeast
500g plain flour
1½ tsp salt
30g caster sugar
6 eggs
350g butter, softened

For lining the mould
30g butter
Flour, to dust

For the glaze
1 egg yolk
1 tbsp milk

This recipe uses plain flour, which has a lower gluten content than strong bread flour, giving the brioche a cake-like texture. For a more bread-like texture, use either strong bread flour or a mixture of plain and strong. Here the brioche is baked in two 500g loaf tins. You can also bake the mixture in a large fluted brioche mould, shaping the dough as described for individual brioches (see below).

1 Pour the milk into a small saucepan and bring to scalding point (see page 133) over a medium heat. Remove from the heat and cool to blood temperature, about 38°C. Pour the milk over the yeast in a small bowl and stir to dissolve.

2 Meanwhile, put the flour, salt and sugar in a large bowl. Lightly beat the eggs and add to the flour along with the milk and yeast mixture. Using a cutlery knife, mix to a very soft dough. Then, using a wooden spoon, beat the dough until smooth and elastic, about 10–15 minutes.

3 Turn the dough onto a work surface and, using your fingertips, work the dough by stretching it to shoulder height; it won't stretch this far until the gluten is fully developed, so keep working it until it does.

4 Cut the butter into walnut-sized pieces. Using the same kneading-stretching technique, work the pieces of butter into the dough one at a time, only adding each when the previous piece is completely worked in. As more butter is worked in, the dough should gradually become more shiny, elastic and glossy.

5 Lift the dough into a clean bowl and cover with lightly oiled cling film. Leave to rise in a warm place until doubled in size, about 2 hours.

6 Tip the dough out onto the work surface and knock back by turning it over with your fingertips a few times. Refrigerate, covered, for at least 3–4 hours (up to 24).

7 To prepare the tins, melt the 30g butter in a small saucepan and remove from the heat. Brush two 500g loaf tins with the butter and set aside in a cool place for the butter to firm up, then brush again with butter and, before the butter sets the second time, dust with flour, tapping any excess out.

8 Divide the dough in half, shape into 2 loaves (see step 7, page 602) and place them in the tins. Cover loosely with lightly oiled cling film and leave to prove at room temperature until risen to the top of the mould. Place in the fridge for 10–15 minutes to firm the dough. Meanwhile, heat the oven to 220°C/gas mark 7.

9 For the glaze, lightly whisk the egg yolk and milk together in a small bowl, then sieve. Brush the risen brioche with the egg glaze, taking care not to let it drip down the sides of the mould.

10 Bake the brioche in the oven for 40–45 minutes until cooked and dark golden brown on top. The finished loaf should be quite dark, but if it appears to be colouring too quickly, lower the oven setting to 200°C/gas mark 6. The brioche should come out of the tin easily and sound hollow when tapped on the base. Transfer to a wire rack to cool.

Variation

Individual brioches Grease and dust 12 small fluted brioche tins. Divide the dough into 12 pieces, roll three-quarters of each piece into a ball and place in the tins. Make a hole in the middle of each with a floured wooden spoon handle (as shown). Roll the remaining pieces of dough into 12 small balls, place in the holes in the larger rounds (as shown), and press the wooden spoon handle through to seal. Place on a tray, cover loosely with cling film and prove as above. Refrigerate as above, then brush with the egg glaze (as shown) and bake for 8–10 minutes.

Cinnamon raisin buns

Makes 8 large buns

250ml milk

20g fresh yeast

100g caster sugar

500g strong plain flour, plus extra
  to dust

½ tsp salt

100g butter, at room temperature,
  plus extra to grease

1 egg

50ml maple syrup

½ tsp ground mixed spice

½–1 tsp ground cinnamon

100g raisins

½ quantity glacé icing (see page 643)

1 Pour the milk into a saucepan and bring to scalding point (see page 133) over a medium heat, then remove from the heat and leave to cool to blood temperature, about 38°C.

2 In a small bowl, cream the yeast with 1 tsp of the sugar and 1 tbsp of the milk.

3 Put the flour and salt in a large bowl. Cut 75g of the butter into cubes and rub into the flour with your fingertips. Stir in 50g sugar and make a well in the middle. Set aside the remaining butter in a warm place to soften.

4 Break the egg into a small bowl and beat with a fork. Add the beaten egg to the well with the creamed yeast mixture and at least three-quarters of the remaining milk. Using a cutlery knife, bring the dough together, adding any remaining milk if needed to make a soft dough.

5 Transfer the dough to a very lightly floured surface and knead for about 5–8 minutes (see step 3, page 602) until smooth.

6 Place the dough in a very lightly oiled bowl and cover with lightly oiled cling film. Leave to rise in a warm place until doubled in size, about 1½ hours.

7 Meanwhile, mix the remaining butter and sugar to a smooth paste with the maple syrup, mixed spice and cinnamon to taste.

8 Transfer the risen dough to the work surface and knock it back, kneading it for 2–3 minutes. Using a rolling pin, roll the dough into a 25cm square. Spread the butter, sugar and spice paste over the dough as evenly as possible, and almost to the edges, then scatter over the raisins. Roll the dough up into a Swiss roll shape, trim off the ends and cut into 8 pieces, 3cm thick.

9 Generously butter a 24cm round cake tin. Arrange 7 buns, cut side up, around the inside edge of the prepared cake tin, leaving a little space between each to allow them to expand as they prove. Place the eighth bun in the middle.

10 Cover with oiled cling film and leave to prove for 25–30 minutes, or until almost doubled in size. Meanwhile, heat the oven to 200°C/gas mark 6.

11 Bake in the oven for 25–35 minutes until risen and golden. Check between the layers for any greyness and continue to cook a little longer if there is any, on a lower shelf to prevent them taking on too much colour. Remove from the oven and turn the whole crown out onto a wire rack to cool. Once cool, drizzle with glacé icing.

Variations

Chelsea buns Omit the maple syrup, replace the cinnamon with an extra ½ tsp mixed spice and the raisins with a mixture of sultanas and currants. Proceed as for the main recipe.

Cinnamon pecan toffee buns Omit the maple syrup and mixed spice and replace the raisins with chopped pecan nuts. Instead of buttering the tin, spread a mixture of 75g softened butter and 75g soft light brown sugar over the bottom and scatter 100g pecan nuts over this before arranging the buns on top to prove, as for the main recipe. The butter, sugar and pecans will create a nutty toffee syrup on the base of the buns. Remove the buns from the tin while still warm (or they may stick) and serve upside down, sticky nutty side uppermost.

Hot cross buns

Makes 8

100ml milk
10g fresh yeast
2 tbsp warm water
30g caster sugar
1 egg
250g strong plain flour, plus extra
  to dust
¼ tsp salt
2–3 tsp ground mixed spice
40g butter, at room temperature
50g currants
1 tbsp chopped mixed peel

For the crosses and glaze

50g plain flour
Pinch of baking powder
2 tsp oil
15–30ml milk
1 tsp caster sugar

1 Pour the milk into a saucepan and bring to scalding point (see page 133) over a medium heat, then remove from the heat and leave to cool to blood temperature, about 38°C.

2 In a small bowl, mix the yeast with the water and ½ tsp of the sugar to create a loose paste. Beat the egg and add it to the yeast mixture.

3 Put the flour, salt and mixed spice in a large bowl. Cut the butter into cubes and rub it into the flour with your fingertips. Stir in the remaining sugar.

4 Make a well in the centre and pour in the yeast mixture and three-quarters of the milk, making sure all the yeast is scraped into the well. Stir with a cutlery knife, then with your fingers, adding enough of the reserved milk to make a soft but not sticky dough.

5 Tip the dough out onto a very lightly floured surface and knead for about 8–10 minutes (see step 3, page 602) until smooth and elastic, using as little extra flour on the work surface as possible.

6 Place the dough in a very lightly oiled bowl and cover with lightly oiled cling film or a damp tea towel. Leave in a warm place to rise for about 1½ hours until doubled in size.

7 Transfer the risen dough to the work surface and knock it back, kneading for 2–3 minutes and adding in the currants and mixed peel (trying to ensure that the currants and peel stay in whole pieces).

8 Divide the dough into 8 equal pieces, shape into buns (see page 604) and place about 2cm apart on a large, oiled baking sheet. Flatten each slightly with the palm of your hand, then cover with oiled cling film and leave to prove. Meanwhile, heat the oven to 200°C/gas mark 6.

9 To make the crosses for the tops of the buns, sift the flour and baking powder into a bowl. Stir in the oil and enough cold water to make a thick but pipeable paste. Once the buns have risen and doubled in size, mix the milk with the sugar and use to brush the buns lightly. Fill a piping bag fitted with a 5mm nozzle with the paste. Using a sharp knife, cut a very shallow cross in the top of each bun, 1mm deep, and pipe a cross on top.

10 Bake for 15 minutes then brush the buns again with the sweetened milk and return to the oven for 5 minutes, or until golden brown. They should feel light and sound hollow when tapped on the base. Transfer to a wire rack to cool and serve fresh with butter, or split in half and toasted.

Note For extra shine, brush the cooked, cooled buns with an apricot glaze (see page 642), or a light stock syrup (see page 138), in place of the milk glaze.

Variation

Cranberry and orange buns Replace the currants and mixed peel with 60g dried cranberries and the mixed spice with 2 tsp ground cinnamon. Add the finely grated zest of 1 orange when adding the sugar.

Blinis

Makes about 15
125g wholemeal flour
125g plain flour
¾ tsp salt
15g butter
375ml milk
3 eggs
25g fresh yeast
1 tsp caster sugar
Sunflower oil for frying

1 Sift the flours and salt into a bowl, tipping in any bran left in the sieve.

2 Melt the butter in a small saucepan. In a separate pan, heat the milk until warm.

3 Make a well in the centre of the flour and add 2 whole eggs and 1 yolk, reserving the leftover white.

4 In a small bowl, combine the yeast, sugar and 2 tbsp of the warm milk; mix well until the yeast has dissolved. Pour the yeast mixture onto the eggs in the well with the melted butter and about three-quarters of the remaining milk. Mix together and add the remaining milk, if needed, to create a smooth batter. The mixture should be a pourable batter rather than a dough.

5 Cover the bowl with lightly oiled cling film and leave to rise in a warm place until at least doubled in size, about 1 hour. The quantity of yeast should make it grow quite considerably and quickly in a warm place. Heat the oven to 120°C/ gas mark ½.

6 Whisk the egg white to medium-stiff peaks (see page 161) and fold it into the blini batter.

7 Lightly oil a non-stick frying pan and place the pan over a low to medium heat. Pour in enough batter to create a saucer-sized blini and cook until bubbles rise to the surface. Flip it over and cook the second side to a golden brown.

8 Transfer the blini to a plate in the low oven and repeat with the remaining batter, lightly oiling the pan between each, and layering the cooked blinis between sheets of greaseproof paper.

Note If you are using an individual blini pan, fill it about one-third full and flip it when bubbles rise to the surface.

Variation

To make small canapé-sized blinis, cook teaspoonfuls of the mixture. This quantity of batter will make 50–60 blini canapé bases.

Topping suggestions

Smoked eel with horseradish cream (see page 318)

Serrano ham, semi-dried figs and mascarpone

Smoked trout, cooked beetroot and a mixture of horseradish and crème fraîche, topped with dill

Smoked salmon, with or without crème fraîche

Cakes

Cake making requires precision. Weighing the ingredients correctly, knowing what to look for at each stage, careful preparation of tins, baking temperature and position in the oven are all important. Air bubbles are incorporated into the mixture during mixing and/or by using a chemical raising agent. Cake making calls for a light touch, so that the air bubbles trapped in the mixture are retained. Avoid over-mixing, which would make cakes heavy and tough.

There are 4 main methods of cake making: rubbing in, melting, creaming and whisking.

Essential ingredients

Fats Of the various options, butter gives the best flavour for cake making. Unsalted butter is often preferred, but if it is used a small pinch of salt should be added to the flour to lend flavour. Although the flavour will not be the same, vegetable margarine is a good alternative to butter, resulting in a light and airy cake. Oils result in a dense, moist texture, which suits certain cakes.

Flours Plain flour is the most common flour to use for cake making. Strong flour, with its high percentage of gluten, would not result in the same tender crumb, and is more suited to bread making.

Self-raising flour should only be used when specified in the recipe; it has an added chemical raising agent, baking powder. If a recipe calls for self-raising flour and you don't have any, then plain flour with the addition of baking powder is acceptable. As a guide, use 2 level tsp baking powder to 225g plain flour.

Raising agents Cakes need air to rise and lighten them or they will be heavy and dense. Air can be incorporated in several ways, the more common methods being sifting the flour, beating or creaming air into fats, or whisking the eggs.

Bicarbonate of soda, or baking soda, is a chemical raising agent which releases carbon dioxide when it comes into contact with liquid, which is then trapped in the uncooked cake mixture. When the cake is baked the mixture rises and sets around the bubbles. Acidity enhances the carbon dioxide reaction, so baking powder is often found in cakes using some form of acidic liquid, such as buttermilk, sour milk or yoghurt, or cream of tartar.

Baking powder comprises bicarbonate of soda, an acid and a starch filler, usually cornflour, which helps to absorb any moisture and keeps the baking powder active.

A note on the temperature of ingredients...
For all baking, you get better results if the ingredients are at room temperature, particularly the eggs, so remove all ingredients from the fridge in time to ensure they come to room temperature. If this is not possible, you can bring eggs up to room temperature by placing them in a bowl of warm/hand hot water for 10–15 minutes, making sure the water is not too hot.

A note on assembling cakes...
If sandwiching two cakes together, you should sandwich the bases together. A cake made in a moule à manque (a tin with sloping sides) can be cut in half, filled and reassembled. It is traditionally served upside down, with the bottom uppermost.

Preparing cake tins

All cake tins should be greased to prevent sticking. Use either melted or softened butter or oil, and apply with a pastry brush to give only the lightest coating and avoid any fat from sitting in the corners. Non-stick cake tins do not need to be greased but it is still a good idea to line the base. You can line the bottom with either greaseproof paper that you grease, or with baking parchment, which is non-stick and does not need greasing.

To base-line round tins For 2 tins, fold a piece of greaseproof paper in half and place a tin on top. Use a pencil to trace around the outside of the tin, then cut inside the line of the circle and trim to size if necessary. Brush the paper with melted butter. Lightly brush the tins with melted butter and place a disc of greaseproof paper in the bottom of each tin. It is essential that the disc is cut to size, as if it comes up the sides of the tin it will prevent the cake having a clean, neat edge.

For whisked cakes Grease the tin and place a disc of greaseproof paper on the base, then grease it again. Dust with caster sugar, shaking it around the tin to coat it evenly, tap out the excess, then dust it with flour and tap out the excess.

To line a shallow rectangular tin To fully line a tin (for brownies etc), take a piece of baking parchment about 5cm bigger on all sides than the tin. Cut diagonally through the corners, about 5cm deep and lay the parchment in the roasting tin, pushing it into the corners. The cuts made through the corners will allow the paper to overlap neatly and line the tin.

Preparing a tin for a fruit cake

1 Cut 2 discs (or squares) of greaseproof paper to fit the bottom of the tin. For the sides, fold a sheet of greaseproof paper in half lengthways, long enough to fit snugly inside the tin all the way round the inside. On the folded edge, fold up about 3cm again. Then, using scissors, make diagonal cuts across the 3cm depth of the folded border all the way along the paper.

2 Lightly grease the inside of the tin, place a disc (or square) of greaseproof paper on the base, then fit the long sheet around the inside the tin, with the border folded towards the middle of the tin. The cuts will overlap to allow you to line the sides of the tin neatly. Make sure the paper fits well into the bottom edge of the tin and trim the top if it protrudes too much over the rim.

3 Place the second greaseproof paper disc on top. Lightly grease the paper base and sides. As fruit cakes are dense and take a long time to cook, it is a good idea to wrap 2 or 3 layers of newspaper around the outside of the cake tin and tie them securely with kitchen string. This will help prevent the outside of the cake from overcooking.

Rubbing-in method

This technique uses the process of rubbing fat into flour (as for pastry), resulting in cakes with a crumbly, moist texture. It uses raising agents: bicarbonate of soda, baking powder or self-raising flour, which has raising agents already added.

Scones

Makes 6–8 scones

225g self-raising flour, plus extra
  to dust
½ tsp salt
60g butter
30g caster sugar
150ml milk
1 egg (optional)

To serve

Clotted cream or butter
Strawberry jam

1 Heat the oven to 220°C/gas mark 7. Sift a little flour over a baking sheet. Sift the flour into a large bowl with the salt. Cut the butter into 1cm cubes and rub it into the flour with your fingertips until the mixture resembles coarse breadcrumbs. Stir in the sugar and make a well in the centre. Pour in the milk and stir briskly using a cutlery knife until the dough starts to come together. Gather the dough with your hands; it should be soft and spongy. Avoid overworking or kneading, which can make the scones tough. Add a little more milk if the dough is too dry, but not too much as a very wet dough results in heavy, dense scones.

2 Place the dough on a lightly floured surface and pat or roll out to no less than a 3cm thickness. Dip a 5–6cm pastry cutter in flour and cut out the scones, getting as many as possible out of the dough. To ensure an even rise, cut firmly and avoid twisting the cutter as you release the scone. Place on the prepared baking sheet. Push the cut dough back together (rather than squash it into a ball), and cut out more scones; these may not be quite as tender as the first rolled batch.

3 For a glossy crust, beat the egg in a small bowl with a fork, sieve it, then use to brush the top of the scones. Alternatively, for a soft crust, sprinkle with flour. Bake in the top third of the oven for 15–18 minutes, or until the scones are well risen and golden brown on top. Transfer to a wire rack. Serve warm or allow to cool, before eating with clotted cream or butter and strawberry jam.

1 Bringing the dough together with your hands.

2 Cutting out the scones, using a floured 5–6cm pastry cutter.

3 Transferring the cooked scones to a wire rack to cool.

Variations

Date scones Add 100g coarsely chopped dates to the mixture before the milk.

Cheese scones Reduce the butter by half and omit the sugar. Add 75g strongly flavoured grated cheese, such as Cheddar, Gruyère or Parmesan, along with a pinch each of English mustard powder and cayenne pepper, before the milk.

Melting method

This method involves heating the fat to melt it before incorporating into the mixture, and results in a very moist cake. The dry ingredients are sifted and mixed with the melted mixture to form a batter. Not a great deal of air is incorporated during the process, so the cake is leavened using a chemical raising agent, such as bicarbonate of soda. Cakes made this way are fairly easy and reliable to make, and because they are so moist, keep well in an airtight tin.

Gingerbread

Makes 20 squares
225g butter, plus extra to grease
225g soft dark brown sugar
70g black treacle
165g golden syrup
300ml milk
350g plain flour
Pinch of salt
1–1½ tbsp ground ginger
2 tsp ground cinnamon
2 tsp bicarbonate of soda
2 eggs

1 Heat the oven to 170°C/gas mark 3. Lightly grease a 30 x 20cm roasting tin with butter and line the base and sides with baking parchment (see page 621).

2 Put the butter, sugar, treacle and golden syrup in a saucepan and melt over a low to medium heat. Remove from the heat, stir in the milk and leave to cool.

3 Sift the flour, salt, ginger, cinnamon and bicarbonate of soda into a large bowl. Make a well in the centre and break in the eggs. Using a wooden spoon, start to stir the eggs, but without forcing flour into the eggs (which can cause lumps); it will be drawn in and incorporated as you stir the eggs.

4 As this mixture becomes thicker, add a little of the cooled butter and sugar mix to loosen it, then continue stirring. Continue like this until all the flour has been incorporated and all the liquid ingredients added. This should take about 5 minutes.

5 Pour the batter into the prepared tin. Bake in the middle of the oven for about 50–60 minutes. Don't be tempted to open the oven door before 45 minutes or the cake may sink. Test by inserting a skewer into the centre; it should come out clean or with only a few moist crumbs clinging to it. If there is uncooked mixture on the skewer, return the cake to the oven to cook for a little longer.

6 Once cooked, turn the gingerbread onto a wire rack to cool before cutting into squares. It keeps very well in an airtight tin, for up to 3 weeks, and even improves with keeping.

A note on weighing syrup...

When weighing syrup, it is best to weigh it onto the top of the sugar that is being added at the same time, to prevent it sticking to the scale pan. To prevent it sticking to the spoon, dip the spoon in hot water for a few seconds, dry it and then use to measure the syrup out.

Creaming method

This involves creaming or beating softened butter and sugar together until they are a pale colour and have a light consistency. The creaming helps to incorporate air into the mixture, but the cake is mainly risen by the use of self-raising flour, which contains a chemical raising agent. This raising agent begins to take effect as soon as it comes into contact with liquid, so working quickly once the flour is added is imperative.

Victoria sandwich

Makes a 20cm round cake
Oil, to grease
225g butter, softened
225g caster sugar, plus extra to dust
4 eggs, at room temperature
225g self-raising flour
1–2 tbsp water or milk
5–7 tbsp raspberry jam

A classic Victoria sandwich uses equal weights of butter, sugar, eggs and flour.

1 Heat the oven to 180°C/gas mark 4. Lightly brush two 20cm sandwich tins with a little oil and line the base of each with a disc of greaseproof paper.

2 Using a wooden spoon or hand-held electric whisk, cream the butter and sugar together in a medium bowl until pale, light and fluffy (as shown). The paler the mixture becomes the better, as it shows that more air has been incorporated, which will help to create a lighter cake.

3 Break the eggs into a small bowl and beat lightly with a fork until broken up. Gradually add the egg to the creamed butter and sugar (as shown), in several additions and beating well after each. Adding eggs that are too cold, or adding them too quickly, can cause the mixture to curdle. If this happens, add 1 tbsp of the flour to help to stabilise the mixture.

4 Once all the egg has been added, sift the flour over the surface and fold it in, using a large metal spoon (as shown). To bring the mixture to a dropping consistency (see page 627), if necessary, fold in 1–2 tbsp water or milk.

5 Divide the mixture between the prepared tins and smooth the tops using a spatula. Bake in the middle of the oven for about 20–30 minutes, or until well risen and golden. They should feel spongy to the fingertips and not leave an indentation when pressed gently.

6 Allow the cakes to cool for a few minutes in the tins, then turn them out onto a wire rack to cool completely before peeling off the lining paper. While the cakes are cooling, put the jam into a small saucepan over a low heat and gently warm through, to make it more spreadable. Sandwich the cooled cakes, bases together, with the jam and dust the top of the cake with caster sugar.

Variations

Coffee walnut cake Dissolve 4 tsp good quality instant coffee granules in 1 tbsp warm water and stir into the mixture before you add the flour. Stir in 75g coarsely chopped walnuts after the flour. You may not need water or milk to achieve a dropping consistency. Omit the raspberry jam. Use coffee butter icing (see page 643) to sandwich and ice the cake.

Chocolate cake Replace half the caster sugar with soft light brown sugar and 55g of the flour with good quality dark cocoa powder, adding ½ tsp baking powder to the flour. Omit the raspberry jam. Use chocolate ganache (see page 647) to sandwich and ice the cake.

Cherry almond cake Replace 55g of the flour with 75g ground almonds and stir in 100g halved glacé cherries after the flour, adding ½ tsp baking powder to the flour. Omit the raspberry jam and use Amaretto butter icing (see page 643) to sandwich and ice the cake.

Fruit cake

Makes a 22–24cm round cake

100g glacé cherries

50g chopped mixed peel

450g raisins

275g sultanas

100g currants

1 lemon

2 tbsp black treacle

200ml beer or sweet sherry

225g butter, softened, plus extra
   to grease

225g soft dark brown sugar

5 eggs

300g plain flour

2 tsp ground mixed spice

100g ground almonds

The fruit needs to be soaked overnight, so start this cake the day before.

1 Halve the cherries, place in a large bowl with the mixed peel, raisins, sultanas and currants. Finely grate the lemon zest and add to the fruit along with the treacle and beer. Stir well, cover and leave overnight in a cool place for the fruit to soak up the beer and become plump.

2 Heat the oven to 170°C/gas mark 3. Grease and line a 22–24cm round, deep cake tin (see page 621).

3 Put the butter and sugar into a large bowl and cream together until pale and fluffy, using a hand-held electric whisk or a wooden spoon.

4 Break the eggs into a small bowl and beat lightly with a fork, just to break them up. Add the beaten egg to the creamed butter and sugar in additions, beating well after each addition (about 5 additions will do).

5 Sift the flour and spice into the bowl and, using a large metal spoon, fold into the mixture. Fold in the ground almonds and finally incorporate the fruit mixture.

6 Spoon the mixture into the prepared tin. Turn a plastic spatula through the middle of the mixture to make a well in the middle, to help to prevent the cake from 'peaking' in the middle.

7 Bake in the lower to middle part of the oven for 2–2½ hours, until risen and golden and a skewer inserted into the middle emerges clean, or with only a few moist crumbs clinging to it. If there is any soft or undercooked mixture on the skewer, return the cake to the oven for a little longer.

8 Once cooked, remove the cake from the oven and allow to cool for 10–15 minutes before turning it out onto a wire rack to cool completely. Leave the cooled cake in the greaseproof paper and over-wrap well in foil until ready to use.

....

A note on storing/maturing...

Fruit cakes can be made several months in advance of eating, and their flavour matures with keeping. To avoid the cake drying out, wrap well with foil and 'feed' the cake with brandy every 2 weeks. Unwrap the foil and insert a skewer into the cake several times, pushing the skewer almost through to the base. Pour about 2–3 tbsp brandy over the entire surface of the cake, allow it to seep in, then rewrap well in the foil.

All-in-one creaming

This is an easy adaptation of the creaming method in which all the ingredients are beaten together at the same time, which gives pretty good results.

Lemon drizzle loaf

Makes a 500g loaf cake
100g butter, plus extra to grease
1 large lemon
2 eggs
2 tbsp milk
125g self-raising flour
1 scant tsp baking powder
100g caster sugar
50g granulated sugar

1 Heat the oven to 170°C/gas mark 3. Grease a 500g loaf tin, then line the base and short sides with a piece of greaseproof paper that extends over the sides. Finely grate the lemon zest and squeeze the juice. Beat the eggs and milk together in a small bowl. Sift the flour and baking powder into a large bowl and stir in the caster sugar. Cut the butter into small cubes and add to the bowl. Add the egg mixture and lemon zest and beat with an electric whisk until smooth, about 1 minute. The mixture should have a dropping consistency (see note).

2 Pour the mixture into the prepared loaf tin and bake for 35–40 minutes, or until the top springs back when pressed lightly. Test by inserting a skewer into the centre; it should come out with a few moist crumbs but no raw mixture.

3 Leave to cool in the tin for 5 minutes before turning it out onto a wire rack to cool a little more. Put the granulated sugar in a small bowl and stir in enough lemon juice to make a runny syrup. Return the cake to the tin while still a little warm and pour the syrup over the loaf. Leave to cool completely, then remove the cake from the tin by lifting the greaseproof paper ends. Cut into slices to serve.

Variation

Lime drizzle cake Use 2 limes in place of the lemon.

1 Checking that the mixture is the correct dropping consistency.

2 Inserting a skewer into the centre of the cake to check whether it is cooked.

3 Spooning the lemon drizzle over the warm cake in the tin.

A note on dropping consistency...

To check the consistency of the mixture, lift a spoonful up; it should hold briefly for a few seconds on the spoon, then fall without any encouragement. If the mixture runs off the spoon, it is too loose. If it doesn't drop at all, or takes longer than a few seconds to drop, it is too stiff.

Whisking method

This method involves whisking eggs and sugar together to create a mousse or foam into which you fold flour and melted butter (although the simplest versions contain no fat). Whisked sponges rise purely due to the air incorporated during the whisking process, so they are more delicate than creamed cakes and take a little more practice to perfect. You can either use a free-standing electric mixer, or a hand-held electric whisk and a bowl set over just boiled water. During whisking, the mixture should easily increase to 4 times its original volume and when ready it should fall from the beaters in a wide ribbon-like trail. A good folding action is needed to incorporate the flour.

Whisked sponge

Makes a 20cm sponge
Oil, to grease
85g caster sugar, plus extra to dust
85g plain flour, plus extra to dust
Pinch of salt
3 eggs
1½ tbsp warm water

To assemble
200ml whipping cream and 250g
  raspberries or halved strawberries
OR
½ quantity buttercream (see pages
  644–5) and 4–5 tbsp raspberry jam

This fatless sponge is best eaten the day it is baked.

1 Heat the oven to 180°C/gas mark 4. Oil and line a 20cm cake tin, then dust with sugar followed by flour, tapping out the excess (see page 621). Sift the flour and salt onto a sheet of greaseproof paper.

2 Break the eggs into a large heatproof bowl, add the sugar and, using a hand-held electric whisk, start whisking on a low speed without moving the whisk through the eggs and sugar until they are combined.

3 Place the bowl over a saucepan of just boiled water, making sure the bowl is not touching the water, and continue to whisk on a low speed for 3–4 minutes. This will help to build up a network of small air bubbles, which will help to stabilise the mixture.

4 Increase the speed and continue whisking until the mixture becomes very pale, fluffy and mousse-like, and is 'to the ribbon', holding about a 5–6 second ribbon (see page 630). Remove the bowl from the pan and continue whisking until the bowl has cooled slightly, a further 1–2 minutes. Lastly, whisk in the water.

5 Sift the flour and salt again over the whisked mixture and, using a large metal spoon, carefully fold it in, trying not to beat any air out of the mixture.

6 Gently pour the mixture into the prepared tin, holding the bowl as close to the tin as possible, to ensure minimal air loss. Give the tin a little tap on the work surface to bring any large air bubbles to the surface.

7 Stand the cake tin on a baking sheet and bake in the middle of the oven for about 30 minutes. After 25 minutes, you should be able to smell the sponge. At this point (not before, or the sponge may sink), open the oven door a little and have a look. The sponge should be risen, golden, slightly shrinking away from the sides and crinkly at the edges. When lightly pressed with your fingertips, it should bounce back and not leave an indentation. If you are close to the sponge you will hear a slight creaking when you press it.

8 Stand the sponge, still in its tin, on a wire rack to cool a little for 1–2 minutes, then carefully invert it and leave upside down on the wire rack, still in the tin, to cool completely.

9 To release the sponge from the tin, run a cutlery knife around the side of the sponge, keeping the knife firmly against the tin. Once fully released, carefully turn the sponge onto a clean hand and gently place back down on the wire rack. Peel off the lining paper. To serve, cut the cake horizontally into 2 layers and sandwich together with whipped cream and berries or buttercream and jam.

1 Shaking the excess flour out of the prepared cake tin.

2 Whisking the eggs and sugar together on a low speed to combine.

3 Whisking the mixture over hot water to encourage it to thicken and increase in volume.

4 Checking that the mixture has reached the correct ribbon stage.

5 Carefully folding in the flour, using a large metal spoon.

6 Gently pouring the mixture into the prepared cake tin.

7 Pressing the sponge gently with the fingertips to test whether it is ready.

8 Inverting the cooked sponge onto the wire rack to cool.

9 Releasing the sponge from the side of the tin.

A note on 'to the ribbon'...

This term is used to describe the thickness of a whisked mixture, such as eggs and sugar. When the beaters are lifted, the mixture should fall from them onto the surface of the mixture in a wide ribbon-like trail and hold itself there for a few seconds before sinking in (see step 4, page 628). When a recipe calls for a 4 or 5 or 6 second ribbon, this refers to the length of time the ribbon trail holds on the surface of the mixture. Normally a 5–6 second ribbon is required, but check the recipe.

Making a Swiss roll

This classic teatime favourite is made using a whisked sponge mixture and is best eaten on the day it is made. Once rolled, store in an airtight container, wrapped in its paper to prevent it from drying out, until ready to serve.

1 Line a 30 x 20cm Swiss roll tin with baking parchment or prepare a paper case: cut 2 sheets of baking parchment to a size 2cm bigger all around than an A4 sheet of paper. Fold up a 2cm edge on each side and fold and clip the corners with paper clips. Place this on a baking sheet.

2 Add 2–3 drops of vanilla extract to the whisked sponge mixture (see page 628) after whisking the eggs and sugar together. Spread the mixture into the prepared tin or paper case, smoothing it to the edges gently, to avoid knocking out the air. Bake for just 12–15 minutes.

3 While the cooked sponge is still warm, lay a piece of greaseproof paper on the work surface and sprinkle it evenly with caster sugar. Invert the warm sponge onto the sugared paper and carefully peel off the paper, using a palette knife to support the cake. Trim off the dry edges.

4 Make a shallow cut across the width of the cake (where you will begin to roll it); this helps to get a well shaped roll. While the sponge is still warm, spread it with 5–6 tbsp raspberry jam **and** start to roll from the cut end.

5 Using the paper under the cake to help, continue to roll the cake up firmly and evenly. Leave the Swiss roll wrapped in the paper to set its shape.

6 To serve, carefully unroll the paper, dredge the Swiss roll with a little more caster sugar and cut into 1–1.5cm slices.

Genoise

Makes a 20cm round cake
Oil, to grease
125g caster sugar, plus extra to dust
125g plain flour, plus extra to dust
55g butter
4 eggs

To assemble
1 quantity buttercream (see
   pages 644–5)
1 quantity praline (see page 648)

A genoise differs from a whisked sponge in that it contains butter, which enriches the cake and also means it will last longer before becoming stale.

1 Heat the oven to 180°C/gas mark 4. Lightly oil a 20cm moule à manqué (tin with sloping sides) or round cake tin and line the base with a disc of greaseproof paper. Lightly oil again. Dust with sugar then flour, tapping out the excess (see page 621).

2 Melt the butter in a small saucepan over a low heat, then set aside to cool.

3 Place the eggs and sugar in a large heatproof bowl and, using a hand-held electric whisk, start whisking on a low speed without moving the whisk through the eggs and sugar. Place the bowl over a saucepan of just boiled water, making sure the bowl is not touching the water, and continue to whisk on a low speed for 3–4 minutes. Increase the speed and continue whisking until the mixture becomes very pale, fluffy and mousse-like, and holds a 5–6 second ribbon (see note, left).

4 Remove the bowl from the pan and continue whisking until the bowl has cooled slightly, a further 1–2 minutes.

5 Pour the melted, cooled butter around the edge of the mixture and fold it in, using a large metal spoon, with just 3 or 4 folds.

6 Sift the flour over the mixture and carefully fold it in, taking care not to beat any air out of the mixture.

7 Gently pour the mixture into the prepared tin, holding the bowl as close to the tin as possible to ensure as little air loss as possible. Give the tin a little tap on the work surface to bring any large air bubbles to the surface.

8 Stand the cake tin on a baking sheet. Cook in the middle of the oven for about 30–35 minutes. After 25 minutes, you should be able to smell the sponge. At this point (not before, or the sponge may sink), open the oven door a little and have a look. It should be risen, golden, slightly shrinking away from the sides and crinkly at the edges. When lightly pressed with your fingertips it should bounce back.

9 Stand the sponge, still in its tin, on a wire rack to cool a little for 1–2 minutes, then carefully invert it and leave upside down on the wire rack, still in the tin, to cool completely.

10 To release the sponge from the tin, run a cutlery knife around the side of the sponge, keeping the knife firmly against the tin (see step 9, page 628). Once fully released, carefully turn the sponge onto a clean hand and carefully place back down on the wire rack. Peel off the lining paper.

11 To serve, cut the cake horizontally into 2 layers and sandwich together with a third of the buttercream. Spread the remaining buttercream over the top and sides and coat the sides with the crushed praline. Smooth the buttercream top decoratively with a palette knife.

Variations

Coffee genoise Dissolve 2–3 tsp good quality instant coffee granules in 2 tsp hot water, leave to cool and add with the butter.

Chocolate genoise Reduce the flour to 85g and add 40g dark cocoa powder.

Lemon genoise Fold in the finely grated zest of 1 lemon with the butter.

Genoise fine Increase the butter to 100g and reduce the flour to 100g. This sponge is richer and lighter, and slightly more difficult to make.

Small cakes

Financiers

Makes about 20
95g unsalted butter
50g skinned hazelnuts or almonds
50g plain flour
100g caster sugar
Pinch of salt
4 egg whites
½ tsp vanilla extract
Small handful of fresh or dried cherries,
  or blueberries (optional)

1 Heat the oven to 200°C/gas mark 6.

2 Melt 20g of the butter in a small saucepan over a low heat. Place 20 large (7cm) barquette moulds on a baking tray and brush each with the melted butter.

3 Melt the remaining butter over a low to medium heat and cook to a deep beurre noisette (see page 114). Remove from the heat and set aside to cool.

4 Grind the nuts to fine crumbs in a food processor. Sift the flour, ground nuts, sugar and salt into a large bowl. In a separate bowl, lightly beat the egg whites until frothy, then fold them into the dry ingredients, adding the beurre noisette and vanilla extract once most of the whites have been incorporated.

5 Fill each mould almost to the top with the mixture and scatter the fruit, if using, over the surface. Bake in the middle of the oven for 10–15 minutes until golden brown and spongy when pressed.

6 Remove from the oven and leave the financiers to cool for a few minutes, before releasing the tops with the tip of a sharp knife. Turn out onto a wire rack and leave to cool completely. These are best eaten the same day, but will keep in an airtight container for a few days.

Note For mini financiers, bake the mixture in mini muffin tins; allow 7–8 minutes.

Madeleines

Makes about 36
180g butter
3 eggs
150g demerara sugar
15g clear honey
150g plain flour
1½ tsp baking powder

1 Melt 30g of the butter in a pan over a low heat and lightly grease a 15–18 hole ridged madeleine tray. (Keep the rest of the melted butter for the second batch.)

2 Melt the remaining 150g butter in a second small pan over a low to medium heat and cook to a beurre noisette (see page 114). Remove from the heat.

3 Break the eggs into a large bowl, add the sugar and honey and whisk together with a hand-held electric whisk until pale and thick. The mixture should just leave a ribbon trail when you lift the whisk (see step 4, page 628).

4 Add the flour to the beurre noisette slowly, beating with a wooden spoon to incorporate fully. Cook, stirring, over a low heat for 1 minute, then remove from the heat and set aside to cool slightly.

5 Stir this beurre noisette and flour mixture with the baking powder into the whisked egg mixture and place in the fridge for 1 hour to firm up. Meanwhile, heat the oven to 200°C/gas mark 6.

6 Place a teaspoonful of the mixture in each madeleine mould. Bake in the middle of the oven for 8–10 minutes until risen and pale golden with a 'peaked' middle.

7 Remove the madeleines from their moulds to a wire rack to cool and repeat with the remaining mixture to cook a second batch. These are best eaten the day they are made, but will keep in an airtight container for a few days.

Note For mini madeleines, bake the mixture in petits fours moulds, allowing just 4–5 minutes in the oven.

Lemon and poppy seed muffins

Makes 12
120g butter
250g plain flour
2 tsp baking powder
½ tsp bicarbonate of soda
Pinch of salt
2 tbsp poppy seeds
2 eggs
120g soft light brown sugar
75ml milk
3 lemons
150g icing sugar

1 Heat the oven to 190°C/gas mark 5 and line a 12-hole muffin tin with paper muffin cases.

2 Melt the butter in a small saucepan over a gentle heat, then set aside to cool.

3 Sift the flour, baking powder, bicarbonate of soda and salt into a large bowl. Stir in the poppy seeds and set aside. Break the eggs into a small bowl and beat lightly.

4 In another large bowl, mix together the cooled butter, sugar, beaten eggs and milk. Finely grate the zest and squeeze the juice from the lemons. Add all the zest and the juice of 2 lemons to the liquid ingredients, reserving the remaining juice.

5 Using a large metal spoon, fold the flour mixture into the lemon mixture, using as few folds as possible. The more the mixture is worked the heavier the muffins, so it needs a light touch. Fill the muffin cases two-thirds full with the mixture.

6 Bake in the middle of the oven for 20 minutes, or until the muffins are well risen and pale golden brown, and a wooden skewer inserted into the centre comes out clean or with a few moist crumbs attached.

7 Transfer the muffins in their paper cases to a wire rack and leave to cool.

8 Mix half the remaining lemon juice with the icing sugar to make a glacé icing. Drizzle over the cooled muffins.

Variations

Lemon blueberry muffins Omit the poppy seeds, use the zest and juice of just 1 lemon and fold in 100g fresh blueberries just after the flour.

Lemon raspberry cheesecake muffins Omit the poppy seeds. Instead of adding the lemon zest to the liquid ingredients, mix it with 150g cream cheese and 50g icing sugar. Fold 100g fresh raspberries into the mixture just after the flour. Half-fill the muffin cases with the mixture, place a generous teaspoonful of lemon cream cheese in the middle of the mixture and top with the remaining muffin mixture.

Apple cinnamon crumble muffins Omit the poppy seeds and lemons. Soak 50g dried apples in 100ml apple juice for 3–4 hours, then drain, finely chop and add to the dry ingredients. Continue as for the main recipe, two-thirds filling the muffin cases. Sift 100g plain flour with a good pinch of ground cinnamon, rub in 75g cold butter, then stir in 50g demerara sugar. Sprinkle this crumble mixture over the top of the muffins before they go in the oven.

Tray bakes and biscuits

Chocolate brownies

Makes 20
200g good quality dark chocolate, minimum 60% cocoa solids
140g butter
225g caster sugar
2 large eggs, plus 1 extra yolk
2 tsp vanilla extract
85g plain flour

1 Heat the oven to 180°C/gas mark 4. Line a 20cm square shallow baking tin with baking parchment.

2 Break the chocolate into pieces and place in a large heatproof bowl. Cut the butter into small cubes and add to the chocolate. Stand the bowl over a pan of gently simmering water, ensuring that the base of the bowl does not come into contact with the water, to melt the chocolate, stirring occasionally.

3 Set aside to cool for 2–3 minutes, then whisk in the sugar using an electric whisk. Beat the eggs and yolk in a separate bowl with the vanilla extract, just to combine.

4 Gradually whisk the eggs into the chocolate mixture and beat until smoothly combined. Sift in the flour and stir in until evenly combined, using a spatula.

5 Pour the mixture into the prepared tin and bake in the middle of the oven for 25–35 minutes, or until a knife inserted in the middle comes out with moist crumbs (not wet batter) clinging to it. It is better to slightly undercook than overcook brownies, as they should still be fudgy in the middle and will become less moist as they cool.

6 Leave to cool in the tin for 2 minutes before lifting carefully from the tin and transferring to a wire rack to cool. Remove the paper before the brownie is completely cold. Cut into 20 squares using a sharp knife. These are delicious served cold or warmed through and served with ice cream as a dessert.

Flapjacks

Makes 16
150g butter, plus extra to grease
100g soft light brown sugar
50g golden syrup
200g rolled oats

1 Heat the oven to 190°C/gas mark 5. Lightly grease a 20cm square, shallow baking tin.

2 Put the butter into a saucepan and melt over a gentle heat. Add the sugar and syrup and stir for 2 minutes to warm through rather than melt. Remove from the heat and add the oats. Stir thoroughly, then spread the mixture evenly in the tin.

3 Bake in the oven for 20–25 minutes, or until golden brown.

4 Remove from the oven and, using a sharp knife, cut into 16 squares while still warm. Leave in the tin to cool for 10 minutes before transferring to a wire rack to cool completely. They will keep for a 4–5 days, stored in an airtight container.

Variations

Dried fruit and seed flapjacks Replace 30g of the oats with 30g mixed seeds (such as sesame, pumpkin or sunflower) and stir in 30g chopped dried fruit (such as apricots, pear or apple) with the oats.

Sour cherry and almond flapjacks Replace 30g of the oats with 30g roughly chopped almonds, and stir in 30g dried sour cherries with the oats.

Shortbread

Makes 8 petticoat tails
100g butter, softened
50g caster sugar, plus extra to sprinkle
130g plain flour
30g ground rice

1 Place a 15cm flan ring on a baking sheet. Put the butter into a medium to large bowl and beat with a wooden spoon until soft, then add the sugar and beat well until fully incorporated. Sift the flour and ground rice into the mixture and stir to a firm, smooth paste. You may need to use the back of the wooden spoon to 'mash' the ingredients together.

2 Press the mixture into the flan ring and smooth into a neat circle, using the back of a cutlery spoon, then remove the flan ring. Crimp the edges of the shortbread with your fingers to create a decorative edge.

3 Mark the shortbread into 8 wedges, scoring deeply, prick evenly with a fork well into the dough and chill until firm. Meanwhile, heat the oven to 170°C/gas mark 3.

4 Sprinkle the shortbread evenly with a little sugar and cook on the middle shelf of the oven for 20–25 minutes, or until a pale biscuit colour with no grey patches in the middle. Remove from the oven and run a palette knife under the shortbread to loosen it from the baking sheet. Leave to cool for 5 minutes before transferring to a wire rack to cool completely. It will keep for a few days in an airtight container.

 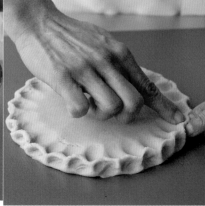 

1 Stirring the shortbread mixture to combine and form a firm, smooth paste.

2 Crimping the edge of the shortbread between the fingers to form a decorative edge.

3 Cutting the shortbread into 8 wedges to shape the petticoat tails before baking.

Variations

Almond shortbread Replace 50g of the flour with 50g ground almonds. For a crunchier texture, you can also stir 10g roughly chopped blanched almonds into the mixture.

Orange shortbread Add the finely grated zest of ½ orange with the flour.

Chocolate chip cookies

Makes about 15

120g butter
60g granulated sugar
90g soft light brown sugar
1 large egg
1 tsp vanilla extract
150g plain flour
¼ tsp baking powder
150g milk chocolate chips

1 Heat the oven to 180°C/gas mark 4. Line 2 large baking sheets with baking parchment.

2 Using an electric whisk, beat the butter and sugars together until pale and fluffy. Beat the egg with a fork in another bowl to break it up and stir in the vanilla extract. Gradually beat the egg into the butter mixture.

3 Sift in the flour and baking powder and stir in well, using a spatula, then stir in the chocolate chips.

4 Drop tablespoonfuls of the mixture onto the prepared baking sheets, spacing them at least 4cm apart as they will spread.

5 Bake in the middle of the oven for 10–12 minutes, or until browning round the edges but still soft and chewy in the middle. Halfway through the cooking time, swap the top and bottom trays around in the oven, and at the same time turn the trays round so the back of the tray comes to the front, to ensure even cooking.

6 Remove from the oven and leave the cookies to set for 1–2 minutes before carefully transferring them to a wire rack to cool. They will keep for a few days, stored in an airtight container.

Variation

Double chocolate chip cookies Reduce the flour to 100g and add 50g sifted good quality dark cocoa powder with the flour.

Oatmeal and raisin cookies

Makes about 20

100g raisins
120g butter
75g caster sugar
75g soft light brown sugar
1 large egg
1 tsp vanilla extract
100g self-raising flour
250g rolled oats

1 Heat the oven to 180°C/gas mark 4. Line 2 large baking sheets with baking parchment.

2 Put the raisins in a small bowl, pour on about 50ml boiling water and set aside to plump up while you make the dough.

3 Beat the butter and sugars together, using an electric whisk, until pale and fluffy. Beat the egg in another bowl with a fork and stir in the vanilla extract. Gradually whisk the egg into the butter mixture.

4 Sift in the flour and stir in well, using a spatula. Add the oats, with a drop of water if the mixture is too stiff to stir easily. Drain the raisins and stir them in too, discarding the soaking liquid.

5 Drop tablespoonfuls of the mixture onto the prepared baking sheets, spacing them at least 4cm apart as the mixture will spread. Pat them down so they are a little flattened.

6 Bake in the middle of the oven for 15–20 minutes, or until browning round the edges but still soft and chewy in the middle. Halfway through the cooking time, swap the top and bottom trays around in the oven, and at the same time turn the trays round so the back of the tray comes to the front, to ensure even cooking.

7 Remove from the oven and leave the cookies to set for 1–2 minutes before carefully transferring them to a wire rack to cool. They will keep for a few days, stored in an airtight container.

Tuiles

Makes 20–25
60g butter, plus extra to grease
2 large egg whites
125g caster sugar
60g plain flour
½ tsp vanilla extract

1 Heat the oven to 190°C/gas mark 5. Lightly grease 2 large baking sheets and a rolling pin. Put the butter into a small saucepan and melt over a low heat, then set aside to cool.

2 Put the egg whites into a bowl and, using a fork, beat in the sugar until just frothy. Sift in the flour, add the vanilla and combine well with a fork. Add the cooled, melted butter to the mixture and stir well. Chill for 10–15 minutes to firm the mixture a little, to make it easier to work with.

3 Place 4 or 5 teaspoonfuls of the mixture, at least 13cm apart, on one of the prepared baking sheets and spread into thin circles, 1mm thick, using a palette knife. (Using a stencil cut out from a plastic ice-cream container lid makes shaping the mixture easier and also ensures the correct thickness.) You need to bake the tuiles in batches of 4 or 5 at a time, to give you enough time to shape them before they cool down.

4 Bake in the oven for about 6 minutes, until pale biscuit in colour in the middle and golden brown at the edges. Remove from the oven and leave to cool for a few seconds, to become pliable. Meanwhile, put a second batch in the oven on the second baking sheet.

5 Lift the cooked biscuits carefully off the baking sheet with a palette knife. Lay them, while still warm and pliable, over the rolling pin, to form them into a slightly curved shape. Once the shape has set, remove them carefully to a wire rack to cool.

6 Repeat with the remaining batches until the mixture is used up. The tuiles will keep for a few days, stored in an airtight container.

Note If the tuiles cool too much before shaping, return them to the oven for a few minutes to soften and make pliable, but be aware that you cannot do this many times or they will eventually become very brittle and break very easily.

Variations

Almond tuiles Scatter 30–40g flaked almonds over the tuiles before baking.

Orange tuiles Stir the finely grated zest of ½ orange into the mixture with the flour and vanilla.

Brandy snaps

Makes 12–15
A little oil, to grease
100g butter
100g caster sugar
90g golden syrup
½ lemon
100g plain flour
Pinch of ground ginger

These round brandy snap biscuits can be shaped into baskets, tuiles or tubes that can be filled with cream.

1 Heat the oven to 190°C/gas mark 5. Line a baking sheet with baking parchment. Lightly oil any moulds you will need: the base of a timbale or jam jar for a basket, a rolling pin for a tuile or the handle of a wooden spoon for a tube.

2 Put the butter, sugar and syrup into a small saucepan, place over a low heat and stir until the sugar and butter have melted. Remove from the heat and leave to cool to room temperature. Squeeze the juice from the lemon and measure 1 tbsp.

3 Sift the flour and ginger into the cooled mixture (if too hot the mixture will turn lumpy), stir well, then stir in the 1 tbsp lemon juice.

4 Place teaspoonfuls of the mixture on the prepared baking sheet, at least 10cm apart as they will spread out considerably. You need to bake them in batches of 4 or 5 at a time; this will also give you time to shape them before they cool down. Bake in the oven for 5–7 minutes, or until an even, deep golden brown.

5 Remove from the oven and leave to set for just 30 seconds. Remove from the baking sheet one at a time, using an oiled palette knife to prevent them sticking, to a second oiled baking sheet for flat biscuits, or over your chosen mould, if shaping. Leave for a few minutes until just set on the moulds, then transfer to a wire rack to cool. You might need to warm the remaining brandy snaps in the oven to make them pliable again if they get too firm to mould.

6 Repeat with the remaining mixture, cooking and shaping in batches. They will keep for a few days, stored in an airtight container.

Langues de chat

Makes about 50
100g butter, softened
100g caster sugar
3 egg whites
100g plain flour

1 Heat the oven to 200°C/gas mark 6. Line 2 or 3 large baking sheets with baking parchment.

2 Put the butter into a medium bowl and add about one-third of the sugar. Cream together using a wooden spoon, then add the remaining sugar in 2 additions, beating until pale and fluffy.

3 Whisk the egg whites until frothy, then gradually mix into the creamed butter and sugar mixture using a spatula, beating well after each addition.

4 Sift in the flour and fold it in carefully with the spatula.

5 Spoon the mixture into a piping bag fitted with a 5–8mm plain nozzle. Pipe straight lines onto the prepared baking sheets, about 8cm long and the thickness of a pencil, spacing them well apart to allow room for spreading. Tap the baking sheets to release air bubbles from the mixture

6 Bake in the oven for 5–8 minutes until the sponge biscuits are slightly risen and golden around the edges. Remove from the oven and leave to cool for a few seconds before carefully lifting the biscuits with a palette knife and transferring them to a wire rack to cool completely. They will keep for a few days, stored in an airtight container.

Macaroons

Makes 50 paired macaroons
200g ground almonds
200g icing sugar
160g egg whites (about 5 medium)
Food colouring of your choice (see below)
75ml water
200g caster sugar

To assemble
Chocolate ganache (see page 647),
  good quality jam or buttercream icing
  (see pages 644–5)

1 Line 2 baking sheets with baking parchment. Thoroughly mix the ground almonds and icing sugar together in a food processor and sift into a large bowl, discarding any coarse pieces of almond remaining in the sieve.

2 Put the almond mixture into a bowl and, using a spatula, mix in 80g unbeaten egg white, to create a smooth paste. Add ¼–1 tsp food colouring, depending on how vibrant you want the colour to be. Set aside.

3 Bring the water and sugar to the boil in a small saucepan to make a sugar syrup (see page 138). Meanwhile, in a large bowl, whisk the remaining 80g egg white to soft peaks using a hand-held electric whisk (see page 161). When the sugar syrup reaches 115°C, pour it over the whisked egg white, avoiding pouring it onto the whisk itself, then continue to whisk to stiff peaks.

4 Using a rubber spatula, stir one-third of this meringue into the almond paste, to loosen the mixture, then carefully fold in the remaining meringue. Continue to fold the macaroon mixture just until it becomes smooth, uniform, gently flowing and a little shiny. Test a small amount on the baking parchment: it should not be stiff enough to leave a peak, nor so soft that it floods excessively.

5 Fill a piping bag fitted with a 5–8mm plain nozzle with the macaroon mixture and pipe little mounds, about 2–2.5cm in diameter, onto the prepared trays. Set aside for 20–30 minutes until a skin forms on the surface. Meanwhile, heat the oven to 160°C/gas mark 2½.

6 To check the macaroons are ready to bake, lightly brush the top of one with the tip of your finger: the batter should not stick to your finger and it should feel slightly leathery. Bake in the oven for 15–20 minutes, or until the macaroons have formed a crisp shell and base.

7 Slide the baking parchment onto a cool surface, to encourage the bases of the macaroons to release from the paper. Leave to cool completely before peeling carefully from the paper. They will keep for a few days, stored in an airtight container. To serve, sandwich the macaroons together in pairs with either a chocolate ganache, jam or buttercream icing.

Colour and flavour variations

Lemon Use yellow colouring. Sandwich the macaroons together with lemon curd (see page 591).

Raspberry Use red colouring. Sandwich the macaroons together with raspberry ganache: mix 100g melted white chocolate with 50g warmed raspberry purée and cool for at least an hour before using.

Chocolate Use brown colouring. Sandwich the macaroons together with chocolate ganache (see page 647).

Coffee Use brown colouring. Sandwich the macaroons together with coffee butter icing (see page 643).

Vanilla Omit colouring. Sandwich the macaroons together with vanilla butter icing (see page 643).

Pistachio Use green colouring. Sandwich the macaroons together with pistachio ganache: warm 50ml double cream with 1 tbsp pistachio paste, add to 100g melted white chocolate, stirring well, then cool for at least an hour before using.

Glazes and icings

A delicious icing, from a simple ganache to a more intricate affair, shows off your baking to best effect. These are a selection of the glazes, icings and fillings we use most often.

Jam glazes

Glazing a fruit tart helps to prevent it from drying out and retain its texture, as well as adding a beautiful shine to emphasise the colour and freshness of the fruit. Some enriched sweet breads are also traditionally glazed with a fruit glaze.

Use a cold glaze for fresh fruit and a warm glaze for cooked fruit. The amount of water you need to add to the jam depends on the jam. You are looking for a light syrupy consistency rather than a thick coarse texture, which would not look attractive on the fruit.

Apricot glaze, because of its pale and neutral colour, is very useful as a general purpose glaze and is best for pale fruits and breads, while a redcurrant glaze works well for red fruits.

Apricot glaze

Makes enough to glaze a 24cm tart
250g apricot jam (not whole fruit)
1 lemon

1 Put the jam into a small saucepan. Using a swivel peeler, pare a strip or two of lemon zest, add to the pan and heat gently over a low heat until the jam has melted, without letting it boil. Avoid stirring the jam too much or too vigorously or you will incorporate air bubbles that can cause it to cloud.

2 Once melted, if the jam is still very thick add 2–3 tbsp warm water to loosen it, then pass it through a fine sieve into a clean bowl, discarding the zest.

3 Adjust the consistency with a little more warm water until the glaze coats a pastry brush evenly and is the consistency of runny honey. It should come off the brush in a single stream for about 2–3cm, then start to drip off. Some jam will not need any water added and some might need more, but take care as too much water will thin the jam too much and it will not adhere properly.

4 When applying glaze, dab it on the fruit or bread rather than brushing or using strokes. This will give a much more even finish, as long as the consistency is correct. As you use the glaze, keep checking the consistency and adding water as necessary, as it will thicken as it cools.

Variation
Redcurrant glaze Replace the apricot jam with redcurrant jelly. Generally, on warming, redcurrant jelly melts to a much looser consistency, so you won't need to add as much water.

Simple icings

These are simple icings and fillings for cakes that can be made relatively quickly.

Glacé icing

Makes enough to ice a 20cm cake
250g icing sugar

Glacé icing is a thin icing used to ice cakes or drizzle over cakes and sweet breads, to glaze them and provide a little additional sweetness.

1 Sift the icing sugar into a large bowl.

2 Add enough boiling water, starting with ½–1 tbsp, to mix to a fairly stiff coating consistency. It needs very little water, so take care not to add too much. The icing should hold a trail when dropped from a spoon but gradually find its own level.

Note Hot water produces a shinier result than cold water and the icing is less likely to crack when it dries.

Coffee butter icing

Makes enough to ice a 20cm cake
125g butter, softened
200g icing sugar
3 tsp finely ground strong espresso coffee
  (powder-fine)

1 Put the butter into a medium bowl and, using a hand-held electric whisk, cream until light and fluffy.

2 Sift in the icing sugar and coffee powder and whisk again for 5–7 minutes, or until the mixture returns to a light and fluffy consistency and the coffee has dissolved into the icing.

Variations

Vanilla butter icing Omit the coffee. Add a few drops of vanilla extract.

Coffee maple butter icing Replace 25g of the icing sugar with maple syrup.

Amaretto butter icing Replace the coffee powder with 2 tbsp Amaretto.

Soured cream and chocolate icing

Makes enough to ice a 20cm cake
250g good quality dark chocolate,
  minimum 60% cocoa solids
225ml soured cream
1–2 tbsp caster sugar

1 Break up the chocolate and put in a heatproof bowl. Place the bowl over a pan of simmering water, making sure the base of the bowl is not touching the water, and place over a low heat.

2 Add the soured cream with sugar to taste, and melt. Stir to combine, then remove from the heat and leave to cool and thicken before using.

Buttercream icings

We use 3 types of buttercreams: custard-, meringue- and mousse-based. Consistency and temperature are the important factors in making buttercreams. As a general rule you should always add a thinner mixture to a thicker one, as they combine more readily, and if either the butter or the base mixture is a little cool then you risk the mixture curdling. To avoid this, make sure the temperature of all your ingredients is similar, and at least at room temperature. Buttercreams must also be kept at room temperature; if chilled, they become too solid.

Custard-based buttercream

Makes enough to fill and top a 22cm two-layered sponge
150g caster sugar
225ml milk
3 egg yolks
150g unsalted butter, at room temperature
150g salted butter, at room temperature

This method involves making a custard and beating it into the butter.

1 Put half the sugar and half the milk into a medium saucepan and bring to scalding point (see page 133) over a medium heat.

2 Combine the egg yolks with the remaining sugar and milk in a medium bowl. Pour over the scalded milk, a little at a time to begin with, to allow the egg yolks to warm a little, then add all the milk and combine well.

3 Return the custard to the rinsed out pan and place over a low heat, stirring with a wooden spoon. Allow the egg yolks to thicken the custard as for a crème anglaise (see page 132). To check the consistency, remove from the heat and draw the back of the spoon through the custard; the custard should coat the back of the spoon evenly, and a finger scraped through it should leave a line. Strain immediately into a bowl and leave to cool, with a piece of cling film in contact with the surface to prevent a skin from forming.

4 Using a hand-held electric whisk or wooden spoon, beat the butters together until soft but not greasy; they should be the same temperature as the custard.

5 Gradually add the cooled custard to the butter, 1 tbsp at a time to start with, beating well after each addition with a wooden spoon or spatula and increasing the amount you add. Once all the custard has been added, gradually stir in your chosen flavouring, if using, see below.

Flavour variations

Chocolate Melt 75g dark chocolate with the milk as it heats, then use to make the custard. You may need to whisk the chocolate into the milk to incorporate it fully.

Lemon, orange or lime Add the finely grated zest of 1½–2 lemons or oranges, or 2–3 limes, to taste, to the finished buttercream.

Coffee Add 3–4 tsp warm very strong coffee or espresso, to taste, at the end. (Alternatively, 40–50ml Camp Coffee can be used.)

Vanilla Add a few drops of vanilla extract to the finished buttercream.

....

A note on curdling...

To avoid curdling, ensure the mixtures you are combining are at the same temperature, and that neither is cold. However, if any of these buttercreams do start to split, they can be rectified if not too badly curdled. Start by whisking very quickly, which often helps to re-combine the ingredients. If necessary, place the bowl over a steam bath and warm the icing a little, without allowing it to melt, then whisk very quickly. If this does not work, start again with 2–3 tbsp softened butter and slowly add the curdled buttercream in teaspoonfuls to begin with, beating well between each addition.

Mousse-based buttercream (crème au beurre mousseline)

**Makes enough to fill and top
a 22cm two-layered sponge**

175g granulated sugar

175ml water

6 egg yolks

100g unsalted butter, at room
  temperature

100g salted butter, at room temperature

This method, which makes a rich, creamy icing, involves whisking a sugar syrup into egg yolks to create a foam, then combining this with the butter.

1 Put the sugar and water into a medium saucepan and dissolve the sugar over a low heat, agitating with the handle of a wooden spoon (see page 138). Once the sugar has dissolved, increase the heat and boil the syrup, without stirring, until it reaches the short thread stage (see page 139), about 108°C on a sugar thermometer. Remove from the heat immediately.

2 Put the yolks in a medium heatproof bowl and, using a hand-held electric whisk, whisk in the sugar syrup, pouring the syrup slowly onto the yolks and taking care not to pour it onto the whisks, or it will stick. Keep whisking until thick.

3 Using a wooden spoon or hand-held electric whisk, beat the butters together in a separate bowl, then check the butter and mousse are similar temperatures. Gradually add the mousse to the butter, whisking slowly after each addition, starting with 1 tbsp and gradually increasing the amount until it is all incorporated. Whisk in any flavouring, see below.

Flavourings

Lemon, orange or lime Add the finely grated zest of 1–2 lemons or oranges, or 3–4 limes, to taste, to the finished buttercream. You can also add a little juice, up to 2 tbsp or to taste, in additions, but be aware that too much may cause curdling or make the icing too loose.

Coffee Add 3 tsp warm very strong coffee or espresso to the mousse before it is added to the butters. (Alternatively, 40–50ml Camp Coffee can be used.)

Meringue-based buttercream (crème au beurre meringue)

**Makes enough to fill and top
a 22cm two-layered sponge**

3 egg whites

175g icing sugar

120g unsalted butter, at room
  temperature

120g salted butter, at room temperature

This method makes a light, soft icing using a meringue to combine with the butters.

1 Put the egg whites and icing sugar in a large heatproof bowl and set over a saucepan of just simmered water (off the heat), making sure the base of the bowl is not touching the water.

2 Whisk until the meringue is thick and holding its shape, using a hand-held electric whisk. Remove the bowl from the pan of water and continue to whisk until the bowl is a little cooler.

3 Using a wooden spoon or hand-held electric whisk, beat the butters in a separate bowl. Gradually add the meringue, beating well after each addition, starting with 1 tbsp, then increasing the amount as you add more until it is all incorporated. Add your chosen flavouring, if using, see below.

Flavourings

Lemon, orange or lime To the finished buttercream, add the finely grated zest and juice of 1 lemon or orange, or 2 limes, to taste (the juice must not be cold).

Coffee Stir 3–4 tsp warm very strong coffee or espresso, to taste, into the finished buttercream. (Alternatively, 40–50ml Camp Coffee can be used.)

Chocolate Melt 75–85g good quality dark chocolate and stir in well, in additions, to the finished buttercream.

Chocolate

Chocolate is very sensitive to heat and can change from melted to scorched quickly over a narrow temperature range, making it potentially tricky to work with. Besides simply melting it for use in cooking, chocolate can also be tempered (which involves heating, cooling and reheating to specific temperatures) to give it a high gloss for use in chocolate work; this is normally the preserve of skilled chocolatiers. In these recipes, tempered chocolate is not required.

Types of chocolate

Those most commonly used in cooking are as follows:

Dark (or plain) chocolate When using chocolate in cooking look for one with 60–70% cocoa solids. The flavour will generally be one that most people enjoy, whereas chocolate with greater than 70% cocoa solids can taste bitter to some.

Milk chocolate With added milk solids and sugar, this has a milder, sweeter flavour. It is important to use a good quality milk chocolate for cooking.

Cocoa powder Use a good quality cocoa powder with a fairly intense flavour.

Storing chocolate

Store chocolate well wrapped in a cool, dry place, ideally about 17°C. If storing in the fridge, wrap it closely to avoid condensation. If the chocolate is stored at too high a temperature a 'bloom' will form on the surface, from cocoa butter rising to the surface. If this happens, the chocolate can still be used for cooking.

Chocolate that is not well wrapped can develop a sugar 'bloom'. Condensation dissolves the sugar in the chocolate and then, when the moisture evaporates, leaves a white crust, or bloom. Again, the chocolate can still be used for cooking.

Melting chocolate

When melting chocolate there are several points to remember:

• If you are not using chocolate drops or buttons, chop the chocolate into small pieces, so that it melts evenly and quickly.

• For small quantities (up to 250g), half-fill a small saucepan with water and bring to a simmer. Remove from the heat and place the chocolate in a heatproof bowl that will sit on the saucepan without the base touching the water.

• For larger quantities, the saucepan can be left over a low heat with the water still simmering, but take care not to overheat the chocolate. It can become dry and crumbly and cannot be brought back.

• Let the chocolate soften, then give it an occasional stir to ensure even melting.

• Avoid getting any water or steam in the chocolate or this may seize it, causing it to become grainy and harden into an unworkable lump.

• You can melt chocolate in a microwave. Use a heatproof bowl and microwave on 50% power for 30 seconds at a time, stirring the chocolate after each 30 second session. Milk and white chocolate can be melted in the microwave at 30% power.

Adding liquid to chocolate

Chocolate will seize if liquid is added as it is melting. If you need to add a little liquid, add it before the chocolate starts to melt. If you need to add a large amount, as a rule of thumb, add at least 15ml to each 50g melted chocolate and try to add the melted chocolate to the liquid, rather than the other way round. Also ensure the liquid is warm, as adding melted chocolate to a cold liquid can cause seizing.

Chocolate ganache

Makes enough to fill two 20cm cakes generously
350g good quality dark chocolate, minimum 60% cocoa solids
250ml double cream

Chocolate ganache is most often used as a filling for cakes. The consistency of ganache depends on the proportion of double cream to chocolate.

1 Chop the chocolate into small pieces, ideally about 1cm in size, and put into a heatproof bowl.

2 Pour the cream into a small saucepan and bring to a simmer over a medium heat. Pour the hot cream over the chocolate and stir gently until the chocolate has melted and the mixture is well combined.

3 Leave to cool until it begins to thicken a little around the edges, then beat with a hand-held electric whisk on a slow speed for 1–2 minutes, until it is has thickened a little but is still creamy. Do not aerate the mixture too much.

Variation

Chocolate truffles Make a ganache as above, but use 250g dark chocolate and 125ml double cream; if the chocolate does not melt fully, place over a pan of simmering water until it is smoothly melted. Stir in 50g unsalted butter, 1 tbsp liquid glucose and 2 tbsp Amaretto, Grand Marnier or other liqueur of your choice, then allow to cool as in step 3 before beating for 1–2 minutes until lightened a little in colour. Leave the mixture to cool until it is a pipeable consistency. Now take a teaspoonful at a time in hands lightly floured in cocoa and gently shape into balls between the palms of your hands; work swiftly to avoid warming the chocolate. Roll the shaped truffles in sifted cocoa powder or finely ground praline (see page 648). Store in a cool place (not the fridge) in a shallow, airtight plastic container lined with baking parchment, and eat within a few days.

Piping icing/chocolate

Piping calls for a steady hand. It's a good idea to practise on a sheet of greaseproof paper first, so that the decoration is applied to the cake with a confident hand.

Making a paper piping bag

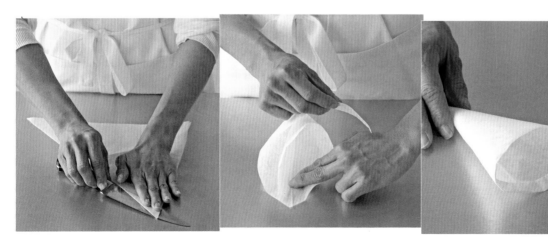

1 Take a piece of greaseproof paper, about 30cm square, and cut it in half diagonally to create a triangle, 2 points having the same angle.

2 Hold the triangle with the 2 same points away from you, then fold them over each other. Work these 2 points, one behind the top point and one in front of it until all 3 points are in line.

3 Pull the paper tightly, then twist the points over each other 2 or 3 times to seal the cone. Snip a little off the pointed end, then insert a piping nozzle into the paper piping bag.

Simple decorations

We often use praline and nougatine to decorate cakes and desserts. They are both made by combining caramel and nuts – traditionally almonds, although potentially any nut could be used. The difference between praline and nougatine is that for praline whole nuts are used and toasted in the caramel, and for nougatine the nuts are crushed and toasted before being added to the caramel. Glucose is also added to nougatine to keep it pliable.

Praline

Makes 300g
150g blanched almonds
150g caster sugar

1 Very lightly oil a baking sheet.

2 Put the almonds and sugar in a heavy-based sauté or frying pan and set over a low heat. As the sugar begins to melt and brown, use a fork to very gently encourage the unmelted sugar to the sides of the pan to melt and caramelise.

3 When the almonds start to make a cracking sound and all the sugar is a rich golden colour, tip the mixture onto the oiled baking sheet and flatten using the fork. Allow to cool completely.

4 Once cooled and hardened, the praline can be broken into pieces or pounded with a pestle and mortar or food processor to a fine or coarse powder, according to how you intend to use it.

Nougatine

Makes about 250g
100g skinned hazelnuts
150g caster sugar
1 tsp glucose syrup

1 Heat the oven to 180°C/gas mark 4 and very lightly oil a baking sheet.

2 Finely chop the hazelnuts, place on a second baking sheet and toast in the oven until pale golden, then remove and keep warm. (The nuts must be warm when they are added to the caramel or the caramel will cool down too quickly and may crystallise.)

3 Put the sugar and glucose syrup in a heavy-based sauté or frying pan and set the pan over a low heat. As the sugar begins to take on colour, use a fork to gently encourage the unmelted sugar to the edges of the pan and achieve an even colouring (see dry caramel, page 141).

4 When all the sugar is caramelised, add the still warm nuts and turn to coat in the caramel. Immediately tip the mixture onto the oiled baking sheet and turn it over with a lightly oiled palette knife, using a half-mixing, half-kneading motion until it is stiffening but still workable.

5 If the nougatine is to be used as a flat sheet, while it is still warm and pliable, roll it as thinly as possible and cut into shapes. Alternatively, allow to cool completely, then break into pieces or pound with a pestle and mortar or food processor to a fine or coarse powder, depending on its intended use.

Special occasion cakes

Celebration fruit cakes are generally covered with marzipan, then royal or fondant icing. We use a cooked marzipan, which is softer and easier to handle than the more commonly found uncooked version.

Marzipan

Makes enough to cover a 22–24cm round cake

½ lemon
175g caster sugar
175g icing sugar, plus extra to dust
2 eggs
350g ground almonds
4 drops of vanilla extract

1 Juice the ½ lemon and sift the caster and icing sugars into a heatproof bowl.

2 Beat the eggs lightly in a medium bowl. Using a hand-held electric whisk, whisk in the sifted sugars, then place the bowl over a saucepan of simmering water and whisk until light and creamy, or until the mixture just leaves a trail when the whisk is lifted. Remove from the heat and continue to whisk until the bowl is cool.

3 Stir in the ground almonds, vanilla extract and 1 tsp lemon juice, mixing until the ingredients come together into a loose ball.

4 Lightly dust a clean surface with icing sugar. Knead the marzipan on the surface until just smooth. Take care not to overwork or oil will be drawn from the almonds, resulting in a greasy paste. Shape into a disc, wrap in cling film and chill until firm.

Covering a cake with marzipan

Lightly dust a clean surface with icing sugar and roll out the marzipan to a circle, about 20cm in diameter, ensuring the marzipan is moving on the surface and not stuck, and there are as few cracks as possible around the edge. If the cake is not level, shave a little off the top.

1 If the cake is still slightly domed, shape a very small amount of marzipan (2–3 walnut-sized pieces) into a thin rope. Secure this around the edge of the cake with a little apricot glaze (to ensure the cake is flat, when turned upside down). Turn the cake upside down and lightly brush the surface (originally the base) and sides with 2–3 tbsp apricot glaze.

2 Place the cake, glazed surface down, in the centre of the marzipan circle and, using your hands, carefully bring the marzipan up against the sides of the cake. Now carefully turn the cake over.

3 Roll lightly across the top of the cake and coax the marzipan down the sides with your hands to the bottom. Roll a jam jar or tin around the sides of the cake, to neaten and smooth the marzipan, ensuring the sides are straight and edges square. Trim to neaten, if necessary. Place on a suitably sized cake board and leave uncovered for at least 3 days for the marzipan to dry out. This prevents the almond oils from staining the icing.

Royal icing

Makes enough to coat a 22–24cm round cake

500g icing sugar
2 egg whites
1–2 tsp glycerine (see note)
1 tsp lemon juice, optional (see note)

1 Sift the icing sugar into a bowl. Put the egg whites into a separate, large bowl and, using a wooden spoon, gradually stir in a little of the icing sugar, about 3 tbsp. Add the glycerine and the lemon juice, if using.

2 Gradually mix in the remaining icing sugar until the mixture is soft and fluffy and will hold its shape; you may not need to incorporate all of it.

3 Cover the surface of the icing with a clean, damp cloth to prevent it drying out, and place in the fridge overnight to allow any air bubbles to rise to the surface.

Note For larger quantities than this, a wooden spoon can be hard work; use a hand-held electric whisk, but try to avoid incorporating too much air when mixing.

Royal icing consistency

A cake usually has 2 coats of icing applied after the marzipan, and is then decorated with either piping or 'run in' work. The consistency of the icing varies for each stage. For the first coating and piping, the icing should be very thick; a teaspoon should stand upright in the icing and the icing should stand up in points when the spoon is lifted out. For the second coat, the icing should be a bit thinner; points should flop over at the tip.

A note on adding glycerine...

Adding glycerine keeps the icing soft so that it doesn't splinter when cut. Without it, royal icing becomes incredibly hard, but if you are eating the cake within 24 hours you don't need to add it. You can add more glycerine to make an even softer icing, but the resulting icing will not be suitable for cakes that are going to be tiered.

A note on adding lemon juice...

It is not essential to add lemon juice to royal icing but it effectively seasons the sugar, so the icing tastes less sweet.

Covering a cake with royal icing

The marzipan-covered cake must be allowed to dry thoroughly for at least 3 days before royal icing is applied.

The layers of royal icing are more easily applied in 2 stages for round cakes and in 3 stages for square cakes. The top is iced first and left to dry for up to 24 hours, before the sides are iced. On a square cake the two opposite sides of the cake are iced and left to dry, then the remaining two sides iced.

Before you begin, carefully lift the cake and place a generous teaspoonful of icing in the middle of the cake board, then lower the cake and leave to dry to ensure the cake is securely fixed to the board.

Applying the first coating

1 Spoon half the icing onto the top of the cake and, using a palette knife in a paddling action which will help remove bubbles, spread the icing over the entire surface of the cake.

2 Using a stainless steel ruler or long palette knife as a paddle, smooth the icing out, working it towards you then away. Start with small strokes and lengthen them gradually until the entire top of the cake is smooth and level. Draw the ruler or palette knife off the cake as level as possible.

3 Using an icing scraper, scrape the excess icing from the sides of the cake, working the scraper downwards with short, sharp strokes, without damaging the top. Allow the icing to dry for 24 hours before icing the sides.

4 For the sides, put the cake, on its board, on a cake stand or an upturned bowl. Using a palette knife, spread the remaining icing evenly around the sides of the cake, if it is round.

5 Using an icing scraper held at a 45° angle to the cake, try to turn the cake around in one movement in order to smooth the icing on the sides as evenly as possible.

6 Carefully scrape any excess icing from the top of the cake using a scraper. (For a square cake, ice 2 opposite sides and leave to set for 24 hours before icing the other two sides.)

The second coating

If the first layer is very smooth, applying a second layer may not be necessary. The cake can be brushed with a clean pastry brush to remove any crumbs before applying icing. Apply the second layer as for the first, but with a slightly thinner consistency icing.

To cover a cake with ready-made fondant icing

For an easy way to ice a celebration cake, you can buy ready-made fondant icing or sugar paste, in a block or ready-rolled form. It gives a good finish, but doesn't have the same flavour as royal icing. The marzipan-covered cake must be allowed to dry thoroughly for at least 3 days before royal icing is applied.

1 On a work surface lightly dusted with icing sugar, roll out the fondant icing to a thickness of about 3–4mm. Carefully lift the icing onto a rolling pin and lay it over the cake.

2 Smooth the fondant icing over the top surface of the cake and then down the sides, making sure you don't create any pleats or folds.

3 Trim off the excess icing with a knife and neaten the bottom edge against the cake board, tucking the end towards the cake if necessary.

Icing special occasion cakes

Royal icing is generally thought to have a better flavour and to be more resilient than fondant, however it takes practice to achieve a really smooth result and bought fondant is much easier to use. If you are making a tiered cake, royal icing will support the layers better than fondant, although upright dowling rods are used with both types of icing to prevent the lower layer(s) collapsing.

Decorating special occasion cakes

Once the cake is fully covered, the icing will need to be left to dry (and harden in the case of royal icing) for a few days before the cake can be decorated.

Making intricate decorations for cakes is a specialist skill, but simple shapes can be moulded from fondant, or cut out from the rolled out icing, using suitable cutters (stars, holly leaves and Christmas trees for festive cakes, for example). There is a huge variety of food colours that can be kneaded into the paste to obtain the appropriate colour, and edible lustre sprays that can be applied to give a metallic or pearlescent sheen. A traditional royal iced cake is often finished with piping, using either white or subtly coloured royal icing for contrast.

Alternatively, a fondant or royal iced cake can look stunning finished with a simple, elegant arrangement of flowers or leaves. Of course, it is important to ensure that the arrangement does not include any toxic foliage or flowers.

Glossary of cooking terms

Acidulated liquid Water with lemon juice or vinegar added, used to keep fruit or vegetables such as pieces of apple or celeriac from turning brown.

Agar agar A vegetarian setting agent made from seaweed, used as an alternative to gelatine.

Al dente Used to describe cooking an ingredient such as pasta or vegetables so that they still have some texture or 'bite' rather than being completely soft (literally, 'to the tooth').

Aromatics Spices, herbs and other fragrant flavourings, such as ginger and garlic, added to impart flavour to a dish while it cooks. Often removed prior to serving.

Bain marie A hot water bath, often a roasting tin filled with water, used to protect a delicate dish from direct heat. Also used to keep food in a pan or bowl warm, such as a delicate sauce, without continuing to cook.

Ball stage, Soft-/Hard- Stages of sugar syrup boiling. To test, a little of the boiled sugar syrup is dropped into cold water. At 115°C it will form a soft ball; at 120°C it will form a hard ball.

Ballotine A boned chicken or portion of chicken (or other poultry, game bird or meat), stuffed and tied into an even shape before cooking. Usually roasted and served hot.

Bard To tie bacon fat or a piece of lard over meat to keep it moist and prevent it from drying out as it roasts.

Baste To spoon juices or fat over food at intervals during cooking, for example while roasting a chicken, to maintain moistness and flavour.

Batons Used to denote vegetables cut into even-sized, medium-thin sticks.

Baveuse A soft, slightly undercooked consistency, generally used to describe the texture of an egg dish, such as a perfectly cooked omelette.

Beurre manié Equal quantities of softened butter and flour stirred together and whisked in small pieces into an unknown quantity of cooking liquor, such as that of a stew, to thicken it.

Beurre noisette Butter cooked until it turns nut brown in colour, which happens when the milk solids caramelise.

Bind To use an ingredient such as a thick white sauce or beaten egg to combine and hold ingredients together, such as beaten egg in fishcakes, stuffings etc.

Blanch To part-cook vegetables quickly in boiling water, usually before refreshing in cold water, to stop the cooking and set the colour before freezing or to make them quicker to cook for serving later. Blanching is also used to loosen the skins of tomatoes, or mellow the flavour and/or reduce the salt in certain foods, such as bacon and sweetbreads.

Blind bake To line a pastry case with a circle of greaseproof paper (a cartouche), fill it with baking beans and bake before the filling is added. The beans help the pastry case to hold its shape as it cooks. They are then removed with the paper and the pastry case is returned to the oven to dry the base (or cook the pastry completely if the filling won't be cooked in the case.)

Blood temperature 37–38°C: the temperature that feels neither hot nor cold to the touch.

Bloom White sugar or fat deposits on the surface of chocolate, often because it has been kept in an environment that is too moist or too warm; the chocolate is still usable.

Boil To cook food submerged in liquid heated so that the bubbles are constant and vigorous.

Bouillon Strained stock.

Bouquet garni Parsley stalks, thyme sprigs and a bay leaf tied onto a length of celery and used to flavour soups, stocks and stews while they simmer, then removed before serving.

Braise To cook poultry, meat, fish or vegetables on a bed of vegetables (known as a mirepoix) with a small amount of liquid in a covered pan.

Brine A salted liquid, sometimes also flavoured with aromatics, used to preserve meat, fish and vegetables.

Brown To fry or roast to achieve colour and flavour as the natural sugars caramelise, such as pieces of beef for a stew.

Brunoise Vegetables cut into small dice.

Butterfly To slit a piece of food almost in half, but leaving it attached so it can be opened out like a butterfly to cook more quickly and/or evenly, for example prawns or sardines.

Caramel Sugar turned to a deep terracotta brown by heating.

Caramelise See Brown (above).

Cartouche A circle of greaseproof paper used dry during blind baking (see left), or wet pressed onto sweating onions or other vegetables under a lid, to maintain a steamy atmosphere which allows the food to soften without browning.

Caul Or crépin. A thin membrane covered in a delicate web of fat, used to wrap meat to hold it in shape. During cooking the fat melts down and bastes the meat.

Chiffonnade To shred soft leaves, such as basil, lettuce, spinach or sorrel.

Chill To cool food down in the fridge or using an ice bath, ideally to 4°C.

Chine To remove the backbone from a rack of ribs, once a butcher has 'chined' the rack, by sawing through the area joining the ribs to the back bone (this is very difficult to do without butchery equipment).

Clarified butter Butter which has been heated and the milk solids removed. This gives it a clear appearance and allows it to be heated to a high temperature without burning, while retaining the flavour of butter.

Clarify To filter a hot liquid, such as stock or a flavoured syrup, through beaten egg white to remove the impurities and produce a clear liquid. This can then be set using gelatine to make a perfectly clear jelly, such as aspic.

Coagulation The setting of protein as a result of heating; usually refers to egg protein once cooked.

Concasse Fine, even dice. Generally describes tomato flesh cut into small squares or diamonds.

Confit To cook something immersed in fat, traditionally duck or goose, which is then preserved in the fat. Other ingredients, such as shallots, can also be cooked in this way.

Coulis A thin purée, usually of fruit with a little sugar syrup.

Court bouillon Water acidulated with vinegar or lemon juice and flavoured with aromatics, used for poaching fish.

Cream To beat together ingredients to incorporate air, typically butter and sugar for a cake mixture.

Curdle When an emulsion separates undesirably into solid and liquid, such as mayonnaise or a cake mixture.

Cut up (or knock up) To cut into the edge of raw layered pastry, holding the knife blade horizontally, to encourage it to rise, and the layers to be more defined during cooking.

Deglaze To add liquid, usually wine or water, to a pan after frying and stirring/scraping to loosen the sediment on the bottom so it can be incorporated into the sauce to add flavour. This resulting liquid is called the déglaçage.

Degorge To remove some of the liquid, usually from vegetables (less commonly fish and meat) by salting to draw out some of the juices. For example, aubergine slices, to allow them to crisp up when frying.

Dégrasse or degrease To remove a layer of fat from the surface of a liquid by blotting with a piece of kitchen paper or skimming with a ladle.

Dépouiller To add a splash of cold water to a hot stock, to encourage fat and impurities to rise to the surface so they can be skimmed off.

Détrempe The base dough of a layered pastry.

Devein To remove the black intestinal thread running down the back of a prawn.

Dropping consistency When a mixture will drop reluctantly from a spoon if it is tapped on the side of the bowl or pan, neither pouring off nor continuing to stick to the spoon.

Duxelles Finely chopped mushrooms or a mushroom and shallot mixture, often used as a stuffing.

Egg wash Beaten egg, sometimes salted, brushed onto pastry or bread to give it colour and shine once baked.

Emulsion A suspension of fat and other liquid. An emulsifier such as egg yolk or mustard is often added to make the suspension more stable, such as in mayonnaise or hollandaise.

Enrich To add cream, butter or a cream and egg yolk mixture to a sauce or other dish to thicken and enhance the flavour.

Farce A stuffing.

Fécule A farinaceous thickening agent such as cornflour or arrowroot.

Finish To complete a dish by adjusting its consistency, flavourings, seasoning and/or applying a garnish or decoration.

Flambé To set light to alcohol in a dish, usually for a dramatic effect. A lit long match is held over the dish to ignite the alcohol, which is then burnt off as the liquid glazes the food in the pan, leaving a mellow flavour.

Flood the plate To coat the base of a serving plate with sauce as part of the presentation. The sauce must be of a light, coating 'floodable' consistency.

Fold To combine two or more mixtures using a large metal spoon or spatula and a lifting and turning motion to avoid destroying the air bubbles. Usually one of the mixtures is more airy and delicate than the other.

Fraiser When making French pastries, to use a palette knife to 'scrape' and combine the ingredients.

Fumet A strong flavoured liquid used to flavour sauces, typically the liquor from cooking a fish which then flavours its sauce.

Galantine Boned poultry, stuffed and tied into shape before poaching. Served cold.

Game A wild bird, fish or animal killed by hunting, shooting or fishing before being cooked.

Gastrique Caramel dissolved in vinegar, used to give a sauce a sweet and sour flavour and a brown colour.

Gelatine A setting agent for sweet and savoury jellies and mousses, available as thin sheets (leaves) or in powdered form, which must be fully dissolved. Made from animal bone/skin, it is not appropriate for vegetarians but agar agar (see left) is a suitable alternative.

Glace de viande A highly reduced brown stock added to sauces to lend depth of flavour and colour.

Glaze To lend a glossy finish. A glaze may be applied before or after cooking. For example, an egg glaze is applied to bread or pastry prior to baking, while an apricot glaze is brushed over the warm fruit in a tart on removing from the oven.

Grain The direction the fibres run in a joint of meat. Cutting across the grain reduces toughness.

Gratiner To sprinkle a dish with breadcrumbs or crumbs mixed with grated cheese and grill until golden brown.

Hang After killing, meat and game is hung on hooks in a cool, airy place to develop the flavour of the flesh and to tenderise the meat, as the fibres start to break down ('mortifier').

Infuse To immerse aromatic ingredients such as herbs or spices in a hot liquid to flavour it.

Julienne Vegetables, fresh ginger or citrus zest cut into thin, matchstick-sized pieces.

Jus or jus de viande The juices that naturally occur when cooking meat. In restaurants jus denotes a thin, intense sauce.

Knead To work a bread dough vigorously in order to develop the gluten and elasticity.

Knock back or knock down To knead or punch the air out of a risen bread dough so that when it rises for the second time it will have a finer, even texture.

Lard To thread strips of fat through a joint of lean meat, such as venison, to moisten the meat as they melt during cooking. A skewer or a larding needle can be used to push the strips through the meat.

Lardons Small strips or cubes of pancetta or bacon cut from a whole piece.

Let down To thin an overly thick sauce with a little liquid, normally stock or water in savoury dishes, to achieve the desired consistency.

Liaison A mixture of egg yolks and cream, used to thicken a sauce. The term can also refer generally to other thickening agents, such as cornflour, a roux or beurre manié.

Lighten To incorporate air into a dish, by carefully folding in egg whites or lightly whipped cream for example.

Loosen When combining whisked egg whites into a heavier mixture, to first stir in a spoonful of the whisked whites before folding in the remainder.

Macedoine Vegetables or fruit cut into small dice.

Macerate To soak food, usually fruit, in a flavoured liquid, to soften it and allow the exchange of flavours, for example orange segments in a cinnamon-flavoured syrup.

Marbling The pattern of intramuscular fat through a joint of meat, especially beef. In general, the more even the marbling, the better the cut is considered to be.

Marinate To soak food in a highly flavoured liquid or coat it with a dry rub of flavourings, from which it absorbs some flavour. Marinades for meat and game are usually acidic, such as red wine, to help to tenderise the flesh.

Mirepoix See Braise.

Mise en place The organisation of equipment and ingredients prior to preparation and cooking. This includes heating ovens, adjusting the position of oven shelves, weighing ingredients and oiling baking sheets.

Monter au beurre To whisk small pieces of butter into a sauce, to enrich, thicken and add shine.

Mousse A savoury or sweet dish, where the air bubbles from whisked egg whites (and also usually cream), make the texture frothy and light.

Mousseline A fine purée of fish, shellfish, poultry or meat, lightened with cream or whisked egg whites and used as a garnish or stuffing. Quenelles of mousseline can be poached and served alone or as a garnish.

Nappé To coat food evenly in a sauce.

Needleshreds Finely and evenly cut shreds of citrus zest, typically used as a garnish.

Noisette A small round, boneless piece of meat or fish, especially loin of lamb and salmon.

Offal The edible internal organs of an animal that are removed before the carcass is cut into joints.

Oven spring The crack along the length of a loaf that is created by the yeast's final activity in the oven before it is killed by the intense heat.

Oyster A small piece of meat found on either side of the back bone of a chicken, which is thought to be the best flavoured flesh.

Panade The thick base mixture of a soufflé or choux pastry. Made from butter, flour and milk or water, it is also used as a binding mixture.

Paner To coat delicate foods with flour, then beaten egg and finally breadcrumbs before frying, to protect them and add texture and colour.

Papillote, en Food cooked in an enclosed greaseproof paper case in the oven. On heating, steam is produced and trapped inside the parcel, effectively cooking the food.

Parboil To part-cook by boiling.

Pass To push a purée or soft ingredients through a sieve to achieve a fine texture.

Pâte The base mixture or paste, such as uncooked pastry, dough or uncooked meringue etc.

Piquer To make small cuts or holes and insert flavourings, such as studding a ham for baking with cloves.

Pavé A square or diamond shape of food for presentation (literally, a slab or block).

Pectin A natural gelling agent, found in varying quantities in fruit and vegetables. It can also be purchased and added to jams, jellies and chutneys, or sugar with added pectin can be used.

Pin-bone To remove all of the small bones found in the flesh of fish, using kitchen tweezers.

Pinch An approximate quantity that can be pinched between the thumb and forefinger, less than 1/8 tsp.

Piquant A robust, sharp, tangy flavour.

Pith The soft white layer directly beneath the coloured zest of citrus fruit. It is invariably bitter in flavour and avoided when zesting the fruit.

Poach To completely submerge food in liquid that is hot yet barely trembling (certainly not bubbling), either on the hob or in the oven. Ideal for cooking delicate food.

Pot roast To roast at a low temperature in an enclosed dish with very little liquid.

Prove The final rise of a bread dough after it has been knocked back. The term also describes rubbing a pan with oil and salt to make it non-stick.

Purée Usually vegetables or fruit, blended and/or sieved until smooth. Purées can also be made from meat and fish.

Quenelle A smooth three-sided oval of mousseline, ice cream or mousse, shaped by passing the mixture repeatedly between two spoons of the same size.

Rechauffer To reheat previously cooked and cooled food to create a hot dish.

Reduce To rapidly boil a liquid, such as a stock or sauce, to concentrate the flavour by evaporating some of the liquid.

Refresh To plunge blanched or boiled vegetables into cold water to stop the cooking and set the colour, before draining.

Relax or rest To set pastry aside in a cool place, usually the fridge, to allow the gluten to relax before baking. This helps to minimise shrinking in the oven. Batters are also left to rest before use to allow the starch cells to swell, which results in a lighter cooked result.

Render To melt solid meat fat by cooking slowly, for example placing a duck breast skin side down in a frying pan to render down the fat under the skin.

Revenir To make ingredients hot again by tossing in hot oil or butter such as blanched and refreshed green beans.

Ribbon stage When a whisked egg or mousse mixture is thick enough to leave a line or ribbon over the surface when the whisk is lifted and some of the mixture falls from it.

Roast To cook uncovered, without added liquid, in the oven.

Roux Equal quantities of butter and flour, cooked together and used to thicken a measured quantity of liquid, such as for a white sauce.

Rub in To rub small pieces of butter into flour with the fingertips until the mixture resembles breadcrumbs.

Sauté To brown small pieces of food in butter or oil over a high heat, shaking the pan or stirring to ensure the ingredients colour quickly and evenly.

Scald To heat a liquid (milk, usually) until on the verge of boiling. At scalding point, steam is escaping and bubbles are starting to form around the edge of the pan.

Score To make shallow or deep cuts in the surface of food with a sharp knife. For example, scoring through pork skin into the fat but not the flesh, for crackling, or deeply scoring bread to create decorative slashes that open out on baking.

Sear To brown the surface of meat over a high heat.

Season Usually simply to flavour with salt and pepper, but it can also involve adjusting acidity with lemon juice or sweetness by adding sugar. The term also describes rubbing a pan with oil and salt to make it non-stick.

Seize To brown the surface of meat, fish or poultry before roasting, or to brown offal such as kidneys to encourage bitter juices to run out. Seize also denotes chocolate becoming hard and unworkable on contact with moisture during melting.

Setting point The stage at which a mixture containing gelatine starts to set. Also the point where the pectin gels in jams and jellies, which should then be removed from the heat.

Simmer To cook food submerged in liquid, heated to a level that ensures small bubbles constantly appear around the edge of the pan.

Slake To mix a thickening ingredient such as cornflour with a little cold water and then whisking the mixture into the sauce to thicken it. Unstable ingredients such as yoghurt should also be slaked into a mixture using a little of the sauce, to prevent curdling.

Spatchcock To remove the back bone and flatten poultry, typically poussin, before cooking.

Sponge Soaking powdered gelatine in a little water until it forms a translucent spongy gel before melting. Fresh yeast is also said to sponge if mixed with a little warm water and left until the yeast is seen to be working and frothing.

Steam To cook food in hot vapour, usually from boiling water. This is a gentle method of cooking food such as fish or vegetables, which sit in a perforated container or permeable bamboo steamer and cook in the steam that surrounds them. Alternatively, in indirect steaming, the food is protected from the steam itself but cooks in the heat created by it; a steamed sponge enclosed in a covered pudding basin is an example.

Stew To cook meat or other food immersed in liquid in an enclosed dish at a low temperature.

Sweat To cook food gently in a little butter or oil, usually in a covered pan, to soften but not brown and release some of the moisture and natural sweetness.

Syrupy The consistency of a sauce reduced down until it just coats the back of a spoon. Similar to warm syrup or honey.

Thread stage An early stage of sugar syrup boiling. To test, a little of the boiled sugar syrup is dropped into cold water, then removed and pulled between the finger and thumb. At 110°C it will form a fine thread as it is pulled.

Tronçon An individual cut taken from across a flat fish, with the bone still in.

Turn To shape vegetables into barrel shapes with smooth, even facets, using a small, sharp knife.

Tunnel boning Removing the bones from a joint, such as a leg or shoulder of lamb, leaving the meat intact so it can be stuffed if required.

Velouté A flour-based sauce where the roux base is cooked to a blond, straw colour before liquid is added, usually stock and some cream.

Well A hollow in a mound of flour in a bowl or on the work surface, created to contain the liquid ingredients before they are incorporated. Used in bread, pastry and batter making.

Wilt To cook leaves such as spinach so they soften, collapse and lose their expansive fresh volume.

Zest The coloured outer skin of citrus fruit used for flavouring, which must be carefully removed from the bitter white pith before it is added. 'To zest' describes the action of finely paring the zest from citrus fruit, using a zester.

Kitchen tools & equipment

We use basic equipment that can be found in any well equipped home kitchen for most of our classes at the school. Here we have listed the most useful items to have in your kitchen. As you move on to more complex recipes, you will probably want to expand your range, but this is a good starting point. Keep in mind that it is worth paying for good quality utensils and equipment: they will perform better and last longer.

Knives

Spend as much as your budget will allow on a really good set of kitchen knives. Each one must be comfortable to hold, not too heavy, but weighty enough. Keep them in a knife block, not a drawer. The following knives are most useful:

Large cook's knife You will use this for most of your food preparation.
Paring knife For cutting small ingredients – to get close to them for more control.
Boning knife A must if you enjoy a bit of butchery. Ideally it should have a rigid blade.
Filleting knife A long knife with a flexible blade used for boning fish.
Pastry knife A long serrated knife, used for breads, cakes and pastries, which cuts through the crumb without tearing.
Turning knife A very short knife with a curved blade, used for peeling, trimming and shaping vegetables.
Small serrated knife This is useful for preparing fruit.
Sharpening steel A durable steel rod with a textured surface for sharpening knives. Get into the habit of 'honing' your knives each time you use them to ensure they maintain a sharp edge.

Utensils

Good quality kitchen tools make work in the kitchen easier and more efficient. The following are ideal:

Measuring spoons
Wooden spoons
Slotted spoons
Basting spoon
Ladles (several sizes)
Fish slice
Kitchen tongs
Rolling pin
Meat mallet
Kitchen scissors (a sturdy pair)
Swivel vegetable peeler
Apple corer
Melon baller
Ice-cream scoop
Pastry cutters
Palette knife
Spatula (heat resistant)
Fine grater
Nutmeg grater
Zester
Kitchen tweezers
Larding needle
Skewers (metal and wooden/ bamboo)

Equipment

Most of the following items are pretty essential! Trays and tins do not need to be non-stick, but should be solid/rigid enough not to warp when they are heated.

Scales (a set of good scales is imperative)
Chopping boards (at least two, for raw and cooked foods)
Bowls (various sizes, glass or stainless steel)
Pestle and mortar
Jugs (including a measuring jug)
Juicer
Baking sheets (lipped and flat)
Shallow baking trays or tins
Roasting tins
Wire cooling racks
Ramekins and soufflé dishes
Pie dishes
Casseroles and lids
Oven gloves
Oven thermometer
Muffin tins
Mini muffin tins
Loaf tins (500g)
Loose-based flan tins or flan rings
Cake tins (sandwich tin, springform tin, deep cake tin, Swiss roll tin)
Silicone moulds (such as madeleine and barquette moulds)
Moule à manqué (tin with sloping sides)
Dariole moulds or timbales (various sizes)
Terrines (metal or ceramic)

Saucepans and frying pans	Paper/lining products	Small electrical equipment

Saucepans and frying pans

A range of good quality pans in different sizes, from very small to large, is ideal. Saucepans do not need to be non-stick, but a large non-stick frying pan is most useful. Choose heavy-based saucepans and frying pans (with lids) as they will provide a more even heat and hold their heat longer. An ovenproof frying or sauté pan is particularly handy. Note that lids are sometimes interchangeable between larger saucepans and smaller frying pans. The following selection will cover your needs:

Saucepans (at least three in a range of sizes, from 18–28cm)
Frying pans (at least two in different sizes, from 16–28cm)
Sauté pan (a deep frying pan, at least 24cm)
Steamer (a perforated container that will fit over one of your saucepans under a tight-fitting lid)
Large stockpot or preserving pan
Griddle
Wok

Paper/lining products

Of the following, the first 4 items are indispensable:

Greaseproof paper
Baking parchment/Silicone paper
Aluminium foil
Cling film
Paper cake cases
Muslin
Non-stick baking mats (re-usable)

Small electrical equipment

These are the most useful labour-saving small appliances:

Hand-held electric whisk
Electric mixer (free-standing)
Food processor
Blender
Hand-held stick blender
Spice grinder
Ice-cream machine

More specialist equipment
These items are beneficial for specific recipes:
Mandolin
Meat thermometer
Sugar thermometer
Blini pans
Bain marie (special purpose)
Pasta machine
Thermomix
Sous-vide

Food hygiene in the kitchen

These basic guidelines should be followed whenever you prepare, cook and store food.

Storage in the fridge
Different foods should be kept apart. Raw meat or fish should be kept on the bottom shelf of the fridge so their juices cannot drip onto cooked food. Eggs keep better if stored pointed end downwards and, as they have porous shells, should be kept away from strong smelling food, as they will absorb the flavour. The fridge should ideally be kept at 4°C, although up to 8°C is considered safe.

Stock rotation
Keep an eye on expiry dates and make sure you use 'older' foods first. Don't mix leftovers, or add the remains of a carton of milk to a new one, as the newer food will then perish faster and any 'use by' date will be incorrect.

Cross-contamination
This is where bacteria from uncooked food are passed to food that will not be cooked further before eating. Most bacteria will be destroyed when cooked to a high temperature and are not any cause for alarm, as long as cross-contamination does not happen. Professional kitchens use separate chopping boards for food that will be cooked to a high temperature and food that will not. At home, scrubbing your chopping boards well and washing all kitchen cloths and utensils between tasks will suffice. Note that vegetables and fruit should be washed thoroughly before being prepared or eaten.

Wrapping
Food should only be loosely covered or not covered at all as it cools. It should then be well wrapped before placing in the fridge or freezer to prevent cross-contamination, drying out and becoming tainted by odorous food. Butter and milk easily take on other flavours, so they should not be left uncovered. Vegetables and fruit keep better unwrapped – or with any plastic wrapping pierced – in a vegetable drawer if the fridge has one, or above any raw meat or fish if not.

Food temperatures
Initially food should be brought to a high temperature, to kill any bacteria. If using a temperature probe, this should register at least 63°C (for commercial purposes the core temperature should reach 70°C for 2 minutes). When cooking at home without a probe, use a metal skewer and insert it into the centre of the food for 10 seconds,

then test it carefully on your wrist, which is more sensitive than fingertips; it should be too hot to keep on your skin.

Particular care must be taken when cooking chicken and minced or cubed stewing beef and lamb, which are more prone to salmonella and need to be cooked properly. If serving meat or fish raw, such as for beef carpaccio or sashimi, it must be of the highest quality, very fresh and from a trusted source.

Food can be kept warm ready to serve for a short while, if it was piping hot to start with and has not cooled to below serving temperature. Food should not be cooked, kept warm, cooled and then heated again to serve.

When reheating food, make sure it is piping hot all the way through and stir to distribute the heat if you can.

Food cooked in advance should be cooled as quickly as possible and then refrigerated or frozen until required. To speed cooling, spread the food over a large surface area or stand a pan in a sink of cold water and stir regularly; don't cover the food as that will slow the cooling process.

Using frozen food
Food should be left to defrost on a plate in the fridge overnight (or longer in the case of the Christmas turkey) so that it defrosts throughout and the outside doesn't get too warm before the middle has thawed. If you use a microwave to defrost, you need to cook the food straight away, as it will have warmed up, and may even have cooked in patches. Frozen cooked food must be thawed before reheating and then checked carefully to ensure it is very hot all the way through. It is not advisable to refreeze food that has already been frozen and defrosted.

Using leftover food
Leftover food must be cooled, then wrapped and chilled as soon as possible. It should be either eaten cold or reheated to at least 63°C for 2 minutes, ideally within 24 hours. Take particular care with leftover cooked rice.

Cooking for vulnerable groups
The elderly, pregnant women, those with underlying illnesses and very young children may have impaired resistance to infection, so attention to hygiene must be meticulous in these cases. It is also sensible to avoid raw or lightly cooked eggs, pâtés and unpasteurised soft ripened cheeses such as Brie, Camembert and blue-veined cheeses, and to reheat cooked chilled meals to piping hot rather than serve them cold. Advice on feeding pregnant women and babies is ever-changing, but current information is available on the NHS website.

Catering quantities

How much food you serve depends on many variables, such as appetites, the type of occasion and what else is being served. However, it is helpful to have a guide, particularly when cooking for large numbers where there is the greatest potential for waste. Quantities in the recipes in this book may differ slightly from those below, depending on other ingredients in the dish. You should allow the full portion per head when plating up individual servings, but can reduce the quantity per head if presenting food on a communal dish, as when helping themselves more people take less than the allotted portion. The quantities below are generous, and when cooking for larger numbers, you can reduce the amount per head. For example, you should allow 225g meat per person when making a stew for 4 people, but 170g per head would be enough when feeding 60.

Soup
Allow approximately 300ml soup per head, depending on the size of the bowl.

Fish and shellfish
Whole large fish Pre-cleaned weight with head on: allow 350–450g per person.
Prawns Allow 60–90g per person as a starter; 150g per person as a main course.

Fried or baked portions of fish or meat
Fish steaks or portions Allow a 140g piece for a starter, 170g for a main course.
Beef, lamb or pork steaks Allow a 170–225g piece per person.
Beef, lamb or pork mince for burgers etc. Allow 170g–200g per person.

Roasts
Chicken Allow 350g per person when cooking a whole bird. An average chicken serves 4–6 people.
Duck A bird weighing 2.7kg will feed 3–4 people; a 1.8kg bird will feed 2 people.
Turkey Allow 450g on the bone per person.
Beef, lamb or pork Allow 350g per person on the bone, 225g off the bone.
Beef, lamb or pork fillet cooked in a piece Allow 170–200g per person.

Stews
Stewed or braised dishes Allow 225g meat or poultry per person.
Fish stews Allow 170g per person.
Mince dishes Allow 100g minced meat per person in a dish such as lasagne, moussaka, ragù sauce for pasta etc.

Rice and pasta
Risotto or pilaf Allow 30g per person (raw weight) for a starter, 60g per person for a main course.
Pasta If using fresh pasta, allow 70–80g fresh pasta per person for a starter, 100–120g per person for a main course. If using dried pasta, allow 50–60g per person for a starter, 80–100g per person for a main course.

Accompaniments
Vegetables (including potatoes) served with a main course: Allow 100–125g each vegetable per person, depending on how many vegetables you are serving, except for French beans or peas, allow about 60g; spinach, allow 350g.
Rice Allow 60g (raw weight) per person.
Salads Allow 1–1½ portions of salad, in total per head, so if only one salad is served, allow a generous helping each and if serving several different salads, allow for less of each. If 100 guests are to choose from 5 different salads, allow a total of approximately 150 portions, ie serve 30 portions of each salad.
Green salad Allow a generous, loose handful of leaves for each person.
Cheese If serving after a meal, choose one blue-veined, one hard and one soft cheese: 75g per person for up to 8 people; 60g per person for over 20 people.
Fruit Allow 100–125g prepared fruit, such as cherries, strawberries or raspberries, per person.

Canapé parties
Allow 10 cocktail canapés per head, or approximately 4–6 per hour.
Allow 14 cocktail canapés per head if served as a meal.
Allow 4–5 cocktail canapés per head with pre-lunch or pre-dinner drinks.

Index